Kylix:

The Professional Developer's Guide and Reference

JON SHEMITZ

apress™

Kylix: The Professional Developer's Guide and Reference
Copyright © 2002 by Jon Shemitz

ISBN (pbk): 1-893115-89-5

Printed and bound in the United States of America 12345678910

Editorial Directors: Dan Appleman, Gary Cornell, Jason Gilmore, Karen Watterson

Technical Reviewer: Ray Lischner

Managing Editor: Grace Wong

Copy Editor: Jennifer Lind

Production Editor: Janet Vail

Compositor: Susan Glinert

Artist: Tony Jonick

Indexer: Nancy Guenther

Cover Designer: Tom Debolski

Marketing Manager: Stephanie Rodriguez

Distributed to the book trade in the United States by Springer-Verlag New York, Inc., 175 Fifth Avenue, New York, NY, 10010

and outside the United States by Springer-Verlag GmbH & Co. KG, Tiergartenstr. 17, 69112 Heidelberg, Germany

In the United States, phone 1-800-SPRINGER, email orders@springer-ny.com, or visit http://www.springer-ny.com.

Outside the United States, fax +49 6221 345229, email orders@springer.de, or visit http://www.springer.de.

For information on translations, please contact Apress directly at 901 Grayson Street, Suite 204, Berkeley, CA 94710.

Phone 510-549-5930, fax: 510-549-5939, email info@apress.com, or visit http://www.apress.com.

The source code for this book is available to readers at http://www.apress.com in the Downloads section. You will need to answer questions pertaining to this book in order to successfully download the code.

Dedication

When you write your first book at 42, you've had plenty of time to imagine dedications. I'm very pleased to finally be able to dedicate this book:

To my grandmother, Peggy, with special thanks for all the books. I wish she were still here to read this.

To my mother and father, for their always inflated opinion of my abilities and for the first rate education they bought for me.

To Carla Freccero, who taught me so much when she was my Daily Themes TA at Yale.

To Jeff Duntemann, who was my editor for so many years, and whose tip on ambiguous its helped make this book clearer.

And, most of all, to my partner, Tané Tachyon, and to our boys Sam and Arthur, for all their love, patience, and encouragement.

Acknowledgments

THIS BOOK REPRESENTS an awful lot of work on my part. However, I didn't do that work in a vacuum—this book wouldn't have been possible without the work of numerous other people.

I'd particularly like to thank my old friend Dan Appleman of Apress, who suggested this book back when Kylix was announced in late 1999. Dan also put me in touch with Paul Bonner, who kindly wrote the *Kylix for Visual Basic programmers* appendix that I didn't have the background for.

Dan's partner at Apress, Gary Cornell, made sure that I had everything I needed to write this book. Gary patiently answered my questions all through the very long writing process, and I think of him as a friend I've never met.

Grace Wong, Apress's managing editor, fielded all my formatting questions and special requests with aplomb and clarity. This book wouldn't be a physical artifact without her. I'd like to thank my copy editor, Jennifer "Scourge of the Which" Lind, for her light touch. Janet Vail and Susan Glinert took the manuscript from Word document to camera-ready copy; Tony Jonick turned my rough sketches into handsome illustrations.

I've received an immense amount of help from Borland and the Borland community throughout the process of researching and writing this book. Danny Thorpe and Chuck Jazdzewski of Borland's R&D department provided authoritative answers to many of my questions. Karen Giles of Borland's Developer Relations arranged inside access while Kylix was under development. Several other members of the Borland team—including one particularly helpful person who wishes to remain anonymous—provided much appreciated answers, insights, and suggestions.

I'd also like to thank Hallvard Vassbotn for his detailed, helpful comments on several chapters. Mark Duncan of Borland's R&D department, Nick Hodges, and Jeroen W. Pluimers also read and commented on various parts of the manuscript. They all helped make the book better, and a free copy doesn't seem like much payment for their time!

Most of all, I'd like to thank Ray Lischner, who did the technical review on this book. As anyone who's read his excellent books can imagine, Ray did an absolutely splendid technical review. His comments were accurate, insightful, and always helpful. Naturally, any mistakes that remain are entirely my fault.

—October 2001,
Santa Cruz, California

Contents at a Glance

Appendixes 849

Contents

List of Tables

CHAPTER 0

Hello Kylix

CHAPTER 0

Hello Kylix

NEWTON FAMOUSLY SAID, "If I have seen farther than others, it is because I have stood on the shoulders of giants." This made a big impression on me as a boy, and to this day I still think that the highest thing one can do is to add something to the store of human knowledge. Spreading some of that knowledge a bit more widely is probably the next best thing. So, when I set out to write a programming book, I don't want to write a book that will be pulped in six months. I want to write a classic like K&R or The Camel Book that will go through multiple printings and multiple editions. When a small bookstore only carries one Kylix book, I want it to be this book.

The hallmark of programming classics seems to be that not only do they have something for everyone, but that they are also worth keeping around for reference. A Kylix classic needs to introduce Kylix to people who've never used Delphi or Borland Pascal, and it needs to introduce Linux programming to experienced Windows programmers. At the same time, it needs to be deep and well organized, so that it's the first place you turn when the on-line help isn't enough.

These are not necessarily easy goals to reconcile. I think I've done a pretty good job, but of course only you can make that decision.

This book is a tutorial or a guide, in the sense that each section assumes nothing but intelligence and a broad programming background. I explain Pascal so that someone who's done lots of programming, but not in Pascal, can understand every detail of the language and how and why to use it. I explain Kylix's tools and libraries so that anyone who's done any GUI programming can understand the architecture and how to use it. I explain Linux programming so that anyone who knows what files and processes are can understand how files and processes work under Linux.

At the same time, this book is a reference in that it's full of details and is organized so as to make it easy to find answers to specific questions. This is a big book, but that's because it covers a lot of material, not because it's full of white space and screen shots. I don't expect you to remember everything you read; I expect you to come away from each chapter and each section with enough of a feel for the material to go out and get in trouble. Then come back to check the details. I've provided lots of tables and a global index to them, and every chapter has a detailed table of contents that lists every section heading.

About Kylix

Kylix is a Linux application development environment. You can't use Kylix to write device drivers or kernel modules, but you can use Kylix to write any type of Linux application. Kylix can do small command line utilities that read standard input and write standard output. Kylix can do system daemons. Kylix can do database apps and web server apps. And Kylix is simply the best and most productive environment in which to write Linux GUI apps.

Kylix is an amazing product. Most programming projects are considered successes if they get one key thing right. Kylix gets a whole basketful right.

- Kylix compiles and links incredibly quickly. The longer an environment takes to compile and link, the more likely you are to make a lot of changes after each test run. The more changes you make, the harder it is to figure out which change caused new problems. Kylix compiles so quickly that it's entirely practical to test each change as you make it. It's not uncommon for Kylix programmers to compile and test tens and hundreds of times a day.

- Kylix has a capable and tightly integrated source code debugger. Combined with fast compiles, debugging with Kylix is almost as easy as debugging with an interpreter. Easier, perhaps, as the GUI environment means that you don't have to keep typing commands.

- Kylix is full of cross-referencing tools that make it easy to understand both applications and the libraries they use.

- Kylix is built on top of Object Pascal, a language that is fully as expressive as C++, but that is much easier to read and that offers stronger protection against careless errors.

- Kylix uses Borland's CLX [Component Library, cross platform] library, a 4th generation GUI object library. The old OWL [Object Windows Library] reflected lessons learned from TurboVision. Delphi's VCL [Visual Component Library] reflected lessons learned from OWL. In turn, Kylix's CLX reflects lessons learned from the five iterations of the VCL. Kylix's CLX is powerful, extensible, clean, and elegant.

- Kylix and the CLX let you write cross-platform applications with a native feel and native capabilities. There's nothing 'lowest common denominator' about the CLX.

Kylix and Delphi users absolutely love their development tool. I think this book will show you why.

About this book

This book is divided into four sections, plus a series of appendices. Section 1, *Object Pascal*, introduces the Object Pascal language as used in Kylix and Delphi 6. While this section is written to be accessible to people who have never programmed in Pascal, or who haven't done so for years and years, even experienced Delphi programmers will find it worth their while to read Section 1. Unlike some other Kylix books, this book is not in any way a "port" of a Delphi book. Section 1 describes Kylix's Object Pascal as an organic whole; it wasn't originally written for a 16-bit Pascal with material inserted for each new feature as it came along.

> *Experienced Delphi programmers will especially appreciate the material on operator overloading and custom variants in Chapter 3.*

Section 2, *Kylix*, describes Kylix as a programming environment and as an object library. Again, while programmers who have never used Delphi can profitably read this section, I also think that very few experienced Delphi programmers will think that they wasted their time in reading Section 2. The material on basic form design in Chapter 5, *Using Kylix*, for example, includes an explanation of "Anchors" that might change the form design practices of anyone who learned Delphi before version 4. Chapter 6, *Visual objects*, explains the fundamentals of widgets and drawing surfaces, as well as detailing what's new in the CLX and how the CLX differs from the VCL. Chapter 7, *Foundation objects*, similarly describes utility code from streams and collections to threads and semaphores for both those who've never used the VCL equivalents and for those who chiefly need to know what's new. Chapter 8 is a wide-ranging overview of *Library procedures* that will surprise anyone who thinks they know their way around SysUtils. Chapter 9, *Component creation*, covers less new ground, but even here there are a few Qt-specific techniques that old hands may find useful.

Section 3, *Linux*, is an introduction to Linux programming: "Linux for Windows programmers", by a Windows programmer. There's probably little here for an experienced Linux or Unix programmer, but Linux newbies will find that Chapter 10, *Unix*, contains what they need to know about files and processes, memory mapping and signals, as well as environment strings and user ids. Chapter 12, *Regexes & scripts*, introduces POSIX regular expressions and their use in Kylix applications, as well as basic shell scripting. Chapter 13, *X & Qt*, contains an architectural overview of X and Qt.

Section 4, *Projects*, contains a couple of extended examples, showing Kylix in action. The first three sections contain plenty of short bits of sample code that illustrate key concepts—and the tarball that you can download from the Apress web site contains the working projects that the sample code comes from—but Section 4 contains two complete applications and detailed walkthroughs of their most interesting features.

What you **won't** find in this book is anything about databases and web servers. Obviously these are key topics, but if I'd covered them well, this book would have been much bigger and much later. If you like this book, let Apress know that you want a companion volume.

Downloading the sample code

There are scores of sample projects in this book. For the most part, I only print the few most interesting lines of each. To run the projects and/or read the code that I don't print, you'll have to download the tarball from the Apress web site, and install it on a Linux machine.

You can get the code by going to the "Downloads" section of the Apress web site, www.apress.com, where you'll find complete download and installation instructions.

I urge you to download the sample code. While I've made every effort to keep the book self-contained, so that you can read it away from a computer, you'll find that some of the more complex examples can best be understood by loading them into Kylix and using some of its powerful cross-referencing tools.

Also, all the sample code—from the code that demonstrates various useful techniques to the utility units in my lib/ directory and the six sample components—is distributed under a license that lets you make any use of the code that you like, so long as you leave my copyright notice in the source code.

> **Note**
>
> *The rest of this chapter is a hands-on, Getting Started tour in a "Click here, type this" style that I don't use elsewhere. Since many people skip prefaces, I don't say anything here that I don't say else-where—but taking the tour should give you some of the feel of actually using Kylix.*

Basic text applications

This seems like a good place to do the traditional Hello World application. We all know that it bears little resemblance to any real program—but as the simplest of all possible programming tasks, it can shed a certain light on the nature of the environment.

If you've downloaded the sample code and installed it as *per* directions on the Apress web site, you'll be able to load the two projects in this section by loading the ch0/console *project group*. You can do this by using the menu command File ➤ Open (ALT+F then O), which will bring up a standard "Open" dialog. Navigate to the ch0 directory and select the "File type" of "Project Group file (*.bpg)". You should see two groups, console.bpg and GUI.bpg, as in Figure 0-1.

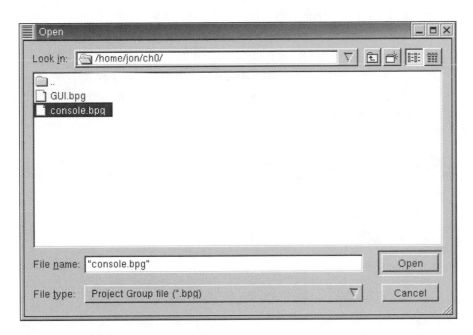

Figure 0-1. The File ➤ Open dialog

Select console.bpg, and click the Open button. If you now do View ➤ Project Manager (CTRL+ALT+F11, if your desktop and/or window manager don't intercept that), you'll see the two projects in the console group, stdout and stdin, as in Figure 0-2.

Select Project ➤ View Source, and you'll see the following stdout project code.

```
program stdout;

{$APPTYPE CONSOLE}

begin
  WriteLn('Hello, world.');
end.
```

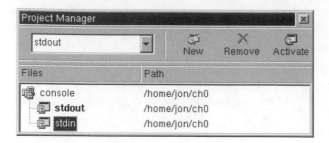

Figure 0-2. The console group

Of course, it's really rather pointless to bother loading a project this simple from the sample code, but I mention it here so that you'll know what I mean in future chapters when I say things like "the stdout project in the ch0/console project group."

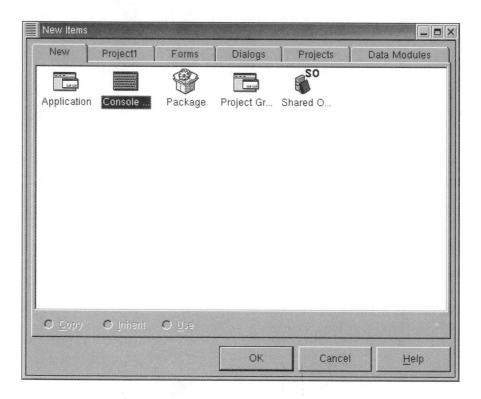

Figure 0-3. New Console Application

Anyhow, you can see that the stdout project is quite simple. In fact, Kylix wrote most of it for me. When I clicked the Project Manager's "New" button and selected "Console Application" as in Figure 0-3, Kylix supplied

```
program Project1;

{$APPTYPE CONSOLE}

29.667 pc

end.
```

I just entered the WriteLn('Hello, world.'); statement, and then did a File ➤ Save Project As[1] to give the project a name.

Standard output

Try running the stdout project. Press F9 or click on the green arrow (Figure 0-4) on the main Kylix window. The caption on the main Kylix window will briefly show "[Running]", but that's about it (unless you launched Kylix by typing startkylix & in a console window that is visible underneath Kylix).
What gives? The program writes 'Hello, world' to stdout, but (unless you launched Kylix by typing startkylix & in a console window that is visible underneath Kylix) you can't see that from within the Kylix IDE.

Figure 0-4. The run button

If you open a console window and run ch0/stdout, you'll see that the program writes to the console. You can see that the program's writing to stdout (and not to stderr or to some weird, non-standard device) by piping it to less, or by redirecting it to /dev/null, as in Figure 0-5.

```
[jon@BlueFat ch0]$ ls -l stdout
-rwxrwxr-x    1 jon      jon         17304 Aug  3 17:31 stdout
[jon@BlueFat ch0]$ ./stdout
Hello, world.
[jon@BlueFat ch0]$ ./stdout > /dev/null
[jon@BlueFat ch0]$ █
```

Figure 0-5. Console output

---

1. As a general rule, you should never change the program clause yourself; you should always change it *via* File ➤ Save Project As. The filename and the program name *must* agree. File ➤ Save Project As will assure that they do, and will also update the Project Manager.

Within Kylix, you can capture stdout and stderr by selecting Run ➤ Parameters and checking Use Launcher Application in the middle of the Local tab, as in Figure 0-6. Once you do this, when you run the stdout project, Kylix will pop up a "KylixDebuggerOutput" window that shows the 'Hello, world'. output then goes away when the application terminates.

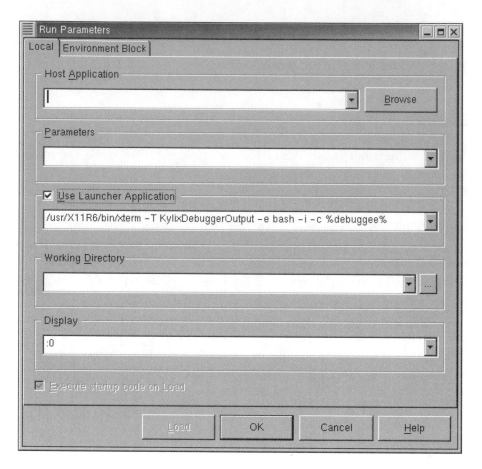

Figure 0-6. The Run ➤ Parameters dialog

You can force the KylixDebuggerOutput window to stay open by adding a –hold to the xterm command line. That is, if you change the Run ➤ Parameters dialog's Launcher Application command line from

```
/usr/X11R6/bin/xterm -T KylixDebuggerOutput -e bash -i -c %debuggee%
```

to

```
/usr/X11R6/bin/xterm –hold -T KylixDebuggerOutput -e bash -i -c %debuggee%
```

the KylixDebuggerOutput window will stay up until you click on the window frame's close button. This lets the output of a run stick around as long as you need it.

In general, all Kylix applications can write to stdout. One way to debug your GUI applications is to add WriteLn statements (see Chapter 8) that write status messages, and capture the messages in a Launcher Application window.

Standard input

Just as WriteLn writes to stdout, so ReadLn reads from stdin. (You can also use these routines to read and write text files. See Chapter 8.) The stdin project in the ch0/console project group

```
program stdin;

{$APPTYPE CONSOLE}

var
  Line: string;

begin
  while not EOF(Input) do
  begin
    ReadLn(Line);  // from stdin
    WriteLn(Line); // to stdout
  end;
end.
```

reads a line at time from stdin, and writes it back to stdout as long as there is data on stdin. If you run this project from within Kylix, be sure to check Run ➤ Parameters / Use Launcher Application so that you can close stdin by typing CTRL+D in the Launcher Application window. If you don't, you'll have to reset the program with Run ➤ Program Reset, or CTRL+F2.

Since the stdout program reads stdin and writes stdout, and since ReadLn ignores the carriage return in Windows-style line breaks, you can use the stdout program to convert Windows text files to Linux text files. ch0/stdout < windows.txt > linux.txt will read a file, windows.txt, with

Windows-style CR-LF line breaks and write it to linux.txt with Linux-style LF-only line breaks.

Kylix console apps are good Linux citizens and small, too: the stdout executable is only 17,304 bytes, and the stdin executable is only 18,672 bytes.

Visual programming

Of course, it's nice that Kylix can produce such compact console apps, and that it can compile them so quickly, but the real point of Kylix is not "Turbo Pascal for Linux" but visual programming and GUI apps. In Kylix, "visual" means much more than a syntax-highlighted IDE. Of course, the editor **does** do syntax highlighting, and of course it's all totally configurable—but that's only the beginning. Kylix is built around *components*, objects that you select from a palette and drop onto a *form* (window) that your users will see, or onto a data module that the rest of your code will use. Components have various *properties* that control their behavior and/or appearance, and you can either use the default values or change them at design time, using the Object Inspector. (Component properties are stored in text files, so that you can manage them with your favorite version control system.) Components also have *events* that fire when various things happen, so that all you have to do to respond to a button press, or to write some cleanup code that's fired when a window closes is to double-click on the event in the Object Inspector and write the appropriate code in the event handler. Not only will Kylix automagically handle all the tedious, mistake-prone, minutiae of creating, placing, and initializing your widgets, it will also do so behind the scenes; you only have to write the parts that actually do something new, and your code isn't cluttered with lots of machine-generated boilerplate.

The best way to experience this is to read this book (at least Chapters 1 through 5) and then just dive in and learn to use Kylix by trying to apply what you've read about. If you'd prefer a bit of a guided tour first, let me take you by the hand and walk you through a GUI "Hello World" application. If you've no taste for such things, you may prefer to skip the rest of this chapter.

Start by selecting File ➤ New Application from the main menu. (Alternatively, you can select File ➤ New, and double-click New Application from the New Items dialog.) This will produce a large window, labeled Form1, colored gray with a grid of black dots. Now click on the Standard tab of the component palette, then on the label component, which has an A glyph. This will make the glyph "stay down" as in Figure 0-7, which indicates that clicking on the form will place a new instance of this component on the form.

Figure 0-7. The label component

Click near the top left of the form's gray, dotted *client area*, which is the part that you have full control over. The A glyph on the Standard tab of the component palette will go back to its usual flat look, and the form will show the text Label1, surrounded (and partly obscured) by eight black boxes. These are grab points; they let you change the visual component's size.

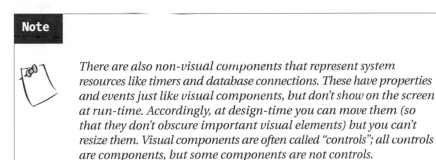

Note

There are also non-visual components that represent system resources like timers and database connections. These have properties and events just like visual components, but don't show on the screen at run-time. Accordingly, at design-time you can move them (so that they don't obscure important visual elements) but you can't resize them. Visual components are often called "controls"; all controls are components, but some components are not controls.

If you move the cursor over one of the label's grab points, the cursor will change shape to show that this is a point that you can grab to resize the label component. If you click and drag (move the mouse while holding down the left button) on one of these grab points, you change the label's size, as in Figure 0-8. The label's size matters if the label's background Color is different than the form's background Color, or if the label's Caption is too big to fit. Similarly, this new form is quite a bit bigger than you need, so you can click and drag on the lower right corner to make it a more reasonable size.

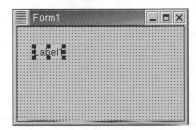

Figure 0-8. A form with a new label

You can load this version as hello1 *in the* ch0/GUI *project group.*

At this point, you have an application that you can compile and run, even if it doesn't exactly meet even our rather pathetically minimal GUI-Hello-World spec. Pressing F9, or selecting Run ➤ Run, or clicking on the green arrow in Figure 0-4 will compile and run the app. Or, rather, it *would* if this were an old, established app with its source code saved to disk. At this stage, the new code and the new form only exist in memory, and when you try to run it, Kylix will popup a dialog asking what name to save Unit1 under. You can accept the default Unit1 name and the default directory, or you can specify a more descriptive name and whatever directory is appropriate. For now, try saving Unit1 as "Main". You may not be able to easily see this, because the form and the next popup may be in the way, but Kylix will automatically change the editor tab labeled "Unit1" to "Main", and it will also change the code in the editor window that says unit Unit1; to say unit Main;.[2] Once you've named Unit1, Kylix will popup the File ➤ Save Project As dialog, to ask what name you'd like to give Project1. Again, you can keep the default Project1 name, or you can give the project a better name. Since the executable's name will be the same as the project name, you should pick your project name with some care. "Hello" or "HelloWorld" might seem sensible enough, but remembering that the Linux file system is case sensitive and that the Unix world historically has favored short, meaningless (or, more euphemistically, "terse") names, we'll name this little app hello. Doing so creates a file, hello.dpr; when Kylix proceeds to compile it, it will create an executable file named hello.

> **Note**
>
>
> *One common mistake on Unix systems is to name a program* test. *The shell has a built-in function that will shadow your executable, unless you specifically call it as* ./test. *Sooner or later, everyone forgets this and wastes several minutes trying to figure out what's going on.*

When you have named the project file, Kylix will compile the application. Depending on your settings (see Chapter 5), this may be silent, or it may popup a status box that will show you the compiler's progress. Regardless, if the compile is successful (and we certainly haven't had any room to make a mistake yet), Kylix will run the new application within its powerful and flexible

---

2. As with program clauses and File ➤ Save Project As, as a general rule you should never change the unit clause yourself; you should always change it *via* File ➤ Save As. File ➤ Save As will make sure that the filename and the unit name agree, and will also update the make information that you can see in the Project Manager and that's saved in the project (.dpr) file.

source code debugger. We don't have any occasion to use the debugger, here; at this stage it just means that we can edit the code while it's running (though this won't have any effect on the running program) and that we will return to the IDE when we close the program by clicking in the close box on the caption.

Since we're only running this application as a test along the way, note the differences between the way the form looks when it's running (Figure 0-9) and when it's in the form designer—no background grid and/or grab points—and then close it up.

Figure 0-9. The same form, as a running app

Note

If you try to run ch0/hello *from a console window, you may get the message "error while loading shared libraries: libqtintf.so: cannot load shared object file: No such file or directory". This means that you haven't set the LD_LIBRARY_PATH environment variable by running the* kylixpath *script, as described in the README file in the directory that you installed Kylix to.*

When you run hello from the IDE and then close it, focus may return to the design-time form. (This depends on your window manager and on whether you ran the application by pressing F9 or by clicking on the green run arrow.) If the design-time form **doesn't** have the focus, click on to give it the focus.

Press F12 to see the code for this window, and press F12 again to get back to the form. If the Object Inspector is not visible, press F11 to bring it up. Click on the label to select it, and press F11 to bring up the Object Inspector. You'll see that the dropdown box at the top of the Object Inspector shows that Label1: TLabel is selected. You can use this dropdown box to select the

Object Inspector	⬜✖
Label1: TLabel	▾

Properties | Events

Align	alNone
Alignment	taLeftJustify
⊞ Anchors	[akLeft,akTop]
AutoSize	True
Bitmap	(None)
BorderStyle	bsNone
Caption	Label1
Color	clBackground
⊞ Constraints	(TSizeConstraints)
Cursor	crDefault
DragMode	dmManual
Enabled	True
FocusControl	
⊞ Font	(TFont)
Height	15
HelpContext	0
HelpKeyword	
HelpType	htKeyword
Hint	
Layout	tlTop
Left	20
Masked	False
Name	Label1
ParentColor	True
ParentFont	True
ParentShowHint	True
ShowAccelChar	True
ShowHint	False
Tag	0
Top	24
Transparent	False
Visible	True
Width	38
WordWrap	False

All shown

Figure 0-10. The Object Inspector

form or any other component on it; you can also simply click on a component to select it. Clicking on a component and hitting ESC will select that component's Parent; every visual component is contained within (clipped to) a Parent, and is only visible when its parent is visible. In this case, the only components are the TForm and the TLabel you dropped on it, and the only Parent is the form itself, but there are controls like panels, group boxes, and tab sheets that can contain (be the Parent of) many other controls.

Now, select the form, and press F11 if the Object Inspector (Figure 0-10) is not visible. You can see that the form has many properties and many events. As you explore Kylix, you'll find that some of these properties and events are common to many different types of components (yes, a form is itself a component), while others are specific to TForm's. For now, all we care about is the Caption property. Click on it, and change it to "Hello, World". You'll see that the Caption changes on the form as you type in the Object Inspector. Now, click on the label, and change its Caption to something like "Kylix makes this easy!". You'll see that the label's text changes on the form as you type in the Object Inspector. You'll also see that the label's size—as shown by the grab points—changes with the text, because the AutoSize property is True by default. If you had changed AutoSize to False (by double-clicking on it or by selecting a value from the combo box that appears when you click on AutoSize) you'd see that the text is clipped if it exceeds the size you've set.

Hit F9 again, and you'll see that—without writing any code—we've created a simple GUI app that pops up a Hello, World message (Figure 0-11).

You can load this version as hello2 *in the* ch0/GUI *project group.*

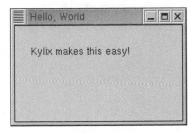

Figure 0-11. Hello, World

Centering and resizing

Of course, even by the low standard of Hello World apps, this trivial app leaves a lot to be desired. For example, unless you very carefully fiddled with the label's Top and Left properties, it probably is somewhere off-center, looking sort of ugly. Select the label, and choose View ➤ Alignment Palette (Figure 0-12) from the main menu. If you move the mouse cursor over the ten buttons on this palette, you'll see tool tip windows that tell you that the buttons control the horizontal and vertical alignment of the selected component(s). The center two are labeled 'Center … in window' and will center the selected component(s) in their Parent window. In this case, that means that they will center the label on the form; if the label were on a compound component like a panel, the alignment buttons would center the label on its Parent panel.

Figure 0-12. The Alignment Palette

If you try this, you'll quickly find that the Alignment Palette only centers the component(s) statically, at design-time. If you change the size of the app's window at run-time, the label stays where you placed it at design-time, despite the increase or decrease in white space to the left and bottom. You can make it dynamically center itself—again without writing a line of code—by following these steps:

1. 'Open up' the label's Anchors property, either by double-clicking on it or by clicking on the plus sign to the left of it. Then set both akRight and akBottom to True (Figure 0-13).

⊟Anchors	[akLeft,akTop,akRight,akB
akLeft	True
akTop	True
akRight	True
akBottom	True

Figure 0-13. The Anchors property

2. Set the label's AutoSize property to False.

3. Set the label's Alignment property to taCenter, and set the label's Layout property to tlCenter.

You can load this version as hello3 *in the* ch0/GUI *project group.*

What this does is to make the label's right and bottom edges keep a constant distance from its Parent's (the form's) left and right edges as the Parent (the form) is resized. (Leaving AutoSize on will defeat this.) Since the text is drawn horizontally and vertically centered within the label's bounding box, this will automatically center the text as you resize the window.

If you wanted the label to stay centered at the top of the form, instead of centered on the form, you would leave the Anchors.akBottom Layout set to False. Then the label would keep a constant height, but its width would float with its Parent's. Clever combinations of variously Anchor-ed and Align-ed (see Chapter 5) controls and panels let you write applications that can exhibit rather sophisticated resizing behavior, without your having to write any code.[3] To be honest, in this case, you could do the dynamic centering without touching the Anchors property, simply by setting Align to alClient. However, an alClient label won't work so well if there were any other controls with the same parent—and I wanted to introduce Anchors as they really simplify many common effects, like buttons that stay in the bottom right of a window as it's resized.

---

3. Of course, that sophisticated resizing behavior does require a lot of code—but it's already been written for you. You inherit it just by using CLX objects. You don't have to clutter your code with lots of complicated (and hard to get right or to change) positioning formulae.

Not resizing

Of course, dynamic centering effects are more than a bit of overkill for a simple popup message box like this Hello World application. It doesn't really make a lot of sense to allow the user to change the size of the window. If you double-click on the form's Constraints property, or click on the plus sign to the left of it, it will 'open up' and reveal four new properties: MaxHeight, Max-Width, MinHeight, and MinWidth. If you set both MaxHeight and MinHeight to Height, and both MaxWidth and MinWidth to Width, you will find that you can no longer resize the window when you run the application.

You can load this version as hello4 *in the* ch0/GUI *project group.*

> **Note**
>
>
>
> *Delphi users may expect to be able to set the BorderStyle property to fbsSingle or fbsDialog to get the non-sizable effect. However, under most Linux window managers, these act no differently than the default fbsSizeable. Future releases of Kylix may fix this, perhaps using the Constraints mechanism to simulate what under Windows is a simple style bit.*

Similarly, it doesn't make a lot of sense for this app to have a minimize or maximize button. However, both border style and frame buttons are a matter of window manager "hints". Kylix can suggest to the window manager that this form should be non-resizable and should only have a close button, but the window manager is free to ignore the request. You should probably set BorderStyle and BorderIcons for the benefit of users with working windows managers, but you should also write code that works well with broken window managers.

Backgrounds, colors, and fonts

By default, the form's background color will be a medium gray. As we all know, black text on a gray background is harder to read than black text on a white background because it has a lower contrast ratio—but it's great for 3D effects, because you can use darker and lighter grays for shadow and highlight colors. Windows stole this idea from NeXT years ago, and it's become a *de facto* standard. However, the Web made colored and bitmapped backgrounds popular, and the 3D effect is less ubiquitous than it was.

If you select the form, and click on the Color property, you'll get a list of color names. Some of these are 'absolute' colors, like clRed, clWhite, and clBlue, while others like clBackground and clForeground depend on system settings. Double-clicking on the Color property brings up a color dialog that allows you to pick any color you like. (You can bring up this dialog from your own programs.)

By default, the "Kylix makes this easy!" label will have the same background Color as its Parent. You can, however, set its Color independently—presumably to some contrasting color—to draw attention to the text. When you do this, the ParentColor property changes to False from its default True.

> **Note**
>
> *If you change a component's Color, all its child controls that have ParentColor = True change Color as well. In turn, all dutiful children of the changed child controls will change Color, and so on. Once the ParentColor is False, changing the Parent's Color will have no effect on a control, even if the two had the same color. To reestablish the automatic link between a control's Color and its Parent's Color, set ParentColor back to True. This will also reset the control's Color to its Parent's current Color.*

If you set the form or the label's color to a relatively dark color, you may find that the default font becomes hard to read. If you open up the form or the label's Font property, you can change the size, color, and font family. If you open up the Font's Style property, you can add or remove the standard bold, italic, underline, and strikeout attributes. The label (and, indeed, all controls) has a ParentFont property that works just like the ParentColor property; when ParentFont is true, changing the parent's font changes the child's font, while when ParentFont is False, the child's font does *not* track changes to the parent's font.

Finally, all Qt controls (TWidgetControl) have a Bitmap property that works just like a Web page's background bitmap; Qt controls can have a tiled bitmap background, as in Figure 0-14, or a solid color background. So, to make our little Hello World app look just like a Web page:

1. Select the form's Bitmap property; click on the ... button; select a bitmap, like ch0/paper.bmp; click OK.

2. Set the label's Transparent property to True.

You can load this version as hello5 *in the* ch0/GUI *project group.*

Figure 0-14. So 1995!

A close button

You might be thinking that it's really pretty lame to have to click on the frame widget to close the app. Let's add an "I know" button that closes the app.

Kylix offers three basic sorts of buttons: TButton, TBitBtn, and TSpeedButton. TButton is a basic, text only button; you can't add a Glyph to it. TBitBtn is basically just like a TButton, except that it can have a bitmapped Glyph. TSpeedButton offers specialized properties that make it useful for graphical versions of radio buttons and check boxes.

These differences are all covered in great detail in the on-line help. For now, just click on the Additional tab of the component palette, and select the TBitBtn icon (Figure 0-15). Place it on the form below the "Kylix makes this easy!" label. It will still be selected, so now hold down the shift key and click on the "Kylix makes this easy!" label. This should select both the button and the label. You'll know that it did, because the dropdown box at the top of the Object Inspector will go blank, and the properties listed will be limited to those that both (all) the selected components have. This can be useful for doing things like setting a group of fonts, or making sure that a series of components all have the same Width, but all we'll do here is use the Alignment palette.

Figure 0-15. TBitBtn is on the Additional tab

Click on the second button from the left on the top row of the Alignment Palette, "Align horizontal centers". This will put all the selected controls on a common center line. Now, click on the middle button on the top row of the Alignment Palette, "Center horizontally in window", to move that common center line to the middle of the window. Finally, click on the middle button on the bottom row of the Alignment Palette, "Center vertically in window" to vertically center the selection.

Undo the multiselect by clicking on an uncovered part of the form, then select the TBitBtn. (Alternatively, you can just select the TBitBtn from the dropdown at the top of the Object Inspector.) Set the Kind property to bkOK. This sets the Caption and ModalResult property, but it also selects a stock bitmap that seems appropriate here. Now, set the button's Caption to "I know". The Kind property will revert to bkCustom, but the Glyph will remain as a green check. If the form still has a bitmapped background, keep things simple by clearing it; select the Bitmap property, click on the ... button, and press the Clear button.

You can load this version as hello6 *in the* ch0/GUI *project group.*

Try running the app now, and pressing the "I know" button. The button will go down, but the app won't close. We need an OnClick handler that calls the form's Close method.

To create an OnClick handler, either double-click the button in the form designer, or click on the Events tab of the Object Inspector and double-click on the OnClick event. Kylix will take you to the code editor, with the cursor right in the BitBtn1Click method. Just type Close; and hit F9. Now, clicking the button will close the app. If you set both the Default and Cancel buttons to True, hitting either Return (Default) or Esc (Cancel) will click the button, and thus close the app.

Anchoring the button

Finally, what happens if the form's Constraints are all 0, so the form can be resized, and the button's Anchors are all True? Will the button float gracefully the way the label did? Try it. Did it act like you expected?

'Positive' anchors are useful for keeping buttons near an edge, or for keeping an edit box a certain offset from the left and right edges as it grows and shrinks, but you can't use them to center a bordered control like a TBitBtn. For that matter, the anchored label would look decidedly strange if it had any BorderStyle besides bsNone.

However, if you set both left and right Anchors to False, a component will shift left or right as its Parent resizes so that the component's center point is always at the same proportional position relative to the Parent. That is, if the component was centered on the form before the resize, it will be centered on the form after the resize. If the component's center was at 25% of the Parent's Width (*eg*, at 100 out of 400) before the resize, it will be at 25% of the Parent's Width after the resize (*eg*, at 125 out of 500). The same is true of Parent Height. Thus, a component that's centered on its parent and that has all Anchors set to False will always be centered on its Parent.

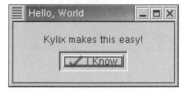

You can load this version as hello7 *in the* ch0/GUI *project group.*

Figure 0-16. Hello7, original size

If you select both the label and the button, and set all their Anchors to False, both controls will maintain their relative position as the form is resized. You may like this 'expanding universe' look (Figure 0-17), but odds are that you'd rather that both the text and the button stay in the center as we resize the form. To do this, we'll have to drop a panel 'behind' them, and then set the panel to stay centered.

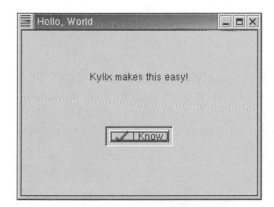

Figure 0-17. Hello7, in 'galactic expansion' mode

To do this, click on the Standard tab (Figure 0-18) of the component palette, and select the TPanel component, which will be the second from the right, unless you've installed third party packages or edited the palette order in Tools ➤ Environment Options. You can just click on the form to add a panel with the default size at the click point, or you can click and drag to set both the top-left and bottom-right corners. Set the Caption to an empty string, and set the BevelOuter to bvNone.

Figure 0-18. TPanel is on the Standard tab

Now for a little magic: press ALT+F12 (or right-click on the form designer, and select "View as text"), to see the form's .xfm file in text mode. At the bottom, you'll see some lines like

```
object Panel1: TPanel
    Left = 12
    Top = 20
    Width = 169
    Height = 77
    BevelOuter = bvNone
    TabOrder = 2
  end
```

Select the lines from object Panel1: TPanel through TabOrder = 2 and cut them out with CTRL+X or SHIFT+DEL. *Don't* cut the end line! Move the cursor to the start of the object Label1: TLabel line, and paste the panel text with CTRL+V or SHIFT+INS. Now, edit the Top and Left lines for the label and the button to something like

```
object Label1: TLabel
    Left = 1
    Top = 2
```

and

```
object BitBtn1: TBitBtn
    Left = 4
    Top = 16
```

You can load this version as hello8 *in the* ch0/GUI *project group.*

so that the controls will be visible in the panel. Press ALT+F12 again, and you will see the label and button *on* the panel. Use the Alignment Palette to center the controls on the panel, and the panel on the form, then set all the panel's Anchors to False. When you run the program now, the label and button will stay in the center as you resize the form.

Note

One man's white magic is another man's black magic. Some people don't like to edit the .xfm file by hand. They would prefer to visually cut the label and the button, drop a panel on the form, then paste the label and the button onto the new panel. I find this more error-prone than .xfm editing—it can be difficult to multi-select a lot of components without selecting components that you didn't mean to—but tastes differ. That's why There's More Than One Way To Do It.

Sharing bitmaps

Now, for one last fillip before we bid this sadly over-built Hello World application *adieu,* let's add back the background bitmap. Go ahead and set the Bitmap property for the form, panel, and button to the same bitmap image. You'll notice when you run the application that Qt handles child controls' Bitmap properties well, so that you don't see a boundary at the top left of the panel where the bitmap is redrawn starting at its top-left corner; rather, the background is continuously tiled across the whole form.

The only problem here is that the executable now contains three copies of the bitmap! Note the size of the executable, then clear the Bitmap property of Panel1 and BitBtn1, and add this OnCreate handler to Form1:

```
procedure TForm1.FormCreate(Sender: TObject);
begin
  Panel1.Bitmap  := Bitmap;
  BitBtn1.Bitmap := Bitmap;
end;
```

Note

Some people are willing to ship code with identifiers like Form1 and Panel1 in it. Most people deprecate this practice. While some go so far as to always *give every component a descriptive name, I think the compromise of* usually *giving every component a descriptive name is probably the most common. The practice I follow is that while I usually set the Name property (Chapter 5) as soon as I drop a component, I'll certainly set it as soon as I find myself writing code that refers to the component. In the interests of keeping the 'Now do this' instructions to a minimum, I haven't done that in this subsection, but I'll do it in the rest of the book.*

You can load this version as hello9 *in the* ch0/GUI *project group.*

The application will act just the same as it did before, but the executable will be smaller, because it will only contain one copy of the bitmap. The running program will also consume fewer system resources, because assigning one bitmap to another simply creates a new reference to the existing data; it doesn't make a new copy of the bitmap.

Section 1

Object Pascal

A language tutorial and reference

KYLIX IS WRITTEN IN OBJECT PASCAL, and you will write your Kylix applications in Object Pascal. This section is primarily intended for those of you who have never used any Pascal; who have never used a Borland Pascal; or who may not have used a Borland Pascal since Turbo Pascal 2 or 3, years and years ago. For that matter, even experienced users of Delphi for Windows may find some useful information or perspective here.

Note

When I say "Kylix" in this book, I mean the applications development system as a whole: the language, the IDE [Integrated Development Environment], and the various libraries. When I speak of "Pascal," I'm referring to "Standard Pascal," the base language as defined by Wirth in 1971. "Object Pascal," or "Kylix's Object Pascal," refers to the particular dialect of Pascal used in Kylix.

This section is a tutorial in the sense that it's meant to be read through as a continuous 'narrative,' but it moves fast and assumes that you have significant programming experience. Most explanations are in terms of how something is done in other languages, not in terms of what is being done, or why you would want to do it. Simultaneously, this section is a reference in the sense that the discussion of each language feature aims to be as complete and self-contained as possible.

Some of you may be looking at Kylix through the distorting lens of a strong pro-C, anti-Pascal religious prejudice. I can only ask you to keep an open mind. Kylix's Object Pascal is *not* the Pascal you think you know. It's a real language—modular, object oriented, and fully capable of twiddling bits and diddling pointers. There's nothing you can do in C++ that you cannot do in Object Pascal. And the Pascal version will be clearer and easier to maintain.

Still, Object Pascal *is* a strongly-typed language. You can use typecasts and untyped parameters to bend the rules, but generally you have to use each piece of data the way you promised to when you declared it. The key to learning to love Object Pascal is to stop thinking "this blasted toy makes me keep saying what I *mean* before I can *say* it" and to think of declarations as a software engineering tool: they make your code clearer and help it evolve gracefully.

C++ pretends that you're infallible.
Pascal knows that you make mistakes.

Scalar datatypes

CHAPTER 1
Scalar datatypes

IN MATHEMATICS, a *scalar* is a quantity that has only magnitude. It's generally described as a contrast to a *vector*, which has both magnitude and direction. Similarly, computer languages like Kylix's Object Pascal often call their simple, primitive datatypes scalars, because they're just a single, bare value. While you may care about a scalar's internal structure under special circumstances, normally you operate on it as a whole, using the primitive operations built into Object Pascal.

Object Pascal's scalar datatypes are roughly divided into *ordinal* types and all the other types. As the name implies, ordinal types are ordered; it makes sense to speak of one being greater than or less than another. Another key feature of ordinals is that they have *unique neighbors*. For example, 4 is the smallest integer greater than 3, just as 2 is the largest integer less than 3. 4 succeeds 3, just as 2 precedes 3. There are no other integers between 2 and 3, or between 3 and 4. This is **not** true of types like *strings* and *floating point* (real) numbers that are ordered but not ordinal. 'Joho' is greater than 'John', but so are 'Johnnies' and 'Johnson'. 3.1416 is greater than 3.1415, but so are 3.14159 and 3.141592654. With the types that are ordered but not ordinal, you can always (up to the limits of string sizes and floating point representations, at least) construct a new value that lies between any two values.

Ordinal types include *booleans, enumerations,* and *subranges,* as well as the familiar *integers* and *characters*. Non-ordinal types include floating point numbers and strings, which are ordered, as well as *pointers* to both data and to code, which are not ordered. (As a special case, the C-style PChar and PWideChar string pointers (below) **are** ordered.)

Ordinal types

As a group, the ordinal types receive special treatment in Object Pascal based on the way that they have unique neighbors.

- There are operators that increment or decrement an ordinal variable and there are operators that return an ordinal value's predecessor or successor, but there are no comparable operators for string or floating point variables or values. The ordinal operators have a syntax that resembles a subroutine call, but they actually generate very efficient inline code. (Operators are covered in Chapter 2.)

- You can use ordinal values as indices to static arrays or as members of sets, but you can't use string or floating point values as static array indices or as members of sets. Static arrays don't have to be indexed by numbers starting at 0 as in C: you can have an array indexed by characters, arrays indexed by enumerations, or arrays indexed from 3 to 75. (Arrays and sets and other data structures are covered in Chapter 3.)

- You can use any ordinal type as a for loop control variable, but you can't use string or floating point types as a for loop control variable.[1] Especially in conjunction with array indexing, it can be very convenient to loop from 'A' to 'Z', or from Red to Blue. (Loops and other control structures are covered in Chapter 2.)

Booleans

Object Pascal, like C++, Java, and recent versions of Visual Basic—but unlike Perl and all but the latest versions of C—has a *boolean* datatype. Relational and logical operators return True or False, not zero or non-zero. Boolean values can be simply the constants True or False; or the results of a relational operation; or the results of boolean expressions, which combine one or more boolean values using *boolean operators* like and, or, and not. Boolean values can be saved in a boolean variable or used in conditional statements.

There are actually four distinct boolean types. The most basic type, Boolean,[2] is the Pascal native type. All relational and logical operators return

---

1. More precisely, you can use any 32-bit or smaller ordinal type, which precludes int64. Additionally, the compiler uses signed integer arithmetic while generating for loop code, so even loops with Cardinal (32-bit unsigned integer) control variables can only include High(integer), or 2^{32}-1 iterations.

2. Pascal is case **in**sensitive. It does not care if you say "boolean", "Boolean" or even "booleaN". In practice, most people use the convention that keywords (type, var, if and so on) are all lower-case, as are the single word fundamental types like boolean and integer. Symbolic names like True and False, Index and Color are usually capitalized like proper nouns. PhrasesRunTogetherWithoutSpaces are done (unlike Java) in "camel caps", where the first letter of each word is capitalized, as in SmallInt and LongWord. This is just convention, and there's nothing at all to stop you from saying something like This AND That when you want the operator to really stand out.

   While I will generally stick to convention in the extended code samples, inline code snippets are monospaced, like <tt> text in an HTML document. Too much of that in a paragraph is ugly and hard to read, so I will often use the normal, proportional font to talk about, *eg*, "the Boolean datatype" or "the Integer datatype" rather than "the boolean datatype" or "the integer datatype". Treating the type name like a proper noun will help make it clear when I'm talking about the programming construct and not the general concept of booleans or integers.

a Boolean, and whenever you need to store a boolean value in your programs, you should declare it as a Boolean.

Boolean is the simplest of all the ordinal types. A boolean value can only be True or False. `True > False`, so the built-in Boolean datatype is basically equivalent to the user-defined enumeration

```
type Boolean = (False, True);
```

One consequence of this is that `ord(False) = 0` and `ord(True) = 1`. (The Ord() operator is covered in Chapter 2.) As in Table 1-1, you can take advantage of these equivalencies to avoid branching by writing expressions that do arithmetic with the ordinal value of a boolean expression. (You should always comment this sort of thing carefully, as it's not the most readable construct in the world.) Similarly, an `array[boolean]` of strings or numbers can often be used in place of branches to make your code smaller, faster, **and** clearer.

Table 1-1. Avoiding branches with boolean expressions

Code	Comments
`var CrLfMode: boolean;` `Inc(Index, 1 + ord(CrLfMode));`	Steps Index by 1 if `CrLfMode` is False and by 2 if it is True.
`const Plural: array[boolean] of string = ('', 'es');` `Format('%d potato%s', [Count,  Plural [Count <> 1]]);`	Returns '1 potato', '2 potatoes', and so on.

The other three boolean types—`ByteBool`, `WordBool`, and `LongBool`—are provided primarily for compatibility with libraries written in languages that use the zero / non-zero convention. They are, in some ways, `ShortInt`, `SmallInt`, and `LongInt` types (that is, signed 1, 2, and 4-byte integers)—except that you can't do arithmetic with them, you can set them to `True` and `False`, and you can use them in conditional statements and boolean expressions as if they were normal booleans. Note, however, that while `Ord(CompatibilityBoolean = True)` will always be 0 or 1, you can **not** rely on `Ord(CompatibilityBoolean)` being only 0 or 1 as with a normal Boolean. While Object Pascal code that sets one of the compatibility booleans to True sets all bits (see Table 1-2), any non-zero value is also interpreted as True. You should only use these three types to interface with other languages; operations on a native Boolean are smaller and faster than operations on the three compatibility booleans.

Table 1-2. The four boolean types

Type	Size	Ord(False)	Ord(True)	Notes
Boolean	1 byte	0	1	The type to use unless you're talking to other languages
ByteBool	1 byte	0	-1	True results from other languages may differ
WordBool	2 bytes	0	-1	True results from other languages may differ
LongBool	4 bytes	0	-1	True results from other languages may differ

Characters

We all know this story: Once upon a time, characters might be 7-bit ASCII or EBCDIC, but they all fit in an 8-bit byte. Lots of code was written on this basis, from 128-byte or 256-byte character translation tables to string code that stepped pointers by 1. This worked fine as long as virtually all the computers in the world were in the USA, but started to get distinctly creaky as Europeans wanted to be able to use characters with accents like é, or national currency symbols like £. Standards came and went, mostly *de facto* standards, like the IBM PC character set. Ultimately, international standards committees agreed on the Latin-1 encoding, which handles most Western European language characters, and is today the default character set for the World Wide Web. Those of us who moved from DOS to Windows programming grumbled a bit about having to swap one extended ASCII for another, but for the most part we adapted.

Of course, there's more to Europe than Western Europe, and there's more to the world than Europe and the Americas. There are many more than 256 glyphs in use, worldwide. Accordingly, the International Standards Organization created ISO 10646, a 32-bit Universal Character Set, or UCS.

There are many ways that 8-bit code can coexist with the 32-bit UCS. For example, Latin-1 is a strict 8-bit subset of the 32-bit UCS. There are also various quoting mechanisms you can use to represent UCS glyphs in the context of strings of 8-bit bytes. For example, Windows uses Multi-Byte Characters Sets [MBCS] to represent Russian or Far Eastern characters. In a MBCS string, some characters are represented by one byte and others by more than one byte. Windows MBCS formats are examples of what the ISO calls "UCS Transformation Formats", or UTF. There are many different possible UTF's; the one that Linux uses is called UTF-8.

You don't really need to be concerned with the details of the transformation format unless you're writing word processing software; most of us just need to know that a string's length may be longer than its display length, while a single keyboard key may take two or three UTF-8 elements to store, and so on. Since both UTF-8 and Latin-1 are ASCII extensions, you should have no problem transferring text files between Windows and Linux machines, so long as they use only 7-bit ASCII; some 'high-bit characters' will need to be converted.

Note

The UTF-8 FAQ says that the lead byte of any multi-byte sequence will be a length byte between #$C0[3] and #$FD, and that the trailing bytes of a multi-byte sequence will all be between #$80 and #$BF. It doesn't say anything about bytes between #$80 and #$BF without a lead byte. I've done experiments with Windows text files saved to a Linux share that seem to indicate that high-bit text that doesn't follow the UTF-8 quoting rules is treated as if it's Latin-1. That is, the high-bit characters look normal when I cat *Windows text files in both text mode (CTRL+ALT+F1) consoles and in GUI terminal windows, and when I open the files in a Kylix code window. I don't think these experiments are conclusive, and urge you to do your own tests and research if you need to share a lot of non-ASCII text files between Linux and Windows. See* http://www.cl.cam.ac.uk/~mgk25/unicode.html, *the "UTF-8 and Unicode FAQ for Unix/Linux" for more information.*

Unicode, as used in Kylix's WideStrings, is a 16-bit subset of the 32-bit UCS. It avoids the issue of mapping from one 8-bit character set to another by having enough room for just about every character and symbol used in written languages and mathematical notation. (It, too, is running out of room, which is why UCS is a 32-bit standard, but as of the middle of 2001, there still aren't any 'high-word characters' defined.) Whether any given application should use 8-bit UTF-8 or 16-bit Unicode depends largely on what it does and where it will be used. If the application is going to be used mostly in America, and for the most part strings are handled as atomic entities (assigned and compared as whole strings; rarely ripped apart character by character), the fact that Unicode takes roughly twice as much room as UTF-8 will probably tip you towards UTF-8. If the application is going to see a significant number of European or Asian characters, and has to do a significant amount of character-by-character processing, the fact that each Unicode character is the same width as every other (*i.e.*, word N is also character N, which is not necessarily true with UTF-8), will probably push you to use Unicode.

---

3. #$C0 is the character corresponding to the hexadecimal number C0, char($C0).

Object Pascal supports both 8-bit `AnsiChar`'s and 16-bit `WideChar`'s. These are known as *fundamental* character types, because the distinction is grounded in the processor architecture. There is also a *generic* character type, `Char`, which you should use whenever you are dealing strictly with old-fashioned ASCII, as it will always be the type that is best suited to the processor and operating system.

Note

 Char is the same as AnsiChar under Kylix version 1, but you should not write code that assumes this is the case: On other Unixes and other CPUs, it may make more sense to handle Char as a WideChar. Use the SizeOf() operator rather than assuming that a Char takes a single byte.

AnsiChar and WideChar are not *assignment compatible*. That is, Kylix will not let you assign an AnsiChar variable to a WideChar variable, or a WideChar variable to an AnsiChar variable. To convert between character types, you need to use a *cast* operator:

```
var
  AC: AnsiChar;
  WC: WideChar = #$1001;

begin
  AC := AnsiChar(WC); // Discards the high byte; AC = ^A
  WC := WideChar(AC); // Adds a null byte; WC = #$0001
end.
```

The above example also illustrates two of the three ways of specifying character values. While you will normally specify 'keyboard character' values as single character strings (unlike C++, Object Pascal uses the same syntax for characters and strings) like `'A'`, this syntax doesn't work well for characters that aren't on your keyboard, or that aren't distinguishable in the font you use for editing. For the traditional ASCII control characters, the most convenient notation is the caret notation, as in `const LF = ^J;`. For other characters, there's a numeric syntax where you can specify a character by prefixing its ordinal value with the # character. That is, `^A` is the same as `#1`, and the Unicode character `'£'` is the same as `#163` or `#$A3`. (`#$A3` uses the Object Pascal hexadecimal notation that you'll see more of in the *Integers* section of this chapter, and in examples throughout the book.)

Enumerations

In many programming situations, you want to be able to refer to a group of values by symbolic names, but you don't really care what bit pattern the computer uses for each value. For example, a font may have Bold, Italic, or Underline attributes. A color might be Red, Green, Blue, or Puce. Your code will be clearer if you refer to these by name instead of arbitrary numeric or character constants, but you don't care if Red is 'really' 0 or 5 or 100—what matters is that it's not Green.

This is where *enumerations* are used. An enumeration (often abbreviated as *enum* in the C world) is a user-defined ordinal type. That is, it has the same properties as all the other ordinal types—each element of an enum is less than subsequent elements and greater than prior elements, and each element (except the first and last) has a unique predecessor and a unique successor—but there is no built-in Enumeration type like the built-in Boolean or Char types. You create new enumerated types by declaring them like

```
type
  Colors = (Red, Green, Blue);
```

In this case, Red < Green and Green < Blue, Succ(Red) = Green as does Pred(Blue), while Low(Colors) = Red and High(Colors) = Blue. (The Succ(), Pred(), Low() and High() *ordinal operators* are covered in Chapter 2.) Sometimes you don't really care about the ordering of your enumerated values, but often you do. For example, the first three elements of a function return enum may be success codes, while the subsequent values are failure codes.

```
type
  BufferFlushCodes = ( bfcNoPages, bfcSinglePage, bfcMultiplePages,
                       bfcDiskFull, bfcHardwareError, bfcOtherError );

const
  LastSuccessCode  = bfcMultiplePages;
  FirstFailureCode = Succ(LastSuccessCode);
```

Given this, any value <= LastSuccessCode is a success code, while any value >= FirstFailureCode is a failure code. Defining FirstFailureCode as Succ(LastSuccessCode) like this means that there is only one point in the code that can get out of synch with the definition of the BufferFlushCodes enum: If LastSuccessCode is valid, so is FirstFailureCode. (See the sections on *Subranges* (later in this chapter) and on *Sets* (in Chapter 3) for other ways of implementing this sort of categorization.)

While you normally don't care what the underlying bit pattern is for each symbol in an enumeration, it's important to realize that the compiler does assign each one a unique numeric value. That is, when you write code like `ThisColor := Green`, the compiler actually generates the same code as if ThisColor was a numeric variable and you had written `ThisColor := 2`. If you wrote

```
type
  Colors  = (Red, Green, Blue);
  Lefties = (Red, Pink, Green);
```

you would have Green in two different positions in two different enums. When the compiler saw Green, it wouldn't know if it should be 1 or 2. Thus, no enum can contain the same symbol as any other enum. (Object Pascal's *units* (see Chapter 4) act somewhat like C++ *namespaces* and Java's *packages* so that you can, in fact, use the same name in two different units, and qualify it with the unit name (*eg*, `ThisUnit.Red` and `ThatUnit.Red`) in case of any ambiguity—but you should try to avoid this.) This is why all the BufferFlushCodes start with bfc—not only does it help you remember that, *eg*, bfcSinglePage is a buffer flush code, it helps prevent collisions with a SinglePage symbol from another enum.

By default, enums are stored in the most compact possible form. That is, an enum with less than 257 values will only take a byte, and an enum with more than 256 values but less than 65537 values will be stored in a word. If you're doing mixed-language programming, you can use the {$Z} pragma (see Chapter 4) to force enums to always be at least 16 or 32 bits.

Assigned enumerations

C and C++ programmers should note that Pascal's enumerations are quite different from C++'s. While C++ does allow you to write code like `if (ThisCode <= LastSuccessCode)`, that's only because it treats enumerations as a sort of collection of constants. There is no C++ analog to `Succ(LastSuccessCode)`, because C++ enumerations can have 'holes' in them. Normal Pascal enums, by contrast, always start at 0—Ord(Low()) always equals 0—and the Ord() of each symbol is 1 greater than its Pred()ecessor's Ord().

Kylix also supports C++ style enumerations, where an identifier can be followed by an equal sign and an integer.

```
type
  Bitmap  = (Foo = 1, Bar = 2, Bleah = 4, AndSoOn = 8);
  Aliases = (Red = 0, Green, Blue, Indigo = 2);
```

This has been done primarily to make it easier to write Qt bindings. I can't recommend strongly enough that you avoid this form, and use it very rarely.

- It changes the concept of ordinal: There are elements besides the last that do not have a valid, named successor. To avoid seeing assigned enumerations as "breaking" the concept of ordinals, you have to think in terms of named and anonymous members of an ordinal range. Some members of the range `Low(Bitmap)..High(Bitmap)` have names; others are anonymous and can only be referred to *via* circumlocutions like `Bitmap(6)`.

- Similarly, if you declare an `array[Bitmap]`, it will have 8 elements (`Bitmap(1)..Bitmap(8)`) in it, not 4. Some of these elements can't be addressed except by casting an integer constant to a Bitmap, or by a loop that runs from Low(Bitmap) to High(Bitmap).

- It's not really a very good match for the C++ semantics. In C++, you can combine enumerated elements with code like `Foo|Bar`. Object Pascal's assigned enumerations are still enumerations—non-numeric ordinals—so you have to write clunky code like `Ord(Foo) or Ord(Bar)`.

Integers

The integers are the most complex of all the ordinal types. In addition to the ordinal operators that we've seen so far, integers can be used with the familiar arithmetic operators (addition, subtraction, multiplication, and division), and they overload the logical operators to do bitwise logic. In addition, like chars and booleans, integers come in several varieties, with similar behavior but different capacities.

Kylix makes the same sort of generic *vs* fundamental distinction with integers as with characters. The `Integer` and `Cardinal` types are the generic signed and unsigned integers. These types represent the best fit to the processor and operating system, and you should use them unless you specifically need a narrow integer to talk to hardware or legacy code, or you need to represent huge numbers, like the free space on a hard drive. In 32-bit implementations like the current Linux and Windows versions, Integer and Cardinal are 32-bit numbers, with the familiar range of –2,147,483,648 to 2,147,483,647 and 0 to 4,294,967,295. Under future 64-bit Kylix's, Integer and Cardinal will presumably be implemented as 64-bit numbers.

The fundamental integer types include signed and unsigned 8, 16, and 32-bit numbers; the only 64-bit integer, `int64`, is a signed type. If you are concerned about code size or speed, you should avoid the 16-bit SmallInt and Word types. Intel chips in their 32-bit modes require an extra byte for each 16-bit instruction, and instruction length is the single most important factor[4] in how long an instruction will take to execute. Similarly, the int64 type is currently implemented as a *double precision integer.* This means that addition and subtraction take two inline instructions, which isn't so bad, but multiplication and division are implemented *via* subroutine calls.

Table 1-3. The fundamental integer types

Type	Bytes	Minimum	Maximum	Generic Equivalent
ShortInt	1	-128	127	
Byte	1	0	255	
SmallInt	2	-32,768	32,767	
Word	2	0	65535	
LongInt	4	-2^{31} ($-2{,}147{,}483{,}648$)	$2^{31} - 1$ ($2{,}147{,}483{,}647$)	Integer
LongWord	4	0	$2^{32} - 1$ ($4{,}294{,}967{,}295$)	Cardinal
Int64	8	-2^{63} ($-9{,}223{,}372{,}036{,}854{,}775{,}808$)	$2^{63} - 1$ ($9{,}223{,}372{,}036{,}854{,}775{,}807$)	

In general, when you do arithmetic with integers, the result will have the type of the widest operand. That is, if you add an Integer and a ShortInt, you'll get an Integer. If you multiply an Integer by an Int64, you'll get an Int64. This behavior can cause problems when the result is too big for the original type. For example, two billion plus two billion is four billion, which is too big to fit in an Integer variable. Kylix offers two sorts of run-time checking to help catch problems like this during development. Arithmetic overflow checks (controlled with the {$Q} pragma—see Chapter 4) will alert you when an intermediate result is too big for the result type, while range checking (controlled with the {$R} pragma) will alert you when the final result is too big for the variable you're trying to store it in. Both can be very helpful, but of course they can only find problems if you actually execute the code with large enough values during testing. The ultimate defense against arithmetic errors is thinking about the possible range of input and result values, as you're coding.

Most integer arithmetic is done in 32-bit registers, using the generic Integer datatype. Smaller datatypes are coerced to 32-bit values as they're loaded into the registers, and the intermediate results are all calculated as 32-bit values. Any overflow checking is done when the result is written back to an 8-bit or 16-bit result variable. That is, you never need to write code like

---

4. Yes, of course it's more complicated than that. Instruction timings vary between processor models, and the bandwidth of both memory and cache affect timings. But, as a *rule of thumb,* "instruction length" is a remarkably good predictor of code speed. A five byte instruction is generally faster than a six byte instruction or two three byte instructions.

```
var
  A:    integer;
  B, C: ShortInt;
begin
  A := integer(B) + integer(C);
end.
```

to prevent overflow and/or loss of the high order result bits, as Kylix does this automatically.

The only times you might need to explicitly force a datatype conversion to avoid arithmetic overflows or errors is when the intermediate results won't fit in a 32-bit register. For example, if you're adding two large integers, you'll probably want to *promote* them to 64-bits to avoid numeric overflow. You can do this by casting one or both of them to an int64. As in the example above, Object Pascal casts look much like function calls, with the name of the type that you're casting to followed by parentheses around the variable or expression that you're casting. Thus,

```
var
  A:    int64;
  B, C: integer;
begin
  A := B + C;        // May well overflow
  A := int64(B) + C; // Can't overflow
end.
```

Finally, although many other languages support binary and octal constant values, Object Pascal only allows you to use decimal and hexadecimal. As you probably expect, a number like 42 without any special radix markers is assumed to be decimal. Leading zeroes are ignored, unlike in C where they mean an octal value. Hexadecimal numbers start with a $, not 0x or &h. Thus, $42 is the same as 66, and 42 is the same as $2A.

*You **can** use octal in inline assembler—see Chapter 2.*

Subranges

Subranges are a Pascal feature that you won't find in languages like C++, Java, Perl, or Visual Basic. A subrange type is a constrained ordinal: You declare it by specifying a high and a low value. (The values must be of the same type, obviously; you can't have a subrange from Blue to 'A', or 37 to '~'.) When you try to assign values to a subrange variable, the compiler does compile-time checks to make sure that the value isn't too small or too large, and can also do the same at run-time. Perhaps more importantly, a subrange type is an ordinal type like any other; you can get its High() and Low() values, you can use it as an array's index type, and so on.

Subranges are declared with a double dot between the low and high values. Thus,

```
type
  LowerCase   = 'a'..'z';
  SevenEleven = 7..11;

var
  Lower: LowerCase = 'a';
  AnyCase: char;

begin
  AnyCase   := Lower;    // This is fine; they're both Char's
  AnyCase   := 'z';
  LowerCase := AnyCase; // This is OK
  AnyCase   := 'Z';
  LowerCase := AnyCase; // This will cause a range check
                        // (exception or runtime error)
end.
```

Subrange variables act just like variables of the 'larger' type, except that assignment to them is range checked, when you throw the right compiler switch. You can always assign a value from a subrange to a larger type; you can assign values between 'intersecting' subranges, provided the values are in range.

```
type
  SevenEleven = 7..11;
  DoubleDigit = 10..99;

var
  Narrow: SevenEleven;
  Wider:  DoubleDigit;

begin
  Narrow := 10;
  Wider  := Narrow; // No type incompatability
  Narrow := Wider;  // ditto
  Wider  := 42;
  Narrow := Wider;  // Will range check
end.
```

Subranges are particularly useful in working with enums. We can improve on the earlier BufferFlushCodes example a bit:

```
type
  BufferFlushCodes = ( bfcNoPages, bfcSinglePage, bfcMultiplePages,
                       bfcDiskFull, bfcHardwareError, bfcOtherError );

const
  LastSuccessCode = bfcMultiplePages;

type
  BufferFlushSuccess = Low(BufferFlushCodes)..LastSuccessCode;
  BufferFlushFailure = Succ(LastSuccessCode)..High(BufferFlushCodes);
```

It's arguably clearer to test that `(ThisCode >= Low(BufferFlushSuccess))` and `(ThisCode <= High(BufferFlushSuccess)` than merely that it's `<= LastSuccessCode`—and it's certainly safer, if the enum might be divided into three or more subranges, like success, partial success, failure, and catastrophic failure. (See the *Sets* section of Chapter 3 for an even better way to handle this sort of test.)

Similarly, a subrange like

```
type
  ExtendedSlots = (Slot1, Slot2, Slot3, Slot4, NoSlot);
  Slots         = Low(Slots)..Pred(High(ExtendedSlots));
```

is particularly useful for the common case where you have an array indexed by Slots, but you need a special flag value for an IndexOf function to return when you search for a value that doesn't exist. Note that defining Slots using Low() and High() instead of actual values means that as your program evolves you can rearrange the Slots, or add new Slots, simply by editing ExtendedSlots. If you defined Slots as `type Slots = Slot1..Slot4`, you'd have to be sure to keep the declaration of Slots definition in synch with the declaration of ExtendedSlots.

One shortcoming of subranges is that Kylix automatically stores them in the smallest possible space. There is no analog to the {$Z} pragma that allows you to force short enums to be allocated 16 or 32-bits. Thus, `type MyWord = 0..$FFFF;` defines MyWord as being exactly equivalent to the standard Word type—right on down to the run-time performance penalty for working with 16-bit data.

Float point types

Intel versions of Kylix have three fundamental floating point types, the IEEE-754 64-bit Double and 32-bit Single precision floats, as well as the 80-bit Extended type, which corresponds to the FPU's internal representation. There is also the generic type, Real, which is currently the same as Double.[5] In addition, there are Comp, a 64-bit integer that uses FPU instructions instead of integer instructions, and Currency, a 64-bit FPU integer that's automatically scaled by 4 decimal places whenever it's used as a floating point number.

Kylix's on other platforms (such as Solaris or OS/X) may have different fundamental floating point types. In particular, while most RISC chips support IEEE Single's and Double's, few or none support the Extended type. Borland suggests that code that aspires to portability should only use the Single and Double types.[6]

Table 1-4. The fundamental floating point types

Type	Smallest	Largest	Significant Digits	Bytes
Single	1.5E-45	3.4E38	7 or 8	4
Double	5E-324	1.7E308	15 or 16	8
Extended	3.64E-495132	1.1E4932	19 or 20	10
Comp	-2^{63}	$2^{63}-1$	0	8
Currency	−922337203685477.5808	922337203685477.5807	4	8

5. In older versions of Delphi, Real's were a 48-bit software float, kept for compatibility with old Turbo Pascal code and data files. (You can still get this behavior with the REALCOMPATIBILITY pragma. See Chapter 4.) New code with a need to read and write old data files can use the Real48 type. No calculations are done in Real48 format; the run-time library contains only enough Real48 code to read it into a Double and to write a Double into a Real48. Doing any extended calculations (involving explicitly stored intermediates) with Real48's is thus very slow. Code that reads and writes Real48's should immediately convert it to a native type and do any calculations using the native types, only writing back to a Real48 for filing.

6. It's likely that Kylix on a processor that only supports 4-byte and 8-byte floats would still support the Extended type, as removing it would not only be much more complicated than simply making it the same as the Double type, but would also break lots of code. Thus, there is something to be said for regarding the Extended type as the "high precision generic".

Fundamental and generic float point types

Most calculations should be done with Double's, either explicitly or *via* the Real generic type. While they can be over twice as slow as Single's, they also have a significantly greater range and more significant digits than the Single type. You're more likely to encounter overflow, underflow, or rounding errors with Single variables, and so you should use them only where speed or memory consumption is of the utmost importance and you've checked that your calculations will not be affected by the reduced range and accuracy.

Conversely, you should only use the Extended type when you're quite sure that you know what you're doing. A 10-byte Extended takes three 32-bit bus cycles to read or write where an eight-byte Double takes only two, so Extended calculations are *ca* 50% slower than Double calculations. You're not necessarily buying all that much with that slowdown. The Extended type corresponds directly to the FPU's internal format—what the FPU converts Single's and Double's to when it loads them onto the FPU stack—but the extra range and precision were intended to assure that Double results are reasonably accurate even after a long series of calculations. Much as in high school science classes, where it makes no sense to do calculations to ten significant digits on measurements only good to two significant digits, the extra significant digits you get with an Extended may be pretty meaningless.

The Comp type is also deprecated, though for rather different reasons. It is a historical artifact from 16-bit implementations where using the FPU for 64-bit integer arithmetic was significantly faster than quad-precision integer arithmetic. In a 32-bit implementation, the double-precision Int64 is faster than the FPU, especially for simple operations like addition and subtraction. In addition, you can't use Comp with ordinal functions like High() or Pred(), nor can you use it with the Inc() and Dec() procedures. (See Chapter 2.)

The Currency type is implemented as a fixed-point (scaled) integer based on the Comp type. That is, it's treated as an integer whose last four digits are considered to be to the right of the decimal place. When you assign a floating point value to a Currency value, it's multiplied by 10,000; when you assign a Currency value to a floating point value, it's divided by 10,000. However, when you do arithmetic with a Currency value, it acts like an integer, which means that there's no rounding error in the last significant digits, and the books for your gigabuck enterprise will be accurate to the last (hundredth of a) penny.

Floating point expressions

Floating point numbers are stored internally much like a binary version of the *scientific notation* of high school chemistry and physics. Just as 3E8 is 3×10^8, so are floating point numbers stored as a *mantissa* and an *exponent*, and interpreted as mantissa $\times 2^{\text{exponent}}$. This allows the 32-bit Single and the 64-bit Double to represent numbers much bigger than 2^{31} and 2^{63}, but it comes at the cost of some lost precision. Two numbers that mathematically should be equal, like 17÷15103 and 18887÷16779432, will actually differ by 1.16E-10 if you do the calculations with Single's. As this unlikely pair of constants may suggest, floating point imprecision is not a huge problem: I had to write a search program to generate this pair. So, if you write code that tests floating point numbers for equality, it might seem to work, at first. Sooner or later, though, it will fail, when real use runs the right numbers through your equations. **Never** compare test floating numbers for equality! Use routines like the Math unit's[7] `CompareValue` and `SameValue` (Chapters 4 and 8) which use tests like `Abs(A - B) < Epsilon` where Epsilon is some small positive constant.

Loss of precision cuts both ways. Numbers that should be the same may actually differ slightly; numbers that should differ slightly may actually be the same. If you add `1E-100 + 1E-100`, the result will be 2E-100—but if you add `Pi + 1E-100`, the result will be Pi. All the significant digits in 1E-100 are too far to the right of the significant digits in Pi to make any difference at all. Any calculation that depends on detecting such a tiny change in value will fail.

Floating point arithmetic follows the same sort of result type rules as integer arithmetic: The result will be the same type as the widest input type. That is, a Single plus a Double is a Double; a Double divided by an Extended is an Extended. Types are automatically converted on assignment, so you can assign a Double value to a Single without any conversion; conversely, you can *not* use typecasts to convert a float point value from one format to another.

This automatic type conversion applies to integers, too. There is no need to explicitly cast an integer to a floating point type to assign it to a floating point variable, or to use it in a floating point expression. Thus, an Integer plus a Double is a Double, and an Integer divided by an Extended is an Extended. Conversely, you can not assign a floating point value to an integer variable; you have to explicitly specify the rounding strategy by calling a conversion function like Trunc or Round (Chapter 8).

Kylix has a number of standard floating point routines, like Sin() and Cos() as well as Int(), Frac(), Trunc(), and Round(). There are far too many of these functions to describe here; consult Chapter 8 for an overview and the online help for details. The standard routines are available to any program at any time, while for historical reasons equally useful functions like Log10() and ArcSin() are in the Math unit. If a math function doesn't seem to be available, it's probably in the Math unit.

---

7. Units are Kylix's module management syntax and are covered in Chapter 4. Briefly, by adding "Math" to the comma delimited `uses` statement in your source code, you will be able to use Math unit routines and constants in your code.

Special values

Not every possible bit pattern is a valid floating point number. The IEEE 754 standard defines two categories of invalid numbers—positive and negative infinity [INF] as well as "quiet" and "signaling" Not A Number [NAN] patterns. Most programs will never encounter these values. You'll never get a NAN or INF result unless you use a NAN or INF input; floating point overflow raises an exception instead of returning an INF value.

The rules which govern operations on infinite values are complex—5.8 - +INF is –INF, for example, while +INF - +INF raises an exception—so if you have some reason to explicitly inject +INF or –INF into your calculations, you should both handle exceptions *and* use the Math unit's `IsInfinite` function to test results.

NAN's are in many ways more interesting than INF's. They are somewhat like `Nil` pointers—a special value that means 'there's nothing here'. You might use a NAN to represent a required value that hasn't been supplied or determined yet, so that any calculations that depend on it are not valid. When you do calculations with "signaling NAN's", you will get a float point exception. However, calculations with "quiet NAN's" do not cause an exception—they simply return another quiet NAN. This allows you to implement spreadsheet-like behavior, where calculations on a #N/A return a #N/A. The `ch1/IEEE754` unit (you can get the sample code for this book from the Downloads section of the www.apress.com web site, if you haven't already done so) contains `QuietNan`, `SignalingNan`, `PositiveInfinity` and `NegativeInfinity` constants as well as an `IsNan()` function.

Note

Kylix's Math unit provides a NaN constant which corresponds to my QuietNan, but no SignalingNan. I also think the IsNan and IsInfinity routines in my IEEE754 unit are clearer than the equivalents in Borland's Math unit.

Strings

In some sense, strings don't belong in this section on scalar datatypes. They are very definitely a data structure, with a length field and an array of characters. At the same time, they are an intrinsic datatype, not a user-defined one, and we often operate on them as a single value (*ie*, not a collection of individual characters).

There are several different string types, just as there are several different integer types and several different floating point types. By default,[8] the generic String is the same as the fundamental AnsiString, a dynamically allocated, reference counted structure that can be up to High(integer), or 2^{32}-1 characters long. WideString is the same as String except that the characters are WideChar's, not AnsiChar's, and so it can only hold just over a billion characters. The older ShortString is a statically allocated structure that can hold strings up to 255 bytes long. Kylix also supports C-style null terminated strings via the PChar and PWideChar types, which have special syntax that simplifies their use and which permits easy mixing of Pascal and C-style strings.

All five string types share much of the same syntax. In general, string values are a sequence of characters in single quotes and control characters specified with the same sort of ^ and # syntax as with characters. Thus, 'string', ^M^J, #13#10, and 'Tan'#$233' Tachyon' are all string values.

There is no general \ escape mechanism as in C, but you can use a '' sequence (as in Table 1-5, below) to include a quote character in a string constant. Unlike in Perl, string constants cannot span multiple lines; the compiler insists on seeing a closing quote before a line break. You can use the + operator to combine multiple strings into a single compile-time string constant.

Table 1-5. Some string values

Code	Characters
'A simple string'	13
'Let''s escape'	12
'Inline'^I'tab'	10
'First line' + sLineBreak + 'Second line'	19 – assuming sLineBreak is a Linux ^J

The Length() function returns the length of any string type. Note that the length is measured in characters, not bytes, and not (necessarily) glyphs. Copying a String to a WideString may change the length. The length of a string that contains UTF-8 escape sequences is the number of character positions in the string, which is greater than the number of glyphs; the length of a WideString is the number of displayable characters.

The three native string types contain a length field, so that Length() is a cheap, constant-time operation. That is, it takes no longer to call Length() on a

---

8.   The {$H} pragma (Chapter 4) allows you to map the generic String to the fundamental ShortString.

long string than on a short one. You can call Length() on C-style PChar and PWideChar strings that do *not* contain a length field, but this is **not** a constant time operation—it takes longer with long strings than with short ones—and it works only because Kylix will automatically translate a PChar or PWideChar when you assign it to a native string variable, or pass it to a native string routine. That is, calling Length() on a C-style PChar and PWideChar string does an implicit conversion to a temporary native string, then calls Length, and then discards the temporary string. In other words, do not use Length() on C-style strings—use the SysUtils unit's StrLen() instead.

Native string types

The generic String type is the type you will use most of the time. It can handle very long strings, so you can do things like load a whole text file into memory, and it is reference counted, so that string assignment and passing strings as parameters are cheap operations that don't involve making copies. The generic String is the same as the fundamental AnsiString; when you need Unicode strings, you should use the WideString type. The WideString type has exactly the same semantics as the String type—the only difference is that each character is a WideChar, not a Char, so a WideString takes twice as much space as a String and is somewhat slower because of the 16-bit data penalty.

You can refer to the string as a whole, or you can use subscript notation to refer to individual characters:

```
var
  Foo:          string = 'foo';
  Bar:          string = 'bar';
  FooBar:       string;
  First, Last: char;
  CStyle:       PChar;     // Pointer to Char
begin
  FooBar = Foo + Bar;      // Strings as scalars
  First := Foo[1];         // For historical reasons, 1st char is [1] -
                           // Foo[0] is a compile-time error
  Last := Foo[Length(Foo)];
  CStyle := PChar(Foo); // Points to the 1st char in Foo
  FooBar := '';            // An empty string, represented by a Nil pointer
  First := FooBar[1];   // A runtime error - range check {$R+},
                           // or dereferencing Nil {$R-}
end.
```

Kylix is not Delphi

The two 'huge string' types, String and WideString, are stored as pointers to a heap block that contains the length and reference count 'to the left of' a null-terminated string.[9] This means that you can always cast a huge string to a null-terminated string, to pass it to an API function or a C library. Do be careful, though—many string expressions in Kylix will actually be WideString expressions, as many CLX string properties are actually WideString's. The compiler will let you cast a WideString to a PChar, but the result *will* generally not be what you expect because most WideString's are full of 0-bytes.

Kylix is not Delphi

> **Note**
>
> *Long-time Delphi programmers may think that while the compiler will let you cast a string expression, like* PChar(Foo + Bar), *the expression result will have a reference count of 0. This would mean that the string value's heap block is on the free list, and might be overwritten by the time the function you called does anything with the PChar. This is no longer an issue: The string expression is saved to an anonymous local variable, so the PChar value is good until the routine returns and finalizes all its string variables.*

A string value can include null characters anywhere in the string. All the native string routines will work properly with nulls and any characters that follow them, and will always keep a null at Length()+1; C-style functions will usually treat an embedded null as the end of the string.

> **Note**
>
> *Empty strings are stored as a Nil pointer, but* PChar('') *is **not** Nil. While I've described PChar(StringValue) as a cast, and it certainly looks and acts that way, it really isn't. It actually involves a function call to a routine that returns the address of the first character if the string is not empty, or the address of a null byte if the string is empty. This allows you to choose between passing an empty C-style string or Nil to functions that distinguish between the two.*

Huge strings are reference counted. This means code like ThisString := ThatString does not make a copy of ThatString's (possibly multi-megabyte)

---

9. Delphi's WideString's are not reference counted the way Kylix's are. This means that WideString's are much 'cheaper' in Kylix than in Delphi.

data. Instead, it simply increments the reference count in the heap block that ThatString points to as it sets ThisString to point to the same address. When either ThisString or ThatString is changed—or goes *out of scope*—the reference count is decremented. When the reference count goes to the 0, the heap block is freed.

Note

There is no commonly accepted term for this process of decrementing the reference count and possibly freeing the data structure. This is unfortunate, as Kylix maintains reference counts for dynamic arrays and interfaces (Chapter 3) as well as huge strings. Since I don't want to keep repeating "decrement the reference count and free the data if the reference count is now 0", I'll speak of finalizing the reference as a shorthand. I think this makes sense, as you have to call the Finalize() procedure (below) in the few cases where Kylix can't do so automatically.

If you change part of a string—*eg*, `ThisString[5] := '*'`—the way Kylix does this for you depends on the reference count of the string. If the reference count is 1, then the variable you are changing is the only one that refers to this string value, so that copy will be changed. If the reference count is greater than 1, then at least one other variable refers to the same value, so Kylix does a *copy on write* operation: It makes a copy for the variable you're changing (with a reference count of 1), decrements the reference count of the original value, and then changes the new value. This all happens transparently, and you don't have to pay attention to it except in two cases:

1. When you cast a string to a PChar and pass it to a C function that may change it, you need to be sure that its reference count is 1. You can do this with `UniqueString(MyString)`.

2. When you use the bulk dynamic memory routines `GetMem()` and `FreeMem()` (Chapter 3 and 8), Kylix does not automatically call the setup and cleanup code for any strings in your data structures. You have to explicitly call `Initialize()` and `Finalize()`. Initialize sets any reference counted variables to Nil, so that explicitly setting them doesn't try to finalize random bit of memory, while Finalize does the same "decrement the reference count and free the data if the reference count is now 0" that is normally done automatically when a reference-counted variable goes out of scope.

Zero-length ('empty') strings are stored as a `Nil` pointer. This saves space, and allows code like `Foo <> ''` to compile to an inline `Ptr <> 0`,[10] but it also means that `Foo[1]` dereferences Nil and will generate a run-time error if Foo is empty. This is why you should write code like `if (Path <> '')` and `(Path[Length(Path)] <> PathDelim)` instead of `if Path[Length(Path)] <> PathDelim`. (This, in turn, is one of the chief reasons why you should be very careful of turning on "complete boolean evaluation" via the {$B} pragma discussed in Chapter 4.)

Standard string routines

There are several standard string routines in addition to Length(); the most ubiquitous are SetLength(),Copy(), Insert(), Delete(), and Pos().

SetLength

`SetLength(StringVar, NewLength)` will, obviously enough, set StringVar to NewLength characters long. If StringVar was longer than NewLength, SetLength will truncate it. If StringVar was shorter, SetLength will copy the old contents, but the value of the new, rightmost characters is undefined. If StringVar was empty ('' or Nil), SetLength will allocate space for a new string. In any case, so long as NewLength is greater than 0, the result is always a unique string (one with a reference count of 1) with a null character at `StringVar[NewLength + 1]`.

Note

`SetLength(S, Length(S))` *is perfectly valid, and guarantees a unique copy that can be passed as a PChar to an external routine that may modify it without any danger of modifying other copies of the same value. However, making a unique string is basically a side effect here: The prime purpose of SetLength is to change the string's length. If what you really want is just to guarantee uniqueness, without changing length, you should use* `UniqueString(S)`.

---

10. `WideString <> ''` is not optimized this way, at least in Kylix 1.0.

Copy

`Copy(StringVal, StartIndex, CopyLength)` returns a string (up to) CopyLength characters long, starting at StartIndex. If StartIndex is greater than Length(StringVal), Copy() will return an empty string, `''`. If StartIndex + CopyLength is greater than Length(StringVal), Copy() will only return Length() – StartIndex bytes. Thus, you will commonly see code like `Copy(S, Index, MaxInt)` (or, equivalently, `Copy(S, Index, High(integer))`) to copy the rightmost part of a string.

Copy() combines the functions of Visual Basic's Left\$, Right\$ and Mid\$ functions.

> **Note**
>
>
>
> *When working with UTF-8 strings, you need to be aware that Copy() assumes that characters are always 8-bit bytes. That is,* `StartIndex` *refers to a byte offset from the start of the string, and* `CopyLength` *is the numbers of bytes to return, not the number of glyphs. It's entirely possible to Copy from the tail-byte of one glyph to the lead-byte of another.*

Insert

`Insert(StringVal, StringVar, InsertAt)` will insert StringVal into StringVar, so that StringVal appears at position InsertAt in the new string. If InsertAt is greater than Length(StringVar), Insert() will simply concatenate the two strings. Note that Insert() is a *procedure* that modifies its StringVar parameter; it is not a *function* that returns the new value. Thus, the StringVal to be inserted can be a string expression, while the StringVar it is inserted into must be a string variable.

> **Note**
>
>
>
> *Insert, like Copy, assumes that characters in a String are always 8-bit bytes. It's perfectly possible to insert into the middle of a UTF-8 escape sequence. Although this may be exactly what you want to do, it's usually a mistake.*

Delete

`Delete(StringVar, Position, DeleteLength)` removes DeleteLength characters from StringVar, starting at Position. If Position is greater than

Length(StringVar), StringVar is not changed. If DeleteLength is greater than Position + Length(StringVar), StringVar will be truncated to the first Position-1 characters. As with Insert(), StringVar must be a string variable because Delete() is a *procedure* that modifies its StringVar parameter; it is not a *function* that returns the new value.

Note

Just like Copy and Insert, Delete works with String variables on a character basis, not a glyph basis.

The fact that Insert() and Delete() are value-less procedures, and not functions that can be used in string expressions, can be quite annoying. One consequence of it, though, is that they are relatively fast. For example,

```
function Replace1( const S:       string;
                   Start, Length: integer;
                   const New:     string ): string;
begin
  Result := S;
  Delete(Result, Start, Length);
  Insert(New, Result, Start);

end;
```

can be as much as 50% faster than

```
function Replace2(const S:       string;
                  Start, Length: integer;
                  const New:     string ): string;
begin
  Result := Copy(S, 1, Start - 1) +
            New +
            Copy(S, Start + Length, MaxInt);
end;
```

depending on the lengths of S and New.

Pos and AnsiPos

Pos(Probe, Value) returns the index of the first occurrence of Probe in Value. It doesn't support UTF-8 (or MBCS, on Windows) and you should generally use the SysUtils function AnsiPos(), instead. Both Pos() and AnsiPos() return 0 if Probe is not found, which makes them less than ideal for the common case of 'popping' the parts of a string to the left of an optional delimiter. In this case, a wrapper function that returns Length() + 1 is more useful.

```
function FirstMatch(const Value, Probe: string): integer; overload;
// Returns AnsiPos(Probe, Value), or Length(Value)+1 on no match
begin
  Result := AnsiPos(Probe, Value);
  if Result = 0 then Result := Length(Value) + 1;
end; // FirstMatch


function PopString(var S: string; const Delimiter: string): string;
// Returns the chars to the left of the Delimiter (or whole string);
// sets S to chars to right of Delimiter (or '')
var
  Index: integer;
begin
  Index := FirstMatch(S, Delimiter);
  Result := Copy(S, 1, Delimiter - 1);          // Return leftmost
  Delete(S, 1, Index + Length(Delimiter) - 1); // Remove from S
end; // PopString
```

Pos() and AnsiPos() always return the first match. Since popping the leading matches off a string involves *heap churning*, they're comparatively expensive. When you're doing a lot of string interpretation, you want to work with Start and Stop indices, and resume searching at the previous Stop point. You can't do this with Pos. You'll need to either use the PChar (C-style) functions (which can be slow with large strings) or use my lib/GrabBag workhorse, FindString.

```
function FindString( const Source, Target: string;
                           Offset: integer = 0): integer;
// Returns index of first incidence of Target, or Length(Source)+1 if not found.
// Starts search Offset chars into Source.
var
  SLen, TLen: integer;
  T1:         char;
  Match:      boolean;
  Index:      integer;
begin
  SLen := Length(Source);
  TLen := Length(Target);
  if (SLen > 0) and (TLen > 0) then
    begin
    T1 := Target[1];
    for Result := 1 + Offset to SLen - (TLen - 1) do
      if Source[Result] = T1 then // Found leading character of Target
        begin
        Match := True;
        Index := 2;
        while Match and (Index <= TLen) do
          begin
          Match := Source[Result + Index - 1] = Target[Index];
          Inc(Index);
          end;
        if Match then EXIT; // Found all of Target
        end;
    end;
  Result := SLen + 1;
end; // FindString
```

Short strings

The ShortString type acts just like a String, with four exceptions:

1. It's limited to 255 characters.

2. It can only hold AnsiChar's, not WideChar's.

3. It is *statically allocated*: It is stored as a length byte plus an array of characters, not a pointer.

4. It is not null terminated, and you cannot cast a ShortString to a PChar.

Otherwise, it is pretty much functionally equivalent to a huge string, in that you can use it with all the string routines discussed above. It is fully assignment compatible with huge strings; assigning a value to a short string that's too long to fit in it will truncate the value, without raising any run-time exception.

Declaring a `var Short: ShortString` allocates 256 bytes. `Short[0]` is the length byte (it is always equal to `Chr(Length(Short))`, while `Short[1]` through `Short[255]` hold the string value. Conversely, `type StringN = string[N]` (where *N* must be less than 256) declares a string type that can hold no more than *N* characters, and that takes *N*+1 bytes.

Note

The fact that a ShortString stores the length byte at offset 0 is why an AnsiString's first character is indexed at 1, not 0. A 0 origin would have been infinitesimally faster, and more consistent with dynamic arrays and open arrays, but would have broken old code.

Because short strings include a statically allocated array of characters, you can never generate a run-time exception by reading or writing a character that's within the array but outside the string (*ie*, beyond `Short[Length(Short)]`). That is, given a `var Short: string[10] = 'Jon'`, you can safely read and write the characters at `Short[4]` through `Short[10]`. However, you **can** get a range check by reading or writing `Short[I]`, when I has any value outside the range 0..10.

If you do need to pass a short string value to a PChar function, you can use the old Turbo Pascal trick of setting `Short[Length(Short) + 1] := #0`. This adds a trailing `#0` to the character array without affecting the length byte at `Short[0]`, so that the short string is simultaneously a valid Pascal string and a C-style string. The compiler won't let you cast a ShortString to a PChar, but you can simply pass the address of the first character—@ `Short[1]` is a PChar.

While the much greater capacity of huge strings makes them the string of choice for most purposes, the ability to declare a compile-time capacity-limited string is one of the reasons to occasionally use short strings even in new code. For example,

```
const SIfNotOne: array[boolean] of string[1] = ('', 's');
```

takes four bytes, not twenty seven[11]. More significantly, static allocation means that they are faster in some circumstances: *eg,* `Inc(Short[0]);` `Short[Length(Short)]` = `NewLastChar` is faster than `Huge := Huge + NewLastChar`.

Another reason to occasionally use a short string is that they are statically allocated, where huge pointers are dynamically allocated. In particular, a record (Chapter 2) that contains a short string contains the actual string value, while a record that contains a huge string contains only a pointer to the actual string. Thus, when you stream a record containing short strings to disk or shared memory, you can do a simple bitwise copy of the whole record. Conversely, when you stream out a record containing huge strings, you need to stream it an element at a time, streaming the huge strings as a length field followed by the actual string data. This means that records containing short strings are much easier to stream in or out than records containing huge strings.

Historically, the hand-crafted assembly language speed and ready availability of the standard string routines tempted many programmers to use short strings for short lists of small values. It's not exactly the world's cleanest coding practice but, I confess, I once wrote a DOS-based multitasker that used short strings for its task lists. However, in Kylix (as in Delphi 5 and 6) short strings are supported as a storage type only, much like the Real48 type. All short strings are converted to long strings before being used in any string expression, and are converted back to short strings on assignment. Short strings still have their uses, but using them does incur a speed penalty.

C-style strings

The dynamically allocated huge strings have a hybrid nature: They have a length field, so that operations on them are efficient, and they are null-terminated, so that they can be passed to C-style functions by casting them to a PChar. In addition, C-style zero-based character arrays like `array[0..N]` `of char` or `array[0..N]` `of WideChar` are treated specially by the compiler, in that they are considered to be 'like' a PChar. That is, you can use the name of a zero-based character array wherever a PChar value is expected and *vice versa*. This equivalence goes both ways, and you can use the index operator `[]` with a PChar just as if it were an array reference:

---

11. Two pointers, two reference counts, and two lengths at four bytes each, plus two trailing null chars and one 's' character.

```
const
  StringConstant = 'C-style string constant';

var
  ZString: array[0..Length(StringConstant)] of char = StringConstant;
  CString: PChar = ZString; // Initialized to Addr(ZString)
  String2: PChar;
  Native: string;
  C:      char;

begin
  Native := ZString; // automatic conversion to huge string
  Native := CString; // ditto
  C := ZString[1];   // '-', *not* 'C'
  C := CString[1];   // ditto
  String2 := CString + 8; // pointer arithmetic
  Native := String2;      // 'string constant'
end.
```

You can assign a C-style string value to a native string type, and the compiler will do the conversion *via* a transparent call to a function that does an inline StrLen() and then effectively calls the standard procedure

```
procedure SetString(var s: string; buffer: PChar; len: Integer);
```

that copies a C-style string of known length to an AnsiString. When you don't know the C-style string's length, simply assigning it to an AnsiString variable is your best way to convert it to an AnsiString. However, you can call SetString directly and, while the inline string length code is rather nicely optimized, calling SetString() directly is obviously more efficient than a simple assignment if you already know the string's length. To copy a native string to a zero-based character array (as opposed to simply casting a huge string to a PChar) you must use either the StrPCopy() function or the (much safer) StrPLCopy() function.

You can also do pointer arithmetic with PChar's. CString + 8 is the null-terminated string starting at the eighth character from CString. (If these were declared in terms of WideChar's, not AnsiChar's, the actual address would be stepped by 16 bytes, not 8.) Conversely, String2 − CString returns the integer 8. This means that String2 points to a spot 8 characters into CString: if String2 and CString were declared as PWideChar instead of PChar, String2–CString would still be 8, although Cardinal(String2) −Cardinal(CString) would be 16.

While there is a full suite of C-style string functions for working with zero-based character arrays, there's not an awful lot of reason to use a zero-based character array for anything except a space for C functions to return a string value. The native string types always 'know' their length, which makes them more efficient; the huge types are dynamically allocated, so you never have to worry about allocating too much or too little room; and you never ever forget to allocate an extra character for the null terminator. Since you can always cast a string value to a PChar to pass to various API functions, there's no need to allocate C-style character buffers to copy string values into before passing them to API functions.

Pointers

Like C, and unlike VB and Java, Object Pascal has full support for pointers. (Perl's references are, in some ways, more like Pascal/C pointers than they are like references in Java, Object Pascal, or C++, but since you explicitly can't do pointer arithmetic with them, it seems fair enough to call them references.) You declare a pointer type as *pointing to* some other type, with a caret on the left of the base type—*eg*, `type PInteger = ^ integer` —and you dereference it by putting a caret to the right of the pointer value—*eg*, `IntVar := IntPtr^ + 5`. By convention, pointer types begin with a capital P, but this **is** just a convention and not a compiler requirement. Standard types like PInteger are predeclared, but the declarations are precisely the same as those you can make yourself; the predeclared PInteger or PCardinal have no syntactic or semantic differences from `type PInteger = ^ integer;` `PCardinal = ^ Cardinal`.

The special value `Nil` means 'no address'—a pointer that contains Nil does not point to data. It happens to be the case that Nil equals pointer(0) — and the popularity of C probably assures that no OS in the foreseeable future will allow 0 to be a valid address in an application's address space— but you should always use Nil, and not pointer(0), just in case. Taking this one step further, the Assigned() operator is exactly equivalent to `<> Nil`, but is slightly clearer and combines better with logical operators—many people find a statement like `if Assigned(This) and (This^ <> 0) then` a bit easier to parse than `if (This <> Nil) and (This^ <> 0) then` simply because it doesn't start with a left parenthesis.

All the usual pointer address *vs* value distinctions apply; a value in a pointer is the address of a value, not the value itself. Reading or writing a pointer value (*ie*, without the caret to the right) reads or writes the address; reading or writing the pointed-to value (*ie*, with the caret on the right) reads or writes the current contents of the address. Fortunately, Object Pascal's *strong typing* means that, in most cases, the compiler can catch the mistake when you use a pointer type instead of a value type or *vice versa*; the code

simply won't compile. For example, you just can't write `IntValue := IntPtr` —
you have to write `IntValue := IntPtr^`. The single biggest exception to this is
that when the pointer is to a record (Chapter 3), you can treat pointers as
references, and write either `Foo^.Bar` or `Foo.Bar` interchangeably. Personally,
I don't like this 'reference-like' syntax and prefer to explicitly use the ^, but I
seem to be in a minority.

Strong typing also means that you can't assign a PInteger to a PCardinal;
they're of different types just as the addresses that they point to are. You can,
of course, explicitly cast a pointer from one type to another: *eg*, `PIntVar :=`
`PInteger(PCardVar)`. In addition, the standard `Pointer` type is an untyped
pointer compatible with all typed pointers. That is, you can assign any typed
pointer value to a Pointer variable, and you can assign a Pointer value to any
typed pointer variable. However, you can only dereference a Pointer value
when you are calling a subroutine with an untyped `var` or `const` parameter
(see the *Routines* section of Chapter 2), or to the right of the @ and Addr()
address operators.

`Addr()` and @ return the address of their argument, and are analogous to
C's & operator. By default, both return an untyped pointer (*ie*, a Pointer) that
is compatible with any typed pointer variable. The {$T+} pragma allows you
to distinguish between Addr(), which returns a untyped Pointer, and @,
which returns a typed pointer. That is, given `var Card: Cardinal; PInt:`
`Integer`, you could write `PInt := Addr(Card)` but not `PInt := @ Card`. Obviously, it
is nice to have both a typed and untyped address operator, and so I advise
you to use {$T+} in your code to enable the typed address operator.

For the most part, the address and dereference operators work together
just as you'd expect. For example, when `PIntVar = @ IntVar`, `PIntVar^ := 5` is
just the same as `IntVar := 5`. However, the way the address operators work
with pointer variables is a bit more complicated, and is an occasional source
of errors. For example, while @ `IntVar` is the address of the integer variable,
@ `PIntVar` is the address of the pointer to an integer variable. If

```
var
  IntVar: integer;
  PInt:    PInteger = @ IntVar;
  PPInt: ^PInteger = @ PInt;
```

`PPInt^ := 5` will not compile—it's `PPInt^^ := 5` that's the same as `IntVar := 5`.
This is all pretty standard—and not very common. Where it can cause particular confusion in the Object Pascal context is with *reference* types that
look like normal variables but are in fact pointers, like huge strings and
Chapter 3's dynamic arrays. Thus, @ `HugeString` is the address of the string
pointer while @ `HugeString[1]` and `PChar(HugeString)` are both the address of
the first character of the string's text.

Pointer arithmetic

Object Pascal allows a lot less pointer arithmetic than C does. The PChar and PWideChar types—which were introduced precisely in order to support C-style strings—are the only pointer types which may be used in conjunction with the + and – operators. On the other hand, Object Pascal has much better support for arrays (see Chapter 3) than C does, so you simply don't have the need for pointer arithmetic in Kylix that you do in a C or C++ environment. While C's pointer arithmetic was a fine fit for the architecture of the PDP-11, the 32-bit Intel architectures we use today include direct support for memory addressing models like `[Base+Offset*ItemSize]` for ItemSize's of 1, 2, 4, and 8 bytes, so that array indexing is, in fact, often faster than pointer stepping.

You can, however, use `Inc()` and `Dec()` (Chapter 2) to step any typed pointer by some multiple of its pointed-to type's size. That is, `Inc(PIntVar)` steps a pointer to a 32-bit integer by 4, while `Dec(PWordVar, 6)` decrements a pointer to a 16-bit word by 12. `Inc(PCharVar)` is exactly equivalent to `PCharVar := PCharVar + SizeOf(Char)`. Note that since the `pointer` type is generic and untyped, you can't use it with Inc() and Dec(). (For the same reason, you can take `SizeOf(TypedPtr^)`, but you can't take `SizeOf(UntypedPtr^)`.)

In rare cases, you need to step a typed pointer by something other than a multiple of its base size. Or, you might really really really want to do some pointer arithmetic in an expression, which the Inc() and Dec() procedures won't let you do. In these cases, you can cast your pointer to a Cardinal or PChar to do your arithmetic, then cast it back to the right type. You should do this rarely and with great caution, as the compiler has no way to check that the type you cast your result to **is** the right type.

Procedural types

Procedural types are pointers to subroutines. I know it's a bit strange to talk about pointers to subroutines before I talk about subroutines, but writing a language specification is full of chicken and egg problems, and procedural types are definitely scalars and a lot like pointers.

The declaration of procedural types is very similar to that of the subroutines they point to. For example, a lot of numeric functions look like ArcSin():

```
function ArcSin(X: Extended): Extended;
```

The corresponding procedural type declarations would be

```
type TMath = function (X: Extended): Extended;
var MathFn:  function (X: Extended): Extended;
```

That is, the procedural type declaration looks just like the corresponding subroutine declaration, except that the subroutine is unnamed. The name to the left of the = or : belongs to the procedural type or procedural variable.

A procedural variable can be set to any subroutine that matches its *prototype*—that is, has the same argument list (or lack thereof) and result type (or lack thereof). Thus, MathFn could be set to ArcSin() or Log10(), but not to StrCopy() or Power(). You set a procedural variable to a 'bare name', without any of the routine's prototype information:

```
begin
  MathFn := ArcSin;
  MathΓn := Log10;
end.
```

> **Note**
>
> *Procedural types can't 'hold' routines (like Sin) declared in the System unit, as many of these are 'magic' and generate inline code instead of function calls.*

Procedural types are dereferenced just as if they were the subroutines they point to. That is, there is no ^ between the variable name and any argument list.

```
var MathFn:  function (X: Extended): Extended = Log10;
    X:       double;

begin
  X := Log10(32);  // 1.50515
  X := MathFn(32); // 1.50515
end.
```

This causes problems when you need to check the contents of a procedural variable. Of course, most of the time all you really care about is whether the variable is set or not, and Assigned() will work here, just as for other pointers. But what if you need to check whether 'this' procedural variable points to 'that' procedure? Just saying if This = That won't compile, as This will be evaluated as to a call to the procedure it points to, which doesn't return a value. To get around this, @ has been overloaded to return the *contents* of a procedural variable, while @@ does what @ does everywhere else, and returns the *address* of the procedural variable. So, you would write if @This = @That, which works because @This returns the contents of the procedural variable named This, while @That returns the address of the procedure named That.[12]

Method types

Procedural types can also be used with object methods, which are covered in chapter 3. The declarations are distinguished from normal procedural types by being suffixed with the keywords of object. For example,

```
type TMathMethod = function (X: Extended): Extended of object;
```

A normal procedural type is a 32-bit pointer, while a method type contains two 32-bit pointers—a pointer to the method and a pointer to the object—bound into a single 64-bit scalar. While you *can* cast this scalar to a method/object record like the System unit's

```
type
  TMethod = record
    Code, Data: Pointer;
  end;
```

a method type *is* a scalar, and has no language-level structure.

Assignment to a method variable requires a object/method pair—*eg*, you would assign var MathMethod: TMathMethod as MathMethod := Foo.Bar. You call 64-bit method pointers just like a normal procedural variable—*eg*, Result := MathMethod(X).

Typecasting

I've shown a few typecasts in some of the examples, so you're probably aware that the general syntax is typename(expr), where *typename* is the type you want to cast *expr* to. The two things that the examples didn't show is that Object Pascal has two different types of typecast—*value* and *variable*—with the same syntax, and that variable typecasts can appear on the left-hand side of an assignment operation.

---

12. Personally, I find this a really annoying exception to Object Pascal's general level of syntactic elegance, but I do have to admit that it's a rare piece of code that doesn't dereference procedural variables far more than it calls @ or @@ on them.

Value casts

When you cast a Byte or an AnsiChar to an Integer, you are converting an 8-bit unsigned value to a 32-bit signed value. This conversion from one size and/or type to another is the hallmark of a value cast. The name comes from the way the value cast preserves the value, as opposed to the bit pattern.

You can cast any ordinal type to any other ordinal type; the compiler will generate the code to sign-extend or truncate the value as necessary. The compiler will always preserve the sign and value when you're casting 'up' to a large enough type. However, when you cast 'down' to a narrower type, the high order bits are discarded. For example,

```
var
  Int: integer = -77; // $FFFFFFB3
  Wrd: word;

begin
  Wrd := word(Int); // $FFB3 = 64759
end.
```

Variable casts

When you cast a Cardinal to an Integer, you are telling the compiler to treat the same 32-bit value in an entirely different way. This change in the interpretation of a bit pattern, without any change in the bit pattern, is the hallmark of the variable cast. The name comes from the way that a variable cast preserves a register or memory variable's bit pattern, and not the value that that pattern represents.

You can cast any type to any other type, so long as they are the same size, except that you can't cast integers to or from floats. For example, when you cast a high-bit unsigned 16-bit value to a signed 16-bit type, the same bits have different values: Word($FF00) is 65,280 but SmallInt($FF00) is −256.

Variable casts can appear on either side of an assignment operator. For example,

```
Ptr := pointer(2000 + 1);
```

is entirely equivalent to

```
integer(Ptr) := 2000 + 1;
```

and you can use whichever you think is clearer. There's not a lot of difference in this example, but with a more complicated expression on the right-hand side, a left-side cast can help a lot.

You can also cast scalars to and from records. (See Chapter 3.) This is commonly used to read and write the low and high words of an integer:

```
type
  DWord = packed record
          Lo, Hi: word;
          end;

var
  Int: integer = $CAFEBABE; // $DEADBEEF doesn't have quite the
                            // panache of 0xDEADBEEF

  Cafe, Babe: word;

begin
  Cafe := DWord(Int).High;
  Babe := DWord(Int).Low;
  DWord(Int).High := 0;
end.
```

The as operator

Finally, the as operator provides a third type of casting that only applies to object and interface references. The principal difference between as and the 'static' casts I've talked about in this chapter is that the static casts are 'blind'. The compiler does no tests to see if you are truncating a bit stream or treating a pointer as a pointer to something it isn't. When you do a cast, you are telling the compiler that you know what you're doing—even if you don't. The as operator, on the other hand, uses run-time type information [RTTI] (see Chapters 3 and 8) to check that the object really is of the type that you're saying it is, and will raise an exception if it is not.

The is operator does the same test as the as operator, but returns True or False, instead of a retyped pointer. I talk about both is and as more in Chapter 3.

Type identity

As you read the Kylix source code, you might find occasional declarations like this one in Classes.pas

```
type
  TComponentName = type string;
```

or these declarations from Qt.pas

```
type
  HANDLE = type Integer;
  HCURSOR = type HANDLE;
  HPALETTE = type HANDLE;
  HFONT = type HANDLE;
```

This is something called *type identity* and is used to create a new, distinct type that acts the same as the old type. Before you get too excited, you should note that it's really not quite as useful as these declarations in Qt.pas suggest. It certainly **looks** like you can't inadvertently assign a HCURSOR to a HFONT like

```
var
  Cursor: HCURSOR;
  Font:   HFONT;

begin
  Font := Cursor; // This is what type identity appears to prevent
end.
```

but, in fact, the code above will actually compile and run without any complaints. Type identity does not create assignment incompatibility.

The new type is distinct from the original type in two 'smaller' and less generally useful ways: Pointers to the new type are not assignment compatible with pointers to the old type, and the new type has different RTTI than the old type.

The different RTTI lets you define a custom property editor (see Chapter 8) for the TComponentName type that's distinct from the generic string property editor, but that's really about it.

The pointer incompatibility manifests itself in two different ways. First, when you use the {$T+} pragma (Chapter 4), you can't assign @ DerivedType to variable of type ^ OriginalType. For example, you can't assign the address of an HCURSOR variable to a pointer to an HFONT:

```
var
  Cursor: HCURSOR;
  Font:   ^ HFONT;
{$T+}
begin
  Font := @ Cursor; // This is what type identity does prevent
end.
```

Second, type identity does create assignment incompatibility with var and out parameters (Chapter 2) that basically pass pointers into subroutines without requiring you to explicitly use the address operator. For example, you can't pass an HCURSOR to a routine that expects a var Font: HFONT parameter.

These are pretty modest safeguards. Many people would **like** type identity to lead to assignment incompatibility, and it's possible that someday it will. Meanwhile, it can't hurt to write your code as if

```
type
  Cookie = type integer;
```

declares a new type, Cookie, that **is** an integer but is not assignment compatible with integers. If nothing else, it lets the reader know that you would like Cookie to be an incompatible type—and someday it may actually work that way.

CHAPTER 2
Primitive operations

CHAPTER 2
Primitive operations

THE SCALAR DATATYPES OF CHAPTER 1 are the atoms that we build our programs out of. This chapter covers the primitive operations that we can do with those primitive datatypes. It roughly follows the history of programming: It starts with basic operations like addition, subtraction, and assignment, moves on to traditional structured programming, and concludes with exception handling.

Operators

Mathematically, an operation is something that you can do with a value. An operator is a specific operation. Object Pascal, like other computer languages, provides a large set of the familiar arithmetic operators, as well as logical operations like *and* and *or*, and a large set of operations that manipulate data representations.

Assignment

Assignment is probably the most basic computer operation there is. CPU architectures vary widely as to what they implement in silicon *vs* what they leave to be done in software, but even the most radically simplified designs have the ability to load a memory location into a register and store it to a different location.

Object Pascal is unlike just about every other computer language in that assignment is done *via* :=, not =. It makes a lot of sense, when you think about it; assignment is an operation, not a test or an assertion, and it doesn't really make sense to use the same symbols for assigning as for testing equality. It makes more sense to define a new sequence for assignment and keep = for equality testing, than to do as C does and wrongly make = into assignment and then create a new sequence, ==, for equality testing. Anyhow, all special pleading aside, you can't use := where you can use = and *vice versa*; the compiler will catch your careless errors and quickly train you to use :=.

Tip

Giving things names can help you keep them straight. Many people refer to the assignment operator as "gets", so A := B *is "A gets B" while* A = B *is "A equals B".*

Another point of difference is that *the assignment operator has no value.* You can't do something like A := B := C or if (A := B) > C then the way you can in C or Perl. Assignments always appear on the left-hand side of a statement; never in the middle of an expression.

Arithmetic operators

In addition to the usual addition, subtraction, multiplication, and division, Object Pascal supports C-style shift and bitwise operators. Unlike C, most of the 'non-calculator' operators use English keywords like mod and xor, rather than bizarre choices of punctuation like % and ^.

Basic arithmetic

The basic arithmetic operations should be familiar enough. Addition and subtraction are done with + and – as you'd expect. The result has the type of the 'widest' operand: *eg*, adding a 32-bit integer to a 64-bit integer results in a 64-bit integer, while subtracting a float point value from an integer gives a floating point result.

ASCII doesn't have the mathematician's symbols × and ÷ for multiplication and division, so Object Pascal uses * and /. Note that / **always** gives a floating point result, even when both the dividend and the divisor are integers. The div operator does integer division, while the mod operator returns the integer remainder, or *modulus*.

There is no exponentiation operator like A ** B to do A^B, though there are functions in the System and Math units to do this.

Table 2-1. Exponentiation functions

Unit	Name	Operation
System	Exp(X)	e^X
Math	Power(Base, Exponent)	$Base^{Exponent}$
Math	IntPower(Base, Exponent)	$Base^{Exponent}$, where Exponent must be an integer

Bitwise operators

Computer programs commonly need to be able to manipulate the pattern of bits that make up a value. Object Pascal supports and, or, xor, and not. Obviously, the first three take two arguments while not takes only one.

Thus, to turn on some bits in an option mask, you would do Options := Options or BitsToSet, while to turn off some bits you would do Options := Options and not BitsToClear. As *per* the Operator Precedence list in Table 2-4, on page 53, not has a higher priority than and, so parentheses are not needed, here—but of course the compiler won't care if you write this as Options := Options and (not BitsToClear).

Shift operators

You can shift integer values left and right to get and set particular bits. For example, you can extract the high nibble from a byte with BitMap shr 4 and $0F. Similarly, you can get the middle four bits from an eight-bit bitmap with BitMap shr 2 and $0F and set them with Bitmap and $C2 or NewBits shl 2. (Note that these examples work because and has the same precedence as shl and shr (Table 2-4) so the expressions are evaluated from left to right. $0F and Bitmap shr 2 is the same as ($0F and Bitmap) shr 2, **not** $0F and (Bitmap shr 2).)

Traditionally, shifts have also been used to quickly multiply or divide by powers of two. A shl 2 is the same as A * 4, while B shl 6 is the same as B div 64. Many—probably most—people convert B shl 6 into B div 64 by counting 2, 4, 8, 16, 32, 64 (or 16, 32, 64) in their head (or on their fingers!), so that an expression using multiplication or division is generally easier to read than the equivalent expression using shifts. The compiler does a very good job of optimizing expressions, using shifts where it's appropriate, so you should generally avoid using shifts where you can use multiplication or division.

In addition to the clarity issue, you should be aware that shl and shr map directly to the Intel shl and shr opcodes. That is, they never use the signed `sal` and `sar`. Shifting a negative number to the right will make it positive, while shifting a positive number to the left may make it negative.

Relational operators

All scalar values can be compared with another of the same or compatible type for equality or inequality. In addition, all of the scalar datatypes except pointers are ordered. That is, you can compare two values of the same or compatible types to see if one is greater than or less than the other. As *per* Chapter 1, the relational operators all return the boolean values True and False.

When it comes to comparisons, Object Pascal divides the scalars into three large classes: Numbers, strings, and enums. You can compare any two numbers—even if one is a Byte and the other an Extended—and the compiler will automatically generate the numeric conversion code to do the comparison at the highest width. You can *not* compare numbers to strings as you can in Perl[1]—you'll have to explicitly convert one or the other, as in `A > StrToInt(B)` or `IntToStr(A) > B`. Similarly, you can not compare two enums of different types; if you're sure that you need to do this, you can use `Ord()` to convert the enums to integers and compare `Ord(A)` to `Ord(B)`.

Comparing numbers and enums uses the same relational operators as comparing strings, unlike languages like Perl which use a different set of relational operators for strings than they do for numbers. Object Pascal uses fairly standard "typewriter" symbols like >= in place of mathematician's symbols like $\geq$, but C++, Java, and Perl programmers should note that the test for equality is =, not ==.

Table 2-2. Relational operators

Pascal Operator	Math Notation	Meaning
<	<	Less than
<=	$\leq$	Less than or equal to
=	=	Equal to
<>	$\neq$	Not equal to
>=	$\geq$	Greater than or equal to
>	>	Greater than

---

1. Chapter 3's Variants are the exception to this rule: arithmetic or comparisons with Variants will convert strings to numbers as necessary.

While you can always compare two pointers of the same (or compatible) types for equality with = or <>, they are not ordered. You cannot ask if pointer A is greater than pointer B, unless they are PChars. Part of the special syntax associated with PChars is that you *can* apply relational operators to PChars, just as you can calculate PChar(A) - PChar(B) in a way that you can't with other pointer types.

Logical operators

Like Visual Basic, but unlike C++ and Java, Object Pascal uses English words for logical operators. That is, you say and and or instead of && and ||; xor and not instead of ^ and !.

Table 2-3. Logical operators

Pascal Operator	C++ Equivalent	Short circuits	Interpretation
and	&&	Yes	True if both sides are true
or	||	Yes	True if either side is true
xor	^	No	True iff one side is true; false if neither or both is true.
not	!	No	True if the right side is false

Iff means "if and only if."

By default, the and and or operators do *short circuit evaluation.* That is, they evaluate the left-hand term first; if there is then no way that the right-hand term can change the operator's result, they will not evaluate the right-hand side. So, if the left-hand side of an and operator is False, the right-hand side will not be evaluated; if the left-hand side of an or operator is True, the right-hand side will not be evaluated.[2] For the most part, this behavior is

---

2. Since True > False as *per* Chapter 1, you can use relational operators as shortcuts for various permutations of and, or, and not. That is, A and not B is the same as A > B, while not A and B is the same as A < B; similarly, A or not B is the same as A >= B, while not A or B is the same as A <= B. The savings are only in the typing; the relational versions are no faster than their logical equivalents (this has been true since the earliest versions of Turbo Pascal) and are harder to read. Most relevantly, here, the relational operators do not do shortcut evaluation the way the logical operators do.

exactly what you want, though there can be rare instances (involving function calls with *side effects*) where you might not want short circuit evaluation. You can use the {$B-} pragma (see Chapter 4) to turn off short circuiting around small sections of code, but you should definitely turn short circuiting back on as soon as possible after disabling it. Not only does it let your code run faster, most Kylix code depends on short circuit evaluation, and will break if it's turned off. For example, if (StringVar <> '') and (StringVar[1] = 'Y') then {…} can deference Nil with short circuiting turned off, because empty strings ('') are represented by a Nil pointer.

You'll have noticed that the logical operators overload the bitwise operators. While it will always be clear from the datatypes whether to use a logical or bitwise operator, the overloading causes problems in that the operations have been given precedence based on their bitwise use. This means that and (a "multiplier") has a higher precedence than or (an "adder"). More importantly, since the bitwise (arithmetic) operators all have higher precedence than the relational operators, an expression like A > B and C < D will be evaluated as (A > (B and C)) < D and **not** (A > B) and (C < D) as you might have expected. Typically, such precedence errors will not compile, just like this example will not compile, but it **is** possible (though unlikely) to have relational expressions compile to code that you did not mean. Be careful, and when in any doubt, use explicit parentheses.

Precedence

In standard arithmetic, multiplication and division always take precedence over addition and subtraction. Thus, A×B+C×D is always evaluated as (A×B)+(C×D). With four operators and two precedence levels, this works pretty well. Most of us manage to get it straight by eighth grade or so.

Computer languages have many more than four operators, though, and the problem becomes much more difficult. The language designers have to decide whether *this* operation has the same precedence as *that* operation or whether it has a higher or lower precedence; language users have to remember where parentheses are needed and where they're not. One or two languages have very sensibly given all operations the same precedence, but few other languages have taken this tack. The C++ standard, for example, has an absolutely ridiculous **seventeen** precedence levels!

Object Pascal takes a reasonably sensible middle-of-the-road approach, restraining itself to four levels. With the exception of giving the logical operators the precedence of their bitwise overloads, the precedence hierarchy generally results in expressions doing what you'd expect, with a minimum of parentheses.

Table 2-4. Operator precedence

Operators	Category	Precedence
@, not	Unary operators	Highest
*, /, div, mod, and, shl, shr, as	'Multipliers'	
+, −, or, xor	'Adders'	
, <>, <, >, <=, >=, in, is	Relational operators	Lowest

All of these have been discussed in this chapter except @ (the address operator), in (a set operator), and is and as (run-time type checking operators for objects). I discuss the in operator in Chapter 3; I covered the others in Chapter 1.

Ordinal operations

Some of the operators we've seen so far may have used words instead of symbols, but they were all traditional-looking prefix and infix operators. The *ordinal operators* in this section are unusual in that they all look like subroutine calls, but they evaluate to inline code just like the other operators.

The ordinal operators include operators that really only apply to an actual value, an ordinal variable or expression, as well as operators that apply to the type as a whole. You can, however, use the type oriented operators on an instance of the type. The value returned will be the same as if you had applied the operator to the type itself. For example:

```
type
  Colors = (Red, Green, Blue);

var
  Color:    Colors;

  LowColor,
  HighColor: Colors;
```

```
begin
  LowColor  := Low(Colors); // Applying Low() to a type to get Red
  HighColor := High(Color); // Applying High() to a variable to get Blue
end.
```

You will often find yourself in situations where you can use an operator like High() or Low() on either a variable or its type. For example, given `var This: SmallInt`, you could write either

```
if (Value >= Low(SmallInt)) and (Value <= High(SmallInt)) then
  This := Value;
```

or

```
if (Value >= Low(This)) and (Value <= High(This)) then
  This := Value;
```

Is there any real difference?

Yes. What happens to the first snippet if the declaration of `This` were to be changed to `var This: word`? Right—it breaks. Whenever you can, you should apply operators like Low(), High() and SizeOf() to variables and not types. That way, if the variable ever changes type, your code changes with it.

The High() and Low() operators

High() and Low() can be applied to an ordinal type or an ordinal variable, as well as to an array type or array variable. (As you'll see in Chapter 3, an array declaration requires either a named ordinal index type or an inline subrange (from *this* ordinal to *that* ordinal) declaration.) Applied to an ordinal, High() returns the highest value the type can take and Low() returns the lowest value the type can take. When applied to an array, High() returns the highest value that can be used to index that array, the High() of the array's ordinal index type, while Low() returns the lowest value that can be used to index that array.

> **Tip**
>
> *High() and Low() of an array return the highest and lowest index—* **not** *the highest or lowest value in the array.*

Table 2-5 gives some examples of High() and Low() on some intrinsic types as well as on a couple of user-defined types..

Table 2-5. Some High() and Low() values

Type	Low(Type)	High(Type)	Comments
(Red, Green, Blue)	Red	Blue	A user-defined enumeration.
Cardinal	0	4,294,967,295	32-bit unsigned integer.
Integer	–2,147,483,648	2,147,483,647	32-bit signed integer.
ShortInt	-32,768	32,767	16-bit signed integer.
SmallInt	-128	127	8-bit signed integer.
1..10	1	10	A user-defined numeric subrange.
Char	#0	#255	Char is 8-bits in this release—but you shouldn't count on that.
WideChar	#0	#65535	A 16-bit (Unicode) character.

The Succ() and Pred() operators

Succ() stands for "successor", and returns the next value in the ordinal sequence, while Pred() stands for "predecessor", and returns the previous value in the ordinal sequence. For example, Succ(Red) is Green and Pred (Blue) is Green; Succ('A') is 'B' and Pred ('Z') is 'Y'; while Succ(42) is 43 and Pred(0) is –1.

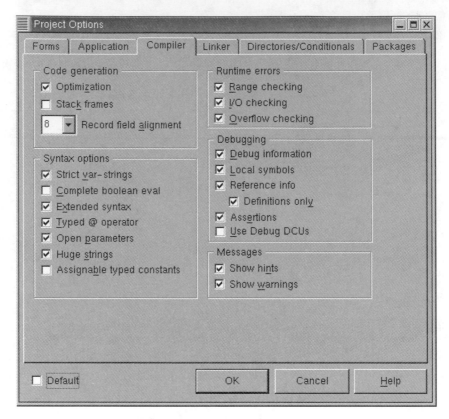

Figure 2-1. The "Project Options" dialog

Pascal offers a rich set of run-time checks that can catch common coding errors. Succ() and Pred() can generate both *range checks* and *overflow errors* if "Range checking" and "Overflow checking" are turned on *via* the Project ➤ Options (SHIFT+CTRL+F11) dialog (Figure 2-1) or *via* the {$R+} and {$Q+} pragmas (see Chapter 4). You get a range check when you assign an out-of-range value to a variable. For example,

```
var
  Value: byte = High(Value);
{$R+,Q+}
begin
  Value := Pred(Succ(Value)); // OK, if weird: Value = High(Value)
  Value := Succ(Value);    // Range checks
end.
```

The statement Value := Pred(Succ(Value)) is OK, though pointless. Since Value is initialized to High(Value), or 255, Succ(Value) is 256, which will fit comfortably in a 32-bit register. `Pred(Succ(Value))` is 255 again, so the assignment causes no problems. However, Succ(255) is 256, which can not be assigned to a `byte` variable, so the second line range checks. Note that if you turn range checking off, Value would get the low-byte of Succ(Value), or 0. Range checking doesn't add all that much to code size and it doesn't slow it down all that much—and it catches errors where they occur, not (potentially) much later in a different module.

Since most ordinal evaluation is done with 32-bit values, overflow checking will catch a smaller class of errors: `Succ(High(integer))` or `Pred(Low(integer))`. These errors, however, are caught at the point of execution, not at the later assignment. For example,

```
var
  Value: integer = High(Value);
{$R+,Q+}
begin
  Value := Pred(Succ(Value)); // Overflows in Succ()
  Value := Low(Value);
  Value := Pred(Value);      // Would also overflow
end.
```

Expressions like `Succ(Blue)` or `Succ(#255)` that can be identified as impossible at compile-time generate a compilation error; this checking cannot be disabled.

Succ() and Pred() can be applied only to an ordinal value, not an ordinal type—what would it mean to ask for, say, the value after the `Colors` type? The value does not, however, have to be the current contents of a variable; you can apply both Succ() or Pred() to either a function call's result or to an expression result, as in `Succ(A + B)`.

The Inc() and Dec() 'procedures'

Inc() and Dec() look like a standard Pascal procedure (see the *Routines* section of this chapter) in that they don't return a value, and so can't be used in an expression the way Succ() and Pred() can. Neither is a real procedure, though, as they always generate inline code and never result in a CALL op code.

They can be used in one of two ways: `Inc(OrdinalVariable)` does the equivalent of `OrdinalVariable := Succ(OrdinalVariable)`, but is smaller and easier to read. `Dec(OrdinalVariable, 2)` does the equivalent of `OrdinalVariable := Pred(Pred(OrdinalVariable))`—that is, the optional second parameter specifies how much to increment or decrement the variable by.

The compiler does no compile-time plausibility checks on the second argument; you can, for example, successfully compile Inc(BooleanVar, 100). (If you have range checking on, this will produce a run-time error, but if you have range checking off, this bizarre Inc() statement will run without complaint.)

Whether or not you supply a second argument, Inc() and Dec() can generate range check and overflow errors, just like Succ() and Pred() can.

As with Succ() and Pred(), Inc() and Dec() can only be applied to ordinal values, not to ordinal types. However, unlike Succ() and Pred(), Inc() and Dec() can only be applied to actual variables, not to expressions, as they change the contents of their first parameter. Inc() and Dec() can also be used with pointers; this was covered in the Pointers section of Chapter 1.

Note

Inc and Dec can't be used with object properties (Chapter 3) because reading or writing a property may involve a subroutine call: a property is not necessarily a 'normal' object field.

The Ord() operator

Ord() is a sort of typecast operator that converts any ordinal value into a number. This is very useful for things like character arithmetic; also, since ord(False) is 0 and ord(True) is 1, you can write expressions involving addition of or multiplication by ord(BooleanExpression) to avoid the conditional jumps of an if statement.[3] For example:

Table 2-6. Some examples of the Ord() operator

Code	Effect
chr(ord(CharVar) or $20)	Force the antepenultimate bit on, to lower case an ASCII character
Ord(N > 0) − Ord(N < 0)	Sign (-1..1) of N
IntVar + 7 * ord(BoolExpr)	Add 7 if BoolExpr is True; add 0 if it is not

---

3. A sophisticated reader might have the same objection to this that one of the people who read the manuscript did: "But Ord(BooleanExpr) still entails a jump!" Not so. The Ord() operator uses a SETcc instruction to map a condition code directly to a 1 or 0 value.

> **Note**
>
>
>
> *Ord(False) is always 0, but Ord(True) is not necessarily 1 for the compatibility booleans ByteBool, WordBool, and LongBool. These are meant mostly to be used for cross-language programming, and True for them is any non-zero value. If you set one of them to True, its Ord() will be −1, but this may not be true for True values from libraries built in C. If you want to be able to rely on Ord() being 0 or 1, do* Ord(CompatBool = True)*. (See Chapter 1.)*

When Ord() is converting a nonnumeric ordinal to a numeric ordinal, the result will almost always be a positive integer. Low() of any normal enum or character type is 0; C++ style assigned enums can have negative ordinal values.

Statements

Object Pascal programs are made from only three classes of things: definitions of types and routines; declarations of variables and constants; and statements, which actually do things with those types and values. Statements can be *simple* or *compound*. You can use a compound statement wherever you can use a simple statement.

A simple statement consists of either a routine call or an assignment. Any whitespace is ignored, as you'd expect. There are a number of different indenting and formatting styles; it really doesn't matter which you use, so long as you're consistent. A 'bare' expression (like A + B or ord(C) or variable name is not a valid statement. Unlike in C, statements *do not* end with semicolons.

> **Note**
>
>
>
> *You should at least look at Borland's official Object Pascal Style Guide at* http://community.borland.com/article/0,1410,10280,00.html.

A compound statement consists of a series of simple statements enclosed in a begin / end block, separated by semicolons. Extra semicolons are treated as if they are separating blank statements, and are ignored. Thus, you do not need a semicolon between the last statement in a block and the end keyword, but it can't hurt—and I strongly recommend that you always do place a semicolon after the last statement in a block. If you don't, you'll get strange compiler errors when you add a statement between the old last statement and the end– and this is something that routinely happens as you bootstrap code from prototype to product, or as you add features to an existing product.

Two common problems for C and Visual Basic programmers

> **Note**
>
>
>
> *The difference between the way C and Pascal handle semicolons is one of the things that gives C programmers the most trouble with Kylix and Delphi. In C, the semicolon is a statement* terminator; *it is required after every simple statement. In Pascal, the semicolon is a statement* separator; *it is only required **between** statements in a* begin / end *block. The way that a semicolon is not needed after the last statement in the block leads to C programmers feeling like a semicolon is sometimes needed and sometimes not, in a really irrational way. Similarly, C and Visual Basic programmers are often surprised when they place a semicolon after the* then *statement in an* if, *leading to their* else *being a syntax error.*

Comments

Object Pascal supports three different styles of comments. The most common, these days, is probably the C++ style comment, where everything between a // and a linebreak is a comment. There are also two block-style comments, which can be used for inline comments; to comment out code; or for extensive comments where you don't want a // at the start of every line. Block comments are anything between a (* and a *) pair, as well as everything between a { and a }. (That's right—the curly braces, which C and Perl and most of the rest of the world use for compound statements are used for comments in Pascal. Deal with it.)

Comments can not be nested, but you can wrap { } comments in (* *) comments and *vice versa*. Many people take advantage of this to make it easier to comment out code without attempted comment-nesting leading to syntax errors. If you always use { } and // for comments, you can always safely comment out code with (* *). (Of course, using conditional compilation lets you comment out code and still get syntax highlighting in the commented-out code.)

Note

Object Pascal pragmas (Chapter 4) are block comments where the first character of the comment is a $ sign—eg, {$R+} and (*$Q-). Almost no one uses (* *) pragmas.*

BASM

The built-in assembler, BASM, represents a special sort of compound statement. It consists of a series of zero or more assembler statements, separated by either newline characters, semicolons, or Pascal comments, and enclosed in an asm / end pair. The assembler is pretty stripped down, with no macros, but it's wonderfully convenient for those few times when you still need assembler; it understands all your type declarations and you don't have to fuss with keeping your Pascal and assembler declarations in synch. In addition, you can generally just refer to a variable by name (*eg*, mov eax, [MyVar]) and it will generate the right code, whether MyVar is a global, EBP-relative local, or a procedure's register-passed parameter.

Kylix's BASM understands mnemonics through the Pentium Pro—including SIMD [Single Instructions, Multiple Data] instructions like Intel's MMX and SSE, and AMD's "Enhanced 3D"— but historically it has often lagged quite a long way behind the leading edge. For example, until Kylix and Delphi 6, BASM only supported 80386-level mnemonics; you needed to use db statements to 'fake' more advanced instructions like RDTSC. (I mention this only by way of deflating any hopes you may have of Kylix 2 or 3's BASM supporting new instructions.)

For the most part, if you know enough assembler to read the object code in Kylix's View CPU window, you'll be able to use BASM after reading a bit of both the online help and the Intel and/or AMD processor documentation. (Be especially careful with register usage: Some registers *must* have the same value at the end of a BASM block as at the start. See the *BASM Quick Reference* appendix for details.) If you don't, this really isn't the place for an assembler tutorial.

Conditionals

Object Pascal has two conditional constructs. An if statement lets you execute a statement when a control expression is true and, optionally, to execute a different statement when the control expression is false. A case statement supports more complicated branching, executing any of a number of statements when their tag matches the value of a control expression.

If

The simplest conditional statement is the if statement. It consists of the if keyword, a boolean expression, a then keyword, and a statement, optionally followed by an else keyword and another statement. For example,

```
if (Path = '') or (Path [Length(Path)] <> PathDelim) then
 Path := Path + PathSeparator;
```

and

```
if A > B
  then Max := A
  else Max := B;
```

There is no "elif" shorthand. Any Pascal statement can appear in an else clause, including another if statement.

Note

C, Java, and Perl programmers should be aware of two things: First, you do not need to put parentheses around the whole boolean expression. Your code will compile just fine if you do, but nobody who 'thinks in Pascal' puts parens around the expressions in if *statements and looping constructs except as necessary to control the order of execution. Second, you do **not** put a semicolon after the* then *clauses's statement—either simple or compound—if you have an else clause. The semicolon ends the if statement, making the orphaned* else *clause into a syntax error.*

The optional `else` clause is always associated with the most recent `if` statement. Thus, in a nested `if` statement like

```
if Test1 then
  if Test2
    then DoThis
    else DoThat;
```

`else DoThat` is part of the `if Test2` statement, and will only be executed if Test1 is True and Test2 is False. If you *want* DoThat to be executed when Test1 is False, you need to either supply the inner (Test2) `if` statement with an empty else clause

```
if Test1
  then if Test2
    then DoThis
    else {do nothing}
  else DoThat;
```

or wrap the inner `if` in a `begin` / `end` pair to 'close out' the if statement.

```
if Test1
  then begin
      if Test2 then DoThis;
      end
  else DoThat;
```

Note

The second form, which uses an explicit begin / end pair, is easier to read and a lot less 'brittle' than the first, with its 'empty else' clause.

As you can see, I think of the `then` and `else` clauses as two parts of the same statement and format them that way. However, most Kylix and Delphi programmers these days seem to follow C conventions, and place any `else` clause on a newline, lined up with its `if` statement.

Optimization

The compiler is quite good at *dead code elimination*. If it can determine at compile time that a given then or else clause can never be reached, it will simply not generate any object code for those clauses. If there is no else clause and the then clause can't be reached, the compiler won't generate any code to evaluate the test, either. In the Kylix IDE, you can tell if a given piece of code has been optimized away because it will not have little bullets next to it in the editor's gutter panel.

Finally, although CPU's are getting better at branch prediction, conditional statements still remain relatively expensive in that they entail a jump around the then clause on test failure and perhaps a jump around the else clause on test success. Where speed really matters, as in loops executed millions of times, you should try to replace if statements with either arithmetic on Ord(BooleanExpr) or lookup in a boolean-indexed array.

Case

Like C and Java, and unlike Perl, Pascal has a multi-way branch statement, case. It is significantly more flexible, less bulky, and easier to use than C's switch statement. It does not support C's 'fall through to the next case when you don't explicitly break' behavior—but since that's more often a source of bugs than of useful behavior, you probably won't miss it.

The general syntax of a case statement is *case Selector of OneOrMoreTaggedStatements [else statement] end*, where a tagged statement looks like *Tag : statement*. You can use any ordinal value—numeric, character, or enum—as the case selector, but you can not use string or floating point values. A case statement must have at least one tagged statement:

```
case Value of
  else DoSomething;
end;
```

is a syntax error. At its simplest, a case tag is just a value of the same type as the case selector

```
case IntExpr of
  1:   ;
  else ;
end;
```

but the tag can also contain subranges and multiple, comma-separated values:

```
case IntExpr of
  1, 3:     ;
  2, 4, 6:  ;
  5, 7..10: ;
  else      ;
end;
```

Naturally, case tags can contain symbolic constants (Chapter 3) as well as constant expressions (also Chapter 3) like Low(ThisSubRange)..High(ThisSubRange) or SomeConstant+1. However, all case tags must be true compile-time constants. You can **not** write code like

```
case IntExpr of
  ThisIntVar: ; // Not legal!
  ThatIntVar: ; // Not legal!
else          ;
end;
```

that matches the case selector against the current value of various variables. (You have to use nested if statements for that.) This also means that you can't use *typed constants* (Chapter 3) in case tags, as they are essentially initialized variables. You can, however, declare a true compile-time constant and use it in both the typed constant initialization and in case tags.

Case statements are very efficient, as branching constructs go. When the compiler can, it will generate a jump table. When it can't, it loads the selector into a register and generates an efficient series of tests on that register. A case statement will generally be both clearer and faster than an equivalent set of nested if statements.

Note

C and Java programmers should be sure to note that Pascal's case *statement is quite different from C's* switch *statement in one key way. A* switch *will proceed from the bottom of one tagged substatement to the top of the next if you don't explicitly* break;. *The tagged substatements in a* case *statement are logically independent: zero or one will be executed, and execution will never fall through to the next tagged statement.*

Assert

Assertions are a special sort of conditional statement designed to help you produce reliable code. They consist of a procedure 'call' with a boolean expression and an optional error message. If the expression is true, nothing happens; if the expression is false, you get a run-time exception. (Exceptions are covered later in this chapter.) For example,

```
Assert( (ThisInt >= 1) and (ThisInt <= 1000),
        IntToStr(ThisInt) + ' not in range 1..1000' );
        // The string expression is only evaluated
        // when the assertion is violated
```

In general, you should use assertions anywhere your code makes assumptions that might be violated: that a particular value is in a certain range; that two arrays are of the same length; that an object passed to you as an instance of an ancestral class is in fact of the right descendant type; and so on. There is a compiler switch to turn off assertions in production code, so you can use them liberally during development without impacting the run-time performance of your finished code. Some people[4] argue that you should leave assertions on to catch critical errors, even in shipping code, but most people prefer to explicitly test for such errors and manually raise an exception if they occur.

Explicitly raising an exception when you detect a critical error leaves you free to use lots of really fine-grained assertions, and to use relatively expensive tests that you wouldn't want to leave in shipping code.

Be careful not to write code that depends on assertions being evaluated! This will break your code when you turn off assertions for the final builds. The easiest way to make this mistake is to assert that a given function call returns a success code, not a failure code. It might be fine to do this test in an assertion and not in an explicit if statement—but be sure that you make the actual function call outside the assertion. In general, any functions you call in an Assert() statement should be simple predicates, as any side effects they may have will be lost when assertions are turned off.

Loops

Object Pascal has the three standard loop constructs that emerged from the "structured programming era": Loop *for* a fixed number of times; loop *until*

---

4.   Like Ray Lischner, in "Delphi In A Nutshell."

some condition is true; and loop *while* some condition is true. The `for` loop is a bit less flexible than its three-term counterpart in C, Perl, and Java, but the syntax is also quite a bit simpler.

for

There are two forms of the `for` loop, depending on whether you want to count up or count down.

```
for IndexVar := StartValue to StopValue do {statement}
for IndexVar := StartValue downto StopValue do {statement}
```

The actual object code varies, depending mostly on whether or not you actually refer to the IndexVar in the body of the loop, but the effect is

1. The IndexVar is initialized to the StartValue.

2. The loop statement is executed if the IndexVar is less than or equal to the StopValue. (Or if it is greater than or equal to, in a downto loop.)

3. The IndexVar is incremented (decremented) by 1, and step 2 is repeated.

Note

Unlike C's `for` *loop, Pascal's* `for` *loop can only step its IndexVar by 1. If you need to step by some other number, you'll have to use a* `while` *{...}* `do` *or* `repeat` *{...}* `until` *loop.*

This means that a loop like `for N := 1 to 1` will execute once. It is not an error for the StartValue to be greater than the StopValue (or less than, in a `downto` loop) —this just means that the loop statement will never be executed. Zero-pass loops like this are commonly encountered in 'list walking' or string processing code: `for Index := 1 to Length(Str) do {...}`. (If the StartValue and the StopValue for a zero-pass loop are both compile time constants, the compiler will eliminate the whole loop as dead code and give you a hint.)

The index variable can be *any* ordinal type except `int64`, including characters and enums. There are four significant restrictions on the index variable:

1. The index variable must be a 'simple' local scalar. It can not be a field of a record or object (see Chapter 3) and it can not be a global variable.

2. The value of the index variable is undefined outside of the loop. It *may* have the StopValue, or whatever value it had when you called `Break` (below), but you should not count on this. The only exception to this rule is that you can rely on the value that a function (*Routines* section of this chapter) will return when you `Exit` out of a `for` loop that uses the function's `Result` variable as its index variable.

3. You can **use** the index variable in the body of the loop (the loop statement), but you can not **change** it.

4. While the index variable can be a Cardinal, you can't have more than High(Integer) iterations in a `for` loop. That is, you can loop from `0 to High(Integer)` or `$80000000` to `$FFFFFFFF` but **not** from `Low(Cardinal) to High(Cardinal)`.

The only way to avoid any of these restrictions is to rewrite your `for` loop as a `while {…} do` or `repeat {…} until` loop.

Finally, many people become confused when they put a breakpoint in the body of their loop and find that sometimes their `for` loop is counting downwards. You **can** trust a `for` loop to walk a list or string in the order you specify; if you refer to the IndexVar in the body of the loop, the object code will indeed initialize it to the StartValue and increment (decrement) it until it's greater (less) than the StopValue. However, if you do *not* refer to the IndexVar in the body of the loop, the compiler generates object code that computes the difference between the StartValue and the StopValue, and uses count-down logic that is faster than the semantically equivalent count-up logic. (Turning off optimizations will force the `for` loop to count in the order that you specify, whether or not you refer to the IndexVar in the body of the loop.)

repeat {…} until

The `repeat {…} until` loop is Pascal's test-at-bottom loop construct. It will always execute the loop body at least once; the loop is executed before the first test, and is re-executed so long as the test is False. The general syntax is

```
repeat
  {zero or more statements}
until BooleanExpr
```

Note

Unlike in C, Java, or Perl, the BooleanExpr does not have to be enclosed in parentheses.

This syntax is slightly strange in that the body of the loop is not a single statement, as it is with the for and while loops. There can be zero, one, or more semicolon-separated statements in the body of a repeat loop. I find it best to think of the repeat keyword as analogous to the begin keyword, and the until clause to be analogous to the end keyword. That is, the whole repeat loop constitutes a single compound statement, just as do the for, if, case, and while statements.

There are no restrictions on the contents of the BooleanExpr in the until clause. It may or may not refer to a variable changed in the loop—the compiler won't even complain if you code repeat until True = False. This is, of course, an infinite loop, and generally you would only write it if you used some sort of structured exit, like Break or Exit, which are covered later in this chapter.

while

The while Test do {statement} is Pascal's test-at-top loop construct. The loop body will not necessarily ever execute; the test is executed before the loop body, which is executed only so long as the test is True. The general syntax is

```
while BooleanExpr do {statement}
```

where the {statement} may be any simple or compound statement.

Note

Unlike in C, Java, or Perl, the BooleanExpr does not have to be enclosed in parentheses.

As with the `repeat` loop, there are no restrictions on the contents of the BooleanExpr in a `while` loop.

Break and continue

Object Pascal supports the now-standard structured exit constructs `Break` and `Continue`. You can use either within any of the three looping constructs: for, repeat, and while. They always apply to the innermost loop; you can not use labels[5] to apply them to an outer loop. The compiler will not let you use break or continue outside of a loop. (There is also an `Exit` statement that returns from the current subroutine.)

`Break` *breaks out* of a loop. It transfers control to whatever statement would normally execute when the loop terminated.

> **Note**
>
>
> *The value of a `for` loop's index variable is officially "undefined" after you break out of the loop. In practice, the `for` loop's index variable will contain the value that it had when the Break was executed. It's always dangerous using officially deprecated features, but both the CLX and the VCL contain code that use the loop control variable after a Break, so you probably shouldn't worry too much about this behavior changing.*

`Continue` skips any remaining statements in the loop body, and jumps to the test. Thus, if this was the last loop iteration, continue has the same effect as break. If there are more loop iterations, control passes to the first statement in the loop with, in the case of for loops, a new index variable.

Routines

Pascal divides routines into two types: *procedures* and *functions*. Procedures never return a result; they are called only for their *side effects*. Functions always return a result, though you are free to ignore it. Both consist of a pro-

---

5. Pascal does, in fact, have labels and a `goto` keyword, but you will never ever need to use them. In fact, this is the only place in the whole book where they'll be mentioned. If you insist on using `goto`, check the online help.

totype (signature) declaration; an optional list of local declarations; and a list of zero or more statements in a begin / end; (or asm / end;) block known as the *body* of the routine.

Prototype

A routine's prototype consists of its name; a list of its arguments, if any; and, for functions, the result type. It may also contain a calling convention and various "hint directives". The prototype looks a lot like the procedural types of Chapter 1, except that the name is in a different location.

```
procedure Beep;
procedure LogTransaction(When: TDateTime; const What, ByWho: string);
procedure SetChangedFlag(Changed: boolean = True);
function Sgn(N: integer): ShortInt; overload;
function Sgn(X: double ): ShortInt; overload;
function Callback(Data: pointer): integer; cdecl;
function NextBusinessDay: TDateTime;
```

These examples illustrate a number of key points:

- An empty parameter list (no arguments) is usually coded without the C-style empty parens.

- Formal parameters use the same *name: type* syntax as variable declarations.

- Parameters can be preceded by a const modifier. There are also var and out modifiers.

- A routine's scalar parameters may have default values.

- A function's result type is separated from its name and parameter list by a colon.

- Routines can be overloaded.

- The calling convention, if any, is separated from the rest of the prototype by a semicolon.

Parameter lists

The parameter list, if any, follows immediately after the routine's name. Empty parameter lists can be totally omitted, *ie* the C-style () is not necessary.

Note

Declarations like procedure Beep(); *and calls like* Beep() *are perfectly valid–but are exceedingly rare.[6] This is because, without the empty parens, a function call looks just like a reference to a constant or a variable. While this "ambiguity" is precisely what C's () requirement is meant to avoid, it actually is incredibly useful as you bootstrap your project from prototype to product: You only have to change the identifier's declaration, not every reference to it. Similarly, not coding empty parens after a function call makes it much easier to change an object method (see Chapter 3) to a property.*

There is no limit to the number of parameters a routine can have—though most people find that an 'excessively' long parameter list is usually a sign that a routine should be split into a family of smaller routines. Multiple parameters are separated by semicolons. When you have several successive parameters of the same type, you can place their comma separated names before a colon and type name, so that name1, name2: type1 is equivalent to name1: type1; name2: type1.

Parameter types

Object Pascal offers the usual "pass by value" *vs* "pass by reference" distinction. The default behavior is pass by value: *value parameters* are, effectively, local variables initialized to a copy of the values that they were passed when the routine was called. You can change a value parameter without changing the calling environment.

When you **want** a routine to be able to change its calling environment, you prefix the parameter's name with the var keyword to specify a *variable parameter* and do a pass by reference. Any changes to a variable parameter will also change the memory location that was 'bound' to the parameter by the routine call.

---

6. To the point where when I first saw Foo() on a whiteboard, I said "Oh, that's C – that won't compile."

> **Note**
>
> *Variable parameters must **be** memory locations—while you can pass a function result to another routine as a value parameter, you cannot pass a function result to another routine as a variable parameter.*

Variable parameters are passed as pointers. While the automatic dereferencing means that variable parameters are somewhat more expensive than value parameters for things that are no bigger than a pointer, like integers, it also means that they are cheaper than value parameters for large structures that are referred to infrequently, where the copying cost overwhelms the dereferencing cost. For this reason, in particularly old code that has been ported to Linux you will occasionally see variable parameters used even where there is no intention of changing the calling environment.

New code should use *constant parameters* for this, instead. The compiler will not let you change the value of a parameter prefixed with const. The compiler will not let you pass a constant parameter as a variable parameter to another routine. In addition, parameters larger than 32-bits are passed *via* a pointer, making constant parameters both efficient and safe. Reference-counted (huge string, interface, and dynamic array) constant parameters are optimized by not incrementing their reference count on entry to the routine and decrementing it on exit.

Constants that aren't

Reference-counted constant parameters are optimized by not incrementing their reference count on entry to the routine and decrementing it on exit. This is not an insignificant optimization, especially for small routines that do only one or two simple things, or that simply pass the parameter on to another routine: It takes four times as long to call an empty procedure that takes a string by value as it does to call an empty procedure that takes a const string parameter. Because of this savings, many people routinely add a const modifier to their reference-counted parameters in just about every routine that doesn't change the parameter.

This is a good practice, so long as you remember that a const parameter really is just a pointer to some other data, which may change 'under your feet', either as a result of something you do or as a result of something that happens in another thread (Chapter 7). The ch2/ConstDanger program illustrates the hazards.

```
program ConstDanger;

var
  Global: string;

procedure ShowDanger(const Copy: string);
begin
  Global[2] := UpCase(Global[2]);
  WriteLn(Copy);
end; // ShowDanger

procedure CauseTrouble(const Copy: string);
var
  Nu: string;
begin
  Global := '';
  Nu := Copy;
  Nu := Nu + 'This is not the string you were passed';
  WriteLn(Nu);
end; // CauseTrouble

begin
  Global :=  'This is a string';
  ShowDanger(Global);
  CauseTrouble(Global);
end.
```

Both the ShowDanger procedure and the CauseTrouble procedure are passed a 'copy' of the Global string. Because they are passed this 'copy' as a const parameter, the Global string has a reference count of 1 in both the top level begin / end. block and within both the procedures. Thus, when ShowDanger does Global[2] := UpCase(Global[2]), the normal copy-on-write semantics don't apply: the run-time library only sees one reference to the string, so it changes the Global string in place. That is, while the Copy parameter still points to a valid string, the ShowDanger procedure has changed both the Global string **and** its 'constant' Copy! WriteLn(Copy) prints not 'This is a string' but 'THis is a string'.

Bad as this is, it's really the least that can go wrong when a const parameter changes underneath you: The CauseTrouble procedure crashes because it changes the actual value of the Global string pointer. Copy is now a tombstoned pointer—a copy of a pointer that has been freed. When the Cause-

Trouble procedure tries to do Nu := Copy, it's dereferencing freed memory, which crashes the program with a Runtime error 203.

> **Note**
>
> *There is absolutely nothing the compiler or the RTL can do to protect you from this. This is just another way global variables are bad and dangerous. As a rule of thumb, "a routine with reference-counted* const *parameters should be* **extremely** *careful when changing global variables of the same type." This always includes true global variables; for local procedures, it includes any locals of the outer procedures; for object methods, it includes any of the object's fields.*

The ch2/ConstDanger program brought its problems upon itself, but an even subtler version of the same problem crops up with threads. Any time a procedure in a thread is passed a reference-counted global (or an object field) as a const parameter, it runs the danger that another thread will change the variable that the const parameter is a 'copy' of, thus potentially turning the const parameter into a tombstoned pointer. This sort of error can be very hard to track down, because the error is not in the thread code which crashes or (worse) works with the wrong data. Because so many library routines use const parameters, simply avoiding const parameters in your threaded code isn't really practical.

Probably the best heuristic for keeping const parameters from undermining your threaded code is to 'copy' any reference-counted global to a local variable before passing it to **any** routine. That is, instead of a procedure like

```
procedure Dangerous;
begin
  DoSomethingWith(SomeGlobal);
end; // Dangerous
```

use a procedure like

```
procedure Safe;
var
  LocalCopy: ReferenceCountedType;
begin
  LocalCopy := SomeGlobal; // Increment the reference count
  DoSomethingWith(LocalCopy);
end; // Safe
```

It may seem like making a 'copy' before calling "any routine" is a bit paranoid, that you really only need to worry about any routine which takes a const parameter or which may (either directly or indirectly) call another routine that takes a const parameter. That is, that you don't need to make a copy before calling simple 'terminal' routines that take a var or value parameter. And, you don't. Today. But one thing you can rely on is that no code is ever static. Today's simple terminal routine may be much more complex tomorrow. By always forcing a copy of a global bit of reference-counted data before calling a routine, you prevent tombstones or variable constants.

....

Out parameters are a specialized variation on variable parameters. Semantically, prefixing a parameter name with out means that the value on entry to a function is meaningless, that the parameter exists only to be set. In fact, the compiler will not complain if you refer to the value of an out parameter before you set it, and within the subroutine there is no effective distinction between variable and out parameters. However, if an out parameter is a reference-counted datatype like a huge string, dynamic array, or interface—or a Variant (see Chapter 3), as is common with CORBA interfaces—it will be cleared by the calling code before the subroutine call.

Value parameters always have a data type, while variable, const, and out parameters **usually** have a data type. However, you can declare non-value parameters as *untyped* by not suffixing their name with a colon and a datatype.

```
procedure Write(const Data; Bytes: Cardinal);
procedure Read(var Data; Bytes: Cardinal);
```

The things you can do with an untyped parameter are relatively limited:

- You can pass it to a generic routine, like FillChar() or Move(), that treats it simply as a stream of bytes.

- You can get its address with @ and Addr().

- You can cast it to a specific type, either explicitly or *via* absolute (see the Local Declarations section, below.)

Default Parameters

Given the prototype

```
procedure SetChangedFlag(Changed: boolean = True);
```

you can call SetChangedFlag with an explicit parameter, as
SetChangedFlag(True) or SetChangedFlag(False). You can also just
call SetChangedFlag and the compiler will automatically add the True
parameter. Default parameters are strictly a compile-time construct:
Default parameters are passed to their routine just as if you coded them,
and there is no way for a routine to tell whether a parameter was defaulted
or explicitly supplied.

Any defaultable parameters must be **after** any parameters that must be
explicit. Conversely, when you call the routine, you can only default parameters 'back to front'; you cannot call a routine as *eg* Foo(This, , That) and get
a default value for the middle parameter.

While you can pass structured types like records and objects (Chapter 3)
as parameters, you can't supply a default value for them. Only the scalar
datatypes may be defaulted.

Array parameters

Object Pascal offers no analog to C++'s variadic functions, where the last
entry in a parameter list can end in ... which stands for 'as many arguments
as the caller cares to supply'. Variadic routines like WriteLn() (chapter 8)
require compiler magic; you cannot write such routines yourself.

Note

*While you can't write variadic functions in Object Pascal, you can
call C library routines that take variable numbers of arguments. See
the online help for the* varargs *directive.*

Object Pascal's does offer something very close to variadic functions,
though, as you can declare any parameter as an *array parameter* (also known
as an *open array*) by prefixing its type with array of. For example, function
Sum(const Values: array of integer): int64 has as its single parameter an
array of integers. This parameter is compatible with the *dynamic arrays* of
Chapter 3, or you can supply a list of values at compile time by enclosing
them in square brackets:

```
Sum([1, 2, 3, 4]);
Sum([1, A, B, C, 2]);
Sum([This, That, Sum([A, B, C])]);
```

The Length() function will return the number of entries in the array, while the Low() and High() functions will return the first and last indices of the array. Thus, the full definition of the Sum function might look like

```
function Sum(const Values: array of integer): int64;
var
  Index: integer;
begin
  Result := 0;
  for Index := Low(Values) to High(Values) do
    Inc(Result, Values[Index]);
end; // Sum
```

> **Note**
>
>
>
> *Under the current implementation, array parameters are actually passed as a pair of parameters: a pointer to the first element, and a length count. Thus, Low() of an array parameter is always 0, and you will often see code that iterates from 0 to High(), or from 0 to Length() – 1. You should avoid this practice! While in all probability the sheer volume of code that counts on Low() equaling 0 prevents any changes, it's always possible that future implementations will pass Slice()s out of larger arrays as start and stop offsets or that the array parameter syntax will be extended to be more like standard arrays, which can have any ordinal as an index.*

A parameter of type `array of const` is a special, heterogeneous array that can hold any type. It's absolutely equivalent to an `array of TVarRec`, to the extent that you don't even have to cast each element of an array of const to a TVarRec to 'crack' it:

```
procedure ShowVType(A: array of const);
var
  Index: integer;
begin
  for Index := Low(A) to High(A) do
    WriteLn(TVarRec(A[Index]).VType); // This compiles and runs
  for Index := Low(A) to High(A) do
    WriteLn(A[Index].VType);          // This compiles and runs, too
end; // ShowVType
```

The TVarRec datatype is a five-byte record consisting of the VType datatype tag and four bytes that either contains the value or a pointer to it. Array of const parameters are mostly used in conjunction with Chapter 8's Format() function, though you may find your own uses for them, such as a routine that writes any number of values of any type to a stream. If you want to write a routine that uses an array of const parameter, the TVarRec datatype is well-documented in the online help. (You can also just type TVarRec in the Kylix code editor, and CTRL+CLICK on it to jump to the record definition.)

The standard function Slice() is used to pass selections from an array to routines that expect array parameters.

Function results

Procedures never return a result; functions always return a result, though you are free to ignore a function's result.[7] The syntax is similar to that of parameters and var declarations:

```
function Name(Arguments): ResultType; {or}
function Name: ResultType;
```

That is, the argument list (if any) is followed by a colon and a result type.

Functions can return any intrinsic or user-defined type. Pointers, floating point numbers, and ordinal values are returned in registers; other result types are returned by passing a pointer to the variable that the caller

---

7. The {$X-} pragma will turn on the Standard Pascal behavior where you **must** use a function result.

assigns the result to. That is, at the object code level, these two bits of code are virtually identical:

```
function ReturnARect: TRect;        procedure SetARect(var Result: TRect);
begin                               begin
end; // ReturnARect                 end; // SetARect


var                                 var
  MyRect: TRect;                      MyRect: TRect;


begin                               begin
  MyRect := ReturnARect;              SetARect(MyRect);
end.                                end.
```

Both 'push' a pointer to MyRect, and then call a routine that sets Result as (if it were) a var parameter. When a function returns a structured type that's used in an expression (like BoundsRect.TopLeft) and has no named storage, the calling code generates temporary storage on the stack and passes the function a pointer to that temporary storage.

In traditional Pascal, you set a function's result by assigning it to the function's name:

```
function One: integer; begin One := 1; end;
```

You can use this syntax in Object Pascal, but generally it's better to use the Result variable which every function has:

```
function Two: integer; begin Result := 2; end;
```

There's no difference between the two in this contrived example, but since Result *is* a local variable like any other, you can read it back after you set it. You can also do things like use it as the index variable in a for loop that scans some sort of list for a particular value; if the loop calls Exit on success, the function's result will be the match's index.

```
function IndexOf(Probe: TValue): integer;
// Searches ValueList. Returns Low(ValueList)..High(ValueList) on success, or
// Low(ValueList)-1 on failure.
begin
  for Result := Low(ValueList) to High(ValueList) do
    if ValueList[Result] = Probe then EXIT;
  Result := Low(ValueList) - 1;
end;
```

Overloading

Overloading is when you use a named subroutine or operator in two or more distinct ways. When these different uses are related in some obvious way, the result is greater clarity; you're taking advantage of people's hardwired ability for metaphor and analogy to make your code self-documenting. For example, the boolean operators and, or, xor and not are overloaded; with boolean arguments, they apply to the value as a whole, while with integer arguments they work in a bitwise manner. Similarly, the + operator is overloaded so that it works with numbers as well as strings and sets (Chapter 3).

These examples of *operator overloading* are all built into the language. Object Pascal only supports custom operator overloading *ala* C++ with Variant values (Chapter 3). However, you can overload any routine or object method. That is, you can have more than one routine with the same name—provided they have different argument lists. The compiler ignores the function result type when resolving overloaded identifiers, so overloading like

```
function Max(A, B: integer): integer; overload;
function Max(A, B: integer): int64;   overload;
```

is **not** allowed, as the compiler would have no way of knowing which function to call. Conversely,

```
function Max(A, B: integer): integer;    overload;
function Max(const A, B: string): string; overload;
function Max(A, B: double): double;       overload;
```

is perfectly fine, as the compiler can always tell which of the three Max functions to call.

All routines that are overloaded must be declared with the `overload`; modifier following the routine's prototype. You can not declare a routine then overload it by declaring a new routine with the `overload` tag: the first routine must be tagged, too.

Overloaded functions can (and often do) have different result types; you can also overload functions with procedures and *vice versa*. Giving two very different routines the same name is just a recipe for confusion but, used in moderation, overloading is a very useful tool to prevent the sort of name space pollution and loss of clarity that separate routines like MaxInt, MaxString, and MaxDouble represent.

Calling conventions

The way parameters are passed to a routine is known as the routine's calling convention, the rules that must be followed to call it properly. Normally, of course, the compiler takes care of this for you, so you only have to worry about calling conventions when you're calling a subroutine from inline assembler code or when you're writing a declaration for a library routine written in a language that uses a different default calling convention.

Under Object Pascal's default `register` convention, the first three parameters are passed in CPU registers, with any other parameters pushed onto the stack by the caller, left to right, and then popped by the routine before it returns. If you want to be absolutely clear which convention a given routine is using (perhaps you are afraid that the default behavior will change 'under' your assembly language function), you can specify the register-passing default behavior by putting the `register`; keyword after the rest of your routine's prototype.

Other calling conventions are less efficient, and are primarily provided for calling libraries written in other languages. The `pascal` calling convention passes all parameters on the stack, pushed left to right and popped by the routine. The `cdecl` calling convention passes all parameters on the stack, pushed right to right and popped by the *caller*. (This bloats the calling code, but is necessary to support `varargs` library routines that can take an indeterminate number of arguments.) The `safecall` and `stdcall` conventions are Windows calling conventions supported under Kylix primarily to minimize the differences between the Delphi and Kylix compilers; there's not much reason to use them in Kylix.

Although any explicit calling convention is separated from the rest of the prototype by a semicolon, the routine's calling convention is part of its prototype. A routine is not compatible with an otherwise identical procedural parameter if the calling conventions don't match. 'Bare' prototypes (as in declarations of procedural parameters, `forward` declarations (later in this chapter), and the `interface` section of units (Chapter 4)) always include the calling convention unless they use the default `register` convention.

Hint directives

A routine's prototype can include the `deprecated`, `library` or `platform` hint directives. Like a calling convention declaration, hint directives are separated from the rest of the prototype by a semicolon. Hint directives don't affect the routine in any way—unlike calling conventions, they have no impact on procedural parameter compatibility—but they do cause a compiler warning, if the routine is actually used. (You can disable these warnings with the {$WARN} pragma—see Chapter 4.)

- The `deprecated` directive means that the routine is obsolete, and being maintained only for backward compatibility; new code should not use deprecated routines.

- The `library` directive means that this routine depends on a particular library, or a particular version of a library. (Borland suggests that `library` be used to flag dependencies on CLX or VCL, but neither Kylix nor Delphi 6 include any `library` directives anywhere in their library source directories.)

- The `platform` directive means either that the routine acts differently in different environments, or that the routine does not exist in all environments. You would typically use this on routines that act mostly the same, but that have slightly different side effects on Linux than on Windows, or that behave differently under certain edge conditions. (For example, in Kylix, SysUtil's RenameFile routine will rename a file even when the new name already exists; in Delphi, SysUtil's RenameFile will fail if the new name already exists.)

Local declarations

Routines can, of course, have local variables. In addition, routines can have local types and constants, as well as local routines.

In general, local variables are allocated on the stack when the routine is called, and are freed when the routine returns. (When optimization is turned on, as it is by default, the compiler does a very good job of keeping most ordinal and pointer locals in the registers.) With two exceptions, there is no initialization of local variables in Object Pascal: local variants (Chapter 3) are set to Unassigned, and variables that can hold (point to) reference-counted data types like huge strings, dynamic arrays, and interfaces are automatically initialized to Nil. If the reference-counted variables weren't initialized, setting them for the first time would try to decrement the (nonexistent) reference count of some random piece of memory.

Local variables are *statically scoped*. That is, they are visible only within the routine that defines them, not to any called routine as in *dynamically scoped* languages like APL and Lisp. Local routines, however, can see any local declarations that precede them; they can use local types and constants, and they can read and write local variables. Note that a local routine can not see **all** its routine's local variables; it can see only the variables declared before it, and it can not see any variables declared after it. (See the *Contrived* example, below.)

Local declarations look just like any other declaration, except that they are placed between a routine's prototype and its body.

```
function Contrived(AnArgument: SomeType): TWhatever;
type
  YoungWhippersnappers = 18..35;
var
  DemographicData: array[YoungWhippersnappers] of Cardinal;

  procedure Local;
  var
    Index: YoungWhippersnappers;
  begin
    // Local can 'see' AnArgument, the Result variable,
    // the YoungWhippersnappers type, and DemographicData.
    // It cannot see Contrived's Index, which is declared
    // after it. Conversely, code in the body of Contrived
    // cannot see Local's Index variable.
  end;

var
  Index: YoungWhippersnappers;
begin
end;
```

One occasionally surprising consequence of the way that local declarations are just like global declarations is that a routine can easily have more than one var block of local variables. They don't have to be separated by a different type of declaration. Usually, of course, one runs all the local variable declarations together, but multiple var blocks can be useful, especially in conjunction with conditional compilation. Multiple var blocks can also help make your intentions clear when you have, say, multiple working sets: a group of variables that are used together in *this* branch, but not used at all in *that* branch.

Unusual constructs

Pascal is one of the few languages that supports local routines but they are very useful, both in breaking long routines up into screen-sized chunks for legibility, and in routines that must perform the same set of operations on some sort of ungrouped data (like three buttons on a form, for example). You should be aware, though, that the utility comes at the cost of access to their 'parent's' local variables being a relatively expensive process that requires walking a chain of stack frames. I don't particularly worry about this issue, preferring clear, simple code to complex, fast code in all but the most frequently executed inner loops, but some people prefer to avoid local routines in favor of external routines with many parameters.

Local (and global) variables can be declared absolute. The name is a bit strange, dating to the early personal computer days when one would often need to do things like assign symbolic names to a BIOS data area or declare the CGA as a 25 by 80 array of character/color pairs absolute $B800:0. The effect of a declaration like

The eponymous numeric syntax of absolute *is no longer supported.*

```
var
  AsReal: single;
  AsLong: LongWord absolute AsReal;
```

is that you can refer to the same 32-bit memory location as a floating point Single or as a 32-bit LongWord, depending on the name you use. It's a sort of permanent cast, and it can be much clearer to use an absolute variable than to keep casting. (You can also use absolute to do things that you can't do with casts, like treat the same 32-bit variable as either a single or a LongWord.) Absolute variables are probably most often used in routines that take untyped var or const parameters, and in callback routines that typically get a 32-bit integer or an untyped pointer argument that they 'know' is really an object reference:

```
procedure Callback(Data: pointer);
var
  ReallyIs: TSomeObject absolute Data;
begin
  // and so on
end;
```

Some people deprecate absolute variables because the optimizer doesn't handle them well. Absolute variables are not kept in registers the way normal variables are. These people prefer to write code like

```
procedure Callback(Data: pointer);
var
  ReallyIs: TSomeObject;
begin
  ReallyIs := TSomeObject(Data);
  // and so on
end;
```

Also, Borland almost dropped all absolute support in Kylix. The outcry this created from the pro-absolute camp probably guaranteed that the symbolic form of absolute will be around forever, but the particularly prudent may prefer to avoid absolute variables entirely.

Another Object Pascal historical oddity is the way it handles local static variables. Recent versions of Delphi—including, of course, Kylix—have allowed global variables to be initialized. In older versions, though, the only way to get an initialized variable was to use a *typed constant*. This is a constant declaration that looks a bit like an initialized variable: const *Name*: *Type* = *Value*;. Such a 'constant' was actually an initialized variable, and could be freely changed at run-time. Now that Object Pascal supports initialized globals, typed constants are generally only used *as* constants—except where you need local static storage. Local typed constants are actually stored as global variables (*ie*, not on the stack) but are only visible inside the routine that declared them. Thus, they act much like static variables in C, in that they can have an initial value but any changes persist across calls to the routine.

```
procedure HasState;
const

{$J+} // allow writeable typed constants
  FirstTime: boolean = True;
{$J-} // restore the unwriteable default

begin
  if FirstTime then
  begin
    // Do some sort of setup
    FirstTime := False;
  end;
  // Do whatever depends on the initialization above
end;
```

One thing to note about this is that the {$J} pragma controls whether or not you can change typed constants. In the default {$J-} state, you can't assign to a typed constants, and you'll have to set {$J+} around any typed constant that you want to use as a static variable.

{$J+} was the default in Delphi 5.

The body

The third part of the routine's declaration is its body, the set of statements that actually do something. The body of a routine can contain *only* statements: Object Pascal does not support C-style block local variables, or any other block local declarations.[8]

Exit

The Exit 'procedure' is a structured exit construct like Break and Continue. Its effect is to jump to the routine's exit code, freeing local storage and returning control to the caller. Because its effect is so radical, I usually put EXIT in all

---

8. Yes, this does mean that all local variables have to be declared at the top of the routine, not at the point where they're actually used. It's an annoyance—and yet another good reason to keep your routines small.

caps to make it stand out. Of course, Pascal is case **in**sensitive, so you don't have to follow this convention if you don't like it.

> **Note**
>
>
>
> Exit *is like C's* return *statement, not like C's* Exit *procedure, which halts the application. The Object Pascal equivalent of C's* Exit *procedure is the* Halt *procedure.*[9] *C programmers should also note that* Exit *cannot set a function's result the way C's* return *can.*

Calling Exit in a function that uses its Result variable as the index variable in a for loop is the *only* time that a for loop's index variable is officially guaranteed to have a meaningful value outside the body of the loop. (As above, Break can be unoffically relied on to leave the for loop's index variable intact.)

Recursion and forward declarations

Pascal has an iron-clad rule that you can't use an identifier until it's been declared. This causes no problems for *self-recursive* routines which call themselves, as of course their prototype always precedes their implementation, but it can cause problems in some cases of *mutually recursive* routines, where A needs to call B and B needs to call A. If A is declared before B, it can't call B.

In situations like this, you can use procedural variables, or you can use a *forward declaration* so that A knows B's prototype and can thus call it. A forward declaration consists of the prototype—and only the prototype—followed by the forward keyword.

```
procedure B(Level: Cardinal); forward;

procedure A(Level: Cardinal);
begin
  if Level > 0 then B(Level - 1);
end;
```

---

9. Do not use Halt in GUI programs once Application.Run has been called. (I discuss the Application global in Chapter 7.) Use Halt only in console applications, or to abort a GUI program during initialization.

```
procedure B;
begin
  if Level > 0 then A(Level - 1);
end;
```

As in this example, the eventual definition can use an abbreviated prototype, consisting of merely the procedure or function keywords and the routine's name. Many people prefer, as I do, for the eventual definition to contain a full prototype, as in a normal definition. If you **do** include a full prototype with the eventual definition it must exactly match the forward definition.

Forward definitions are more common in 'straight' Pascal than in Object Pascal. This is because Object Pascal's unit structure (Chapter 3) requires you to declare prototypes for all of a module's public routines in the interface section. These public routines are then visible to any other module that uses the unit—and to every routine in the unit's implementation section. Thus, two mutually recursive public routines do not need forward declarations to call each other, nor does a private routine need a forward declaration to call a public routine whose definition comes later in the source file.

Hints and warnings

The compiler will warn you if there is any path through a function which could result in the Result not being set. The warning is generally right, but there **are** cases where it is not, like

```
type
  Colors = (Red, Green, Blue, Black);

function BadWarning(Color: Colors): boolean;
begin
  case Color of
    Red, Blue:    Result := True;
    Green, Black: Result := False;
    else          begin
                  Assert(False, 'Code rot?')
                  Result := False;
                  end;
  end;
end; // BadWarning
```

I always want my code to compile with no hints or warnings, so I'm generally willing to put in seemingly needless code like the `else` block in this example. You could turn off warnings around this function, but I find that an awfully drastic—and potentially dangerous—solution. You could also just say 'Well, the compiler's wrong, here'—but then someone's going to have to go check that line every time they do a build, to make sure that it's the compiler at fault and not the program. (You can add a {$message} (Chapter 4) to the effect that you're quite sure that the warning's wrong, but I consider this a cure that's almost worse than the disease.)

> **Note**
>
> *Given the definition of Colors in the example above, the else block in the BadWarning function's case statement will not be executed unless you do something pathological like call* `BadWarning(Colors(-1))`*—and that would be caught by {$R+} range checking. However, what if you added a new identifier to the Colors enum, but didn't update the BadWarning function? Suddenly, the warning would be valid, but you wouldn't get it because it was suppressed by the 'spurious' assignment to Result. That's why there's also an Assert(False) in the block. You want to know if execution* **does** *make it into the else block.*

There are one or two other more unusual scenarios where the compiler will falsely warn you about a possible unset Result (see, for example, Chapter 7's `lib/LThreads` unit) but for the most part you should take compiler warnings about unset results seriously.

The compiler will also warn you if you use any local variables before you set them, and will give you a hint whenever a particular assignment or variable is never used. These hints and warnings are generally reliable, with only a few known scenarios that can cause false warnings, so you should pay attention to them. Sometimes it can look at first as if the compiler **is** wrong, but such situations usually turn out to hinge on a subtlety and to resolve in the compiler's favor.

There are cases, though, like

```
procedure BadWarning3(A: boolean);
var
  B: boolean;
begin
  if A then
    B := A;
  // ...
  if A then
    WriteLn(B); // Warning: Variable 'B' might not have been initialized
end; // BadWarning3
```

where the compiler is wrong. Or, at least, not quite right. Its analysis of code paths shows, quite rightly, that B is only set if A is True; that there's a path through the code that results in B not being set. So, it will generate a warning WriteLn that B might not have been set before the WriteLn reads it. *It doesn't see that B is only being used under conditions where B has already been set.* That is, its code path analysis doesn't look at the content of the tests that govern which paths are followed; it merely notices that it's possible that B hasn't been set before the second if statement.

You have three basic choices in cases like this. The first choice is bad: Don't do anything, and just ignore the warning each time it comes up. This is a bad choice because most hints and warnings **are** meaningful; hints and warnings are the hallmarks of bad, potentially buggy code. You might know which warnings are bogus—but everyone who inherits your code will have to satisfy himself. The second choice is to add a {$message} to the effect that the compiler's message really is wrong. This is a little better than the first choice but is still not ideal, both because it doubles the number of messages and also because everyone who inherits your code will still have to check that you're right. Generally, the third choice is best: Change your code to eliminate the compiler message. For example, in BadWarning3, inserting

```
B := False;
```

before

```
if A then
    B := A;
```

eliminates the warning. This does have a modest run-time cost, but not really enough to matter in 99.999% of all cases.

Note

I don't want to give the wrong impression with these examples of bad hints and warnings. The compiler is almost always right. While there are some classes of code that it misunderstands, you should generally assume that a hint or warning points to an error in your code, not in the compiler.

Assembler routines

While any routine can include a BASM asm / end block, you can also have special, all-assembler routines where the routine's body is replaced with an asm / end block. Assembler routines are perfectly normal routines in just about every way—they can have local variables, local types, and even local routines—except that their whole body is implemented in BASM and not in Object Pascal. In addition, if an assembler routine has no locals, and if all of its parameters (if any) and its Result (if any) are passed in registers, the compiler will optimize away its stack frame, making calls to the routine particularly fast.

Kylix generates pretty good code, so that you certainly won't need to use assembler routines in most projects, but there are still special cases where you will need to. For example, the assembler routine MulDiv2 is about 32 times as fast as its Pascal equivalent MulDiv1

```
function MulDiv1(A, B, C: integer): integer;
begin
  Result := int64(A) * B div C;
end; // MulDiv1

function MulDiv2(A, B, C: integer): integer;
asm
  imul edx // eax:edx := A {eax} * B {edx}
  idiv ecx // eax := eax:edx div C {ecx}
end; // MulDiv2
```

because it doesn't have to use multiple-precision subroutines for its 64-bit temporary value.

Exceptions

Exceptions allow you to simplify your code. There are many operations, like writing a file or sending data over a socket, that **usually** succeed but that sometimes fail. You could write your programs so that all such operations return a status code, but these operations are usually nested inside others. Your routines become cluttered with statements that check status codes and either continue or pass a failure code to their caller. Exceptions allow you to write code that assumes all sub-operations succeed, and that concentrates all error handling in one place. So, instead of checking each operation when you, for example, stream a data structure to or from disk, you simply have an exception handler that gets invoked automatically on any error, even if it occurs two or a hundred routines 'down'.

There are three exception handling statements in Object Pascal.

1. Raise 'throws' an exception object, which unwinds the subroutine call stack until it finds an except statement.

2. Except statements 'catch' the exception. You can either handle it completely, re-raise it, or raise a new exception.

3. Finally statements allow you to do cleanup, like freeing memory or closing files, no matter how you pass out of them.

Raise

You can raise any object instance (see Chapter 3) as an exception. However, the default exception handling that displays an alert box on any unhandled exception raised within an event handler requires that the object be an Exception object or one of its descendants, so almost all Object Pascal exceptions are Exception's of one sort or another.

The syntax of the raise statement is raise *ExceptionObject* or raise *ExceptionObject* at *Address*. The second form is almost never used; consult the online help for more information. A common mistake is to try to code raise Exception, which will not compile; Exception is a *class*, and you can only raise an *instance*. You need to do something like raise Exception.Create('This is an exception'). Create() is the simplest and most commonly used of Exception's constructors, but there are many others, appropriate for special situations. All Exception's have a Message member which is set in the constructor, and which you can display or otherwise process in the except handler. You can define Exception descendants with more members, if your applications require more extensive information about what went wrong.

When you raise an exception within a block with an exception handler, that handler gets the first chance to 'trap' the exception. If the handler can't handle the exception, or the exception is raised outside of a block with an exception handler, the current routine Exit-s, finalizing any local strings &c. If the aborted routine was called within a block with an exception handler, it will try to handle it; otherwise that routine, too, will call its cleanup code, and the process will repeat until control reaches an active exception handler that knows how to handle this particular exception.

What happens if the exception isn't handled depends on what type of program it is, and where the exception was raised. In the most normal case, where the exception was raised from an event handler in a GUI application (see Chapter 5), the run-time library will popup an alert box with details of the exception. (As a special case, EAbort exceptions are not visible in this way.) The program continues to run, but any of the event handler's code that would have followed the exception is not executed. Unhandled exceptions in GUI initialization code abort the program with a "Runtime error 230", while unhandled exceptions in console (non-GUI) applications write an error message to the standard error device, ErrOutput. Multithreaded code has special rules about unhandled exceptions: see Chapter 7.

Exception objects are freed when they are handled in an except statement. If you need to pass the object 'upstream' for further handling, a bare raise statement will "re-raise" the current exception instance, and pass control to the next exception handler on the stack frame.

Except

Except statements look like

```
try
  // Zero or more statements
except
  // Zero or more exception handling statements
end
```

That is, you can think of an Except statement as a compound statement with two parts. The Try block is just like a begin / end block. If it finishes normally, the Except block is skipped. If an exception is raised inside the Try block, or inside any routine called from it which does not have an exception frame of its own, control passes to the Except block.

At its simplest, the Except block consists of zero or more normal statements, which are executed on any exception. Thus, `try RiskyOp except end` is a very dangerous piece of code, with an empty Except block that will simply "'eat" any exception that RiskyOp may raise.[10] Similarly, `try RiskyOp except TellUserItDidntWork end` calls `TellUserItDidntWork` on any exception, no matter what.

Usually you need to tailor your response to the exception. Thus,

```
try
  // Whatever
except
  on EIntOverflow do HandleIntegerOverflow;
  on EMathError do HandleFloatError;
  on E: EAppError do HandleAppError(E);
  else HandleAllOtherErrors;
end;
```

uses `on` / `do` to call one of three specific exception handlers before giving up and calling the `else` handler. On entry, the Exception block will first check to see if the current exception matches the exception class named in the first `on` statement. If it does, it will execute the accompanying `do` statement, and then pass control to the first statement after the Except block. If the current exception doesn't match the first type, the second `on` statement is checked. If no `on` statements matches, the `else` statement is executed. If there's no else statement, an unhandled exception is passed on to the next active exception handler.

> ### Note
>
>
>
> *In general, you should be very wary of* else *clauses in Except blocks, and of 'swallowing' an exception. You want to be sure that the top-level code that called 'you' has a chance to know that the operation failed!* On / do *statements should be as narrow as possible, and utility code should only swallow an exception when it can safely continue despite the error. Top-level code needs to decide whether the error is fatal and the application should be shut down; whether the operation can safely be retried, either now or at some scheduled later time; or whether the user needs to alerted.*

---

10. This sort of code is unfortunately not uncommon. (I've been guilty of it.) People examine RiskyOp and say 'Oh, it will either succeed or throw an EConvertError. I'll set a valid default and just eat the EConvertError.' This is a bad practice for two reasons: First, at some future point, RiskyOp may be changed, and start also raising an ENewError, that you're **not** prepared for. Second, it's not impossible that bad memory will raise a hardware exception that you really **don't** want to eat. You should only eat specific, expected exceptions.

If your handler needs to use some of the fields of the exception object, you can use the on *Name: Exception* do syntax to give the exception instance a name. You can read or write any fields[11] of the exception object and you can call any of its methods, or you can re-raise it *via* raise *Name*. You can also always use a bare raise to re-raise the current exception. Re-raising an exception prevents the object from being freed, and passes it to the next active exception frame. Note that you can only re-raise the exception within the Except block itself, not from within any subroutines that you may pass the exception instance to.

Do not be fooled by the case-like syntax: Exception frames are relatively expensive to setup, and exceptions are relatively expensive to catch. It can be tempting to use exception handling for routine program control, but this is generally not a good idea. However, exception handling can make your code that 'usually' succeeds much simpler and less cluttered, and can centralize error handling for multiple related operations in a single place.

Finally

Finally statements are also compound statements with two parts, like Except statements.

```
try
  // Zero or more statements
finally
  // Cleanup code
end
```

The cleanup code in the Finally block is guaranteed to execute, regardless of whether control passes out of the Try block normally, *via* a routine's Exit statement, or as a result of an exception. The cleanup code generally does things like free memory, close files, or reset a flag.

---

11. For example, it's sometimes useful to replace a generic exception Message with a more verbose one that includes error reporting instructions for the end-user.

> **Note**
>
> *Object Pascal does not call objects' destructors when the objects go out of scope, the way C++ does for automatic objects that 'live' on the stack. Thus, Object Pascal code typically uses try / finally statements for the sort of cleanup operations that C++ code puts in destructors. You can think of using a try / finally block as being somewhat analogous to protecting a dynamic object with an* auto_ptr<>.

It's relatively common to Create and Free an object (Chapter 3) within a single routine. Whenever you do this, you should use a Finally block to be sure to Free the object. A common idiom for this is to use a with statement to Create, use, and Free the object anonymously:

```
with SomeObject.Create do
try
  // use it
finally
  Free;
end;
```

Freeing the object within a Finally block guarantees that it's freed, even if some of the statements in the Try block raise an exception. A good habit to get into is to code the try finally Free; end as soon as you code the Create, and to then go back and fill in the code that actually uses the new object. This helps keep you from making the mistake of creating an object without freeing it.

Try / finally statements can not be merged with try / except statements into a single try / finally / except statement. You have to nest them, like

```
try
  try
    // Doubly protected code
  finally
    // Cleanup, even if an exception is thrown
  end;
except
  // Handle any exceptions
end;
```

or

```
try
  try
    // Doubly protected code
  except
    // Handle exceptions while objects still exist
  end;
finally
  // Cleanup after any exceptions have been handled
end;
```

You do *not* need to use a try / finally statement to release reference-counted data structures like strings, interfaces, and dynamic arrays. These structures have a sort of automatic try / finally block that guarantees that the reference count will be maintained properly whether they go out of scope *via* normal routine return, Exit, or an exception. You only have to use an explicit Finally statement for resources that you explicitly Create or open. Changing your code so that you access files, say, through an interface (Chapter 3) instead of *via* explicit file handles eliminates a whole class of failure points, reducing the need for vigilance on your part.

CHAPTER 3
Data structures

CHAPTER 3

Data structures

CHAPTER 1 COVERED PRIMITIVE scalar datatypes, while Chapter 2 covered structured programming constructs. This chapter returns to data, and all the ways that scalars can be combined into compound data structures.

Basic structured data

Like C++ and unlike Java, Object Pascal is built upon an older, non-object oriented language. Thus, there are 'flat' data structures that often have routines designed to manipulate them, but no methods that are a part of them.

Unlike C++, the addition of objects didn't change the existing language: Objects are objects, and records are records. In C++, the big difference between a `struct` and a `class` is that a structure's default visibility is `public` while an object's default visibility is `private`. This just isn't true in Object Pascal. While the objects are as full-fledged as you could like—supporting encapsulation, polymorphism, single inheritance, and interfaces—records have no methods and no visibility modifiers.

This chapter covers the 'flat' data structures and the details of variable and constant declarations, then it covers objects, and Object Pascal's Variants. Variants are dynamically typed data structures, like Perl's scalars. Kylix allows you to define *custom variants* which implement *operator overloading*, and the section on Variants includes a detailed walkthrough of a custom variant list class.

Records

Pascal's notion of `record` includes both what C calls a `struct` and what C calls a `union`: a collection of named *fields*, each of which can be of any type. That is, a record's fields may be any of the simple scalar datatypes of Chapter 1, or any of the compound data structures of this chapter, including object references and other records.

```
type
  PPoint = ^ TPoint;
  TPoint = record
             X, Y: LongInt;
           end;
  TLine  = record
             Start, Stop: TPoint;
           end;
  PLine  = ^ TLine;
```

By convention, record and object type names start with a capital T. Of course, this is only a convention, and the compiler does not enforce it in any way.

Records are commonly declared along with an associated pointer type, which usually starts with a capital P. A pointer declaration can reference a *base type* which hasn't yet been defined—so long as the definition comes in the same `type` block.

You can deal with records as a whole or in part. If you have two records of the same type, A and B, `A := B` does a byte-by-byte copy of record B, so that every field of A equals the corresponding field of B.[1] When you pass a record to a routine by value, you actually pass a pointer, and the routine's preamble code copies the record (does an assignment) to a local variable.

Note

*Each record type declaration creates a unique type, and two different record types are **not** assignment compatible with each other, even if their field lists are 100% identical. You can use a cast to get around this, subject to the usual* caveat *that casting is a way of telling the compiler that you know exactly what you're doing—even if you don't.*

As *per* Chapter 2, when a function returns a record, the calling code passes a pointer to the record that receives the Result record. The called code treats this pointer as if it were an invisible parameter, `var Result: ` *record*. That is, functions that return records write directly to the caller's storage;

---

1. This is a bit of an oversimplification. When the record contains no reference-counted datatypes, the compiler does a simple, inline bulk copy. When the record does contains reference-counted datatypes, the compiler uses a subroutine that copies the data and increments each reference count. The effect is the same, however.

they don't create a new record, fill it in, then copy it to the caller's copy of the record. If the result is being ignored, the calling code creates an anonymous local which is filled in by the called code and then discarded. When you pass the result of a function that returns a record to a routine that takes a record by value (*ie*, not as a var parameter),

```
RectRoutine( Rect(Left, Top, Right, Bottom) ); // Passing an anonymous record
```

the compiler creates an anonymous local before calling the function, fills in the anonymous local in the function, and then copies the anonymous local in the routine's preamble code. If the record is a const parameter, the final copy is skipped; the routine simply uses the passed pointer to the anonymous record.

Individual fields are accessed as *RecordName.FieldName*. Thus, given var Point: TPoint; Line: PLine, we can read and write Point.X or Line^.Start.Y. When a record contains another record as a field, that field's name acts as the record name, so that the dot notation is recursive and we refer to Line^.Start.Y or Line^.Stop.X.[2] If we had a var TwoLines: record Top, Bottom: TLine; end, we could refer to TwoLines.Top.Start.X and TwoLines.Bottom.Stop.Y, and so on.

You can use the record / end notation to declare single instances of records in a var block, but you can not use it in a formal parameter list. You can only declare record parameters to be of an explicitly declared type. Note that the rule about each declaration being a unique type means that you can only pass a 'direct typed' record variable like var Point: record X, Y: LongInt end; to a routine that expects a record type like TPoint by casting it to TPoint, even though the field layouts are 100% identical.

Variant records

A *variant record* is the Pascal analog to a C union, a data structure which has more than one name (and type!) for the same bytes. All Pascal records can contain both an invariant 'header' and a variant 'footer'. This is the primary difference between Pascal's records and C's structs and unions: in C, a struct never has any variant parts and a union never has any invariant parts.

---

2. As *per* Chapter 1, you can omit the ^ (*caret*, or sometimes *hat*) when dereferencing pointers to records. Though I recommend that you don't, I feel I ought to mention that those who favor omitting the carets make much the same sort of argument that I do about omitting the optional empty parentheses after procedures or functions with no arguments. Just as omitting the empty parentheses makes it easier to turn an object method into a property, so omitting the carets makes it easier to turn a dynamically allocated record into an object.

The invariant header looks like the records we've seen already: a list of zero or more *FieldName: FieldType* pairs following the record keyword, and separated from each other with semicolons. The variant part starts with the case keyword, which is followed either by *TagFieldName: TagType* of or *TagType* of, and then all the variant definitions. The *TagFieldName: TagType* syntax yields a *tagged variant*, while the bare *TagType* syntax yields an *untagged variant*. The only difference between tagged and untagged variant records is that the tagged variant has an invariant field *TagFieldName* of type *TagType*, which presumably somehow identifies the format of the succeeding variant part. There is absolutely no difference in a tag field and a normal field in the invariant part before the case keyword, except that the *TagType* can only be an ordinal type. That is, both

```
type
  TVariant1 = record
                Float: double;
                case Tag: integer of
                  2: (Lo, Hi: word);
                  4: (Int:  integer);
                end;
  TVariant2 = record
                Float: double;
                Tag:  integer;
                case integer of
                  2: (Lo, Hi: word);
                  4: (Int:  integer);
                end;
```

are valid, but

```
type
  TInvalid  = record
                Float: double;
                case Tag: double of // TagTypes must be ordinals
                  2: (Lo, Hi: word);
                  4: (Int:  integer);
                end;
```

is not.

Everything between the of and end keywords is the variant part of the record. It consists of one or more *Tag: (FieldList)* entries, separated by semicolons. The *Tag*'s are not stored as part of the record, and are not used to select one variant part or another. They are simply used to distinguish one variant part from another at compile time. Nonetheless, each *Tag* must be of the *TagType*, and it must be unique. Often, the *Tag*'s are chosen to have some connection with the *FieldList*, as in the above examples where the 4: entries contained a 4-byte Integer, while the 2: entries contained a pair of 2-byte Words corresponding to the low and high words of the Int field.

Note

You may have noted a bit of syntactic weirdness, here. A variant record has only a single end—*there's no* end *to match the* case, *followed by a second* end *to match the* record. *One way to look at this is that an* end *for the* case *would suggest that the variant record is at least potentially a sort of invariant-variant-invariant 'sandwich', which it's not: the variant part must be the end of the record.*

You cannot have reference-counted field types like huge strings and dynamic arrays in the variant part. This is because of the automatic finalization of reference-counted fields when a record that contains them is freed or goes out of scope. If a variant record has overlaid other data on top of a reference field, then the compiler can not know if the data in the reference-counted field is really a reference or is really something else. Not finalizing a reference-counted object is a memory leak; trying to decrement the reference count on something that's not really reference counted leads to data corruption or a segmentation violation. So, the compiler just won't allow reference-counted field types in a variant part.

You refer to variant fields just as you refer to invariant fields. Thus, given a var `This: TVariant1`, you can read and write `This.Float`, `This.Tag`, `This.Lo`, `This.Hi`, and `This.Int`. Each entry in the variant part (the *FieldList*) shares space. That is, the first field of each list starts at the same offset from the start of the record. Changing `This.Lo` or `This.Hi` changes `This.Int` and *vice versa*. The SizeOf () a variant record is the size of the invariant part, if any, plus the size of the largest variant part.

In 'classic', or Standard, Pascal there is no typecasting, and variant records like this were the only way that you could refer to the same byte stream as both an integer and a pair of smaller Hi and Lo parts. Object Pascal, of course, allows you to cast any value to a same-size record to 'crack' its byte-stream, so this type of variant record is much less common. Most variants are like

```
type
  TQuiteDifferent = record
                      Name:      string;
                      SSN:       TTaxNumber;
                      Birthday: TDateTime;
                      case Salaried: boolean of
                        False: (PerHour:  double);
                        True:  (Salary:   double;
                                Benefits: TBenefitLevel;
                                Vested:   boolean)
                    end;
```

where the variant fields overlay each other but are essentially unrelated.

Packing and memory layout

There is a one to one correspondence between field name order and field position in the record. That is, in Kylix 1, a record like

```
type
  DWord = record
          Lo, Hi: word;
          end;
```

takes four bytes, and has the Lo word as the low order word and the Hi word as the high order word. This makes it a useful type to cast 32-bit numbers to when you need to 'crack' the byte-stream and read or write the 16-bit words separately.[3]

But the Intel 32-bit architecture places a relatively high penalty on accessing multi-byte data that starts at odd[4] offsets. By default, the compiler will insert pad bytes so that each field is optimally aligned. For example, SizeOf()

---

3. This assumes, of course, an Intel, "little-endian" architecture, where the Least Significant Byte [LSB] of a multi-byte value is the first byte, and the Most Significant Byte [MSB] is the last byte. If Borland ever ports Kylix to a "big-endian" machine, where the MSB is the first (leftmost) byte and the LSB is the last (rightmost) byte, this record probably wouldn't work.

4. Yes, "odd" both as in odd numbers (N mod 2 = 1) and in the colloquial sense. The CPU acts like it pauses for a moment to say "that's odd" when you ask it to load or store a value at an odd offset.

```
type
  EightBytes = record
                 First:  word;
                 Second: LongInt;
                 end;
```

is 8, not 6, because access to 32-bit data is fastest when the offset of the first byte is a multiple of 4. (See Figure 3-1.)

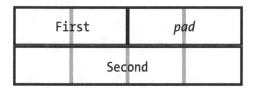

Figure 3-1. DWord alignment for the Second field requires pad bytes

Historically, the default alignment policy has often changed between releases, tracking the alignment requirements of the newest processors. On a future 64-bit platform, the DWord record might take 6 or 10 bytes, not 4, and would thus no longer be suitable for cracking a 32-bit value. Similarly, a change in alignment strategy might break programs that need to transfer records (*via* disk files, shared memory, or sockets) to programs compiled under different versions of Kylix.

Thus, Kylix allows you to declare packed records, which have no pad bytes. In a packed record, the size of the record is always the sum of the size of the fields, while in an aligned record, the size of the record is always **at least** the sum of the size of the fields. Thus, changing the definition of the DWord record to

```
type
  DWord = packed record
            Lo, Hi: word;
            end;
```

guarantees that it will always be a 4-byte type that can be used to crack 32-bit datatypes.

Packing only applies to individual record types. If you need to declare a large block of packed types, you can use the {$A-} pragma (Chapter 4) to turn the default alignment on and off. In Kylix 1 and Delphi 6, the default {$A+} state uses some complicated rules (see Chapter 4) to assure that every field is optimally aligned. Most of the time, you should use the default alignment, as that will make for the fastest access to data. That is, packed records offer predictability and portability at the expense of performance.

Dynamic allocation

Traditionally, records were heavily used in conjunction with dynamic memory allocation; just about each heap block would be a record of some type. However, now that we have objects and dynamic arrays, this is just not true any more. Few Kylix programs use GetMem and FreeMem, and probably even fewer use New and Dispose, but the old constructs are still there, and still worth knowing a little about.

New and Dispose are typed memory managers. If you pass New() a typed pointer (*ie*, any pointer except an generic `pointer` or a procedural variable), it will allocate enough bytes to hold the variable, clear any references (pointers) it may contain to reference-counted data like strings and dynamic arrays, and set the variable to point to the newly allocated object. Conversely, when you Dispose() of a pointer you got from New(), any reference-counted data will automatically be finalized, and the memory will be returned to the free list. (See Chapter 8 for more information on Kylix's memory management.) When you use New and Dispose with the deprecated "old-style objects" (below), New takes an optional constructor call parameter, and Dispose can call a destructor.

GetMem, FreeMem, and ReallocMem are untyped, or bulk, memory managers. GetMem(PtrVar, Bytes) will allocate Bytes bytes (plus an invisible header to the 'left' of the allocated memory), and set PtrVar to point to the heap block— or raise an exception, if there's not enough memory. FreeMem(PtrVar) releases the memory, using the block size stored in the block header. (In older code, you will sometimes see FreeMem used with a second argument—which Kylix ignores.) ReallocMem() changes the size of an existing block, either by adding or removing bytes at the 'right' end of the block, or by copying the old data to a new block and then freeing the old block.

You're probably most likely to use the bulk memory routines with raw byte-streams like audio or video samples; if you *do* use them with records, you need to remember that they are bulk routines that do no initialization or finalization of the memory they allocate. That is, any records you allocate will be filled with garbage. If the record contains any reference-counted fields, the first time you set them the RTL [Run Time Library] will try to decrement the reference count on the value that's currently stored there. This will either damage data in your address space or cause a segmentation fault. Conversely, when you FreeMem the records, the reference counts of any valid references will not be decremented, and you will have a memory leak. The solution to both problems is simply to call Initialize on any record pointer after you GetMem it, and Finalize before you FreeMem it.

The Initialize procedure assures that all reference-counted fields are set to Nil, so that the initial assignment doesn't try to finalize a (non-existent) previous value. The Finalize procedure finalizes all reference-counted fields, preventing memory leaks. These are exactly the operations that are done automatically when entering or leaving a procedure with a local record; the only difference is that when you use the bulk memory routines you have to explicitly Initialize and Finalize your records.

Both Initialize and Finalize have to step through compiler-generated descriptions of the record structures to find reference-counted fields. This is not exactly a free operation. The only way to get around calling Finalize is to manually set every reference-counted field to Nil. I recommend that you not even *think* about doing this, as it's both tedious and error-prone. You can, however, avoid calling Initialize if you fill the heap block with 0's as soon as you allocate it. This will set all reference-counted fields to Nil, just as Initialize will, but without having to walk the record structure's description.

The easiest way to fill the heap block with 0's is to use the SysUtil's function AllocMem. The following example shows both approaches.

```
program getmem_demo;

uses SysUtils; // for AllocMem

type
  TStringRecord = record
    This: string;
    That: string;
  end;
  PStringRecord = ^ TStringRecord;

var
  P: PStringRecord;

const
  RecCount = 2;

begin
  // When you GetMem, you need to Initialize
  GetMem(P, SizeOf(P^) * RecCount);
  Initialize(P^, RecCount);

  Finalize(P^, RecCount);
  FreeMem(P);
```

Both Initialize and Finalize can take an optional repeat count parameter.

```
    // When you use SysUtils.AllocMem, you don't need to Initialize
    P := AllocMem(SizeOf(P^) * RecCount);

    Finalize(P^, RecCount);
    FreeMem(P);
end.
```

The with statement

When records contain records that contain records, referring to the innermost fields can get complex and hard to read. Something like `This.That.TheOther.Field` is hard to read, at best; when you have statements like `This.That.TheOther.Field := This.That.TheOther.Field * 42`, "opaque" becomes a polite way to describe your code.

This is what the `with` statement is for. The basic syntax is `with Structure do Statement`, and the effect is to temporarily create a new, most-local scope. (Figure 3-2.) This modifies name lookup so that the *Structure* is the first place that the compiler looks for every name it encounters in the *Statement*. That is, you can rewrite something like `This.That.TheOther.Field := This.That.TheOther.Field * 42` as `with This.That.TheOther do Field := Field * 42`, which is smaller and clearer.

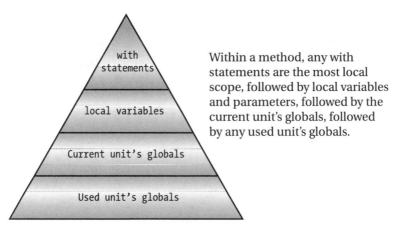

Within a method, any with statements are the most local scope, followed by local variables and parameters, followed by the current unit's globals, followed by any used unit's globals.

Figure 3-2. With statements create a temporary, most-local scope

When you are using with to open up nested records like this, it's a simple compile-time construct. The generated code is no different than it would be if you used the full, nested name for each field. However, the *Structure* clause can include pointer dereferences or array lookups to refer to a particular item in a large and complex data structure. When the *Structure* clause thus implies address generation, the with statement stores the generated address in an invisible local, and uses that for references to the structure within the *Statement* part. That is, statements like

```
with Foo^.Bar^ do ThisField := ThatField / TheOtherField;
```

or

```
with ArrayOfRecords[Index] do ThisField := ThatField / TheOtherField;
```

are not just smaller but are also faster than the corresponding

```
Foo^.Bar^.ThisField := Foo^.Bar^.ThatField / Foo^.Bar^.TheOtherField;
```

or

```
ArrayOfRecords[Index].ThisField :=
  ArrayOfRecords[Index].ThatField /
  ArrayOfRecords[Index].TheOtherField;
```

Since with is just another statement type, you can of course nest one with statement inside of another.

```
with Foo^ do
  with Bar^ do ThisField := ThatField / TheOtherField;
```

You can use with Foo^, Bar^ do as a shorthand for this nested with statement. Note that the comma syntax is *exactly* equivalent to the nested syntax: Bar^ can be either an independent structure that you want to access in parallel with Foo^, or it can be (as it is here) a field of Foo^ that was exposed by the with Foo^ to its left.

Used with care, with can make your code smaller, clearer, and more efficient. Used carelessly, it can also cause hard-to-find bugs, by *shadowing* identifiers that would normally be in scope behind an identifier of the same name from a structure that you've opened up. This shadowing behavior causes with to be the language feature most deprecated by Pascal novices. A similar, subtler bug occurs when changes to a structure defined *here* break code that uses that structure in a with statement over *there*. For example, a TStructure might be defined as

```
type
  TStructure = record
    Foo: integer;
  end;
```

and you might use it in a routine like

```
procedure WillBreak(Structure: TStructure);
var
  Bar: integer;
begin
  with Structure do
    Bar := Foo;
  // Do some more
end; // WillBreak
```

The WillBreak procedure copies Structure.Foo to a local variable, Bar. No problem. But, imagine that you (or someone else, like a component vendor) changes TStructure to

```
type
  TStructure = record
    Foo, Bar: integer;
  end;
```

Suddenly, the WillBreak procedure is not copying Structure.Foo to a local variable, it's copying Structure.Foo to Structure.Bar. If you're lucky, you'll get a warning about an unset variable; if you're unlucky, the code will break without any warning at all.

The way to keep with from being a benefit and not a drawback is twofold: Be careful with your use of short, common field names like Tag and Caption—you're less likely to have name collisions when you use long, detailed names—and keep your with statements as small and as localized as possible. Don't forget, too, that you can always use a fully qualified name within a with block—you don't **have** to use the shorthand.

Finally, you can always use CTRL+CLICK (Chapter 5) to debug your with statements. If doing a CTRL+CLICK on an identifier in a with statement doesn't take you where you expect, you're either shadowing an identifier or doing something like *expecting* the 'opened' component to have an Enabled property when it really doesn't.

Sets

Sets are officially defined in a rather abstruse and mathematical way, as an 'unordered collection of values.' There is no inherent order to the values in a set, and a given value is either in the set or not: It can't be included twice.

This is true enough, but doesn't necessarily give as good an idea of their utility as these alternate formulations:

- You can look at a set as a sort of array of Boolean values, indexed by an ordinal. That is, any given value is either in the set or not. This makes for a great way to classify values.

```
function IsAlphaNumeric(AsciiChar: char): boolean;
begin
  Result := AsciiChar in ['A'..'Z', 'a'..'z', '0'..'9'];
end;
```

- You can also ignore the semantics, and just focus on the implementation. Sets are an excellent way to manipulate individual bits in a bitstream.

You can have a set of any ordinal type, but sets are never bigger than 32 bytes and can thus never have any more than 256 members. In addition, the Ord() of each value must be in the range 0..255; the compiler will not generate code to map, say, 1000..1255 to 0..255. These are some occasionally annoying restrictions that **may** be lifted in future versions of Kylix, but sets are still quite useful, even so. (The Classes unit's TBits class can be used to work with larger collections of bits.)

Sets are declared as set of *BaseType*, where the *BaseType* can be either an existing ordinal type or a subrange. Thus,

```
type
  TSetOfChar  = set of char;
  TTeens      = set of 13..19;

  TFlagColor  = (fcRed, fcWhite, fcBlue);
  TFlagColors = set of TFlagColor;

const
  AlphaNumeric: set of char = ['A'..'Z', 'a'.. 'z', '0'..'9'];

var
  ConditionsSatisfied: set of TConditionCodes {an enum} = [];
```

[] is the *empty set*, which is compatible with all sets. Set values consist of zero or more values of the base type, enclosed in square braces and separated by commas. Subranges (*eg*, This..That) are acceptable, and mean that all the values from This to That are included in the set. The same value can appear more than once—`set of char = ['A'..'Z', 'A'..'Z']` is perfectly legal—but the duplication has no effect: a value can only be in the set once.

You use the `in` operator to see if a single value is in the set or not: for example, `ThisChar in AlphaNumeric`. More complicated operations overload the +,–, * and relational operators.

Table 3-1. Set operators

Overloaded operator	Name	Example	Bitmapped interpretation
+	union	A + B	A or B
-	difference	A - B	A and not B
*	intersection	A * B;	A and B
=	equality	A = B	A = B
<>	inequality	A <> B	A <> B
<=	subset	A <= B	A and B = A
>=	superset	A >= B	A and B = B

Note

>= *and* <= *are supported, but* **not** > *and* <.

In addition to the infix operators of Table 3-1, you can use the Include() and Exclude() procedures to add or subtract individual values somewhat faster than the equivalent + [Value] and - [Value] operations.

For sets that take four bytes or less, assignment is done *via* inline code, while assignment of larger set values involves procedure calls. Similarly, sets that take four bytes or less can be passed to a routine in the registers, just like ordinals. In the interests of efficiency, sets are not normalized at all: That is, a set of 7..10 will take two bytes, just as a set of 0..15 would, but the values of bits 0..6 and 11..15 are undefined.

Static arrays

Object Pascal supports two different types of arrays. Dynamic arrays are resizable at run-time, and always live on the heap. A dynamic array variable is actually just a pointer to a reference-counted heap block, much like a huge string. By contrast, a static array can not change size at run-time (though there are tricks you can play with 'template' declarations and GetMem) and static array variables take up space where they're declared; they can live on the heap, but they can also live either in the global data area or on the stack.

Static arrays are declared as array[IndexType] of ElementType, where the *IndexType* can be any ordinal type and the *ElementType* can be any type at all. Unlike C, arrays do not have to be indexed by numbers, and they don't have to be based at 0. It's perfectly legal to have an array[char] or an array[1..10]. The only restriction on the IndexType is that SizeOf() the array must be less than or equal to MaxInt ($7FFFFFFF) bytes. As with records, you can assign one array to another of the same type (or pass an array by value) and the compiler will do a bytewise copy. (If the array contains reference-counted data, an array copy will increment the reference count of each datum.)

> **Note**
>
>
> *The same rule about unique type definitions applies to arrays as to records: two different array types are **not** assignment compatible with each other, even if their definitions are 100% identical.*

You can use High() and Low() on static array types and values, just as with the open array parameters of Chapter 2. As with open arrays, High() and Low() return the high and low **index**, not the highest or lowest value in the array.

The compiler will always catch a static attempt to read or write a nonexistent element (*ie*, an index less than Low() or greater than High()). With range checking turned on, any dynamic attempt to read or write an index will result in a range check. That is,

```
{$R+}

var
  AnArray: array[1..10] of integer;
  AnIndex: integer;

begin
  AnIndex := 11;
  WriteLn(AnArray[AnIndex]); // will range check
  WriteLn(AnArray[11]);      // won't compile
end.
```

Performance issues

It's not uncommon to find that some data can be represented as either an array of records or a record of arrays. While this is at least partly a matter of personal preference, there are some tradeoffs. Kylix takes full advantage of Intel CPU's array indexing modes, so that arrays of 1, 2, 4, or 8 byte base types are particularly fast. Thus, if your code routinely accesses single scalars from multiple records, a record of arrays may be faster than an array of records. On the other hand, if your code will usually need to deal with several fields of any given record at the same time, you can do the address calculation once, either using with or @ or by passing the record as a const parameter, and so an array of records may be faster.

A related performance issue has to do with the way that C programmers are very used to doing pointer arithmetic to scan strings or walk arrays. While you can do exactly the same thing in Object Pascal, something like

```
function FindFirstChar1(const Target: string; Probe: char): integer;
begin
  for Result := 1 to Length(Target) do
    if Target[Result] = Probe then EXIT;
  Result := Length(Target) + 1;
end; // FindFirstChar1
```

is simultaneously smaller, clearer, safer **and** faster than

```
function FindFirstChar2(const Target: string; Probe: char): integer;
var
  Ptr:    PChar;
begin
  Ptr := PChar(Target);
  for Result := 1 to Length(Target) do
    if Ptr^ = Probe
      then EXIT
      else Inc(Ptr);
  Result := Length(Target) + 1;
end; // FindFirstChar2
```

as Target[Result] will load the character in a single operation that costs very little more than Ptr^, and avoids the overhead of stepping Ptr along with Result. Thus, C programmers should make a conscious effort to use arrays instead of pointer arithmetic.

Multidimensional arrays

While most arrays are "one dimensional", with a single index, Pascal supports higher-dimensional arrays. The general syntax is thus array[*IndexList*] of *ElementType* where *IndexList* is one or more comma-separated ordinal types. There is no requirement that the indices be of the same type: you can have, *eg*, an array[char, word] if that makes sense in your application. Again, the only real restriction on the *IndexList* is that SizeOf() the array must be less than or equal to MaxInt bytes.

An array[TypeA, TypeB, TypeC] of BaseType is *exactly* equivalent to an array[TypeA] of array[TypeB] of array[TypeC] of BaseType. Both are laid out the same way, and both can be addressed either as Arr[A, B, C] or Arr[A] [B] [C].

```
var
  A1: array[1..2, 1..3, 1..4] of byte;
  A2: array[1..2] of array[1..3] of array[1..4] of byte;
begin
  A1[2, 3, 4] := A1[1] [2] [3];
  A2[2, 3, 4] := A2[1] [2] [3];
end.
```

Similarly, you can get the address of a subarray—*eg*, @ A1[1] or @A1[1, 2]—even when you haven't declared the array as an array of arrays.

The equivalence of a multidimensional array to an array of arrays means that multidimensional arrays are laid out in row-major order. That is, the rightmost addresses vary fastest, as in Figure 3-3. I mention this primarily because multidimensional array indexing is a bit slower than linear array indexing. Calculating the position of a particular element means adding the column index to the row index multiplied by the number of columns, perhaps adding that to the plane index times the number of elements in a plane, and so on. This position then has to be multiplied by the element size to get an offset. With multidimensional arrays, C-style pointer arithmetic may be faster than repeated array subscripting.

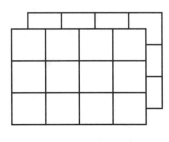

1,1,1	1,1,2	1,1,3	1,1,4
1,2,1			
1,3,1			
2,1,1			
2,2,1			
2,3,1			2,3,4

logical layout of
array[1..2, 1..3, 1..4]

physical layout of
array[1..2, 1..3, 1..4]

Figure 3-3. Logical and physical layout of multi-dimensional arrays

No open-ended arrays

Some dialects of Pascal support what you might call "open-ended arrays", where you specify a low index but not a high index: Any index greater than the low value is valid. These are used for dynamically allocated lists of variable length. Kylix's Object Pascal does not. The *dynamic arrays* of the next section are a good solution for most in-Kylix variable length arrays, but they don't work quite as well when you have to pass structures with fixed headers followed by variable length data to a non-Kylix library, or where you might need to treat a given sample stream as either a stream of bytes, words, or dwords.

These situations are among the few where you'll still need to use the bulk memory routines. The general idea is that you declare a large 'template' like

```
type
  TTemplate = array[0..High(integer) div SizeOf(BaseType) - 1] of BaseType;
  POpenEndedArrayOfBaseType = ^ TTemplate;
```

and then GetMem (or AllocMem) an actual heap block that only has room for ten or a hundred elements, instead of the millions or billions that the template declaration calls for.

```
// Allocate unfilled memory & Initialize
function Allocate1(Elements: Cardinal): POpenEndedArrayOfBaseType;
begin
  GetMem(Result, SizeOf(Result^[0]) * Elements);
  Initialize(Result^, Elements); // Kylix will tell you if you DON'T
                                  // need to Initialize()
end; // Allocate1

// Allocate cleared memory
function Allocate2(Elements: Cardinal): POpenEndedArrayOfBaseType;
begin
  Result := AllocMem(SizeOf(Result^[0]) * Elements);
end; // Allocate2
```

Some people implement open-ended arrays by declaring the template as an array[0..0]. This is wrong, because this says that 0 is the only valid index. If you use this template with range checking turned on—and you should, as range checking can catch a large class of careless errors—you'll get a range check whenever you try to read or write anything but the first element. The best solution is to declare a huge template type indexed from 0..High(integer) div SizeOf(BaseType) - 1. The range checking code won't be able to detect when you try to index a entry that you didn't actually allocate memory for, but at least you will be able to leave range checking turned on for the errors that it *can* catch.

Dynamic arrays

A major drawback of static arrays is, of course, that they *are* static. While they are faster and clearer than linked lists when you need random access to variable length data, they present an undesirable tradeoff between allocating too little room and writing code that breaks when faced with too much data, or allocating too much room and wasting precious space. Typically, you declare a huge array type, as in the previous section, then allocate space for it on the heap, resizing it as necessary. You then have to keep track of the amount of memory allocated, be sure to Finalize() and free it when you're done, and Move() data around as the array changes size. That's a lot of boiler-plate code, with many possible failure points.

Object Pascal's dynamic arrays do away with the boilerplate code.

You declare a dynamic array as an `array of BaseType`. That is, the syntax of a dynamic array declaration is the same as the syntax of a static array declaration except for the missing `[IndexType]`. You access individual elements of a dynamic array just as you access individual elements of a static array, except that dynamic array indices are always numbers starting at 0. When range checking is enabled, trying to read or write an element at a position greater than or equal to the array's Length() will cause a range check. When range checking is not enabled, accessing an element in a dynamic array generates exactly the same efficient code as accessing an element in a static array *via* a pointer, as in `ArrayPtr^[Index]`. That is, while resizing a dynamic array is not a cheap operation, element-by-element access very definitely **is** cheap.

Dynamic arrays are implemented much like huge strings:

- Just as with huge strings, a dynamic array variable is actually a pointer to a heap block with a length field and a reference count 'to the left of' the first byte of the array that the pointer points to.

- Assignment (including pass-by-value into a routine) increments the reference count and copies the pointer, not the array. When a dynamic array variable goes out of scope, the reference count is decremented. When the reference count reaches 0, the actual array is freed.

- You can call Length() to get the number of elements in a dynamic array, or SetLength() to change the length. Increasing the length copies all the existing array entries, while decreasing the length discards the last entries.

- You can use Copy() to extract sub-arrays.

- Empty (zero length) dynamic arrays are represented by a Nil pointer.

- Just as you can always cast a string variable to a PChar, so you can always cast a dynamic array variable to a pointer to the array's BaseType, or to a pointer to a static array of BaseType.

However, there are also three major differences between dynamic arrays and huge strings. The first is that you can't use High() and Low() with huge strings, while you can use High() and Low() with dynamic arrays. The second is that the first character of a huge string is accessed as HugeString[1] while the first item in a dynamic array is accessed as DynamicArray [Low(DynamicArray)].[5]

The third difference is the most significant, in that not being aware of it can cause you to write buggy code. String variables hold *values*; dynamic array variables hold *references*, which **look** like values but **act** like pointers. That is, as *per* Chapter 1, huge strings have "copy on write" semantics. If StringVar points to a value that's shared with (an)other string variable(s), changing StringVar[N] makes a new copy of the string value; the other variable(s) are not affected.

```
var
  A, B: string;
begin
  A := 'value';
  B := A;      Assert(PChar(B) =  PChar(A));
  B[1] := 'V'; Assert(PChar(B) <> PChar(A));
end.
```

By contrast, dynamic arrays explicitly do **not** have copy on write semantics. Assignment creates a new reference to the array, not a new value. Changing the copy changes the original, and *vice versa*.

Note

This applies to a routine's value parameters, too. Normally, changing a value parameter has no effect on the 'outer' value. This is not true with dynamic array parameters. A routine that changes elements of a dynamic array parameter has an effect on the calling environment, even if the parameter is not declared as a value parameter—and the compiler will not warn you. Similarly, declaring a dynamic array parameter as a by reference (var) parameter effectively makes the parameter a pointer to a pointer, and should be avoided unless you're sure you know what you're doing.

---

5. I'm making a point, here. As currently implemented, Low() of a dynamic array is **always** 0, and you'll often see code like for Index := 0 to High(Arr), or even for Index := 0 to Length(Arr) - 1. But it's not impossible that the syntax of dynamic arrays will be extended to make them more like static arrays—*ie*, with indices of any ordinal type, and not necessarily starting at 0—so I think it's poor practice to write code that assumes that Low(DynamicArray) = 0.

On the other hand, calling SetLength() on a dynamic array **does** guarantee a unique copy (one with a reference count of 1), just as with strings—even if you don't change the length in the process. Thus, assigning one dynamic array to another merely creates an alias, but as soon as you set the length of either you will have two independent arrays. Note that this means that a routine that appends to or deletes from a dynamic array parameter must declare that parameter as var for the changes to affect the calling environment.

```
var
  A, B: array of string;
begin
  SetLength(A, 1);
  A[Low(A)]    := 'this'; Assert(A[Low(A)] = 'this');
  B            := A;       Assert(pointer(B) =  pointer(A));
  B[Low(B)]    := 'THAT'; Assert(pointer(B) =  pointer(A));
                          Assert(A[Low(A)] = 'THAT');
  SetLength(B, 1);        Assert(B[Low(B)] = 'THAT');
  B[Low(B)]    := 'this'; Assert(pointer(B) <> pointer(A));
                          Assert(A[Low(A)] = 'THAT');
                          Assert(B[Low(B)] = 'this');
end.
```

Yes, this can be a bit confusing and may seem arbitrary. Just remember: Changing an element changes all 'copies' of the array. Changing the length changes only 'this' particular 'copy'.

The standard "unique type" rules apply to assignment compatibility of arrays and Copy()ed sub-arrays. For example,

```
var
  Bar: array of integer;
  Baz: array of integer;

begin
  SetLength(Bar, 5);
  Baz := Copy(Bar, 2, 2); // not legal
end.
```

will not compile, because each array of integer declaration creates a unique type. Use code that either declares the source and destination arrays together, or that uses a common type declaration:

```
type
  TArrayOfInteger = array of integer;

var
  Bar: TArrayOfInteger;
  Baz: TArrayOfInteger;

begin
  SetLength(Bar, 5);
  Baz := Copy(Bar, 2, 2);
end.
```

```
// Alternatively:

var
  Bar, Baz: array of integer;

begin
  SetLength(Bar, 5);
  Baz := Copy(Bar, 2, 2);
end.
```

Finally, dynamic arrays are inherently one dimensional, but you can nest them, as in an `array of array of string`. As with multidimensional static arrays, you can access individual elements of a multidimensional dynamic array as either `Arr[I, J]` or `Arr[I][J]`. With multi-dimensional dynamic arrays, a normal SetLength operation will set the length of the first (major) dimension—the one indexed as I in expressions like `Arr[I, J]`. You can also set the size of the whole array, using multiple arguments to SetLength. Of course, a multidimensional dynamic array can easily be 'triangular'; unlike multidimensional static arrays, there's no requirement that each row (or plane, or whatever) be the same size as every other.

```
var
  Foo:   array of array of string;
  Index: integer;

begin
  // A triangular array
  SetLength(Foo, 4);
  for Index := Low(Foo) to High(Foo) do
    SetLength(Foo[Index], Index + 1);

  // A rectangular array
  SetLength(Foo, 4, 5); // 4 rows of 5 strings each
  Assert(High(Foo) = 3);
  Assert(High(Foo[High(Foo)]) = 4);
end.
```

Mixing dynamic and static arrays

A dynamic array variable points to the first element of the array. The length and reference count are 'to the left of' the first byte, at negative offsets from the address in the variable. Thus, you can always cast a dynamic array to a pointer to a static array of the same base type. For example, given

```
type
  TDynamic = array of string;
  TStatic  = array[word] of string;
  PStatic  = ^ TStatic;
var
  Strings: TDynamic;
```

you can use PStatic(Strings)^ just as if it were actually a TStatic array.

The converse is not true. That is, you can't take a pointer to a static array and safely cast it to a dynamic array, because the dynamic array code expects to find a length and reference count to the left of the pointer.

This is somewhat analogous to the relationship between PChars and huge strings: You can cast a huge string to a PChar because a huge string is a C-style string with some extra information to the left, but assigning or casting a PChar to a huge string takes a little compiler magic to build that hidden header. The difference is that where Kylix does do the magic to convert C-style strings to huge strings, current implementations won't let you assign or cast a static array to a dynamic array.

Mixing dynamic and open arrays

Dynamic arrays and open array parameters are similar in some ways. Neither has a fixed size; they're both indexed only by numbers, starting at 0; and you can pass a dynamic array to a procedure that expects open array parameter of the same base type.

However, you cannot assign an open array to a dynamic array, even when they have the same base type. That is, dynamic arrays can be assigned to open arrays (by passing them as parameters) but not *vice versa*.

More significantly, open array parameters *can* be passed by value. If a routine changes one or more elements of an open array parameter, it has no effect on the calling environment, unless the open array is a var (variable) parameter.

Dynamic array type declarations and an open array parameter declarations look alike, and the difference can be confusing. For example,

```
type
  TArrayOfInteger = array of integer;
```

declares a dynamic array type, while

```
procedure TwoArrays( DynamicArrayParameter: TArrayOfInteger;
                     OpenArrayParameter:     array of integer );
begin
  // The next statement is legal
  Setlength(DynamicArrayParameter, Length(DynamicArrayParameter) + 1);

  // The next statement is NOT legal and will not compile
  Setlength(OpenArrayParameter, Length(OpenArrayParameter) + 1);
end;
```

declares two different types of parameters. DynamicArrayParameter is a dynamic array, and can **only** be passed a TArrayOfInteger dynamic array, while OpenArrayParameter is an open array, and can be passed **either** a dynamic array **or** an open array **or** a static array. That is,

```
var
  DynamicArray: TArrayOfInteger;

begin
  // These calls will compile
  TwoArrays(DynamicArray, [1, 2, 3, 4]);
  TwoArrays(DynamicArray, DynamicArray);

  // This call will NOT compile
  TwoArrays([1, 2, 3], [1, 2, 3, 4]);
end.
```

What's more, despite the way that open array parameter declarations not only look like dynamic array declarations but that you can also pass a dynamic array to an open array parameter, the open array parameter is **not** a dynamic array. This shows up in the way that open array parameters are true value parameters (changing them doesn't change the calling environment) and in the way that you can call SetLength on a dynamic array parameter but not on an open array parameter.

Variables

The var keyword is used to declare both global variables and local variables. The syntax should be pretty obvious from the examples so far. A block of variable declarations consists of the var keyword followed by one or more variable declarations, separated by semicolons. The block must be separated from type or const blocks, procedure declarations, or code statements by a semicolon. Each variable declaration consists of one or more variable names, separated by commas, followed by a colon and either a type name or a type expression. Type expressions are the same sort of array, record, and set descriptions that are valid in type statements.

Note

The same rule about unique type declarations applies to 'on the fly' record and array definitions as to multiple type declarations. A variable of type TArrayOfChar = array[char] of char *and a* var ArrayOfChar: array[char] of char *are not assignment compatible.*

Variables declared within a routine are local. They come into existence when the routine is called, and they are destroyed when the routine exits. Pascal locals are statically scoped: They are visible to routines defined after the local, but within the same routine as the local. They are not visible to routines called by the routine that declares them, as in dynamically scoped interpreted languages like Lisp and APL. Most local variables are never initialized: The only two exceptions are that references to reference-counted data (strings, dynamic arrays, and interfaces) are initialized to Nil, so setting them to an actual value doesn't try to decrement the reference count of some random area of memory, and that any Variant locals are initialized to Unassigned. Uninitialized locals are filled with garbage on entry to a routine; the compiler will warn you if you use an uninitialized local before you've set it.

All variables declared outside of a routine are global, and exist throughout the life of the program. The scope of a global variable depends on where they are declared. Variables declared in the public (interface) section of a unit (Chapter 4) are visible to all units that use their unit, while variables declared in the private (implementation) section of a unit are visible only within their unit. You can specify initial values for global scalars and simple structured types like strings, records, and arrays, but you can't specify initial values for dynamic arrays, objects, interfaces, or variants. Any global that you don't initialize is cleared (all bytes set to 0). This sets all numbers (including floating point numbers) to 0; booleans to False; and pointers to Nil. Since empty strings and dynamic arrays with a Length() of 0 are implemented as Nil pointers, a global dynamic array is initially empty (has a Length() of 0) and any uninitialized global string will equal ''.

Initialized variables

When you are declaring an initialized variable, you cannot use the syntax that allows you to declare more than one variable of the same type at once, by separating the names with commas. You have to declare one variable at a time, using the alternate syntax

```
var
  VarName1: VarType1 = Value1;
  VarName2: VarType2 = Value2;
```

You can mix initialized and uninitialized variables in the same var block; the only restriction is that only uninitialized variables can use the comma-separated list of variables of the same type. This is just like with parameter lists, where you can have more than one parameter of the same type, separated by commas, but where if you want to supply a default parameter for more than one parameter, each has to be a discrete *ParamName*: *ParamType* = *ParamDefault* entry in the list.

```
var
  This, That: integer;
  IsTrue: boolean = True;
  IsAlphaNumeric: set of char = ['A'.. 'Z', 'a'.. 'z', '0'.. '9', '~'];
  TheOther: integer;
```

> **Note**
>
> *If you declare an uninitialized variable but never use it, the compiler will give you a hint. However, 2001-release Delphi's (Kylix 1 and Delphi 6) do **not** give you a hint about unused initialized variables.*

Initialized records follow a slightly more complicated syntax, where the value to the right of the equals sign consists of a series of *FieldName*: *FieldValue* pairs, separated by semicolons and enclosed in parentheses. The FieldName's must appear in the same order as in the record declaration. While you normally supply a value for every field, any trailing fields that you don't specify will simply be initialized to 0.

```
type
  TSimpleRecord = record
                    This, That: integer;
                  end;
  TComplicated  = record
                    Simple:   TSimpleRecord;
                    TheOther: integer;
                  end;
```

```
var
  Simple: TSimpleRecord = (This: 5; That: 6);
  Partial: TSimpleRecord = (This: 5); // Partial.That = 0
  Another: record
             ThisIs, HardToRead: string;
           end =
           ( ThisIs:     'So you should avoid defining and';
             HardToRead: 'initializing a record in a single statement.');
  Complicated: TComplicated =
                 (Simple: (This: 1; That: 2);
                  TheOther: 3);
```

Initialized arrays are handled much as if they were records with no field names. The array value consists of a series of comma-separated values, one for each element of the array, enclosed in parentheses.

```
var
  CostVector: array[0..3] of double = (1.5, 2.7, -3.4, 5);
```

Multidimensional arrays are initialized as if they were declared as an array of arrays. That is, each column is initialized like a simple, one-dimensional array, with a series of comma-separated values, enclosed in parentheses. Each row, in turn, consists of a comma-separated series of column values, enclosed in parentheses, while 'pages' are just a comma-separated series of rows, enclosed in parentheses, and so on.

```
var
  Diagonal: array[0..1, 0..1] of integer =
            ( (1, 0),
              (0, 1) );
```

Reference-counted variables

Reference-counted variables—strings, dynamic arrays, and interfaces—receive special handling. When you create one, either 'bare' or as part of a record or object, it's set to Nil, so that when you do set it, the RTL won't try to decrement the reference count of a random piece of memory. Conversely, when you destroy a reference-counted variable, the RTL automatically decrements the reference count of any non-Nil variables, freeing the object if its reference count is now 0. This automatic *initialization* and *finalization* happens for local variables when you enter and exit a routine, and it happens for heap variables when you SetLength() a dynamic array or call New() and Dispose().

> **Note**
>
> *Remember, automatic initialization and finalization does **not** happen when you call the 'bulk' memory routines, GetMem() and FreeMem(), and you must explicitly call Initialize() and Finalize() whenever you do so.*

Do be aware that using SetLength to shorten a dynamic array finalizes any elements that it disposes of. If you're treating the array as a stack, and simply deleting the last entries, this is fine. However, if you are emulating the string Delete() routine,[6] and shifting the rightmost elements leftward over (a) deleted element(s), you have to be sure to

1. Finalize any 'internal' elements that you are deleting.

2. Clear any duplicated elements on the right before trimming the array, so that automatic finalization doesn't wrongly free any reference-counted structures they may point to.

---

6. I'm not privy to Borland's plans. Kylix 1 does not support Insert() or Delete() for dynamic arrays, though Borland's certainly aware that people want this. If you can use Delete() with dynamic arrays by the time you read this, you can just ignore the next few paragraphs, except to appreciate what a lot of trouble you've been saved.

For example, the following snippet will dump core, because it trims an array of string improperly.

```
var
  S: array of string;

begin
  SetLength(S, 5);
  S[0] := 'The first string';
  S[1] := 'The second string';
  S[2] := 'The third string';
  S[3] := 'The fourth string';
  S[4] := 'The fifth string';
  Move(S[3], S[1], SizeOf(S[4]) * 2); // Mem leak:
                                      // S[1] and S[2] are 'orphaned'
  SetLength(S, 3); // S[3] and S[4] are freed, even though we mean
                   // them now to be S[1] and S[2]
  WriteLn(S[0]);
  WriteLn(S[1]); // Does not work as expected
  WriteLn(S[2]); // Does not work as expected
end.
```

The following program, ch3/DeleteStrings, works as desired because it uses a Delete routine that explicitly finalizes the elements that are about to be deleted **and** clears the elements that have been shifted to prevent premature finalization.

```
program DeleteStrings;

type
  TArrayOfString = array of string;

procedure Delete( var DynamicArray: TArrayOfString;
                  Index: integer; Count: integer = 1 ); overload;
var
  NewLength: integer;
const
  ElementSize = SizeOf(DynamicArray[0]);
begin
  NewLength := Length(DynamicArray) - Count;

  Finalize(DynamicArray[Index], Count);
  Move(DynamicArray[Index + Count], DynamicArray[Index], ElementSize * Count);
```

```
  FillChar(DynamicArray[NewLength], ElementSize * Count, 0);
  SetLength(DynamicArray, NewLength);
end; // Delete

var
  S: TArrayOfString;

begin
  SetLength(S, 5);
  S[0] := 'The first string';
  S[1] := 'The second string';
  S[2] := 'The third string';
  S[3] := 'The fourth string';
  S[4] := 'The fifth string';

  Delete(S, 2, 2);

  WriteLn(S[0]);
  WriteLn(S[1]); // Works fine
  WriteLn(S[2]); // Works fine
end.
```

> **Note**
>
> *The ElementSize constant in the Delete routine has been declared in terms of SizeOf(DynamicArray[0]). This allows the same routine to be used as a template to delete elements from any dynamic array: Just change the type of the DynamicArray parameter, and the code will cleanly delete elements from a different type of array. If the new array type doesn't need finalization, Kylix will tell you so, and will optimize away the call to Finalize(). It will, however, always use FillChar to clear the 'tail' elements, even when this is not necessary.*

Absolute variables

As *per* Chapter 2, Object Pascal supports a sort of variable aliasing, or 'permanent typecast', through the absolute keyword. The syntax is

var *VarName*: *VarType* **absolute** *OtherVariable*;

This allows you to declare any global or local variable 'over' any *OtherVariable* that's visible at that point in the code. Some people like to declare one record variable `absolute` another record variable of another type, to avoid the complexities of variant record declaration. This practice is only safe if the absolute record is no bigger than the 'base' record—and of course the compiler has no way of checking that for you. If you declare a record variable absolute over a smaller record variable, writing to the overlaid record will trash unrelated memory.

Probably the most common use of `absolute` is to assign a type to an untyped parameter.

```
procedure Callback(Data: pointer);
var
  ReallyIs: TSomeObject absolute Data;
begin
  Assert(TObject(Data) is TSomeObject);
  // ...
end;
```

is one line shorter and, hence, arguably clearer than

```
procedure Callback(Data: pointer);
var
  ReallyIs: TSomeObject;
begin
  Assert(TObject(Data) is TSomeObject);
  ReallyIs := TSomeObject(Data);
  // ...
end;
```

Note

 Some people think the second form is clearer. I don't: you'll have to decide for yourself. The second form is certainly a little faster, though, as the optimizer can't handle absolute *variables.*

Constants

The const keyword is used to declare both global and local constants, with scoping rules exactly like those for variables. Constants declared in the interface section of a unit are visible from that point on in the unit, and in any code that uses that unit; constants declared in the implementation section of a unit are visible only from that point on in the unit; while constants declared within a routine are visible only from that point on in the routine, and are visible to any subsequent local procedures.

Simple constants

Most simple (untyped) constants occupy no storage, and are copied literally into the object code every time they are referenced. The two exceptions are float point constants and strings. Float point constants are stored as anonymous Extended globals. String constants are also stored as anonymous globals, with a reference count of –1 which 'tells' the string code that these strings are constants and should not be reference counted.

This means that assigning a string constant (or a string literal, which is basically just an anonymous constant) to a string variable acts quite differently from assigning one string variable to another. Specifically, where string assignment (including value parameter binding) is normally just a matter of incrementing reference counts, assigning a string constant to a string variable makes a copy of the constant. The copy is a perfectly normal string value, with a reference count of 1.

The compiler will make a reasonable effort to fold identical string and float point literals into a single anonymous global, even when you don't use symbolic names for them. This optimization is done on a per-unit basis; using the same literal in two or more units will result in an anonymous global in each unit that uses it. Note that giving the literal a symbolic name (*eg*, something like const SymbolicConstant = 'this is a string constant') doesn't change this; if you refer to SymbolicConstant in two different units, the compiler will act exactly as if you had used the string literal, and will create an anonymous global in each unit. You **can** force the compiler to use a single copy of the string constant by declaring it as either a typed constant or a ResourceString (below).

Kylix's "reasonable effort" at constant folding doesn't stretch as far as algebraic simplifications; an expression like X * 3.3 + Y * 3.3 will compile to two multiplications by the same anonymous constant and then an addition. Similarly, the object code for an expression like X * 3 + Y * 3 for integer X and

Y will use the same clever `lea eax,[eax+eax*2]` trick twice, rather than doing
`(X + Y) * 3`.[7]

Set constants

Set constants are handled in a particularly interesting[8] way. When the set has
'enough' disjunct elements, the object code for an `in` test will use the `BT`
instruction, just as for an in test against a set variable. However, for 'simple
enough' sets, with only a few disjunct elements, the object code will consist
of a test for a match with the first set element or range, followed by a test for
a match with the second set element or range, and so on. This is actually
slower **and** larger than the equivalent typed constant code, and it's hard to
imagine that this is anything but an artifact of code archaeology.

For example, the ch3/SetConstants project benchmarks `I in` *SetConstant*
for six different set constants, with from 1 to 6 terms. As you can see if you
examine the object code (set a benchmark and press CTRL+ALT+C or select
View ➤ Debug Windows ➤ CPU,) `I in [42]` all the way up to `I in [6, 12, 40,
42, 67]` does successive tests against I, almost like in a `case` statement. It's not
until the set constant has six terms—`I in [6, 12, 40, 42, 67, 74]`—that the
compiler finally switches to using a BT instruction. This makes for bulky
code, and you can see that the two, three, four and five term tests are actually
slower than the six term test.

Typed constants

Kylix is not Delphi 5

Object Pascal also supports *typed constants* which are basically a special sort
of initialized variable. Typed constants can be either truly constant or just a
sort of initialized variable declared with the `const` keyword instead of the `var`
keyword. The {$J} pragma (Chapter 4) controls this behavior. By default,
typed constants are truly constant. You can use {$J+} around typed constants
that you're using as local static variables, but should then use {$J-} to disable
changes to typed constants. {$J+} was the default in Delphi 5, but {$J-} is the
default in Kylix and Delphi 6.

---

7. Rearranging code in this way could change the behavior of the program, which is
    something that an optimizing compiler shouldn't do. For example, if `X * 3 > MaxInt`,
    the expression will overflow, while if Y is 'close enough' to –X, `(X + Y) * 3` will not
    overflow. While overflowing less **and** executing faster are two nice side effects of the
    rearrangement, this sort of thing is your responsibility, not the compiler's.

8. Also known as "bizarre" and "seemingly senseless".

> **Note**
>
> *Regardless of the $J state, you can't use the value of a typed constant in compile-time* constant expressions *like type declarations or case selectors.*

Typed constants are useful where the data type of a constant makes a difference in the object code—Single or Double constants are faster than the default Extended constants, though the effect can be nearly swamped by code alignment issues—but their chief use is with structured types like records and arrays. Record typed constant records are declared just as initialized records are, as a series of *FieldName: FieldValue* pairs, separated by semicolons and enclosed in parentheses. Similarly, array typed constants are declared just as initialized arrays are, as a series of comma-separated values enclosed in parentheses.

Array typed constants are probably more common than initialized array variables. They are used for table driven programming, which is often faster, smaller, easier to read, and easier to maintain than its 'decision tree' alternatives. In addition to all the examples so far of avoiding branching by using Boolean-indexed arrays, you can use arrays of Format() (see Chapter 8) strings to handle cases where you want to format the same information differently under various circumstances.

```
type
  TCardinality = (cZero, cOne, cMore);

function Cardinality(Number: Cardinal): TCardinality;
begin
  case Number of
    0:   Result := cZero;
    1:   Result := cOne;
    else Result := cMore;
  end;
end; // Cardinality
```

```
function YouHaveMail(New, Old: Cardinal): string;
const
  //                  --- New ----  --- Old ----
  Formats: array[TCardinality, TCardinality] of string =
          (('You have no mail',
            'You have no new mail and 1 piece of old mail',
            'You have no new mail and %1:d pieces of old mail'),
          ('You have 1 piece of new mail',
            'You have 1 piece of new mail and 1 piece of old mail',
            'You have 1 piece of new mail and %1:d pieces of old mail'),
          ('You have %d pieces of new mail',
            'You have %d pieces of new mail and 1 piece of old mail',
            'You have %d pieces of new mail and %d pieces of old mail'));
begin
  Result := Format(Formats[Cardinality(New), Cardinality(Old)], [New, Old]);
end; // YouHaveMail
```

You can also use a similar multi-dimensional array of strings to handle common situations like validating user input and displaying a diagnostic message: The input might be invalid in several ways, but you only want to display a message about the most pressing. An array with multiple Boolean indices lets you cover every point in the 'error space' with a single table, which makes this technique more reliable than a decision tree. 'Coloring' regions of the error space with a particular error string has the effect of making some error indicators more important than others, in the sense that the user gets the same message until she clears that error condition, regardless of how many other changes she makes. Using this technique can take careful formatting and lots of comments, but changing a few array entries is a lot faster and safer than changing a decision tree—consider how easy it is to miss a branch of the decision tree, or perhaps to place a test where it can't be reached.

For a simple example, imagine that you only have two tests. The first is the more important: If it fails, then you want to display a message telling the user to correct it. The second is less important, and you only want to display a message if the first test succeeds. The following MsgTable contains an error string to display in each case, with a ' ' string meaning No Error:

```
const
  OK = '';
  M1 = 'Please correct THIS important error';
  M2 = 'Please correct THAT less important error';

                  {Test 1} {test 2}
  MsgTable: array[boolean, boolean] of string =
                  {T2: False} {T2: True}
    {T1: False} (( M1,        M1        ),
    {T1: True}   ( M2,        OK        ));
```

As you can see, MsgTable contains M1 whenever T1 is False; M2 only where T1 is True but T2 is False; and OK only where both tests succeed.

Constant expressions

Object Pascal supports a reasonably wide range of constant expressions that can be used wherever a constant value is appropriate. This includes both the obvious places, like const statements and initialized variables, and some not so obvious places like subrange and/or array index declarations and even case tags.

Constant expressions are evaluated at compile time, and so can not refer to the value of any variable or typed constant. (You can define a true constant, and then use it both to initialize a variable or typed constant and in a constant expression.) Constant expressions can use any of the operators in Chapter 2, as well as typecasts and set constructors. Constant expressions may not use function calls, except to the 15 low-level standard functions in Table 3-2.

Table 3-2. Functions you may use in constant expressions

Abs	High	Low	Pred	Succ
Chr	Length	Odd	Round	Swap
Hi	Lo	Ord	SizeOf	Trunc

SizeOf

The SizeOf operator returns the size of a variable or type. This is particularly useful in conjunction with low-level memory operations like Move() and FillChar() (Chapter 8) as well as GetMem(). You should also use SizeOf any time you're casting a pointer to a Cardinal or PChar to do pointer arithmetic. Doing all this low-level memory work in terms of SizeOf an element insulates you from changes in record definition or alignment, and from changes in the implementation of generic types like Integer, Char, or Real.

As with the High() operator in Chapter 1, when you have a choice, it's generally safer to use SizeOf on the variable than on its nominal type. If the variable's type changes, SizeOf the variable will still give you the right value.

Note that SizeOf any pointer will give you the size of the pointer variable itself, or 4 bytes in 32-bit Kylix's. To get the size of the 'pointed to' type, you use `SizeOf(PtrVar^)`. Similarly, SizeOf a dynamic array variable will return the 4-byte size of the pointer, while SizeOf element 0 will return the element size.

```
type
  TRecord = record
    A, B: integer;
  end;
  PRecord ^ TRecord;
  TArrayOfRecord = array of TRecord;

var
  RecordPtr: PRecord;
  ArrayVar:  TArrayOfRecord;

begin
  Assert(SizeOf(RecordPtr) = 4);
  Assert(SizeOf(RecordPtr^) = SizeOf(TRecord));

  Assert(SizeOf(ArrayVar) = 4);
  Assert(SizeOf(ArrayVar[0]) = SizeOf(TRecord));
end.
```

> **Note**
>
> `SizeOf(RecordPtr^)` *doesn't actually dereference RecordPtr. RecordPtr can be Nil or filled with garbage, and it won't matter. Similarly, you can refer to* `SizeOf(DynamicArrayVar[0])` *even if* `Length(DynamicArrayVar) = 0`.

Resource strings

Resource strings are declared like any other string constant, except that they are declared as a ResourceString, instead of a const. They follow exactly the same scoping rules as any other constant, and are true constants that can't be assigned to. Where they differ from other sorts of constants is that they are stored in the executable file in the "resource fork", in much the same way that GUI forms (Section 2) are.

This has two consequences. The lesser consequence is that every time you refer to a resource string, it is read from the executable file. This means that it takes much longer to copy a resource string than it does to copy any other string. Applications that use a lot of resource strings may want to follow a strategy of confining at least the most common ones to a unit (Chapter 4) that reads them into global variables at program startup.

The more important consequence is that you can extract all the resources in a program with the resbind (in the Kylix bin directory) utility, and send the resulting resource file to a translation shop (or department) for localization. You can then use the resbind utility to merge the translated resource strings back into a copy of the executable, to create a localized version.

Hint directives

The hint directives of Chapter 2—deprecated, library and platform—can also be applied to any variables, constants, or type declarations. As with the 'tagged' routines in Chapter 2, every use of a tagged identifier will produce a warning that the identifier is problematic in some way.

Where the hint directives for routines are syntactically like the calling convention modifiers—*ie*, they're separated from the rest of the prototype by a semicolon—for types, constants, and variable declarations the hint directives comes between the declaration and the terminating semicolon. For example,

```
var
  UntypedHook: pointer deprecated;
```

```
type
  QtInfo = record
    Version: string;
    Supports: set of QtOptions; // Needs QtOptions to be declared somewhere ...
  end library;
```

```
const
  MinKernel = '2.2.4' platform;
```

Note

Merely compiling declarations that contain hint directives won't produce any warnings. You only get the warning when the tagged identifiers are actually used. You can disable these warnings with Chapter 4's {$warn} pragma.

Objects

Object Pascal is, of course, an object oriented language. It supports encapsulation, polymorphism, and inheritance. It does *not* support multiple inheritance as C++ does, but it does have Java-style interfaces, which come to almost the same thing.

There are actually two different object models, using the `object` and `class` keywords. The officially deprecated "old style" objects are much like C++'s 'structs with methods': They can be either statically or dynamically allocated, and when you include one in another data structure, you get all its field's 'inline', just as if it were a record. New style object classes are always dynamically allocated, and variables that hold a `class` object are actually references—data structures that look like values and act like pointers. While the old style objects still have their uses, the class model offers many features that the object model does not, including `class of` metatypes that greatly simplify things like recreating objects from a saved stream. Much of the material in this section applies to both classes and objects, but the focus is primarily on the new-style classes; I will use "object" to refer to an instance of a "class" of objects, while the unique features of the old-style objects are covered in their own subsection.

Class values are actually references

Objects have fields, just as records do, and the basic class syntax is much the same as record syntax.

```
type
  TSimple = class
            This, That: integer;
            end;
```

There are several differences between this class and the analogous record, but the single biggest difference is that a variable of type TSimple is a *reference* to a TSimple, not an actual TSimple. That is, as in `var` parameters that are "passed by reference", a reference variable is a pointer to a data structure that acts syntactically like the data structure itself—you don't need to (and can't) use a ^ to dereference a reference variable.

Note

*Don't be confused: Object variables are actually references, but object references are **not** reference counted the way strings and dynamic arrays are! If you create an object in a routine, it will not be freed when the object returns and its reference goes out of scope; if you explicitly Create it, you have to explicitly Free it. There are only two exceptions to this rule. First, interface references (see the subsection on* Interfaces *later in this section)* **are** *reference counted. If you create an object and refer to it **only** through its interfaces, then it will be automatically freed when the last interface reference goes out of scope. The RTL is responsible for managing the lifetimes of reference-counted data; you are responsible for managing the lifetimes of object instances. Second, if you create a* component *(Chapters 6 and 7) that is* owned *by another component, the owner will Free its property when it is itself freed. You **can** explicitly Free owned components, but you don't need to.*

Global variables and class fields are always initialized to 0, and `pointer(0)` = `Nil`, so code like

```
var
  Simple: TSimple;

begin
  Simple.This := Simple.That;
end.
```

is wrong because Simple = Nil, and you will get a segmentation fault when you try to read Simple.That. Generally, you need to explicitly Create() an object before you can do anything with it, and you should always Free an object when you are done with it.[9]

Thus, the above example should actually be written more like

```
var Simple: TSimple;          // or:

begin                         begin
  Simple := TSimple.Create;     with TSimple.Create do
  try                             try
    Simple.This := Simple.That;     This := That;
  finally                         finally
    Simple.Free;                    Free;
  end;                            end;
end.                          end.
```

Finally, since class variables are references, or syntactically privileged pointers, all that is copied with a value parameter is the pointer, not the object. Procedures can change objects that are passed by value, even if the parameter is tagged as const. All that a const class parameter means is that you can't change the parameter to point to a different instance of the class; you are still free to change instance fields, or to call instance methods that change the object's internal state.

Passing a class variable as a var parameter is passing a pointer to a pointer. The double dereferencing is more expensive than normal dereferencing, even though it is done transparently, and you should only pass class variables by reference when you need to change the reference in the calling code.

Constructors and destructors

Create is something like a *class method*. I'll cover class methods in more detail in the next subsection; for now, what it means is that you can call

---

9. Linux will free your process's memory when it terminates, so it may seem like your application doesn't need to Free objects when it terminates. However, it's a good idea to always do so anyway, as many objects' destructors have important side effects like flushing buffers, closing files, or closing conversations with remote systems. If you Free only the objects that 'you know you need to', you run the risk of missing one; if you always Free all objects, you'll always Free all the ones that really need to be freed.

Create even before you have an instance of the class. More specifically, Create is a *constructor*, which means that it allocates space for a new object, initializes it, and then returns a reference to it. All objects *inherit* a default constructor from TObject, the root of the class tree, which allocates space and initializes all fields to 0.[10] Descendant classes usually declare their own constructors, which initialize fields as needed. In particular, object fields are not created by the default constructor; you need to explicitly Create them in the 'owning' object's constructor. For example,

```
type
  TThis = class
  end;

  TThat = class
    This: TThis;

  constructor Create;
  destructor  Destroy; override;
  end;

constructor TThat.Create;
begin
  This := TThis.Create;
end; // TThat.Create

destructor TThat.Destroy;
begin
  This.Free;
  inherited;
end; // TThat.Destroy
```

The *destructor* is the inverse of the constructor: It's responsible for freeing any space the object allocated, closing any files that may still be open, saving any necessary state, and so on. All objects inherit a *virtual* destructor, Destroy, from TObject, so the destructor must be declared as an override method. (I cover virtual methods and overriding later in this section.) Except in a few very rare circumstances, the last thing that every destructor does is to call the inherited destructor, to allow the ancestral object to do any cleanup.

You will rarely—if ever—call Destroy directly. Instead, you call an object's destructor by calling its Free method, which all objects inherit from

10. Strictly speaking, this is done by the invisible *preamble code*, not by TObject.Create, which has an empty body.

TObject. What's special about Free is that it checks to be sure that it hasn't been called with a Nil, or unassigned, object reference, before it calls Destroy. Thus, you can write cleanup code like that in TThat.Destroy that always calls This.Free. It's safe to call This.Free, even if TThat.Create never created the This object; it's **not** safe to call This.Destroy if This = Nil!

People are occasionally surprised that Free does *not* set the reference to Nil. This is partly because Free is a perfectly ordinary method, with no compiler magic enabling it to change the variable it was called from, and partly because it's not uncommon for the same object to be referred to in several different places. It doesn't do an awful lot of good to reset one reference to Nil if there are several 'tombstoned' references scattered throughout various data structures. Nonetheless, the standard procedure FreeAndNil() will reset a single reference to an object and then Free it.

It's generally safe not to use FreeAndNil in a destructor, but you should be sure to FreeAndNil any class variable (whether a local variable or a part of a larger data structure) that will stick around after you Free its contents. One reason to use FreeAndNil in a destructor is that a large and complex object may contain object fields that refer back to their owner and some of its other object fields. If the destructor for field A refers to field B, and you have already freed B without Nil-ing it, you will get unpredictable behavior. If you set B to Nil when you freed it, you'd consistently get a SIGSEGV when A's destructor referred to B. People who have been burned by this pattern often use FreeAndNil every time they Free an object.

> **Note**
>
> *Raising an exception in a constructor will call the destructor on the partially constructed object. Thus, code in destructors—and any code that might be called from destructors—should always test that an object field is Assigned before doing anything but calling Free on it. (See the* Destructors *section, below.)*

Fields

The fields of an object are quite analogous to the fields of a record. In fact, aside from the fact that records offer no visibility control (below), the only real difference is that you can't have a 'variant object'. The case syntax is not supported at all for objects. Typically, you use inheritance (below) instead of variants. Rather than having one type with fields that can be referred to 'this' way or 'that' way, you'd have two or more distinct types, each with a unique name for each field.

Unlike C++, where the only real distinction between structs and objects is the default visibility, Object Pascal draws a strong distinction between records and objects. Records can never have methods or inherit from another record type; objects can, and can never have a variant part.[11]

While a record with a record field contains an instance of the 'inner' record, the same is not true of a class with a class field. Class fields, like class variables, are references. Pointers that look like values. While you can refer to *Field.Subfield* just as if *Field* were a record type, you have to be sure to either set *Field* to refer to an existing object—or Create *Field* in the object's constructor and Free *Field* in the object's destructor.

> **Note**
>
>
>
> *A good discipline is to always write the parts of an object's constructors and destructor that Create and Free object fields first, as soon as you declare the object. Whenever you declare a new object field, be sure to add the Create/Free lines to the constructors and destructor. Then, whatever else your object might do wrong, it won't generate segmentation faults and it won't leak memory.*

As a general rule, you should **never** refer to an object's fields anywhere except in an object's methods. Not setting an object's field allows it to maintain data integrity. If 'this' field depends on 'that' field in some way, that knowledge is embedded in the method(s) that set 'that' field, not scattered all over the application. Not reading an object's fields allows you to change its implementation freely, so long as you hold its interface constant. You can and should declare an object's fields `private` (see the *Visibility* section, below) to the object, which means that only the object's methods can set them. (There are some exceptions, which I discuss in the *Visibility* section.)

Object Pascal supports *properties* (below) that combine the convenience and clarity of simply reading or writing a value with the above benefits of encapsulating your data by only calling an object's methods.

---

11. When a record has a variant part, all the variant parts are present in the record. You can write a field that belongs to one variant part, and read the same data under a different name and type from a different variant part. This is not true of objects. When object types B and C both descend from object type A, all they have in common are A's fields and methods. If B adds a field, you can't refer to it in a object of type C, and *vice versa*.

Methods

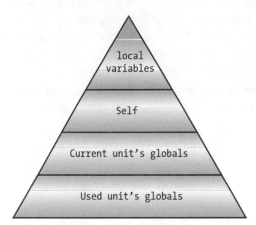

Within an object method, any local variables and parameters are the most local scope, followed by Self, followed by the current unit's globals, followed by any used unit's globals.

Any with statements are layered on top of (are more visible than) the local declarations.

Figure 3-4. Scope in object methods

You can think of objects as records that 'know how to' operate on themselves. They can have *methods*, which are special routines that have an invisible parameter, Self, which refers to the object. You call a method as if it were a procedural field of the object, and within the method can call any method or read and write any field of that object. All methods get an invisible parameter, Self, and act as if a with Self do is inserted between the method name and the method's prototype and local declarations. (Figure 3-4.) That is, you don't have to refer to Self.This to call the This method or to read or write the This field; you can just refer to This. You only need to qualify a name as Self.Name if you have a local identifier with the same name as an object identifier. For example,

```
type
  TTrivial = class
          private
            fThis: integer;
          public
            procedure SetThis(Value: integer);
            function GetThis: integer;
          end;
```

```
procedure TTrivial.SetThis(Value: integer);
begin
  fThis := Value;
end; // TTrivial.SetThis

function TTrivial.GetThis: integer;
begin
  Result := fThis;
end; // TTrivial.GetThis
```

Any code that creates a TTrivial can call GetThis and SetThis. This 'outside' code doesn't 'know' that they operate by getting or seeing fThis, and it doesn't care. You can change the way that TTrivial implements GetThis and SetThis without affecting any code that uses it—provided, of course, that GetThis and SetThis continue to act the same way.[12] This is what's known as *encapsulation* and is, of course, a powerful tool for isolating the effects of changes as code evolves, by keeping a change 'here' from breaking code 'there'.

All method declarations must follow all field declarations. An object can be divided into multiple sections (see the *Visibility* subsection, below), but within each section all field declarations must preceed all method declarations.

The syntax of a method implementation differs from that of a normal, 'flat' routine only in that the method's name is *qualified* with the class's name and a dot. Like Java —and unlike C++, which uses :: to qualify names within objects and namespaces—Object Pascal uses the same *This.That* dot notation for object and module names as for records. Otherwise, method prototypes look just like flat routine prototypes; they can have any number of value, variable, or constant parameters, and you can overload methods so long as the compiler can tell them apart by their signatures.

A method's code can freely read and write the fields of the Self object. All references to Self are generally implicit, but sometimes (like in a with statement) it can make sense to explicitly say something like Self.fThis := Value. There is absolutely no difference in the object code for Self.fThis := Value and fThis := Value—unless, of course, Self.fThis and fThis are actually different fields.

Constructor and destructor details

Constructors and destructors are special methods responsible for allocating and initializing memory for an object, and then for finalizing and freeing that

---

12. This sort of "getter" and "setter" pair is very common in C++ and Java. You can use this idiom in Object Pascal, if you like, but most Delphi programmers would actually use explicit "properties" here. Properties are covered later in this chapter.

memory. In C++, a constructor must have the same name as the class, while the destructor must be named ~ClassName. Object Pascal doesn't impose these naming restrictions on you; instead, you use the keywords `constructor` and `destructor` to declare constructors and destructors, instead of procedure or function.

Note

*Older code, ported from Windows, will often have multiple names for multiple constructors. Newer code generally overloads Create() for all its constructors, if only to simplify calling Pascal code from C++Builder. Somewhat similarly, while you **can** name a destructor anything you like, in practice most of the library code won't work properly unless your destructor overrides Destroy.*

Constructors

A constructor call looks somewhat like a class function (below) in that you typically call it as `Instance := TClassName.Create`. However, there are two things that distinguish constructors from class functions. First, they don't set a Result as true functions do. Second, within the body of the constructor, the implicit Self parameter refers to the (new) object instance and not to the whole class, as it would in a true class method.

Visual Basic programmers: I explain virtual methods in the Polymorphism *section, below.*

An object's constructor is responsible for two different type of setup. The compiler takes care of allocating space for the object, and setting the Virtual Method Table [VMT—in C++, this is known as a *vtable*] pointer so that virtual methods can be dispatched properly. The compiler's share of the work is all done before any of your code executes. Thus, unlike C++, virtual method calls work correctly in both constructors and destructors.

Your constructor code needs to properly initialize all the fields that the compiler allocated space for. When a class descends from some class besides TObject, it will probably have fields that need to be initialized by a call to `inherited Create`. Unlike C++, though, you have absolute control over *when* in the constructor you call the inherited constructor. Usually, it doesn't matter, and in most constructors the first line of code is a call to `inherited`.

Sometimes it does matter, though, and it's nice to be able to do some setup before the ancestral setup. For example, the ancestral class might declare a field of some abstract type, and descendant types might need to instantiate some particular descendant type before the ancestral constructor does anything with it.

As a general rule, you should **always** call an inherited constructor. It may seem like a waste of processor time to call `inherited Create` when an object descends directly from TObject, whose constructor has an empty body, but doing so will prevent bugs if the ancestor is ever changed.

> **Note**
>
>
> *Object Pascal's "inherited" keyword has no real analog in C++. It can be used to call an ancestral method, or to read or write an ancestral* property. *In C++, you have to use* AncestralType:: *to call ancestral methods. This is not as safe as Object Pascal's inherited, because it requires your method's implementations to make assumptions about the class's parentage. It's not uncommon for parentage to change—adding another level of abstraction between the root and the leaves, or even moving an object to a wholly different branch—which breaks code that makes assumptions about its ancestors. You can use a class-local typedef to localize that assumption close to the point where the parentage is declared, but you do have to not only make that extra declaration but also keep it up to date. Inherited is always present and always valid.*

When an object is allocated, all its fields are filled with $00 bytes. This corresponds to a 0 for all numeric types, zero-length strings and dynamic arrays, False for booleans, Low() for enums, [] for sets, and `not Assigned()` (*ie*, Nil) for pointers as well as object or interface references. If an object needs some other initial values, the constructor must set them. (As you've already seen, initializing the object's object reference fields involves creating the 'sub-objects'.)

If a particular object type needs no special initialization, then you don't have to define a constructor. You can just use an ancestral constructor, and the new object will get the size and VMT pointer appropriate to its class from the class you specify in the call to Create. That is, code like

```
type
  TSimple = class
    A: integer
  end;

begin
  with TSimple.Create do
  try
    Assert(A = 0);
  finally
    Free;
    end;
end.
```

will create a TSimple object with an A field initialized to 0, even though TSimple is using the default constructor it inherits from TObject.

Normally, a constructor returns a reference to the new object. If you raise an exception in a constructor, either directly or by calling a routine that raises one, the exception will propagate out of the constructor, just as it would out of any normal function call. Thus, the instance variable will not be set, which is why a sequence like

```
try
  ThisInstance := ThisClass.Create;
finally
  ThisInstance.Free;
end;
```

will give you a warning that "Variable 'ThisInstance' might not have been initialized"—any error in Create will result in ThisInstance.Free being called before ThisInstance was set. (Global variables and object fields are initialized to 0; local (automatic) variables are **not**.) The proper sequence is

```
ThisInstance := ThisClass.Create;
try
finally
  ThisInstance.Free;
end;
```

If this code should raise an exception in Create, the try finally block will not be executed.

Destructors

Destructors are the converse of constructors: Your code does any necessary cleanup—freeing object fields, closing files, and so on—and then the compiler's code frees the object's memory. While the compiler will let you name a destructor anything that you like, in almost every instance you should override Destroy rather than creating a new destructor. First, virtually all Kylix code uses the Free procedure instead of calling a destructor, because it is safe to call Free on a Nil (unassigned) reference. Since Free in turn calls the virtual destructor Destroy, almost all Kylix code overrides Destroy rather than creating a new destructor. Second, many internal routines call Destroy directly. If your destructor is not an override of Destroy, it won't get called. There *may* be some special cases where you want to use a destructor that's not an override of Destroy—but I can't think of any.

As with constructors, you must call inherited Destroy to clean up any fields inherited from ancestral types. Also as with constructors, you can do this at any point in the destructor. Usually, of course, you want to do any cleanup while any inherited fields are still valid, so you do 'local' cleanup before calling inherited, but under some special circumstances you may need to call inherited **first**. (See Chapter 13 for an example.)

If an exception is raised in a constructor, Destroy is called—even though the constructor didn't finish. Most destructors do nothing but Free any object fields, so this is not an issue: Calling Free on an unset (Nil) object reference is perfectly safe. However, destructors that do anything besides free a data structure created in the constructor need to be aware of the possibility that the constructor might not have terminated cleanly. For example, this constructor / destructor pair

```
var
  // A global used only by the TInstanceCounted class - Object Pascal does
  // not have class variables the way C++ does.
  InstanceCounted_Instances: Cardinal = 0;

constructor TInstanceCounted.Create;
begin
  inherited; // Could be written as "inherited Create;"
  Inc(InstanceCounted_Instances);
end; // TInstanceCounted.Create

destructor TInstanceCounted.Destroy;
begin
  inherited; // Could be written as "inherited Destroy;"
  Dec(InstanceCounted_Instances);
end; // TInstanceCounted.Destroy
```

is safe enough, by itself. But, if the constructor were to raise an exception before Inc(InstanceCounted_Instances)—perhaps a descendant type's constructor ran some code before calling inherited—the instance count would be decremented by the destructor but not incremented by the constructor. A safer approach is to keep track of what part(s) of the object are valid, as in the fuller TInstanceCounted example in the next subsection, so that the destructor doesn't do any damage.

Class methods

Most methods operate on an object, an instance of a class. Their invisible Self parameter refers to the object. *Class methods*, on the other hand, operate on classes, not objects. They can be called even before any instances have been created, and their Self parameter is a class reference—*eg*, a class of TWhatever (see the *Class references* section, below), as opposed to a TWhatever—and not a reference to an instance of the class. Thus, the chief restriction on class methods is that they can not refer to any instance variables (object fields) the way that normal methods can.

All classes inherit a number of class methods from TObject, like ClassType and ClassName. You might define your own class methods to keep functions that return information about a class syntactically bound to the class, as opposed to freely floating nearby with no necessary connection. For example,

```
type
  TInstanceCounted = class
                       private
                         Created: boolean;
                       public
                         constructor Create;
                         destructor  Destroy; override;
                         class function Instances: Cardinal;
                       end;

var
  InstanceCounted_Instances: Cardinal = 0;

constructor TInstanceCounted.Create;
begin
  inherited; // Could be written as "inherited Create;"
  Inc(InstanceCounted_Instances);
  Created := True; // Safe to Dec() in Destroy
end; // TInstanceCounted.Create
```

```
destructor TInstanceCounted.Destroy;
begin
  inherited; // Could be written as "inherited Destroy;"
  if Created then // Constructor made it at least as far Inc()
    Dec(InstanceCounted_Instances);
end; // TInstanceCounted.Destroy

class function TInstanceCounted.Instances: Cardinal;
begin
  Result := InstanceCounted_Instances;
end; // TInstanceCounted.Instances

var
  A: TInstanceCounted;

begin
  WriteLn(TInstanceCounted.Instances); // 0
  A := TInstanceCounted.Create;
  WriteLn(A.Instances);                    // 1
  with TInstanceCounted.Create do
  try
    WriteLn(Instances);                    // 2
  finally
    Free;
  end;
  WriteLn(TInstanceCounted.Instances); // 1
  A.Free;
  WriteLn(TInstanceCounted.Instances); // 0
end.
```

The TInstanceCounted class keeps track of how many instances currently exist. Its constructor delegates basic TObject setup to the inherited constructor *via* the call to inherited Create, then increments the global counter. Its destructor delegates basic TObject cleanup to the inherited destructor *via* the call to inherited, then decrements the global counter. The class function returns the current value of the global.

C++ programmers would most naturally declare InstanceCounted_Instances as a *class field*. This is a field that's not allocated once for every instance; there's a single instance, for the whole class. In effect, a class field is a special global variable that's associated with the class.

Object Pascal does not support class fields; the only way to implement them is the way TInstanceCounted does, as 'associated' data, accessible *via* class methods. If this were real code, TInstanceCounted's type declaration would be in the public part of a unit (Chapter 4) while the InstanceCounted_Instances variable would be in the private part of the unit, along with the method implementations. Thus, any code that used the module would not be able to see InstanceCounted_Instances, and would only be able to access it through the class function.

As in the above instance counting example, you can call a class method as either *ClassName.MethodName* or as *Instance.MethodName*.[13] In both cases, the Self parameter will be a pointer to the VMT and other class information. The difference between the two forms is that *ClassName.MethodName* uses a compile-time constant for the class pointer while *Instance.MethodName* gets the class pointer from the instance. This latter has two consequences:

1. The Self parameter will be the actual class of the object that called the class method. This will always be either the class that contains the class method or one of its descendants. Calling Self.Create will create a new instance of the class that actually called the method, not the class that the method belongs to.

2. Calling a class method from an uninitialized reference is an error that may—or may not—result in a segmentation fault. Even if the code runs without causing a segmentation fault, Self will not actually point to the object class.

As per point 1, within a class method Self refers to the class that was actually used to call the method. Thus,

```
type
  TParent = class
    class function New: TParent;
  end;


class function TParent.New: TParent;
begin
  Result := Self.Create;
end;


type
  TChild = class (TParent)
  end;
```

---

13. You can also call class methods from a *class reference* variable. See the section on *Class references*, below.

```
begin
  with TChild.New do
  try
    WriteLn(ClassName);
  finally
    Free;
  end;
end.
```

will print 'TChild', not 'TParent'.

Visibility

C++ has three levels of object visibility: private, protected, and public. Kylix does too, and adds a published level, which is not only public but also generates Run Time Type Information [RTTI].[14] A class's private members can only be seen by the code in the same unit (module) as the class. Protected members can be seen by code in the same unit and by methods of descendant classes. Public members can be seen by any code that *uses* the unit.

> **Note**
>
>
> *In C++,* private *means private: only a class's member functions can see its private members. It takes an explicit declaration of friendship for one class to be able to play with another class's privates. Borland is a California company, though, and classes 'live with' any other code in their unit: that code can not only see them naked but can also reach out and touch them, too. (I think that what works just fine for humans in hot tubs isn't so sensible for programs. I don't like Object Pascal's 'automatic friendship' rule, but that's the way it is.)*

You specify visibility with a 'bare' private, protected, public, or published keyword: the visibility keywords are not followed by colons, as in C++. The various visibility levels do not have to appear in any particular order (like

---

14. There's also an automated visibility level, but this is mostly supported to ease porting of old Delphi code: in Kylix, automated is basically the same as public.

private before public) and the same visibility modifier can appear more than once.[15] You can, in fact, place an explicit visibility modifier before every class member, though I can't say that I've ever actually seen anyone do so. Typically they are used to group members into sections, and they are lined up with the class name, two spaces in from the margin, while the members in the group are indented two spaces from the visibility keyword, or four spaces in from the margin.

If you don't specify a visibility level, Object Pascal defaults to `public`, as C++ does with structs. The {$M+} pragma changes the default visibility to `published` for any objects declared in the {$M+} state **and** for all their descendants. When you drop a component on a form (which is an object derived from TForm) in the IDE, Kylix adds a field declaration for that component to the first part of the class's declaration, before any visibility modifiers. TForm descends from TPersistent, which is declared in the {$M+} state, so these components are part of the form's published members. At compile time, Kylix uses the resulting RTTI to save your forms' components' design-time state into the executable file, and at run-time to load this information from the executable to recreate that state.

Inheritance

Encapsulation is one of the three key attributes of an object oriented language, but in many ways it's just a bit of syntax that makes it easier to follow what was already good practice: Keep your code modular, and spare 'this' part from any knowledge of how 'that' works. Program to the interface, not the implementation.

Inheritance and polymorphism were the two more radical legs of the OOP revolution, and of course Object Pascal supports them.

Inheritance is the notion that a new object often 'is' an old object, with extra attributes. Thus, a square might be defined by its top left and bottom right points, while a filled square would add a fill color. The root of a widget hierarchy may know how to stream itself to and from storage and how to 'talk' to a widget editor; the descendant types might be as different as check boxes, directory browsers, and spread sheets.

Syntactically, an object declares its parentage as

```
type DescendantClass = class (AncestralClass) {new members} end;
```

---

15. You can have, *eg*, two or more private sections in the same object, if that helps group fields and methods better. These multiple sections have no semantic significance, though: a method declared in one private section can 'see' members declared in any other private section.

That is, the only syntax difference between a class with an explicit ancestor and one that descends directly from TObject is that the class with an explicit ancestor has (*AncestralClass*) immediately after the class keyword. (A class that descends directly from TObject can say so explicitly—type TThis = class (TObject) {whatever} end—but this is not necessary. There is absolutely no behavioral difference between a class that doesn't specify an ancestor and one, like TThis, that explicitly descends from TObject.)

Note

Object Pascal supports only single inheritance. *That is, a class can have one and only one ancestral class, unlike C++, where a class can have two or more parents and inherits everything from each. While there is no doubt that multiple inheritance is occasionally very useful, there is also no doubt that it makes it particularly easy to shoot yourself in the foot. Most people really like the way that Kylix's can protect you from so many careless errors, and are willing to accept the tradeoff of safety* vs *multiple inheritance—especially given that Object Pascal* **does** *support interfaces, which give most of the benefit of multiple inheritance at a fraction of the cost.*

Descendant classes are not nested, the way records with record fields are. Rather, both new and inherited members have first class, top-level status. For example,

```
type
  TParent = class
    A, B: integer;
  end;
  TChild  = class (TParent)
    C: integer;
    end;

begin
  with TChild.Create do
  try
    A := 1; B := 2; // All members of TParent are members of TChild.
    C := 3;         // There is no syntactic difference between new
                    // and inherited members.
  finally
    Free;
  end;
end.
```

Descendant classes can *reintroduce* a member that appears in an ancestral class. Reintroduced fields shadow the ancestral fields, and the descendant class's methods can only read or write the shadowed field if they're willing to cheat a bit. (See the *Peeking at your parents* sidebar if you're interested.) You can access (the most immediately) shadowed *properties* (see the Properties section, below) and methods *via* inherited and, of course, reintroduced virtual methods are the basis of *polymorphism*, which is the subject of the next section.

Peeking at your parents

If one of your classes shadows an ancestral public identifier but still needs to access it, it can do so by casting Self to the parental type.

```
type
  TParent = class
  public
    Age: integer;
    constructor Create;
  end;

  TChild = class (TParent)
  public
    Age: integer;
    constructor Create;
  end;

constructor TParent.Create;
begin
  Age := 42;
end; // TParent.Create

constructor TChild.Create;
begin
  inherited;
  Age := 12;
  Assert(TParent(Self).Age = 42);
end; // TChild.Create
```

It is not possible to take "everything except …" from an ancestor. Inheritance is all or nothing. In object oriented analysis, one often hears that an instance of child class *is* also an instance of the parent class. Finding yourself wanting to inherit some but not all of a class is usually a sign that you should split that class into two classes: A new ancestral class which has only what your new class needs, and the old class which now just adds the unwanted (in its new sibling) members to the new common ancestor.

The object oriented analysis use of "is" has been brought into the language in the form of the `Reference` is `ClassType` operator. An object reference "is" of a particular class type if the object is of that type or of a *descendant* type. That is, a TParent object is not a TChild, while a TChild object is a TParent. If the *Reference* equals Nil, is will return False: Nil means 'no object' which certainly isn't any object class in particular, even TObject.

The as operator is a dynamic typecast operator specifically for object references. `Reference` as `ClassType` does an implicit `Reference` is `ClassType`. If the *Reference* is not a *ClassType*, as will raise an exception. If the *Reference* is a *ClassType*, `Reference` as `ClassType` acts just like the static cast, `ClassType(Reference)`. Because as thus has a run-time cost, you'll often see code like

```
Assert(This is That);
with That(This) do {whatever};
```

instead of with This as That do {whatever}. The development time effect is exactly the same, but the debugged code does not incur the run-time cost of the is operator.

Polymorphism

Polymorphism was the third leg of the OOP revolution. Most basically, it's the notion that the 'same' method might work very differently in one member of an object hierarchy than in another. An ancestral class's methods form a sort of contract that all descendant types will adhere to, but a button widget might implement its GetCaption method quite differently than a text editing widget does.

Polymorphism relies on reintroduced methods. If

```
type
  TParent = class
    procedure Method;
  end;
  TChild  = class(TParent)
    procedure Method;
  end;

var
  Parent: TParent;
  Child:  TChild;

begin
  Child  := TChild.Create;
  Parent := Child;
end.
```

Parent.Method would call TParent.Method, while Child.Method would call TChild.Method. This sort of static polymorphism has its uses, but it relies on the calling code knowing what type of object it is calling. Typically, we don't want that. We want to have a reference to some object that descends from TParent and honors its contract, but to get the specialized implementation of that contract, whether this particular TParent is actually a TParent, a TChild, a TGrandChild, or whatever.

This is where virtual methods come in. With

```
type
  TParent     = class
    procedure Method; virtual;
  end;
  TChild      = class(TParent)
    procedure Method; override;
  end;
  TGrandChild = class(TChild)
  end;

var
  Parent: TParent;
  Child:  TChild;

begin
  Child  := TChild.Create;
  Parent := TGrandChild.Create;
end.
```

Child.Method would still call TChild.Method—but so would Parent.Method. Polymorphism means that each descendant of a class can implement the virtual methods of that parent class however it is appropriate, and a call to that virtual method through a generic reference to the parent class will always call the most recently overridden method.

The virtual keyword introduces a new virtual method, and creates a new slot in the class's Virtual Method Table [VMT]. The override keyword says that this method is the current class's implementation of an ancestral virtual method, the one to use when that method is called on an instance of this class. If you define a new method with the same name as an ancestral class's method, the new method "hides" the ancestral method (static polymorphism). Hiding a virtual method will generate a compiler warning; the reintroduce directive allows you to hide an existing virtual method with a new one of the same name without generating a compiler warning.[16]

Class methods can be virtual, too. A class reference is implemented as a pointer to the VMT, so the class reference contains all the information needed to properly dispatch virtual class methods. Thus,

```
type
  TParent = class
    class procedure Method; virtual;
  end;
  TChild = class (TParent)
    class procedure Method; override;
  end;
  CParent = class of TParent;

class procedure TParent.Method;
begin
  WriteLn('TParent.Method');
end; // TParent.Method

class procedure TChild.Method;
begin
  WriteLn('TChild.Method');
end; // TChild.Method
```

---

16. When you use reintroduce to hide a virtual method, the new method does not have to itself be virtual.

```
var
  ClassVar: CParent = TChild;

begin
  ClassVar.Method;
end.
```

will print 'TChild.Method'.

Abstract methods

It's common for a class to introduce a virtual method that descendant classes will call *via* `inherited`, or that some descendants will not override. That is, the 'root method' in the 'virtual method tree' will actually be executed. Other times, though, the class is merely defining a set of behaviors that descendant classes will implement in very different ways. For example, a circle and a square may both be geometric figures that can draw themselves on a canvas within a bounding rectangle, but they do so very differently and without ever calling the ancestral `inherited` Draw method. The root method will never be executed.

This is what *abstract* (or "pure virtual") methods are for. Following a virtual method's declaration with the `abstract` directive means three things:

1. The compiler will not expect to (and will expect not to) find any implementation of the abstract method, not even an empty `begin end` method body.

2. If you call an abstract method (perhaps *via* the `inherited` keyword, below), you will get a run-time error.

3. You will get a compiler warning if you ever Create a class that has abstract methods.

Inherited methods

Often, though not always, a descendant's method wants to do everything that its parent's method does, as well as something extra. The bare `inherited` statement will call the ancestral method, passing along any parameters, if and only if there *is* an ancestral method with the same signature. That is, it's safe to call `inherited` if there is no ancestral method of the same name and signature. It's not *always* safe to call `inherited`, though: calling an abstract method will cause a run-time error, and the compiler will not warn you at compile time. (This last is no longer true in Delphi 6, and thus presumably will not be true in Kylix 2. It's still true in Kylix 1, though.)

A virtual method can only override an ancestral method with the same signature, but static methods can overload ancestral methods and need not have the same signature. (If TChild reintroduces a static method of TParent with a different signature, it does not need to declare this as an `overload` method. You only have to explicitly `overload` methods when you have two or more methods in the same object with the same names and different signatures.) When a TChild thus reintroduces ancestral methods, it can call the shadowed TParent method by using the `inherited` keyword to qualify the method name.

```
type
  TParent = class           procedure Foo(Bar: integer); end;
  TChild  = class(TParent) procedure Foo(Bar: char);    end;


procedure TParent.Foo(Bar: integer); begin end;


procedure TChild.Foo(Bar: char);
begin
  inherited Foo(7);
end; // TChild.Foo
```

> **Note**
>
>
> *TChild can call TParent.Foo via either* inherited Foo(7) *or* TParent(Self).Foo(7). *Using* inherited *is better, because it doesn't assume that Self is a TParent, or that TParent is the immediate ancestor.*

Dynamic methods

Virtual methods are implemented very efficiently. The first four bytes of every object is a pointer to its VMT, which consists of an array of pointers to virtual methods. Each new virtual method gets its own slot in the VMT, and a call to a virtual method involves dereferencing the object reference to get the VMT pointer, then doing an indirect call through the proper entry in the VMT. That is, something much like `Instance^^[SlotNumber]()`. See Figure 3-5.

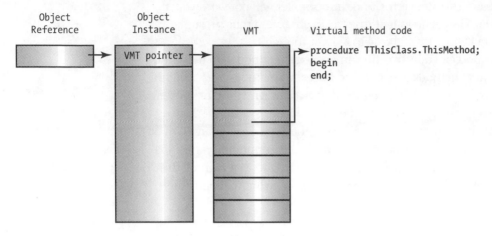

Figure 3-5. Calling the 4th virtual method

The only drawback to this is that in a large object hierarchy, with many virtual methods and many descendant classes, the VMT's can take up a lot of room. This really isn't a very big issue in a 32-bit program running on a machine with significant fractions (or even multiples) of a gigabyte of RAM, but it did pose an issue for 16-bit implementations of Object Pascal where all the VMT's had to share a 64K data segment with the global data. *Dynamic methods* solved this problem.

Dynamic methods act just like virtual methods, but they have a different lookup mechanism. Each new dynamic method gets a unique method number, much as each new virtual method gets a unique slot in the VMT. Every class has a pointer to its Dynamic Method Table [DMT] in the class information area 'to the left of' the VMT. The DMT consists of a pointer to the ancestral DMT, a list of method numbers, and an associated list of method pointers. While a class's VMT contains entries for each virtual method in the class, even if that method is actually inherited from an ancestral class, each class's DMT only contains entries for methods actually declared in that class. If a class does not override an ancestral dynamic method, its DMT contains no entry for that method.

When you call a dynamic method, the compiler actually first calls a function that looks up the method address. This function gets the class's DMT address from the VMT, then looks up the method number in the DMT. If it finds it, it returns the appropriate method pointer; if it doesn't, it repeats the lookup on the ancestral DMT, if any.

Dynamic method dispatch is thus significantly slower than virtual method dispatch. The memory savings only begin to amount to anything when you introduce methods near the root of a large hierarchy (scores or hundreds of descendants) that are rarely overridden. Don't use dynamic methods unless you are quite sure that the memory savings overbalance the performance cost.

Message methods

Message methods are a special sort of dynamic method that allow you to specify the method number. Under Delphi, message methods are very important, as you can handle any Windows message simply by declaring a method for it. Qt uses a different message passing mechanism (see Chapter 6) so message methods are much less important, but you can declare a message method and invoke it *via* the object's Dispatch() method.

Properties

Properties are an Object Pascal language feature without any real analog in any other language except C#. Properties look and act just like fields, but you specify their read and write behavior. A property's read or write specifier can be simply an underlying field, in which case the property is just a sort of public alias for a private field, and accessing the property generates exactly the same fast (no CALL) code as accessing the field would. A property's read or write specifier can also be the name of an *access method*, which allows you to create synthetic properties (built out of several underlying fields or other pieces of system state) or to enforce data consistency by updating 'this' field whenever you update 'that' field. You can also have read-only or write-only properties, simply by omitting a read or write specifier.

The basic syntax of a property is

```
property PropName: PropType read ReadSpec write WriteSpec;
```

You can have read-only or write-only properties by omitting either a `write` clause or a `read` clause, but you have to have at least one of them: You can't say something like `property Foo: integer`. When the *ReadSpec* or *WriteSpec* refer to an actual field of the object, convention dictates that this field name start with an F, as in *FPropName*. When the *ReadSpec* or *WriteSpec* refer to methods, convention dictates that read methods start with Get while write methods start with Set.

Note

Kylix's code completion feature allows you to simply type the property declaration, then press CTRL+SHIFT+C. Kylix will then automatically generate private declarations for any fields that you referred to but didn't declare, as well as private method declarations and empty implementations for them. If you simply type property Name: Type;, *CTRL+SHIFT+C will automatically add a private read field and a private write method.*

When a property refers to an underlying field, the reference may be to any part of a larger structure that's of the same type as the property. That is, in

```
type
  TSimple = class
  private
    fIntField: integer;
  public
    property IntProperty: integer read fIntField write fIntField;
  end;

  TComplex = class
  private
    fStructure: array[0..1000] of record
                  A, B: integer;
                end;
  public
    property IntProperty: integer read fStructure[1].A write fStructure[1].B;
  end;
```

both TSimple and TComplex contain valid declarations of IntProperty. In general, the field specifier can include any expression that refers to the object's fields and that can be resolved at compile-time. As you can see, the compiler will even allow the read and write specifiers to refer to different memory locations! I can't really imagine any situation where this last wouldn't be a bug, and suspect the compiler should issue a warning on declarations like read fStructure[1].A write fStructure[1].B or read fStructure[1].A write fStructure[2].A.

A read function must always return a value of the same type as the property. A write procedure must take a parameter (usually called Value) of the same type as the property.

Because reading or writing a property may be mapped to a method, not a field, you can only write code that refers to a property's value. You can't write code that refers to a property's address. That is, you can't take @ or Addr() of a property;[17] you can't pass a property as a var or untyped const parameter; and you can't Inc() or Dec() a property.

The principles of modularity and encapsulation apply within classes just as they do between classes. You should avoid referring to a property's underlying field except within the property's get and set methods. Read or write the property, not the field; the interface, not the implementation. Writing the property and not the field means that any data integrity rules stay in the setter and are not scattered throughout the class's methods. Reading the property and not the field means that changing a property's read specifier from a field reference to a get method doesn't require changes throughout the method.

Following this principle is generally pretty easy when it comes to reading property values. Many—probably most—property reads do map to a field read, so you pay no cost for reading the property, not the field. The principle can be a bit harder to follow when it comes to writing properties and not the underlying fields. Especially in visual components, property setting methods may be relatively expensive. They may involve a visual update, or some database or network activity that keeps the object's state in synch with other objects or the Real World. However, properties can be private or protected just as fields and methods can, and you can almost always decompose an expensive externally accessible setter method into references to private properties with relatively little effort.

For example,

```
type
  TExample = class
  private
    fVisible: string;

    procedure FullSideEffects;
    procedure SetVisible(const Value: string);
```

---

17. This is actually not totally true. You **can** apply @ and Addr() to a property whose read specifier is a field, not a function. I recommend that you not take advantage of this 'feature', as it seems to violate the spirit of the other restrictions, and may thus go away in some future release.

```
    procedure SetPrivateVisible(const Value: string);

      property PrivateVisible: string read fVisible write SetPrivateVisible;
    public
      property Visible: string read fVisible write SetVisible;
    end;

procedure TExample.FullSideEffects;
begin
  // Update UI or whatever
end; // TExample.FullSideEffects

procedure TExample.SetPrivateVisible(const Value: string);
begin
  // Do whatever it takes to maintain internal consistency,
  // but don't do the expensive side effects
  fVisible := Value;
end; // TExample.SetPrivateVisible

procedure TExample.SetVisible(const Value: string);
begin
  PrivateVisible := Value; // Maintain internal consistency
  FullSideEffects;         // Show the world
end; // TExample.SetVisible
```

Array properties

You can have properties that look like arrays. While true arrays can only be indexed by ordinal values (and dynamic arrays can only be indexed by 0-based integers, as in C) array properties can be indexed by any value, including strings and object references.

This unique ability comes from the fact that array properties are always accessed *via* access methods; you can not have an array property mapped directly to an array field. The syntax of an array property is like that of a simple property, with the addition of an array specifier.

```
property PropName[IndexList]: PropType read ReadFn write WriteProc;
```

The *IndexList* looks much like a routine's parameter list—a semicolon separated list of one or more Names: Type groups—and can include var and const (and even out)[18] modifiers. The *IndexList* can have more than one value, which creates an array property that looks like a multidimensional array. An important difference between a multidimensional array and a multidimensional array property is that while you can always access an element of, for example, a two-dimensional array as a 'true' two-dimensional array (`Arr[I, J]`) or an array of arrays (`Arr[I][J]`) regardless of whether you define it as an `array[IType, JType]` or an `array[IType] of array[JType]`, you must always access a multidimensional array property as a 'true' multidimensional array. That is, all the parameters that are passed to the access method must go within a single pair of square brackets, `Arr[I, J]`.

An array property's read method consists of a function returning a value of the same type as the property and whose parameter list exactly matches the property's *IndexList*. An array property's write method consists of a procedure whose parameter list exactly matches the property's *IndexList*, with a final parameter (usually called Value) of the same type as the property. This syntax means that the setter function is roughly modeled on array element assignment—*Arr[IndexList] := Value*.

Note

This assignment model is a good one to follow for your own routines. A routine that sets one or more var *parameters based on some other parameters should be modeled on assignment, and have the* var *parameters first, followed by the other parameters*—Results := Op(Parameters). *A routine that sets some aspect of system state based on some parameters should have the 'subscripts' first, followed by the 'values', to the 'subscripts' right*—State[Params] := Values.

Every object can have one default array property. This is declared by adding the default; directive **after** the semicolon that terminates the rest of the property declaration. What this means is that you can omit the property name, and index the object reference directly.

---

18. You might be tempted to use var or out parameters to create a indexed property that can use some of its index parameters to return status codes. Resist this temptation, for in that way lies obscure and unmaintainable code! If you need to call an object method that changes its parameters, then you should call it explicitly.

```
type
  THash = class
  private
    function GetValues(const Key: string): string;
    procedure SetValues(const Key: string; const Value: string);
  public
    property Values[const Key: string]: string read GetValues write SetValues;
           default;
  end;

// method definitions elided

var
  Hash: THash;

begin
  Hash := THash.Create;
  try
    Hash.Values['this'] := 'that'; // Explicit property reference
    Hash['this'] := 'that';        // Default property reference
    finally
    Hash.Free;
  end;
end.
```

Indexed properties

Indexed properties are, in some sense, the converse of array properties. They rely on access methods that look just like the access methods for an array property indexed by a single integer (that is, the get function takes a single integer parameter, while the set procedure takes an integer parameter followed by a Value parameter), but you specify the index parameter at compile time. You typically have more than one property using the same access methods with different indices. This is often used to 'crack' more fundamental properties that consist of an array of elements, and give each array slot a symbolic name. For example, instead of referring to SubItems[2], you could refer to SizeColumn.

The syntax is like that of a simple (non-array) property, with the addition of an index clause **before** the read and write specifiers.

```
property PropName: PropType index IntIndex read ReadFn write WriteProc;
```

The *IntIndex* can be any value from Low(Integer) + 1 to High(Integer), and can be a literal constant or a symbolic const. Using symbolic constants is, of course, a good idea here as elsewhere, as it allows the access methods to use the same symbolic constants as the property definition. It's generally a good idea to add an Assert() or two to the access methods to check that the *IntIndex* contains a sensible value.

You **can** mix array and index properties to create an indexed array property. The index will be passed to the read and write routines as the last parameter. For example,

```
const
  MangoIndex = 111;

type
  TMango = class
  private
    function GetMango(M, A, N, G, O, Index: integer): integer;
  public
    property Mango[M, A, N, G, O: integer]: integer index MangoIndex
                                                 read   GetMango;
  end;

function TMango.GetMango(M, A, N, G, O, Index: integer): integer;
begin
  Assert(Index - MangoIndex);
  // Whatever
end;
```

You can also use the same access methods to provide named access to individual slots of an array as well as indexed access to individual elements. For example,

```
type
  TSomeList = class
  private
    // GetElement/SetElement map any Index<0 to the last element
    function  GetElement(Index: integer): integer;
    procedure SetElement(Index: integer; Value: integer);
  public
    property List[Index: integer]: integer read  GetElement
                                           write SetElement; default;
```

```
    property First: integer index  0 read GetElement write SetElement;
    property Last:  integer index -1 read GetElement write SetElement;
end;
```

The imaginary TSomeList class has a List property that's indexed in the normal way, except that any index less than 0 is mapped to the last element. It takes advantage of this to give names to two special positions, First and Last.

Note

*One annoyance of indexed properties is that they **must** be indexed by an integer value. You can't index by an enumeration or other non-integer ordinal, the way you can with arrays. You can, however, use any constant expression as an index specifier. So, you can use Ord() to turn an enum into an integer, and use code like* index ord(ieFirst) *and* index ord(ieLast) *instead of* index ieFirst *and* index ieLast.

Inherited properties

When a property has the same name as a property in an ancestor class, it can either *shadow* or *override* the ancestral property.

A property that overrides an ancestral property does not have a type declaration. Property overrides can be used to increase a property's visibility, to change an access specifier, to change the default value of a property (below), or to change the default array property. For example, the THash type in the array properties section might have been more simply implemented as

```
type
  THash = class (TStringList)
  public
    property Values; default;
  end;
```

A property that shadows an ancestral property has a complete property declaration. It can be of a different type than the ancestral property—though this is generally a bad idea which leads to confusion—or it can be of the same type as the ancestral property. Shadowing can also be used in components (Section 2) derived from other components, where you might need to hook an event but still want to supply that event to users of your derived component—though components derived from CLX ancestors will usually do this by overriding the dynamic method that calls the event handler.

Whether the ancestral property is shadowed or overridden, you can always access the ancestral property *via* inherited:

```
type
  TRatherContrived = class (TStringList)
  private
    function GetText: string;
    procedure SetText(const Value: string);
  public
    property Text read GetText write SetText;
  end;

function TRatherContrived.GetText: string;
begin
  Result := inherited Text;
end; // TRatherContrived.GetText

procedure TRatherContrived.SetText(const Value: string);
begin
  inherited Text := Value;
end; // TRatherContrived.SetText
```

Properties are statically bound. If you create a THash or a TRatherContrived and assign it to a TStringList variable, you will get the TStringList behavior of the Text property and the TStringList default property (which is Strings, not Values). Thus,

```
var
  Hash: TStringList;

begin
  Hash := THash.Create;          // this is fine, of course
  Hash.Values['this'] := 'that'; // no problem
  Hash['this'] := 'that';        // will not compile
  Hash.Free;
end.
```

However, you *can* get polymorphic behavior merely by making the access methods virtual.

```
type
  TAncestor = class
  protected
    function GetUserName: string; virtual;
  public
    property UserName: string read GetUserName;
  end;

  TDescendant = class (TAncestor)
  protected
    function GetUserName: string; override;
  end;

var Ancestor: TAncestor;
```

Here, the value of the Ancestor.UserName property will depend on whether it was set to a TAncestor or a TDescendant, even though it's the same statically bound property in either case.

Storage specifiers

While any class can have properties, and they can be quite useful in general programming, it's probably true that most properties are associated with Kylix components. The final property directives relate to the way that Kylix saves property values in form files. (See Section 2.)

The default directive allows you to declare a default value for the property, one that is set in the constructor. If the property's value is the same as this default value (either you never set it, or you did set it but then changed it back to the default), Kylix will not store the property value in the form file. This makes the form file—and hence your application—smaller. It also means that you can create an instance of the form a bit faster, as there is that much less to process in the resource stream.

Note

 *The default directive does **not** actually set the default value. You still have to do that in the object's constructor. All that the default directive does is prevent values that match the default from being saved in the form file.*

The nodefault directive allows you to override the default value of an ancestral property without substituting a new default value: All values are stored.

The stored directive takes a Boolean argument: Either a constant True or False; or the name of a Boolean field; or the name of a niladic function that returns a Boolean value. If there is no stored directive, or if the Boolean is True, the property is stored whenever it differs from its default value. If stored is False, the property is not stored, even when it differs from its default value This is most useful with properties that are related in a way that lets a stored False property be recreated from the value(s) of stored True properties.

With with objects

You can use with with objects as well as with records. While opening up a record with with is just a sort of syntactic shorthand, a sort of macro operation, opening up an object with with can result in more efficient code, just as with array references. For example, every Kylix form is an object that has a Canvas property that is an object, and this Canvas object has a Brush object. A statement like Canvas.Brush.Style := bsClear; is equivalent to Self.Canvas.Brush.Style := bsClear;, which generates code as if the references were really pointers, or Self^.GetCanvas()^.Brush^.SetStyle(bsClear). Now, pointer dereferencing is a lot cheaper than it used to be, so this operation isn't particularly expensive, but we still don't really want to do something like

```
Self^.GetCanvas()^.Brush^.Style := bsClear;
Self^.GetCanvas()^.Brush^.Color := clNone;
```

If we were faced with code like this, we'd tend to create a temporary Brush variable, and do something more like

```
Brush := Self^.GetCanvas()^.Brush;
Brush^.Style := bsClear;
Brush^.Color := clNone;
```

This is pretty much what

```
with Canvas.Brush do
begin
 Style := bsClear;
 Color := clNone;
end;
```

175

does: The with statement creates an invisible local variable, saves a reference to Self.Canvas.Brush in it, and then does one dereference for each of the assignments, instead of three. While the savings here are rather minimal, you can readily see that with more statements in the with block, or with deeper nesting and/or more property read functions, the savings can be substantial.

Class references

The usual way to create an object is to call something like TThisClass.Create. This hardwires the creation of a TThisClass into the code, but in most cases that's just what we want to do. There are special cases, though, where we really don't know at compile time what class we want to create. One example is an object streaming system, where the same code needs to be able to create objects of just about any type.

Similarly, while usually we want to test an object's type with something like ThisObject is TClassName, there are times when we'd like to be able to parameterize the test. In some circumstances, we want to check that ThisObject is a TThisClass, while in others we want to test that ThisObject is a TThatClass.

Class references, or meta-classes, let us handle these special cases in a clean way. Class references are variables that hold class type values. You can use a class reference in many of the same ways you use a class name: to the left of a constructor or class method call, and to the right of is and as. (In fact, outside of class declarations and method definitions, a class name is pretty much syntactically equivalent to a class reference constant.) You can call **only** constructors or class methods with a class reference. You can't use a class reference to call a normal (instance) method or to refer to an instance's fields, any more than you could do so with a class name.

Class reference types are declared using a class of syntax.

```
type CThisClass = class of TThisClass;
```

In the same way that a pointer to a TThis is commonly named PThis, I usually give a class of TThis the name CThis.

Given an (initialized!) var ThisClass: CThisClass, you can substitute ThisClass.Create for TThisClass.Create, and ThisInstance is ThisClass for ThisInstance is TThisClass. The difference, of course, is that ThisClass can hold a reference to TThisClass or to any of its descendants, so that the object you create or the class you test for can vary at run-time.

The assignment compatibility rules for class references follow the assignment compatibility rules for instance references. That is, you can assign a reference to a descendant class to an ancestor class reference variable, but you can't assign a reference to an ancestor class to a descendant class reference variable. So, given that all classes, including TThisClass, descend from TObject,

```
var
  Generic:  TClass     = Nil; // TClass = class of TObject
  Specific: CThisClass = Nil;

begin
  Generic  := Specific; // Legal
  Specific := Generic;  // Not legal
end.
```

The binding rules for calling constructors and class methods from a class reference also follow the binding rules for calling normal methods from an instance reference. That is, regardless of the actual value of the class reference variable, the method called depends on the type of the class reference variable, and on whether that method is declared as virtual in that class. Thus, `Generic.Create` would call `TObject.Create`, while `Specific.Create` would call `TThisClass.Create`. If `Specific` actually referred to a TThisClass descendant class, `Specific.Create` would only properly initialize an object of that descendant class if the constructor `TThisClass.Create` is declared as virtual. In other words, you must use virtual constructors whenever you plan to do generic construction *via* an ancestral class reference.

Class registration

One of the main uses of class references is saving objects to a stream and later recreating them from that stream. A valid class reference and virtual constructors allow you to recreate a class from a stream. Of course, getting a valid class reference isn't as straightforward as reading a 32-bit pointer from the stream. Two different programs (or two different versions of the same program) may use the same class, but they will almost certainly place the VMT in a different location, which will change the appropriate value of the class reference.

The usual solution is to use the ClassName method that every class inherits from TObject to stream the class name instead of a class reference. Now all you need to do is to get a valid class reference given the class name. If your classes descend from TPersistent, then you can use the standard routines RegisterClass and FindClass. You typically call RegisterClass in the initialization section of every unit that defines a streamable class, and call FindClass in the streaming code.

In some cases, you may want a streamable class hierarchy that's not based on TPersistent. (I know that I've done this at least twice, mostly to avoid the 'semantic violence' of saying that each of my streamable objects "is" a TPersistent.) Since you can't use RegisterClass and FindClass, a good solution is to create a TStringList (see Chapter 7) in a unit that's used by the streaming code and by all the units that contain streamable objects. To register TThisClass, you would use

```
List.AddObject(TThisClass.ClassName, TObject(TThisClass));
```

A class's name acts much like a class reference constant, so that `TObject` `(TThisClass)` returns the same value as `TObject(TThisClass.Create.ClassType)` would—a class reference typecast to an instance reference for assignment compatibility with AddObject's TObject parameter—without leaking memory.

To map a streamed-in class name to a TClass that you can use to recreate the object, you would use code like

```
function LookupClassName(const ClassName: string): TClass;
var
  IndexOf: integer;
begin
  List.Sorted := True; // Force binary search
  IndexOf := List.IndexOf(ClassName);
  if IndexOf < 0
    then Result := Nil // not found
    else Result := TClass(List.Objects[IndexOf]);
end; // LookupClassName
```

ClassType

All classes inherit a ClassType method from TObject that returns a reference to the actual run-time class of an instance. This can be used to clone any member of a class hierarchy, using a virtual constructor and a virtual Assign method. ClassType can also be used to check if a particular object is of one specific type, and not any of its descendants. That is, `Descendant is TAncestor`, but `Descendant.ClassType <> TAncestor`.

What ClassType actually does is to simply return the pointer to the VMT that is the first field of every object. That is, a class reference is implemented as a reference to the class's VMT.

InheritsFrom

Class references can not appear on the left-hand side of an `is` or `as` operator. That is, while you can test whether or not `ThisInstance is TThisClass`, you can't test whether `TThisClass is TThisClass`. To do this test, you have to use the TObject class function, InheritsFrom: `TThisClass.InheritsFrom(TThisClass)` or `TThisClass.InheritsFrom(ThisClassReferenceVariable)`.

Interfaces

Object Pascal supports Java-style *interfaces*. An interface is something like an ancestral object with no fields and only abstract methods—a pure contract. You can make virtual method calls through a variable of an ancestral class without knowing whether the methods are implemented in the particular descendant class that the variable refers to, in the ancestral class, or somewhere in between. Similarly, you can make method calls through an interface reference, without knowing which object implements the interface.

In C++ you would implement this with multiple-inheritance; an interface would just be a pure virtual class that some particular class happens to inherit from. C++ programmers might therefore be wondering why this technique merits a special name, and why Object Pascal doesn't just implement multiple inheritance, instead. One reason, of course, is that interfaces are a lot easier to implement than full-fledged multiple inheritance. By supporting interfaces, Kylix can have many of the benefits of multiple inheritance while still offering the world's fastest compilation. Another reason is that by not supporting multiple inheritance, Kylix doesn't force the programmer to deal with all of C++'s *virtual base class* headaches.

There are other advantages to interfaces besides implementation simplicity, though.

1. With interfaces, your code can be even further removed from implementation details. You only know that 'this' object can do 'that'; you don't know what type of object it is. You program to the interface, not the implementation.

2. Paradoxically, interfaces also 'specificize' your code. Passing an object reference passes a reference to all its fields and all its methods. Passing an interface reference passes a reference to only the abilities you are actually using.

3. Interfaces are often a better model of the semantics of a problem than multiple inheritance. Inheritance is a strong, "is a" relationship: Inheriting from a hypothetical TStreamer class so that you can pass the object to generic code that calls SaveToStream or LoadFromStream means that this object "is a" TStreamer. By contrast, supporting an interface is a weaker, "can do" relationship. Implementing a hypothetical IStreams so that you can pass the object's IStreams interface to generic code that calls SaveToStream or LoadFromStream means only that this object "can do" IStreams.

4. Interfaces support querying of capabilities, which multiple inheritance doesn't. (At least, multiple inheritance as implemented in C++ doesn't support querying.) If you have a reference to an object's *IThis* interface, you can use the as operator (or the various Supports() functions) to see if the same object also supports an *IThat* interface.

5. Object Pascal's implementation of interfaces is reference counted. Objects automatically keep track of how many references there are to one of their interfaces. When the last such reference goes away, the object automatically frees itself. That means less boilerplate code, which in turn means fewer points of failure.

Declaring interfaces

Interface declarations look a lot like class declarations, with the keyword class replaced with interface.

```
type
  ISimple = interface
    procedure DoThis;
    procedure DoThat;
    function GetTheOther: integer;
    procedure SetTheOther(Value: integer);
    property TheOther: integer read GetTheOther write SetTheOther;
  end;
```

Interface definitions can **not** have any fields or visibility modifiers (like public and private); an interface consists entirely of public methods, and properties with method read/write specifiers. Interface methods can be overload-ed, but since interfaces represent a contract, not an implementation, the virtual, abstract, dynamic and override routine modifiers are not allowed.

By convention, interface types start with a capital I. As with other naming conventions, the compiler will allow you to break this convention, but anyone who reads your code will probably complain loudly.

As with classes, interfaces can inherit from other interfaces. The syntax is exactly analogous:

```
type
  IDescendant = interface (ISimple)
    procedure Added;
end;
```

and acts much the same as class inheritance. IDescendant contains all the methods and properties of its ancestor, ISimple. Note that there is one key difference between interface inheritance and class inheritance: Where a class only has to implement the methods it declares, a class that implements a derived interface has to implement *all* the methods of both the base (ancestral) and derived interface.

Just as all classes inherit from TObject whether they say so or not, so do all interfaces inherit from IInterface, whether they say so or not.

```
type
  IInterface = interface
    ['{00000000-0000-0000-C000-000000000046}']
    function QueryInterface(const IID: TGUID; out Obj): HResult; stdcall;
    function _AddRef: Integer; stdcall;
    function _Release: Integer; stdcall;
  end;
```

IInterface *vs* IUnknown

Microsoft has wholeheartedly adopted interfaces, to the extent that you can't do COM programming without at least some familiarity with interfaces. As a result, some Delphi programmers have come to associate Delphi's interface support with COM support. Borland doesn't see it that way. Interfaces in Object Pascal are a platform-independent language feature, just as they are in Java.

Kylix is not Delphi 5

Under Windows, every interface derives from IUnknown, at least through Delphi 5. In Kylix, Borland introduced IInterface and made it the root of the interface inheritance tree, with IUnknown defined as a derivative type IUnknown = IInterface. Borland chose to turn IUnknown into a mere alias for IInterface to drive home the point that interfaces are not tied to Windows. Delphi 6 follows Kylix's lead, here.

When you are declaring interfaces that have nothing to do with Windows COM, you should derive from IInterface. You should reserve IUnknown for those parts of a cross-platform program that are Windows specific.

The string literal in square brackets, ['{00000000-0000-0000-C000-000000000046}'], is a more-or-less human readable representation of a 16-byte GUID, or Globally Unique Identifier. GUID's are generated by a complex algorithm involving the current time and the hardware number in your network card (if any) to yield a number that's extremely unlikely to ever be duplicated, and are thus rather reliably Globally Unique.[19] You can generate a GUID in the Kylix IDE by pressing CTRL+SHIFT+G.

An interface doesn't need a GUID, but without one, QueryInterface can't tell if a given object implements the interface. You can always statically cast an object reference to an interface reference, but of course this suffers from the standard problem with static casts: *viz*, if you miscast, your program will probably crash, preferably sooner but all too often much later. QueryInterface lets you ask an object or an interface if it supports a specific interface. You can pass the GUID as either an initialized TGUID record or as an interface name. The result, in the out parameter, is either the interface you asked for or Nil.

---

19. Much like the name Jon Shemitz, in fact.

Global TGUID records and typed constants can be initialized directly from a '{xxxxxxxx-xxxx-xxxx-xxxx- xxxxxxxxxxxx}' string

```
var
  ThisGuid: TGUID = '{B0A01BE0-91C7-11D5-B010-444553540000}';
```

```
const
  ThatGuid: TGUID = '{B0A01BE1-91C7-11D5-B010-444553540000}';
```

or you can use the SysUtils StringToGUID function,

```
ThisGuid := StringToGUID('{B0A01BE1-91C7-11D5-B010-444553540000}');
```

which returns either a TGUID record or raises an exception.

Kylix wraps QueryInterface in the as operator. You can explicitly call QueryInterface, or you can say something like ThisObject.Create as IInterfaceItSupports. (You can use as only with interface names: A TGUID record can't appear on the right side of the as operator.) Again, if IInterfaceItSupports doesn't have a GUID, you can't use it with as, nor can you use QueryInterface to see if the object supports it.

You can use as/QueryInterface with interface references. That is, if you already have an interface reference, you can use as to get other interfaces that that object also supports.

Using as to check capabilities is not a good idea, as the as operator acts with interfaces as it does with objects; it either returns the right type of interface or raises an exception. You can use QueryInterface to check capabilities without raising an exception, but this can be clunky. If all you want is a boolean test, some of the overloaded SysUtils Supports() routines are generally your best choice.

Just as you will rarely call QueryInterface directly, so you will almost never directly call _AddRef and _Release. These are called automatically by Object Pascal's reference counting mechanism. Whenever you assign an interface reference to a variable (or pass it to a routine's as a value parameter), the RTL calls _AddRef. Whenever that variable goes out of scope or is overwritten, the RTL calls _Release.

Note

There is a bug in Kylix (and Delphi 6) such that global *interface references are not finalized when the program terminates. Any state-saving or cleanup that you might have placed in your interfaced object's destructor will not be called at program shutdown if there are outstanding global references. This bug does not affect local interface references, or those contained in any objects that you Free: it only affects global interface references. The bug will be fixed in future releases, but for now you should be sure to explicitly set any global interface references to Nil in the* finalization *clause (Chapter 4) of the unit that declares them.*

Implementing interfaces

Implementing interfaces looks a lot like multiple inheritance. That is, a class that implements interfaces looks like

```
type
  ISomethingElse = interface
    procedure DoSomethingElse;
  end;

  TSimple = class (TInterfacedObject, ISimple, ISomethingElse)
  private
    // ISimple
    procedure DoThis;
    procedure DoThat;
    function  GetTheOther: integer;
    procedure SetTheOther(Value: integer);

    // ISomethingElse
    procedure DoSomethingElse;
end;
```

A class that implements interfaces must always explicitly derive from a base class; it cannot implicitly derive directly from TObject by omitting the (TObject) the way a class that doesn't implement interfaces can. A class can implement more than one interface, merely by including them in the comma-delimited list in parentheses after the class keyword.

You might be wondering why TSimple doesn't declare QueryInterface, _AddRef, and _Release. Have I been slack, and not tested every snippet in this book? Nope.

When I said above that "a class that implements a derived interface has to implement *all* the methods of both the base (ancestral) and derived interface" I was ever so slightly overstating. While it's true that the class has to implement all the methods in the interface, it does not have to do so directly. It suffices to inherit from an ancestor that implements them. Thus, all components already implement IInterface, and you can base non-component objects on TInterfacedObject to use its implementation of IInterface.

Method resolution clauses

Normally, class methods are bound to interface methods by name and signature. Thus, TSimple's DoThis procedure implements ISimple's DoThis procedure, its DoThat procedure implements ISimple's DoThat procedure, and so on. In some cases, an object may implement two or more interfaces that have methods with identical names and signatures, so that this name-based binding can not work. In these cases, you can use a *method resolution clause* to explicitly bind class methods to interface methods.

```
type
  IThis = interface
  ['{B0A01BE2-91C7-11D5-B010-444553540000}']
    procedure Foo;
  end;

  IThat = interface
  ['{B0A01BE3-91C7-11D5-B010-444553540000}']
    procedure Foo;
  end;

type
  TThisAndThat = class (TInterfacedObject, IThis, IThat)
    procedure IThis.Foo = ThisFoo;

    procedure ThisFoo;
    procedure ThatFoo;

    procedure IThat.Foo = ThatFoo;
  end;
```

A method resolution clause consists of the procedure or function keyword, followed by the qualified name of an interface method, an equal sign, and a method in the current class. A method resolution clause can cite a class method either before or after the method is declared.

Delegation

Objects routinely contain references to other objects. An object that claims to implement an interface can in, fact, *delegate* that implementation to one of its properties, which must be either an interface of the right type or a class that implements it.

Delegations pose special problems with regard to mixing reference types (see the next section) and you should always delegate to a special 'inner' object that descends from either TAggregatedObject or TContainedObject.

```
type
  IThis = interface
  ['{B0A01BE2-91C7-11D5-B010-444553540000}']
    procedure Foo;
  end;

  IThat = interface
  ['{B0A01BE3-91C7-11D5-B010-444553540000}']
    procedure Foo;
  end;

  TInner = class (TAggregatedObject, IThis)
    procedure Foo;
  end;

  TDelegates = class (TInterfacedObject, IThis, IThat)
    fInner: TInner;
    fThat:  IThat;

    // Obviously, this class needs a constructor to set fInner and fThat!

    property Inner: TInner read fInner implements IThis;
    property That: IThat   read fThat  implements IThat;
  end;
```

Usually, you'll use TAggregatedObject for delegation. The difference between TAggregatedObject and TContainedObject is that TAggregatedObject acts normally with respect to interface querying. That is, code that gets an interface that's been delegated to a TAggregatedObject can also get other interfaces that the "controlling" object supports. If you don't want this behavior, and would like to restrict interface querying to only those interfaces that the 'inner' object supports, you'd use TContainedObject.

When a class delegates interface implementation to a class property as TDelegates does with fInner and IThis, the compiler must be able to bind interface methods to class methods by name. That is, an inner object can not use method resolution clauses.

Mixing reference types

Object references and interface references are two very different sorts of data types. An object reference is basically just a pointer to the object. Nothing special happens when it comes in and out of scope, nor when you change its value. Interface references, on the other hand, are automatically initialized and finalized, and setting an interface reference changes the reference count in the object that implements the reference.

Objects operate under the "Free what you Create" rule, while interfaces free themselves. Normally, you will deal with any given object only as an object or only as an interface. If you Create it and assign the value to an object reference, you will deal with it as an object until you Free it. If you Create it and assign the value to an interface reference, you will deal with it as an interface until it Free's itself.

There are times, though, when you need to mix the two. For example, a TForm may implement an interface, and you want to pass the form's interface to a routine that has an interface reference parameter. This could be dangerous! Your object may have one or more object references scattered throughout the system, but its interface reference count is 0. When you pass the reference to the procedure, parameter binding will increment the interface reference count to 1. In the course of the procedure, the interface reference count may grow and shrink, but when the procedure returns, the interface reference count goes back to 0—and your object will free itself. If you're lucky, the method that called the routine that did the damage will bomb, but the segmentation fault may come far downstream.

Since it's not uncommon to want to add interface support to a TForm or to various components, the TComponent class (Chapters 5 and 6—all forms and components descend from TComponent) has a special implementation of IInterface that does no reference counting. This means that the only special issue you face is that you must not Free a component or Release a form (Chapter 6) that has any outstanding interface references. If you do, finalizing the form when the interface references are changed or go out of scope will attempt to refer to freed memory. (It's not that TComponent._Release doesn't get called when an interface is finalized; it's just that TComponent._Release will never free the component.) You must explicitly clear any outstanding interface references by setting them to Nil before freeing a component or releasing a form.

In addition to being careful not to Free any object with outstanding interface references, if you need to mix interface and object references to an object that **doesn't** descend from TComponent, you want to be sure that the object won't disappear when the routine that sees it as an interface returns. To do so, you should explicitly call _AddRef before you first treat the object as an interface if you don't want your object to disappear when the routine that sees it as an interface returns. This will ensure that it never frees itself, and that it will persist until you Free it in the normal way.

Note

You should think long and hard before you mix interface and object references to any object that doesn't descend from TComponent. It's really just asking for trouble.

Old-style objects

Object Pascal actually supports two object models. The `class` model I've discussed so far is newer and has many advantages, while the older `object` model is deprecated[20] and in some (probably slight) danger of being removed at some point. In fact, if you look at all the things that old-style objects *can't* do, you might wonder why you would ever want to use an old-style object.

1. Old-style objects don't support RTTI; they can't have a published section.

2. Old-style objects can't have class methods.

3. Old-style objects can't have class references.

---

20. Borland has also decided that they will no longer fix any bugs that are discovered in old-style objects.

4. Old-style objects can't have properties.

5. Old-style objects can't implement interfaces.

The answer is that the old model is significantly simpler, and has three key points in its favor:

1. Old-style objects are like C's 'struct's with methods'.

2. Old-style objects can be statically allocated.

3. Old-style objects that have no virtual methods have no VMT; their memory layout is just like that of a record that has the same fields.

One thing you can do with old-style objects is to define extensible 'records': A core object may contain key fields, while an extended version contains extra fields that you don't always need. With records, you'd have to either redeclare all the fields of the core record in the extended record, or to nest the core record in the extended record as a Core field. With old-style objects, you simply derive the extended object from the core object, and automatically get a flat 'record' with all the core fields before all the extended fields.

```
type
  TCore = object
    This: integer;
    That: integer;
  end;
  TExtended = object (TCore)
    TheOther: integer;
  end;
```

The method-less objects TCore and TExtended are basically indistinguishable from the 'equivalent' records. In particular, if you have a TExtended variable, it will take up twelve bytes in the global data area or on the stack; if you have a TExtended field in another record or object, it will take up twelve inline bytes. That is, like records, old-style objects can be statically allocated. This means they come and go faster than new-style objects that require dynamic memory, and access might be slightly faster.

Old-style objects *are* objects, of course. That is, they can have methods, and act like records that know how to operate on themselves, instead of being passive records that must be manipulated by essentially unrelated routines. Whenever you find yourself declaring a record type and a suite of 'flat' routines that take the record as a parameter, you ought to consider using old-style objects, instead. Whenever you find yourself calling routines on elements of an array of records, you ought to consider using an array of old-style objects, instead.

Similarly, old-style objects can be particularly useful in reading or writing a byte stream shared with another program that consists of a series of heterogenous records. Typically, each one will start with some sort of identifier, which specifies the number and type of subsequent fields. This is a natural fit to an object hierarchy: The base object contains only the identifier field and any common methods. Derived objects contain more fields and more methods. Rather than passing a pointer to each record to a flat routine, you can cast it to a pointer to an old-style object, and then call that object's methods to read and write the data stream.

While old-style objects can be dynamically allocated and do support virtual methods, by and large this is the point where you should switch back to new-style classes. Old-style objects are primarily useful because they can be statically allocated and because you never get any fields that you didn't declare. If you never declare any virtual methods in your old-style object hierarchy, you can treat them just like as smarter versions of records; as soon as you have virtual methods, you **have** to call a constructor to initialize them, you can't cast arbitrary data to them, and so on.

Variants

The scalars in Chapter 1 are all *statically typed*. A variable's type is determined at compile time, and you can't assign a float point value to an integer variable, or a string value to a character variable. This is a distinct contrast to the behavior of other languages, like Perl, that feature *dynamic typing*: Any Perl scalar can hold any value. A variable can be a string one moment and a number the next. This offers great flexibility, but is also inherently slower than static typing. Not only does every operation on every variable have to check what the current datatype is, but also every operation has to check that this combination of datatypes is legal. That is, with static typing, the compiler simply won't allow you to compile code that tries to multiply a number by a street address; with dynamic typing, the run-time library has to check for that possibility. Computers these days are more than fast enough to deal with this, of course, and there are plenty of times where the time it takes to write a program is much more important than the time it takes to run the program. Accordingly, Kylix includes the Variant datatype, which gives you dynamic typing in a compiled environment.

Internally, a Variant is a 16-byte variant record that contains a datatype tag and subsequent overlaid fields. Syntactically, none of the internal structure is visible; a Variant is just a variable that can hold a scalar (except pointers) or an array. You can mix Variants and other types in expressions: A + B will work as expected if A is a Variant and B an Integer, or if A is a Double and B is a Variant.

As in Perl, Variants feature automatic type conversion. Thus, while

```
var
  S: string = '1000';
  I: integer = 1;

begin
  I := S + I;
end.
```

is illegal and won't compile,

```
var
  V1, V2: Variant;
  I: integer;

begin
  V1 := '1000';
  V2 := 1;
  I := V1 + V2;
end.
```

will compile—and run without errors. Note that the conversion is only from string to number: If V1 holds the string 'The answer is ', the expression V1 + 1 will generate a type conversion exception instead of the string 'The answer is 1'. That is, while the compiler will disallow attempts to concatenate strings and numbers at compile time, illegal Variant operations are often not caught until run-time. In one sense, of course, this is no different from the way statically typed variables work. A div B works just fine when B is not 0, but raises an exception when B is 0. The difference is that there is a much larger class of exceptional operations with Variants than with statically typed variables: with Variants, A div B can fail because B is '0' or 'Zero', not just 0.

As you might expect, a run-time library that can add a string and a number can also handle other type conversions. If you assign a Variant to a statically typed numeric or string variable, or if you pass a Variant to a routine that expects a statically typed parameter, the Variant's value will be automatically converted if necessary. You can also explicitly cast a Variant value to, say, an integer for use in expressions where you want to control the datatype of any intermediate results.

Special values

Global Variants cannot be initialized the way global scalars can. That is,

```
var
  CantDoThis: Variant = 'Wouldn''t it be nice';
```

is not legal code. Instead, every Variant—including local variables—is initialized to the special value, Unassigned. You can set Variants to Unassigned, but using an Unassigned value in any other operation generates a run-time error.

This is something like a signaling NAN (Chapter 1): Just as using a signaling NAN anywhere except the right side of an assignment—even in a equality test—results in a SIGFPE, so any expression except assignment that uses an Unassigned value generates a run-time error. Thus, you can write `ThisVariant := Unassigned` (and you might do so, if it contained a large array that you no longer need) but you can **not** write `if ThisVariant <> Unassigned then {...}`. To test if a Variant is Unassigned, you have to use the VarIsEmpty function.

Just as NAN's come in two flavors, signaling and quiet, so do the special variant values. The special value Null is analogous to a quiet NAN in that any operation—except a comparison—that involves a Null value will have a Null value. As with the Unassigned special value, you should always use the VarIsNull function instead of writing code like `if ThisVariant <> Null then {...}`. While the inline test will compile, VarIsNull is slightly faster[21] – and, more importantly, evaluating `ThisVariant =Null` or `ThisVariant <> Null` raises an exception if ThisVariant is Unassigned.

---

21. It's more than a little crazy to worry about efficiency when you're dealing with Variants, but I can't quite stop myself from pointing out that Null is not a constant but a function that returns a Null value. Since a Variant is a record, internally, and functions that return records actually operate on a pointer to the result, an expression like `ThisVariant := Null` has to reset any existing value in ThisVariant, which might be a string or an array. The same Null function is called whether you're assigning to an anonymous temporary variable (as in `ThisVariant = Null`) or whether you're assigning to an existing, populated variable. By comparison, the VarIsNull function only has to examine the internal type code. Thus, `VarIsNull(ThisVariant)` is slightly faster than `ThisVariant = Null`.

Variant arrays

Variant arrays offer great flexibility. They can be homogeneous arrays of scalars, where each element is of the same type, or they can be heterogeneous arrays of Variant's, where each element can be of a different type. Variant arrays of Variant's can even include elements which are themselves arrays, allowing you to build LISP-like recursive data structures.

Homogeneous variant arrays are included in Delphi for passing arrays to other programs *via* OLE Automation. They have their uses in Kylix, in that they're dynamically typed and self-describing—a single routine can handle **any** variant array—but they're considerably slower than Kylix's native dynamic arrays. Kylix's management of dynamic arrays extends only to dynamic sizing and reference counting: actual element-by-element access is done by small and fast inline code. By contrast, element-by-element access to variant arrays requires calls to run-time library procedures that have to lookup the array's datatype &c. Also, even when the array is homogeneous and contains, say, only integers, reading or writing each element is done *via* Variants. (See the *Custom variants can't use subscript notation* sidebar.)

If you want to investigate homogeneous variant arrays despite my deprecation, be sure to look into the VarArrayLock and VarArrayUnlock routines (Table 3-3), which allow for fast access to the actual homogenous array.

Table 3-3. Some key variant array routines

Name	Description
VarArrayCreate	Creates a homogenous array of a specified type, which may include variants.
VarArrayOf	Creates a one-dimensional array of variants, from an open array parameter.
VarArrayLock	Locks the array–guaranteeing that it won't move–and returns a pointer to the data.
VarArrayUnlock	Unlocks the array.

Internals

It's not uncommon for an application to use Variants in only one or two subsystems, and to use normal static typing in all other subsystems. While you can trap EVariantError exceptions generated when you try to assign, say, an address string to a date variable, generally the interface between the dynamically and statically typed subsystems needs to be able to tell what datatype a given Variant contains.

The VarType function returns the internal datatype tag. This is a variable of type TVarType, which is (can be) a hashed value. The low bits, `VarType()` and `VarTypeMask`, contain a type code, while the high bits may signal `varArray` or `varByRef`. (varByRef is a Windowsism that you're not likely to see much of in Linux.) Scalar variants—those that do not have the varArray bit set—contain their value within the last eight bytes of the variant record.

Variant arrays—those that have the varArray bit set—contain a pointer to a "safe array" in the VArray member. All elements of the safe array are of the same type—`VarType()` and `VarTypeMask`–though this type can itself be varVariant. That is, at this internal level, homogeneous arrays are distinguished from heterogeneous arrays only in that heterogeneous arrays are arrays of Variants, while homogeneous arrays are arrays of some static type.

The VarType function works by casting the Variant to the TVarData type, and returning the VType field. TVarData is the variant record that gives names to the various internal fields of a Variant. It's used extensively by the function in the Variants and VarUtils units, and you need to deal with TVarData records to implement custom variants.

Custom variants

Kylix is not Delphi 5

Unlike older versions of Delphi, Kylix allows you to define custom variants. (Delphi 6 followed Kylix's lead on this.) These can then be used in expressions just like any other variant. That is, you can use your custom datatype with infix arithmetic operators like `A := B + C` instead of having to make function calls like `A := Add(B, C)` or `A := B.Add(C)`. Obviously, this sort of *operator overloading* can make your code much clearer if you're working with matrices and vectors, or with huge integers. Less obviously, since all your arithmetic will be piped through the variant dispatch machinery, your code will be much slower than if you stick to explicitly calling functions or object methods.

You define a custom variant by creating an object class that descends from either TCustomVariantType or TInvokeableVariantType and creating a single instance of it.[22] This registers your custom variant with the run-time library, and gives you a new VarType code.[23]

Note

*Your custom variants are **not** objects; they are variant records that get passed to the methods of the CustomVariant object that implements your custom variant. This can get confusing: We have a type of custom variant which is manipulated by the singleton instance of a TCustomVariantType class! To try to minimize this confusion, I refer to the actual data as "custom variants" and to the object that manipulates them as "the CustomVariant object".*

Every custom variant type needs at least one "factory function" that creates it. This will typically be a method (that returns a Variant) of the CustomVariant class that implements this particular custom variant. The factory function needs to do two things: set `TVarData(Result).VType :=` `VarType` to mark this particular Variant as one of your custom variants, and use some or all of the last eight bytes of the TVarData record (*ie,* `TVarData(Result).varDouble` &c) to represent this particular custom variant's value.

When you use a Variant that's produced by one of these factory functions, the run-time library will read the custom VType code, and will call various methods of the registered CustomVariant object to manipulate TVarData records. (Note that the CustomVariant object **is** a full-fledged object: It can have private or protected methods that are used by the public methods that implement a custom variant type, and you can use inheritance to simplify the implementation of a suite of related custom variant types.)

---

22. The basic TCustomVariantType lets you define a custom variant that acts like a scalar: It has a value and that's that. TInvokeableVariantType is a TCustomVariantType descendent that adds methods that let you define Variants that *act like* objects: They can have properties and methods, though you have to supply methods that look up a method or property name and call the appropriate code.

23. You generally Create the CustomVariant object in the initialization section of the unit that defines it, and will not Free it until the finalization section. If you **do** Free a CustomVariant object before program shutdown, its VarCode is not reused, but instead is marked as a CInvalidCustomVariantType. This lets the run-time library generate an exception if you try to use a custom variant whose CustomVariant object has been freed—instead of calling the methods of a different CustomVariant object.

Implementing a custom variant is actually rather complex, and I imagine that there are aspects of it that I haven't run into in my explorations. Still, the example I present below is rather complex, and should constitute a pretty good introduction to the subject.

The very first step is to create a new unit that: uses Variants; that publishes an object type that descends from TCustomVariantType; and that creates and destroys a single instance of it, like this unit from the ch3/Templates project in the ch3/Variants project group.

```
unit BasicCustomVariantTemplate;

interface

uses
  Variants;

type
  TCustomVariant = class (TCustomVariantType)
  end;

var
  CustomVariant: TCustomVariant;

implementation

uses
  SysUtils, VarUtils;

initialization

  CustomVariant := TCustomVariant.Create; // Register, get VarType code

finalization

  FreeAndNil(CustomVariant);

end.
```

Of course, since you had the good sense to buy this book and download[24] the demo code, you can save yourself a bit of time by opening ch3/CustomVariantTemplate.pas or ch3/InvokeableVariantTemplate.pas, renaming TCustomVariant and CustomVariant as necessary, and then doing a Save As into your project directory.

The next step is to override the virtual methods that you'll need, the ones the run-time library will call to manipulate your custom variant.

```
TCustomVariant = class (TCustomVariantType)
  protected
    function LeftPromotion(const V: TVarData; const Operator: TVarOp;
      out RequiredVarType: TVarType): Boolean; override;
    function RightPromotion(const V: TVarData; const Operator: TVarOp;
      out RequiredVarType: TVarType): Boolean; override;
    function OlePromotion(const V: TVarData;
      out RequiredVarType: TVarType): Boolean; override;
    procedure DispInvoke(var Dest: IVarData; const Source: TVarData;
      CallDesc: PCallDesc; Params: Pointer); override;
  public
    function IsClear(const V: TVarData): Boolean; override;
    procedure Cast(var Dest: TVarData; const Source: TVarData); override;
    procedure CastTo(var Dest: TVarData; const Source: TVarData;
      const AVarType: TVarType); override;
    procedure CastToOle(var Dest: TVarData; const Source: TVarData); override;

    procedure Clear(var V: TVarData); override;
    procedure Copy(var Dest: TVarData; const Source: TVarData;
      const Indirect: Boolean); override;

    procedure BinaryOp(var Left: TVarData; const Right: TVarData;
      const Operator: TVarOp); override;
    procedure UnaryOp(var Right: TVarData; const Operator: TVarOp); override;
    function CompareOp(const Left, Right: TVarData;
      const Operator: TVarOp): Boolean; override;
    procedure Compare(const Left, Right: TVarData;
      var Relationship: TVarCompareResult); override;
  end;
```

---

24. If you haven't downloaded the demo code yet, visit the Downloads section at www.apress.com.

This looks daunting, I know. InvokeableVariants are even worse, as they add another four methods that you may have to override.

```
function DoFunction(var Dest: TVarData; const V: TVarData;
  const Name: string; const Arguments: TVarDataArray): Boolean; override;
function DoProcedure(const V: TVarData; const Name: string;
  const Arguments: TVarDataArray): Boolean; override;
function GetProperty(var Dest: TVarData; const V: TVarData;
  const Name: string): Boolean; override;
function SetProperty(const V: TVarData; const Name: string;
  const Value: TVarData): Boolean; override;
```

Nonetheless, while implementing a custom variant is not trivial, it's not as bad as this looks. My demonstration variant, VarLists.pas in the VariantsTest project of the ch3/Variants project group, implements a "list" class.

```
type
  List = type Variant;
```

This is a one-dimensional array of variants, with overloaded addition (List + List and List + Scalar) and subtraction (List - List and List - Scalar) operators. Casting a list to a number gives you its length, while casting it to a string gives you a debug dump of the list contents. This comes to nearly five hundred lines of code, with comments and white space, of course, but I only needed to implement nine out of the above eighteen methods: RightPromotion, Cast, CastTo, Clear, Copy, BinaryOp, and CompareOp, as well as DoFunction and DoProcedure.

Which ones do you need? I recommend overriding **all** of them, and then watching which ones get called as you exercise various features of your custom variant. When you see which operations lead to a method's being called, you can use the F1 help for TCustomVariant and TInvokeableVariantType to see what the default handler does, and thus decide whether you need to override the default. When your custom variant is done, you can go back and delete any methods whose inherited behavior proved to be sufficient or that were never called.

You can watch the methods by setting breakpoints on the first line of each method, but you'll find that a lot of breakpoints slow the IDE down quite a bit on even moderately old machines. Unless you have a rather fast machine, you may prefer to raise an exception in each overridden handler.

Custom variants can't use subscript notation

ch3/VarLists.pas, in the VariantsTest project in the ch3/Variants project group, implements a one-dimensional array of variants, with overloaded addition and subtraction operators. Initially, it looked like the way to implement this was as a custom variant type (obviously) with the varArray bit set. This meant that my CustomVariant methods created and manipulated the VArray safe array, just like the standard variant array routines do. After a few hours, I had code that could create a list and that could add two lists together. I could cast to a number to get length, and cast to a string to see the contents.

Good, good, very good.

But then I tried to subscript my list—to read List[0]—and ran into a major limitation of Kylix's custom variant system. *It's only designed for scalars.*

TCustomVariantType has all sorts of methods that you override to copy and cast values to and from your custom type, and to do various arithmetic and comparison operations on your custom variant, but it doesn't have any methods to subscript an array of your custom variants. Instead, all variant subscripting goes through a single routine in the Variants unit, _VarArrayGet, which assumes that a variant with the varArray bit set is either a heterogeneous array of VarVariant or a homogeneous array of some static data type that takes 8 bytes or less. (This listing is seriously abbreviated—I stripped error checking and some cleanup code—both to save space and make the logic clearer.)

```
function _VarArrayGet(var A: Variant; IndexCount: Integer;
  const Indices: TVarArrayCoorArray): Variant; cdecl;
var
  LVarArrayPtr: PVarArray;
  LArrayVarType: Integer;
  P: Pointer;
  LResult: TVarData;
begin
  LVarArrayPtr := GetVarArray(A);

  // use a temp for result just in case the result points back to source, icky
  LArrayVarType := TVarData(A).VType and varTypeMask;
  if LArrayVarType = varVariant then
  begin
    SafeArrayPtrOfIndex(LVarArrayPtr, @Indices, P);
    _VarCopy(LResult, PVarData(P)^);
  end
```

```
    else
    begin
      SafeArrayGetElement( LVarArrayPtr, @Indices,
                            @TVarData(LResult).VPointer );
      TVarData(LResult).VType := LArrayVarType;
    end;

    // copy the temp result over to result
    _VarCopy(TVarData(Result), LResult);
end;
```

Now, of course, my list variants were heterogeneous arrays of VarVariant, but I couldn't use a VType code of `VarVariant` or `varArray`, as then my CustomVariant methods would never get called! _VarArrayGet would see my `VarType` or `VarArray` code and conclude that it wasn't an array of Variant—and so would try to load the static data into the second (data) half of a Result Variant. Not only did this end up loading the VType field as if it were data, it trashed memory when SafeArrayGetElement(, , @TVarData(…).VPointer) wrote sixteen bytes starting at the 9th byte of the TVarData record.

That nearly killed my example code right there. I wouldn't run into this problem if I didn't set the varArray bit—because you wouldn't be able to subscript the list at all.

But as I was writing a sidebar about "The example that got away", I wrote that last sentence and said "So? There's a law that says you **have** to be able to use subscript notation with a list?" There needs to be 'outboard' functions (or *invokeable methods*) to scan the list and extract sublists anyhow—what's so horrible about SetElement() and GetElement() functions, too? So, I went back to the code, stripped out every bit of code that set the varArray bit, and the code worked fine.

The bottom line is that you can create a custom variant that uses the SafeArray machinery, but you **can't** set the varArray bit that lets you use subscript notation to get and set individual elements. Annoying, but not crippling—and future releases will probably not have this problem.

A secondary conclusion is that you should avoid using safe arrays in your code. They're slower and more cumbersome than Object Pascal native arrays; they can't hold varString (AnsiString) Variants (you have to be sure to replace any varString Variants with varOleStr (WideString) Variants); and their only real point is supporting varArray Variants. Since you can't have custom varArray Variants, you don't need to bother with them. The first working version of my custom variant example, the OldVariantsTest project in the ch3/Variants project group, uses safe arrays to implement my list Variant. Replacing that code with a dynamic array of Variant saved about 100 lines and made the code faster, too.

A custom variant example

I suppose the place to start is at the beginning, with a factory function.

```
function TVarList.New: List;
begin
  TVarData(Result).VType  := VarType;
  SetListLength(TVarData(Result), 0);
end; // TVarList.New
```

This function creates an empty list. It sets the VType field to the VarType that Kylix generated in TVarList.Create,[25] then calls SetListLength to populate the VPointer field. SetListLength and GetListLength work by casting the generic `pointer`, TVarData.VPointer, to an ArrayOfVariant. (Remember, a dynamic array variable is actually just a pointer to the array.)

```
procedure TVarList.SetListLength(var V: TVarData; Value: integer);
begin
  SetLength(ArrayOfVariant(V.VPointer), Value);
end; // TVarList.SetListLength
```

```
function TVarList.GetListLength(const V: TVarData): integer;
begin
  Result := Length(ArrayOfVariant(V.VPointer));
end; // TVarList.GetListLength
```

A slightly more complex factory function creates a list from an open array of Variants.

```
function TVarList.New(const A: array of Variant): List;
var
  Index: integer;
begin
  TVarData(Result).VType := VarType;
  SetListLength(TVarData(Result), Length(A));
  for Index := Low(A) to High(A) do
    GetAddr(TVarData(Result), Index - Low(A))^ := A[Index];
end; // TVarList.New
```

---

25. There's an overloaded form of Create that lets you specify the VarType code. While you **might** want to use this if you store binary representations of custom variants on disk and want to be sure that they will work with future versions of your program, in general you're better off letting Kylix assign you a VarType code.

Safe arrays and AnsiString Variants

You may find it interesting to compare TVarList.New to its counterpart from the OldVariantsTest project, which uses safe arrays.

```
function TOldVarList.New(const A: array of Variant): List;
var
  Safe:  array of Variant;
  Index: integer;
  Wide:  WideString;
begin
  SetLength(Safe, Length(A));
  for Index := Low(A) to High(A) do
    // Can't let an AnsiString into a SafeArray!
    if Variants.VarType(A[Index]) <> varString
      then Safe[Index] := A[Index]
      else begin
           Wide := A[Index];
           Safe[Index] := Wide;
           end;
  CopyArray(TVarData(Result), Safe);
end; // TOldVarList.New
```

It turns out that if you copy a Variant containing an AnsiString (*aka* a normal Object Pascal string) into a safe array of Variants, you'll get SIGSEGV's when you free the array: Safe arrays can't contain AnsiStrings. So, this code scans the array of Variant, and converts any AnsiStrings to WideStrings.

This more complex function sets the VType field, creates a list of the right size, and copies each element into the list. It's important to note that it does an element-by-element Variant assignment rather than a bulk Move() (REP MOVS) operation. Variants have complex string handling code to get around the fact that variant records can't have reference-counted types (like strings) in them. Doing the element-by-element copy assures that each Variant is copied properly, without memory leaks or tombstoning.

The factory function uses the GetAddr() function, as does much of the rest of the code. It should be pretty obvious what's going on here:

```
function TVarList.GetAddr(   const V: TVarData; N: integer): PVariant;
begin
  Result := @ (ArrayOfVariant(V.VPointer)[N]);
end; // TVarList.GetAddr
```

The flip side of the factory function is the Clear method. This method is responsible for resetting your custom variant and making it into an Unassigned Variant. Clear is an abstract method, so you **have** to supply it. If your custom variant is self-contained—it keeps the whole value in the TVarData record, without doing any memory management—you can just call the SimplisticClear method that the F1 help talks about. However, if you trace through the code, you'll see that this eventually just calls VariantInit, so it's hard to see why you shouldn't just call VariantInit.[26] TVarList, of course, is not self-contained, so it has to be sure to finalize its dynamic Array Of Variant.

```
procedure TVarList.Clear(var V: TVarData);
begin
  Assert(V.VType = VarType);
  ArrayOfVariant(V.VPointer) := Nil;
  VariantInit(V); // Make it Unassigned
end; // TVarList.Clear
```

The other abstract method that you have to override is the Copy method, which is responsible for copying one custom variant to another. Note that the Copy method creates a new dynamic array, as dynamic arrays do not use copy-on-write semantics, the way strings do, and we *do* want our list values to be independent of each other.

```
procedure TVarList.Copy(var Dest: TVarData; const Source: TVarData;
  const Indirect: Boolean);
var
  Len, Index: integer;
begin
  Assert(Source.VType = VarType);
  Dest.VType := VarType;
  Dest.VPointer := Nil; // Dest may be filled with garbage
  Len := GetListLength(Source);
  SetListLength(Dest, Len);
```

---

26. I suppose SimplisticClear **may** offer some more portability than a Win32 function like VariantInit, but Borland seems committed to maintaining a Windows-like API to their Portable Variants to maximize compatibility between Windows and non-Windows platforms.

```
    for Index := 0 to Len - 1 do
      GetAddr(Dest, Index)^ := GetAddr(Source, Index)^;
end; // TVarList.Copy
```

These basic methods allow you to create, destroy, and copy list variants. They are the foundation upon which we can erect operator overloading. The next function to implement is BinaryOp, which handles addition and subtraction for the list variant.

```
procedure TVarList.BinaryOp(var Left: TVarData; const Right: TVarData;
  const Operator: TVarOp);
begin
  case Operator of
    opAdd:      Add(Left, Right);
    opSubtract: Subtract(Left, Right);
    else        inherited;
  end;
end; // TVarList.BinaryOp
```

TVarOp is defined in System.pas, and includes symbolic names for all the operations that BinaryOp and CompareOp will be asked to perform. This custom variant only implements addition and subtraction, and passes all other operation requests on to the inherited method, which raises an EVariantError. Thus, List + List returns a new List; List * List or List div List raises an exception. The Add and Subtract methods do pretty much what you'd expect, and I don't think there's a lot of point to printing them.

Similarly, CompareOp implements only the = and <> comparisons, and passes any ordered tests on to the inherited method, which raises an EVariantError,

```
function TVarList.CompareOp(const Left, Right: TVarData;
  const Operator: TVarOp): Boolean;
begin
  case Operator of
    opCmpEQ: Result := Equals(Left, Right);
    opCmpNE: Result := not Equals(Left, Right);
    else     Result := inherited CompareOp(Left, Right, Operator);
    end;
end; // TVarList.CompareOp
```

The Equals method is pretty straightforward, and worth printing only to point out the way that it uses standard Variant (in)equality testing, which means that the list (12, '13', 14) equals the list ('12', 13, '14').

```
function TVarList.Equals(const Left, Right: TVarData): boolean;
var
  LLen, RLen, Index: integer;
begin
  Result := False; // unless ListLength's are equal and so is each element
  LLen   := GetListLength(Left);
  RLen   := GetListLength(Right);
  if LLen <> Rlen then EXIT;
  for Index := 0 to LLen - 1 do
    if GetAddr(Left, Index)^ <> GetAddr(Right, Index)^ then EXIT;
  Result := True; // Length's are equal and so is each element
end; // TVarList.Equals
```

Both BinaryOp and CompareOp can assume that both arguments are list variants, because the default behavior is to "right promote" a mismatched argument to the type of the left argument. You can control this by overriding RightPromotion.

```
function TVarList.RightPromotion(const V: TVarData; const Operator: TVarOp;
  out RequiredVarType: TVarType): Boolean;
begin
  case Operator of
    opAdd, opSubtract, opCompare, opCmpEQ, opCmpNE:
      begin
        RequiredVarType := VarType;
        Result := True;
      end;
    else Result := False;
    end;
end; // TVarList.RightPromotion
```

Note that I didn't really have to override RightPromotion—this implementation is really only a sort of optimization: "Right promote only for operations that we can handle; don't bother for ones that will raise an exception." Note also that this implementation is arguably wrong, as it means that TVarList.New(12) = 12. That is, the list variant (12) equals the scalar variant 12, which perhaps shouldn't be true.

In any event, when RightPromotion says that Kylix should cast a different type Variant to your custom variant, your Cast method is called to do so. By now, my list variant's Cast method probably looks pretty straightforward.

```
procedure TVarList.Cast(var Dest: TVarData; const Source: TVarData);
begin
  Dest.VType  := VarType;
  case Source.VType of
    varEmpty,
    varNull:  SetListLength(Dest, 0);  // an empty list
    else      begin
              Assert(Source.VType <> VarType);
              SetListLength(Dest, 1);
              Assert(Source.VType <> varString);
              VarDataCopy(PVarData(GetAddr(Dest, 0))^, Source);
              end;
    end;
end; // TVarList.Cast
```

As you can see, Cast is doing an *active cast*, creating a new value with the same 'meaning' as the old value. It's **not** doing a simple reinterpretation of the bit patterns. That is, it's more analogous to the cast string(PCharValue) than to the cast pointer(IntValue).

This Cast function examines the VType field, and turns Unassigned and Null variants into empty lists. It turns every other variant type into a one-element list containing a copy of the Variant. It's important to use the inherited VarDataCopy method, not the similar VariantCopy function from the VarUtils method, as VarDataCopy can copy other custom variants and VariantCopy can not.

Cast converts other variants to your custom variant, while CastTo is responsible for converting your custom variant to other standard types. TVarList's CastTo is highly repetitious; this is just an extract. As you can see, you're passed a desired format and must set the appropriate data field of the Dest record: you don't need to set Dest.VType.

```
procedure TVarList.CastTo(var Dest: TVarData; const Source: TVarData;
  const AVarType: TVarType);
begin
  case AVarType of
    varInteger: Dest.VInteger  := GetListLength(Source);
    varOleStr:  WideString(pointer(Dest.VOleStr)) := Format(Source);
    end;
end; // TVarList.CastTo
```

Does that `WideString(pointer(Dest.VOleStr)) := Format(Source)` line look strange? Do you know why I can't just say `Dest.VOleStr := Format(Source)`?

TVarRec is a variant record. Variant records can't contain reference-counted data like strings, as the run-time library can't know if the variant record actually contains a reference-counted object that needs to be dereferenced (or which type—string, dynamic array, interface?) or if it actually contains some non-reference-counted data. So, instead, the Variants and VarUtils units are full of this idiom which casts a generic pointer to a WideString and does an assignment to it. This cast assignment increments the WideString's reference count; Variant cleanup code takes care to do a corresponding `WideString(pointer(Dest.VOleStr)) := ''` to finalize the WideString.

Invokeable variants

That's 'all' I had to do for a simple, 'flat' custom variant. Your mileage may vary.

If you want to create a custom variant that looks like an object, with methods and/or properties, you need to base your CustomVariant object on TInvokeableVariantType instead of TCustomVariantType. This adds four IVarInvokeable methods—DoFunction, DoProcedure, SetProperty, and GetProperty—which are passed a string representing the name of the "property" or "method", and VarData records representing the values or arguments.

```
IVarInvokeable = interface
    ['{1CB65C52-BBCB-41A6-9E58-7FB916BEEB2D}']
    function DoFunction(var Dest: TVarData; const V: TVarData;
      const Name: string; const Arguments: TVarDataArray): Boolean;
    function DoProcedure(const V: TVarData; const Name: string;
      const Arguments: TVarDataArray): Boolean;
    function GetProperty(var Dest: TVarData; const V: TVarData;
      const Name: string): Boolean;
    function SetProperty(const V: TVarData; const Name: string;
      const Value: TVarData): Boolean;
  end;
```

Each of the four IVarInvokeable methods is a Boolean function that returns True if it supports the named method or property and False if it doesn't. If any of these functions return False—including SetProperty and GetProperty—Kylix raises an EVariantError with the slightly misleading message "Variant method calls not supported". This is misleading, of course, because what it really means is "*This particular* Variant property or method call not supported."

Anyhow.

DoFunction and GetProperty expect you to fill in the Dest Variant with the function result or property value. DoProcedure and SetProperty, obviously, do not. You'll note that all pass in the Arguments and property Value as TVarData records, not as actual Variants. This presumably has something to do with the implementation of the dispatch mechanism but shouldn't unduly complicate matters for you, as you can always cast a TVarData to a Variant or a Variant to a TVarData.

> **Note**
>
>
> *If you're like me, you worry about 'breaking' reference counting by casting a TVarData to a Variant or a Variant to a TVarData. If you think it through carefully, though, you'll see that this is not a problem. Casting a TVarData to a Variant to read it is always safe, as reading a reference-counted value never touches the reference count. Casting a TVarData to a Variant to set it is always safe, as this will finalize the current contents if necessary, and will automatically increment the new the value's reference count if necessary. In fact, the only operation that's **not** 'reference count safe' is doing a simple assignment of a varString (or varDispatch) value from one TVarData to another.*

My DoProcedure and DoFunction methods are both implemented on the same pattern, so one listing will pretty much cover both.

```
function TVarList.DoProcedure(const V: TVarData; const Name: string;
  const Arguments: TVarDataArray): Boolean;
begin
  Result := True;
  case Procedures.IndexOf(Name) of
    piSetElement: begin
                Assert(Length(Arguments) = 2);
                Assert(VarDataIsNumeric(Arguments[0]));
                SetElement(V, Variant(Arguments[0]), Arguments[1]);
                end;
    else        Result := False;
    end;
end; // TVarList.DoProcedure
```

I set Result True before the case statement, so that I don't have to do it in each branch. I use a TStringList (see Chapter 7) that I created and initialized in the CustomVariant's constructor to lookup the Name. When one of the DoX case statements matches a Name tag, I check the parameters and call a private method that implements it.

```
const
  ProcedureNames = 'SetElement';
  piSetElement   = 0;

  FunctionNames  = 'SubList,GetElement,Contains';
  fiSubList      = 0;
  fiGetElement   = 1;
  fiContains     = 2;

constructor TVarList.Create;
begin
  inherited Create;
  Procedures := TStringList.Create;
  Procedures.CommaText     := ProcedureNames;
  Procedures.CaseSensitive := False;

  Functions  := TStringList.Create;
  Functions.CommaText      := FunctionNames;
  Functions.CaseSensitive := False;
end; // TVarList.Create
```

Setting the string lists' CommaText property breaks the list of names at the commas, so that Functions.IndexOf('GetElement') returns 1, meaning that it matched the 2nd element (origin 0) in the list. (I define the "pi" and "fi" constants with the list of names, because it's important that they stay in synch.) As it happens, Kylix 1 passes the IVarInvokeable functions UpperCase()d names like 'GETELEMENT', so I *could* save a few cycles by setting the Names list to all-uppercase and specifying a case sensitive search—but that's not the sort of behavior that I think it's prudent to rely on.

CHAPTER 4
Program structure

CHAPTER 4

Program structure

PREVIOUS CHAPTERS HAVE MOVED from simple, scalar data to basic operations to data structures of all sorts. This final chapter on Object Pascal syntax returns to code. It starts with an overview of pragmas that control code generation, and then moves on to cover *units*, Object Pascal's module syntax; executable programs; sharable libraries; and *packages*, which are basically libraries with type information.

Pragmas

Pragmas are compiler directives. They allow you to control how strictly some syntax rules are observed, to control how various constructs are translated to object code, or to have code that is compiled in some circumstances and not others.

Most pragmas can be set for the project as a whole. Normally, you'd set global pragmas *via* the Compiler tab of the Project Options dialog (SHIFT+CTRL+F11, or Project ➤ Options). When you're using the command line compiler, dcc, you can put global pragmas in a file named dcc.conf, or set them *via* command line switches. You can also put project-wide pragmas in an include file that you {$I} in every module. Global pragmas affect all modules compiled during a particular make or build. You can also set pragmas on a per-file basis, which is what this section is concerned with. Pragmas in your source code override the global pragmas, and control the compiler environment for the current module. Source pragmas affect only the current module; they do not affect other modules, which will be compiled under the compiler environment set by the global pragmas.

Object Pascal pragmas are specially formed comments: either {$*pragma*} or (*$*pragma**). That is, they consist of a comment block (either a {} or (**) comment - //$ is **not** a pragma) with a $ sign and a pragma immediately after the { or (*, with no whitespace. { $*pragma*} does not count as a pragma, and putting a space between the open curly brace and the dollar sign is a common way to turn off a pragma without deleting it, so that you can turn it back on easily.

Note

The pragma parser is rather stupid. It does not take the attitude that 'a comment is a comment', and that only properly formed pragmas should receive special treatment: Any comment block that starts with a $ sign is assumed to be a pragma. If what follows the dollar sign is not a legitimate pragma, you'll get a syntax error. Thus, {$ pragma} is a syntax error while { $pragma} is a 'commented out' pragma. This sounds worse than it is, really. The only practical consequence of this shortcut is that you have to be careful commenting out pragmas … and hexadecimal constants. (*$CAFEBABE*) is a syntax error, while (* $DEADBEEF *) is a legitimate comment.

Several pragmas have both a short form, like {$R+} or {$R-}, and a long form, like {$RANGECHECKS ON} or {$RANGECHECKS OFF}. You might be surprised to hear this, given the way I'm always harping about clarity, but I actually recommend that you use the short forms. This is because the {$IFOPT} pragma (see the *Conditional Compilation* section, below) only supports the short forms. You'll find it easier to use and read {$IFOPT} if you routinely use the short forms than if you have to translate {$IFOPT R-} to 'if {$RANGECHECKS OFF}'.

Note

When I describe the short form of a pragma, that means that you can use it with {$IFOPT}. When I describe the long form of a pragma, that means there is no short form and you cannot use it with {$IFOPT}.

Kylix has a lot of pragmas. I'm not going to try to provide an exhaustive list, here. You can always use the online help for that, and some of the options are only important in easing porting of particularly old code. What follows are the pragmas that are the most important, the pragmas that you are the most likely to actually use.

I've grouped these pragmas into three broad groups: pragmas that control syntax options, pragmas that control object code generation, and pragmas that control source code handling. Some of the last group are what might be called 'text oriented', in that they control what gets compiled, but most pragmas are what might be called 'symbol oriented', as they affect the meaning or use of program identifiers. The symbol-oriented pragmas can be further divided into those that affect a symbol's *definition* and those that affect a symbol's *use*. A pragma like the alignment directives of Chapter 3 affects the symbol's definition; a symbol carries the alignment it was defined with, even when it is used in a structure that uses a different alignment. By contrast, the pragmas that control the various run-time checks all affect a symbol's use; the same array might be subject to run-time index checks *here* but not *there*.

Compiler options

The smallest set of pragmas turns various compiler options on and off. These don't affect code generation *per se*: they affect what the compiler considers legal code.

Writeable typed constants

Older versions of Delphi didn't support initialized variables, and even today local typed 'constants' are the only way for a routine to have local static storage. While you can always use a global variable declared just in front of the routine, and so only visible to routines further down in the same unit, most people don't like to do this. A variable should only be global if it's **meant** to be global; if multiple routines are meant to read or write it. Turning a local static into a global opens us up to namespace collisions, invites careless errors, and forces those who inherit our code to waste time trying to decide if this particular variable is truly meant to be global or if someone just didn't like using a const as a var.

So, typed constants are still the best solution when you need local static storage. This (and the desire not to break old code) is why Delphi 5 defaulted to letting you treat typed constants as initialized variables and change their values at run time. The default behavior has been changed in Kylix and Delphi 6—now typed constants **are** constants. You can use {$J+} to override this, temporarily, when you need to use typed constants in the old way, as (misnamed) static variables.

The {$J} pragma affects the compiler's definition of symbols in much the same way that the alignment pragmas do. That is, when you declare a typed constant in the {$J+} state, you can always use it as a variable. You only have to place the typed constant declaration in a {$J+} wrapper, not the whole routine.

The following function illustrates a common pattern for functions that return information that is relatively expensive to compute but that doesn't change from call to call. It saves the result in a static string, initialized to ''. If the static string equals '', the function has never been called, so it computes the result. If the static string does not equal '', the function has already been called at least once, and can just return the previous result. (A non-string variation on this pattern involves a static boolean named FirstTime, initialized to True.)

```
function WhoAmI: string;
const
{$J+}
  IAm: string = '';
{$J-}
begin
  if IAm = '' then
    IAm := getlogin; // The getlogin function is in the Libc unit
  Result := IAm;
end;
```

You may have noticed a problem with this code, though I prefer to think of it as a political statement. The code always leaves the compiler in the {$J-} state, even if it was in the {$J+} state before compiling the WhoAmI function. You can use {$ifopt} (below) to write code that senses (some of) the compiler state and restores it after making changes, but I firmly believe that there is only one right state for writeable typed constants, just as there is only one right state for hints and warnings. Code that enables writeable typed constants should always re-disable them as quickly as possible, just as code that disables hints and warnings should always re-enable them as soon as possible.

Typed pointers

By default, Addr() and @ both return an untyped `pointer` datatype, which is assignment compatible with all pointers. You can use {$T+} to make @ return a typed pointer, while Addr() still returns an untyped pointer. I recommend that you use {$T+}—it catches many careless errors, and you can always use Addr() in the very few places where you really do want an untyped pointer.

Code generation

The second group of pragmas affects how the compiler generates code. Some of these pragmas control the semantics of the language (what your code means) while others merely turn on and off various run-time checks or optimizations (how your code performs).

Complete boolean evaluation

The rarely used {$B} and {$H} pragmas are the sort of pragmas that can change the meaning of your code. By default, statements like if A and B then are evaluated like C's if (A && B): If A is False, then B is not evaluated at all. Usually this is exactly the behavior you want: Without short-circuiting, statements like if (This <> '') and (This[1] <> PathDelim) then would dereference Nil when This is '' and This[1] is evaluated. Occasionally, though, you do want all the terms in a boolean expression evaluated. For example, the terms are functions that have side effects, and while you care if all (or any) returned True or False, you do want them all to be executed. In cases like these, you can either rewrite your code so it runs properly in the default {$B-} state or you can simply set {$B+} for a line or two.

Porting aids

By default, the string keyword declares a reference-counted, long (up to 2 gigabytes) string. In 16-bit Delphi, and in all Borland and Turbo Pascals, though, it referred to a 256-byte ShortString, with a length byte and up to 255 characters of AnsiChar data. While these ShortStrings still have their uses, new code generally should explicitly declare them. However, when you are porting old, 16-bit code, it can be convenient to force string to mean ShortString, *via* the {$H-} pragma.

The new strings are much better in just about every way—higher capacity, and cheaper to copy to routine parameters and function results—but porting can be a real pain. With short strings, Str[0] is the length byte; with long strings, Str[0] is a syntax error. With short strings, indexing beyond the current Length() is safe, so long as it is within the actual statically allocated string; with long strings, indexing beyond the current Length() can cause a segmentation fault. For frequently used code, porting is worth the effort. For infrequently used code, it can make sense just to slap a {$H-} at the start of the unit and leave it at that.

> **Note**
>
> *While the ShortString syntax is still available, they are actually implemented as huge strings. That is, they are stored in the same old format (an array of char, with a length byte at position 0) but they are converted to and from huge strings for most (not all) operations. Thus, while it can be convenient to include eg, a* string[80] *in a record that you read and write directly from and to disk, you're paying a pretty hefty price for that convenience. You should really think twice, or maybe even thrice, about using old-style short strings in new code.*

Similarly, while the `real` keyword now specifies the generic float point type, and is implemented as a Double, in older versions of Delphi it was the old Turbo Pascal 6-byte float format. As with short strings, Kylix only supports Real48 as a storage format—values are converted to Double's before you do any arithmetic with them, and converted back to Real48's on assignment—so using the Real48 type is particularly expensive. Nonetheless, when porting infrequently used code, or code that reads and writes records from and to disk, it can be convenient to throw the {$REALCOMPATIBILITY ON} switch and have `real` mean Real48, not Double.

Range checking

When you enable range checking, the compiler will check every assignment to an enum, integer and subrange variable, and will raise an exception on any assignment that's out of range. It will also check every array access, similarly raising an exception on every invalid index. This can catch at least some careless errors, and adds surprisingly little overhead. Typical GUI applications grow by less than 1% with range and overflow checking enabled and, given the sheer speed of modern processors, the effect on most program's responsiveness is hard to detect.

Every program should be developed and tested with range checking on. Some programmers even argue for leaving it on in shipping code—surely it's better to generate a run-time error than to die mysteriously or just hang—and, given the low cost, it's really rather hard to argue against this. Coding practices that don't work with range checking enabled—like declaring open-ended arrays as an `array[0..0]` instead of an `array[0..MaxInt div SizeOf(BaseType) - 1]`, or using typecasts to treat pointers as dynamic arrays[1]—should be avoided.

Still, there are places where you legitimately need to turn off range checking, like a loop that's already been tested and which is executed tens of thousands, or even millions of times per second. {$R-} will turn off range checking, and {$R+} will turn it back on.

Numeric overflow checking

Object Pascal's numeric type rule is quite straightforward: The result type of a computation is the result type of the largest operand. Thus, if you add two integers, the result will always be an integer. If you add two billion to two billion, the result will be four billion mod 2^{32} (treated as a 2's complement signed number, or –294,967,296), which may be what you expected—but probably is not.

Enabling overflow checking will catch these errors at run-time. Obviously it can only catch them if you exercise your program hard enough to cause these values to pop up, so run-time checking is no substitute for a little design time analysis, but overflow checking can still catch some careless errors for you.

As with range checks, you may need to turn overflow checking off in tight loops. There are also a wider class of programming practices that quite legitimately call for overflow checking to be turned off than call for range checking to be turned off. Examples include incrementing a byte, knowing it may go from $FF to $00, or various hashing algorithms. {$Q-} will turn off overflow checking, and {$Q+} will turn it back on.

Alignment

As *per* Chapter 3, Kylix normally will insert pad bytes into record and object definitions so that each field is optimally aligned. You can turn this off on a *per* record and *per* object basis with the packed keyword, or you can turn off the default alignment policy with the {$A-} pragma which turns off default alignment, effectively making every structure a packed structure.

---

1. You can cast a pointer to a static array to a dynamic array of the same base type only with range checking turned off because, with range checking turned on, the range checking code will look for an array length 'to the left of' the first element.

{$A+} restores the default alignment policy. In addition, Kylix lets you specify 1, 2, 4, or 8 byte alignment ({$A1}, {$A2}, {$A4}, and {$A8}) to simplify sharing data structures with non-Kylix libraries that use different padding rules. ({$A1} is currently the same as {$A-}, and {$A8} is the same as {$A+}. In future releases, the default alignment, {$A+}, may be {$A16} or something else besides {$A8}.) Because Kylix's rules are bit complicated—as *per* Table 4-1, Kylix will align word fields on two-byte boundaries even in the {$A4} and {$A8} states, and Kylix will align integer fields on 4-byte boundaries even in the {$A8} state—you may still need to manually add some pad bytes to share data with libraries that use different rules.[2]

Note that record alignment is a function of the structure. That is, a record (or old-style object) declared with {$A2} (2-byte) alignment will always have 2-byte alignment, even if it's later used as a field in a larger record or class with a different alignment.

Table 4-1. Field alignment

Field size	A2 alignment	A4 alignment	A8/A+ alignment	Examples
1	1	1	1	AnsiChar, Boolean, Byte, SmallInt, 1-byte sets
2	2	2	2	WideChar, Word, ShortInt, 2-byte sets
4	2	4	4	Integer, Cardinal, Single, 4-byte sets
6	2	4	8	Real48
8	2	4	8	Double, Int64
10	2	4	8	Extended
-	1	1	1	Short strings, large sets

---

2.   I had to do this, once, and it was **not** fun. The library insisted on word alignment in the interests of a common code base between its 16-bit DOS and Windows versions and its 32-bit Windows version. It kept acting 'weird', and it kept being a disagreement between its structures and the Pascal records I was mapping them to. If you ever need to share structures with a non-Kylix library, consider writing an automatic header conversion tool. It might only take about as long as making a single manual conversion pass through a large header file, and even an imperfect one will probably save you days and days of frustrated bug hunting.

Enum size

Normally, Object Pascal will store an enum in the smallest possible space. Thus, a typical enum with less than 257 values will only take a single byte, while a larger enum with less than 65,537 values will take two bytes. This can cause problems with libraries compiled by compilers that treat enums as integers and store them in words or dwords. If Object Pascal writes a single-byte enum to a multi-byte field, it will only write a single byte. It will not set the high order bytes, and so they will be filled with garbage.

The {$Z2} pragma allows you to force enums to take at least two bytes, regardless of the size of their range, while the {$Z4} pragma forces enums to be stored in four byte dwords. Note that the {$Z} pragmas affect the enum definition: An enum declared {$Z2} will take two (or more) bytes even if it is allocated as a var or declared in a record declared {$Z1} or {$Z4}.

```
type
  E1 = (Foo1, Bar1);
  {$Z2}
  E2 = (Foo2, Bar2);
  {$Z4}
  E4 = (Foo4, Bar4);
  {$Z1}

var
  V1: E1;
  V2: E2;
  V4: E4;

begin
  WriteLn(SizeOf(V1): 2, SizeOf(V2): 2, SizeOf(V4): 2);  // 1 2 4
end.
```

Note that the {$Z} pragma affects only the enumeration's *minimum* size. Each instance of a 257-element enumeration will take 2 bytes, even in the {$Z1) state; each instance of a 65537-element enumeration will take 4 bytes, even in the {$Z1) or {$Z2}states. Also, the {$Z} pragma, like the alignment and writeable typed constant pragmas, modifies the symbol's definition. An enum declared as {$Z2} will always take (at least) 2 bytes, even when used in structures declared {$Z1} or {$Z4}.

Note

{$Z2} should only be used for cross-language compatibility, as 16-bit enums are slower than 8-bit or 32-bit enums. Using {$Z4} to push an enum with 257..65536 elements to 32-bits will improve performance.

Assertions

As *per* Chapter 2, assertions are a sort of conditional statement that look like a procedure that takes a boolean expression and an optional string expression. If the boolean expression evaluates to True, the string expression is not evaluated. If the boolean expression evaluates False, though, the string expression is evaluated, and added to the text of an exception that also contains the file name and line number where the exception occurred. Assertions are commonly used to express—or assert—the assumptions that underlie various pieces of code. If the assumptions have not been violated, then all is well. If they have, then you don't want to proceed.

Assertions are thus a development aid, and are commonly turned off in production code. This is usually done globally, *via* the Project Options dialog or a dcc switch, but you can also turn them off in a particular source file, or part of a source file, with {$C-}. You might do this once you're confident of a particularly tricky routine that has so many assertions that it's significantly slower with assertions on, but this is rare. The most common use for the {$C} pragma is in conjunction with {$ifopt C+}—you might have variables that are only set for use with various assertions, and you want to avoid the hints about unused variables and/or assignments by not declaring the variables when assertions are off.

Optimization

While Kylix isn't going to win any prizes for optimization, it does do a pretty good job. It moves local variables into registers, rearranges code, removes dead code, and eliminates some common subexpressions. This can make it hard to step through the code, at times, as the debugger reports that this or that value has been eliminated by the optimizer. The {$O-} pragma will allow you turn off optimization on a per-routine basis.

> **Note**
>
> *There are a few, exceedingly rare, cases where code works with optimization off but not with it on, or vice versa. While the odds are pretty overwhelmingly high that any particular bug is your fault, not Borland's, when all else fails, you can try turning optimization off. If that does change the behavior of your program, be sure to report it to Borland.*

Compiler control

The final group of pragmas controls both how the compiler reacts to dangerous or non-portable coding practices, and what the compiler 'sees' within a source file.

Filtering compiler messages

There are three pragmas that control what sort of messages the compiler generates when it compiles your source code. The {$hints} and {$warnings} directives allow you to turn hints and warnings on and off, while the {$warn} directive allows you to suppress each of the five class of messages that the hint directives deprecated, library, and platform (see Chapters 2 and 3) can produce.

The {$hints} and {warnings} directives are the most important of these three pragmas. By default, the compiler provides hints and warnings whenever it detects syntactically legal but semantically dubious code. For example, the compiler will give you a hint if you declare a variable but never use it, or if you set a variable but then never use the value. The compiler will give you a warning if you use a variable before you've set it, or if it's possible that a function's result will not be set.

I cannot urge you strongly enough to keep hints and warnings on and to **eliminate every hint and warning from your code**. While hints generally result from sloppy or poorly maintained code, warnings generally mean bugs. While the compiler will optimize away many of the things that it hints about, it's generally worth fixing your code to eliminate the hints, if only so the warnings don't get buried in a blizzard of hints. While there are occasional cases where warnings are just plain wrong (see the *Hints and warnings* section of Chapter 3) these are few and far between. The vast majority of warnings represent real problems with your code.

Nonetheless, there *are* special cases where you want to turn off hints, and even warnings, for small parts of your code. For example, the following function normally results in a hint that the value assigned to DeliberatelyIgnored is never used:

```
function StrIsInt(const Str: string): boolean;
var
  DeliberatelyIgnored, ErrorLocation: integer;
begin
  Val(Str, DeliberatelyIgnored, ErrorLocation);
  Result := ErrorLocation = 0;
end; // StrIsInt
```

While of course it's perfectly true that DeliberatelyIgnored is not used, the function does what it's supposed to do—ensure that a string can be passed to the StrToInt function without raising an exception—and most of us would really rather not have to ignore the hint every time we build the program, and we'd just as soon not force everyone who takes over our code to have to check that the hint is harmless. If we use the {$hints} pragma, we can turn hints off for this one function.

```
{$hints off}
  function StrIsInt(const Str: string): boolean;
  var
    DeliberatelyIgnored, ErrorLocation: integer;
  begin
    Val(Str, DeliberatelyIgnored, ErrorLocation);
    Result := ErrorLocation = 0;
  end; // StrIsInt
{$hints on}
```

Similarly, the compiler will give you a hint if an object has a private method or field that is not used. If this is a debugging aid that goes in and out of use, you may tire of ignoring the hint and prefer to suppress the hint by wrapping the declaration in a {$hints off} / {$hints on} pair. You can similarly control warnings with the {$warnings} pragma, but should do so much more carefully: I generally only use the {$warnings} pragma to ensure that warnings are on.

Filtering hint directives

The {$warn} pragma allows you to turn off the messages generated by the hint directives, deprecated, library, and platform. New code shouldn't use constructs that the compiler tells you are deprecated, as deprecated constructs may disappear in future releases, or may contain bugs that will never be fixed. But, if a project includes some old, working code that relies on deprecated constructs, you might decide that the benefit of eliminating the use of deprecated constructs does not justify the cost—and danger[3]—of rewriting working code. Having made this decision, you probably don't need to be reminded of it every time you build the project. Similarly, while it's good to know that some particular construct limits your code's portability, that doesn't mean that you shouldn't use it, especially when the program might be bound to a particular platform or library in many other ways. Again, once you decide to use a non-portable feature, you generally don't need or want constant reminders.

The {$warn} pragma allows you to turn off these messages, on a category-by-category basis. Currently, there are five message categories, and all are displayed by default. The {$warn} pragma's syntax is {$warn *category* on} or {$warn *category* off}, where *category* is one of the five keywords in Table 4-2.

Table 4-2. {$warn} pragma categories

Category	Warnings about
SYMBOL_DEPRECATED	Code that uses deprecated symbols.
SYMBOL_LIBRARY	Code that uses symbols declared as being library dependent.
SYMBOL_PLATFORM	Code that uses symbols declared as being platform dependent.
UNIT_LIBRARY	Code that uses units declared as being library dependent.
UNIT_PLATFORM	Code that uses units declared as being platform dependent.

Although the hint directives are a part of the symbol itself, they generate warnings when the symbols are used, not when they're defined. Accordingly, the {$warn} pragma applies to the point of use, not to the symbol definition. For example,

---

3. "Don't fix it if it ain't broke."

```
{$warn symbol_deprecated off}

type
  TThis = record
    A, B: integer;
  end deprecated;

var
  This: TThis;

begin
  This.A := 1; // no warning
{$warn symbol_deprecated on}
  This.B := 2; // warning
end.
```

generates a warning on the line that sets This.B even though This and TThis are declared in the {$warn symbol_deprecated off} state, because *that particular line* is compiled in the {$warn symbol_deprecated on} state.

When you turn off hint directive warnings in specific sections of your code, bear in mind that there will be times when you will want to turn them **all** back on again. For example, you might want to check for newly deprecated constructs as new releases of Kylix come out, or you may want to enable all portability warnings when you try to port code from Kylix to Delphi, or from Delphi to Kylix. One approach is to put all ten {$warn} pragmas into their own *include file* (below), so that you can turn all the hint directive warnings back on simply by changing the include files and rebuilding your application(s). Another approach is to wrap all {$warn} pragmas in an {$ifndef warn} *conditional compilation* block (also below) so that you can turn them on and off easily. Which approach you use is up to you, but even though

```
{$i symbol_deprecated.on}
```

is not self-contained because it involves an 'outboard' file, it's shorter and cleaner than

```
{$ifndef warn}
  {$warn symbol_deprecated on}
{$endif}
```

and is harder to get wrong, too.

Custom compiler messages

The {$message} pragma allows you to generate custom compiler messages. You might use this so you don't forget to return to incomplete or fragile code (it's harder to miss a warning than a to-do list item) or to flag code that may be dependent on the behavior of a particular Kylix release.

Table 4-3. {$message} syntax

Example	Generates	Usage
{$message 'string'}	A hint.	A dubious coding practice.
{$message HINT 'string'}	A hint.	A dubious coding practice.
{$message WARN 'string'}	A warning.	Probably an error.
{$message ERROR 'string'}	An error.	Definitely an error.
{$message FATAL 'string'}	A fatal error.	An error so bad that you should stop compilation.

That is, {$message} must be followed by a string in single-quotes. You cannot use a named string constant, or a string expression. ({$message 'foo' + 'bar'} will generate the hint 'foo'.) By default, {$message} generates a hint; you can insert the special 'keywords' hint, warn (**not** warning), error, or fatal between the {$message and the quoted string to generate warnings, errors, and fatal errors. (Naturally, these message-type keywords are not case sensitive.)

Custom hints and warnings can be turned off with the {$hints} and {$warnings} pragmas, just like the compiler-generated hints and warnings. Custom error messages can **not** be suppressed.

Any error message will prevent linkage: You won't be able to run the program within the IDE, and the executable file won't be replaced. The difference between an "error" and a "fatal error" is that you can get multiple error messages, but the first fatal error will stop compilation.

Include files

You can *include* one source code file in another with the {$I *filename*} pragma, which compiles the contents of the *filename* as if it were a part of the file that includes it. The *filename* is **not** quoted the way the {$message} string is: use {$i this.inc}, not {$i 'that.inc'}. The filename can include a path specification, but this must be a fully expanded pathname: shell shortcuts like {$i ~/lib/deprecated.on} are **not** supported. Filenames that don't include a full path must be in either the current project directory or in one of the paths specified in the same Project Options "Search path" that Kylix scans for other source code.

I recommend that you limit your use of include files to lists of pragmas that you want to include in multiple modules to maintain a standard compilation environment, or that you change from time to time. You *can* use include files for things like sharing declarations between a library (below) and the program that uses it, but most of Kylix's cross-referencing tools (Chapter 5) like CTRL+CLICK and SHIFT+CTRL+UP or SHIFT+CTRL+DOWN don't really work very well when the source code is in include files.

Conditional compilation

Object Pascal supports four conditional compilation pragmas, {$ifdef}, {$ifndef}, {$ifopt}, and {$if}, as well as the conditional symbol pragmas {$define} and {$undef}.

{$define *Name*} defines a conditional symbol, *Name*. This exists only during compilation of the module it's defined in (you can define global symbols *via* either the Project Options dialog; a dcc switch; or an include file that you {$I} in every module) and exists in its own name space. That is, actual code can't see or refer to *Name*, and the existence or non-existence of the conditional symbol *Name* has nothing to do with any Object Pascal variables, types, or constants. The only use for a {$define}d name is conditional compilation.

Note

Conditional symbols either exist or they do not exist. They can never have a value *or a datatype, unlike C and C++ where you can* #define Symbol 1.

You can delete (or *undefine*) a {$define}d name with {$undef Name}. It is not an error to {$define} a name that already exists, or to {$undef} a name that does not exist. Naturally, conditional symbols are not case-sensitive. If Foo is defined, then so is FOO and foo.

The compiler defines a few standard conditional symbols that you may have occasion to test.

Table 4-4. Predefined conditional symbols

Symbol	Meaning
Linux	"Toto, I have a feeling we're not in Kansas anymore."
MsWindows	**Not** defined in Kylix; for use only in portable programs. Only defined in Delphi 6 or higher.
Win32	**Not** defined in Kylix; for use only in portable programs. Is roughly synonymous with MsWindows in Delphi 5 and 6, but in future Delphi releases will serve to distinguish 32-bit Windows from 64-bit Windows.
Ver140	Kylix 1 or Delphi 6. Ver140 specifies the *compiler version*–see also RTLVersion in table 4-5.
Console	This application is being defined as a console app, not a GUI app.
PIC	This unit is being compiled in Position Independent Code [PIC] mode. In addition to the normal register conventions, assembler code needs to preserve EBX, and restore it before it terminates and before **any** CALL instruction. See the *BASM Quick Reference* appendix.
ConditionalExpressions	You can use {$if}.

{$ifdef}

{$ifdef *Name*} is the most basic conditional compilation construct. If *Name* has been defined, either globally or locally by a {$define *Name*} in the same module, the code between the {$ifdef} and the matching {$endif} will be compiled. If *Name* has not been defined, the code will not be compiled. There can be an {$else} clause, and you can nest conditional compilation constructs.

```
{$ifdef This}
  {$ifdef That}
  {$endif}
{$else}
{$endif}
```

In addition to the obvious uses in maintaining multiple versions or turning experimental code on and off, conditional compilation is particularly useful in commenting out code. If you comment out some code with a (* *) comment block, you will have trouble if the code already contained a (* *) block—and all the code will be syntax highlighted as a comment. However, if you comment it out with an

```
{$ifdef OBSOLETE}
{$endif}
```

block, you have no comment nesting issues and the code is syntax highlighted normally. (This is useful when you want to keep old code around for a reference while you radically rework a routine or three, but keeping dead code like this in your production code is a bad idea that will just confuse people.)

Note

*If you use {$ifdef} to isolate Linux or Windows dependent parts of portable programs, be sure to use* positive logic. *That is, never assume that if it's not Linux it must be Windows, or that if it's not Win32 it must be Linux. Kylix or something like it may run on Solaris or OS/X someday, and there will certainly be Win64 versions of Delphi. If some bit of code requires Linux, put it in its own* {$ifdef Linux}, *not in the* {$else} *of an* {$ifdef MsWindows}.

{$ifndef}

{$ifndef *Name*} will compile the code that follows it if *Name* is **not** defined. It's thus the exact converse of {$ifdef}, and is just a syntactic shorthand, intended to be clearer than

```
{$ifdef Name}{$else}
{$endif}
```

{$ifopt}

{$ifopt} allows you to write code that 'senses' the state of the single letter (short form) pragmas. The 'argument' is a single pragma code letter—no curly braces or dollar signs are allowed—followed by a + or a -. You can only test a single pragma at a time. That is, while {$ifopt R+,Q+} is legal, the Q+ part is completely ignored and the pragma acts exactly the same as {$ifopt R+}.

One common use of {$ifopt} is writing code that only compiles when assertions are turned on during development:

```
{$ifopt C+}
var
  AssertTemp: integer;
{$endif}
```

Another common use is to save and restore the compiler state around code that changes it in some way.

```
{$ifopt R+} {$define RPlus} {$endif}
  {$R-}
  // some code that really needs to be {$R-}
{$ifdef RPlus} {$R+} {$undef RPlus} {$endif}
```

{$if}

{$if *Expr*} is the most flexible of the conditional compilation constructs. Unlike {$ifdef}, it can do multiple tests—if this is defined and that is not, for example—and it can refer to Object Pascal constants. This allows you to do things that are very hard otherwise, like write a piece of utility code that compiles properly under all Delphi versions. (For example, the int64 datatype wasn't introduced until Delphi 4; older code had to use the FPU comp type wherever it needed 64-bit range.) Given that the VerXXX symbol is a single symbol, detecting what version of the compiler was in use took a long series of lines like {$ifdef Ver100} {$undef ThisFeature}{$endif}—and the code still might not work properly with a new version.

{$if} circumvents these limitations by allowing you to refer to constants from the code's namespace, not just the conditional symbol namespace. Thus, you can say something like {$if RtlVersion >= 14.0}. You can also use logical operators, just as in the if statement, to write conditional statements like

```
{$if Defined(This) and not Defined(That) and (High(ThisType) > $7FFF)}
```

Within an {$if} statement, you can use two new special functions, Defined() and Declared(). Defined() returns True if you pass it an identifier that has been defined with {$define}: {$if Defined(Foo)} is almost exactly the same as {$ifdef Foo}. Declared() returns True if the Pascal identifier you pass it has been declared and is in scope. You can use this to write code that checks for datatypes added in a future release (so that your code can still compile under Kylix 1.0) or that acts differently if a certain unit has been used than if it hasn't.

Note

C and C++ programmers should note that the key difference between the Object Pascal pragma processor and the C and C++ preprocessor is that pragma evaluation is part of the compilation process, not a preprocessing step. On the minus side, this means that you can't write macros that rewrite the source code. (Given the problems this can cause, many people would actually count this as a point in Object Pascal's favor.) On the plus side, a preprocessor can't offer anything like the Declared() function, nor can it make conditional compilation decisions based on the values of a program's symbols.

Table 4-5. Some key constants to test in {$if}

Constant	Meaning
GPL	If this symbol is Declared(), you are using the Kylix Open Edition's version of the run-time library – the symbol's value does not matter.
RTLVersion	The Ver140 (Table 4-4) conditional symbol is defined in both Kylix 1 and Delphi 6. The RtlVersion constant is similar but more specific: In Kylix 1, RtlVersion = 14.0, while in Delphi 6, RtlVersion = 14.1. In general, you should avoid testing for specific versions ({$if RtlVersion = 14.0}) and should instead check for versions before or after a specific feature was added ({$if RtlVersion < 15.0} or {$if RtlVersion >= 16.1}).
CompilerVersion	**Not** Declared() under Kylix–equals 14.02 under Delphi 6.

Note

Anything you can do with {$ifdef} or {$ifndef} you can do with {$if}, and often in a smaller and clearer way. The only reason that {$if} isn't a wholesale replacement for {$ifdef} and {$ifndef} is that it is new in Kylix 1 and Delphi 6. Thus, you can't use {$if} in code that is meant to be portable between Kylix and older versions of Delphi.

{$if} blocks can also have {$elseif} clauses as well as {$else} clauses, which lets you write conditional code somewhat like a case statement. An {$if} / {$elseif} chain can be followed by a single {$else} clause, which will be evaluated if none of the {$if} or {$elseif} tests succeeded. (You can have an {$else} following an {$else} (at least in Kylix 1) but such 'secondary' {$else} clauses have no effect.)

You have to be careful using {$else} with {$if} in code that needs to work under Delphi 5 or earlier. If you wrap your {$if} in an {$ifdef ConditionalExpressions}, older compilers will see the {$else} as applying to the {$ifdef ConditionalExpressions}.

```
{$ifdef ConditionalExpressions}
  //  The INTENT is that Kylix/D6 version see this branch
  {$if Foo > Bar}
    // This code compiles only if (CompilerVersion >= 14) and (Foo > Bar)
  {$else}
    // PROBLEM: D5 (and earlier) see this as applying to the
    // {$ifdef ConditionalExpressions}
  {$ifend}
{$else}
  // The INTENT is that D5 (and earlier) should see this
{$endif}
```

To avoid this problem, don't use {$else} with an {$if} nested inside an {$ifdef ConditionalExpressions}. Use {$elseif True}, instead:

```
{$ifdef ConditionalExpressions}
  //  Only Kylix/D6 (or later) see this branch
  {$if Foo > Bar}
    // This code compiles only if (CompilerVersion >= 14) and (Foo > Bar)
  {$elseif True}
    // This code compiles only if (CompilerVersion >= 14) and (Foo <= Bar)
  {$ifend}
{$else}
  // Only D5 (and earlier) see this branch
{$endif}
```

> **Note**
>
> *Where {$ifdef}and {$ifndef} blocks are ended with an {$endif}, {$if} blocks **must** end with an {$ifend}.*

Units

Units are Object Pascal's program modules. Unlike C++, which relies on a convention about putting public declarations in a .hpp file which is then #include-d by both the .cpp file which implements the module and by any module which uses it, Object Pascal has explicit syntax for specifying both visibility and module usage. See Listing 4-1. Unit syntax.

Listing 4-1. Unit syntax

```
unit UnitName;

// Comments and conditional compilation pragmas

interface

uses ThisUnit, ThatUnit;

// Public declarations

implementation

uses TheOtherUnit;

// Implementations of routines and methods, private declarations

initialization

// optional setup code

finalization

// optional teardown code

end.
```

Every unit begins with the `unit` keyword, followed by the unit name and a semicolon. Other modules use a unit by its name, and you can refer to shadowed names as *UnitName.Shadowed,* just you refer to record and object fields. Under Windows, the unit name is case-insensitive, like the rest of Pascal, though the IDE will preserve any case you type in the unit and file name. Linux, though, has a case-sensitive file system, which Kylix has been forced to accommodate. When you use a unit in Kylix, you must capitalize it just as it is capitalized in its own unit statement (which in turn must match the filename).[4]

> **Note**
>
>
>
> *The* uses *clause is the only case-sensitive part of Object Pascal. If a unit's name is* Foo, *it must appear in any* uses *clauses as* Foo. *However, any other references to the unit–such as a qualified name like* foo.bar–*are case-insensitive.*[5]

You cannot have any declarations or routines between the unit statement and the interface keyword, but you can have any comments or pragmas (including conditional statements) that you like.

The interface section

The interface keyword means much the same as an object's public keyword. Every declaration in the interface section of a unit is visible to all code that uses the unit. (Of course, the private and protected sections of objects declared in the interface section are not *accessible*, even though they **are** visible.) The interface section can include any type, var, const or resourcestring statement, as well as routine prototypes and any pragmas. It can **not** contain any actual code.

An interface section can include a uses statement. If it appears, it must be the first statement in the interface section. The uses statement consists of the uses keyword followed by one or more comma separated unit names, followed by a semicolon. A unit with no uses statement in its interface section can only use identifiers that are built into the language, or that are declared in the System and SysInit units, which every unit uses implicitly. A unit with

---

4. The unit name and the filename will always match if you use File ➤ Save As to change the unit name, instead of doing it by hand.

5. Strictly speaking, it's not that the uses clause itself is case-sensitive so much as that the unit lookup code uses the name as it appears in the source code. On a case-insensitive file system, Kylix's uses clause is just as case-insensitive as Delphi's. (For that matter, if This unit uses both That unit and TheOther unit, and That unit also uses TheOther unit, it doesn't matter how This unit capitalizes TheOther–it's already been loaded by That unit.) However, since most Linux file systems are case-sensitive, you should generally act as if uses clauses are case-sensitive in Kylix.

a uses statement in its interface section can use those standard declarations plus any declarations made in the interface section of the units it uses.[6]

Note

Uses statements are not transitive.[6] That is, if unit A uses unit B, which uses unit C, unit B can depend on types declared in unit C— but unit A can not, unless it also uses unit C.

The interface section contains only declarations, not code. Thus, a public object's `type` definition belongs in the interface section, but the actual code for its methods belongs below, in the `implementation` section. Similarly, routines may be declared in the interface section, but their bodies belong in the implementation section.

The way you declare public routines in a unit should look pretty familiar. It's just a bare prototype—the procedure or function keywords, the routine's name, any argument list and/or result type, a semicolon, an optional calling convention, and optional hint directives—without a begin/end block or any local declarations. This is just like the way you declare methods inside of an object (Chapter 3), though without any modifiers like `virtual` or `override`. It's also just like a forward routine (Chapter 2), without the `forward` keyword. Because declarations in the interface section are visible to the implementation section as well as to any code that uses the module, routines that are declared in their unit's interface section can call each other (mutual recursion) without having to use any forward declarations.

The implementation section

The implementation section is everything that follows the `implementation` keyword. It includes both the code to implement objects and routines declared in the interface section, as well as any private declarations needed to do so. Any declaration made in a unit's implementation section is visible to any code that follows it in the source file, but is not visible to any code that uses the unit.

An implementation section can include a `uses` statement, too. If it appears, it must be the first statement in the section. A unit can only be used once by any other unit. That is, it may not appear two or more times in either uses statement, and it may not appear in both the interface and implementation

---

6. Uses statements were transitive in Delphi 1 and earlier Borland/Turbo Pascals.

uses statements. Apart from this ban on multiple use, the uses statement in the implementation section does not depend in any way on the uses statement in the interface section. Any unit can have 0, 1, or 2 uses statements, and if the unit has only 1 uses statement, it can be in either section. The uses statement in the implementation section means that any code in the implementation section can use any declarations made in the interface section of the used units. The fact that the uses statement appears in a unit's implementation section does not give it any magic power to see into other units' implementation sections!

Uses statements in the interface section cannot have any circularity. That is, if This unit uses That unit, then That unit cannot use This unit. This restriction on mutual usage applies **only** to uses statements in interface sections. If one or both of the mutual uses statements are in the implementation section, then there's no problem.

Initialization and finalization

The unit structure is something like that of a routine: a public interface, some private declarations, and some code. The last piece of a unit is a `begin end.` block of setup code that is executed when the program (or library) loads, before it starts to run.

> **Note**
>
>
> *Note the period after the* end, *not a semicolon. Declarations are terminated with semicolons while modules are terminated with periods. This is (very!) roughly analogous to English grammar, with declarations being clauses in a long list, and modules being whole sentences.*

A unit's setup block is where you can create objects, collect various pieces of the system status, and otherwise assure that your units have the environment they need to run properly. Initialization is optional, and if your unit doesn't need any, it can simply have an `end.` statement after the last procedure or method body.

You can replace the `begin` keyword with the `initialization` keyword. "Initialization" is a lot more to type than "begin", and it seems (to me) to be seriously affected compared to something like "setup", but that's the language we have to work with. Despite the clunkiness, almost all units use an `initialization end.` block instead of a `begin end.` block because when you use `initialization` you can also use `finalization`, which means "tear down" or "knock off".[7] Just as initialization code is executed as the program or library is loading, so finalization code is executed as the program is shutting down. It's an opportunity for your units to save their state, free memory, close files and network connections, and so on. It's a sort of `finally` block for the unit, and you can't have a `finalization` block without an `initialization` block any more than you can have a `finally` block without a `try` block.

The initialization and finalization order is determined by the uses statement in the program or library. The first unit listed is initialized, then the second, and then the third, and so on. Initializing a unit means initializing the units in its interface section's uses statement, if any, then initializing the units in the implementation section's uses statement, if any, and then executing the code in the initialization block. (You may be comfortable with thinking of this as a depth-first traversal of the uses tree.) Any given unit will be initialized once and only once, even if it's used by more than one unit.

Finalization occurs in exactly the opposite order. The last unit initialized is the first unit finalized, while the first unit initialized is the last unit finalized. This ordering ensures both that all units are initialized before any unit initialization code that may depend on them executes, and that no code will be called after its unit has been finalized.

Units as modules

You may have noticed that units are similar in some ways to objects. Each has public and private parts; each can contain both data and code that operates on it; you can use the same *Name.Member* notation to refer to elements of each. There are also two big differences. There are often lots of copies of any given object type, while there is only one copy of each unit *per* program or library, and there is no analog of inheritance or polymorphism for units.

This similarity between units and objects is no accident; program modules were the first wide-spread application of the doctrine of encapsulation, which predates inheritance and polymorphism by a few years. The notion of programming to the interface and not to the implementation is not new; rather, it's one of the pioneering insights of software engineering. By focusing on what a unit does, not how it does it, we reduce the chance that a

---

7. Another reason to use `initialization` instead of `begin` is that the IDE can get confused when there is a `begin` at the bottom of the source file that doesn't belong to a routine or method.

change *here* will break code over *there.* Objects took the concept of modules and made it much finer grained.

A unit represents a system or subsystem of the program as a whole, a collection of related code. A good test for whether or not two pieces of code belong in the same unit is to ask yourself if you are ever likely to want to use one without the other. Generic code to restore an application's visual state at startup probably belongs in the same unit as code to read and write other configuration data at startup and shutdown, but not in the same unit as some generic file access routines that you may happen to use to read and write your configuration.

When we get to the visual aspects of Kylix in Section 2, you'll see that Kylix maps forms (windows) to objects, and places each form and its object in a single unit. (In fact, you can't have more than one form in a unit, which is occasionally annoying.) Kylix will write and maintain a good deal of this code for you, but you remain free to add your own code to the unit and/or the form object, and to hand-edit any Kylix-generated code.

External routines

An *import unit* is a specialized sort of unit that exists primarily to allow Object Pascal code to call code which resides in a dynamically linked library and which may be written in other languages. It's just a bit of stub code that hides the fact that the routines it declares aren't actually statically linked into the program that calls them.

Libc.pas is a prime example of an import unit. Its interface section consists of a series of declarations translated from various .h files, and a large number of routine prototypes—but its implementation section contains no code.

Rather, every routine is declared external. External routines can be statically linked to an assembly or C routine in a .o file, but more commonly they are dynamically linked to routines in a shared library. If you want to use a new library in one of your Kylix programs, you'll need to find or write an import unit for it.

Translating C or C++ header files into Pascal is pretty straightforward, if you know both C++ and Object Pascal, though there are some C++ constructs like templates that can be difficult or impossible to map. A few things to keep in mind are

- Struct/record packing. It can be hard to tell when you don't have this right.[8] If the library works as documented, some of the time, but seg faults or acts strangely at other times, you should check that the records you are passing to and from the library are aligned properly. Remember, Kylix has some slightly strange notions of what dword and qword alignment mean when it comes to 16-bit and 32-bit data. If the library you are calling uses different conventions than Kylix, you may have to manually add pad fields.

- C-style strings. You should almost always translate a `char *` as a `PChar`, not a `^ Char`. PChar's are syntactically privileged, so that you can easily pass Object Pascal strings to the library and automatically convert C-style output strings to Object Pascal style strings.

- Enum size. Object Pascal normally packs enumerations so that they take no more room than necessary. Thus, a typical enum with less than 257 values will be stored in a single byte. If the library represents enums as words or dwords, you will have problems (over and above alignment issues) when Object Pascal only writes a single byte, leaving random garbage in the high order bytes. You can use the {$Z2} and {$Z4} pragmas to resolve these issues. (By default, `gcc` uses 32-bit storage for all enums, *ala* {$Z4}. There **is** a relatively little-used flag which forces the equivalent of {$Z1} behavior.)

- `Var` and `const` parameters. Remember that these are implemented as pointers. (Except that `const` parameters which can fit in a 32-bit register are passed by value.) Your bindings should use pointer parameters only where these are optional (*ie*, the library allows them to be passed as NULL.) Required pointers should be bound as `var` or `const` parameters. Not only does this enforce the "required" semantics, passing a reference is usually syntactically cleaner than passing a pointer. (`Foo(Bar)` instead of `Foo(@ Bar)`.)

- Calling conventions. Object Pascal defaults to the `register` convention, even for external routines. While this is very efficient, it's unlikely to work correctly with a library compiled by gcc or any other non-Borland compiler. Usually you'll have to use `cdecl`.

- External C routines with ... parameters can be declared with the `varargs` directive.

---

8.   You can know you have it **wrong** if the SizeOf() your Pascal translation does not match the sizeof() the C original. However, matching sizes is not a guarantee of matching declarations: it's not impossible to have two alignment mismatches that result in identically sized structures with very different notions of where each field 'lives'.

Programs

In Pascal, a `program` compiles to an executable file. Where unit source is stored in .pas file, in Kylix, a program file has the extension .dpr, for Delphi Project.[9] Its syntax is modeled on a routine:

```
program Name;

// declarations

begin
  // code
end.
```

Note that, like a unit, a program has a `begin end.` block, not a `begin end;` block. The declarations can and usually do start with a uses statement; many Kylix programs contain no declarations in the program file, and contain only a uses statement and a begin end. block. For that matter, Kylix will generate a great deal of the code in the .dpr file of a GUI application automatically (when you add a form to a project, or make changes to the Forms and Application tabs of the CTRL+ALT+F11 Project Options dialog) and many GUI applications contain no user-written code in the .dpr file.

Note

*While the code that Kylix writes for you **is** perfectly ordinary Object Pascal and Kylix makes an effort at working around any manual changes you make to the .dpr file, it's not really very good at it. That is, Kylix may get confused if you add some code to handle a splash screen or to ensure that only a single instance of the program should be running at any one time. Sometimes this confusion is no worse than bad indenting; other times it can actually break code. Most people try to avoid placing code in the .dpr file. Unit* initialization *blocks are often a very good alternative.*

When you write traditional, non-GUI Linux applications of the sort that have complicated command line options and that read stdin and write

---

9. Yes, the product is called Kylix, not "Delphi for Linux". But Delphi for Linux is certainly a good way to describe it—and changing file extensions would have needlessly complicated maintaining cross-platform code.

stdout, you will do more hand-editing of the .dpr `program` file than when you write GUI apps. Good programming practice suggests that you place only the highest-level code in the program file, but Kylix doesn't write this for you the way it does for GUI apps. When you create a new console app by clicking on File ➤ New, and selecting Console Application in the dialog, Kylix will write the boilerplate for you, but that's about it.

Libraries

Figure 4-1. The File ➤ New dialog

The Object Pascal `library` keyword creates a Linux *shared object*, which is very similar to a Windows DLL [Dynamic-Link Library]. You can create a new library by clicking on File ➤ New, and selecting Shared Object from the dialog. (See Figure 4-1.) Kylix will open a file that has all the boilerplate necessary to create a minimal shared library as well as some advice about sharing exceptions between executables and libraries.

Note

Delphi applications and libraries need to both use ShareMem *to share strings, because Delphi layers a memory sub-allocator (see Chapter 8) on top of the Windows memory manager. Using* ShareMem *assures that both application and library use the same sub-allocator. Kylix applications and libraries do **not** need to use* ShareMem, *as they use a system-supplied sub-allocator in Libc. However, Kylix applications and libraries **do** need to use* ShareExcept *in a way that Delphi applications and libraries do not.*

Kylix is not Delphi

A library is somewhat of a cross between a program and a unit. Like a program, it can pull together multiple units into a single object file. Like a unit, it's not meant to be run directly by users, but instead provides service that a program can call. Libraries have a begin end. block just as programs do, but this is actually initialization code that's executed when the library is first loaded.

Note

As of this release, at least, you cannot use the same initialization *and* finalization *syntax with libraries that you can with units. If you have any extra finalization that should be done when you use a unit in a library that you don't need to do when you use it in a program, you need to add a new unit with the extra finalization.*

Libraries can have public, *exported* routines as well as private routines that can not be called from other programs but that can be used to implement the public behavior. Routines are exported by including them in an exports statement. This consists of the exports keyword, followed by a list of one or more, comma separated *export clauses*, followed by a semicolon. The most basic export clause is simply the name of a routine. This leads to the routine being available to external programs under its true name. You can also export a routine under an assumed name with *TrueName* name 'Alias', which leads to external programs calling *TrueName* as *Alias*. This is especially useful when exporting overloaded routines, as you can give each overloaded routine a distinct alias. When you do this, you need to follow the *TrueName* with a parameter list, so that the compiler will know which overloaded routine to bind to which alias.

Export statements can be in the library module, in the units it uses, or both. When a unit includes an exports statement, it can be in either the interface or implementation sections. Any given routine may appear in more than one exports clause, or even more than once in the same export clause: This creates multiple entries in the libraries export table for the same routine. Exports statements in a unit have no effect when a unit is linked into a program.

Any global variables in your library are only visible within the library: The code that loads the library cannot see them. Globals are created on a *per* process basis, not *per* library. That is, every time another process 'loads' a library that's already in memory, Linux creates a new data 'page' for it; a library cannot use its global variables to do any sort of inter-process communication.

Note

In particular, the VMT for a class declared in a library resides in that library. Even if the program and the library–or two different libraries– use the same object code, *they are effectively creating distinct object types. That is, you'll get a different value if you call the ClassType function on a TFoo created by library code and on a TFoo created by process code. This means that* FooCreatedInALibrary is TFoo *will return False when executed in the program or a different library. Packages (see the* Packages *section below) do not have these problems.*

Dynamic linkage

When you use a library, you have a fundamental choice. You can use an import unit, or you can dynamically load and unload the library. Using an import unit like Libc is easier in many ways, as you simply call routines with `external` declarations and don't have to write code that may or may not find the library and that may or may not find particular routines within the library—but using an import unit is also inflexible. Your application cannot run if that library is not present. If the library is present, but doesn't contain some of the routines you use, your application will crash when it tries to call the missing routines. (You can use the techniques in this section to identify missing routines.)

Using dynamic loading techniques allows you to write applications that function whether or not an optional library is present. Your application might try to take advantage of libraries installed with some distributions and not others, or it might be written to allow for optional add-ons. (See the *Packages* section, below, for a better way to do this with all-Kylix code.)

The Libc dynamic loading API includes the functions dlopen(), dlclose(), *and* dlsym(). *You can use these in Kylix if you're already familiar with them, but Borland has adopted the Windows* LoadLibrary(), FreeLibrary() *and* GetProcAddress() *API as a cross-platform dynamic loading API which they'll also implement on future Kylix/Delphi platforms, so that's what I describe here.*

The LoadLibrary function

```
function LoadLibrary(ModuleName: PChar): HMODULE;
```

loads a library by name. If the ModuleName parameter does not include a fully rooted path (*ie*, one that starts with a /) the system will look for the library in /lib or /usr/lib, the /etc/ld.so.conf directories, or any of the directories listed in the LD_LIBRARY_PATH environment variable. Unlike Windows, LoadLibrary will **not** look in the 'application directory' before checking the PATH or any of the system directories. (See Chapters 8 and 10 and the Deployment appendix for more details.)

Linux is not Windows

If it can load the library, LoadLibrary returns a valid module handle that you use to find individual routines. If the LoadLibrary call fails, it returns 0. If LoadLibrary succeeds, you must be sure to ultimately call FreeLibrary

```
function FreeLibrary(Module: HMODULE): LongBool;
```

to decrement the library's reference count and allow the system to release the resources it commits to an open library. Don't call FreeLibrary while you're still using the library! The best place to call FreeLibrary is generally in the finalization section of the unit that opened the library with LoadLibrary.

While you have the library open, you can use the GetProcAddress function

```
function GetProcAddress(Module: HMODULE; Proc: PChar): Pointer;
```

to lookup a routine by name. GetProcAdress returns Nil on failure, and non-Nil on success. The Pointer result is an untyped pointer, which you typically assign to a procedural variable of the right type: Kylix has no way to check that the routine you find with GetProcAddress actually has the same prototype as the procedural variable that you assign it to.

A trivial example

The following trivial example from the ch4/DynamicLoading project group
may help this make sense.

```
library DynamicLibrary;

procedure FindMe;
begin
  WriteLn('you found me');
end;

exports FindMe;

begin
end.
```

The DynamicLibrary exports a single routine, called FindMe. (In a real
library, the exported routines would usually 'live' in a unit that the library uses.)

```
program DynamicLoader;

uses
  SysUtils;

var
  LibraryName: string = 'libDynamicLibrary.so';
  Module:      HModule;

  FindMe:      procedure;

begin
  LibraryName := IncludeTrailingPathDelimiter(GetCurrentDir) + LibraryName;
  Module := LoadLibrary(PChar(LibraryName));
  if Module <> 0 then
  try
    FindMe := GetProcAddress(Module, 'FindMe');
    if Assigned(@ FindMe) then
      FindMe;
  finally
    FreeLibrary(Module);
  end;
end.
```

The DynamicLoader program uses LoadLibrary to find the `libDynamicLibrary.so` in the current directory.[10] This trivial example follows the Linux convention that the filename of shared objects starts with `lib` and has a .so extension, but you do not have to do so. The SHIFT+CTRL+F11 Project Options dialog lets you change both the lib prefix and the .so extension if you wish to conceal the fact that your application uses shared objects from the sort of user who knows just enough to be dangerous.

If the LoadLibrary call succeeds, the DynamicLoader program uses GetProcAddress to try to find the FindMe procedure. It assigns the result to the `var FindMe: procedure` procedural variable, and uses `Assigned(@ FindMe)` to test for GetProcAddress success. If FindMe **is** Assigned(), the program calls the FindMe procedure.

In real code, all the LoadLibrary / GetProcAddress / FreeLibrary details would typically be hidden inside a unit that simply exported procedural variables like

```
var
  FindMe: procedure;
```

for every routine that might be dynamically loaded from the library. The code that uses this dynamic import unit might always do the `if Assigned(@ FindMe)` before every use, but most people would prefer to also export boolean variables like

```
var
  LibraryLoaded: boolean;
  Found_FindMe:  boolean;
```

that are set by the LoadLibrary and GetProcAddress code. The code that uses the dynamic import unit would then replace code like

```
if Assigned(@ FindMe) then
  FindMe;
```

with code like

```
if LibraryLoaded and Found_FindMe then
  FindMe;
```

which hides the details a bit.

---

10. In general, you should **not** look for libraries in the user's current directory, as that probably isn't where the application and its libraries are—but the LoadLibrary search order is a complex matter that I'd prefer to ignore in this example of dynamic loading. See Chapters 8 and 10 and the Deployment appendix for more details.

Position Independent Code

You should be aware that the same source code will run faster in a program than in a library. This is because Linux shared libraries have to contain Position Independent Code [PIC] which contains no absolute offsets to routines or variables, but instead refers to all global addresses as an offset from a pointer in the EBX register.[11] This in itself isn't so horrible, but it does mean that the compiler cannot use EBX as a general purpose register, the way it can for 'normal' code. Since the compiler generally does a fine job of keeping local variables in registers, cutting the pool of registers by 14% has a significant effect on program performance.

In addition to reserving EBX for the global offset address, in PIC mode every routine's preamble will (re)set EBX. For short routines, this preamble code may provide more of a performance hit than taking EBX out of circulation does. Library-private routines can eliminate this EBX-setting preamble code by adding the `local` directive in the same place that calling conventions and hint directives are added: after the semicolon that terminates the prototype and before the routine's body and any local declarations. You can only use the `local` directive with unit-private routines—routines that appear only in the `implementation` section of a unit. Object methods and routines that appear in the `interface` section of a unit and routines that are defined in the main `library` module can not be made `local`.

When Kylix compiles a unit to normal, 'absolute' code, it creates a .dcu [Delphi Compiled Unit] file with the same filename as the unit. That is, *unitname.pas* compiles to *unitname.dcu*. (Kylix's use of a proprietary object format is one reason that it can link executables so incredibly quickly.) By default, the object files get placed in the same directory as the source files, but you can specify a "Unit output directory" on the Project Options dialog.

By contrast, when Kylix compiles a unit to PIC code, it compiles *unitname.pas* to *unitname.dpu* [Delphi PIC Unit.] So, when you compile a library, all the units in it get compiled to .dpu files. If you have units that are used in both executables and libraries, you will see both .dcu and .dpu files in the unit output directory.

If you are seeking to provide services to programs that may be written in other languages, you have little choice but to use a shared library. However, you should probably consider the PIC performance hit when deciding how to structure your Kylix apps. Under Windows, the code in a dll is the same as the code in an exe. The only performance hit related to using libraries comes

---

11. This isn't strictly true: The loader **can** handle non-PIC shared objects, but the load time is much worse. In any event, Kylix `library` modules always generate .so files that contain PIC.

with the cross-module linkage,[12] which makes calling a library routine about 33% more expensive than calling an in-exe routine. This is no big deal, and it can make sense to structure a large system as an exe and a number of dlls, for ease in selling different versions, upgrading, and so on.

However, a Linux app that follows this strategy will be slower than a Linux app that keeps all the code in a single executable. It might also be slower than an app that is structured as multiple communicating processes. My point here is simply that Linux's process and library architecture is significantly different from Windows, and you should think a bit about how it affects your program when doing a port in either direction.

Packages

If you do decide to use Kylix libraries within your Kylix app, you could of course create an import unit for each library. You'd redeclare[13] all the types your library needs so that your program can use them, too. Then you'd collect prototypes for all the exported routines, and write external declarations for them. Or you could use packages.

Packages are cool.

There's nothing like packages in any other mainstream programming environment.

Packages are separately compiled, run-time loaded, library modules that look just like normal, statically linked units. You can read and write variables declared in the interface section of a unit that 'lives' in a package just as if it were a part of the main program. (There is a slight performance hit involved in this.) You can use all the types and classes and routines declared in the interface section of any unit in a package, without having to write an import unit or any exports statements. You can move units between packages

---

12. Unless Windows cannot load the DLL at the image base address, in which case the DLL's code is not shared.

13. You might think that you'd put any declarations that the library needed to export in units that just contained the declarations. Then the units in the library that implement the exported routines would use the declarations units, as would the import unit. However, since interface visibility is not transitive, if *This* unit uses *That* unit which uses *Another* unit, *This* unit can see only what *That* unit exports in its interface section. While *That* unit's interface section can rely on declarations made in *Another* unit, the units that use *That* will not see *Another* unit's interface unless they explicitly use it.

Thus, an import unit that just uses a bunch of declarations unit would not work. You'd have to copy the exported types into the import unit. And that, of course, is just asking for trouble when the copied declarations get out of synch.

You **can** avoid copying declarations by moving the shared declarations into include files—but Kylix's cross-referencing tools (Chapter 5) don't really work well with include files.

and the main program without changing a single line of code, just by making a few changes in the package editor.

Perhaps the most important thing about packages is the way they merge the address space of the process and the library. Where a library's globals exist in a separate address space, so that the calling process can't see the library's globals, a package's global variables are merged in with the applications, just as if the package were part of the program. This means that public variables of a package-resident unit act just like public variables of unit linked into the main program. Probably more importantly, the merged type and address spaces mean that each class is declared only once—not once in the library and again in an import unit—and has only a single VMT. This in turn means that, *eg*, a TFoo created by package code and a TFoo created by process code return the same ClassType; a TFoo is a TFoo, regardless of where it is created. This is something that is not true with traditional libraries.

Code that uses a unit contained in a package doesn't look any different from code that uses a unit linked into the program in the normal way. Similarly, code in a package that use units contained in another package doesn't look any different from code that uses a unit contained in the same package.

Packages cannot link against the program file. If a unit in a package uses a unit that's not in the package, it must find it in another package. This is called *requiring* the package that contains the missing unit.

You can move units in and out of packages by using the package editor that pops up when you double click on a package in the CTRL+ALT+F11 Project Manager. You can change the list of packages that your program uses on the Packages tab of the SHIFT+CTRL+F11 Project Options dialog. When you compile a program, any unit you use that's not contained in one of the packages you specified gets linked into your executable file. Changing the list of packages, or changing one of the packages' contents, will automatically change the list of units that get statically linked into your app.

This makes it very easy to change your *partitioning* decisions, or to postpone them until an application has been developed and is ready to deploy. It's common to want to break your application into a relatively small main program and multiple add-on modules. This lets you distribute multiple versions of an application, each with different levels of functionality. It's also faster to download updates to a single module than to download updates to a single monolithic application. However, the most logical partitioning may keep changing as the program evolves, or may not even be particularly obvious until the application is nearly done. Packages make this easy: Whether a particular module 'lives' in the application itself or in a package is a simple, link-time decision.

Package syntax

Package syntax is a bit more spartan than that of other Object Pascal modules. A package can contain only a `package` statement, some pragmas, a `requires` statement, a `contains` statement, and an `end.`. Packages cannot contain any code or declarations, nor can they have an initialization or finalization block.

```
package Name;

// See online help for package-related pragmas

requires OtherPackages;

contains SomeUnits;

end.
```

The `package` statement is required. It names the package, just as `unit`, `program`, and `library` statements name their modules. Package source has a .dpk extension, while compiled packages will normally have a .so extension. The SHIFT+CTRL+F11 Project Options dialog lets you add a prefix or suffix and a custom file extension to the package *Name*, just as you can do for 'regular' library files. These options map to various package-specific pragmas, but you should use the Project Options dialog to edit the prefix, suffix, and extension, rather then editing the .dpk file by hand.

The `requires` statement is optional. If it's present, *OtherPackages* is a comma separated list of package names.

The `contains` statement is also optional, though it's hard to imagine uses for an empty package. *SomeUnits* is a comma separated list of units contained in the package. No package can contain a unit that a package it requires contains. All packages used, directly or indirectly,[14] in a package will be contained in a package. If a package indirectly uses a unit which is not explicitly contained in the package or in one of the packages that it requires, it will be included in the package anyhow, and you'll get a warning. As with all warnings, you should take actions to eliminate the warning, by explicitly adding the unit to the package.

Every package must contain an `end.` statement. The `end.` statement may not be preceded by `begin` or by `initialize`.

---

14. If a package `contains` *This* unit but not *That* unit, and *This* unit `uses` *That* unit, the package is using *That* unit indirectly.

Design time packages

The preceding discussion has treated packages as run-time constructs, which of course they are. But it has talked about them only in the context of static linkage. Just as you can statically link libraries *via* an import unit and external declarations or dynamically *via* LoadLibrary, so you can load packages either statically or dynamically. (Chapter 8 has an example of dynamically loading "plugin" packages.) Kylix is written in Kylix, and makes extensive use of this ability to allow your *components* to have custom *property editors* that live in design time packages that are completely separate from the run-time component code.

At design time, all the components that you might place on a form (see Section 2) live in a design time package. However, if you don't use run-time packages, the component code is statically linked into your application's executable file. To make it easier to do this sort of link-time partitioning, when you compile a package, all the units it contains are compiled to both 'absolute' (.dcu) and PIC (.dpu) code. In addition, the package is compiled to both a .so shared object file and to a .dcp [Delphi Component Package] file,[15] which contains both the object code and a binary version of the interface section of all the units contained in the package.

There is also an Open Tools API that relies on packages, which lets you add various experts and wizards to the Kylix environment. The popular GExperts (www.gexperts.org) add-in is a large open source collection of these tools for Delphi; a Kylix version may be available by the time you read this.

---

15. The package editor shows .dcp files in its 'Requires tree'.

Object Pascal

Postscript

THIS SECTION HAS COVERED Object Pascal from the most primitive operations and datatypes that map directly to the hardware to highly abstract constructs like object oriented dynamically loaded library modules. I hope I have managed to make it more than a dry list of bones and their names. I hope that I have managed to convey some of why I love Object Pascal.

Object Pascal is a low-level language that lets you get down to bits and bytes when you need to. Object Pascal is a high-level language that is easy to read and replete with features that help protect you from careless errors. Software engineers can write modular, data-hiding programs in Object Pascal easier than they can in just about any other language. Unashamed hackers can get down to the hardware as easily in Object Pascal as in C. Novice programmers get a consistent, predictable, *elegant* syntax, while experts get power and efficiency.

But wait, there's more!

Kylix is more than an Object Pascal compiler. Kylix is a visual development environment with an amazing array of tools for writing and maintaining boilerplate code, cross referencing, and quickly and clearly building GUI applications. The next section covers Kylix as a programming environment.

Section 2

Kylix

The World's Best
Programming Environment

KYLIX IS MORE THAN an Object Pascal compiler. Kylix is a visual development environment with an amazing array of editing tools for writing and maintaining code, visualization tools for cross referencing, and interface tools for quickly and clearly building GUI applications. Kylix is a large, clean object hierarchy that covers everything from files to widgets in a surprisingly consistent way.

This section is a top-down tour of Kylix as a programming environment.

"Using Kylix" somewhat resembles a burrito—a good, tasty helping of basic form design, bulked up with miscellaneous tips for using the various tools and wrapped precariously in a thin skin of The Basics. "Visual Objects" is an overview of the control, drawing, and window API. "Foundation Objects" provides essential background on the non-visual objects used in every Kylix program, while "Library Routines" introduces you to the foundation's foundation and shows you where to look for the details. The section concludes with a quick look at "Component Creation", which is Kylix's way of letting you extend the programming environment—in Kylix.

I cover a lot of material in this section, and it may get overwhelming at times. If you're having trouble seeing the forest for the trees, put the book down and try to do some of the things I talk about. I know that you'll quickly find that Kylix does an amazing job of making most things easy, and a great job of making the rest doable.

Then pick the book back up and read on.

CHAPTER 5

Using Kylix

CHAPTER 5

Using Kylix

LEARNING TO USE KYLIX is a joy. Things do pretty much what you'd expect, and there's a rich array of tools that you might not have expected but that you will find useful and well-designed. There's extensive online help, so you can generally figure out how things work just by trying them. This chapter, therefore, makes no attempt to provide a comprehensive, feature-by-feature tour. Rather, it focuses on providing an overview that will help you get started, and mentions some of the more useful 'hidden' features.

Experienced Delphi programmers will find little new in this chapter. They may wish to skim through the *Basic Form Design* section, looking for the "Kylix is not Delphi" margin notes that highlight discussion of differences. They may also find the final section, *Growing with Kylix* to be useful.

Other readers should read the whole chapter, though the impatient may want to skip over the *Configuration* section that covers various environment options. The *Visual programming* section is an overview of Kylix programming techniques, while *Basic form design* contains the information you need to do GUI programming with Kylix. The *Editing tools* summarizes some of the most useful editing shortcuts, and the *Debugging* section introduces key debugger features. Finally, *Growing with Kylix* provides a few tips on keeping up with Kylix as it grows from release to release.

Configuration

Kylix is very configurable. You can change colors, layouts, and various behaviors. For the most part, this is all pretty self-explanatory, so this section is just a brief tour of what's possible along with a few of my favorite settings.

Options dialogs

Most of the configuration is done in four tabbed dialogs. For the most part, the defaults are fine, but there are a few settings that perhaps no one likes but that Borland leaves as they are "because after all it's configurable". What follows in this Configuration section has a very personal flavor—it's full of statements like "I like" and "I change"—but these preferences are based on years of using Kylix and its ancestors. I think you'll find my preferences to be pretty sensible. I certainly seem to have met more people who share my preferences than who don't.

Environment options

Tools ➤ Environment Options brings up a dialog that allows you to configure most of the global aspects of how Kylix works. There are so **many** editor and debugger settings that they each have their own dialog, as do the per-project settings. The Environment Options dialog has five tabs, but most of what I'll talk about is on the first, or Preferences, tab (see Figure 5-1).

The Preferences tab

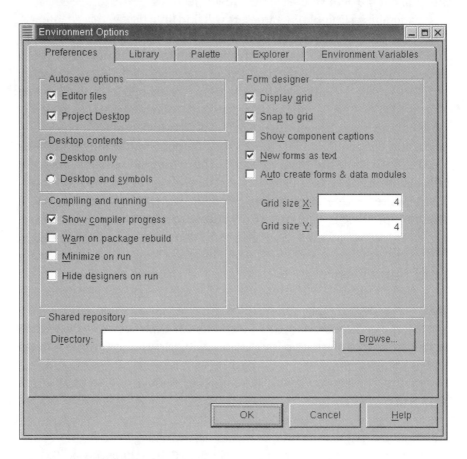

Figure 5-1. My Environment Preferences tab

By default, both "Autosave options" are off, or unchecked. I recommend that you turn them both on. Autosaving editor files means that Kylix saves all changes every time you run your program, instead of only when you explicitly save, or when you exit and Kylix asks you if you want to save your changes; this protects you from programs that crash so badly that you have to `kill` both your hung process and Kylix. Autosaving the Project Desktop means that when you start Kylix in the morning, you come back to just where you left off the night before; otherwise, you get a blank, new project every time, and have to reopen the last project you were working on.

I leave the "Desktop contents" setting at Desktop only. The symbols file is large, and it seems to take less time to regenerate that information (*via* CTRL+F9) than to load the file.

In the "Compiling and running" group, I always check "Show compiler progress" and turn the others off. Kylix compiles very quickly, but it's not instantaneous (especially when it's linking a large application) and I like to see what it's doing. Conversely, hiding any of the design-time windows at run-time just seems 'busy' and 'flashy', to me.

In the "Form designer" section, I turn off "Auto create forms & data modules". The default is to auto create, which means that every form will be loaded from the form resources when the program starts up. Using auto create, the forms appear very quickly once the program is loaded, but startup can take a while and the program can consume a lot of memory keeping prepared versions of infrequently used dialogs around. You can control exactly which forms and data modules get auto-created in the Project Options dialog; this setting just changes the default from create-at-startup to create-on-demand.

In the same section, I set the grid size to 4 units, instead of 8. This just seems to be a better grid size: 8 pixels is just a bit too big.

The Palette tab

I generally leave the Library tab alone. The Palette tab lets you customize the component palette on the main window. (See the *Visual programming* section of this chapter for information about using the component palette.) When you're working on a big project, you may find that you use some types of components quite a lot and others not at all; other projects will have different requirements, and a different working set of components.

The Palette tab of the Environment Options dialog lets you place commonly used components on the left, where they're easy to get to, and to banish the components you're not using to the far right. You can move the tabs left and right; you can add, delete, and rename tabs; and you can move components from one tab to another. It's really all pretty self-explanatory; the important thing is to know that you can do it, and where to go to do it when you need to.

The Explorer tab

I generally leave the Explorer tab pretty much alone, too. This lets you set options for the module tree-view that by default appears next to a code window. I've never really found this all that useful, so I just turn off the "Automatically show Explorer" option and have a wider code window. I can always use SHIFT+CTRL+E to bring the Explorer back when I need it.

Environment variables

The Environment Variables tab allows you to set variables to use in the IDE without making you set them globally, in your ~/.bashrc (or equivalent) file.

This can be useful, because most of the dialogs that let you set string values—like Project ➤ Options ➤ Directories/Conditionals—let you refer to environment variables with a ${VARIABLE} syntax, as in shell scripts. For example, many of the sample projects in the tarball that you can download from www.apress.com use units from a library directory, like lib/GrabBag, and set the search path to ${JLib} so that they can find the library units. On my system, I use the Environment Variables tab to set JLib to /home/jon/lib— depending on where you installed the sample code, you might set JLib to something like /home/yourname/shemitzbook/lib or /apress/kylix/lib. Using the Environment Variables tab lets you change the path for all projects simply by changing the environment variable.

Of course, you **could** set the JLib environment variable globally, but then you're adding that to the environment of every program you run—and you would have to shut Kylix down and restart it for any changes to take effect.

Editor options

Tools ➤ Editor Options brings up a dialog that allows you to configure many aspects of the way the code editor looks and works. Like the environment options dialog, this dialog has five tabs, but I generally only touch three of them.

The General tab

I always turn on "Smart tab". This does two things for you: First, when you hit tab, the cursor will line up under the next text following white space on the first non-empty line above. That is, it uses the word-breaks for tab-stops. This is very useful for creating tables of constants in a legible way, or for indenting code like

```
if Condition
  then begin
      // code
      end
  else begin
    // code
    end;
```

The second thing that "smart tab" does for you is to automatically insert one of its soft tabs when you hit return. That is, when you hit return at the end of a line, you automatically start the next line under the first column on the previous line. Without smart tabs, you have to manually indent.

I also always turn on "Undo after save". This lets me make changes, run a program (which automatically saves the changes), and then still undo the changes if I don't like them. Very handy! Note that undo is only during a Kylix session, and only so long as you have the file open: If you close the file, you lose your undo buffer. Changing projects closes all files, so you will lose your undo buffer(s) when you change projects, even if they have the same file(s) open.

Finally, I generally set "Block indent" to 1, not 2. Kylix lets you indent and un-indent blocks (see the *Editing tools* section of this chapter) with CTRL+SHIFT+I and CTRL+SHIFT+U (with the default keymap; other keymaps use different keystrokes): This setting controls the number of characters that each keystroke adds or subtracts. I set it to 1 because I **do** indent like

```
if Condition
  then begin
      // code
      end
  else begin
    // code
    end;
```

and so sometimes have code lined up on odd columns. This is a decidedly non-standard way to indent, these days, and you may prefer to leave block indent at 2.

The Display tab

On my Redhat 7.0 machine, the editor defaults to a Courier font that I find really rather ugly and hard to read. The best "Editor font", for me, is "Luci-datypewriter", but the list of available fonts will depend on your distribution and on whether you've changed the set of fonts it installed.

The "Editor font" dropdown will display all monospaced fonts that Kylix can use, while the "Size" dropdown will display all available sizes for the font you select.

The Color tab

I like syntax highlighting. I like it a lot. I find that bold keywords and italic comments give code a 'rhythm' that makes it easier to read than unhighlighted code. When code won't compile because I misspelled a keyword, the misspelled keyword does not become bold. This makes it easier to spot my mistake.

Similarly, I like the editor to really shriek at me if I have an awful lot of inline numeric or string constants in my code. So, on the Color tab, I select "String" elements and make them bright red, and select "Number" elements and make them bright purple.

Debugger options

By default, the integrated debugger will stop and let you examine the program state whenever your program raises an exception. While the debugger options lets you set a lot of things, the single most important is the Language Exceptions tab, which lets you turn off this stopping behavior for specific exceptions. Thus, if your program routinely handles, say, EConvertError exceptions, you can tell the debugger to not stop on them. You can also tell it not to stop on any language exception but to only stop at explicit breakpoints that you set. (See the *Debugging* section of this chapter.)

The integrated debugger does slow down your application's execution a bit. If you want your application to run at full speed, and you also want the control over the application's parameters and run-time environment that running your app from within Kylix gives you, uncheck the "Integrated debugging" check box.

Visual programming

In Kylix, "visual" means much more than just a syntax-highlighted IDE. Kylix is built around *components*, objects that you select from a palette and drop onto a *form* (window) that your users will see, or onto a data module that the rest of your code will use. Components have various *properties* that control their behavior and/or appearance, and you can either use the default values or change them at design time, using the Object Inspector. (Component properties are stored in text files, so that you can manage them with your favorite version control system.) Components also have *events* that fire when various things happen, so that all you have to do to respond to a button press, or to write some cleanup code that's fired when a window closes, is to double click on the event in the Object Inspector and write the appropriate code in the event handler. Not only will Kylix automagically handle all the tedious and mistake-prone minutiae of creating, placing, and initializing your widgets, it will also do so behind the scenes; you only have to write the parts that actually do something new, and your code isn't cluttered with lots of machine-generated boilerplate.

Drop components

Kylix puts a number of windows on your desktop. When Kylix first comes up, it will open up its *main window*, a *code editor*, a blank *form*, and the Object Inspector. There are other windows that you will find useful at different times. For example, I almost always have the Alignment Palette and the Project Manager open, while secondary code editors and various debug windows come and go. Closing the main window closes Kylix; conversely, you can close all of the windows except the main window without shutting Kylix down. Kylix will save your window configuration as part of the project's settings, so that it will restart looking just as it did when you shut it down; switching projects can make for a totally different window complement.

Forms and windows

GUI applications are built with *windows*, usually rectangular screen regions where the application places images, text, and/or various controls. Kylix applications are built with *forms*, which are objects that correspond to run-time windows. You may well wonder why Kylix code works with forms and not windows, and why Kylix programmers work with a *form designer* and not a window designer. Kylix uses forms because Delphi does. The short answer to why Delphi uses forms is probably that Visual Basic does. A somewhat longer answer is that under Windows, anything with a window handle is "a window". Top level windows, push buttons, and edit controls all differ only in a few parameters to the CreateWindow() API call. So, calling the top-level window object a TWindow would be about as accurate as calling it a TWidget under Qt.

Each form in your project requires two source code files. (Of course, Kylix creates these automatically.) The .pas file contains the source code that declares each component on the form as a field of the form object, and also contains all the event handler and support code that you write. The .xfm file normally contains a text representation of the various component properties that you've set in the Object Inspector. Optionally, you can have the .xfm file contain a binary representation of the component properties, but this makes it harder to use a version control program.

The main window has the flaming Kylix icon, and is captioned "Kylix - currentproject", where *currentproject* is whatever you are actually working on. The main window contains the main menu, various configurable toolbars, and the component palette (see Figure 5-2). The palette is a tab control, with component icons on each tab. These component icons are actually flat buttons—*ie*, when you move the mouse cursor over them, Kylix draws a raised button frame around the icon. If you move the mouse over a component icon and let it *hover* there for a moment, Kylix will popup a tool-tip window with the name of the component. If you click on the button, it will *stay down*. While it's down, you can press F1 to read the help on that component, or you can click on a form to drop the component on the form.

Once you've dropped the component on a form, the button will pop back up to its flat state, leaving you in the normal form editing mode, where clicking on a component or a form selects it into the Object Inspector. If you click on a component and then decide that you don't want to use it after all, just click on a different component, or on the arrow icon that's always to the left of the component icons. You can easily drop several components of the same type onto a form by *shift clicking* (hold down a shift key while you click) on a component icon; the icon's button will stay down until you click on the arrow icon or on another component.

Figure 5-2. The component palette

If you simply drop a component on a form, the component will be placed with its top-left corner at the point you clicked. For non-visual components like timers or database access, this is the only placement option. However, visual components like buttons and edit boxes have a *bounds* rectangle. If you simply drop them on the form, they will give themselves a default size. You can move components after you drop them by simply clicking on the component and *dragging* (moving the mouse with the left button held down). You can resize a component after you drop it by clicking on any of the eight black *grab points* that surround the currently selected component and dragging the grab point. A newly dropped component is always selected; you can change the selection by simply clicking on a different component.

If you like, you can drop a component on a form **and** set the size in a single operation by clicking where you want the top-left corner to be and dragging to where you want the bottom-right corner to be. For that matter, you can drag up and left, not just down and right; Kylix will do the right thing.

You can always press F12 to toggle between the form designer and the code for that form. When you start Kylix or create a new form, you will get a blank form, whose code will look like:

```
unit Unit1;

interface

uses
  SysUtils, Types, Classes, QGraphics, QControls, QForms, QDialogs;
```

```
type
  TForm1 = class(TForm)
  private
    { Private declarations }
  public
    { Public declarations }
  end;

var
  Form1: TForm1;

implementation

{$R *.xfm}

end.
```

Each component you drop on this form will add a member to the *published* section of the class declaration, which is the part between the class(TForm) and the private. For example,

```
  TForm1 = class(TForm)
    Label1: TLabel;
  private
```

In general, you should not edit this published section. There are special circumstances where you will want to manually edit the published section, and I'll go into them in the *Two Way Tools* subsection, but you have to do this carefully and deliberately. If the declarations of the form's members are out of synch with the form description resource (the .xfm file), the form may not work properly and may even cause exceptions when you try to load it.

Containers

Some components, like panels, group boxes, and page controls are containers. They are visual components in their own right, with a bounds rectangle and a customizable appearance, but they can also have other visual components placed on them. The contained components are only visible and enabled when their Parent component is visible and enabled. Similarly, contained components are clipped to their container's bounds rectangle, just as components placed on a form are clipped to the form's bounds rectangle.[1] Components placed too close to their Parent's right or bottom edges will be only partially visible; components placed beyond the edge will not be visible at all.

When you drop a component on the form, its Parent is the form. When you drop a component on a container, its Parent is the container. If you select a component by clicking on it and then press Esc, the component's Parent will be selected. (Thus, no matter where you click on a form, if you press Esc enough times, you will eventually 'get to' the form.)

A component's position is always specified relative to its Parent. Thus, while a form's Top and Left will reflect its position on the screen, the Top and Left of components on the form do not change as the form is moved about on the screen. Similarly, a panel near the top-left of the form might have a Top and Left of 4, while a component near the top-left of the panel might also have a Top and Left of 4. One way to say this is that every component has its own *coordinate space* (where [0, 0] is the control's top-left) and that every component's Top and Left are specified relative to its Parent's coordinate space. Every visible component has methods that can transform coordinates from its own coordinate space to and from both screen (or *absolute*) and Parent coordinates.

There's no really straightforward way to change a component's Parent once you've placed it. You can, however, *cut* (*via* Edit ➤ Cut; or by right-clicking and choosing Cut from the Edit submenu; or by pressing CTRL+X, though this convenient shortcut may be intercepted by your window manager or desktop) it off the form and then *paste* it into a different container. You can cut more than one component at once by making a multiple selection before issuing the cut command. Select the first component by clicking on it, then select additional components by holding down the shift key as you click on them. You can also do a multiple selection by clicking and dragging around the components you want to select.

---

1. A form, of course, is a container component, too. In fact, any TWidgetControl (a component that represents a Qt widget, or window) can be the Parent of any other TWidgetControl. Of course, controls that basically just frame an area and leave the interior blank make more natural containers than controls that fill their interior with text and graphics. What distinguishes a container component from a normal visual component is that the component designer gave it a csAcceptsControls style that lets you drop other visual components on it at design time.

Note

When you cut components from one container and paste them into another like this, all their properties remain unchanged. In particular, the Top and Left properties will not normally be changed; the component(s) will have the same location in the new container as in the old container. The only exception to this rule is that Top and Left **will** *be changed if the component(s) would not be visible in the new location. This can lead to multiple components overlapping each other, clumped in the lower-right corner of their new container.*

Naturally, you can cut a component off of one form and paste it onto another. In addition to cutting, you can also copy one (or more) component(s) to the clipboard, and then paste them. You can paste copies onto a new form or container—or you can paste a copy to the same form or container as the original. If you've used the Object Inspector to change the component's Name (or any other) property, cutting and pasting will keep the property values you've chosen. This is mostly true for copying, too; however, no component may have the same name as any other component on its form, so the copy (copies) will be given new names (Label1, Edit3, or whatever) just as if you'd just dropped them off the component palette.

Object Inspector

Components are objects, and can have methods, members, and properties at various levels of visibility. Properties with a `published` visibility are shown in the Object Inspector for you to set at design-time. As far as Object Pascal is concerned, a property is a property, but the Object Inspector has two tabs, which split the properties into 'data' Properties and procedural Events. The Properties tab controls how a form *looks* while the Events tab controls how a form *acts.*

As a general rule, published properties deal with a component's behavior and appearance, and you set them at design time to affect how your applications look and act. (You can, of course, also change published properties at runtime.) Un-published properties reflect or control the actual data your application's user is working with, and it doesn't make sense to set them at design-time.

Whenever you have a component selected in the form designer, its published properties and their values will be listed in the Object Inspector. You can change the object displayed in the inspector by selecting it in the form designer.

Conversely, you can change the component selected in the form designer by choosing a different component from the drop down list at the top of the Object Inspector.

Every component you can drop will have at least two properties: Name and Tag. When you drop a component on a form, it's given a default name based on its class name and the number of components on the form of that type with default names. Thus, the first TLabel you drop on a form will be named Label1. If you promptly give that label a more descriptive name, the next label you drop on the form will also be named Label1. If you don't rename Label1, the next label will be Label2. And so on.

The Tag property is an integer that you can use in any way you like. Common uses include distinguishing one button from others that share the same OnClick handler, and marking members of a group of controls (like menu items) for special treatment by code that steps through the group. Just bear in mind that the Tag property is, in essence, a global variable available to all parts of your program that can 'see' the form that the component is on; if one part of your program uses the Tag property one way and another part uses it a different way, you can end up with bugs that may be very difficult to track down.

Property editors

The part of the Object Inspector that lets you set a property's value is called a *property editor*. Many property editors are simple edit boxes that you type new values in, like the property editors for the Name and Tag properties. Others are more complicated.

For example, the property editor for enumerated types, like Align, is a combo box: You can type one of the acceptable values, or you can select one from a dropdown list. Double clicking on the value selects the next element in the list. (Thus, when the enumerated type is boolean, which can only be True or False, double-clicking toggles the property's state.)

Other properties, like Bitmap, bring up special dialogs when you double-click on their values. These **usually** have a ... button to their right when you select them, but the component writer has wide discretion as to how the property editor will behave, so there are occasional exceptions. For example, Color properties look and act much like ordinary enumerated type editors—you can type a value or select one from the dropdown list—but if you double-click, they pop up a color picker dialog that lets you select any possible color.

Some properties will have a little boxed plus sign to the left of their name (see Figure 5-3). This indicates that you can click on the plus sign, or double-click on the property name, to 'open up' the property and display subproperties. When the property value to the right consists of zero or more values in square brackets, like [akLeft, akTop], this is a *set property* (see Figure 5-4), and opening it up will reveal an indented list of boolean properties, one for each value the set can hold. When the property value to the right consists of a name in parentheses, like (TFont), this is an *object property*, and opening it up will reveal an indented list of all its published properties.

Figure 5-3. An object property; closed

⊟ Anchors	[akLeft,akTop]
akLeft	True
akTop	True
akRight	False
akBottom	False

Figure 5-4. A set property; open

Filtering and grouping

By default, the Object Inspector shows all properties and all events in alphabetical order. Some components have dozens of published properties, and it can be hard to find the ones you're interested in, especially on a small screen where the property list may scroll. This is why Kylix lets you hide properties that you're not interested in, and to group them hierarchically.

If you right-click on the Object Inspector, the context menu includes View and Arrange submenus. The View submenu lets you turn off groups of properties that you're not interested in; the Arrange submenu offers you a choice between the normal alphabetical listing and a hierarchical listing that lets you open and close the various groups.

Multiple selection

If you have more than one component selected, the Object Inspector will show only those properties that both (all) components have. Any visible property values are those that all the selected components share; a blank property value means that there are at least two different values for this property in the set of selected components. If you select one of these properties, the Object Inspector will show the value of the **first** component you selected. If you then hit return, that value will be assigned to (all) the other component(s). Conversely, any changes you make to a property will affect all selected components. This can be useful for things like making sure that all of a set of edit boxes have the same Width, or that they all line up.

Events

Every form consists of two files, a .xfm file with property values and a .pas file with program code. Similarly, the Object Inspector has two tabs, Properties and Events. If you click on the Events tab, you will see a list of all the selected component's published events and their current handlers, if any. Most components will have more properties than events. All components have at least two properties, while there are a few components that have no events at all.

The Events tab looks a lot like the Properties tab, and in fact event handler names are stored in the .xfm file as simple string properties. The property editor for an event property lets you either create a new event handler, select an existing event handler, or rename an existing event handler. If you double click on an event with no handler, Kylix will create a new handler, and put you in the code editor with the cursor on the first line of the blank handler. (The next subsection covers event handlers and what goes in them; this subsection is only concerned with the mechanics of using the Object Inspector.) Kylix will always put a new event handler at the bottom of the .pas file, but you can move it about to keep your code organized as you choose: Kylix will be able to find the handler after you've moved it.

Note

Organizational styles differ. Some people don't bother at all, simply leaving their methods in whatever order they were created in. While this pains me, I have to admit that Kylix has such wonderful cross-referencing tools that this really isn't as horrible as it would have been ten years ago. Borland developers follow a style guide that calls for method implementations to be in alphabetical order, but this really strikes me as little better than random. I prefer to group methods functionally, with all the public functions together, all the setup and teardown functions together, all the event handlers of a given type together, and so on.

If you double click on an event that already has a handler, Kylix will put you in the code editor with the cursor on the first line of the existing handler. When you click on the dropdown's down arrow, Kylix will display a list of all event handlers on the current form that have the right prototype—the type of all parameters—for this event. This list might be empty, or it might be quite long. If you choose a handler from this list, Kylix will replace the current event handler with the one you selected.

Note

Two or more events can share the same handler.

If you type over the name of an event handler, Kylix will rename that handler for you, automatically changing any other event handlers that may share it. If you have given your components sensible names, you will probably find the default event handler names to be pretty reasonable. For example, the `OnClick` handler for a `CloseBtn` will be named `CloseBtnClick`. However, when more than one event shares a handler, you'll probably want to give the handler a more appropriate name: `ValidateInput` instead of `NameChange`, for example.

Note that Kylix will **not** delete 'orphaned' event handlers. They will stay in your .pas source file, and you can reattach them to an event at any time. (You should be aware that event handlers are `published` methods so that the form loading code can find them with Run Time Type Information [RTTI]; one consequence of this is that they will be linked into your executable whether they are used or not. Don't worry about this too much—Kylix programs link in a lot of library code, and a handful of unused methods aren't going to make a big difference—but don't let it get out of hand, either.) On the other hand, Kylix **will** (usually) delete empty event handlers when you compile your program. This is generally a good behavior, as it's relatively easy to inadvertently double click and create an event handler you didn't want, and it does make it easy to delete an event handler—just delete the code you added, and Kylix will handle the rest. However, it can cause a problem if you create a set of related (*eg*, OnMouseDown and OnMouseUp) handlers at the same time and then only fill in part of one before you first compile: put in a // comment to keep Kylix from erasing the blank handlers.

Write event handlers

As you saw if you read Chapter 0, you can control a lot of your applications' appearance and resizing behavior without writing a line of code. The data aware controls also give you a lot of functionality just by dropping some components and setting some parameters in the Object Inspector. But, clearly, real programs require you to write some real code. While some code will get called in `initialization` and `finalization` blocks, most code in most GUI apps gets called from an event handler.

While some event handlers are quite long and involved, most event handlers are relatively short, just a few lines that link components together in a way that can't be done in the Object Inspector. This OnChange handler for an edit box is reasonably typical:

```
procedure TConfigurationGUI.UserNameChange(Sender: TObject);
begin
  OkBtn.Enabled := Trim(UserName.Text) <> '';
end; // TConfigurationGUI.UserNameChange
```

If OkBtn.Enabled is set to False at design-time, the user simply can't press the Ok button until the dialog contains valid information. Of course, a real app will probably need more stringent validation than simply 'non-blank string', and a well-designed UI will not just prevent users from entering invalid data, but will tell them what it doesn't like about what they have entered so far. If TConfigurationGUI.ValidateInput is a function that returns a string explaining the most important (or at least the first) error, or ' ' if there are no errors, the previous event handler might be shared by several different controls, and look more like:

```
procedure TConfigurationGUI.UserInputChange(Sender: TObject);
var
  ErrorMsg: string;
begin
  ErrorMsg         := ValidateInput;
  OkBtn.Enabled    := ErrorMsg <> '';
  StatusLbl.Caption := ErrorMsg;        // Show error msg
end; // TConfigurationGUI.UserInputChange
```

The Sender parameter

By convention, every event handler's first parameter[2] is the `Sender: TObject` parameter. The Sender is the component that the event happened to. When

---

2. This is definitely true for the Borland components that come with Kylix, but this is a **convention**, not a **requirement**. Don't be too surprised if you find a third-party component or two that breaks this rule.

two or more components share a common event handler, examining the Sender parameter allows you tell which of them triggered the event.

For example, a dialog might have two buttons, Apply and Accept. The only difference between the two might be that the Accept action should close the dialog after doing an Apply. If doing an Apply takes a lot of code, or if the difference between Accept and Apply comes to more than a line or two of code, you'd probably do this *via* two separate event handlers that each call an Apply method. (You might also have the AcceptClick event handler simply call the ApplyClick event handler.) In simple cases, though, you will often just use a shared event handler that looks something like

```
procedure TDialog.ApplyAndAcceptClick(Sender: TObject);
begin
  // Common "apply" code

  // Close iff Accept
  if Sender = AcceptBtn then
    Close;
end; // TDialog.ApplyAndAcceptClick
```

Avoid taking any action in the `else` clauses in any tests you make on Sender; always positively identify the Sender. There is absolutely nothing preventing you (or whoever inherits your code five years from now) from calling an event handler directly—after all, they're perfectly ordinary Object Pascal methods. Some people always pass Nil as the Sender for an application-generated event; others pass the Sender of the current event handler. **Never** assume that the only components that might be an event's Sender are the two that you set at design-time, so that if it's not the one it must be the other!

In a similar vein, many event handlers share the same TNotifyEvent prototype (`procedure (Sender: TObject) of object`), which makes it easy to assign the wrong handler to an event. If you expect, say, a TComboBox, to be the Sender, test that this is the case before casting Sender.

```
procedure TDialog.ComboBoxSelect(Sender: TObject);
begin
  Assert(Sender is TComboBox); // Catch design-time errors during development
  with TComboBox(Sender) do ;  // A free runtime cast
end; // TDialog.ComboBoxSelect
```

```
procedure TDialog.ComboBoxChange(Sender: TObject);
begin
  with Sender as TComboBox do ; // Does error-checking even in deployed code
end; // TDialog.ComboBoxChange
```

Some people use as for this, but I prefer to use an assertion followed by a 'blind' cast: the chances are good that testing will catch any misassigned event handlers, and the deployed code doesn't have the overhead of checking the Sender is the right type. Obviously, this overhead is negligible for something like a button push, but it can be less so for something like a custom draw handler that may be called many times in a single paint operation. As *per* Chapter 3, an is or as test will fail if the Sender is Nil.

Types of event handlers

All the event handlers I've talked about so far are simple notifications that let you take action when something happens. Many event handlers pass you more parameters than a simple Sender object, but still give you no control over the way the component processes the event. While these simple notifications are the majority of event handlers, there's also an important class of event handlers that might be called 'hooks' or 'callbacks'.

These event handlers have var parameters that let you change the default behavior. The components are typically written so that they work perfectly well if you don't handle a hook event, or if you do but don't change any of the parameters. On the other hand, changing one of the parameters might prevent the form from closing (OnCloseQuery), suppress a keystroke (the various OnKeyXxx events), or customize the tooltip hint depending on where in a control the mouse is (Application.OnShowHint).

For example, this OnCloseQuery handler

```
procedure TAreYouSureFrm.FormCloseQuery(Sender: TObject;
  var CanClose: Boolean);
begin
  CanClose :=
    Application.MessageBox( 'Do you really want to close this window?',
                            'Are you sure?',
                            [smbYes, smbNo], smsInformation, smbYes )=smbYes;
end; // TAreYouSureFrm.FormCloseQuery
```

pops up a dialog box with Yes and No buttons (see Figure 5-5) and only allows the window to close if the user presses the dialog's Yes button.

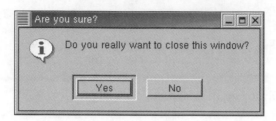

Figure 5-5. An "Are you sure" dialog

As a general rule, if an event handler has a var parameter, you can change the default response by changing the parameter.

Long running event handlers

It doesn't take many CPU cycles to close a window or to disable a widget or twelve. You can do quite a lot in an event handler before your application's responsiveness starts to suffer. However, the Qt event loop (which is ultimately responsible for calling all your event handlers) runs only in your application's main thread. This means that your application can run only one event handler at a time. If an event handler takes a long time—perhaps iterating over thousands of list items, or running a database query—you will notice that your application doesn't respond to other events until it's done. Buttons don't go down or toggle their state when pressed; dropdowns don't drop; list boxes don't change their selection; and so on.

Yes, just like Windows 3.0.

The simplest solution to maintaining responsiveness throughout a long-running event handler is to periodically call Application.ProcessMessages. If there are no pending Qt events, this procedure will return relatively swiftly. Still, if you call Application.ProcessMessages too often, your already long-running operation will be even longer. Conversely, if you don't call Application.ProcessMessages often enough, your application's responsiveness will suffer.

> **Note**
>
> *Of course, you can create threads to handle long-running computa-tions. However, Kylix's version of Qt is compiled in the unthreaded mode, so you can't touch the screen from a thread: You have to use the Thread.Synchronize (Chapter 7) method, or create a custom Qt event (Chapter 6).*

If there are any pending events, they will be processed before Process-Messages returns. Thus, while `Application.ProcessMessages` gives the **appearance** of multiple events being processed simultaneously—allowing button presses to be handled while you work your way through a big list, say—the reality is that only one event is being processed, while another event is suspended. In some ways, this is rather nice: For the most part, you don't have to worry about synchronization issues as you do with simulta-neously executing threads. Only one event handler is executing at a time.

You do have to pay attention to reentrancy, though. For example, if a long running button press handler calls `Application.ProcessMessages`, the button won't go up until the event handler returns—but the user can still press it, and generate a new OnClick event. If you don't call `Application.ProcessMessages`, your event handlers don't have any reentrancy issues, but as soon as you do call `Application.ProcessMessages`, you have to be aware of the possibility that your event handler might interrupt itself. You have three ways to deal with event handler reentrancy: First, of course, you can write the event handler so that it can safely interrupt itself. Second, you can simply disable the control that sent the event until the event handler is about to return. This will prevent the event from firing again. Third, you can add an InEvent flag to the `private` section of the form object. The first thing the event handler does is to check this InEvent flag.

```
procedure TExample.LongRunner(Sender: TObject);
begin
  if InEvent then EXIT;
                // Many people find EXIT clearer than enclosing all the rest
                // of the routine in a begin/end block.
  InEvent := True;
  try
    // Long-running code goes here
  finally
    InEvent := False;
  end;
end; // TExample.LongRunner
```

If this is a recursive call, it exits; if it's not a recursive call, it sets the flag, and does all the long running processing in a try / finally block that resets the InEvent flag before the event handler returns.

One other thing to be aware of is what happens if the user presses the close button on the window frame (or she presses one of your buttons whose event handler calls the form's Close method) while your application is running a long event that calls `Application.ProcessMessages`. The form won't actually close until the long event terminates, but it will stop normal repainting. Be sure to set a Terminate flag in the OnCloseQuery handler, and check that in your long op, after the `Application.ProcessMessages` call.

Two way tools

Everything I've discussed so far has been pretty mouse-oriented: Drop this; drag that; click here and type. After all, this is a section on Visual Programming. But one of Kylix's many strengths is the way it splits the difference between visual programming and traditional text programming in a way that few, if any, other environments can match.

You know by now that pressing F12 will toggle between the form designer and the code editor. With the form designer active, try pressing ALT+F12. This will close the form designer (see Figure 5-6), and will replace the Unitname.pas file in the code editor with Unitname.xfm, a text representation of the form (see Figure 5-7).

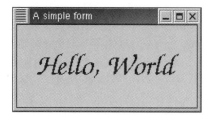

Figure 5-6. A simple form; visually

The text representation includes all the components on a form and their *non-default properties* in a somewhat Pascal-like syntax. This corresponds rather directly to what is stored in the resource section of your program's executable file, which is streamed in at runtime to recreate your form. That is, a form resource consists of a series of component names, along with parentage information, and any non-default properties and their settings. Since components can declare default values for their various properties, Kylix can

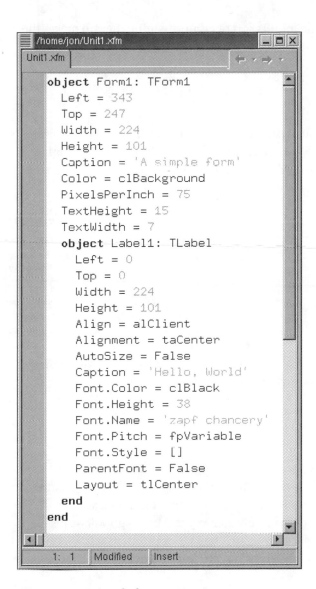

```
/home/jon/Unit1.xfm                      _ □ ×
Unit1.xfm                              ⬅ ·  ➡ ·

object Form1: TForm1
  Left = 343
  Top = 247
  Width = 224
  Height = 101
  Caption = 'A simple form'
  Color = clBackground
  PixelsPerInch = 75
  TextHeight = 15
  TextWidth = 7
  object Label1: TLabel
    Left = 0
    Top = 0
    Width = 224
    Height = 101
    Align = alClient
    Alignment = taCenter
    AutoSize = False
    Caption = 'Hello, World'
    Font.Color = clBlack
    Font.Height = 38
    Font.Name = 'zapf chancery'
    Font.Pitch = fpVariable
    Font.Style = []
    ParentFont = False
    Layout = tlCenter
  end
end

1: 1    Modified    Insert
```

Figure 5-7. A simple form as text

save both (load) time and (executable) space by not storing and restoring default values.

You can edit the xfm representation, then press ALT+F12 and see the changes. For example, if you edit a component's Top or Left property, it will move the component just as if you had dragged it, or edited the Top or Left property in the Object Inspector. If you delete a property setting, this will cause it to revert to its default value; conversely, you can add a line to set a non-default value. In general, though, it's best to use the Object Inspector and the Alignment Palette for this sort of editing; editing the xfm makes the most sense for things that are difficult or impossible to do visually.

Editing long captions

If you have a long caption, it can be very difficult to edit it in the Object Inspector, where you only see a few characters at a time. (For that matter, how would you include a newline character?) In the xfm representation, you can see the caption as a whole

```
object Label1: TLabel
    Left = 440
    Top = 40
    Width = 103
    Height = 193
    Alignment = taRightJustify
    AutoSize = False
    Caption =
      'This is some nice long, right-aligned word-wrapped text.'#10#10'This s' +
        'hould be the second paragraph.'
    Layout = tlCenter
    WordWrap = True
  end
```

and you can edit it freely, including inserting special characters *via* the # mechanism (see Chapter 1; note that you can't use the ^ form in the xfm editor). Long text will be broken into a series of concatenated sublines, without any attempt at breaking between words: The + sign will be just inside the 80-character gutter. You **don't** have to conform to this wrapping when you make changes; your lines can be shorter or longer, and Kylix will deal with it. For example,

```
    Caption =
      'This is some nice long, right-aligned word-wrapped text.'#10#10 +
      'This should be the second paragraph.'
```

is just fine. If you press ALT+F12 twice, the wrapping will be in the middle of "should" again.

Changing a component's type

It will sometimes happen that as you work with a form, you will realize that you actually chose the wrong sort of component. Perhaps you dropped a TStringGrid, but as your code evolved, it became obvious you never use the Cells property and that a TDrawGrid would have been better.

You can, of course, drop a new component next to the old one, and copy property and event values one-by-one. But that's tedious and error-prone, and if the old component is not alNone Align-ed, it can be hard to slip a new component in its place without doing a lot of other surgery. The easy way is to just change the type name in the xfm editor. (*Eg*, change `object Grid:` `TStringGrid` to `object Grid: TDrawGrid`.) When you press ALT+F12 to return to the form designer, Kylix will notify you of any properties that were explicitly set and that don't exist in the new component. Just tell it to Ignore these.

> **Note**
>
> *You don't **have** to change the matching declaration in the published section of the form object—the next time you compile, Kylix will ask you if it should do so automatically. On the other hand, if you choose to program defensively and to explicitly change the declaration in the .pas file, too, you'll be doing what I do.*

Changing a component's parentage

Changing a component's type like this is relatively rare. It's probably more common to need to change a component's parentage. For example, you might want to move a (group of) component(s) off the form itself and onto a panel, or you might want to move a (group of) component(s) from one panel to another or even back to the form. Just as with a type change, recreating the components in their new location is tedious and error-prone. Ideally, you'd just do something like select a different Parent in the Object Inspector and have all the other properties transfer unchanged to the new location.

You can't do that in Kylix,[3] though, so you have to do a bit of cut-and-paste in either the form designer or the .xfm representation. Now, whenever I try to multi-select a lot of components, I find myself clicking off of a component, and selecting a container that I didn't mean to select. That's why I

---

3. Delphi 6 does have a nice "Object TreeView" that lets you drag controls from one container to another. Presumably, Kylix 2 will have this, too.

find that it's usually easier and safer to edit the .xfm representation than to use cut-and-paste in the form designer. Within the xfm representation, a container/contained relationship is shown by having the contained components appear 'inside of' the object end pair, just before the end. For example, a panel with a top-aligned label might look like

```
object DemoPnl: TPanel
  Left = 472
  Top = 272
  Width = 213
  Height = 181
  TabOrder = 0
  object DemoLbl: TLabel
    Left = 1
    Top = 1
    Width = 211
    Height = 13
    Align = alTop
    Alignment = taCenter
    AutoSize = False
    Caption = 'Demo Panel'
  end
end
```

So, to move another component onto the panel, just cut out its representation, and paste it before the final end line.

```
object DemoPnl: TPanel
  Left = 20
  Top = 28
  Width = 213
  Height = 181
  TabOrder = 0
  object DemoLbl: TLabel
    Left = 1
    Top = 1
    Width = 211
    Height = 13
    Align = alTop
    Alignment = taCenter
    AutoSize = False
    Caption = 'Demo Panel'
  end
```

```
object Grid: TStringGrid
  Left = 416
  Top = 80
  Width = 281
  Height = 189
  TabOrder = 1
end
end
```

Note

As with the wrapping of long strings, you don't have to worry about the indenting—unlike Python, Kylix doesn't care about that, and the xfm will be automatically reformatted next time you go from the form designer to the xfm editor.

If you press ALT+F12 now, to see your changes in the form designer, you might be dismayed. Where did the Grid go? It's not where it was, and it doesn't appear to be on the panel you thought you placed it on. The key to this mystery lies in the

```
Left = 416
Top = 80
```

lines. Remember, Top and Left are coordinates in the Parent's client rectangle; they're not (necessarily) relative to the form's client area, and they're certainly not absolute screen coordinates. A component at [416, 80] is not visible on a panel that's only 213 by 181—it's totally clipped. The easiest solution to this is to just trim the Top and Left lines to single digits after pasting

```
Left = 4
Top = 8
```

and then visually move the component into the right place on its new parent, using the form designer in the usual way.

Cross-mode copy and paste

Finally, you've already seen that in the form designer you can copy a component or group of components, and then paste copies of them onto the same or different form or onto a different container. What happens if you copy a component or group of components in the form designer, and then paste it in the xfm editor? Or, if you copy a component or group of components in the xfm editor, and then paste it in the form designer?

Pretty much The Right Thing, which is pretty slick.

If you copy a component visually and paste it textually, you will paste the text representation. If you copy a component textually and paste it visually, you will paste the visual representation.

There are some caveats, though:

- If you copy textually and paste visually, Kylix will insert declarations in the form object for the component(s) as named; it will **not** rename components as necessary, the way it would if you do a visual copy and paste.

- If you copy visually and paste textually, Kylix will **not** automatically insert declarations in the form object. You'll have to do that manually. If you are pasting a copy onto the same form as the original, you will have to rename the copy by hand; Kylix will not do this for you.

Help (F1)

Part of what Kylix makes Kylix self-explanatory is the help. You can press F1 just about anywhere and get a few paragraphs of hypertext explaining an object, method, library function, keyword, or tool. Most help pages have green underlined links to other pages; you can answer most questions by following a few links from the first page you find.

Component help

As you've already seen, selecting a component from the palette and pressing F1 will bring up the main (or root) page for that component. This page will have a brief overview of what the component does, as well as a few standard links.

Hierarchy

The **Hierarchy** link will have a dashed (or broken) underline: This indicates that clicking on it will pop up a small window, but will not take you to a new page. The Hierarchy popup will list the object's ancestors, all the way up to TObject. This information is useful when you want to base a new component on an existing one: You can look at the inheritance chart to see where the properties and methods you need are introduced. In addition, because the hierarchy popup contain links to all of a component's ancestral classes, the popup is an easy way to jump to the help page for the ancestor that introduces a particular property or method.

Properties

The **Properties** link brings up a "Topic Groups" window that lists the component's public, published, and protected properties. Clicking on a link in the main (yellow) part of this window will open up that page in the main help window. The first link in the Topic Groups (gray) header is the name of 'this' component. You can always click on this component-name link to get back to the main page for the component; this is particularly useful when you've been reading about properties introduced in ancestral classes, and want to get back to the component you're really interested in.

By default, the properties page is organized hierarchically: The properties introduced in 'this' component are listed alphabetically at the top of the page, followed by the properties introduced in the component's ancestor, then the ancestor's ancestor, and so on down to TObject. If you click on the **Alphabetically** link in the Topic Groups header, you'll get the same list, alphabetically by property name. While it might seem that the flat alphabetic view makes more sense, the lists can be very long. Since the properties you're most likely to lookup are those specific to a component—*ie*, those introduced in the component—or one of its immediate ancestors, the default **By object** grouping really does make the most sense.

Many of the properties will have little glyphs next to them that indicate whether they are published or protected, and whether they're read-only at run-time or not. (The **Legend** popup link explains the glyphs). A property with no glyph is neither published nor protected: this is a public property that you can read (and often write) *via* code at run-time, but that you can't set at design-time *via* the Object Inspector. Sometimes this is because you are trying to use the component in a way that the author simply never thought of, but more generally there are three main reasons why a property might be unpublished and run-time only:

1. The property refers to an ephemeral state of a component that you simply wouldn't want to set at designtime. For example, where the caret is in a TMemo.

2. The property is meant for programmatic access to an aspect of the component that's already exposed in a visual way. For example, you can **see** the components on a form, and so don't need direct design-time access to the Components array.

3. The author didn't want to write a custom property editor. This may be why you can't set a TStringGrid's Cells property at design-time, and have to set even invariant captions at run-time.

Methods

The **Methods** link on the main help window's header strip brings up a "Topic Groups" window that lists links to the component's public and protected methods. There will only be one of these Topic Groups windows open at a time; if you already have a Properties list open, the Methods list will replace it. The Methods list can be displayed either Alphabetically or By Object, just as the Properties list can.

As *per* Section 1, the distinction between a property and a method is that a property is a value (set of values) that you can read and/or write, while a method is a procedure or function that you can call. The actual implementation of reading or writing a property may use a private method, but that's transparent, irrelevant, and subject to change: Private methods are not documented in the online help.

Events

The **Events** link on the main help window's header strip brings up a list of links to the component's events. Again, this normally displays By Object, but can be switched to an Alphabetical listing.

As *per* the above subsection on writing event handlers, events are special properties that always hold procedure ({...}) of object values. These are 8-byte values that contain a pointer to an object and a pointer to one of its methods. When the component encounters the right conditions, it will use code like

```
if Assigned(OnFoo) then
  OnFoo(Self {perhaps some other params});
```

to call any handler that you may have set. The help page will detail both the conditions that trigger this event and any special handling that you may be able to do within the event handler. For example, some event handlers have var parameters that you can set to override the component's default behavior.

Other help entry points

In the code editor, pressing F1 will take you to the help page for the word the cursor is on. If the cursor is on a component name, pressing F1 will take you to the same page as if you selected that component from the palette and pressed F1. Of course, the CLX contains plenty of objects—let alone subroutines—that don't appear on the palette but are still documented. Pressing F1 in the editor is a good way to jump directly to the help for objects like TBitmap and subroutines like Now.

Note

Pressing F1 on a keyword that has a man *page will bring up an* xman *window with the man page.*

Often, of course, you want help on an identifier or keyword that's right in front of you, so it's easy to just click on it and press F1. Similarly, the cross-reference tools like CTRL+CLICK (see the *Cross Referencing* section of this chapter, below) will take you right to an identifier's declaration, where it's easy to click on a field's type name and press F1. However, I often find that I know just what keyword I want help on, and so will type it in the editor and press F1, erasing the keyword I just typed once I'm done.

If it bothers you to type 'garbage' in your code that you never plan to execute or compile, relax. Kylix is a shining exemplar of the There Are Many Ways To Do It school of user interface design. Select Help ➤ Kylix Help from the main menu, and you'll get the help contents dialog, open to its index tab. Just start typing the keyword you want to lookup, and the list of keywords will scroll as you type. Double-click on the word you want, or select it and hit return, or select it and click on the Display button.

Finally, there are times when you don't know what keyword you want. You need to do some string manipulation, say, but you don't know the name of the appropriate function. If you have a help window open, just click on the Help Topics button (select Help ➤ Kylix Help from the main menu, if you don't) then select the Find tab. This lets you do a full-text search on the contents of the help pages.

Basic form design

Every Kylix GUI app starts with a form. The CLX [Component Library, Cross-platform—more or less] offers a wide range of components to help you fill in that form with both standard and custom elements. This section will provide an overview of basics, such as providing a keyboard interface, resizing gracefully, and changing in response to user input, as well as the more advanced topics of form inheritance and frames.

Keyboard Interface

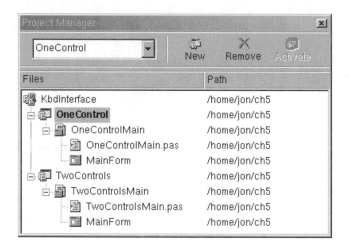

Figure 5-8. The Kdbinterface project group

Let's start with a simple example that will show some of the main issues. The ch5/KbdInterface.bpg project group in the tarball that you downloaded from www.apress.com contains a couple of projects. Load the project group (*via* File ➤ Open or the open file button), then bring up the Project Manager *via* View ➤ Project Manager. The active project will be shown in bold: Make sure One-Control.dpr is active (double click on it, or use the up/dn keys and press return) and expand the outline by clicking on the plus sign on the box (see Figure 5-8). Load OneControlMain into the editor and form designer by double clicking on the name. As you can see, this project has one form, with one button (see Figure 5-9) and one event handler, TMainForm.CloseBtnClick, that calls MainForm.Close to close the form and hence the application.

Note

Every GUI project has a main form. When the main form is closed, the application is closed. The main form can open up other, secondary forms; the application does not close when these secondary forms are closed.

Figure 5-9. One Control

Tab stops

If you run OneControl, you'll find you can close the application by clicking on the Close button, or by pressing Space, or by pressing Return. This is because the CloseBtn is the first (and only) control. If you now select and run TwoControls, you'll find that Space and Return press the Popup button instead; and that Tab will move the visible focus to the Quit button, which means that Space or Return will now push it.

In the TwoControls project, if you turn off either button's TabStop you will find that Tab no longer cycles the visible focus between the buttons. The TabStop property controls whether or not a control is part of the 'tab cycle'. This lets you decide whether the user can Tab through all controls, or whether the tab cycle is limited to the most important controls—*eg*, a data entry form might restrict TabStop to the required fields and the Post button, making keyboard access to optional fields depend on explicit keyboard shortcuts (see below).

The TabOrder property lets you control the order that TabStop controls appear in the tab cycle. By default, controls are placed at the end of the tab cycle—they will have a higher TabOrder than any other control in their container. You can edit the tab order by changing individual components'

TabOrder property (any negative number will move it to the top, while any 'sufficiently large' number will move it to the bottom) but it's generally easier to use the Edit Tab Order dialog, which you can bring up by Edit ➤ Tab Order or by selecting Tab Order from the right mouse button's context menu.

When a form has containers (like panels and group boxes) that contain TabStop controls, the container's tab cycle is 'spliced into' the outer tab cycle. (See Figure 5-10.) For example, if a container with four tab stop controls (Alpha, Beta, Gamma, and Delta) is second in a cycle that starts with One and ends with Three, the tab cycle will be One, Alpha, Beta, Gamma, Delta, Two. (The container itself can have TabStop set True, but there's not an awful lot of reason to do this.)

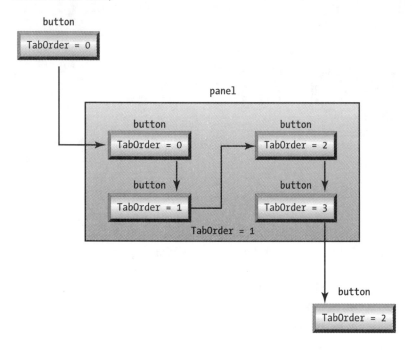

Figure 5-10. A 'nested' tab cycle

Active control

In these rather contrived examples, the programs always start with the keyboard focus on the first tab stop on the form. If this isn't what you want, you can set the form's ActiveControl property at design-time. This will determine which control has the keyboard focus when the form opens.

You can read ActiveControl while your program is running, to see which control currently has the focus. Similarly, you can set it at runtime, to change which control has the focus. Generally, of course, users are very surprised and disconcerted when the keyboard focus jumps around "randomly". You should probably avoid changing ActiveControl programmatically except in those special cases where the former ActiveControl is no longer visible because of a tab change, or a BringToFront operation, or something of the sort. (See the *Page controls* and *Dynamic regions* sections, below.)

Keyboard shortcuts

Cycling from one control to the next is fine for hard-core data entry applications, where the user does the same thing day after day, and an absolute minimum of keystrokes makes for a high throughput. But most applications are used by people who often don't know them all that well, and they jump from this control to that, as they spot what they need. The mouse, of course, is good for this, but many people prefer keyboard shortcuts—and as they get familiar with your app, the keyboard shortcuts save time.

Kylix handles keyboard shortcuts in a perfectly standard way: If the Caption has an ampersand in it, the next character is underlined, and that underlined character is the shortcut. For example, a caption that shows in the Object Inspector as '&Close' will show onscreen as Close, and ALT+C is the shortcut character.

For button controls, typing the keyboard shortcut is the same as clicking on the button. The situation is a bit more complicated for edit controls, list boxes, and other controls that can get the keyboard focus (be tab stops) but that don't have a Caption property and a click action. These controls generally need a label next to them with an & (and, hence, a shortcut) in its Caption. TLabel's have a FocusControl property that you set at design-time. When the user types the label's shortcut, the FocusControl gets the keyboard focus, just as if the user had tabbed to it.

Tip

There's a difference between typing a button's keyboard shortcut and typing the keyboard shortcut of a label whose FocusControl points to the button. Typing the button's shortcut presses the button; typing the label's shortcut highlights the button as if you'd tabbed to it, so that you can press it by typing Space or Return.

Be careful with keyboard shortcuts. When you have a large form, it's easy to have conflicting keyboard shortcuts—and there's no way to find this out except to try each shortcut and make sure it does what you expect. In the case of a conflict, it's load order—not tab order—that matters. That is, when a form is created at runtime, components are read from the form resource and created in the order that they appear in the ALT+F12 text view. If you have two components that share a shortcut, the one that appears first in the ALT+F12 text view will be the one that responds to the shortcut keystroke.

Default and Cancel buttons

Buttons have Default and Cancel properties. These give the buttons extra shortcut keys that are particularly useful for the OK and Cancel buttons of dialog boxes.

A default button—a button whose Default property is True—looks and acts somewhat differently than a non-default button: when the user presses Return, the default button is clicked. Well, most of the time. There are two caveats:

- Any button that is currently selected is temporarily the default button. Pressing return clicks the selected button, not the default button.

- Various controls—like multiline edit controls (TMemo)—can 'eat' the Return.

In other words, the default button is clicked when the user presses return—unless another control that 'wants' the return key has the focus.

Cancel buttons—a button whose Cancel property is True—are similar, except that they're clicked when the user types Esc instead of Return. This is, of course, a common shortcut for 'close this and discard any changes I made'.

Just as you can have duplicate keyboard shortcuts, so you can have more than one default or cancel button. This is generally a mistake, just as are duplicate keyboard shortcuts: Only the first default or cancel button in the tab order will be clicked when the user presses Return or Esc.

Tip

Don't put any effort into remembering which conflict is resolved by load order and which by tab order. (Hey, I didn't know until I wrote this section.) Conflicting shortcuts are a mistake, as are conflicting default or cancel buttons.

Resizing gracefully

Some forms consist only of controls like checkboxes and radio buttons. They get no benefit from being resized and, in fact, you don't want the user to be able to resize them. Others may have some fixed-size controls along an edge or two, but also have controls that can usefully grow to allow the user to see more data at once. These are common UI issues, and Kylix has built solutions into the CLX library; you can handle most sizing issues at design-time, by setting various properties in the Object Inspector. You'll almost never have to explicitly reposition controls in an OnResize handler.

Constraining resize

Every TControl has a Constraints property that allows you to specify a minimum and maximum height and width. While you can set the Constraints for any control on a form, the effects of setting a control's Constraints are not as easy to see as the effects of setting the form's Constraints.

Every form's Constraints default to 0 for MaxHeight, MaxWidth, MinHeight, and MinWidth. 0 means 'no constraint'—the form can assume any size the user cares to give it. If you set a minimum value, the form simply won't get any smaller; if you set a maximum value, the form won't get any larger. Thus, if you set MinHeight and MaxHeight to Height, and MinWidth and MaxWidth to Width, the user won't be able to resize the form at all.

> **Tip**
>
> *Delphi programmers may expect that setting the form's BorderStyle property to fbsSingle or fbsDialog will keep the form from resizing, but this will not necessarily work. Under Linux, the form can only ask the window manager to set the border style—there's no guarantee that it will get what it asked for. (The same applies to BorderIcons: many window managers insist on putting minimize and maximize buttons on frames even when you ask them not to.) If your form should not be resizable, don't rely on BorderStyle: set the Constraints.*

Kylix is not Delphi

Many forms will have a minimum size but no maximum size. They may have some fixed-size controls that need to be visible, and some variable-size controls that aren't usable unless they're big enough. For example, a memo field may need at least enough room for one line of text and a couple of scrollbars. Similarly, a grid or list view may need enough room for three columns and a header row and a couple of data rows.

The ConstraintsAndAnchors project in the ch5/Resizing.bpg project group illustrates this. It's a file viewer that consists of a TMemo and a button on the bottom right that opens a file dialog and loads the selected file into the memo. The form's minimum size constraints have been set big enough to show a very tiny configuration file, but the form can grow to fill the entire screen. If you load this project and play around with it a bit, you'll notice that the Constraints apply at design-time as well as at runtime.

Anchors

If you try the ConstraintsAndAnchors project, you'll probably be struck by something else: As you change the form size at design-time, the memo resizes and the button stays in the bottom right, just as they do at runtime. This is done by the Anchors property. You can anchor a control to any or all of the four sides of its container (which may be a form). Anchoring a control to a side of its container means that it will keep a constant distance from that side when the container is resized.

The default anchor is [akLeft, akTop], which means that the control stays in place when the container is resized. If you change this to [akRight, akTop], the control is anchored to the top-right corner; its Left property will change as the container's Width changes, but the Top property will stay constant. If you anchor a control to the bottom-right, [akRight, akBottom], both Top and Left will change as the container changes size, with the control maintaining a constant distance from the bottom-right corner, as the button does in the ConstraintsAndAnchors demo. Of course, if you anchor a control to the bottom-left, [akLeft, akBottom], only Top will change as the container changes size, with the control maintaining a constant distance from the bottom-left corner. In short, controls anchored to a pair of adjacent sides—a corner—'float' with that corner.

When you anchor to two opposing sides, whether Left and Right or Top and Bottom or both, the control maintains its distance from both sides. This means that the control grows and shrinks with its container. Thus, a control anchored left and right gets wider or narrower as its form changes size. A control anchored to all four sides grows and shrinks in both dimensions, as the memo component does in the ConstraintsAndAnchors demo.

The situation is a bit more complex when you anchor to only one side, or when you don't anchor to any sides. When a control is not anchored along one dimension, Kylix will keep the control's midpoint at a constant relative position. A control that was a quarter of the way in before the form was resized will still be a quarter of the way in after it the form is resized. A control that was exactly in the middle will stay exactly in the middle. This strikes me as rather marginally useful—something added rather than forcing controls to be anchored at least one way in both dimensions—but you may find a use for it.

Alignment

Controls also have an Align property that is in some ways complementary to the Anchors. Just as Anchors default to [akLeft, akTop], which means that the control just sits still, not doing anything when its container resizes, so Align default to alNone, which means the same thing. You can also make a control Align itself to any of its container's four sides, or to fill the space available. For example, a left aligned control (Align = alLeft) has a constant width but its height varies with its container's.

This may sound just like setting Anchors to [akLeft,akTop,akBottom], but there are three key differences:

1. Setting Align at design-time will make the control resize itself to fit the space. This is a lot easier than setting Top and Left to 0, and setting Height or Width to match the containers.

2. An aligned control fills the space available; an anchored control can leave a constant width border around itself.

3. An aligned control is sensitive to the behavior of its neighbors. It will resize when they do, even if the container itself doesn't resize. Anchored controls are only sensitive to changes in container size.

The last of these is clearly the most important. As you can see from the AnchorsVsAlign project in the ch5/Resizing project group, an aligned control adjusts itself to changes in the size of its neighbors at both design-time and run-time. This is very useful both in conjunction with programmatic size changes—if one control resizes itself in response to, say, a data change, its neighbors adjust automatically—and when used with a splitter control, which lets the user adjust the relative size of two controls (or containers).

Note

The Anchors property is a lot newer than the Align property. Anchors was introduced in Delphi 4, while Align has been around since Delphi 1. Many older Delphi programs use nested panels to get the behavior that you can now get with Anchors; for example, anything on a right aligned panel that's on a bottom aligned panel will act as if it's bottom-right anchored. The EmulateFrm of the AnchorsVsAlign project illustrates this technique. You should use Anchors rather than write new code that uses this technique—those two panels slow form creation and consume system resources—but you will probably encounter nested panels if you ever have to maintain old Delphi code that has been ported to Kylix.

Form regions

Many forms consist of a few distinct regions. The ConstraintsAndAnchors project is a degenerate example of a familiar sort of window, with a large text or tree view on the left and some buttons in the top-right and bottom-right. Kylix's edit window is another, with its SHIFT+CTRL+E Code Explorer on the left and its tabbed edit windows on the right, separated by a splitter that lets you change the relative widths. We've seen some 'effective' regions, where controls stay together by virtue of common Anchors; this section will introduce 'explicit' regions, where the form is divided between a few containers and large controls.

Containers

In Kylix, the TPanel and TGroupBox are the basic containers. (Page controls are also containers; they're discussed separately, below.) The big difference between the two is in where the Caption is displayed, and in the appearance of their borders. A panel's Caption, if any, is always vertically centered, though it can be left, right, or center aligned. A group box's Caption, if any, is always at the top-left of the frame. A panel's frame is controlled by its Border-Style, and an inner and outer "bevel"; a group box just has the BorderStyle, though its BorderStyle property can have a greater range of values than a panel's. Otherwise, though, the two act pretty identically, and your choice of one over the other will be governed by whether you want the group box's Caption at top-left or not.

Note

TGroupBox's don't have a BorderStyle property under Delphi, where they always have an 'incised' border, like Kylix's BorderStyle = bsEtched. In general, CLX offers a wider range of BorderStyle's than Delphi's VCL does; Delphi programmers may be particularly surprised to find that TLabel's now have a BorderStyle property, letting labels have the sort of frame that requires a panel or TBevel in Delphi.

Kylix is not Delphi

There are four main reasons to use containers:

1. You want a functional group of controls to be visually distinct from the rest of the form. (When you don't also need the resizing and/or parenting properties of a container, you can use a TBevel control for visual grouping. A bevel control uses less system resources than a container.)

2. You have more than one set of radio buttons on a form. Radio buttons are grouped by Parent; only one radio button with the same Parent can be Checked at a time. When you click on a radio button, any other radio button with the same Parent is un-Checked. To get two or more sets of buttons to operate independently, you need to give them different parents. You can do this by placing one or both on their own container; the container is then the Parent, not the form. See the RadioButtons project in the ch5/Containers project group for an example. (Note that this is not an issue with radio buttons placed on different tabs of a page control (below); the various tabs are the radio buttons' parents.)

3. You need a group of small controls to 'hold their own' on a form where other controls have an alignment besides alNone. (The ch13/vfind project group contains examples of this.) Similarly, you may have a region with a number of controls that should be effectively anchored to a slider. You get this effect when they are anchored to a panel that's resized by the slider.

4. You have a group of controls that should be disabled or hidden *en masse*, in response to some user action. Containers let you do this, as a control is not Visible or Enabled unless its Parent is. 'Stacking' two or more identically sized containers at the same point lets you have a region that changes its control set, depending on the state of other regions. (See *Dynamic regions*, below.)

Forms can be thought of as containers, too, and they act the same as containers in the way that Enabled and Visible propagate to all controls on them. Containers and forms have somewhat different clipping behavior, though. By default, if some of the controls on a form extend beyond the form's ClientRect, the form will display scroll bars that let you pan about. You can turn this AutoScroll behavior off, and then controls that extend beyond the edge of the form will only be partially drawn, while controls that are wholly off the form will not be visible at all. Containers, by contrast, have no AutoScroll property, and always clip controls that are not contained within their ClientRect.

Forms and containers both have a Controls list, which you can examine at runtime. This contains a reference to all the controls that have that form or container as their Parent. In addition, forms have a Components list, which is a list of all components on the form, whether directly or via intermediate containers, and which includes any non-visual components on the form. (See Chapter 6 for more information on these lists, as well as a detailed discussion of the difference between a "component" and a "control".)

It's important to note that there is a difference between "parentage" and "ownership". All components on a form are owned by the form—their Owner property points to the form—which means that the form will Free them when it is itself freed. Similarly, all components on a form are fields of the form's object. You would write the same code to refer to FileTextMemo whether it was placed directly on the form, or on a group box on a panel on a page control; you never have to refer to contained controls *via* code like `Self.Container.Container.Contained`.

Splitters

Splitters are pretty straightforward controls to use. They always divide two controls, one of which must be top, bottom, left, or right aligned, and the other of which must be client aligned. To use a splitter, first drop the edge-aligned control and set its Align property. Then drop the splitter (located on the Additional tab) and set its Align property to match the edge-aligned control; the splitter to defaults to alLeft Align. Finally, drop the 'other' control, and set its Align to alClient.

> **Note**
>
> *Unlike anchors and alignment, the splitter will **not** work at design-time. You'll have to change the height or width of the edge aligned control* via *the Object Inspector.*

That's all you **need** to do, but you'll probably want to change some defaults. First, the default height of a horizontal splitter and the default width of a vertical splitter is 100 pixels! Somewhere between 4 and 10 is generally much better. Second, I find a Beveled splitter stands out much better than the default flat bevel. Finally, at least in Kylix 1.0, you'll generally want to use a ResizeStyle of rsUpdate: the default rsPattern and rsLine styles are buggy, and leave garbage on many alClient-aligned controls.

Page controls

Page controls allow you to create tabbed dialogs. Tabbed dialogs are great for folding a lot of controls into a limited space, or for reducing complexity by letting only one functional group be visible at a time—but you have to take care to keep the tab count low, and to keep the grouping logical and predictable.

The first thing to note is that Kylix has two different tab icons on the Common Controls tab. The first, TTabControl, is just a tab set with events that let you respond to the user's selection of different tabs. For example, you might load different data into a common set of controls.

Most of the time, what you'll want is the second, or TPageControl. This is a collection of pages that you can populate at design-time. When the user clicks on a tab, the associated page is "brought to the front", making the controls on it visible and hiding all other controls on all other pages.

When you drop the page control on a form and size it appropriately, it will look a lot like a panel: a blank, gray, control with a raised edge. To add a tab, right-click on the page control and select New Page. Once you've added tabs, there are three different design-time ways to select them:

1. You can set the page control's ActivePage property from the drop-down list.

2. You can use the right-click context menu to scroll through the pages.

3. You can click on the tab.

To edit a tab in the Object Inspector, just select it, and then click anywhere on its 'content' part; to edit the page control itself in the Object Inspector, click on the blank part of the tab row to the right of any tabs, or select a tab and press Esc. The page control is the Parent control of each of the tab sheets, and so pressing Esc takes you from the child to the parent, just as with any other container.

You can put an icon on every tab. Select a TImageList from the Common Controls tab and drop it on the form. Set the image list's Width and Height to the height you want your icons to be—the default is 16x16, which is more standard on Windows than on Linux, and no longer very common even there. Set the page control's Images property to point to the image list, and the tab heights will adjust automatically. You can control the icon that appears on each tab by editing the tab sheet's ImageIndex property.[4]

Note

The image list does not have to be on the current form. It is, in fact, quite common to centralize all of an application's image lists onto a single form.[4] At design-time, the Images dropdown will show all image lists on all forms the current unit uses. *To access the image list(s) on a form in a* CommonImages *unit, just add* CommonImages *to the* uses *clause in the* implementation *section of the current unit.*

Tab sheets are unusual controls in some ways. For one thing, they have a Visible and a TabVisible property. Setting Visible to False will not do anything you might expect—use the TabVisible property to hide a tab. (Setting Tab-Visible to False will hide the tab at design-time as well as at run-time. You will only be able to select it by setting the page control's ActivePage property or by using the right-click context menu to scroll a page at a time.) For another thing, you don't add a tab sheet to a page control at runtime in the normal way. As we'll see in Chapter 6, normally you'd create a control at runtime with code like

```
NewSheet := TTabSheet.Create(Form);     // create the control
NewSheet.Parent := DynamicPageControl; // set its Parent
```

but to create a tab sheet you'd actually use

---

4. It takes just as many CPU cycles to extract an image from a list with a few images as from a list with a lot of images, and multiple image lists take longer to load and consume more system resources than a single image list. While you may need multiple image lists for a few controls that have multiple image lists properties (like the TPageControl's Images and HotImages) but only one ImageIndex property, you should otherwise consolidate all your 16x16 images into one list, all your 32x32 images into another, and so on.

    This has the side benefit of making it easier to hand off your clip-art to a Real Artist for touch-up or replacement.

```
NewSheet := TTabSheet.Create(Form);           // create the control
NewSheet.PageControl := DynamicPageControl;   // set its PageControl,
                                              // not its Parent
```

At run-time, you can change the active tab by setting the PageControl's
ActivePage property. It's a good idea to do this every time the form is loaded but
before it's visible—*ie*, in an OnCreate or OnShow event handler—so that the
form doesn't come up with the last page you were working on selected. You can
also change the TabOrder by setting the tab sheet's PageIndex property.

Frames

Frames are a sort of light-weight component, a form that you can place on
another form, either at design-time or at run-time. Frames are a good
solution to a number of common problems:

1. You are building wizards to walk users through the creation of an
   object. You also want to give your users tabbed property sheets, so
   that they have random access to the object's properties and don't
   have to go through each step of the wizard to change a single property. The only real difference between a wizard and a property sheet
   is that a wizard walks the user from one page to the next (and will
   only allow them to move on when each page contains valid data)
   while a property sheet allows the user to access pages in any order
   they like. That is, the tabs of a property sheet contain the exact
   same view of a part of the object as the pages of a wizard. If you can
   use the same code for wizard pages as for property sheet tabs, there
   is no possibility of the two getting out of synch.

2. You have objects that can appear in more than one context. For
   example, a Person may be an Employee and an Employee's Supervisor. If you can use the same code to display the supervisor record as
   to display the employee record, you can save code and, again, eliminate the possibility of the two getting out of synch.

3. You are part of a team developing a large and complicated tabbed
   dialog. Because it is so big, the team has decided to put several people to work on the same dialog, with each person working on one or
   more of the tabs. Rather than always merging changes into a single
   humongous unit, you would like each tab to 'live' in its own unit.
   This will keep you from stepping on each others' toes, and it will
   also keep the code clearer and more focused.

object hierarchy, and you need a form that lets your

/or change any member of the hierarchy. Some things

all members of the hierarchy; other actions are only

me members of the hierarchy. You would like to have

ith the controls appropriate to the common actions.

vill add the specialized controls appropriate to each

change them as you change objects.

by typing File ➤ New Frame, or by bringing up

cking on the New Items button (see Figure 5-11),

nd selecting Frame (see Figure 5-12). This will

form designer, looking much like a blank form

show the grid dots. You can place anything on a frame

you can place on a form, and of course the frame can have any event

handlers it needs. Because a frame is itself an object, just as components and

forms are, you can add any `public` methods that you might need to populate

the frame with data or to control its behavior and/or appearance.

Figure 5-11. The New Item button

Once you've created a frame, you have a few options as to how you can
use it.

- The simplest way is to just click on the Frames component icon, which is
  the first icon on the Standard tab of the Component Palette. This will
  stay down in the normal way; when you click on a form, you will get a
  dialog box showing all the frames available in the current project. This
  is generally the best approach for frames that are only being used in a
  single project.

- You can add the frame to the Component Palette by right-clicking on
  the frame and selecting Add To Palette. This will bring up a little dialog
  that will let you specify where the frame will appear. When you click
  OK, the frame will appear on the palette, ready to be added to a form
  just like any other component.

- You can add the frame to the Object Repository by right-clicking on
  the frame and selecting Add To Repository. This will also bring up a
  little dialog, which will let you specify where and how the frame will

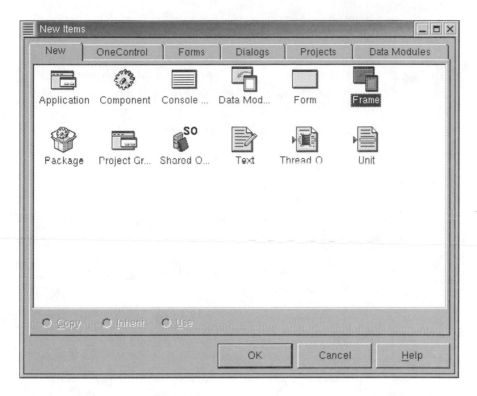

Figure 5-12. The New Items dialog

appear. When you click OK, the frame will be added to the appropriate tab of the Object Repository, ready to be copied or used as the starting point for a more complex frame when you type File ➤ New ... or click on the New Items button.

Regardless of the method you use to add a frame to a form, once you have done so, it will appear on your form as a sort of compound component. You can click on the background to set properties of the frame as for other containers—Color, Anchors, Align and the like—and you can select individual components on the frame to change their properties, including event handlers. Note that you **cannot** add or subtract components to a frame that's been placed on a form. Conversely, changing the frame itself will affect all instances of it. That is, if you create a frame, place it on a form or two, then go back and add a component to the frame, the new component will appear in all instances of that frame.

Because frames are objects just like any other component, adding a frame to a project adds a single new field to your form object. This means that a control on the frame named Jack won't conflict with a control on the form named Jack. It also means that you have to write code like `FrameName.ControlName` to refer to controls on a frame. This can make for long, hard-to-read code that—as *per* Section 1—is a **bit** slower than references to controls placed directly on the form. Use `with`—or follow good Object Oriented practice and never touch frame internals from outside the frame except through the frame's public methods.

By now, it may be obvious how frames can be applied to the four scenarios at the start of this section:

1. Your wizards and your property sheets would simply use the same frames. The frames might all descend (see Form Inheritance, below) from an ancestral frame that declares a public, virtual, validation function for the wizard to use to enable and disable the Next button.

2. If the frame 'knows how' to load data and save any changes, you can use it in as many places as you like.

3. You can just create the tabbed dialog and drop one frame on each page on it. The dialog unit will be very small, with perhaps only some OnChanging event handlers, but will always be up-to-date as the frames evolve. Again, you will probably want each tab frame to descend from a common ancestor, so that each has a standard suite of public methods.

4. Your object editing form would have a panel that you can place the appropriate frame on at runtime. You will probably want to have the object itself tell you which frame to use to edit it. The function would return a `class of TFrame` variable (again, you'd probably use a specialized descendant of TFrame that knows how to do what the editor wants) that you'd use to Create an instance of the frame, then set the parent to the panel:

```
with CurrentObject.EditingFrame.Create(Self) do
begin
  Parent := EditingFrame; // Set parent as for any other
  Align  := alClient;     // manually created control
end;
```

> **Tip**
>
> *For a somewhat dated but more in-depth look at the uses for frames that I've mentioned in this section, you might want to read my 1996 book chapter "Models, Views, and Frames" at* www.midnightbeach.com/jon/pubs/ModelsViewsAndFrames.html. *In particular, that chapter includes a wizard / property page framework that can easily be adapted to use frames. (The chapter was written before frames were added to Delphi: The "Frames" in the title actually refers to a container that you can drop a form (or "View") into.)*

Dynamic regions

I've mentioned a couple of times now that a control is not Visible or Enabled when its Parent is not Visible or Enabled. You can use this to hide or disable groups of controls *en masse.* You might want to do this because, for example, the "Blues Jr" guitar amp comes in black and blond and can be bought with or without a bundled foot switch, while the "BFX25" guitar amp only comes in black, and has no optional packages. You'd want to hide or disable controls that don't have any meaning for the current selection. See the Dynamic project in the ch5/Containers project group for an example.

The Dynamic project in the ch5/Containers project group has routines like

```
procedure TDynamicRegionsFrm.DisableAsAppropriate;
begin
  DisableTab_OptionsPnl.Enabled :=
    DisableTab_Products.ItemIndex = 0;
end; // TDynamicRegionsFrm.DisableAsAppropriate
```

and

```
procedure TDynamicRegionsFrm.HideAsAppropriate;
begin
  HideTab_OptionsPnl.Visible :=
    HideTab_Products.ItemIndex = 0;
end; // TDynamicRegionsFrm.HideAsAppropriate
```

While real projects would obviously need much more sophisticated tests, I'd like to point out that both are using **boolean expressions**. You can use a boolean expression anywhere you can use a boolean constant or a boolean variable. Code like `Visible := State = Desired;` is smaller, clearer, and faster than code like

```
if State = Desired
  then Visible := True
  else Visible := False;
```

which is common in the Object Pascal code of people with significant experience in other languages.

Whether it's better to hide or disable controls that are currently inappropriate is partly a matter of taste, and partly a function of the problem space. If the controls change state often, having them come and go is flashy and distracting; toggling the Enabled property is probably better. However, if the controls are usually inappropriate, and only occasionally would be Enabled, then it's probably better to simply hide them whenever they're not appropriate.

BringToFront

Hiding and disabling controls works fine when you have a binary situation: a control (or group of controls) is either appropriate or not. In more complex, multi-state situations (as on the BringToFront tab of the Dynamic project in the ch5/Containers project group, which adds a new product, the "XB-100" bass guitar,[5] which comes in four different colors) you might need to select from several groups of controls.

One way to do this is to place each group on a panel, which are all the same size and all placed at the same position on the form (see Figures 5-13 through 5-15). You can switch between them at design time by typing Edit ➤ Bring to Front and Edit ➤ Send to Back (or the equivalent choices from the right-click context menu's Control submenu).

When you need to make one visible at run-time, you call its BringToFront method:

---

5. In case you're wondering: yes, I have a Washburn® XB-100 bass guitar in natural mahogany. At the time I was writing this, I was worried about damaging my SO's Fender® Blues Jr guitar amp by playing my bass through it, so I was looking at bass amps. The Crate® BFX25 looked good, on paper, but I ended up with a cheaper, simpler Ibanez® "Sound Wave 25".

```
procedure TDynamicRegionsFrm.BringToFrontAsAppropriate;
begin
  case btfTab_Products.ItemIndex of
    0:  btfTab_OptionsPnl.BringToFront;
    2:  btfTab_ColorsPnl.BringToFront;
    else btfTab_BlankPnl.BringToFront;
    end;
end; // TDynamicRegionsFrm.BringToFrontAsAppropriate
```

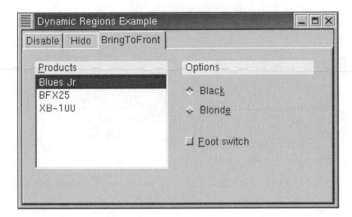

Figure 5-13. The options panel in front

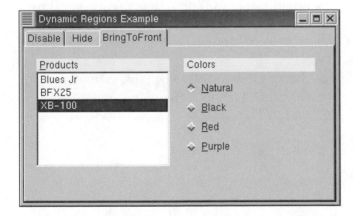

Figure 5-14. The colors panel in front

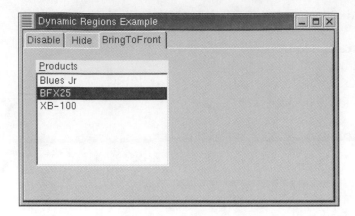

Figure 5-15. The blank panel in front

You could, of course, get a similar effect by hiding (`Visible := False`) the current panel and showing the right one. However, using BringToFront is simpler and smaller, and as a single operation is likely to be faster than a pair of operations.

ActivePage

This 'stacked panels' approach works, but it's a bit messy. You have to play complicated games with multi-selecting the panels and using the Object Inspector to copy one panel's position to the other panels, and you have to fiddle about with Edit ➤ Bring to Front and Edit ➤ Send to Back every time you need to change any of the panels. The ActivePage project in the ch5/ Containers project group takes a simpler approach that uses a PageControl with TabVisible set to False.

The code is virtually identical. Instead of calling BringToFront, the BringToFrontAsAppropriate method sets the PageControl's ActivePage property.

```
procedure TDynamicRegionsFrm.BringToFrontAsAppropriate;
begin
  case apTab_Products.ItemIndex of
    0:    DynamicPages.ActivePage := btfOptionsPage;
    2:    DynamicPages.ActivePage := btfColorsPage;
    else DynamicPages.ActivePage := btfClearPage
    end;
end; // TDynamicRegionsFrm.BringToFrontAsAppropriate
```

Setting ActivePage does a bit more than just bring the active page to the front but if you step into the code with CTRL+CLICK &c, you'll find that TPageControl.ChangeActivePage does do a Page.BringToFront.

> **Note**
>
>
>
> *Using a PageControl is easier, here, but the BringToFront technique is more fundamental. Using stacked controls and BringToFront is especially appropriate in any situation where you create the stacked controls at run-time, as the design-time messiness isn't a factor, and it's particularly easy to be sure that all the stacked controls have the same size and location.*

Menus, action lists, and tool bars

All of the sample projects so far in this chapter have been pretty simplistic. They've been intended to demonstrate one or two points, and so it hasn't mattered if there's been no user interface to speak of. Of course, your real apps need menus and tool bars and all the other paraphernalia of a modern app—and, of course, Kylix makes it easy to look good.

Menus

To add a menu to a form, just select the MainMenu component from the Standard tab and drop it on your form. The form's Menu property will automatically 'point' to the menu you've just dropped down, and will draw a blank menu at the top. The menu component[6] itself has a few properties worth noting:

- AutoHotKeys defaults to maAutomatic. In this state, you don't need to declare keyboard short-cuts for your menu entries—Kylix will do this automatically. This can be very convenient—and is a real timesaver when you're working with dynamic menus, whose entries come and go. If you set AutoHotKeys to maManual, you have to set shortcut keys by putting an & in the Caption of each menu item, as with labels.

---

6. All controls are components, but some components are not controls. Visual components are generally referred to as "controls", while non-visual components are usually referred to as the more generic "components".

- The menu can have a Bitmap, as with most Qt controls. This Bitmap is used both for the menu bar and for the menus as they popup. Using a bitmap that complements the form's is a good way to distinguish the menu bar from the rest of the form, and to make your menus easy to read.

- The menu's Images property 'points' to an ImageList; each menu item that has an ImageIndex that's not equal to –1 will have an image from the list to its left. As with tab sheets, menu items will automatically adjust to the image size.

- The Items property represents the top-level menu, the menu items that appear in the menu bar at the top of the form. To edit the menu, select Items and click on the … button—or double-click the menu component. This will bring up the menu editor.

The menu editor itself (see Figure 5-16) is pretty self-explanatory. To add a new item below an existing one, just click on the blank menu item and fill it in. To create a divider—a horizontal line that groups a menu into sections—set the Caption to ' - '. To move a menu item up or down, or from one dropdown to another, just drag it to where you want it. To create a submenu, press CTRL+RIGHT, or select Create Submenu from the right-click Context Menu.

Figure 5-16. The menu editor

You can, of course, select a menu property and press F1 to read about it. Accordingly, I won't talk about properties like Checked, RadioButton, and GroupIndex, except to strongly urge you to give each menu item a descriptive Name if you plan to write any code that toggles their Checked, Enabled, or Visible properties. (I also strongly urge you to read the section on *Action Lists*, below, before you do any such thing! Action lists allow you to update all the many ways a user might trigger an action by changing a single action component.)

Menu items have an OnClick event handler. The menu items in the Menus project in the ch5/Actions project group, which illustrates many of the things I've talked about in this section, all have OnClick event handlers, but you really should only set these for very trivial applications. Real applications should use action lists, and the menu item's Action property.

Finally, menu items have a Shortcut property that allows you to assign a keyboard shortcut to a menu. The shortcut is displayed on the menu, to the right of the Caption, and thus painlessly trains those of your users who are inclined to use such things. Note that you can select one of many common shortcuts from the dropdown list, but you can also just type in a shortcut. The list is long and tedious to page through, and it doesn't include common shortcuts like SHIFT+CTRL+*Letter*. Obviously, you should make some effort to be sensible in your shortcut selections: SHIFT+CTRL+Y should be an action related to, but perhaps 'stronger' or less common, than CTRL+Y. If there's no connection between the two, your users will find it harder to learn your shortcuts.

Context menus

Your applications can have right-click context menus. To create one, just select a PopupMenu from the Standard tab and drop it on your form. Unlike a MainMenu, your form will not automatically use a PopupMenu. You have to manually set the PopupMenu property of each component that should display a given menu when the user right-clicks.

Note that you can have more than one PopupMenu on a form, and that different components can 'point to' different PopupMenus. That's why they're called "context menus"—the menu you get depends on the context you're in.

You can, of course, change the menu contents at runtime—this is covered in Chapter 6.

Action lists

The Perl Slogan *There's more than one way to do it* applies to user interfaces, too—or, it should. Some people never use anything but menus; others want everything on a configurable tool bar; others learn every keyboard shortcut, and almost never touch the mouse. (The majority, of course, are probably somewhere in the middle.) Good programs cater to all these styles, and this poses the pair of issues that action lists are designed to solve. First, as soon as you have multiple ways of invoking the same action, it's possible for them to be out of synch. The bitmaps on the buttons and the menus may differ; the hints may differ; the default Checked state may differ; and so on. Second, actions have various states that can change. They may be available (Enabled) or not; they may represent options that are on or off; and so on. When you have multiple ways of invoking actions or setting options, you have multiple controls that need updating. This bloats your code—and provides an excellent opportunity to make mistakes.

Action lists provide a single, centralized place to declare everything about a user action—from the event handler to the bitmap, keyboard shortcut, menu Caption, hints, and initial state. Instead of manually replicating this information on menu entries and various buttons, you simply set the menu and button's Action property to an action list entry—and the action information is filled in automatically and changed, too, as you update the action, both at design-time and at run-time. If you disable an action, all the controls that are linked to it are disabled; if you set the action's Checked property to True, all its linked controls are checked or drawn as 'stay down'.

You create an action list by selecting the ActionList icon from the Standard tab of the component palette and dropping it on a form. Set its Images property, then double-click the component icon on your form to open up the action list editor. The editor allows you to group your actions into categories. These are purely a design-time convenience, and they have no run-time effect at all.

Actions have three events: OnExecute, OnHint, and OnUpdate. OnExecute, obviously, is the analog of a menu's or button's OnClick. OnHint gives you the opportunity to modify the hint just before it's displayed—perhaps to reflect the application's current state.

Note

 Controls linked to an action will be disabled unless the action has an OnExecute handler, no matter what you set their Enabled property to.

OnUpdate gives you a chance to centralize your state updating code. That is, *this* action may affect the state of *that* action. If it's the only action that does so, it may make sense to put the code that affects *that* action in *this* action's OnExecute handler. However, *this* action and *that* action may be on different forms, and you may rightly hesitate to write code in one object that reaches into another object and changes it. Or, there may be a lot of things that affect *that* action's state. OnUpdate handlers are called when the application enters the idle state—*ie*, every time it finishes processing a Qt event, and has no more events waiting. An action's OnUpdate handler can examine any relevant aspects of the system state, and make any changes to its Enabled or Checked (or other) properties that are necessary. In essence you are trading simplicity and reliability for efficiency: Applications that do a lot of OnIdle processing can be sluggish.

Tool Bars

You can add configurable toolbars, much like the ones in Microsoft Office or the one in Kylix itself, to your apps. Select the ControlBar from the Additional tab of the component palette and drop it on a form. You'll probably want to top-align it. Then, select the ToolBar from the Common Controls tab of the component palette, and drop one or more onto the control bar. You can drop just about any control onto a toolbar, but most of the time you will use ToolButtons, which you create by right-clicking on the toolbar and selecting New Button. Set the toolbar's Images property and the toolbutton's Action property, play around with the Bevel properties, and the button's ready to go.

At run-time, the user can drag the toolbars around on the ControlBar. This will be strictly a one-time change—which won't make you look good—unless you save and restore any position changes yourself. The ToolBar project in the ch5/Actions project group (see Figure 5-17) has some generic code that you can use for this. It also shows how to add a ControlBar context menu that lets your users turn toolbars on and off. I've left user-configuration of the toolbar contents as An Exercise For The Reader.

Figure 5-17. The ToolBar project

If you set the controlbar's AutoSize property to True, users will be able to resize the controlbar by dragging toolbars below the current bottom row. If your form handles resizing gracefully, the whole effect is very slick and professional. ToolButtons are sized by default for 16x16 images, but they can easily handle larger images; set the toolbar's AutoSize property to True, or manually resize it. If you use big buttons and leave the ControlBar's RowSnap property True, be sure to set the RowSize to match the toolbar's Height.

Menus on tool bars

It doesn't look all that good to have both a menu bar and a top-aligned control bar. Applications that have control bars usually put their main menu onto a toolbar. This looks better, and can save space; the menu and a few toolbars can fit in the same space the menu bar alone would have taken up.[7] Kylix doesn't really have direct support for putting the main menu onto a toolbar—but it's 95% there, and you don't have to add much glue to get it to work as it should.

To start, build your menu as a series of popup menus, one for every top-level menu entry, instead of as a single main menu. Set a menu bar's ShowCaptions property to True (otherwise, the tool buttons on it will be blank) and create a tool button for every top-level menu entry. Set the button's Caption appropriately (you'll have to set the shortcut key explicitly with & because toolbars don't have an AutoHotKeys property) and attach the popup menus to the tool button's DropDownMenu property.

If you try to run your app now, you'll find that clicking on the menu buttons doesn't work. If you set a button's Style to tbsDropDown, you'll get a button that looks like the Open or Run buttons—there will be a vertical line and a down pointing arrow to the right of the glyph or Caption. At run-time, clicking on the down pointing arrow will dropdown your menu, but this isn't what you want. Set the button's style back to tbsButton and give it (and all the other menu buttons) an event handler that drops down the menu when the button is clicked (see Figure 5-18), like this one from the Toolbar project in the ch5/Actions group.

---

7. **You** may be very happy with your 1600x1200 flat panel display—but don't forget that some of your users will still be using old laptops or 14" monitors that can't go beyond 800x600.

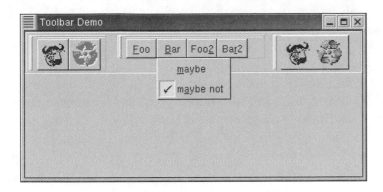

Figure 5-18. A menu on a toolbar

```
procedure TToolbarDemoFrm.MenuBtnClick(Sender: TObject);
begin
  Assert(Sender is TToolButton);
  Assert(Assigned(TToolButton(Sender).DropDownMenu));

  with TToolButton(Sender) do
    with Parent.ClientToScreen(Point(Left, Top + Height)) do
      DropDownMenu.Popup(X, Y);
end; // TToolbarDemoFrm.MenuBtnClick
```

Note

Remember, you only need one copy of this method. All your menu buttons can share the same event handler.

The routine starts with a couple of assertions. The first Assert() simply makes sure that this event handler has been attached to a TToolButton. Remember, a large majority of all event handlers share the same TNotifyEvent (`procedure` (Sender: TObject) `of object`), and it's easy to select the wrong handler from the dropdown list. It's best to **always** be sure that the Sender is who you think it is; certainly, you should do so before doing a blind cast. The second Assert() will abort the event handler with an error message if the tool button doesn't have a DropDownMenu property. It seems appropriate to use an Assert() here—as opposed to an exit on not assigned statement—because this handler should only be attached to a menu button, and a menu button without a menu is an error, not something to be gracefully ignored.

The TPopupMenu.Popup procedure needs an X and Y location for its top-left corner—in *screen coordinates*, where (0, 0) is the top-left corner of the desktop work area. The menus should popup left aligned with and flush under the button, or (Left, Top + Height)—but a tool button's coordinates are relative to its tool bar. These are called *client coordinates*, and all controls have a method, ClientToScreen, that converts a TPoint in their client coordinates and returns a TPoint with those coordinates converted to screen coordinates.

Note

Controls also have a ScreenToClient method that converts screen coordinates to child coordinates. To convert a point from this *control's client coordinates to* that *control's client coordinates, you write That.ScreenToClient(This.ClientToScreen(Point)). The common special case of converting to and from Parent coordinates is also supported via the ClientToParent and ParentToClient methods.*

Is it clear why I call Parent.ClientToScreen() and not ClientToScreen()? Inside the `with`, the 'raw' ClientToScreen is the tool button's ClientToScreen. A control is always at (0, 0) in its own client coordinates; its Top and Left are always expressed in terms of its Parent's client coordinates. Accordingly, we popup the dropdown at `Parent.ClientToScreen(Point(Left, Top + Height))`. Using the wrong coordinate system is a common source of errors!

Finally, you can, of course, assign ClientToScreen's TPoint result to a variable, and then use the two fields individually. However, it's quite common to only need each field of the TPoint result once, as where we pass them right on to Popup() as X and Y parameters. The `with ClientToScreen()` idiom is awfully useful, here, as with most functions that return a record.

Form inheritance

Kylix forms are objects. Objects can descend from other objects. Kylix forms can descend from other Kylix forms. Simple, yes? Powerful, yes?

Form inheritance lets you do a number of things. You can have all your application's forms descend from a root form that supplies some standard functions, like saving each form's size and position to a configuration file, as in the ToolBar project in the ch5/Actions group. You could give your application a distinctive look, a recognizable brand, by having all forms descend from a form with a logo on the side. You may have two or more forms that have some features in common. Basing these on an ancestor that has all the common features makes it a lot easier to have those features look and act consistently.

Further, since frames can inherit from other frames, you can have something like multiple inheritance for forms. The forms themselves can inherit from other forms, and/or can include frames that inherit from other frames.

The Inheritance project in the ch5/Inheritance group illustrates a few of these concepts. It consists of a base form that the main form inherits from, a base frame, and a derived frame that inherits from the base frame and makes a couple of changes (see Figure 5-19). The main form moves inherited elements around and adds elements to the base form—some labels, and an instance of the base frame and the derived frame—and yet it is still linked to its ancestor form. If you change the Caption of a label on the base form or the base frame, that change will be reflected on the main, derived form.

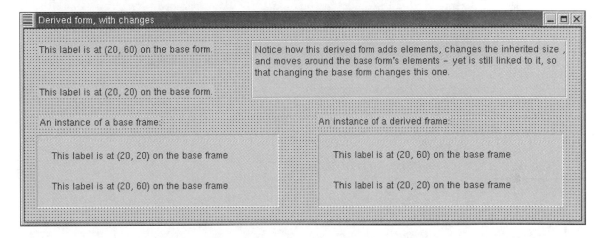

Figure 5-19. A derived form, with frames

It's easy to create a new form or frame that inherits from another form or frame in the current project. When you click on the New Item button, or type File ➤ New …, the second tab will have the current project's name on it (see Figure 5-20). It will show every form and frame in the current project. If you select one, you will get a new form or frame identical in just about every respect to the ancestor. If you were to click on the MainFrm, you would get a new form that looked exactly like the current MainFrm, except that the Caption would be MainFrm1. The TMainFrm1 form object might look a bit strange:

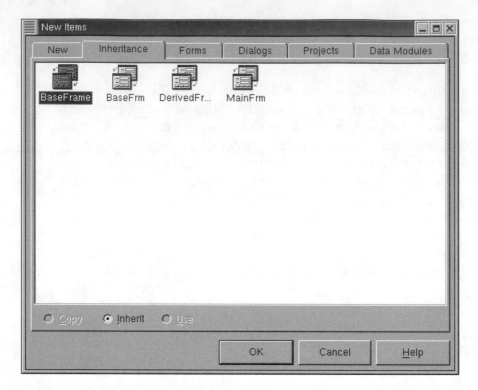

Figure 5-20. The Inheritance tab

```
type
  TMainFrm1 = class(TMainFrm)
  private
    { Private declarations }
  public
    { Public declarations }
  end;
```

class(TMainFrm) instead of class(TForm) is the first surprise—but, of course, that's just normal Object Pascal class inheritance syntax. The bigger surprise may be that the object is empty. Where are the declarations of all the controls that you can see on the form? Again, this is just normal Object Pascal class inheritance: TMainFrm1 inherits all its controls from TMainFrm. In other words, while this class declaration may look surprising at first, it's really exactly what you'd expect if form inheritance worked just like any other sort of object inheritance.

In fact, about all that's new is the xfm file. If you do ALT+F12, the first line usually looks like

```
object BaseFrm: TBaseFrm
```

However, if you do ALT+F12 on the MainFrm, the first line will read

```
inherited MainFrm: TMainFrm
```

That one keyword difference is enough to tell the runtime form loader to go load the base form, first, and then apply any changes and additions. Similarly, if you move or otherwise change properties of an inherited component, they will appear as `inherited` rather than `object`, and the properties shown will only be those changed from the parent object—just as normal xfm's only show non-default properties.

Note

Kylix will not let you do ALT+F12 on any form with open derived forms. Just close the derived form(s) and their source code window(s). You don't have to remove them from the project or anything similarly radical.

Remember, derived forms have access to any methods or members added to their parent form's `public` or `protected` sections, just like any other derived object.

Changing a form's ancestry

Tinkering with your object hierarchy is routine in object-oriented development. You realize that *this* class needs the functionality that *that* sibling has, and decide to push that functionality up to a new common ancestor. Or you realize that Adrian 'is' really a Girl, not a Boy. This sort of change is easy: Just change the `class()` declaration.

Changing a TForm so that it derives from, say, TAppRootFrm is almost as easy. Just change `class(TForm)` to `class(TAppRootFrm)`, then type ALT+F12 and change `object Form1: TForm1` to `inherited Form1: TForm1`. If you don't change the xfm, your form will inherit any code you added to the parent form, but none of the visuals.

Changing the form that a form descends from is similarly straightforward: Just change the `class()` declaration. (Be sure, of course, that the new form's unit appears in the new descendant's form `uses` clause.) The form designer won't be updated until you do ALT+F12 twice, or close the form and reopen it—but you'll see the changes if you press F9 to run the program.

Object Repository

The New Items dialog has four tabs after the New tab and the current project tab: Forms, Dialogs, Projects, and Data Modules. These are known as the Object Repository, and Kylix ships with a few standard entries on each tab. You can use these as starting points for your applications, but the more interesting use of the Object Repository is to build up a library of generic code within your development team.

For example, the Persistent unit in the ToolBar project in the ch5/Actions group is something that would be useful in any project that wants to open its forms where they were when they were last closed, or that maintains any other sort of per-user state information. Forms that inherit from TRootForm automatically save and load their size and position, as well as the state of any toolbars. The Configuration object can easily be extended to save any other information you want, in the same ~/.AppName.ini file that the form states are stored in. (See the vfind projects in Chapter 13 for an example.)

When you start a new project, you could just seek out a copy of the Persistent unit in some other project, copy it into the new project, and strip out the old project's persistent data. But that's tedious and, besides, these generic frameworks have a way of evolving over time. For example, my first versions of the Persistent unit didn't use POSIX regular expressions to decode integer streams saved with `Format('%d %d %d %d', [Left, Top, Right, Bottom])`, didn't handle toolbars, and had the Configuration variable in a separate unit from the TRootFrm. If you just use old projects as templates, you might find that the first few you open up are actually old versions, without the latest functionality.

However, if you always put the latest and greatest copy of the unit into the Object Repository, you can simply copy it into a new project, without having to strip out anything from the old project.

Adding to the Object Repository

To add a form to the Object Repository, just right-click on the form designer and select "Add to Repository …". You'll get a dialog that lets you specify how the new item should appear. You can add the form to an existing page or you can create a new page.

Note

By default, anything added to the Object Repository is only visible to the user who added it. See the INSTALL file in the directory you installed Kylix into for instructions on how to share the Object Repository between developers. Be sure to set the Shared Repository directory in Environment Options to point to the shared directory.

Note that adding to the Object Repository doesn't copy what you added to the Object Repository directory. It stays right where it was; all that adding it to the Object Repository does is to create a database entry that puts it on the New Items dialog. If you change the object after you placed it in the Object Repository, you change the object that's 'in' the Object Repository. This will affect any other projects that "use" or "inherit" the object you changed.

Using what's in the Object Repository

To use an object (like a form) that you've placed in the Object Repository, bring up the New Items dialog and select an object. You'll notice that the Copy / Inherit / Use radio buttons change as you move from tab to tab. On the New tab, they're all disabled. On the current project tab, only Inherit is enabled. On the Projects tab, only Copy is enabled, while on the Forms, Dialogs, and Data Modules tabs you can choose from Copy, Inherit, or Use.

- You would Copy a form and unit like the TRootForm and its Persistent unit. This will copy the contents of the unit into your new project, for you to add new fields to the TConfig template. Within your application, you would then derive forms from the copy of TRootForm that will now appear on the current project tab. If you change the template, your copy will not be affected.

- You would Inherit a form if you wanted your new item to be linked to the original in another project. Changing the original would change your derived form, just as if you'd inherited from a form in the current project. Your new unit would not include copies of any code in the template (like Persistent's TConfig) but would instead list the template in its uses clause, so that the new unit could refer to anything in the template's interface, like Persistent's Configuration.

- You would Use a form if you wanted to add the form from another project to the current project. (This is exactly analogous to selecting Add … from the Project Manager's context menu.) Changing the form in either project will affect both projects.

Editing tools

The Borland manuals and the online help document Kylix's code editor, of course, but there are a few particularly useful features that can be hard to discover. This section is a flying tour through these obscure gems.

Editor commands

When we're young and inexperienced, it's easy to pick up a new editor. But after a while, those keystrokes are encoded in your synaptic patterns, and it's not so easy to change. Accordingly, Kylix lets you select key bindings that mimic several popular editors.

The following tables apply to the "default" key bindings, which are basically a large superset of the standard Windows Notepad keys: move the cursor with the shift key held down to select; CTRL+C or CTRL+INS to copy; CTRL+X or SHIFT+DEL to cut; CTRL+V or SHIFT+INS to paste; and so on.

Table 5-1. Mark and cut word or line

Keystrokes	Action
CTRL+T	Delete to end of word. Like Word's Ctrl+Del.
CTRL+KT	Mark current word. Like double-clicking on the word.
CTRL+Y	Delete line.
SHIFT+CTRL+Y	Delete to end of line.

Table 5-2. Block operations

Keystrokes	Action
SHIFT+CTRL+I	Indents marked block—*ie*, shifts it to the right. You can set the number of characters in Environment Options
SHIFT+CTRL+U	Unindents marked block—*ie*, shifts it to the left.
CTRL+OU	Toggle case. *Eg*, change 'This to 'tHIS'.
CTRL+KE	Change to lower-case.
CTRL+KF	Change to upper-case.

Table 5-3. Bookmarks and macro

Keystrokes	Action
SHIFT+CTRL+<N>	Creates one of ten bookmarks - <N> is any of the keys from 1 to 0. Bookmarks are shown in the gutter to the left of the program text. Bookmarks are **not** saved with the file.
CTRL+<N>	Jump to bookmark N. Bookmarks are *per* file, not *per* tabbed edit window. That is, you can have up to 10 bookmarks in each file you have open, and jumping to one will never move you to another file.
SHIFT+CTRL+R	Record macro. Records all keystrokes until next Shift+Ctrl+R. There's only one macro at a time, which can be used in any edit window. Not saved.
SHIFT+CTRL+P	Playback macro. You can use macros to do all sorts of things, like make tables of constants line up neatly, convert a series of C #define's to Pascal, and so on.

Table 5-4. Miscellaneous editor commands

Keystrokes	Action
CTRL+UP	Scroll up one line.
CTRL+DOWN	Scroll down one line.
CTRL+Q[	If the carat is on a paired delimiter (*ie*, parens (), square braces [], or curly brackets {}), finds the matching delimiter. Documented as looking forward, but actually looks either way to find matching delimiter. Useful in nested procedure calls, or complex array expressions.
CTRL+Q]	Same as Ctrl+Q[, actually.
SHIFT+CTRL+G	Generates a new GUID and inserts it at the caret— useful for Interface type declarations.

Code Insight

Code Insight™ is Borland's generic term for all the various tools they've built into the editor to make it easier to write code and to keep track of where you are in a large project.

Code parameters

Code parameters, or parameter hinting, is a truly wonderful feature. Whenever the caret is on a subroutine parameter, you get a little yellow tool-tip box that shows you the names and types of all the routine's parameters. The current parameter is highlighted in bold type, which changes as you move the caret. This even works for overloaded and Libc (Linux API) calls.

Normally, the tool-tip comes up automatically, after a brief pause. If it doesn't, or if you have it turned off, just press SHIFT+CTRL+SPACE to bring it up. If SHIFT+CTRL+SPACE doesn't seem to work, you almost certainly have a syntax error somewhere in your code.

Symbol insight

Symbol insight is a related feature. When you 'hover' the cursor (ie, the mouse cursor, not the blinking caret that indicates the editor's insertion point) over an identifier, Kylix will popup a tool-top window with declaration information.

> **Note**
>
>
> *Code parameters have changed the way I think about 2-state parameters. Before parameter hinting, I used to avoid using boolean parameters, preferring to declare a new two-element enum. This was "self documenting"—SendDocument (UseStrongCrypto) **is** a lot clearer than SendDocument (True)—but a bit verbose and tedious to code. With Code parameters, you can just put the caret on the ambiguous boolean parameter, and you'd see that it was UseStrongCrypto: boolean. The enum form is still clearer on paper—but code doesn't live on paper, code lives in Kylix.*

Code completion

I find code completion a bit less wonderful than code parameters, but still awfully useful. Pressing CTRL+SPACE will popup a list of all identifiers that you can insert at the current point in the code. Without any context, this can be a **very** long list, but Kylix will winnow it down when it can. On the right-hand side of an assignment operation, or when a parameter is expected, Kylix will show only the values that are syntactically appropriate.

Class completion

I don't think that Borland actually classifies Class Completion as a Code Insight feature, but it's so closely related to Code Completion that it makes sense to talk about it here.

One of the less appealing features of both C++ and Object Pascal is the need to **declare** an object *here* and **implement** it *there*. C++ is a lot more annoying about this than Object Pascal, with its .hpp/.cpp convention as opposed to OP's interface / implementation syntax, but OP's annoying enough. When you add a method to the interface, you have to go and redeclare it, with a slightly different syntax, in the implementation section. If you split some common code into a private method, you have to go back up to the interface section and declare it—again with a slightly different syntax. Understanding the logic of it doesn't make it any less of a pita.

Class completion automates the process. If you press SHIFT+CTRL+C within a class declaration, Kylix will generate empty method bodies for any methods that you've declared but not implemented. Conversely, if you press SHIFT+CTRL+C within the (syntactically correct!) body of a method that's not in the object declaration, Kylix will add a method declaration to the object's `private` section.

Furthermore, class completion can generate a lot of the boiler-plate associated with properties. If a class has a property declaration like

```
property ZOrder: integer read GetZOrder write SetZOrder;
```

and it doesn't have protoypes for the access routines GetZOrder and SetZOrder, SHIFT+CTRL+C will generate both the prototypes

```
private
  function GetZOrder: integer;
  procedure SetZOrder(Value: integer);
```

and the empty method bodies.

Note

Class completion is not perfect—just nearly so. It can be badly confused by syntax errors, or by files with carriage returns.

Templates

Some people really like Kylix's templates, but I have to confess I'm not one of them—I type my code, and only use templates for inserting copyright notices, or for inserting complex HTML tags when I'm using Kylix to edit a web page.

You can define templates on the Code Insight tab of Editor Options dialog, and insert them into your code by pressing CTRL+J and selecting from the list. Typing after the CTRL+J will do an incremental search of the list, so you can often insert a template by typing just CTRL+J, a few letters, and return.

Cross referencing

Kylix offers a rich array of tools to help you make sense of your code. Some of them work always; others require you to compile and link first.

Ctrl+Click

Holding down the CTRL key will turn any identifier into a hyperlink—it will be underlined in blue. CTRL+CLICK will take you to where that identifier is declared, whether in the current project or in library code. Thus, you can CTRL+CLICK on one of your variable names and jump right to its declaration, then CTRL+CLICK on the type name, and jump straight into the CLX source. Similarly, you can jump right from a declaration like TDerived = **class**(TAncestor) to the declaration of the TAncestor class.

Shift+Ctrl+Up, Shift+Ctrl+Down

SHIFT+CTRL+UP and SHIFT+CTRL+DOWN let you quickly toggle back and forth between a method's (or 'bare' routine's) declaration and implementation. (Though they seem to be a pair of complementary commands, like CTRL+Q[and CTRL+Q] they're actually synonyms for a single 'toggle' command.) Pressing SHIFT+CTRL+UP (or SHIFT+CTRL+DOWN) within a routine will take you to the declaration; pressing SHIFT+CTRL+DOWN (or SHIFT+CTRL+UP) within a declaration will take you to the implementation.

Code Explorer

By default, the Code Explorer is docked to the left of the code editor. If you've closed it, or if you've used the Explorer tab of Environment Options to tell Kylix not to always show it, you can bring it back with SHIFT+CTRL+E or View ➤ Code Explorer.

The Code Explorer is an outline view of the contents of the current unit. As you move from file to file in the code editor, the Code Explorer changes with you. If you double-click on an identifier, or select it and press Return, the identifier will scroll into view. Press tab, and the blinking caret will be on the identifier you selected.

Browser

The Browser—View ➤ Browser or SHIFT+CTRL+B—is a clever little dialog that offers a lot of information about what's in your project and where it's used.

I think it's really pretty self-explanatory, so only mention it here to urge you to give it a try.

> **Note**
>
> *The Browser will (among many other things) show you a list of all the units that are explicitly used in your project, and what units they use. What it will **not** do by default is to show you a list off all the units that get linked into your executable—every unit that's used by a unit that you explicitly use. To get it to show you that list, you need to set "Browser Scope" on the Explorer tab of the Tools ➤ Environment Options dialog to "All symbols" (see Figure 5-21). You can also get this information from the .map file—see the Linker tab of the Project ➤ Options (SHIFT+CTRL+F11) dialog.*

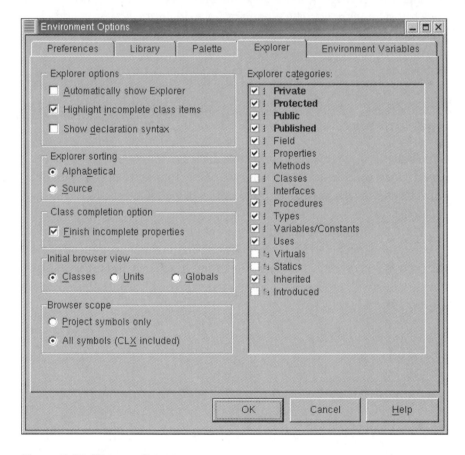

Figure 5-21. Browser Scope

Debugging

Kylix has a wonderfully capable source-code debugger. You can single-step; set conditional and unconditional breakpoints; examine variables, registers, and stack frames; and generally do anything you've grown used to in any other debugger.

Debugging under Gnome

Kylix is, for the most part, quite admirably desktop-neutral. However, if you are running Gnome, you may encounter a problem with its session manager interface that requires you to debug your applications without a session manager.

What happens is that Gnome applications are responsible for connecting themselves to the session manager. This is done automatically, when the window opens. However, if you set a breakpoint in an OnCreate event handler, you are halting the process between the point where it has connected to the session manager and the point where it is able to respond to messages from the session manager. This will subject you to a steady stream of "No response to the SaveYourself command" windows, which are guaranteed to do wonders for your concentration. Apparently, it's only Gnome that has this problem—other window managers use a different architecture—and Borland unofficially recommends that you work around Gnome's bug by debugging your applications without a session manager.

To do this, select the Environment Block tab of the Run ➤ Parameters dialog (see Figure 5-22). Select SESSION_MANAGER from the System Variables listbox, and click on the Add Override button. Set the Variable Value to anything but what it should be: '<nothing>' is fine, as is an empty string. This will keep your application from connecting to the session manager as you debug it, so that the session manager won't send it any messages that it can't respond to.

> **Note**
>
> *This doesn't seem to have any effect on the app being debugged except to eliminate some annoying Gnome behavior. Nonetheless, you're running it in an unusual situation, so you should only override the SESSION_MANAGER variable when you get the "No response to the SaveYourself command" message. (I have only had this problem when debugging OnCreate handlers, but it's possible that it can be triggered under other circumstances, too.) When you no longer need the override, be sure to Delete it.*

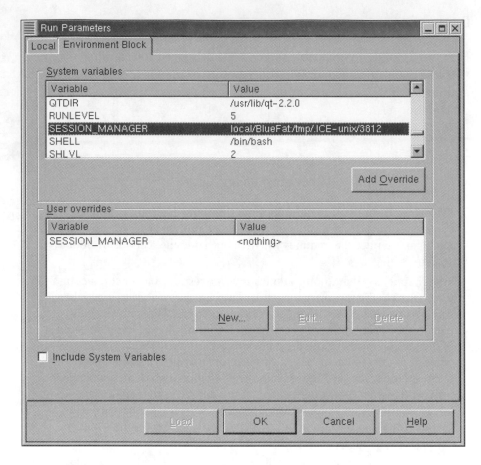

Figure 5-22. The Environment Block tab of the Run Parameters dialog

Be sure you don't set the override in the identical-looking Environment
Variables tab of the Environment Options dialog. This will affect **all** applications you debug, and could have an effect on Kylix itself. Setting the
override in the Run ➤ Parameters dialog ensures that only the app being
debugged is affected.

Breakpoints

The simplest breakpoint is a one-shot, 'run to here' breakpoint. Press F4 on a line of code, and the program will run until it reaches that line.

Note

A Pascal statement commonly spans more than one line, yet you can only set a breakpoint on one of them. Kylix shows you where it 'sees' a 'line of code' by putting little blue dots in the "gutter" to the left of the code. You can only set a breakpoint on a line with a blue dot.

To set a more permanent breakpoint, push F5. This will highlight the line in red; the debugger will stop here every time execution gets to this line. Pressing F5 on a breakpoint will toggle it off.

If you right-click in the gutter next to a line with a breakpoint, you can disable it. This can give you a convenient trail of lines that have been and may continue to be troublesome—but it's most useful for conditional breakpoints. Pressing F5 on a conditional breakpoint discards any conditions you set, but disabling the breakpoint preserves the conditions for future use.

To create a conditional breakpoint, first press F5 to create a breakpoint, then right-click in the gutter next to the breakpoint and select Breakpoint properties. You can set the breakpoint to trigger after a certain number of passes, or when an arbitrary expression is True. (You probably won't be particularly surprised to find that your program runs much more slowly with conditional breakpoints enabled than without any conditional breakpoints enabled.) This lets you skip over all the times the line runs fine, and only stop just before it's about to do the wrong thing.

For particularly hard-to-debug code, you can divide your breakpoints into named groups, and turn the groups on and off *en masse*. The View ➤ Debug Windows ➤ Breakpoints window (CTRL+ALT+B) lets you see and control all the breakpoints in your project.

Single stepping

F7 will single-step by individual code line. If the current line contains a sub-routine call, F7 will take you into that call. The 'granularity' of the step depends on the current window. If you're currently in the code editor, F7 steps by source lines as marked with blue dots in the gutter. If you're currently viewing assembler code (see below). F7 steps by individual instructions.

F8 is similar, but will step over subroutine calls. Use it for a top-level tour of a routine—F7 can involve some incredible detours that will give you new respect for your computer's speed.

Monitoring the program state

'Hovering' the mouse cursor over an identifier while you're debugging will show you its current value, just as you can get declaration info when you're not debugging. This works for local and global variables as well as object fields. The debugger is rather capable, here. You can get most property values even when they involve function calls. Sometimes the debugger can't show you the value and will tell you so—this **usually** means that the value is stored in a register, and it either hasn't been set yet or it has already been reused.

If you need to continuously monitor a value, you can set a Watch on it by pressing CTRL+F5. You have a fair degree of flexibility in how the value is formatted, and you can even watch the results of various expressions, like `Copy(This, 10, 20)`.

As a related alternative, View ➤ Debug Windows ➤ Local Variables (CTRL+ALT+L) will show all local variables in the current routine in a window that can be docked below the code window. This can be much more convenient than setting watches or hovering over an identifier as you step through code.

The other entries on the View ➤ Debug Windows menu are all useful at various times. The call stack shows you exactly how you got where you are. The CPU and FPU windows allow you to examine registers and generated code; to set breakpoints on individual instructions, and to single-step by instructions. (The CPU and FPU windows are disabled when you're not actually debugging.)

Optimization

As you can see by looking at the generated code with the CPU window, Kylix does a remarkably decent job of turning your source code into a stream of CPU instructions. It makes good use of registers, generates optimal code for a lot of language constructs, and eliminates some common subexpressions. There are better code generators—but none that compile as quickly as Kylix does.

There are rare circumstances—usually involving heavy 'register pressure', where your code has a large number of local variables simultaneously active— where optimization generates the wrong code. They are very rare though, and any bugs are almost certainly going to be your fault. If you suspect the compiler, though, try building a project with and without optimization and seeing if it makes any difference. If you do find a routine that acts differently when optimized than when not optimized, you can either try to rewrite it so it works under optimization—which may well improve the clarity and even the performance—or you can simply turn off optimization for that routine *via* the {$O-} pragma.

A much more common reason to turn off optimization is to simplify debugging. With optimization on, you commonly can't view the values of a local variable once you pass the last line where it's used. This is because one of the key optimizations is to store local variables in registers, not on the stack, and once the register has been reassigned, the old value is obviously no longer available. Rebuilding with optimization off—or simply recompiling with a {$O-} pragma before the routine you're trying to debug—can make it much easier to watch local variables.

Trace statements

Probably the oldest and simplest way to debug code is to add special *trace statements* to it. A trace statement is just a bit of debug code that prints out a message like "Got here" or "Foo(True) called at 12:34". This can be a great way to see if things are happening in the order that you expect, as long as you don't add so many trace statements that you're swamped in details.

All Kylix applications, even GUI applications, can write to standard output with a simple WriteLn command. (See Chapter 8 for details.) `WriteLn('Got here')` will write "Got here" to the standard output, as will `WriteLn(Output, 'Got here')`. Similarly, `WriteLn(ErrOutput, 'Got here')` will write to standard error.

Kylix is not Delphi

If you start Kylix from a terminal window by typing the `startkylix &` command, the application's output will go to the window. This may or may not be visible behind the Kylix windows—and if you started Kylix from the system menu, you won't see the application's output at all.

Kylix's "Launcher Application" is a good way to capture your applications' output. Select "Use Launcher Application" from the Run ➤ Parameters dialog, and Kylix will open a terminal window to capture all output.

> **Note**
>
> *It's actually a good idea to use a launcher application even when you don't use trace statements: You really want to know if your application is making Qt or other library code print messages on standard output or standard error!*

Growing with Kylix

I'm going to make a daring prediction: Future versions of Kylix will have lots of features that Kylix 1.0 does not. Some of them will apply to edge conditions that you rarely encounter; others will be primarily for types of programs that you don't normally write; others will be as generally applicable as the addition of Constraints and Anchors in Delphi 4.

So, how do you keep up? How do you avoid turning into a dinosaur, using only what you used years ago? How do you stay on the leading edge, not the bleeding edge?

This is a general problem, of course, and I can only offer some modest, Kylix specific suggestions.

- When a new version comes out, open up old projects. Look for new form properties in the Object Inspector. Click on various components and look for new properties. If you see something novel, read about in the online help. Be sure to check the Methods list of familiar components.

- Look for new components on the Component Palette.

- If you found a particular component cumbersome, be sure to look for changes to it. Others might have had the same experience.

- Pay attention to low-level units like System, SysUtils, and Math. New utilities are regularly added. They may turn code that you wrote as idiomatic sequences into a single call, or they may parallel utilities you wrote. You should make an effort to switch over to the new utilities. They may be more general than yours; they're probably more thoroughly tested; and using them may make for smaller executables, as many of the utility functions get used by library code, and so are being linked in anyway.

- Look for new language features. For example, interfaces and assertions were added in Delphi 3; dynamic arrays were added in Delphi 4; and portable variants with operator overloading were added in Kylix 1. It's generally worthwhile to make an effort to learn how new language features work: they can often make your code smaller, clearer, and more failsafe.

CHAPTER 6
Visual objects

CHAPTER 6

Visual objects

THE BASIC FORM DESIGN SECTION of the previous chapter covered what you need to know about form layout and the design-time behavior of visual controls. It was, however, rather short on code. This chapter is about writing code that deals with controls, forms, and other visual objects.

Controls

Everything that's visible on your applications' windows at run-time is a control. The form's themselves are controls. The buttons, scrollbars, menus, and edit boxes are controls. The control bars and the static text are controls. (See Figure 6-1.)

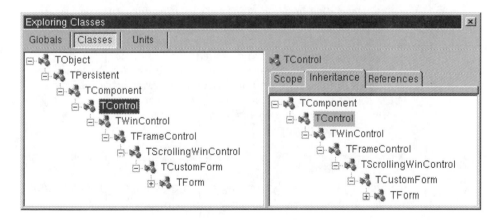

Figure 6-1. Control inheritance

In object terms, every control *is* a component. Every component *is* a persistent object. This means that there are some things that are true of all controls. Obviously, there are also plenty of things that are *not* true of all controls, and these are the details that you'll have to master to work with a particular control, but you'll find it a lot easier to master the specifics once you understand the basics.

Components vs controls

I've said it before: All controls are components, but some components are not controls. All components have the published Name and Tag properties; all components have an Owner. The Name property isn't particularly important at run-time—you're much more likely to refer to a component named Joe by the Pascal identifier Joe, a reference to the object, than by the string 'Joe'—but the Owner is. While you'll very rarely write code that explicitly refers to Owner, you implicitly set the Owner every time you create a component at runtime; the AOwner parameter to the Create() constructor becomes the new component's Owner.

It's important to get the Owner right. When a component is freed, it frees all the components it owns. If you pass the wrong Owner to Create(), your component may be freed when you don't expect it. This in turn can lead to segmentation violations as your application tries to refer to memory that has been released.

Kylix is not Delphi

> **Note**
>
>
>
> *Delphi and Kylix use somewhat different memory management strategies. Delphi uses an internal sub-allocator, which requests relatively large blocks from the operating system, and then splits them into smaller pieces to satisfy requests that are 'too small' to pass on to the OS. This means that dereferencing a 'tombstoned' pointer— one that points to memory that has already been freed–is not guaranteed to cause an exception. Kylix uses an external sub-allocator, that 'lives' in* libc.so.6. *As with Delphi, dereferencing freed memory may or may not raise an exception. See the* Memory *section of Chapter 8 for more information.*

Fortunately, there are really only two common choices for component ownership, so the chances that you will get it wrong are slim.

1. When dynamically creating a component as part of a form, the Owner should be the form itself. Within an event handler or other form method, you'd refer to the form *via* the Self pointer. For example, NewDialog := TOpenDialog.Create(Self);

2. When manually creating a form, as you might do if it is not used regularly, you would typically set Owner to Application. (See the *TApplication* section of Chapter 7.) This assures that the form is destroyed cleanly, allowing it to close files or do any other necessary cleanup, when the application closes.

Unowned components

There is one common special case where you might set Owner to Nil. Many components and forms are created and destroyed within a single procedure. If an Open File dialog is only occasionally needed, you may prefer to create it on the fly, rather than slow form creation and consume extra system resources by dropping it on the form and having it always available.

```
with TOpenDialog.Create(Nil) do
try
  Title  := 'Dynamic!';
  Filter := 'My files (*.my)|All files (*)';
  if Execute then
    {do something with FileName};
finally
  Free;
end;
```

Similarly, if a dialog like an About box is rarely invoked, you might also prefer to create it on the fly, rather than create it at run-time and/or waste system resources by keeping it around after the user closes it.

```
with TAboutBox.Create(Nil) do
try
  ShowModal;
finally
  Release; // Note that we Release a form, not Free it
end;
```

In both these examples, Owner is set to Nil, by passing Nil to Create. This means that the component has no Owner, and will never be automatically freed. This is obviously risky, so you should only do it where the component is freed in a try/finally block that immediately follows the call to Create. Why might you want to write such risky code? It's an optimization: When you Create an owned component, its Owner adds it to a list of components it owns. When you Free an owned component, the Owner removes it from its list of owned components. Creating and freeing an unowned component is a little faster than creating and freeing an owned component.

Note that components are special in being owned; objects that are **not** components are not owned, and must be explicitly freed.[1] Forms that have object fields (bitmaps, semaphores, and so on) typically Create them in their OnCreate event handler and Free them in their OnDestroy event handler. Non-form objects that have object fields typically Create them in a constructor and Free them in a destructor.

Components property

Every component has a Components array property, and a ComponentCount property. At run-time, the ComponentCount contains the number of components this component owns, and the Components array contains a reference to every component this component owns, indexed from 0 to ComponentCount – 1. Obviously, most components' ComponentCount is 0. A form or a frame's Component's array, however, contains references to every component on the form or frame.

You would write code that walks the Components array if you wanted to do something to every instance of a certain type of component on the form, but didn't want to hardcode the list of which components those were into your application. Walking the list may be slower, but it can be smaller and it is certainly safer. For example, suppose you want to change the color of all the TEdit's on a form in response to various state changes.

```
procedure TGarishFrm.Recolor(Color: TColor);
var
  Index: integer;
begin
  for Index := 0 to ComponentCount - 1 do
    if Components[Index] is TEdit then
      TEdit(Components[Index]).Color := Color;
end; // TGarishFrm.Recolor
```

---

1. The general rule is "Free what you Create", but there are a number of exceptions:
    - You don't need to free owned components.
    - You Release forms, you don't Free them.
    - You don't need to free objects that you refer to only *via* interface references.

Parent

Anything you can drop on a form is a component, but anything that you can see at run-time is a control. Controls are components that have a number of new methods and properties, including a bounds rectangle—Top, Left, Height, and Width—and a Parent.

A control's Top and Left are always relative to its Parent, whether this is the form itself or a container nested twelve levels deep. (A form doesn't have a Parent; a form's Top and Left is always relative to the desktop work area, which is the part of the screen not covered with system panels and task bars.) A control is only Visible and Enabled when its Parent is Visible and Enabled; if a container has been obscured by another container being brought to front over it, all the controls on the obscured container are hidden as well.

There is a difference between parentage and ownership. All controls on the form are owned by the form, regardless of their parentage. Only some of the controls that a form owns are its direct children; some are children of container controls whose Parent is the form, and some are children of container controls whose Parent is a container control whose Parent is the form, and so on.

When you create a form in the form designer, Kylix will automatically set the Parent of all the controls you drop on it. When you create them at run-time, the library code gets parentage information from the form resource, and properly sets the Parent of all controls on the form. However, if you create a control at run-time, you have to be sure to set its Parent. If you don't set the control's Parent, it won't be visible.

Tip

Not setting Parent when you create a control dynamically is a common mistake made by people new to Kylix.

When you create a control at run-time, its Top and Left will be set to 0, and it will be created with a default Height and Width. (The default varies from control to control.) You will generally either set Align to alClient, to have the new control fill its container, or you will explicitly set both Top and Left, and perhaps Height and Width.

For example, one common use of dynamically created controls is to drop one of several different possible frames into a container like a panel or a group box. You might need to do this in a property editor for a word processor that allows you to include several different types of objects, like HTML's <ul>, <ol>, <table>, and <script> elements. Each object would be modeled by a different Pascal object, and each Pascal object would be able to tell you what frame to drop into the editing container to edit the object's properties. Thus, you would free any old frame, create the new frame, and set its Parent as

```
FreeAndNil(CurrentFrame); // Safe even if CurrentFrame = Nil
// Using FreeAndNil means that CurrentFrame always holds either a valid value
// or Nil, even if CurrentObject.EditFrame.Create raises an exception.

CurrentFrame := CurrentObject.EditFrame.Create(Self);
// EditFrame returns a "class of TFrame" result

CurrentFrame.Parent  := EditPnl;
CurrentFrame.Visible := True;
// Cheap if already Visible, and necessary if not
```

and you would set the size and position as either

```
CurrentFrame.Align := alClient;
```

or something like

```
CurrentFrame.Top     := Inset; // Some constant
CurrentFrame.Left    := Inset;
CurrentFrame.Height  := EditFrame.ClientHeight - Inset * 2;
CurrentFrame.Width   := EditFrame.ClientWidth  - Inset * 2;
CurrentFrame.Anchors := [akLeft, akRight, akTop, akBottom];
```

Kylix is not Delphi

> **Caution**
>
>
>
> *Delphi programmers may be used to doing something similar to this, except with forms instead of frames. This will not work on Linux, due to differences in the windowing model. You'll have to convert any form-in-form code to use frames.*

Containers

At design-time, there's a strong distinction between containers and other controls. Containers are controls whose constructor adds csAcceptsControls to the ControlStyle set.[2] When you drop a control on a container, the form designer sets the new control's Parent to the container, and sets Top and Left relative to the container. However, if you drop a control on a non-container, you've just created a control that (partially) obscures another control. The non-container doesn't become the new control's Parent.

This distinction is **not** enforced at run-time. If you create a control and set its Parent to a non-container, the new control will appear on top of its new Parent, and will be clipped to it. While this may be what you want in some special cases, it's generally a typo.

There are controls and then there are controls

Just as some components are not visual controls, so some controls are not windowed controls. Where a TWidgetControl (also known as TWinControl, to simplify porting of Delphi code) represents a Qt widget, and is thus a screen window that can have child windows, a TGraphicControl is not. A TGraphicControl exists only as a Kylix object that multiplexes Paint events and translates mouse events into local coordinates. Because a TGraphicControl does not have an underlying screen window, it has no Handle, cannot be the Parent of another control, cannot receive keyboard focus—and it consumes fewer system resources. Speed buttons and bevels are graphic controls.

Most controls, though, are widget controls. Just as every component has a Components property that lists the components it owns, so every widget control has a Controls array and a ControlCount property that lists all its children. At run-time, the ControlCount contains the number of child controls this control has, and the Control array contains a reference to each one, indexed from 0 to ControlCount – 1. Again, most controls' ControlCount is 0: Only forms, frames, and containers like panels have child controls.

---

2. The ControlStyle set controls various aspects of a component's design-time and run-time behavior. You'll never need to pay any real attention to it except when writing components.

Note

Be sure to note the difference between Controls and Components. Every control on a form is in the form's Components array, but only those controls whose Parent is the form itself are in the form's Controls array. Conversely, controls on a container are in the container's Controls array but not in its Components array.

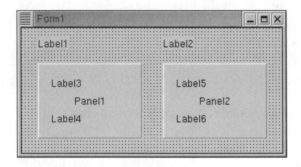

Figure 6-2. Eight components on this form

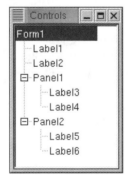

Figure 6-3. The Controls hierarchy

For example, Figure 6-2 shows a small form from the ControlHierarchy project in the ch6/Control project group. This form has two labels placed directly on the form, and two panels, with two more labels each. All eight components are owned by the form, and appear in the form's Components array. However, Panel1 is the Parent of Label3 and Label4, and they appear in Panel1's Controls array. Similarly, Panel2 is the Parent of Label4 and Label5, and they appear in Panel2's Controls array. (See Figure 6-3.)

You would write code that walks a Controls array if you needed to change or examine only the controls in a particular container. For example, this function from lib/QGrabBag.pas (see the RadioButtons project of the ch6/Controls project group for a silly example) returns the Checked radio button on a container control, if any.

```
function CheckedButton(Container: TWidgetControl): TRadioButton;
var
  Index:   integer;
  Control: TControl;
begin
  for Index := 0 to Container.ControlCount - 1 do
  begin
    Control := Container.Controls[Index];
    if Control is TRadioButton then
    begin
      Result := TRadioButton(Control);
      if Result.Checked then EXIT;
    end;
  end;
  Result := Nil; // No Checked radio button on this Container
end; // CheckedButton
```

Mouse events

All controls can respond to mouse events. Usually, of course, you only care about the standard response to mouse events—whether the button was pushed, or the selection changed, and so on—but sometimes you care about where on the control the button was pushed, which button was pushed, whether any shift keys were held down, and so on. For example, you might want to synthesize a shift-click event. Or a graphical editor for music notation, org charts, or circuit diagrams would need to be able to know where on the control the mouse was pressed, so it could translate that to a click on a particular piece of data.

In either case, you would begin by handling the OnMouseDown event for the graphical editor, which might be a TPaintBox. The OnMouseDown events is a

```
TMouseEvent = procedure(Sender: TObject; Button: TMouseButton;
    Shift: TShiftState; X, Y: Integer) of object;
```

You'll get this event on right clicks and middle clicks as well as left clicks, so your first task is to check which Button is generating the event. If it's the button you want, you may or may not care to check the Shift state; some apps distinguish between a shift-click and an unshifted-click, while others don't.

Kylix is not Delphi

> **Note**
>
> *If you do examine the Shift state, be sure to do so defensively: Write tests like* if ssShift in Shift *rather than* if Shift = [ssShift] *or* if Shift = [ssShift, ssLeft]. *While both Qt documentation and the QControls.pas source code suggest that,* eg, *a left SHIFT+CLICK should generate a MouseDown event with* Shift = [ssShift, ssLeft], *what you actually get is just* [ssShift]. *The MouseUp event gets the Shift = [ssShift, ssLeft]. This directly reflects the information in X11 mouse button up and down events; it's just a tad … unfortunate … that it's exactly the opposite of the way Delphi acts. Note, though, that Kylix's mouse events* **do** *act like Delphi's in that they do show "chording". That is, if you hold down the left button and press the right button, the OnMouseDown for the right button press will show* ssLeft in Shift.

To synthesize a left click, you'd just need to check Button and Shift. In the graphical editor example, if the Button and the Shift tell you that this is the event you care about, you also need to check the X and Y parameters to make sure that the user clicked on a piece of data, not on white space. Fortunately, the X and the Y parameters are both in client coordinates of the control receiving the event, so you just have to walk a list of the data you're drawing on the screen, seeing if the click point is in any of its bounding boxes.

Of course, a mouse down is only half of a click. The user also has to release the mouse on the control she pressed it on, or it doesn't count. This poses a problem: Just as your control only gets a mouse down event when the mouse pressed over the control, so it normally only gets a mouse up event when the mouse is released over the control. The solution is "mouse capture", a request for **all** mouse events, until you release the capture.

If you're writing a custom component, you can use the protected MouseCapture property. When you set it to True, the control has mouse capture until you set it False. This option is not available to you when you're writing an event handler, so you have to set Mouse.Capture to the control you want to own the mouse. Whichever approach you take, be sure to free the mouse when you're done!

So, the following two schematic events are what you need to create your own customized click events:

```
procedure TSynthesizer.ControlMouseDown(Sender: TObject; Button: TMouseButton;
  Shift: TShiftState; X, Y: Integer);
begin
  if ThisIsTheRightClick then
    Mouse.Capture := CapturingControl;
end; // TSynthesizer.ControlMouseDown
```

```
procedure TSynthesizer.ControlMouseUp(Sender: TObject; Button: TMouseButton;
  Shift: TShiftState; X, Y: Integer);
begin
  if Mouse.Capture = CapturingControl then
  begin
    Mouse.Capture := Nil;
    if ThisIsTheRightRelease then
      SyntheticClickAction;
  end;
end; // TSynthesizer.ControlMouseUp
```

The ThisIsTheRightRelease test would check that the mouse cursor was in the right rectangle. For a GUI editor, you'd need to check the bounding box of the datum that was clicked on. For the simpler shift-click synthesis, you'd just need to be sure that the click point is still in the control's bounding box: `PtInRect(Rect(0, 0, Width, Height), Point(X, Y))`.

Note

While the OnMouse events include the cursor position, the OnClick event is a simple TNotifyEvent—procedure (Sender: TObject) of object—that doesn't include click location information. When you need that, you can read the Mouse.CursorPos *property. (See Chapter 7 for more information about the* Mouse *global.)*

Keyboard events

As with mouse events, you have a choice between 'raw' and 'cooked' keyboard events. Most controls have an OnKeyPress event, which gives you the keypress info cooked to a standard ANSI character. The cooked character is perfectly adequate for entering filenames, email, or program source, but if you need to respond to non-character keys, like the cursor movement keys, function keys, or combinations like SHIFT+CTRL+INSERT, you need to handle the raw keyboard events, OnKeyDown and/or OnKeyUp.

These events pass you both a shift state map, Shift, and a numeric key code, Key. For the standard Latin-1 characters (*ie*, #32 to #255), the Key code is the Ord() of the character. (Alphabetic keystrokes are all implicitly uppercase. That is, if the B key is pressed, Key will equal Ord('B'), or 66.) The keys that produce Latin-1 characters are also named in Qt.pas, with the English alphabet keys being Key_A through Key_Z and the 'European' alphabet keys having longer names. See the sidebars on pages 358 and 361 for Key_ names for punctuation and 'European' alphabet characters.

Kylix is not Delphi

Any Delphi code that uses Windows' VK_ key names will have to be rewritten to use Qt's Key_ names.

For keys like F1 through F12, the cursor keys, functions keys, pad, and the other non-visual keys, you have to rely on the Key_ names. These are summarized in the sidebar on page 359. Strangely, you can distinguish between the two Enter keys, but you cannot distinguish between the left and right Shift, Ctrl, or Alt keys, nor can you distinguish between 'cursor pad' and 'number pad' keys. (You can tweak your xmodmap settings a bit so that you can distinguish these keys, but obviously you can't rely on a user's having a customized /etc/X11/XModmap unless you're selling turnkey systems.)

Note that the (English) alphabet keys are handled a bit differently than non-alphabet keys. When you press the B key, you get a Key_B event, and ssShift is not in Shift. When you hold down the shift key and press the B key, you get a Key_Shift event, followed by a Key_B with ssShift in Shift. That is, you get the same Key_ code for 'b' and 'B'. However, when you press the 6 key you get a Key_6 event, while SHIFT+6 gives you a Key_Shift event, followed by a Key_AsciiCircum. That is, the key codes have been translated to match the glyph's on the user's keyboard.

The KbdLookup project in the ch6/Controls project group will let you explore these behaviors on your own.

KeyPreview

Keystrokes go to the control with keyboard focus. This means that, by default, form-wide keyboard event handlers will never fire. If you set the form's KeyPreview property to True, the form will 'see' keyboard events before the event with the keyboard focus.

Setting the Key code to 0 suppresses further processing. If you do this in an OnKeyDown handler, for example, you'll still get an OnKeyUp event when the key is released, but you will **not** get an OnKeyPress.

Table 6-1. ASCII punctuation and Key_ codes

Glyph	Decimal	Hex	Key_ code
	32	20	Key_Space, KeyAny
!	33	21	Key_Exclam
"	34	22	Key_QuoteDbl
#	35	23	Key_NumberSign
$	36	24	Key_Dollar
%	37	25	Key_Percent
&	38	26	Key_Ampersand
'	39	27	Key_Apostrophe
(	40	28	Key_ParenLeft
)	41	29	Key_ParenRight
*	42	2A	Key_Asterisk
+	43	2B	Key_Plus
,	44	2C	Key_Comma
-	45	2D	Key_Minus
.	46	2E	Key_Period
/	47	2F	Key_Slash
:	58	3A	Key_Colon
;	59	3B	Key_Semicolon
<	60	3C	Key_Less
=	61	3D	Key_Equal
>	62	3E	Key_Greater
?	63	3F	Key_Question
@	64	40	Key_At
[	91	5B	Key_BracketLeft
\	92	5C	Key_Backslash
]	93	5D	Key_BracketRight

Table 6-1. ASCII punctuation and Key_ codes (Continued)

Glyph	Decimal	Hex	Key_ code
^	94	5E	Key_AsciiCircum
_	95	5F	Key_Underscore
`	96	60	Key_QuoteLeft
{	123	7B	Key_BraceLeft
|	124	7C	Key_Bar
}	125	7D	Key_BraceRight
~	126	7E	Key_AsciiTilde

Table 6-2. Non-visible characters and Key_ codes

Key_ code	Produced by
Key_Escape	Esc
Key_Tab	Tab
Key_Backtab	Shift+Tab
Key_Backspace	Backspace
Key_Return	'Normal' Enter
Key_Enter	Number pad Enter
Key_Insert	Insert
Key_Delete	Delete
Key_Pause	Pause / Break
Key_Print	Print Screen / SysRq
Key_SysReq	?
Key_Home	Home
Key_End	End
Key_Left	'Inverted T' left
Key_Up	'Inverted T' up
Key_Right	'Inverted T' right

Table 6-2. Non-visible characters and Key_ codes (Continued)

Key_ code	Produced by
Key_Down	'Inverted T' down
Key_Prior	PgUp
Key_PageUp	PgUp
Key_Next	PgDn
Key_PageDown	PgDn
Key_Shift	Right or left Shift
Key_Control	Right or left Ctrl
Key_Meta	Shift then Alt, but not Alt then Shift. On some–but not all–distributions, the Windows key produces Key_Meta.
Key_Alt	Right or left Alt
Key_CapsLock	Caps Lock
Key_NumLock	Num Lock
Key_ScrollLock	Scroll Lock
Key_F1	F1 (etc)
Key_Super_L	?
Key_Super_R	?
Key_Menu	?
Key_Hyper_L	?
Key_Hyper_R	?
Key_Help	?
Key_unknown	Number pad 5

Notes:

1. Keys "Produced by" ? are not produced on a standard US 104-key keyboard with a standard Redhat 7.0 /etc/X11/Xmodmap. Other distributions may differ.

2. Though you can distinguish between the two Enter keys, you cannot reliably distinguish between the left and right Shift, Ctrl, or Alt keys, nor can you distinguish between 'cursor pad' and 'number pad' keys. This depends on xmodmap, and varies from system to system and from distribution to distribution.

3. Under Gnome, at least, the three Windows keys come through as Key code 0 by default. I edited my /etc/X11/Xmodmap so I could assign the three Windows keys to Gnome events: Don't expect to be able to detect these keys.

Table 6-3. Latin-1 'European' characters and Key_ codes

Description	Glyph	Decimal	Hex	HTML name	Key_ code
Non-breaking space		160	A0	nbsp	Key_nobreakspace
Inverted exclamation mark	¡	161	A1	iexcl	Key_exclamdown
Cent sign	¢	162	A2	cent	Key_cent
Pound sign	£	163	A3	pound	Key_sterling
Currency sign	¤	164	A4	curren	Key_currency
Yen sign	¥	165	A5	yen	Key_yen
Broken vertical bar	¦	166	A6	brvbar	Key_brokenbar
Section sign	§	167	A7	sect	Key section
Spacing diaresis	¨	168	A8	uml	Key_diaeresis
Copyright sign	©	169	A9	copy	Key_copyright
Feminine ordinal indicator	ª	170	AA	ordf	Key_ordfeminine
Angle quotation mark, left	«	171	AB	laquo	Key_guillemotleft
Negation sign	¬	172	AC	not	Key_notsign

Table 6-3. Latin-1 'European' characters and Key_ codes (Continued)

Description	Glyph	Decimal	Hex	HTML name	Key_ code
Soft hyphen	-	173	AD	shy	Key_hyphen
Circled R registered sign	®	174	AE	reg	Key_registered
Spacing macron	¯	175	AF	hibar	Key_macron
Degree sign	°	176	B0	deg	Key_degree
Plus-or-minus sign	±	177	B1	plusmn	Key_plusminus
Superscript 2	²	178	B2	sup2	Key_twosuperior
Superscript 3	³	179	B3	sup3	Key_threesuperior
Spacing acute	´	180	B4	acute	Key_acute
Micro sign	µ	181	B5	micro	Key_mu
Paragraph sign	¶	182	B6	para	Key_paragraph
Middle dot	·	183	B7	middot	Key_periodcentered
Spacing cedilla	¸	184	B8	cedil	Key_cedilla
Superscript 1	¹	185	B9	sup1	Key_onesuperior
Masculine ordinal indicator	º	186	BA	ordm	Key_masculine
Angle quotation mark, right	»	187	BB	raquo	Key_guillemotright
Fraction 1/4	¼	188	BC	frac14	Key_onequarter
Fraction 1/2	½	189	BD	frac12	Key_onehalf
Fraction 3/4	¾	190	BE	frac34	Key_threequarters
Inverted question mark	¿	191	BF	iquest	Key_questiondown
Capital A, grave accent	À	192	C0	Agrave	Key_Agrave
Capital A, acute accent	Á	193	C1	Aacute	Key_Aacute

Table 6-3. Latin-1 'European' characters and Key_ codes (Continued)

Description	Glyph	Decimal	Hex	HTML name	Key_ code
Capital A, circumflex accent	Â	194	C2	Acirc	Key_Acircumflex
Capital A, tilde	Ã	195	C3	Atilde	Key_Atilde
Capital A, dieresis or umlaut mark	Ä	196	C4	Auml	Key_Adiaeresis
Capital A, ring	Å	197	C5	Aring	Key_Aring
Capital ΛE diphthong (ligature)	Æ	198	C6	AElig	Key_AE
Capital C, cedilla	Ç	199	C7	Ccedil	Key_Ccedilla
Capital E, grave accent	È	200	C8	Egrave	Key_Egrave
Capital E, acute accent	É	201	C9	Eacute	Key_Eacute
Capital E, circumflex accent	Ê	202	CA	Ecirc	Key_Ecircumflex
Capital E, dieresis or umlaut mark	Ë	203	CB	Euml	Key_Ediaeresis
Capital I, grave accent	Ì	204	CC	Igrave	Key_Igrave
Capital I, acute accent	Í	205	CD	Iacute	Key_Iacute
Capital I, circumflex accent	Î	206	CE	Icirc	Key_Icircumflex
Capital I, dieresis or umlaut mark	Ï	207	CF	Iuml	Key_Idiaeresis

Table 6-3. Latin-1 'European' characters and Key_ codes (Continued)

Description	Glyph	Decimal	Hex	HTML name	Key_ code
Capital Eth, Icelandic	Ð	208	D0	ETH	Key_ETH
Capital N, tilde	Ñ	209	D1	Ntilde	Key_Ntilde
Capital O, grave accent	Ò	210	D2	Ograve	Key_Ograve
Capital O, acute accent	Ó	211	D3	Oacute	Key_Oacute
Capital O, circumflex accent	Ô	212	D4	Ocirc	Key_Ocircumflex
Capital O, tilde	Õ	213	D5	Otilde	Key_Otilde
Capital O, dieresis or umlaut mark	Ö	214	D6	Ouml	Key_Odiaeresis
Multiplication	×	215	D7		Key_multiply
Capital O, slash	Ø	216	D8	Oslash	Key_Ooblique
Capital U, grave accent	Ù	217	D9	Ugrave	Key_Ugrave
Capital U, acute accent	Ú	218	DA	Uacute	Key_Uacute
Capital U, circumflex accent	Û	219	DB	Ucirc	Key_Ucircumflex
Capital U, dieresis or umlaut mark	Ü	220	DC	Uuml	Key_Udiaeresis
Capital Y, acute accent	Ý	221	DD	Yacute	Key_Yacute
Capital THORN, Icelandic	Þ	222	DE	THORN	Key_THORN

Table 6-3. Latin-1 'European' characters and Key_ codes (Continued)

Description	Glyph	Decimal	Hex	HTML name	Key_ code
Small sharp s, German (sz ligature)	ß	223	DF	szlig	Key_ssharp
Small a, grave accent	à	224	E0	agrave	Key_agrave_lower
Small a, acute accent	á	225	E1	aacute	Key_aacute_lower
Small a, circumflex accent	â	226	E2	acirc	Key_acircumflex_lower
Small a, tilde	ã	227	E3	atilde	Key_atilde_lower
Small a, dieresis or accent	ä	228	E4	auml	Key_adiaeresis_lower
Small a, ring	å	229	E5	aring	Key_aring_lower
Small ae diphthong (ligature)	æ	230	E6	aelig	Key_ae_lower
Small c, cedilla	ç	231	E7	ccedil	Key_ccedilla_lower
Small e, grave accent	è	232	E8	egrave	Key_egrave_lower (grave_lower)
Small e, acute accent	é	233	E9	eacute	Key_eacute_lower (acute_lower)
Small e, circumflex (ligature)	ê	234	EA	ecirc	Key_ecircumflex_lower (circumflex_lower)
Small e, dieresis or umlaut mark	ë	235	EB	euml	Key_ediaeresis_lower (diaeresis_lower)
Small i, grave accent	ì	236	EC	igrave	Key_igrave_lower
Small i, acute accent	í	237	ED	iacute	Key_iacute_lower

Table 6-3. Latin-1 'European' characters and Key_ codes (Continued)

Description	Glyph	Decimal	Hex	HTML name	Key_ code
Small i, circumflex umlaut mark	î	238	EE	icirc	Key_icircumflex_lower
Small i, dieresis or umlaut mark	ï	239	EF	iuml	Key_idiaeresis_lower
Small eth, Icelandic	ð	240	F0	eth	th_lower
Small n, tilde	ñ	241	F1	ntilde	Key_ntilde_lower
Small o, grave accent	ò	242	F2	ograve	Key_ograve_lower
Small o, acute accent	ó	243	F3	oacute	Key_oacute_lower
Small o, circumflex umlaut mark	ô	244	F4	ocirc	Key_ocircumflex_lower
Small o, tilde	õ	245	F5	otilde	Key_otilde_lower
Small o, dieresis or umlaut mark	ö	246	F6	ouml	Key_odiaeresis_lower
Division	÷	247	F7		Key_division
Small o, slash	ø	248	F8	oslash	Key_oslash
Small u, grave accent	ù	249	F9	ugrave	Key_ugrave_lower
Small u, acute accent	ú	250	FA	uacute	Key_uacute_lower
Small u, circumflex accent	û	251	FB	ucirc	Key_ucircumflex_lower
Small u, dieresis or umlaut mark	ü	252	FC	uuml	Key_udiaeresis_lower

Table 6-3. Latin-1 'European' characters and Key_ codes (Continued)

Description	Glyph	Decimal	Hex	HTML name	Key_ code
Small y, acute accent	ý	253	FD	yacute	Key_yacute_lower
Small thorn, Icelandic	þ	254	FE	thorn	Key_thorn_lower
Small y, dieresis or umlaut mark	ÿ	255	FF	yuml	Key_ydiaeresis

> **Note**
>
>
> *The key codes for the characters from 232 to 235 ('decorated' lower case e's) are declared in Qt.pas without the leading Key_e. Eg, 232 is declared as* grave_lower, *not* Key_egrave_lower. *This may be fixed in later releases, or in a patch to release 1.*

Owner draw

Some controls have events that let you draw them—or parts of them—yourself. These "owner draw" controls include list and combo boxes, string and draw grids, tab and page controls, and list, icon, and tree views. All of these except the draw grid **can** draw themselves; owner draw is an override, for when you want to add a state graphic or custom font.

The date picker component of Chapter 9 uses an owner draw grid for a calendar. The OwnerDraw project in the ch6/Controls project group (Figure 6-4) is a simpler example, with an owner draw dropdown that uses each font name as an example of itself. If you run that program, you'll see that it's actually a rather bad example—rendering each font means that the dropdown is very slow—but it's a **simple** example, as I don't have to obscure the logic with any bogus state generation. The key routine is this FontsDrawItem event handler, which draws each font name in itself.

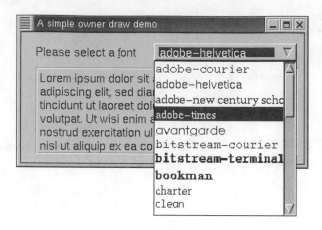

Figure 6-4. An owner draw dropdown

```
procedure TOwnerDrawFrm.FontsDrawItem(Sender: TObject; Index: Integer;
  Rect: TRect; State: TOwnerDrawState; var Handled: Boolean);
var
  Dropdown: TComboBox;
  ThisFont: string;
begin
  Assert(Sender is TComboBox);
  Dropdown := TComboBox(Sender);

  with Dropdown.Canvas do
  begin
    ThisFont  := Dropdown.Items[Index];
    Font.Name := ThisFont;
    TextRect(Rect, Rect.Left + 1, Rect.Top + 1, ThisFont);
  end;
  Handled := True;
end; // TOwnerDrawFrm.FontsDrawItem
```

This should seem pretty straightforward.[3] First, I check that the Sender is indeed a TComboBox, and cast the Sender to a TComboBox. Then, I 'open' DropDown.Canvas (see the *Canvas* section of this chapter, below) with a `with` statement. The Index parameter tells me which item in the combo box's Items list I need to draw (see Chapter 7 for a discussion of Items' TStrings class), so I make a local copy of the string to avoid having to index Dropdown.Items twice. `Font.Name := ThisFont` sets `DropDown.Canvas.Font` to the current font—that's

---

3.   It's sure lucky I don't have to pay royalties on the phrase "pretty straightforward", isn't it?

all I need to do to change fonts. Then, I call TextRect to draw the font name string, clipped to the Rect that was passed in. Note that this Rect is in the Sender's coordinates, not form or screen coordinates.

Owner draw vs application styles

Owner draw relies on the form's event handlers to do the custom drawing. While you can easily have two or more controls on the same form share an event handler, sharing event handler code across forms is more cumbersome. You can push the code into a routine that's called by different event handlers. Or, you can try risky tricks like setting the event handler for a control on *this* form to an event handler on *that* form in *this* form's OnCreate handler. Basically, though, owner draw controls are best restricted to displaying custom data.

If you want to give your application a distinctive look and change the way **all** buttons or all list boxes look, you should use Application.Style. See the *Application* section of Chapter 7.

Drag and drop

Kylix makes it easy for you to add drag and drop to your applications. All controls[4] have a DragMode property and four drag events: OnStartDrag, OnDragOver, OnDragDrop, and OnEndDrag. Normally, DragMode is dmManual, which means that you have to initiate drag and drop activity by calling BeginDrag, typically in an OnMouseDown handler. If you set DragMode to dmAutomatic, StartDrag is called automatically whenever the user drags the mouse more than Mouse.DragThreshold pixels from the click point.

OnDragOver

Once you start dragging a control, the two key events are OnDragOver and OnDragDrop. OnDragOver is called often as you drag a control over a form or over other controls. OnDragOver is called when the cursor enters a control's bounding box; when the cursor leaves a control's bounding box; and whenever the cursor moves about inside of a control's bounding box. The point of the OnDragOver event is setting its Accept parameter to True or False. If you drag a control over a control that doesn't have an OnDragOver event handler, or if

---

4. Well, "almost all". TBevel, for instance, doesn't have a DragMode property and drag events.

that handler sets Accept to False, the cursor will (by default—you can set your own cursors) be a slashed circle: You can't drop here. (See Figure 6-5.) If the OnDragOver event handler sets Accept to True, the cursor will (again, only by default) be a normal drag cursor. (See Figure 6-6.)

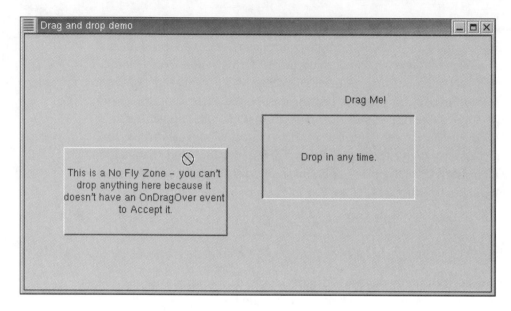

Figure 6-5. Can't drop here

The OnDragOver event handler has, as usual, a Sender parameter. It also has a Source parameter, which is also a TObject. The Sender is, as usual, the control that's sending the event, the one the event handler belongs to. In other words, the Sender is the control that's being dragged over. The Sender is being asked whether or not to Accept the control that's being dragged over it, the Source.

Real apps might have relatively complex tests to determine which controls they'll accept and where, but the DragAndDrop project of the ch6/Controls project group is very simplistic. It will Accept anytime Sender <> Source. (If it blindly sets Accept to True, it could end up trying to drop a control onto itself.)

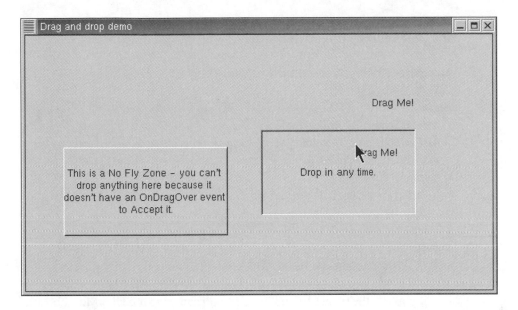

Figure 6-6. Can drop here

```
procedure TDragDropDemoFrm.VeryAccepting(Sender, Source: TObject; X, Y: Integer;
  State: TDragState; var Accept: Boolean);
begin
  Accept := Sender <> Source;
end; // TDragDropDemoFrm.VeryAccepting
```

If you run the DragAndDrop project, you'll see that you can drag all three labels, but that you can't drop onto the 'No Fly Zone' with the raised wall around it. That's because the form and the DropIn label share the above VeryAccepting OnDragOver event handler, but the NoFlyZone label does not have an OnDragOver event handler.

OnDragDrop

When the user drops a control over a control that will accept it, the receiving control gets an OnDragDrop event. If it doesn't handle this event, nothing will happen except that the cursor changes back to normal. Kylix mediates a protocol for you, but it's up to you to make anything happen. In the OnDragDrop event, as in the OnDragOver event, the Sender is the control whose event handler is being fired, the drop target, while Source is the control that's being dropped, and X and Y are the drop location in Sender's coordinates. Thus, the DragAndDrop project moves controls where you drop them:

```
procedure TDragDropDemoFrm.ReparentOnDrop(Sender, Source: TObject;
  X, Y: Integer);
begin
  Assert(Sender is TWidgetControl, 'Sender is ' + Sender.ClassName);
  Assert(Source is TControl,       'Source is ' + Source.ClassName);
  with TControl(Source) do
  begin
    Parent := TWidgetControl(Sender);
    Left := X;
    Top  := Y;
  end;
end; // TDragDropDemoFrm.ReparentOnDrop
```

If you run the project, you'll see that you can drop the DragMe label onto the DropIn label; if you then drag the DropIn label, the DragMe label will move with it. If you drag the DragMe label off the DropIn label, it will no longer move with the DropIn label.

Of course, a real project would typically have a more complicated OnDragDrop event handler than this one. For example, you don't have to use drag and drop to move controls; you might drag and drop the 'contents' of one control into another, or you might use drag and drop to let users reorder a list.

TDragObject

The default drag cursor isn't very enlightening. It doesn't show **what** you're dragging, and it doesn't show **where** the cursor is in relationship to the object you're dragging. The OnStartDrag event lets you create a TDragObject descendant that can help with this. If you don't set the event handler's DragObject parameter, Kylix will automatically create a TDragObject for you that produces the default cursor &c. However, if you create a customized descendant of TDragObject and assign it to the DragObject parameter, you can specify the image that's being dragged as well as its "hot spot", which is the point in image coordinates that should be under the cursor as it's dragged. This lets you both tailor the drag image to what's being dragged, and to give some indication of where it will be placed when dropped. If you create a TDragObject, be sure to Free it in an OnEndDrag event handler.

The DragAndDrop project sets DragObject for the DragMe label, but not for either of the two bordered labels. This is why dragging DragMe shows the text being dragged, but dragging the other labels just shows the default drag cursor.

The DragMe label's OnStartDrag handler creates a specialized descendant of TDragControlObject, which is what you'd typically use for simply dragging a whole control. When you use a TDragControlObject, the Source parameters of the OnDragDrop and OnDragOver events are the control you're dragging, just as if you hadn't set a DragObject. If you use a drag object that descends directly from TDragObject, the Source parameter is the TDragObject itself, which is a bit more complicated but can simplify things when several different controls might be drag sources. They'd all create the same type of DragObject, which the OnDragDrop and OnDragOver events would know what to do with.

The TextDragObject I create in the DragAndDrop project doesn't do anything so subtle, but it does illustrate how to create a custom drag cursor. The constructor saves the Source label's Caption in a Text field, and the GetDragImageIndex method adds an image to the global DragImageList and returns the index of the new image.

```
function TextDragObject.GetDragImageIndex: Integer;
var
  Bitmap: TBitmap;
begin
  Bitmap := TBitmap.Create;
  try
    with DragImageList do
    begin
      Bitmap.Height := Height; // just so we have Canvas &c
      Bitmap.Width  := Width;
      Width  := Max(Width,  Bitmap.Canvas.TextWidth(Text));
      Height := Max(Height, Bitmap.Canvas.TextHeight(Text));
               // The Max() fn is in the Math unit
      Bitmap.Height := Height;
      Bitmap.Width  := Width;
      Bitmap.Canvas.TextOut(0, 0, Text);
      Result := DragImageList.Add(Bitmap, Nil);
      ImageIndex := Result;
    end;
  finally
    Bitmap.Free;
  end;
end; // TextDragObject.GetDragImageIndex
```

This function is a bit longer than some of the others I've presented so far, but it should be obvious enough. I create a TBitmap (see below) to draw on, because we can Add a bitmap to an image list, or Replace an existing one, but we can't directly modify an image in an image list. I set the new bitmap's Height and Width to the image list's current Height and Width, so that I have a valid Canvas which can calculate TextHeight and TextWidth. I resize the global drag image list so it will fit the text image I want to Add to it, then draw text on the bitmap with TextOut. I then Add the bitmap, which gives me the image index I need to return, and save that index in a field of the TextDragObject so that I can remove it from the global drag image list in the TextDragObject's destructor. Once I've added the bitmap to the image list, I no longer need the bitmap, so I Free the bitmap, and return.

In the OnStartDrag handler, I create the TextDragObject and assign it to the DragObject parameter. Kylix will not automatically Free a DragObject that we explicitly Create, so I save a reference to the DragObject in a field of the form object, and Free it in the OnEndDrag event handler.

```
procedure TDragDropDemoFrm.StartTextDrag(Sender: TObject;
  var DragObject: TDragObject);
begin
  Assert(Sender is TLabel);
  DragObject := TextDragObject.Create( TLabel(Sender),
                                       TLabel(Sender).Caption);
  fDragObject := DragObject; // 'cause Kylix doesn't Free it by itself
end; // TDragDropDemoFrm.StartTextDrag

procedure TDragDropDemoFrm.EndTextDrag(Sender, Target: TObject; X,
  Y: Integer);
begin
  FreeAndNil(fDragObject);
end; // TDragDropDemoFrm.EndTextDrag
```

Canvas

I've used a Canvas a few times now, and it should be obvious what's going on: A Canvas is a drawing surface. Forms have a Canvas property, as do bitmaps and all controls with owner-draw abilities. Container controls typically don't have a Canvas property, but you can drop a PaintBox component (from the Additional tab) onto a container if you need to draw on it.

> **Note**
>
> *Paint boxes and other graphic controls are drawn before—or, visually underneath—windowed controls like labels and buttons.*

Canvases have three basic drawing tools—a pen, a brush, and a font—and a variety of basic two-dimensional graphics primitives.

Drawing tools

Designers of graphics primitives have two basic choices: They can fully parameterize every call, so that drawing a line requires you to specify color and line style along with end points, or they can use a concept of "drawing tools", so that before you can draw a line you have to setup the tools, but then you only have to specify a pair of end points. The fully parameterized approach makes for fewer system calls, at the expense of each call being more complex. The drawing tools approach requires system calls to configure the tools, but each call is simpler—and faster overall, as often you will draw several items using the same border, interior, or font.

Kylix's Canvas takes the drawing tools approach. Primitives that draw a line or outline a region use the Canvas' Pen, which has Color, Width, and a couple of drawing mode properties. Primitives that fill a region use the Canvas's Brush, which has Color, Bitmap, and Style properties. Primitives that draw text use the Canvas' Font, which has the same font Name, Color, Size, and Style properties that you've seen already.

Drawing tools Assign() on assignment

A Canvas' Pen, Brush, and Font tools are all objects in their own right. This means that when you want to set a Canvas's properties, you can set the various tools' properties one by one, or you can simply write code like `ThisCanvas.Pen := ThatPen` to change all the Canvas' Pen's properties to match ThatPen's.

Does this look dangerous to you? Like you've changed ThisCanvas's Pen property to point to a new object, without freeing the old one? Or that ThatPen might now have two 'owners' who might think that they ought to Free it?

Good.

The assignment is safe, though, because CLX objects that expose drawing tool objects do so *via* write methods like

```
procedure TCanvas.SetPen(const Value: TPen);
begin
  FPen.Assign(Value);
end;
```

TFont, TPen, and TBrush all descend from TGraphicsObject, which in turn descends directly from TPersistent (see Chapter 7). This lets them stream in from a form resource; it also gives them an Assign() method. The default Assign() implementation in TPersistent just raises an exception, but descendants override it to make themselves functionally identical to the object they're Assign()ed. Thus, when you say ThisCanvas.Pen := ThatPen, pointer(ThisCanvas.Pen) does not change; rather, the Canvas's Pen object copies ThatPen's Color, Mode, Style, and Width properties.

You can—and should—use this technique in your own objects that expose object properties.

```
property Pen: TPen read fPen write fPen;
```

can lead to memory leaks and/or crashes, while

```
property Pen: TPen read fPen write SetPen;
```

where SetPen does an Assign(), is safe and convenient.

....

Pen

You can set a Pen's Color to a TColor. There are many named colors (available in the Object Inspector's dropdown for a Color property) which can be grouped broadly into "absolute" colors like clRed, clBlue, and clBlack, and "functional" colors like clButton, clShadow, and clBase. In addition to these named colors, you can use any 32-bit integer from 0 to $00FFFFFF as a RGB value. The standard function ColorToRGB will convert a named TColor to its RGB values.

Kylix's RGB encoding is "little endian"—the low (or first) byte is the Red component, the second byte is the Green component and the third byte is the Blue component—and thus the reverse of HTML's more hexadecimal friendly RRGGBB. The following functions from my lib/QGrabBag may be useful:

```
function RGB(Red, Green, Blue: integer): TColor;
const
  Mask = $000000FF; // Mask off all but low-byte
begin
  Result := Red   and Mask         or
            Green and Mask shl  8 or
            Blue  and Mask shl 16  ;
end; // RGB


function TColorToHtml(Color: TColor): string;
begin
  Result := IntToHex( Color and $00FF0000 shr 16 or
                      Color and $0000FF00          or
                      Color and $000000FF shl 16, 6 );
end; // TColorToHtml


function HtmlToTColor(const Color: string): TColor;
begin
  Result := StrToInt('$' + Color);
  Result := Result and $00FF0000 shr 16 or
            Result and $0000FF00          or
            Result and $000000FF shl 16 ;
end; // HtmlToTColor
```

It should be obvious what these functions do. I'll only make two quick notes. First, these functions rely on the rather dubious Object Pascal operator precedence (Chapter 2) notion that "bitwise and" and the shift operators are "multipliers" and so have a higher precedence than "bitwise or", which is an "adder". Some people would prefer to use parentheses to make the order of execution explicit. Second, the HtmlToTColor function converts a hexadecimal string to an integer by prepending a '$' character—thus making it look like a hexadecimal constant in Object Pascal source—and calling StrToInt. The lower-level Val() procedure also supports this '$' notation.

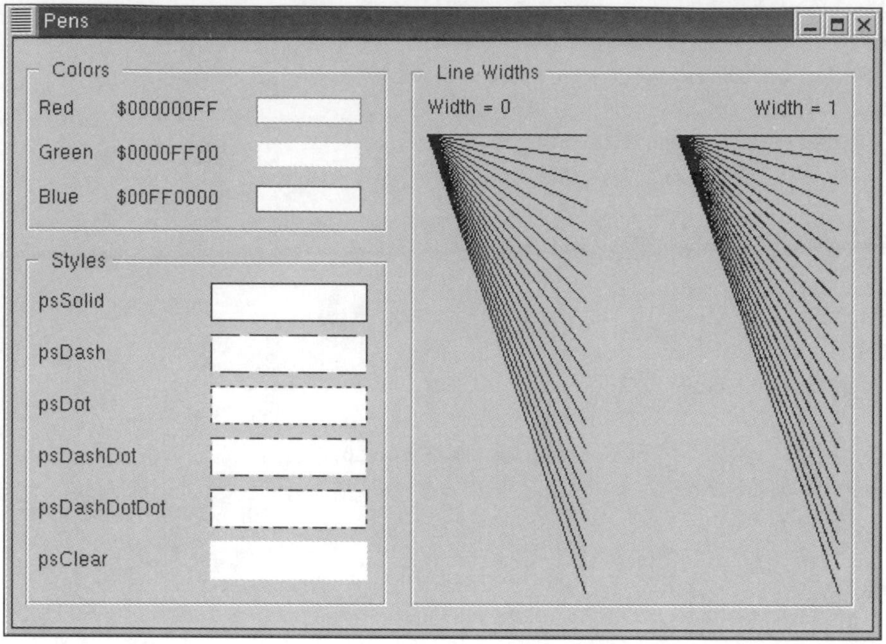

Figure 6-7. The Pens project

You can find the Qt documentation at www.trolltech.com.

The Pens project in the ch6/Canvas project group (Figure 6-7) illustrates color encoding, as well as the Width and Style properties. The Width of a pen is measured in pixels, except that a Width of 0 is special. The Qt documentation says a line width of 0 "draws a 1-pixel line very fast, but with lower precision than with a line width of 1. Setting the line width to 1 or more draws lines that are precise, but drawing is slower." This obviously won't affect horizontal or vertical lines, but it does affect diagonal lines (as you can see from the Pens project) and ellipses. I'm not sure that I would characterize the Width = 1 behavior as more "precise" so much as "heavier" —it seems to be drawing pairs of points near places where the Breshenham algorithm's error term is about to roll over—but I guess it doesn't really matter what you call it, so long as you know that the difference exists.

The Style property lets you draw dashed and dotted lines. This is of relatively little utility, except for drawing selection "marquees". Most of the time, you will use either psSolid or psClear. Note that when you draw with a psClear Pen, your drawings have no outline, and the Brush is used to paint the whole region; normally, the Brush is only used for the interior.

The Mode property controls how the Pen color interacts with the current screen color. This lets you "undraw" black lines by redrawing them with a pmXor Mode. Combining other colors is considerably more complicated: If you need to do this, you're on your own.

Brush

Any time you use a graphics primitive that draws a region with an interior, the Brush is involved. A Brush has a Color, which can be any named TColor or RGB integer, just like a Pen's Color. A Brush's Style controls how the Color is used to fill the region. A Brush can also have a bitmap, which overrides the Color; a Brush with a non-Nil Bitmap pays no attention to its Color or Style properties.

> **Note**
>
> *Delphi programmers should be sure to note that the CLX's Brush.Bitmap is considerably more useful than the VCL's: Window's brushes only use the top-left 8x8 pixels of their bitmap, while Qt's brushes use the whole bitmap.*

Kylix is not Delphi

The Ellipses program in the ch6/Canvas project group is an almost cool demonstration of bitmapped brushes. It loads all the .bmp, .png, or .jpg files in /usr/share/pixmaps/backgrounds/tiles—or any directories you list on the command line—and draws random ellipses, each filled with a random bitmap. As you can see if you run it, small, low-color Brush.Bitmap's are faster than big, high-color ones.

The Brushes program in the ch6/Canvas project group (Figure 6-8) is a more comprehensive demo of the interactions of various Brush Style's, Color's, and Bitmap's. There are several things worth noting in its code. In the OnPaint event handler,

```
// Solid Blue
Color := clBlue;
PaintRect(SolidBlue);

// Clear
Style := bsClear;
PaintRect(Clear);

// Bitmap
Bitmap := BrushBitmap.Picture.Bitmap;
PaintRect(Bitmapped);
```

note that a Style of bsClear supercedes the Color. The interior of the Clear rectangle is left untouched, despite the fact that Brush.Color is still clBlue.

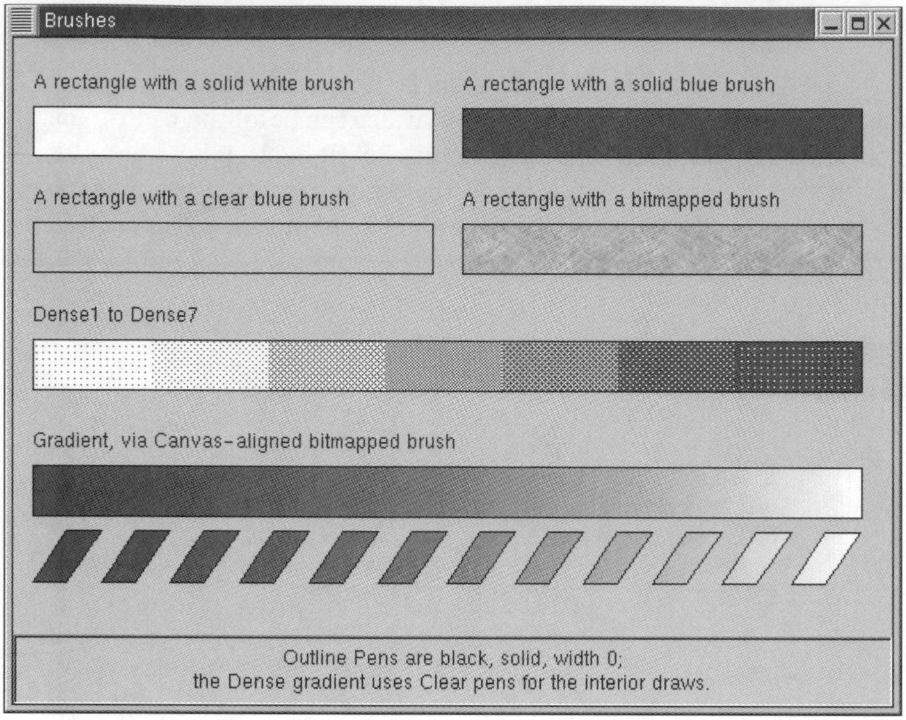

Figure 6-8. The Brushes project

Similarly, the Bitmap supercedes the Color and Style; the interior of the Bitmapped rectangle is filled with the 'paper' bitmap, despite the fact that Brush.Color is still clBlue and the Brush.Style is still bsClear.

In the DenseX code, note how the TBrushStyle's that are neither bsSolid nor bsClear blend the two behaviors. The patterned brushes draw some of the pixels in the interior in the current Brush.Color, while leaving others untouched. Thus, I draw the DenseSpectrum rectangle as a (coarse!) gradient from white to blue by drawing the interior of the rectangle in solid blue, then overlaying it with progressively less dense white.

```
// DenseSpectrum
Bitmap := Nil;
Style  := bsSolid;
Color  := clBlue;
Top    := DenseSpectrum.Top + DenseSpectrum.Height + 8;
Bottom := Top + RectHeight;
```

```
Width   := (Right - Left - 2) div 7;
Rectangle(Left, Top, Right, Bottom);

Pen.Style := psClear;
Color     := clWhite;
for Index := 0 to 6 do
begin
  Style := TBrushStyle(ord(bsDense1) + Index);
  Rectangle( Left | Width * Index + 1, Top + 1,
            Left + Width * (Index + 1) + 1, Bottom - 1 );
end;
```

Note also that the psClear Pen.Style for the interior rectangles draws no outline, and fills the whole rectangle with the brush. This is why the second Rectangle() call in the above snippet—the one that draws the white DenseX interiors—uses Top + and Bottom − 1. If it didn't, it would overwrite the rectangle's black frame.

Finally, perhaps the coolest part of this little demo program is the "Canvas-aligned bitmapped brush" at the bottom, which uses a bitmap I build in the form's OnCreate handler. Because the Brush's Bitmap is Canvas-aligned—*ie*, implicitly tiled over the whole Canvas, with its top-left corner at the top-left of the Canvas—I didn't have to reset the Brush between polygons to draw the slashed 'windows' 'onto' the bitmap: I just drew a dozen polygons, all using the same Brush.

```
for Index := 0 to 11 do
  Polygon( [ Point(Left + Width * Index + Width div 2, Top),
            Point(Left + Width * (Index + 1),          Top),
            Point(Left + Width * Index + Width div 2, Bottom),
            Point(Left + Width * Index,               Bottom) ]);
```

Of course, this Canvas-alignment is a bit of a double-edged sword. You might well **want** the top-left edge of the bitmap to be in the top-left corner of the area you're filling. For example, the Brushes project had a bug at first: the gradient color bar was drawing a solid blue bar at the far right. I was building a bitmap exactly as wide as the rectangle, and since it was tiled from the top-left of the Canvas, I was losing the leftmost pixels of the gradient, and getting them on the right.

For this simplistic demo, I just made the bitmap a bit wider, and left the leftmost pixels undefined. More generally, you might want to use a PaintBox to get a new Canvas, whose top-left is just where you want the top-left of the bitmap to be.

Alternatively, you can use the Qt function QPainter::setBrushOrigin to control where the top-left corner of the bitmap is placed. For example, the Brushes project actually builds two bitmaps, and calls

```
QPainter_setBrushOrigin(Canvas.Handle, Left, 0);
```

so that it doesn't have to have Left unused pixels in the second bitmap.

Font

When you draw text on a Canvas, you use the Canvas's current Font. A Font has four key properties—Name, Color, Size, and Style—and four minor properties—CharSet, Pitch, Height, and Weight. Unfortunately, the Font object doesn't include any methods or properties that can tell you if a given font is a nice, high-quality scalable font or some crufty old bitmapped X font that hasn't looked good since someone built it by hand at MIT in 1985—see the "TFont *vs* QFont" sidebar for more information on how to do this with Qt calls.

....

TFont *vs* QFont

Linux programmers are used to it, but Windows programmers are in for a real shock: Linux font handling is pretty poor. Under Windows, you can easily[5] tell if a font will scale smoothly. If it's a True Type font, it scales smoothly. If it's a bitmapped font, it scales poorly. You can easily tell if a font is a True Type font; you can choose to only 'see' True Type fonts. Not under Linux!

The Fonts project in the ch6/Canvas group illustrates some of the difficulties, as well as some lib/QGrabBag code that you can use to access the Qt QFontInfo and QFontDatabase classes.

When you set a TFont's properties, Qt tries to find the exact match for the Name, CharSet, Pitch, Size and so on. If it can't find an exact match, it will give you the best match it can come up with. This might not be a very good match! (This is true under Windows, too, but not only does Windows generally do a better matching job than X, most developers limit their exposure to this issue by specifying only the standard fonts that are found in all Windows versions. There are **no** standard fonts found in all Linux versions.)

However, the quality—or lack thereof—of the best-match font won't be reflected in the TFont. (This is true of Delphi, too.) TFont passes property

---

5. Well, actually, users can install font handlers for Postscript &c, and this does complicate matters. But you can still write code that only sees TrueType fonts.

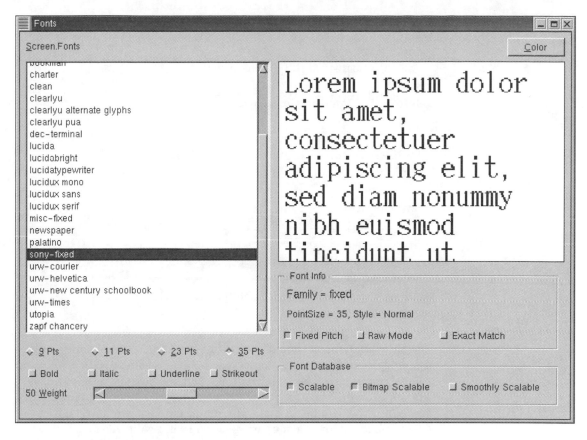

Figure 6-9. A poorly scaled bitmap font

read requests on to Qt, which simply returns the last value you set. To get the actual values, you need to use QFontInfo. The Fonts project does this: It allows you to specify only odd sizes, like 9, 11, 23, and 35 points to increase the chances that Qt won't be able to find an exact size match.

The QFontInfo class will not tell you how a given font family scales. You need to use QFontDatabase, which offers three methods: isScalable, isBitmapScalable, and isSmoothlyScalable. To complicate things, these functions do not apply to a whole font family, but to a font family, with a given combination of style (bold, italic) attributes, and a particular character set. The following abbreviated snippet from the Fonts project shows how to call these functions:

```
procedure TFontsFrm.FontChange(Sender: TObject);
var
  Info:  IFontInfo;
  Family, Encoding, Style:    WideString;
begin
  Info := FontInfo(LoremIpsum.Font);

  Family := LoremIpsum.Font.Name;
  Style  := FontDatabase.StyleString(LoremIpsum.Font);
  QFont_encodingName(@ Encoding, Info.CharSet);

  Scalable.Checked :=
    FontDatabase.IsScalable(Family, Style, Encoding);
  BitmapScalable.Checked :=
    FontDatabase.IsBitmapScalable(Family, Style, Encoding);
  SmoothlyScalable.Checked :=
    FontDatabase.IsSmoothlyScalable(Family, Style, Encoding);
end; // TFontsFrm.FontChange
```

The Family parameter should be the same as TFont.Name, a name that might appear in Screen.Fonts. Screen.Fonts is generated by QFontDatabase::families, which returns a name as "foundry-family" when a family exists in several foundries. (Hence names like 'adobe-courier' and 'urw-courier'.) QFontInfo::Name strips off the foundry-part: If you use a QFontInfo Name for a Family parameter, you will get the info for **a** family with that name, but not necessarily the one you want.

The Style parameter can be 'Normal', 'Bold', 'Italic', or 'Bold Italic'. Rather than build these strings myself—and risk possible future incompatibilities or locale issues—I prefer to use the QFontDatabase::styleString function to describe an existing TFont.

Similarly, I don't think it wise to hardcode locale names into my apps. QFont::encodingName returns a Qt-legible string version of the Qt locale enum I get from the QFontInfo::charSet.

Once I gather this information and call isScalable, isBitmapScalable, and isSmoothlyScalable, things are … still complicated. Some fonts (like 'avantgarde', on my system) that **do** scale smoothly are reported as not scaling smoothly by any of the three functions; others ('zapf chancery') are only reported as scaling smoothing with an 'Italic' style; while others ('adobe-courier') that manifestly **don't** scale smoothly are reported as doing so!

I urge you to run the Fonts project and draw your own conclusions, but I'd suggest this rule of thumb: Avoid fonts that are not smoothly scalable, and fonts that are bitmap scalable.

Key properties

TFont.Name selects a font or, more properly, a font family. Most font families include fonts for different sizes, styles, and character sets. If the font Name you select is on the user's system—*ie*, is in Screen.Fonts—that's the font you'll get. If the font doesn't exist, Qt will do its best to find a plausible font. See the Qt documentation (www.trolltech.com) for details.

TFont.Color can be any named TColor, or RGB value.

TFont.Size is a positive integer that is supposed to represent the font's height in "points", which is a traditional printer's measure: There are 72 points to an inch. Kylix passes Size requests straight through to Qt, which presumably[6] uses the same display size information it exposes in QPaintDeviceMetrics to convert heights in points to heights in pixel.

Note

*When you read Font.Size, Kylix passes the request on to Qt, which returns the last Font.Size that you set. When you change the font family, if the font is not "smoothly scalable" Qt may not give you the exact font size that you asked for; it may choose an actual size that's as much as 20% bigger or smaller than what you asked for. Reading the Font.Size property, however, will give you what you **asked for**, not what you actually **got**. To find out what Qt gave you, you need to use QFontInfo.*

TFont.Style property is a `set of TFontStyle`, which means it can be any combination of fsBold, fsItalic, fsUnderline, and fsStrikeOut. Note that because the set is a property, not a public field, you can't use the system procedures Exclude and Include with Font.Style. You have to write code like `with ThisFont do Style := Style + [fsBold]` or `with ThisFont do Style := Style - [fsItalic]`.

Minor properties

Naturally enough, TFont.CharSet selects the character set. Some font families will be designed to have a similar feel across character sets, so you might have a font named "Globalization" that has faces for Latin-1 as well as Greek,

---

6. Yes, I am in a state of sin: I'm writing a book about programming on an Open Source operating system, using an Open Source widget library—and I'm making inferences about how Qt does things, based on the public API, instead of reading the Source.

Russian, Japanese, Chinese, Korean, Thai, and so on. The default value, fcsDefaultCharSet, means that Kylix will ask Qt what CharSet is appropriate for the user's locale. This is usually fine, but may well cause problems in Latin-1 applications running on machines that default to an Asian language.

Note

English-only Delphi apps running on NT4 machines with a DBCS [Double Byte Character Set] locale have problems if they use DEFAULT_CHARSET, Delphi's equivalent of fcsDefaultCharSet. Their English text gets transcribed to the machine's default character set. To make sure that the text displays correctly even on machines that aren't set to an ANSI locale, you have to explicitly set the Font's CharSet to ANSI_CHARSET. I've done simple tests that don't show a similar problem–but I wasn't using any text that contained UTF-8 escape sequences (see Chapter 1).

TFont.Pitch allows you to specify whether the font is proportional (an 'i' is narrower than an 'M') or fixed pitch (all characters are the same width). This is significantly less useful than it might seem. Setting Pitch to fpFixed will **not** make a proportional font use fixed-width character cells as if it were a fixed-pitch font, nor will setting Pitch to fpVariable make a fixed-pitch font into a proportional one. Qt's font matching algorithm gives more weight to the Name and CharSet than to the Pitch, so changing the Pitch of a selected font will have no effect. The only time Pitch will make a difference is when the font family Name doesn't exist on the current system, and Qt has to select the best match based on CharSet, Pitch, Size, Weight, and whether or not fsItalic is in the Style set.

TFont.Height is just like Size, but is measured in pixels, not points. Delphi programmers should note that Font.Height is always positive under Kylix, which does not use negative Height's to indicate the size *sans* internal leading.

TFont.Weight is a sort of generalized Bold attribute. Bold actually translates to a standard Weight, fwBold, while non-Bold is fwNormal. You can, at least in principle, get light or extra-bold fonts by setting Font.Weight—but few Linux fonts look any different with a Weight of 1 than with a Weight of fwNormal, or any different with a Weight of 100 than a Weight of fwBold. Note that adding and removing fsBold to and from the Style set **has no effect** if Weight is neither fwNormal nor fwBold. If the Weight may be non-standard, be sure to set Weight to fwNormal or fwBold before toggling the fsBold Style attribute.

Kylix is not Delphi

Drawing operations

The drawing operations use the drawing tools to draw on a Canvas. Drawing operations can be roughly divided into geometric operations that use the Pen and Brush, text operations that use the current Font, and bitblts that transfer rectangular pieces of an image from one Canvas to another.

Geometric operations

The geometric operations are all really pretty straightforward. I've used some of them in example code already and, of course, they're well documented in the online help. In fact, I'll just reiterate the basic point that the geometric operations outline with the Pen and fill with the Brush, and talk a bit about the operations that take open array parameters.

Graphics primitives like PolyLine and Polygon take an `array of TPoint` parameter. Perhaps the most straightforward way to supply this array is the way I did it in the Brushes project: an open array of calls to the Point function.[7] As *per* Section 1, Kylix allocates space for the array on the stack, and passes offsets into it to each call to the Point function, which fills in each Point Result record. Kylix passes a pointer to the first Point, and an invisible Length parameter, to the PolyX function, and then deallocates the array when the function returns. All this is done automatically; it's incredibly convenient and reasonably efficient.

However, open arrays like this are also assignment compatible with both dynamic arrays and regular, static arrays. This means that you can pass static arrays and dynamic arrays to the PolyX routines that take open array parameters. You usually draw figures (in every OnPaint event) many more times than you change them (when you create, destroy, or move an element). Therefore, if a given figure is relatively expensive to compute (perhaps involving perspective transforms, or z-order decisions), you may want to store the vertices in a static or dynamic array. Then, your OnPaint handler could pass the drawing primitive the pre-calculated array of vertices, instead of recalculating them every time.

For example, in this snippet

---

7. I also use this approach in the FL3 project in the ch6/Canvas group. I won't talk much about this project—a Kylix port of a Delphi 1 port of a Turbo Pascal 4 project—but I will mention it again in the section on Printing. For a detailed walkthrough of FL3, please see my magazine article about it at http://www.midnightbeach.com/jon/pubs/3D_Fractal_Landscapes.html.

```
const
  Triangle: array[1..3] of TPoint = (
    (X: 10; Y: 20), (X: 100; Y: 100), (X: 30; Y: 200)
  );
  Arbitrary: array of TPoint = Nil;

procedure TForm1.FormPaint(Sender: TObject);
begin
  Canvas.Polygon(Triangle);
  if Assigned(Arbitrary) then
    Canvas.Polygon(Arbitrary);
end;
```

Canvas.Polygon() works just as well with static arrays like Triangle and dynamic arrays like Arbitrary as with an inline array: `Canvas.Polygon(Triangle)` is functionally equivalent to `Canvas.Polygon([Point(10, 20), Point(100, 100), Point(30, 200)])`, but clearer and a bit faster.

Tip

The Slice() function allows you to select a few elements from a larger array.

Text operations

Two basic routines draw text on a Canvas in the current Font: TextOut and TextRect. These routines differ in two ways: TextOut simply takes a position and a string, and draws the string at the position, without clipping or wrapping, and without much alignment control. You can use the TextAlign property to control whether the Y parameter is the top-line or the bottom-line, but that's about it. TextRect, on the other hand, allows you to specify a clipping rectangle and to use the full complement of Qt alignment flags, including word wrap and vertical and horizontal alignment.

Delphi programmers should note that where Kylix's TextOut is basically identical to Delphi's, Kylix's TextRect adds an optional TextFlags parameter that allows you to use any combination of the Qt TextAlign flags in Table 6-4.

Kylix is not Delphi

Table 6-4. Qt TextAlign flags

Qt.pas name	Interpretation	Notes
AlignmentFlags_AlignLeft	taLeftJustify	Combining with AlignRight or AlignCenter will give unpredictable results.
AlignmentFlags_AlignHCenter	taCenter	
AlignmentFlags_AlignRight	taRightJustify	
AlignmentFlags_AlignTop	tlTop	Combining with AlignVCenter or AlignBottom or will give unpredictable results.
AlignmentFlags_AlignBottom	tlCenter	
AlignmentFlags_AlignVCenter	tlBottom	
AlignmentFlags_AlignCenter	ord(AlignmentFlags_AlignLeft) or ord(AlignHCenter)	You can only have one horizontal and vertical flag; AlignCenter counts as one of each
AlignmentFlags_SingleLine	Treat all white-space as space; don't break or wordwrap.	
AlignmentFlags_DontClip	Ignore the bounds rectangle if necessary.	Can draw where you don't want it to.
AlignmentFlags_ExpandTabs	Honor ^I characters.	
AlignmentFlags_ShowPrefix	& underlines next character; && is an un-underlined &.	
AlignmentFlags_WordBreak	Wrap long lines at word boundaries.	Can be combined with ExpandTabs.
AlignmentFlags_DontPrint	Don't draw on the Canvas.	Not particularly useful in Kylix, as TextRect doesn't return the modified bounds rect. Use TextExtent instead.

Unfortunately, the combination of a verbose mechanical translation that turned Foo::Bar into Foo_Bar and the decision to treat C++ assigned enums as non-numeric ordinals condemns us to some long-winded and unreadable code when it comes to Qt constants like these. Where a C++ programmer would combine these flags as *eg* `AlignCenter | WordBreak | ExpandTab`, we're forced to use `ord(AlignmentFlags_AlignCenter)` or `ord(AlignmentFlags_WordBreak)` or `ord(AlignmentFlags_ExpandTab)`. Ugh.

Finally, it's not uncommon to need to know how many pixels a given piece of text will take to display. Perhaps we need to display some text using multiple fonts, or we want to trim the text to the space available, or to adjust various controls to make room for the text. TextWidth returns the pixel width of a given string, without any word wrapping, & underlining, or tab expansion. Similarly, TextHeight returns the pixel height of a given string, also without any word wrapping, & underlining, or tab expansion.

If you want to specify these alignment flags, or you want both height and width, you should use TextExtent. This is available in two overloaded versions: One is a function that returns a TSize—which is just like a TPoint except that the fields are CX and CY, instead of X and Y—while the other is a procedure that modifies a TRect parameter. Use whichever is more convenient. The function calls the procedure, but the speed difference is not significant and, of course, it's always possible that this may be different in future implementations.

Kylix is not Delphi

As with TextRect, Delphi programmers should note that where Kylix's TextHeight and TextWidth are basically identical to Delphi's, Kylix's TextExtent adds an optional TextFlags parameter. The Text project of the ch6/Canvas project group illustrates this difference. TextHeight and TextWidth report the unwrapped size: The pixel width of the longest paragraph, and the height of five lines of text. By contrast, I use the form of TextExtent that allows me to pass in the same flags that I pass to TextRect, and I get the wrapped size: The pixel width of the longest wrapped line, and the height of all the wrapped lines.

Bitblts

The bitblt—or Bit Block Transfer—is the basic workhorse of GUI windowing systems. It moves a rectangular block of pixels (bits) from one portion of the screen to another, or from one off-screen bitmap to another, or between the screen and an off-screen bitmap. It's used for everything from drawing text to drawing pictures to moving windows. Paradoxically, because of its very ubiquity, Kylix programs rarely need to do many bitblt's themselves; it's built into some of the higher-level primitives and into key components like TImage and TImageList. Of course, "rarely" is not the same as "never", and so Kylix canvases include bitblt support, *via* the CopyRect procedure. (To copy a whole image—perhaps loaded from a file—onto a Canvas, you'd typically use the Draw (or StretchDraw) procedure. See the *TBitmap* section, below.)

CopyRect takes three parameters: a destination rectangle, a source Canvas, and a source rectangle. The Canvas that 'does' the CopyRect is the Canvas that's copied to. *Eg*,

```
ThisCanvas.CopyRect(ThisRect, ThatCanvas, ThatRect);
```

copies ThatRect from ThatCanvas to ThisRect on ThisCanvas. The use of a destination rectangle is actually a bit misleading: Only the Left and Top fields are used. That is, bitblts are neither clipped nor stretched when the destination rectangle is not the same size as the source rectangle. Under Kylix 1, the transfer will always be the size of the source rectangle; this may change in future releases, if Qt implements a StretchBlt function.[8]

---

8. If you really need StretchBlt abilities now, you can always synthesize them, *via* the following four step process: 1) Create a temporary TBitmap the size of the source rectangle. 2) Copy the source rectangle to the temporary bitmap. 3) StretchDraw the temporary bitmap to the destination rectangle. 4) Free the temporary bitmap.

You can use CopyRect to move an image (or part of an image) from any Canvas to any other. CopyRect can also copy from one part of a Canvas to another, as in

```
ThisCanvas.CopyRect(ThisRect, ThisCanvas, ThatRect);
```

When you do a 'self copy' like this, there is no requirement that ThisRect and ThatRect not intersect. That is, you can do bitblt's that overwrite (part of) the source. See the BitBlt project of the ch6/Canvas group for an example.

Normally, CopyRect simply replaces every pixel of the destination with the appropriate pixel of the source. In some cases—combining layers, and so on—this isn't what you want. The Canvas.CopyMode property allows you to specify one of sixteen different ways to combine the source and destination bits.

Kylix is not Delphi

> **Note**
>
> *Delphi programmers should note that Kylix's CopyMode is different from Delphi's. In Delphi, CopyMode is a 32-bit integer that allows you to specify any possible Win32 "ternary raster ops". The Borland defined copy modes like cmSrcCopy are simply named constants. In Kylix, CopyMode is an enum; if you have existing code that uses custom copy modes, you'll have to rewrite it.*

One common use for copy modes is transparent bitmaps. You use various copy modes to define a mask bitmap, a monochrome bitmap with 1's where the transparent bitmap has non-background pixels and 0's where the transparent bitmap has background pixels (or *vice versa*). You then use this mask to "cut out" this destination rectangle—*ie*, force every pixel that's going to be replaced to be black—then "drop in" a masked source rectangle. You can do this in Kylix, of course—but you shouldn't, as the TBitmap class has already done it for you. (See the *TBitmap* section, below.)

ClipRect

Normally, of course, you want to be able to draw on the whole Canvas. Sometimes, though, you don't. For example, one of my recent contracts needed to draw a "letterhead" at the top of a scrolling sheet of "paper". When the paper was scrolled down only a little, some of the letterhead showed and some didn't. Knowing how far the paper had scrolled, I could just draw the letterhead at a negative Y position, and some would appear and some wouldn't. But, the customer also wanted a decorated margin all around the paper. Undoubtedly, I could have layered one TPaintBox on top of another, but the simplest solution was to just set Canvas.ClipRect to not overwrite the decorated margin. Then, I could just write the letterhead at the top of the "paper", and the system would take care of only drawing the parts that were actually visible.

Qt actually supports clip *regions*, which are pretty comparable to Windows regions. You can create simple regions with operations analogous to drawing rectangles, ellipses, and polygons, or you can convert a transparent bitmap into a region. You can combine simple regions into compound regions with union, intersection, subtraction, and xor operators. As under Windows, you can use these regions to clip, or for hit detection *via* the QRegion::contains() function. Also as under Windows, Kylix allows you to call these functions (Qt.pas contains QRegion_ bindings for all QRegion:: member functions) but does not provide Object Pascal wrappers.

TBitmap

Naturally enough, the TBitmap class represents bitmapped images. Several components—in particular TImage and the various classes like TSpeedButton and TBitBtn with a Glyph property—have TBitmap properties, and you can of course create your own instances of TBitmap at runtime. TBitmap includes methods to load from and save to files and streams, and it has a Canvas so you can create complex drawings off-screen. You can Draw or StretchDraw a whole bitmap onto any Canvas, and you can use CopyRect to extract pieces of a bitmap.

When you Assign() one bitmap to another, all that's copied is some descriptive information. The actual image information—which can be quite large—is reference counted by Qt, in much the same way as strings are by Kylix, so that copying takes very little time or memory.

Note

See Chapter 7 for a discussion of loading bitmaps from your executables' resource section.

File formats

To load a bitmap from a file image, you call its LoadFrom or LoadFromFile methods. To save a bitmap to file, you call its SaveTo or SaveToFile methods. (You can also load from and save to a *stream*; see Chapter 7 for more on Kylix's streams.) You can control the output format by setting the Format property before calling SaveTo.

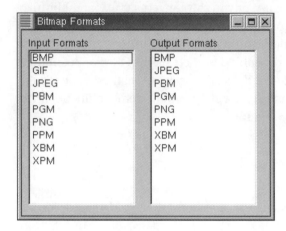

Figure 6-10. File formats

The Bitmap project in the ch6/Canvas project group illustrates how simple this can be.

```
if OpenDialog.Execute then
begin
  Image.Picture.Bitmap.LoadFromFile(OpenDialog.FileName);
  ClientHeight := Image.Top + Image.Height;
  ClientWidth  := Image.Width;
end;
```

OpenDialog.Execute pops up the open file dialog, and returns True if the user clicked "Open". The FileName property contains the complete path to the selected file. The TImage can hold a variety of different Picture types, so I use Image.Picture.Bitmap to specify that it's a bitmap file that I want to load. Kylix and Qt do all the work of checking and decoding the file format.

The Bitmap project also shows how to get the current list of supported formats. (See Figure 6-10.) This may change from release to release, as new formats come along or various legal issues ruin old standards. Under Kylix 1, for example, you can read GIF files but you can't write them.

```
procedure TBitmapFormatsFrm.FormCreate(Sender: TObject);
var
  List:    QStringListH;
begin
  List := QStringList_create;
  try
    QImage_inputFormatList(List);
    CopyQStringListToTStrings(List, InputFormats.Items);

    QImage_outputFormatList(List);
    CopyQStringListToTStrings(List, OutputFormats.Items);
  finally
    QStringList_destroy(List);
  end;
end; // TBitmapFormatsFrm.FormCreate
```

LoadFromFile and SaveToFile figures out what file format to use from the file's extension. If you are loading from or saving to an anonymous stream, you need to explicitly set the Format property to one of the values in the input or output formats list.

While Qt offers control over image quality (*eg*, JPEG compression), Kylix doesn't wrap this. To control the space/quality tradeoff, you need to make a raw Qt call, as in this function from lib/QGrabBag:

```
type
  TQtQuality = -1..100;



function SaveBitmap(        Bitmap:    TBitmap;
                    const Filename: WideString;
                    const Format:    string;
                          Quality: TQtQuality = -1): boolean;
begin
  Result := QPixmap_save(Bitmap.Handle, @ Filename, PChar(Format), Quality);
  // Quality of -1 is default quality, the same as you get from Kylix.
  // 0 is low quality (small file); 100 is high quality (big file).
end; // SaveBitmap
```

Draw and StretchDraw

Draw and StretchDraw are Canvas methods that draw any TGraphic on a Canvas. TBitmap is the most important type of TGraphic; others include TIcon and TDrawing. With Draw, you specify an X, Y position and a graphic; the graphic is drawn full sized, with the top left at [X, Y]. With StretchDraw, you specify a rectangle and a graphic; the graphic is stretched or shrunk to fit into the rectangle. Note that since a TBitmap has a Canvas property of its own, you can Draw *This* bitmap onto *That* bitmap: `That.Canvas.Draw(X, Y, This)`.

Transparency

All TGraphics have a boolean Transparent property, and Draw and StretchDraw both honor transparency. When you load a bitmap from a file with transparency information, the bitmap will, naturally, be transparent. If you want to make a normal bitmap transparent, you have to specify the transparent color.

Bitmaps have three transparency related properties: Transparent, TransparentColor, and TransparentMode. TransparentMode has two different values: tmAuto and tmFixed. tmAuto is the default, and means that the color of the bottom-left pixel will be used as the transparent color. That is, if you set Transparent to True, the TransparentColor property will be set to the color of the bottom-left pixel, and all pixels of that color will be Transparent. If you set TransparentMode to tmFixed, you can set the TransparentColor to whatever you like. (Conversely, if you do set TransparentColor, TransparentMode will automatically change to tmFixed.) Specifying a TransparentColor allows you to have bitmaps where the bottom-left pixel is not transparent.

> **Note**
>
>
> *Delphi programmers need to be aware that the CLX TBitmap is rather different from the VCL TBitmap. In particular, the CLX TBitmap has no MaskHandle property.*

Kylix is not Delphi

Low-level manipulation

Most programs draw on bitmaps just as they draw on any other canvas, with TextOut, Rectangle, Polygon, and the like. But some of the time, you need low-level pixel-by-pixel access. For example, it would have been impossible to create the gradient bitmap in the Brushes example without setting pixels one by one. Similarly, applying any sort of graphics filter to a bitmap requires reading and writing individual pixels. Since there can be hundreds of thousands of pixels in even a relatively small image, it's important that pixel-by-pixel access is very fast.

TBitmap provides both a PixelFormat property that allows you to get and set the bit-depth of each individual pixel, and a ScanLine property which gives you access to each row of the image as an array of pixels. The PixelFormat is of type

```
TPixelFormat = (pf1bit, pf8bit, pf16bit, pf32bit, pfCustom);
```

but probably most programs that manipulate pixels force it to pf32bit, as an array of 32-bit integers is a lot easier to work with than a "high color" array of 16-bit integers, a palletized array of 8-bit bytes, or (especially!) a monochrome bit-stream. (You're not likely to see pfCustom except with uninitialized bitmaps; pfCustom basically means 'unexpected result from QImage::depth()'.)

The ScanLine property is an array property that returns an untyped `pointer` to the first pixel in the row. It's your responsibility to cast it to something like a `^ array[word] of LongWord` as in this relatively long bit from the Brushes project:

```
type
  TInterpolateRec = record
                    Start, Delta, Steps: integer;
                    end;


function InterpolateRec(Start, Stop, Steps: integer): TInterpolateRec;
begin
  Result.Start := Start;
  Result.Delta := Stop - Start;
  Result.Steps := Steps;
end; // InterpolateRec


function Interpolate( const InterpolateRec: TInterpolateRec;
                        Step:           integer ): integer;
begin
  with InterpolateRec do
    Result := Start + Delta * Step div Steps;
end; // Interpolate


const
  StartColor = clBlue;
  StopColor  = clWhite;
```

```
procedure TBrushesFrm.FormCreate(Sender: TObject);
type
  ArrayOf32Bit = array[word] of LongWord;
var
  cbLeft, cbRight: integer;
  Colors, Index:   integer;
  R, G, B:         TInterpolateRec;
  ScanLine:        ^ ArrayOf32Bit;
begin
  ColorBar := TBitmap.Create;

  cbLeft   := 0;
  cbRight  := Bitmapped.Left + 250 - 1;

  Colors := cbRight - DenseSpectrum.Left;
  R := InterpolateRec( StartColor and $FF,
                       StopColor  and $FF,);
  G := InterpolateRec( StartColor and $FF00 shr 8,
                       StopColor  and $FF00 shr 8, Colors);
  B := InterpolateRec( StartColor and $FF0000 shr 16,
                       StopColor  and $FF0000 shr 16, Colors);

  ColorBar.Height      := 1;
  ColorBar.Width       := cbRight - cbLeft;
  ColorBar.PixelFormat := pf32bit;
  ScanLine := ColorBar.ScanLine[0];
  for Index := 0 to Colors do
    ScanLine^[Index + DenseSpectrum.Left + 1] :=
      pf32RGB( Interpolate(R, Index),
               Interpolate(G, Index),
               Interpolate(B, Index) );
end; // TBrushesFrm.FormCreate
```

The first line of FormCreate creates the bitmap and saves a reference to it in a private field of the form object. (The OnDestroy event handler frees it.) I calculate the bitmap Width from the position of various labels … after all, this is just a quick demo. Real code would probably bury those calculations in a single, maintainable method. The bitmap is only 1 high, and I force the PixelFormat to pf32bit. The Interpolate() and InterpolateRec() functions use a straightforward mul/div idiom to calculate each pixel's RGB components.

The real work is done in the for loop, which sets each pixel in turn. Note that it uses pf32RGB, not the TColor returning RGB function I showed earlier. pf32bit pixels use a different encoding than TColor does; their R and B com-

*ScanLine is **not** an array of TColor values, even in pf32bit mode.*

ponents are switched. Thus, the low (or first) byte is the Blue component, the second byte is the Green component, and the third byte is the Red component—or xxRRGGBB in 'pseudo-hex'.[9]

Pixmaps

Delphi programmers are familiar with the VCL's TBitmap.HandleFormat, which allows you to switch between fast, device-dependent bitmaps [DDB], and editable device-independent bitmaps [DIB]. The CLX's TBitmap doesn't work that way. Each bitmap exists both as an Image, which corresponds more or less to a DIB, and a Pixmap, which corresponds more or less to a DDB. The Image is what gets loaded and saved, and the Pixmap is what gets drawn to the screen. Kylix keeps the two in synch, and you rarely have to pay attention to the implementation details.

Kylix is not Delphi

However, you do need to keep the implementation in mind when you are working with the ScanLine property. You can use a ScanLine pointer to read and write the Image side of the bitmap. Before a changed image can be displayed, any changes have to be reflected on the Pixmap side. Unfortunately, there's no way to tell Qt 'I just changed this rectangular region of this Image; please migrate those changes to this Pixmap'—you have to regenerate the whole Pixmap.

The ScanLine property's read function—QGraphics.TBitmap. GetScanLine—handles this by calling FreePixmap before returning a pointer to the first pixel. This means that the next time you Draw the bitmap or do anything else that requires a Pixmap, Kylix will automatically regenerate one. For simple applications like the Brushes project, this poses no real concerns. I built a bitmap pixel by pixel, and it worked just fine when I assigned it to a Brush.

However, if you are doing some long operation on a large bitmap and wish to show your progress, line by line, you have to pay attention to this issue. Each time you get the ScanLine of a new row, Kylix calls FreePixmap. If you haven't done anything that required a QPixmap since the last read of the ScanLine property, this has no real effect. However, if you've gone and done a CopyRect of the updated line to the screen, you've created a new Pixmap. This took a while, which means your line-by-line processing is limited by the need to keep recreating (and freeing) Pixmaps of the whole image.

---

9. The high, or 'xx' byte represents an optional "alpha channel". If you've enabled the alpha channel, this allows you to specify the transparency of each pixel, which obviously can be very useful for layering images on top of each other, as programs like PhotoShop do, or for fading from one slide to the next. If you want to experiment with alpha channel effects, see the Qt documentation (www.trolltech.com) for QImage::setAlphaBuffer.

The best solution is to maintain a one-row working bitmap, and manipulate its ScanLine[0], then Draw or CopyRect it to the large bitmap and to the screen. Remember, you'll need to FreePixmap at the start of each row, either by reading ScanLine[0] again or by explicitly calling FreePixmap.

Printing

Printing under Kylix is reasonably straightforward. Use the QPrinters unit to get access to the Printer function. This returns a reference to a global TPrinter object that lets you select printers from the list of printers attached to the system. It also provides information about the printers, and provides a Canvas you draw on just as you'd draw on any other Canvas. The FL3 project in the ch6/Canvas group provides a simple example.

Printer.Printers is a TStringList of available printers that you can use to let users select a printer. Set Printer.PrinterIndex to select a printer from this list; by default, you print to the system default printer, or Printer.PrinterIndex = -1.

You have to call Printer.BeginDoc before you start using Printer.Canvas, and you have to call Printer.EndDoc before the page will print. Printer.PageHeight and Printer.PageWidth allow you to scale your drawings to fit the page.

Delphi programmers will note the absence of TPrintDialog and TPrinterSetupDialog from the Dialogs tab of Kylix's Component Palette. Qt does provide a dialog that pretty much combines the two, but it's a tad … quirky. (Presumably that's why Borland didn't wrap it for Kylix 1.) To bring up the Qt print dialog, use

Kylix is not Delphi

```
if (Printer.PrintAdapter as TQPrintAdapter).ExecuteSetup then {print};
```

QPainter

If you look at QGraphics.pas, you can see that TCanvas is actually a fairly thin wrapper for Qt's QPainter. Most Canvas operations are implemented as QPainter operations, using only a few lines of code. This means that dealing with Qt via the Canvas layer isn't all that much slower than dealing with Qt directly. It also means that you can call any QPainter functions that Borland doesn't wrap.

For example, QPainter includes a rich set of coordinate transformations that make it easy to rotate, scale, and translate drawings. If you want to draw rotated text, just about all you need to do is to call QPainter_rotate, as in this OnPaint event handler from the QPainter project (Figure 6-11) in the ch6/Canvas project group.

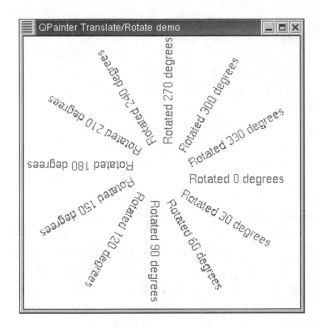

Figure 6-11. Rotated text

```
procedure TQPainterFrm.PaintRotatedText(Sender: TObject);
const
  Steps = 12;
var
  Index: integer;
begin
  Canvas.FillRect(ClientRect);
  Canvas.Font.Color := clBlue;

  // Move 0,0 to the center of the form
  QPainter_translate(Canvas.Handle, Width div 2, Height div 2);
  for Index := 0 to Steps - 1 do
  begin
    Canvas.TextOut( 35, 0,
                    Format('Rotated %0.f degrees', [Index * 360 / Steps]));
    // Rotate clockwise
    QPainter_rotate(Canvas.Handle, 360 / Steps);
  end;
end; // TQPainterFrm.PaintRotatedText
```

There are five things worth noting, here. First, you have to pass Canvas.Handle as the first parameter to the QPainter_ calls that expect a QPainterH. Second, the call to QPainter_translate() moves the coordinate system's *origin* from the top left of the form to the point we want to rotate around, the center of the form. This makes it much easier to place our rotated text, as rotation affects not just the way the text is drawn but the very meaning of the coordinates we pass to TextOut. (Try commenting out the call to QPainter_translate() and see if you can get all twelve strings to draw on the form.) Third, we can freely mix "raw" QPainter_ calls with Canvas operations like TextOut. Fourth, QPainter_rotate() takes an angle measured in **degrees** (not radians!) and rotates **clockwise**. Fifth, we don't need to call QPainter_save and QPainter_restore to protect other drawing operations from our coordinate transformations. Kylix brackets OnPaint event handlers with Canvas.Start and Canvas.Stop operations, which in turn call QPainter_begin and QPainter_end, which implicitly save and restore the coordinate system. You can, of course, use QPainter_save and QPainter_restore to push and pop coordinates during complex drawings, but you don't need to 'put things back as they were'.

The QPainter project in the ch6/Canvas project group has an action list that calls DrawRotatedText when you press CTRL+D. Outside of the different color, DrawRotatedText isn't very different from PaintRotatedText:

```
procedure TQPainterFrm.DrawRotatedText(Sender: TObject);
const
  Steps = 12;
var
  Index: integer;
begin
  Canvas.FillRect(ClientRect);
  Canvas.Font.Color := clRed;
  // Outside of a Paint handler, bracket QPainter_ calls with a Start/Stop
  Canvas.Start;
  try

    // Move 0,0 to the center of the form
    QPainter_translate(Canvas.Handle, Width div 2, Height div 2);
    for Index := 0 to Steps - 1 do
    begin
      Canvas.TextOut( 35, 0,
                      Format('Rotated %0.f degrees', [Index * 360 / Steps]) );
      // Rotate clockwise
      QPainter_rotate(Canvas.Handle, 360 / Steps);
    end;
  finally
    Canvas.Stop;
  end;

end; // TQPainterFrm.DrawRotatedText
```

All QPainter drawing operations have to be bracketed by a QPainter_begin and a QPainter_end. Kylix wraps this in Canvas.Start and Canvas.Stop, and calls Start and Stop around every Canvas drawing operation. In the OnPaint event handler, I didn't have to explicitly call Canvas.Start and Canvas.Stop, because Kylix wraps those around the event handler. But Kylix **doesn't** wrap most event handlers with Canvas.Start and Canvas.Stop because that would be inefficient, and because it has no way of knowing which Canvas you might draw on. So, when we call raw QPainter routines outside of an OnPaint event (or if we are modifying a QPainter from within another QPainter's OnPaint handler) we have to call Canvas.Start and Canvas.Stop. If you comment out the Canvas.Start and Canvas.Stop lines in DrawRotatedText, the text will not be rotated or translated, and all twelve strings will be drawn on top of each other in the top-left of the form.

Note that Canvas.Start and Canvas.Stop are implemented using a "start count" approach that means that you can safely nest Start/Stop pairs. Thus, the Start/Stop within Canvas.TextOut doesn't affect the Start/Stop around the translation and rotation. Similarly, the QPainter project would work just fine if you set the form's OnPaint handler to DrawRotatedText, which explicitly calls Canvas.Start and Canvas.Stop, instead of PaintRotatedText, which doesn't.

Note

*It's a good idea to call Canvas.Start and Canvas.Stop around **every** operation that calls QPainter_ directly, even if it's in an OnPaint event handler. The incremental cost is very modest, and you can then use the same code in paint and other event handlers. (Not to mention that people reading your code–which might be you in five years–don't have to wonder why you call Start/Stop here but not there.) I deliberately don't call Start/Stop in PaintRotatedText because I want to contrast PaintRotatedText and DrawRotatedText–PaintRotatedText is hardly an example of Best Practices!*

Finally, it's probably obvious that I've only scratched the surface of what you can do with QPainter coordinate transformations. The Qt documentation includes an example of how easy coordinate transformations make drawing a clock. Similarly, translation and scaling would simplify any line or bar charting.

Shearing does translation along one axis by an amount that increases linearly with another axis; it looks as if your drawing was composed of layers that slide over each other. It's a standard coordinate transform—Windows and Java offer shearing, too—but I suspect that this is because it's mathematically trivial, not because it's incredibly useful. You can use shearing to synthesize an (ugly) italic font from an upright font (as in the CTRL+S action of the QPainter project), but shearing's neither a perspective transform nor a z-axis rotation transform.

I've included an Object Pascal wrapping of the coordinate transformation parts of the QPainter API in lib/QGrabBag. (See the ITransform interface, and the Transform() function.) You can use the raw QPainter_ calls if you like, but I think you'll find that my thin object layer makes for clearer code—look at the difference between the rotated and sheared text procedures, where code like

```
QPainter_translate(Canvas.Handle, Width div 2, Height div 2);
```

gets replaced by

```
QPainter.Translate(Width div 2, Height div 2);
```

Forms

So far in this chapter, I've talked a lot about controls and canvases, but not much about the forms they sit on. This section is all about forms.

Opening and closing forms

When you or your users run a Kylix application, the Main Form (as defined on the Forms tab of the Project Options dialog) is shown. If you want any other forms to show, you have to make that happen.

Forms can be shown either modally or modelessly. Modal forms take precedence over other forms; when a modal form is open, none of the other forms in the application can be activated (brought to the front and given keyboard focus) until the modal form is closed. When a modeless form is active, you can activate other modeless forms. Modal forms are useful for

About boxes, yes/no popups, and some configuration dialogs, while modeless forms are more suitable for the various parts of an application that you may need at any time but not all the time. (The various windows in the Kylix IDE—the main window, Code Editor, Object Inspector, Project Manager, Alignment Palette, and the various debug windows are all modeless forms.)

The same form can be modal or modeless at different times. What controls modality is how you make the form visible. When you call ShowModal, the form is opened modally, and control doesn't return to the calling code until the form is closed. When you call Show, or set Visible to True, the form is opened modelessly; control returns to the calling code as soon as the new form is visible. Modal forms are a bit easier to deal with, as the same routine can open them and proceed to deal with any information entered on them. The Execute procedure of the standard dialogs is basically a wrapper for ShowModal that returns True when the OK or Open buttons are pressed.

If you ever need to know whether a particular form is modal or modeless, you can examine its FormState: if `fsModal in FormState`, then the form is modal. If not, it's modeless.

Modal forms can be closed by calling their Close method, by the user clicking on the frame's close button, or by setting their ModalResult property to a non-zero value. (TButton's and TBitBtn's can be configured to set their form's ModalResult automatically.) ShowModal is a function, which returns the ModalResult property of the form. Thus, you can write either

```
ThisForm.ShowModal;
if ThisForm.ModalResult = mrOK then {whatever};
```

or

```
if ThisForm.ShowModal = mrOK then {whatever};
```

Modeless forms can be closed by calling their Close method, by calling their Hide method, by setting Visible to False, or by the user clicking on the frame's close button. The visual effect of all these is the same, but Hide doesn't invoke the OnCloseQuery and OnClose event handlers. The OnCloseQuery event lets you prevent a form from being closed (perhaps it contains invalid required data) and the OnClose event lets you control *how* the form is closed.

Note that there is a difference between closing a form and freeing the form object! Normally, when a form is closed, that's all that happens. The GUI window goes away, but the object stays there, with all its data still valid. You can call the object's methods to extract data from it; you can bring it up again.

The form's OnClose event handler lets you control what happens when the form is closed, no matter how it's closed. The default is to just close the form, but you can set the `var Action: TCloseAction` parameter to either prevent the form from closing, minimize instead of closing, or close and then free the form object. Note that you will normally use this last, caFree close action only with modeless forms—code following a ShowModal often extracts some data from the form object, and it can't do this if the object has been freed—but Kylix has no mechanism to keep you from setting `CloseAction :=` `caFree` in a modal form's OnClose event handler.

It's common for infrequently used popups to be created and destroyed in the routine that shows them modally. This sort of code often uses the idiom I used in the Bitmaps project in the ch6/Canvas project group:

```
class procedure TBitmapFormatsFrm.Popup;
begin
  with TBitmapFormatsFrm.Create(Nil) do
  try
    ShowModal;
  finally
    Release;
  end;
end; // TBitmapFormatsFrm.Popup
```

Note the way that the `with TBitmapFormatsFrm.Create(Nil) do` allowed me to create a form without declaring a form variable. This is a mildly controversial practice. The vocal minority who find with statements confusing are rendered apoplectic by this "anonymous object". Most find it perfectly clear, and appreciate the avoidance of boilerplate code. For what it's worth, Borland uses this "with Create" idiom throughout the CLX and VCL.

Note

More importantly, note how I call Release, *not* Free. *You should always call Release to free a form object, not Free. Release waits for all event handlers on the form or its components to finish executing before freeing the form object. Using Free with a form may lead to intermittent SIGSEGV's.*

When you Release an open form, it will be closed before it's freed. This will trigger the OnClose event. Be careful never to use an OnCloseEvent handler that sets `Action := caFree` in a form that will be explicitly Release()d: freeing an already free form is just as much of an error as re-freeing any another sort of object.

Finally, notice how TBitmapFormatsFrm.Popup is a class procedure of the form itself. This keeps the knowledge of what's involved in popping up the form (which, admittedly, isn't much in this case) local to the form object—and saves code, if Popup is called from two or more places.

Form variables

Whenever you create a form, Kylix creates a form variable for it. A form named Foo has a form object type named TFoo and a form variable of type TFoo named Foo. By default, all forms in a project are created at load time, and their form variables are set to point to them. Only the main form is made visible, but all the others are ready to Show or ShowModal. Thus, you can bring up the form named Foo from the main form (or any other form) by including its unit in a uses clause in the other form's unit, and coding `Foo.Show` or `Foo.ShowModal`.

This is wonderfully convenient for small, simple apps, but it can make for excessively long load times for larger apps. Large apps can also end up wasting a lot of system resources on windows that are only brought up infrequently. Thus, you can control the list of auto-create forms on the Project Option dialog, and you can choose in Environment Options to change the default new form behavior to manual create. If you select manual creation, only the first form in an application is auto-created.

When a form besides the main form comes and goes a lot, it can make sense to create it the first time it's needed, and then leave it around. Thus, you'll sometimes see code like

```
if not Assigned(Frequent) then
  Frequent := TFrequent.Create(Application);
Frequent.ShowModal;
```

Similarly, one commonly needs to assure that there is no more than one instance of a form (or other object) at a time. This "singleton pattern" is usually implemented by replacing the public form variable with a form function that refers to a hidden (implementation section) form variable:

```
var
  FSingleton: TSingleton;

function Singleton: TSingleton;
begin
  if not Assigned(FSingleton) then
    FSingleton := TSingleton.Create(Application);
  Result := FSingleton;
end; // Singleton
```

However, manually created forms often don't use the form variable at all. For example, most About boxes are created using the anonymous object idiom I just used in TBitmapFrm.FormatsBtnClick. Similarly, many modeless forms are created and shown in a single operation as `TModeless.Create(Application).Show`, and rely on a caFree CloseAction to Release their memory when done.

Tip

If you don't use the form variable, you should go ahead and delete it. This will save four whole bytes of global data space and (much more importantly) reduce possible confusion.

One time where you need to be especially careful with form variables is when you have multiple copies of a form. (Kylix's "New Code Window" is an example; you can have as many different tabbed code editors open as you can keep track of.) Just as with any other object class with multiple instances, each form copy shares code but also has its own form object. Most code in event handlers and such will refer to Self, and so will have no problem with multiple instances, but you do want to be sure that you don't do something stupid like assign each new instance to the form variable as you create it. Generally, you would delete the form variable, and store references to each form in a variable length list (see Chapter 7).

Inter-system differences

Windows is a much more uniform environment than Linux. Under Delphi, when you maximize a window, it will not cover the system tray, and in fact you have to go through some contortions to get a true full-screen window. Under Kylix, your form's maximize behavior will depend on the user's window manager. That is, on some systems, windows will maximize as on Windows, and not cover system windows like panels and task bars. On other systems, windows will maximize to the full-screen size.

Kylix is not Delphi

This is just one more of those things, like BorderStyle and BorderIcons, that you can't count on.

One thing that you **can** count on is that Screen.PixelsPerInch (see Chapter 7) will vary from system to system. (According to the Qt documentation, this is "usually" a function of dot count divided by monitor size—but I found that my PixelsPerInch changed when I upgraded from Redhat 6.1 to Redhat 7.0 and installed a different set of X fonts.) This matters, because your design time PixelsPerInch is saved in the form resource if the form's Scaled property is True. At load time, Kylix will attempt to resize your Scaled forms so that they look about as big on the users' monitor as they did on yours. Thus, if you design a 300 pixels wide form on your 75 PixelsPerInch monitor, it will come up as 384 pixels wide on a 96 PixelsPerInch monitor.

The controls usually scale just fine. However, fonts never scale as smoothly. The closest match to the scaled font size may actually be bigger or smaller than the scaled size, so the text may be proportionately bigger or smaller than it was at design time. This may not matter for very simple forms. You can just leave enough white space that a 20% jump in relative font size (see the *Font* section, above) won't break things. That's a lot of white space, though, and is usually not possible on more complex forms.

Most people set Scaled to False on all but the simplest dialogs. This means that their forms look smaller on high dot count monitors than on low dot count monitors, but users are used to that, and it's generally better than having either tiny text or huge, clipped text.

Form events

Like any other component, forms have events. Some are completely generic, like the OnMouseX events. Others are generic but behave slightly differently on forms than other controls, like the OnKeyX events; others are unique to forms, like OnCreate. This sub-section is about the events that are unique to forms, with a brief description of keyboard events at the end.

A form's OnCreate and OnDestroy events are analogous to its constructor and destructor,[10] and essentially complementary. You can put setup and teardown code in either the constructor and destructor or in the OnCreate and OnDestroy events, but you generally choose either one or the other, not both. Most people use the OnCreate and OnDestroy event handlers, not the constructor and destructor, simply because it's easy to jump to them from the Object Inspector. About the only time you really will use a form's constructor is when you need something to happen **before** the `inherited Create`. This is not a very common event.

The OnCreate event is a good place to populate various components, like the ch6/Fonts project's `ScreenFonts.Items := Screen.Fonts`. The OnCreate event is also a good place to Create any non-component objects, like string lists or semaphores. Just as with class constructors and destructors, I try to always create an OnDestroy event at the same time I create an OnCreate event, and always add a Free line to OnDestroy as I add a Create line to OnCreate. This small bit of self-discipline goes a long way toward preventing memory leaks.

The OnShow and OnHide events are called when a form is opened (whether by calling Show or ShowModal or by setting Visible to True) and closed (whether by calling Hide or Close or by setting Visible to False). If a form is freed as soon it's closed, it doesn't much matter whether you put setup code in OnCreate or in OnShow. However, if a form is closed and re-opened, OnCreate will be called once, while OnShow will be called several times. It thus makes sense to restrict OnCreate to initialization (creation of non-components, and population of components that won't change) while OnShow should be used only for re-initialization (resetting any state that might change while the form is open).

When you show a form, OnActivate is called after OnShow. It's then called whenever control is transferred to this form from another form in the application. That is, imagine you have two modeless forms open, *This* and *That*, with *This* being active, the one with the keyboard focus and the highlighted caption bar. When you click on *That*, it becomes active: *This*'s OnDeactivate event fires, then *That*'s OnActivate event fires.

---

10. For that matter, OnCreate is called from TCustomForm.Create, while OnDestroy is called from TCustomForm.Destroy.

Note

Kylix distinguishes between a transfer of activation within the application, and a transfer of activation from another application. A form's OnActivate is only fired on an intra-application transfer; on inter-application transfers, the Application.OnActivate event is fired, instead. (See the Application *section of Chapter 7.)*

Finally, I've already mentioned the OnClose and OnCloseQuery events, which are called whenever the form is being closed. The OnCloseQuery event allows you to abort the close operation; the OnClose event allows you to control how the form is closed. If neither interferes with the closing process, they are followed by an OnDeactivate event, an OnHide event, and then (if CloseAction was set to caFree) by an OnDestroy event.

KeyPreview

Normally, keyboard events go to the form's ActiveControl. If you want to see keystrokes in a form-wide event handler, you need to set the form's KeyPreview property to true.

Under Delphi, this works no matter what BorderStyle you have selected. However, Qt has this strange notion that borderless windows are not interactive, and so don't get the keyboard focus. Fortunately, you can override this simply by including the line

Kylix is not Delphi

```
QWidget_setActiveWindow(Handle);
```

in the form's OnShow handler. (See the date picker component in Chapter 9 for an example.) Note that you only need to do this if BorderStyle = fbsNone! I suspect that it can't hurt to call QWidget::setActiveWindow in other cases, but I think of this as a hack and a kluge that limits portability, and prefer to use it only where necessary.

Enter as tab

One common reason to use KeyPreview is to treat the Enter key like the Tab key, and use it to move to the next active control. This is a common requirement in heavy-duty data entry applications, where the operators will be using the application day in and day out, and every keystroke counts. Particularly when using the number pad, it can be a lot faster to press Enter than to reach over and press Tab. This code from the EnterAsTab project of the ch6/Forms project group will do the trick:

```
procedure TEnterAsTabFrm.FormKeyDown(Sender: TObject; var Key: Word;
  Shift: TShiftState);
begin
  // Only works if KeyPreview is True!
  if (Key = Key_Return) or (Key = Key_Enter) then
  begin
    Key := 0;
    SelectNext(ActiveControl, not (ssShift in Shift), True);
  end;
end; // TEnterAsTabFrm.FormKeyDown
```

Note the way it sets Key to 0, to suppress further handling. The OnKeyUp event will still be called when the key is released, but the OnKeyPress event will **not** be called with a Key = ^M.

Forms are objects

One unfortunate aspect of both Kylix and Delphi is that controls are part of the published interface of the form object. This means that they're visible to code in any unit that uses the form's unit. You'll sometimes see people write code like ThisForm.Edit1.Text := ThatForm.Edit1.Text.

Don't do this!

Remember that forms are objects, and **maintain encapsulation**. Pretend that the controls aren't really visible, and read and write any data *via* public properties and methods. This is good for the same reason that encapsulation is good: It limits the effects of changes. If you change the way a particular datum is presented on the form, you only have to change one access function, not all the code throughout the system that relied on object internals.

For example, if both ThisForm and ThatForm had a

```
public
  property CurrentFilename: string read  GetCurrentFilename
                              write SetCurrentFilename;
```

which was implemented *via* the private routines

```
function TThisForm.GetCurrentFilename: string;
begin
  Result := Edit1.Text;
end; // TThisForm.GetCurrentFilename

procedure TThisForm.SetCurrentFilename(const Value: string);
begin
  Edit1.Text := Value;
end; // TThisForm.SetCurrentFilename
```

code like `ThisForm.Edit1.Text := ThatForm.Edit1.Text` could be replaced
by `ThisForm.CurrentFilename := ThatForm.CurrentFilename`. Even if the
"Edit1" control had a more descriptive name, the code that reads the form
property is simpler and clearer than the code that reads a property of a
control on the form. And, of course, if TThisForm needed any changes to
Edit1 to be mirrored *here* or *there*, it's better to do this mirroring in one place—
the SetCurrentFilename method—than all throughout the application.

Class methods

How far do you take encapsulation? Sure, public properties are an abstraction of
the data in the controls, a contract with the rest of the system that's less likely
to change than the specific controls on the form, but doesn't reading and/or
writing a handful of properties constitute embedding a lot of knowledge
about the object into the rest of the system?

Frankly, I go back and forth on this. I do find that when a particular
dialog has a narrow purpose—perhaps getting a Yes/No answer, or a name
and password—that it makes a lot of sense to provide public access to the
form through a class procedure or a class function which is responsible for
both creating and popping up the dialog, and which returns the results
either as a function result or *via* var parameters.

Note

A simple example of this is the `class procedure`
`TBitmapFormatsFrm.Popup` *(in the ch6/Bitmaps project) that
I listed in the section on* Opening and closing forms, *above.*

This means that the code that invokes this dialog knows only the one or two functions that pop it up, not the handful of properties that configure it and the handful of properties that represent the results. The calling code is smaller and clearer and, if the dialog itself changes, the narrower interface is less likely to get out of synch than a handful of inter-related properties.

Internal modularity

Forms are funny objects. Where other objects are tightly focused, modeling a single entity or presenting a single service, forms have diffuse responsibilities. They're a visual representation of often heterogeneous data, and they need to be able to read and write data models; they have UI methods, and often they have various bits of UI state data. This is unavoidable. What belongs together on a form is what makes the application easiest to use. Just as object modeling can be difficult because what initially seems a natural unit may actually be an ensemble of related concepts, so the clean modular lines of a good model may not have much correlation with what belongs together in an intuitive user interface.

Your first response to this issue should be to maintain a distinction between a *data model* and a *view* of the model. The data model is the set of objects that represent the real world phenomena that you're modeling; your user interface is a view of that model. Don't write event handlers that modify your data model directly; call methods, or read and write properties of the model's objects. Maintaining this distinction yields the same benefit that encapsulation always does: if the internals of the model change, you only have to change the access points, not part of *this* dialog and part of *that* dialog.

Maintaining a model/view distinction still leaves the view with a lot of unrelated UI code and state data. The event handlers on *this* tab aren't going to fire when *that* tab is visible; the UI state data for *this* tab is never going to have any correlation with the UI state data for *that* tab. The best response to this muddle seems to me to be to remember that in some ways object oriented languages just provided syntax to make easy what was already good practice: Modularize. Break your code into subsystems, and don't let the left hand know what the right hand is doing. Don't give *this* functional group knowledge of how *that* functional group works: Create a private method for it to call.

This is a hard subject to write about, because you really can't illustrate complexity with simple examples. So, I'm mostly going to wave my hands about and hope you understand. The way the vfind projects in Section 4 decompose routines into private methods is a partial example, as is the PrivateProperties project in the ch6/Forms project group. This is a rather useless little demo program with a couple of unexceptional private methods:

```
function TPrivatePropertiesFrm.GetPanelText(N: integer): string;
begin
  Result := StatusBar.Panels[N].Text;
end; // TPrivatePropertiesFrm.GetPanelText

procedure TPrivatePropertiesFrm.SetPanelText(N: integer;
  const Text: string);
begin
  StatusBar.Panels[N].Text := Text;
end; // TPrivatePropertiesFrm.SetPanelText
```

What's interesting about these methods is these three property declarations in the private section:

```
property Filename:  string index 0 read GetPanelText write SetPanelText ;
property FileLines: string index 1 read GetPanelText write SetPanelText ;
property Caret:     string index 2 read GetPanelText write SetPanelText ;
```

These declarations give names to the various status bar panels. As the form state changes, routines like

```
procedure TPrivatePropertiesFrm.ShowCaret;
begin
  with Memo.CaretPos do
    Caret := Format('%d:%d', [Line + 1, Col + 1]);
end; // TPrivatePropertiesFrm.ShowCaret
```

can update the status bar without 'knowing' that that's what they're doing. If I need to change the panel assignments, I just have to change the index constants in the property declarations.

I find that I use this approach whenever I have a paneled status bar. You can also use this indexed property approach to give names to the various parts of any other indexed component: the header row of a string grid, the columns of a list view, and so on. More generally, this is an example of hiding the details of how one part of the form works from the other parts, thus increasing legibility and conserving flexibility.

Interfaces and forms

Forms can implement interfaces, just like any other object can. By default, however, they implement them **without reference counting**. This is done to avoid the problems of mixing object and interface references that I discussed in Chapter 3. If you create an interface reference to a form that implements an interface, the form will not Free itself when the interface reference goes away.

I think this is a sensible default behavior, and of course we're still free to add reference counting when that's the behavior we want. For an illustration of some of the differences between normal forms and reference counted forms, see the InterfacesAndForms project of the ch6/Forms project group. (See Figure 6-12.)

Figure 6-12. The InterfacesAndForms project

Interfaced forms in Delphi

"Old" Delphi programmers may be familiar with the problem of adding interfaces to forms; forms (all components, for that matter) implement the three methods of IUnknown (which is called IInterface in Kylix), but the implementation relies on a VCLComObject property that's normally Nil. If you add an interface to a form without supplying a VCLComObject or overriding this implementation, your applications will generate Access Violations (SIGSEGV, in Linux-speak) as soon as you try to execute Form as IUnknown.

Supplying a VCLComObject is not totally trivial, so most people just cribbed some code from TInterfacedObject to create a TInterfacedForm. You could then have reference-counted forms, or (carefully!) mix object and interface references.

Familiar, yes? But out of date. Since Delphi 4, controls without a VCLComObject implement IUnknown without reference counting. That is, the reference count is always –1,[11] and neither _AddRef nor _Release ever change it—nor does _Release ever call Free. (Kylix, of course, does this the same way.) This means that there are no problems mixing object and

---

11. Just as it is for string constants.

interface references for TComponents. You can pass a direct descendant of TForm (that implements one or more interfaces) to any routine that expects one of those interfaces as a parameter, without having to manually _AddRef to avoid a disaster when the procedure returns. If you **want** a reference-counted form, you can still use TInterfacedObject-based code—but you no longer have to.

The main form is just a normal TForm that implements the ISetCaption interface—**class**(TForm, ISetCaption)–yet it can call (Self **as** ISetCaption).SetCaption without courting disaster by not calling _AddRef first. The main form isn't reference counted.

The "normal" form isn't reference counted, either. Each time you click on the Create Normal button, you create a new form. Assigning a new value to the Normal interface variable **does** dereference the old value, but this doesn't free the object. Similarly, clicking on the Release Normal button has no visible effect.

```
procedure TForm1.CreateNormalBtnClick(Sender: TObject);
begin
  Normal := TFormWithInterface.Create(Application) as ISetCaption;
  Normal.SetCaption('A normal form, with an interface');
end; // TForm1.CreateNormalBtnClick

procedure TForm1.ReleaseNormalBtnClick(Sender: TObject);
begin
  Normal := Nil;
end; // TForm1.ReleaseNormalBtnClick
```

The code behind the "Interfaced" buttons is virtually identical[12] but since the "interfaced" form **is** reference counted, the buttons act very differently. Each time you click on the Create Interfaced button, you get a new form that replaces any existing Interfaced form; when you click on the Release Interfaced button, the form goes away.

---

12. Yes, that does mean "I don't think it's worth killing trees to print it."

Splash screens

Many applications have splash screens. These are a window that comes up while the application is initializing, often with a cool graphic, that go away by themselves after a few seconds. These pose a modest difficulty for Kylix applications.

The first auto-create form is the Main Form. When the main form closes, the application closes. The process is terminated, and any other open windows are closed. If we make our splash screen the main form, we can hide it (without closing it) when we're done, but then we've lost the main form semantics; when we close the true main form, the application itself doesn't close. We could probably fiddle around with the Application object (see below) but this is unappealing. Such fiddling has a way of being dependent on the internal workings of a particular version. We don't want to have to rewrite our splash screen code every time Borland redoes some framework code. Similarly, we could have the 'real' main form close the splash screen when it closes, but while this is better, it's still a bit fragile (what if the main form changes?) and it requires that the main form know about the splash form. The simplest solution would keep all the 'magic' in the splash screen unit itself.

The SplashScreen project in the ch6/Forms project group illustrates just such a simple solution that you can drop into your own projects. It's based on an ancestral splash form in lib/GenericSplashscreen.pas, which supplies almost all the actual splash screen logic. All you need do to create your own splash screens is to inherit from TGenericSplashFrm and add the look you want, and then add a couple of lines at the bottom of your new splash screen's unit like

```
initialization
  TSplashFrm.Create(Application).Show;
```

Unit initialization blocks run before the main program block in the program (.dpr) file, so this is functionally equivalent to editing the .dpr file (Project ➤ View Source) file, and adding the Create().Show line before the normal `Application.Initialize` first line

```
begin
  TSplashFrm.Create(Application).Show;
  Application.Initialize;
```

as some Delphi splash screen code you'll find on the Net suggests. However, not only do most people prefer to leave the .dpr file alone as much as possible (some of the automatic editing that Kylix does to it can get confused if you've changed it yourself), I think it also makes a lot of Software Engineering sense to keep the special splash screen code as self-contained as possible. Why spread it through three files when two will do?

Calling TSplashFrm.Create instead of Application.CreateForm (TSplashFrm, SplashFrm) means only that the first form created with CreateForm—the main form—will **be** the main form. That is, the only difference between an auto-create form, created in the .dpr file *via* Application.CreateForm(TFormName, FormName) and a form manually created *via* FormName := TFormName.Create(Application) is that CreateForm is responsible for setting Application.MainForm.

The GenericSplashscreen unit is responsible for making sure that the main form doesn't come up until the splash screen times out. It's pretty short, so I'll include the whole file here:

Listing 6-1. GenericSplashscreen.pas

```
unit GenericSplashscreen;

interface

uses
  SysUtils, Types, Classes, Variants,
  QGraphics, QControls, QForms, QDialogs, QTypes,
  QExtCtrls, QStdCtrls;

type
  TGenericSplashFrm = class(TForm)
    Timer: TTimer;
    procedure TimerTimer(Sender: TObject);
    procedure FormCloseQuery(Sender: TObject; var CanClose: Boolean);
    procedure FormClose(Sender: TObject; var Action: TCloseAction);
  private
  public
  end;

implementation

{$R *.xfm}

procedure TGenericSplashFrm.TimerTimer(Sender: TObject);
begin
  Timer.Enabled := False; // allow form to close
  Close;
end; // GenericSplashFrm.TimerTimer
```

```
procedure TGenericSplashFrm.FormCloseQuery(Sender: TObject;
  var CanClose: Boolean);
begin
  CanClose := not Timer.Enabled;
end; // GenericSplashFrm.FormCloseQuery

procedure TGenericSplashFrm.FormClose( Sender: TObject;
  var Action: TCloseAction);
begin
  Action := caFree;
  Application.MainForm.Show;
end; // GenericSplashFrm.FormClose

initialization
  Application.ShowMainform := False;
end.
```

The first thing to note in GenericSplashscreen.pas is actually the penultimate line of the file, in the initialization block:

```
Application.ShowMainform := False;
```

Setting ShowMainForm to False means that Application.Run won't automatically Show Application.MainForm, the way it normally does. It will still be created as normal—and it can do any initialization it needs to do—and it will still be the MainForm, but it won't appear on the screen until the splash screen times out and calls `Application.MainForm.Show`.

That's the only real 'magic' here. The Timer starts running when the splash screen shows, just like any other TTimer. At the end of the Timer's Interval, it fires off its OnTimer event, which sets Enabled to False and Close's the form. Setting Enabled to False turns the timer into a one-shot event; it won't fire again until Enabled is set True. In this case, that doesn't matter, because Enabled is being used only to avoid having to declare a special TimerTicked flag for the OnCloseQuery event. I use Timer.Enabled to answer the close query. (This doesn't matter with borderless splash screens like the one in the ch6/SplashScreen project, but you could easily have a bordered splash screen if you wanted to.)

The OnClose event handler sets the close action to caFree, and calls Application.MainForm.Show, which then comes up as normal. When you close the main form, the application shuts down as it should.

Asynchronous processing

Delphi programmers—and Windows programmers in particular—are used to the Windows message-driven model. Just about all events are ultimately traceable to a message that Delphi receives and massages for us; we control the behavior of controls like the edit and rich edit controls by sending messages, and we post messages to ourselves when we want to do asynchronous processing. If we have a lengthy operation that we want to start after OnShow and the first OnPaint, we PostMessage a custom message, and handle it with a `message` procedure. The message goes to the end of the queue, and gets processed once the app is up and running. Similarly, we commonly post update messages from thread code, for the foreground thread to display the results of a threaded calculation.

Kylix is not Delphi

There's no PostMessage in Kylix.

Fortunately, Qt does have a message loop, and Qt does let us create custom messages. With just a little work, we can do the same sort of asynchronous, message-based processing in a Kylix app that we can do under Windows. This work is embedded in the lib/QMessages unit that the Asynch project in the ch6/Forms project group uses. My QMessages unit defines some functions to send and post messages to a form's Qt event loop, and a form that receives these messages. To use the QMessages framework, just create a new form that inherits from my TMessageForm.

QMessages declares procedures to post pointers, integers, strings, and interfaces, as well as routines that directly emulate the Windows SendMessage/ PostMessage API, which allows you to send a wParam and an lParam. They all work similarly, so I'll just walk through a basic PostPointer and how it gets passed to its `message` handler, and leave you to read the code more closely if you like.

Caution

As under Windows, SendMessage dispatches the event, and returns the result code. The event is handled within the thread that calls SendMessage. Do not call SendMessage from a non-GUI thread! Use the various Post procedures to pass data from background threads to the GUI thread. You can always be sure that posting data will result in a message *handler being called asynchronously in the GUI thread.*

Qt's QCustomEvent allows you pass a numeric type code and a 32-bit pointer to the event loop. The PostQtPointer function constructs a QCustomEvent, then posts it (indirectly) to a form's event queue.

```
function PostQtPointer( Handle: QObjectH;
                        Msg: SimpleMessages; Data: pointer): boolean;
var
  CustomEvent: QCustomEventH;
begin
  Result := True;
  CustomEvent := nil;
  try
    CustomEvent :=
      QCustomEvent_create( QEventType(Cardinal(QEventType_User) + Msg),
                           Data );

    MessageQueue.Post(Handle, CustomEvent);
  except
    if Assigned(CustomEvent) then
      QCustomEvent_destroy(CustomEvent);

    Result := False;
  end;
end; // PostQtPointer
```

Now, it turns out that QApplication::postEvent is not thread-safe. The simplest way to make it thread-safe and retain the benefits of letting background threads run at full speed (*ie*, not wait for TThread.Synchronize to return) is to add another thread. MessageQueue.Post uses a critical section to add the Handle/Event pair to a queue in a thread safe way, and then sends a signal (*via* a TSimpleEvent) to the new thread. This new message queue thread spends most of its time waiting on the TSimpleEvent. When the event is signaled, the message queue thread uses Synchronize to call a method that posts each message in the queue. Since the synchronized method runs in the GUI thread, there's no danger of its calling QApplication::postEvent while Qt itself is. The only real consequence of this new message queue and its thread is Synchronize runs very slowly when integrated debugging (Tools ➤ Debugger Options) is turned on; applications that use QMessages will run much faster from the command line (or when integrated debugging is turned off) than when they run within Kylix's debugger.

PostQtPointer is a hidden (implementation section) function. You call it indirectly through the TMessageForm.PostPointer function or one of its siblings.

```
function TMessageForm.PostPointer(Msg: SimpleMessages; Data: pointer):
  Boolean;
begin
```

```
  Result := PostQtPointer(Handle, Msg, Data);
end; // TMessageForm.PostPointer
```

Now, under Windows, message handling is a more fundamental part of
GUI programming than under Qt. Where Windows controls send messages
to applications whenever anything happens, Qt controls use a *slot* and *signal*
approach (see Section 3) that means that they don't send messages: they call
the application directly. Because messages are less fundamental under Qt,
the messages that we send ourselves with QApplication::postEvent don't
automatically get dispatched to a message handler the way that messages that
we send ourselves with PostMessage() do under Windows. Rather, we have to
override the form's EventFilter function, and catch the type code there.

TMessageForm does this, and puts the type code and 32-bit Data into a
record that it then hands to Dispatch. As *per* the Borland documentation,
Dispatch then looks for a message handler with an identifier that matches the
type code, and passes the record to it. Here's a somewhat abbreviated version:

```
function TMessageForm.EventFilter(Sender: QObjectH;
  Event: QEventH): Boolean;
var
  PointerMessage: TPointerMessage;
  EventType:      QEventType;
begin
  Result := True;
  EventType := QEvent_type(Event);
  case EventType of
   QEventType_CMPostSimpleLow..QEventType_CMPostSimpleHigh:
    begin
      PointerMessage.Msg  := Cardinal(EventType) - Cardinal(QEventType_User);
      PointerMessage.Data := QCustomEvent_data(QCustomEventH(Event));
      Dispatch(PointerMessage);
    end;
    else Result := inherited EventFilter(Sender, Event);
  end;
end; // TMessageForm.EventFilter
```

This EventFilter function means that forms that descend from
TMessageForm only have to declare a message method, and call PostPointer()
to pass a pointer to that method asynchronously. That is, the PostPointer call
will return, and the calling code can do whatever else it has to do, and the
message handler will be called as soon as any messages ahead of it in the
queue are processed. Importantly, the message handler will be called in the

GUI thread, not in whichever non-GUI thread may have called PostPointer(), which means that the message handler can safely make GUI calls. (Threaded code can't do this; see Chapter 7.)

The following extracts from the ch6/Asynch project may make this a bit clearer

```
const
  qt_Pointer   = qtm_Simple + 3;

type
  TAsynchFrm = class(TMessageForm)
    Status: TLabel;
    PostPointerBtn: TButton;
    procedure PostPointerBtnClick(Sender: TObject);
  private
    procedure qtPointer(   var Msg: TPointerMessage);   message qt_Pointer;
  end;

procedure TAsynchFrm.PostPointerBtnClick(Sender: TObject);
begin
  inherited;
  PostPointer(qt_Pointer, pointer(Self));
end; // TAsynchFrm.PostPointerBtnClick

procedure TAsynchFrm.qtPointer(var Msg: TPointerMessage);
begin
  Status.Caption := 'Posted pointer was $' + IntToHex(integer(Msg.Data), 8);
end; // TAsynchFrm.qtPointer
```

Caution

Message *methods require only that their single parameter be a* **var** *parameter. They don't do any type checking.* You *are responsible for making sure that you post a pointer to a method that expects a TPointerMessage, or an integer to a method that expects a TIntegerMessage.*

Posting reference counted objects

Strings, interfaces, and dynamic arrays are actually just pointers to a reference counted data block, so we can Post them, too. This is a bit trickier than passing data that's not reference counted, because the data is dereferenced when the Post function returns, and without a bit of hackery it may not still be around when the message handler gets fired. To make sure that the data doesn't get freed, we have to increment the reference count before we post a pointer to the event queue.

With interfaces, of course, we can just use AddRef. Borland doesn't supply anything equivalent for strings, but the String_AddRef and String_Release functions in my lib/GrabBag are pretty straightforward. (See the sidebar for details.)

....

String_AddRef and String_Release

```
function String_AddRef(const S: string): pointer;
// increments ref count, returns pointer(S)
var
  Reference: string;
begin
  Result := pointer(S);       // Typically used where storing a raw pointer
  Reference := S;             // Increment reference count, unless < 0
  pointer(Reference) := Nil; // DON'T deref Reference on exit
end; // String_AddRef
```

The first line just assigns the address of the first character (if any—the string may be '') to the Result. This is just a convenience feature, since the most typical use of this function will be to pass a string *via* an untyped pointer, as we're doing here; to a callback function's Data parameter; or to a TCustomViewItem's Data parameter. (For an example, see the TMessageForm.PostString procedure in lib/QMessages.)

The real work of the function is done in the next two lines. Copying the string to a local variable increments the reference count, if any. (Empty strings aren't reference counted, obviously, nor are string constants.) By casting the local to pointer, we bypass the reference counting mechanism; by setting the pointer to Nil, we assure that the string will not be dereferenced when the function exits and the string goes out of scope.

```
procedure String_Release(const S: string);
var
  Reference: string;
begin
  pointer(Reference) := pointer(S); // Assign without changing reference
                                    // count; reference will be derefed on
                                    // exit, unless ref count < 0
end; // String_Release
```

Again, by assigning to pointer(Reference) and not simply to Reference, we bypass the reference counting mechanism. The effect is to set the local string to the passed in string. When the procedure exits, the string goes out of scope, and the string is dereferenced.

> **Note**
>
> *String constants are stored in the application's code pages with a reference count of –1. This is a special value that means that the string constant doesn't live on the heap as other strings do. String constants are not reference counted the way string values are: The reference count is never incremented, however many copies are made; nor is the reference count ever decremented when a copy goes out of scope. Because the string constant doesn't live on the heap it doesn't ever need to be freed.*

It's not possible to write code that works with any dynamic array, so QMessages doesn't offer any PostArray support.

The code to Post an interface is

```
function TMessageForm.PostInterface(Msg: SimpleMessages;
  const Data: IInterface): Boolean;
begin
  Data._AddRef; // So it doesn't get destroyed before EventFilter sees it
  Result := PostQtPointer(Handle, Msg, pointer(Data));
end;
```

and the corresponding bit from the TMessageForm.EventFilter case statement is

```
QEventType_CMPostInterfaceLow..QEventType_CMPostInterfaceHigh:
begin
  InterfaceMessage.Msg  := Cardinal(EventType) - Cardinal(QEventType_User);
  pointer(InterfaceMessage.Data) := QCustomEvent_data(QCustomEventH(Event));
  Dispatch(InterfaceMessage);
end;
```

Explicitly adding a reference means that the strings and interfaces 'know' that there's a reference to them in the event queue. QMessages defines separate message code ranges for strings, interfaces, and "simple" 32-bit data; this lets the EventFilter know if a given 32-bit value needs to be assigned to a string or interface message record. As in the String_AddRef and String_Release routines, these assignments are *via* pointer casts that don't touch the reference count. You can think of the EventFilter code as redeeming the pledge made by the explicit _AddRef in the Post call, or you can think of it as the Post call making an assignment to a record in the EventFilter.

CHAPTER 7

Foundation objects

Foundation objects

THE PREVIOUS CHAPTER was all about objects that you can see: controls, canvases, and forms. Some of the sample code in that chapter referred to various non-visual objects: the Items property of various components, the Application and Mouse variables, and so on. Accordingly, in good top-down fashion, this chapter will cover the key non-visual, or foundation objects. It starts with three global variables in the QForms unit—Application, Screen, and Mouse—and then moves on to collections, streams, and the system clipboard, before concluding with a long discussion of threads.

Visual helpers

The Application, Screen, and Mouse fill a somewhat ambiguous ecological niche. They're not visual objects that you can manipulate at design time in the same way as controls or forms, but neither are they out and out intangible in the same way as lists of strings. This ambiguity makes it somewhat arbitrary whether they should be the last section of the *Visual objects* chapter or the first section of the *Foundation objects* chapter. In the end, the sheer length of the *Visual objects* chapter pushed these QForms globals forward.

Application

All Kylix GUI applications have an Application variable, a global instance of the TApplication class. The Application variable is slightly different in Apache DSO's than in desktop applications; console applications have no Application variable. This section is about the Application variable in normal, GUI apps.

The Application variable fills two different roles. It's both a wrapper for the Qt QApplication class (Application.Handle is a QApplicationH) and a repository for Delphi-derived application-wide properties, methods, and events. These two roles are not totally distinct, both because Qt is very Delphi-like to start with, and because some standard Delphi methods, like Application.ProcessMessages, are just passed straight on to Qt.

One key role that Application fills is being the primary owner of forms. Just as controls on a form are owned by the form, which means that they are freed when the form is, so forms are usually owned by Application, which means that the forms are freed when the Application object is freed at application shut-down time. All auto-create forms—the forms that Kylix creates at application start-up time, which are shown in the left-hand list box of the Forms tab of the Project ➤ Options dialog—are owned by Application. Any forms that you manually create (by explicitly calling TFormType.Create()) that may stick around until the application shuts down should also be owned by Application: TFormType.Create(`Application`). The only exception should be forms that you Create, ShowModal, and Release in a single routine, perhaps using the `with Create` idiom. Giving these an owner just slows creation and destruction, so they will often have no owner at all: TFormType.Create(`Nil`).

Properties

As in other sections, I have no intention of competing with or replicating the documentation that comes with Kylix. Table 7-1 is not an exhaustive list of Application properties—for that you can see the online documentation and the QForms source—so much as a brief overview of the most important properties.

Table 7-1. Key Application properties

Property	Commentary
Active	Application.Active is defined to be True when one of the application's forms has the keyboard focus, and False when some other application has keyboard focus. You can use this to act differently when the app doesn't have the focus than when it does, but be aware that it's subject to false positives. A timer event, for example, will set Application.Active to True.
ExeName	Application.ExeName contains the full filename of the application's executable file. May not be equal to ParamStr(0): Kylix's RTL gets ParamStr(0) from the shell, which may or may not expand invocations like ./appname to reflect the full path. ExeName, by contrast, first asks the Linux program loader to tell it the app's name. If that fails, it inspects /proc.

Table 7-1. Key Application properties (Continued)

Property	Commentary
Font	Application.Font is the font used by forms whose ParentFont is True. Note that setting this does **not** allow you to change all forms at once. Forms will only change their base font when they change their ParentFont property from False to True.
Handle	Application.Handle is the QApplicationH value that you need to pass to any non-static QApplication member function.
Hint	Application.Hint is the hint being displayed during an Application.OnHint event. (See below.) You can examine Application.Hint to display part of the hint on a status bar.
Icon	Delphi programmers will expect Application.Icon to control the icon that appears in the task list at the bottom of the screen. However, at least under some desktops and window managers, this will be the Icon of the individual forms, if they have one.
KeyState	Application.KeyState is the current state of the shift keys, which may not agree with the shift state parameter to various events, if their processing was delayed.
Palette	You can query Application.Palette to get the actual colors for various color "roles" and for "mapped" colors like clNormalText. Setting the palette will change the "stock" brushes used to paint Qt controls (TWidgetControls).
ShowHint	Setting Application.ShowHint to False overrides the ShowHint properties of individual forms.
ShowMainForm	When Application.ShowMainForm is True, as it is by default, the main form is shown on application startup. When you set this to False before Application.Run is called, the MainForm will not show until you explicitly Show it. This can be used for splash screens (as in Chapter 6) or for applications that should remain invisible until some specific condition is met.
Style	Application.Style allows to you customize the appearance of various widgets on an application-wide basis. See the Syles section, below.

Kylix is not Delphi

Kylix is not Delphi

Table 7-1. Key Application properties (Continued)

Property	Commentary
Title	As with Icon, Delphi programmers will expect Application.Title to control the text that appears in the task list at the bottom of the screen. However, at least under some desktops and window managers, this will be the Caption of the individual forms, if they have one.

Methods

As in the Properties section above, these are just the most commonly used Application methods.

Table 7-2. Key Application methods

Method	Commentary
BringToFront	Brings the application's current window to the top of the z-order, which can be useful for alerting the user when a long-running process has finished, or an error has occurred. This can be very disruptive for the user, who may be typing away in another application when suddenly her keystrokes start going somewhere else. It's probably a **very** good idea to make your application's use of Application.BringToFront a user settable option. Also, some window managers may suppress this, just as some versions of Windows do.
MessageBox	Application.MessageBox brings up a generic dialog box with the caption, text, and button set you specify. It's not only more general than ShowMessage, it's also available without adding QDialogs to a uses clause.
Minimize	Despite the documentation, Application.Mimimize seems to just minimize the current form; any other of the application's visible modeless forms are not affected.
NormalizeTopMosts	This is **supposed** to temporarily strip the fsStayOnTop attribute from any stay on top forms—but fsStayOnTop doesn't seem to work with many window managers.

Table 7-2. Key Application methods (Continued)

Method	Commentary
ProcessMessages	Handles any pending messages in the Qt event queue. If you call Application.ProcessMessages periodically during a long-running operation, your application will respond to mouse clicks and key presses. Calling Application.ProcessMessages too often will slow down an already slow operation; not calling Application.ProcessMessages often enough will render your application unresponsive. Threads (see the *Threads* section of this chapter) can be a better solution, but pose various synchronization issues.
Restore	Converse of Application.Minimize, and subject to all the same caveats.
RestoreTopMosts	Converse of Application.NormalizeTopMosts, and subject to all the same caveats.
Terminate	Application.Terminate shuts down your GUI application gracefully. **Do not** call Halt in a GUI app except in unit initialization clauses. Once Application.Run has been called (in the .dpr file—Project ➤ View Source), use Application.Terminate instead of Halt.

Events

There are several application-wide events that are useful in various applications. Unfortunately, Kylix 1.0 does not include Delphi's ApplicationEvents component, which replicates Application events to any form that cares about them, and allows you to set event handlers at design time. By the time you read this, you may be able to download or buy a replacement, and Borland will probably add the ApplicationEvents component in a future release of Kylix. If not, however, you'll have to install handlers for these events in OnCreate handlers, and will have to handle replication yourself if two or more forms are interested in, say, the OnShowHint event.

Kylix is not Delphi

Table 7-3. Key Application Events

Event	Commentary
OnActivate	Fires when the application gets the focus back from another application. Note that the current form does **not** get an OnActivate event in this case. That only happens when focus changes within the application. To do something whenever a form gets focus, it's necessary to handle both the form's OnActivate event and the application's OnActivate event.
OnDeactivate	The converse of OnActivate. Fires when the application loses the focus to another application. Again, the current form does **not** get an OnDeactivate event in this case.
OnEvent	OnEvent is fired on **every** Qt event that Application receives. You can set its Handled parameter to True to suppress further processing. Be careful with this event—doing too much on every event can make your app very slow.
OnException	OnException is fired on any exception not caught by a try … except block. You can handle this event to change the default exception display behavior; to log errors; or even to automatically contact you over the net.
OnHint	Fired whenever a tool-tip window pops up. You can use this to display a longer help message on a status bar or in a help label. See "GetLongHint" in the Borland documentation.
OnIdle	Called whenever the event queue goes empty. You can use this for simple background processing; for updating the state of various Actions, you should use their OnUpdate event.

Table 7-3. Key Application Events (Continued)

Event	Commentary
OnShowHint	This is perhaps the most useful of all the Application events. At a minimum, this allows you to customize the size and duration of the tool-tip window. Its greatest utility, though, is that you can use it to give a different hint depending on where the mouse is in a control. That is, instead of a single hint like "This tree represents your document's structure", you can have different hints depending on which part of the structure the mouse is over. Or, you can use it to display the full value of items that were chopped off by a narrow column. See the plugin demo project in Chapter 8 for an example.

Styles

The Application.Style property represents a Qt QStyle object. As such, it allows you to change the look of your whole app; you can change the appearance of every control by setting Application.Style appropriately. The bplAppComponents.so project in the ch7/Application project group contains a TApplicationStyle component that simplifies this process by allowing you to set Application.Style properties at design-time.

Perhaps the most useful part of Application.Style is the DefaultStyle property, which allows you to select between the default MotifPlus look (Figure 7-1) and a Windows 95 look (Figure 7-2). You can also select CDE, though I can't imagine why you'd want to, as well as the more appealing Platinum (Figure 7-3) and QtSGI looks (Figure 7-4). The Styles project in the ch7/Application project group will let you quickly experiment with DefaultStyle.

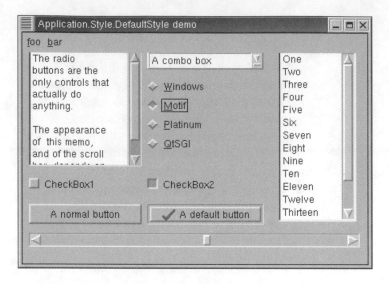

Figure 7-1. The MotifPlus style

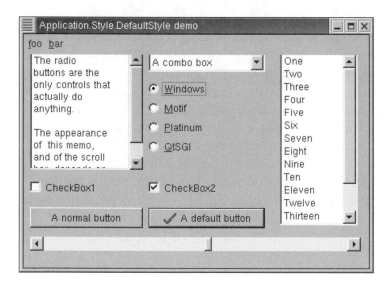

Figure 7-2. The Windows style

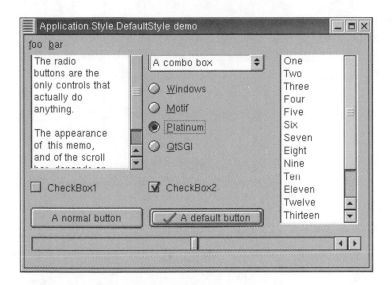

Figure 7-3. The Platinum style

Figure 7-4. The QtSGI style

Beyond that, there are properties to control the sizes of various elements, and event handlers that let you draw components. These are much like owner-draw controls, except that you can install a single handler to draw all the Qt controls of a certain type throughout your application.

Note

Unfortunately, Style support in Kylix 1.0 is really rather wobbly, as is Qt's QStyle object. Play with Application.Styles at your own risk. Doing much but setting DefaultStyle can be an exercise in frustration, with some events firing for one and only one DefaultStyle and so on.

Kylix 1.0 does not support desktop themes.

Screen

All Kylix GUI applications have a Screen variable, a global instance of the TScreen class, that 'lives' in the QForms unit. Unlike Application, Screen does not have a Handle property that corresponds to a Qt object; it's more of a pure-Kylix construct, which primarily represents the screen that your application is running on. You can read Screen to get information about the screen size and installed fonts, and you can write to Screen to set the current cursor and help font. Curiously, Screen also has some functionality that might seem to more naturally belong to Application; the Forms property is an array of all active forms, and the two Screen events concern transfer of focus within your application.

Screen information

Screen.Height and Screen.Width are the physical size of the user's screen. On some systems, this is the size of a form with WindowState = wsMaximized, while on other systems forms maximize to fill what Windows calls the "work area", the part of the screen that's not covered with system windows like panels and task bars. There does not appear to be any reliable way to determine the size of this work area. Calling QWidget_frameGeometry(Application.Desktop, {…}) as I do in the ScreenInfo project of the ch7/QForms project group, **may** give you work area information that differs from the screen size, or it may not. As with so many of these frustrations, it all depends on the user's window manager.

Screen.PixelsPerInch is "usually" calculated as the Screen.Height divided by the monitor's physical display height.[1] On some systems, the display size is gotten straight from the monitor, *via* hardware handshake protocols. On LCD displays, this is going to be pretty accurate, but of course CRT's have controls that let users stretch or shrink the display, so the display height may be only approximate. With older monitors, the display size may be only a guess, or may be derived from a (fallible) user setting. In other words, Screen.PixelsPerInch is a pretty rough value, which is another good reason to be wary of using forms with Scaled set True.

Screen.Fonts is a TStrings list (see below) of all font families available on the current system for the user's locale. The list comes straight from QFontDatabase::families, and contains only the font families' names. For more information on a particular font, see the discussion of fonts in the previous chapter, or QFontInfo in the Qt documentation.

Screen control

Screen.HintFont lets you change the font used for all tool-tips windows in an application.

Setting Screen.Cursor changes the current mouse cursor, as in this procedure from the ScreenCursor project in the ch7/QForms project group.

```
procedure TScreenCursorFrm.SpecialZoneMouseMove(Sender: TObject;
  Shift: TShiftState; X, Y: Integer);
begin
  if Mouse.Capture = Nil
    then begin // now entering the Special Zone - dum ba de bum da
        Mouse.Capture := SpecialZone;
        Screen.Cursor := crCustom;
        end
    else with SpecialZone do
        if not PtInRect( BoundsRect,
                        ClientToParent( Point(X, Y), Parent )) then
        begin // now leaving the Special Zone
        Mouse.Capture := Nil;
        Screen.Cursor := crDefault;
        end;
end; // TScreenCursorFrm.SpecialZoneMouseMove
```

---

1. As *per* Chapter 6, it seems to depend on X font settings more than the Qt documentation implies.

Screen.Cursor is of type TCursor, which is actually a SmallInt, or –32768..32767. Values like crDefault and crHourGlass are predefined constants that refer to standard cursors, but you can create an arbitrary QCursor, using Qt calls, and associate it with a TCursor value by assigning to Screen.Cursors.

```
const
  crCustom = 1;

procedure TScreenCursorFrm.FormCreate(Sender: TObject);
var
  QBitmap: QBitmapH;
  QCursor: QCursorH;
begin
  with TBitmap.Create do
  try
    LoadFromResourceName(HInstance, 'CustomCursor');
    QBitmap := QBitmap_create;
    try
      QBitmap_from_QPixmap(QBitmap, Handle);
      QCursor := QCursor_create(QBitmap, QBitmap, 8, 20);
    finally
      QBitmap_destroy(QBitmap);
    end;
  finally
    Free;
  end;
  Screen.Cursors[crCustom] := QCursor;
end; // TScreenCursorFrm.FormCreate
```

The predefined cursor constants are all between 0 and –22. They are not privileged in any way; assigning to Screen.Cursors will change any of the stock cursors, including crDefault. crCustom is set to 1, because I don't want to overwrite any of the standard cursors.

Note

There is no requirement that you use contiguous cursor numbers. Screen.Cursors is implemented with a linked list, so using a cursor number 10,000 doesn't waste space on 'slots' for blank cursors from 1 to 9,999. Feel free to use some sort of encoding scheme where these *cursors are numbered from 100 while* those *cursors are numbered from 200 and so on. Just make an effort to not populate Screen.Cursors with custom cursors that you don't actually use, as each additional cursor increases (modestly) the average time that setting Screen.Cursor takes.*

The FormCreate method loads a bitmap (Figure 7-5) from the application's 'resource fork' (see the *TResourceStream* section, below) then creates a QBitmap and copies the bitmap's Handle property (a QPixmap) to the QBitmap. It then calls the form of QCursor_create that allows it to specify an image and a mask bitmap, which lets the cursor be transparent. (Real code would almost certainly use different bitmaps for the image and the mask, so as to put a white border around the cursor.) The 8, 20 parameters position the hotspot on the 'hook' of the J; negative parameters center the hotspot on the image, while hotspot values that are too large can cause X errors or even hang Linux.

Figure 7-5. A vanity cursor

Note

Qt 2.2 supports only static, monochrome cursors. You cannot have animated or colored cursors as under Windows.

Table 7-4. QCursor Image and Mask interaction

		Bitmap	
		Color 0	Color 1
M a s k	Color 0	Transparent	Undefined
	Color 1	White	Black

Table 7-4 follows the QCursor documentation in that it is couched in terms of "color 1" and "color 0", not "black" and "white". The meaning of "color 0" and "color 1" seems to depend on how you create the QBitmap. When I first wrote this sample, I used the version of QBitmap_Create that reads an external .png file, and had to use a reverse-video (white on black) image. When I found the QBitmap_from_QPixmap routine that lets me generate a QBitmap from a TBitmap, the cursor was suddenly reverse video, and I had to toggle the bitmap file that I link into the application's resource fork. In other words: Be prepared for a bit of experimentation with cursor image formats!

Finally, note that you still own the custom cursor after you assign it to Screen.Cursors, and are responsible for calling QCursor_destroy(); the Screen variable does not free custom cursors at application shutdown.

```
procedure TScreenCursorFrm.FormDestroy(Sender: TObject);
begin
  QCursor_destroy(Screen.Cursors[crCustom]);
end; // TScreenCursorFrm.FormDestroy
```

Application information

The Screen.Forms and Screen.DataModules act much like a control's Controls array; Screen.FormCount is the number of forms the application currently has instantiated (closed forms appear in the Forms array), and the Forms array is indexed from 0 to FormCount - 1. The Forms array has a rough correspondence with the intra-application z-order: When the user brings a form to the front by clicking on it, it moves to the front of the Forms array. However, programmatic changes to the z-order (*via* calls to BringToFront and SendToBack) do not affect the Screen.Forms array. Note that the Forms array does **not** represent ownership; all instances of all application forms are listed in it, whether they are owned by Application or not. (Presumably, this is why the Forms array is in Screen, and not in Application.)

The Screen.CustomForms array is very similar to the Screen.Forms array. However, where the Forms array lists only forms that descend from TForm, the CustomForms array also lists forms that descend from TCustomForm but not from TForm, like TReplaceDialog.

Data modules are special objects that look like forms at design time, but are invisible at run time. They contain data access components (or any other non-visual component), and can be used to share "business rules" across all forms in an application, or between applications. The Screen.DataModules array and Screen.DataModuleCount are just like Forms and FormCount, except for data modules.

The Screen variable also has a whole suite of ActiveXxx members—ActiveControl, ActiveCustomForm, ActiveForm, and ActiveWidget—that track the part of the application that currently has the keyboard focus, if any. The OnActiveControlChange and OnActiveFormChange allow you to install application-wide hooks that are fired whenever focus changes.

Screen.OnActiveFormChange is very much the converse of Application.OnActivate and Application.OnDeactivate; Screen.OnActiveFormChange is called only when focus changes within your app, while Application.OnActivate and Application.OnDeactivate are called only when focus moves to or from your app and another app.

Mouse

The Mouse variable is much simpler than the Application or screen variable. It has no public methods or events, and only four properties: Capture, CursorPos, DragImmediate, and DragThreshold.

I've already used Mouse.Capture in several places, including the ch7/ScreenCursor project. When you set Mouse.Capture to a TControl, that control will get all mouse messages—including ones that it normally wouldn't get when the mouse is outside of its BoundsRect—until you release the mouse by setting Mouse.Capture to Nil. If you don't reset Mouse.Capture to

Nil, the user will lose mouse-clicks and such, so be sure to reset Mouse.Capture when you're done with it.

Mouse.CursorPos is a TPoint property that will give you the mouse's current position—in screen coordinates—when you read it. Note that you **can** set Mouse.CursorPos, as in the Mouse project in the ch7/QForms project group. The Mouse project moves the mouse to a random location every five seconds, which is very annoying and rather pointless except as a demonstration. You might set Mouse.CursorPos to place the mouse over a default control, but many users will find this very annoying and you should definitely make it optional behavior.

Mouse.DragThreshold is the number of pixels that the user has to drag the mouse to trigger a dmAutomatic drag and drop operation. It only matters if Mouse.DragImmediate is False; when DragImmediate is True, any drag starts a dmAutomatic drag and drop operation.

Lists

Kylix has a set of standard list classes. All have similar interfaces that differ mostly in the data type that the list holds. That is, TList holds generic pointers and you can Add pointers to the Items[] array of pointers; TInterfaceList holds interfaces and you can Add interfaces to the Items[] array of interfaces; and TStringList holds strings and you can Add strings to the Strings[] array of strings.

All the list classes store pointers—not actual data—in an array that is 'chunked' to minimize reallocations. Thus, both additions and random access are cheap. While insertion and deletion are more expensive, they're not particularly dear in absolute terms; it just doesn't take all that long to Move() even a few thousand pointers one 'slot' left or right.

Several components directly expose TStrings as a Lines or Items property, like TMemo and TComboBox. Other components hide TLists behind a Count property and a type-safe array, like TComponent's Components and ComponentCount, or TScreen's Forms and FormCount. You can also use the list classes in your own code, either **as** lists or just as intermediate steps in some algorithm that takes advantage of, say, a TList's sorting capabilities or a TString's associative array abilities.

There is some overlap between the list classes and dynamic arrays, but most of the time it will be fairly clear which is better to use.

Common interface

All the list classes share a certain core functionality. All these core methods and properties work the same, whether the list contains pointers, interfaces, objects, or strings.

Table 7-5. Core list functionality

Type	Name	Role
function	Add	Adds its argument to the **end** of the list, returning its index within the Items array.
procedure	Clear	Deletes all entries in list, and releases the memory the list used. The interface and string lists Finalize their lists before freeing them, thus dereferencing all interfaces and strings added to the list.
procedure	Delete	Deletes a single item, by Items index. The interface and string lists finalize the list entry.
procedure	Exchange	Swaps the positions of two list items; used in sorting. Unlike Move, both items stay in the list.
function	IndexOf	Looks up a value in the list, returning its index or –1. Normally does a linear search; some lists can be maintained in a sorted order, in which case IndexOf does a binary search.
procedure	Insert	Inserts an item at a specific index, pushing other items to the right. The insertion point **must** be between 0 and Count - 1.
procedure	Move	A combination of Delete and Insert that moves an item from the Source index to a Target index. Unlike Exchange, the Target item is not moved to the old Source position: The Source item is deleted and inserted before the Target.
function	Remove	Deletes an item by value, returning its old index.
procedure	Assign	Copies the contents of one list to another. TList adds optional boolean operations.
property	Capacity	The number of 'slots' in the underlying pointer array. You can set this before a lengthy series of additions to minimize heap churning.

Table 7-5. Core list functionality (Continued)

Type	Name	Role
property	Count	The number of values in the list. Indices **always** run from 0 to Count – 1.
property	Items / Strings	An array of values, indexed from 0 to Count – 1. TLists have Items; TStrings have Strings. Both are their class's `default` property, so you can refer to either `MyList[Index]` or `MyList.Items[Index]`.

Functions that return lists

The list classes all share a core problem. They are classes, and someone has to be responsible for freeing them. The general rule, of course, is "Free What You Create", which is all very well when "You" are a class with a constructor and destructor, or a form with an OnCreate and an OnDestroy event—but what about when "You" are a service, a utility function that gets called from anywhere in the system?

The danger of creating a list (or any) class in a function and returning it as the Result is that this hides the process of creation. However carefully you document that the caller is responsible for freeing the result—even if you name the function something like CreateListOfWidgets—**someone** will call the function and forget to free the Result. That someone might be you, whether tomorrow or eighteen months after you wrote the code; it might be the guy five years from now who inherited your code from the guy who inherited it from you; but it **will** happen.

Whatever the converse of Best Practice is, writing functions that create and return objects is it. Don't do it. And, if you have to be bad, do make it a local function that can't get called outside its unit, and only use it in code like

```
with CreateListOfWidgets do
try
  // whatever
finally
  Free;
end;
```

But don't do it, please. Write a procedure that takes a list class as a parameter and populates it. That leaves creation and destruction under the control of the caller, which is a much safer pattern.

For example, see the TWidgetControl.GetTabOrderList method, which populates a TList. Similarly, the QTypes unit's CopyQStringListToTStrings procedure reads a Qt QStringList and populates a Kylix TStrings, while the TIniFile ReadSection methods copy parts of a .ini file to their TStrings parameters.

If you really need a function that returns a list, write a function that returns a dynamic array or an interface. There are no "ownership" issues with dynamic arrays and interfaces; they're reference counted, and they free themselves when the last reference to them goes away.

TList

TList holds untyped pointers. As such, it's useful both as is, and as the base class for a type-safe list class that holds either Integers, or a specific type of pointer, or a specific type of object. A type-safe list class is just a thin wrapper around TList; it redeclares Items as, say, an array of integers and redefines methods like Add and IndexOf so that they can only take integer values. Using a type-safe wrapper class means that you don't have to cast values to and from the generic pointer type every time you use the list, which reduces both clutter and the chances of a careless error. Kylix defines a few such wrappers in the Contnrs unit; you can use them as they are, or use them as a template for defining your own wrappers for more specialized objects.

TList adds a few methods and properties to the core functionality in Table 7-5. The First and Last functions can be useful in stacks and queues. The List property gives you the address of the list of pointers, which can be passed to external functions or used in the rare list traversal that is too time-critical to be passed through the Items property. The Sort procedure does a QuickSort of the pointer list, using a comparison function that you pass in.

TList also has a Notify procedure that is called whenever a value is added, extracted, or deleted. (Extract is the same as Delete in TList, but you might define a wrapper class—like Kylix's TObjectList—that can 'own' the objects placed in it, and Free them when they're deleted. In that case, you'd want to be able to distinguish between delete-and-free and extract-and-transfer-ownership.) Notify does nothing in TList, but it's a virtual procedure that descendant list classes can reimplement as necessary.

Kylix is not Delphi 5

The Assign method is significantly different in TList than it is elsewhere in the Kylix class hierarchy (and, for that matter, significantly different from Delphi 5's TList.Assign.) By default, Destination.Assign(Source) will copy the contents of Source into Destination, just as you'd expect. However, Assign actually has two optional parameters that allow you to combine the Source and Destination lists, or to set the list that's actually doing the Assign to the combination of two other lists. That is, Destination.Assign(Source, *op*) sets Destination to Destination *op* Source, while Result.Assign(Destination, *op*, Source) sets Result to Destination *op* Source.

There are six possible operations:

Table 7-6. TList.Assign operations

Name	Effect
laCopy	This is the default; it simply copies the source list to the destination list. (Note that A.Assign(B, laCopy, C) sets A to C, without affecting B.)
laAnd	Only those elements in both lists. Duplicate elements in the destination list are only removed if they're not present in the source list. Duplicate elements in the destination list that are also in the source list are left in place. That is, 112233 laAnd 135 = 1133.
laOr	Any element that's in either list. Duplicate elements in the destination list are not removed, but duplicate items in the source list are only added once. That is, 112233 laOr 334455 = 11223345.
laXor	Any elements that are in only one list. Duplicates in either list are preserved. That is, 112233 laXor 223344 = 1144.
laSrcUnique	Only those elements in the source list and not in the destination list. Duplicates are not removed. That is, 112233 laSrcUnique 3445 = 445.
laDestUnique	Only those elements in the destination list and not in the source list. Duplicates are not removed. That is, 112233 laDestUnique 3445 = 1122.

TThreadList

The TThreadList is basically just a combination of a TList and a critical section, so that you can be sure that only one thread is reading or writing the list at once. You **cannot** use it to combine multiple simultaneous read access with sequentialized write access.

It provides wrappers for Add and Remove, but for all other TList operations you must call LockList. This sequentializes access *via* the critical section, and returns a reference to the TList. You can then do whatever you like with this TList, but be sure to call UnlockList when you're done, using a framework something like this:

```
with ThreadList do
  with LockList do
    try
      {do whatever you need to do with the TList result of LockList}
    finally
      Unlocklist;
    end;
```

> **Note**
>
> *Thread lists use "recursive" mutexes (PTHREAD_MUTEX_RECURSIVE), which means that the same thread can lock the mutex more than once (so long as it unlocks it each time). This in turn means that it's safe to call LockList, so that other threads can't access the list during a compound transaction, then call the TThreadList versions of Add and Remove, which call LockList internally.*

Thread lists also have a Duplicates property, that allows you to specify the behavior when you add a duplicate list entry. You can allow duplicates; suppress the duplicate without raising an exception (which is the default behavior); or raise an exception.

> **Note**
>
> *The Duplicates setting is only honored when you call TThreadList.Add. If you call TThreadList.LockList and then call Add or Insert on the returned TList, the Duplicates setting is ignored.*

TInterfaceList

The IInterfaceList interface basically replicates the TList functionality (*sans* Assign), with IInterface substituted for generic pointers. That is, an object that implements IInterfaceList can Add() an interface to the list; Remove() an interface from the list; look up an interface with IndexOf();offer random access *via* Items[]; and so on.

The TInterfaceList is a TInterfacedObject that uses a private TThreadList field to implement IInterfaceList. I put it this way to emphasize the point that unless you need the sequential access of a TThreadList, you may prefer just to use TInterfaceList as a model of how to implement IInterfaceList in a way that manages reference counts properly; the locking overhead may be excessive in a single-threaded application.

If you write your code to use IInterfaceList, not TInterfaceList, it will be easier to switch between TInterfaceList and a (hypothetical) TUnlockedInterfaceList. That is, any methods that take an IInterfaceList parameter will work with any implementation of IInterfaceList, and you only have to change the one line

```
InterfaceList := TUnlockedInterfaceList.Create as IInterfaceList;
```

that actually creates the list. Contrarily, any methods that take a TInterfaceList parameter would have to be changed to work with TUnlockedInterfaceList.

Contnrs unit

The CLX "Contnrs" unit implements various standard containers using TList's. You can save yourself a few minutes by using these instead of rolling your own.

Table 7-7. Classes implemented in the Contnrs unit

Class	Job	Notes
TObjectList	Type-safe TList of TObject's.	Can own the objects placed in it, and Free them when deleted or when the list is freed.
TComponentList	TObjectList that can only hold TComponents.	
TClassList	Type-safe TList of TClass's.	`type TClass = class of TObject;`

Table 7-7. Classes implemented in the Contnrs unit (Continued)

Class	Job	Notes
TOrderedList	Base class for TStack and TQueue.	
TStack	Base class for TObjectStack.	You could derive from this to create a stack of integers or generic pointers.
TObjectStack	Type-safe stack of TObject's.	
TQueue	Base class for TObjectQueue.	You could derive from this to create a queue of integers or generic pointers.
TObjectQueue	Type-safe queue of TObject's.	

TStrings

TStrings is an abstract class: It doesn't actually contain any code to save and retrieve the strings you place in it. You'll never Create an actual TStrings—it exists solely to provide a common ancestor for the TStringList objects that you will Create, and for the specialized TString classes that represent Kylix's interface to the lines of a memo or list box, the choices in a combo box, or the rows and columns of a string grid. As this partial list of descendants may suggest, though, you'll use descendants of TStrings all the time, so it's important to understand them.

TStrings add quite a lot to the core list functionality in Table 7-5. I've broken this new functionality down into five functional groups, which makes it easier to present and should also make it easier to grasp.

Associated objects

TStrings is actually two lists in one. Alongside the list of strings is a list of TObjects.[2] Count and Capacity apply to both; the idea is that every string has a TObject associated with it. You can read and write the Objects array with the same 0..Count-1 indices that you use for the Strings array, or you can add strings and objects simultaneously with AddObject and InsertObject. You can look up entries in the Objects list with IndexOfObject, just as you can look up entries in the Strings list with IndexOf.

---

2. In actuality, TStringList is implemented as a single list of string / object records. However, this is **not** true of TStrings descendants which represent control contents, so it's best to think of a TStrings as a pair of lists.

This is awfully useful, in several different ways.

- You can use a TStringList as a sort of dictionary, or directory. Each of a set of objects has a name, and you can find the objects by name (IndexOf) or find the names by object (IndexOfObject).

- Similarly, you can use the Objects array to associate an object with every line in a control with an Items: TStrings property, like a list box or combo box. This might be anything from a TBitmap to display in an owner-draw control to an object that the user's next action will apply to. Similarly, the OwnerDraw project in the ch6/Controls project group might have used the Dropdown.Items.Objects array to cache TFont's, if it weren't for the fact that Qt does that for us.

- You can use casts to store any 32-bit value in the Objects array. This might be a raw `pointer`, a TClass (`class of`) value, an integer, or even a LongBool.

The caveat here is pretty much the same as with components' Tag property. An Items.Objects array is a global resource. Be sure you don't try to use it in two different ways!

TObject is also a very generic type. You'll almost certainly need to cast each value to something more specific before you use it. Be sure to check that it's what you expect it to be, using `is` or `as`.

Note

*The default TStrings implementation of the Objects array does not store the values you assign to Objects[Index]. That is, Objects[Index] will always be Nil, no matter what you set it to. **Most** TStrings descendants override this and provide a functional Objects array—but some, like TMemo's Lines property, do not. The reasoning is presumably that lines in a user-editable memo are much more volatile than entries in a list or combo box, which can only change under program control.*

Associative arrays

TStrings can also act as a sort of associative array. You can write code like `List.Values['this'] := 'that'` or `StringVar := List.Values['this']`. **This** works in addition to the Objects array; you can use IndexOfName to find the position of a given index into the Values array, and read or write the corresponding entry in the Objects array. The TStrings' Names array, indexed by the same 0..Count-1 indices as the other arrays, lets you read all the Names in the list. (Names is read-only; you can't change the Name of a Value by setting Names[Index].)

The way this works is by looking for Strings array entries of the form Name=Value. If there is a string `'this=that'` in the list, `Values['this']` will equal `'that'`. If there isn't, `Values['this']` will equal `''`. Similarly, if there is a string `'this=that'` in the list, doing `Values['this'] := 'the other'` will change the string to `'this=the other'`, while if the line didn't exist, the Values assignment will add it. If Strings[Index] doesn't have an = sign in it, Names[Index] will equal `''`. (That is, Name=Value strings can coexist in the same list as strings that don't have any = sign in them.)

You can take advantage of this implementation of associativity to rename a Value as in this procedure from the Associative project in the ch7/Lists project group:

```
procedure RenameValue(Strings: TStrings; const NewName, OldName: string);
var
  Index: integer;
begin
  Index := Strings.IndexOfName(OldName);
  if Index < 0 then EXIT;
  Strings.BeginUpdate; // Try to minimize flicker
  Strings.Values[NewName] := Strings.Values[OldName]; // Copy
  Strings.Delete(Index);                              // erase OldName
  Strings.EndUpdate;
end; // RenameValue
```

Finally, the name=value format is, not coincidentally, the format for ini-files, or .ini configuration files. The TMemIniFile class in the CLX IniFiles unit contains methods to copy all the Names in an inifile section into a string list (ReadSection) and to copy all the name=value pairs in an inifile section into a string list (ReadSectionValues). See the vfind projects in Chapter 13 for an example.

Text

Though the strings in a string list are stored as individual strings, the Text property allows you to treat the whole list as a single document, with each line separated by a sLineBreak (#10, or ^J) string. Reading the Text property will concatenate all the strings; setting the Text property will break the Text at line breaks, and replace any existing Strings. (String lists do not own their Objects; setting Text will reset all elements of the Objects array to Nil, without freeing any existing Objects.)

This can be very convenient. If you need to process a text file line by line, it's easier to read it into a TStringList and process the Strings than to write your own line-breaking code. (Obviously, this is inefficient for very large files—each string has a 12-byte overhead (heap block size, string length, string reference count), and each entry in the list takes another eight bytes for the string and object pointers—but there's a power law at work, here. Most files are **not** very large.)

The LoadFromFile method will open the file, read its contents into Text, and then close the file. LoadFromStream is similar except that, obviously, it reads a stream. (See the *Streams* section of this chapter, below.) Similarly, SaveToFile and SaveToStream will save the Text directly to a file or a stream.

Structured text

The Text property treats the string list as a collection of lines separated by sLineBreak's. This corresponds directly to a standard text file format, but Kylix also makes it easy to read and write common structured text files like comma separated values (CSV) and tab separated values.

The CommaText property lets you read and write the lines in a list as a series of values separated by commas, with values containing commas enclosed in quotes. This corresponds directly to a single line of a CSV file, which is generally the lowest common denominator spreadsheet format. Thus, you can easily write the contents of a string grid to a CSV file as in this procedure from the StructuredText project of the ch7/Lists project group.

```
procedure TStructuredTextFrm.SaveAsCsvBtnClick(Sender: TObject);
var
  Index: integer;
begin
  with TStringList.Create do
  try
    for Index := 0 to Grid.RowCount - 1 do
      Add(Grid.Rows[Index].CommaText);
    SaveToFile(Filename.Text);
  finally
    Free;
  end;
end; // TStructuredTextFrm.SaveAsCsvBtnClick
```

This routine is very simple since the TStringGrid's Rows and Cols properties return a TStrings corresponding to the row or column. It just creates a TStringList (see below), populates each line with the row's CommaText, and then writes it to a text file. This file can then be read directly by Excel and other spreadsheets.

Reading it back is almost as simple, though this routine ignores complexities like the possibility of Grid's ColCount not matching the file's.

```
procedure TStructuredTextFrm.LoadCsvBtnClick(Sender: TObject);
var
  Index: integer;
begin
  with TStringList.Create do
  try
    LoadFromFile(Filename.Text);
    Grid.RowCount := Count;
    for Index := 0 to Grid.RowCount - 1 do
      Grid.Rows[Index].CommaText := Strings[Index];
  finally
    Free;
  end;
end; // TStructuredTextFrm.LoadCsvBtnClick
```

LoadFromFile broke the CSV file up into a series of lines, so the Count property corresponds directly to the line count. Setting CommaText parses each line into a series of values, which the Rows string list copies into the appropriate columns.

Finally, CommaText is actually just a special case of DelimitedText. You can read and write tab separated text by setting the Delimiter property to a Tab, ^I, and reading or writing the DelimitedText property. You can also customize the quoting behavior by setting the QuoteChar property.

Other TStrings

You can always Assign() one TStrings to another. This.Assign(That) makes the calling TStrings, This, an exact copy of the argument TStrings, That. Both Strings[] and Objects[] are copied. Components that expose a TStrings property generally do so behind a write method that turns Items := List into Items.Assign(List).

Note

Assign can handle different types of TStrings. You can Assign a TStringList to a TMemo.Lines, or a TListBox.Items to a TComboBox.Items, and so on.

This.AddStrings(That) adds the contents of That TStrings—Objects[] and all—to This TStrings, without overwriting the contents of This. *Eg*, if This.Count is 12 and That.Count is 11, after This.AddStrings(That), This.Count will be 23.

This.Equals(That) returns true iff all Strings in This match the corresponding Strings in That; Objects are not checked.

BeginUpdate

In TStrings itself, BeginUpdate and EndUpdate do nothing. But in the TStrings that represent a control's contents (the various specialized TStrings behind Items, Lines, Rows, and Cols properties), BeginUpdate lets you make a series of changes to a control. The control won't show these changes until you call EndUpdate. This not only reduces flicker, but also makes your transaction faster.

See the Associative project in the ch7/Lists project group (in the above *Associative Arrays* section) for a simple example.

TStringList

TStringList is the single most important of the various TStrings descendant types, if only because it's the only one that you would normally Create outside of a component. In addition to all the normal TStrings functionality, TStringList has some extra functionality that's well worth knowing about.

Table 7-8. Functionality unique to TStringList

Type	Name	Comments
procedure	Sort	Sorts the list according to the current locale's collation sequence. Pays attention to the CaseSensitive property.
procedure	CustomSort	Sorts the list according to a comparison function that you pass in.

Table 7-8. Functionality unique to TStringList

Type	Name	Comments
property	Duplicates	Allows you to specify whether the list may contain duplicates, or whether it should just ignore any attempt to Add a duplicate, or whether it should raise an exception on an attempt to Add a duplicate. **Note**: Only matters if Sorted is True.
property Property	Sorted	Setting this True will call Sort. It will also keep the list sorted as you Add to it. (It can be cheaper to add a lot of strings with Sorted = False and then set Sorted to True than to add a lot of strings with Sorted = True.) When the list is Sorted, IndexOf uses a binary search; when the list is not Sorted, IndexOf uses a linear search.
property	CaseSensitive	Controls the behavior of Sort and IndexOf.
event	OnChange	Called **after** a change.
event	OnChanging	Called **before** a change.

You might wonder what the point of an OnChange or OnChanging event is in a non-visual object like a TStringList. After all, you don't need to be told when the user changed it—you're doing it yourself!

There are two points, really. The first is that this non-visual component might be exposed by a component as a property. If the list of strings in something like a TRadioGroup changes—whether at design-time or at run-time—the component needs to react to it. The second is that it simplifies your code, and removes a whole class of failure points. You might change the list in five or six different places. Instead of having to follow each change with the OnUpdate code, with dire consequences if you (or the guys who come along five years later) miss a change point, you just install an event handler, and your OnUpdate logic is called automatically.

Collections vs *dynamic arrays*

How do you choose between a list class and a dynamic array? Let's begin by looking at the advantages and disadvantages of each.

	Advantages	Disadvantages
Lists	• Lists support insertion and deletion, and can easily be reordered. • As objects, they have many generally useful auxiliary functions (IndexOf &c) 'built in'—you don't have to use in-line code or stand-alone procedures. • You can build "virtual lists", whose contents reflect the current state of a system object like a TMemo. • The list classes separate Capacity from Count, which can improve performance when the lists grow and shrink.	• As objects, you have to be sure to Free them. Who owns the list? What about functions that return lists? • TList's store pointers; TObjectList's store TObjects. You usually have to write a type-safe wrapper class—or do an awful lot of typecasting.
Arrays	• Dynamic arrays have a nice, clean syntax. No type-casts, no method calls: just inline array subscripting. • Dynamic arrays are reference-counted, which eliminates the whole ownership issue. There are no issues with returning an array from a function. • Arrays aren't limited to pointers. A dynamic array of records is much more efficient than a TList of pointers to records: One heap block, instead of Count+1.	• It's hard to insert or delete with a dynamic array, except at the end. Dynamic arrays are sort of stack-like. • It's hard to concatenate two dynamic arrays. • It's hard to sort a dynamic array.

In short, list classes are more flexible and extensible; dynamic arrays are simpler and cleaner. Use dynamic arrays when the list is "like a value": something that you may pass around; something that you will iterate over; but basically something that you don't need to change much once you've created it. Use a list class when you need more control over the order; when you need the 'magical' abilities of a 'virtual list' like in TMemo; or when you have a lot of operations on the list that you want to be part of the list class, not floating freely.

Streams

Streams are a familiar programming construct. Just as the notion of "files" and "file systems" generalized all the different sorts of mass storage device back in the 1970's, so "streams" generalized input and output back in the 1980's. Streams are particularly good at representing variable length data, where a fixed length header is followed by a variable set of data, each element of which may itself be variable.

Object Pascal doesn't offer C++'s convenient >> and << notation, but it does offer several otherwise full-featured stream classes. Any operation that you can do on a TStream you can do on any of its descendants. (This is, of course, a basic tenet of Object Oriented Programming.) Thus, you can use the same routine to stream a bitmap to and from file, to and from memory, or to and from a database BLOB field—just by passing in a different type of stream.

Conceptually, streams are very simple. They have just two key properties: Size, or the number of bytes in the stream; and Position, the current read or write pointer. Similarly, they have just three key methods and a handful of specialized methods: Read copies bytes from the stream to an untyped buffer and advances the Position; Write copies bytes from an untyped buffer to the stream and advances the Position; and Seek sets the Position to a specific offset from either the current Position or the beginning or end of the stream. In addition, CopyFrom allows you to copy (portions of) any stream to any other stream.

It's generally a good idea to seek to the beginning of the stream before you start to read it. Not only is it safer—your routine will work, even if the calling code left the Position at the end of the stream—it makes for smaller code if the called routine seeks to 0 than if all the calling code does.

Table 7-9. lib/GrabBag stream routines

Write	Read	Notes
StringToStream	StringFromStream	Writes (reads) a 4-byte length then the text.
ByteToStream	ByteFromStream	Writes (reads) a 1-byte value.
WordToStream	WordFromStream	Writes (reads) a 2-byte value
LongToStream	LongFromStream	Writes (reads) a 4-byte value.

It probably goes without saying, but a stream is a *queue*, not a *stack*. If you write a data set in the order A, B, C, then you have to read it in the order A, B, C. SaveToStream and LoadFromStream routines consist of a parallel series of operations that read a data structure in the exact same order it was written. (Many streams consist (mostly) of a series of tags that identify the next chunk of data, and which may appear in any order[3]. However, you still have to obey the queue law within these tagged sections.)

Whenever you read and write custom data to a stream, you are (at least implicitly) defining a file format. As such, you should **always** be aware of the way that programs change, and the way that data that they need to persist changes with them. Every stream should have a header that contains some sort of stream identifier (so the reading program can be sure that this file contains the data that it expects) and a format version number. That way, even if subsequent versions of the program change the stream format, they can detect old streams, and respond appropriately.

Note

*Portability of stream formats isn't a big issue between Kylix and Delphi—both are 32-bit Intel (Little Endian) implementations—but looking forward to Kylix on Solaris, you'll need to be aware of differences in numeric representation. Either just specify that all numbers in the stream are Little Endian, or consider alternatives such as a header flag that specifies endianness or all-text streams (similar to the way that Kylix stores .xfm files as text, by default, even though this **is** bulkier and slower than a binary representation).*

TStream

TStream itself is an abstract class. It doesn't implement certain key methods, and the compiler will warn you if you try to Create an instance of it. It exists to provide a contract that routines that take a TStream parameter can expect every actual instance of a TStream descendant type to follow. That is, write your routines to take a TStream parameter, but only actually Create TStream descendants. The three most important TStream descendants are

---

3.   This allows the WriteToStream routine to be based on a list of program elements that (may) need to write to the stream, without having to worry at all about the order in which the program elements get added to the list. This in turn vastly simplifies maintenance. Program elements can be added to the list in unit `initialization` blocks, and the order in which unit `initialization` blocks get called can change from build to build.

TFileStream, TMemoryStream, and TStringStream. TResourceStream is **mostly** used by Kylix form's loading code, though of course you can use it in application code to load resources from your application's .res 'fork'.

TFileStream

A TFileStream represents an open file. When you Create a TFileStream, a file is opened (and possibly created). When you Free a TFileStream, the file is closed. Obviously, you don't want to keep a TFileStream around any longer than necessary! Syntactically, TFileStream differs from TStream only in that it adds a constructor that allows you to specify a file name; a file open mode; and, optionally, the file's access rights, which only matter if you are creating a file.

The file name is just a file name, though Windows programmers need to remember here as elsewhere that Linux has a case-sensitive file system.

The file mode specifies the read/write access you need and, optionally, the file sharing you want to allow. That is, the file mode is one of the fmOpenX values fmOpenRead, fmOpenWrite, and fmOpenReadWrite, optionally or-ed with one of the fmShareX values fmShareExclusive, fmShareDenyWrite, and fmShareDenyNone. Specifying fmShareDenyNone is the same as not specifying any fmShareX value - *ie*, just an fmOpenX value.

Note

*While the fmOpen values are defined in terms of the standard Linux O_ values in Table 7-10, the fmShare values are actually indices into a hidden table. You **can** specify the FileMode as, say,* `O_RDONLY`, *but you **cannot** specify it as* `O_RDONLY` **or** `F_WRLCK`—*you'd have to use* `O_RDONLY` or `smShareExclusive` *or, more naturally,* `fmOpenRead` or `smShareExclusive`.

Table 7-10. File mode Open constants

Kylix name	Linux name—open()
fmOpenRead	O_RDONLY
fmOpenWrite	O_WRONLY
fmOpenReadWrite	O_RDWR

Table 7-11. File mode Share constants

Kylix name	Linux name—fcntl(F_SETLK)
fmShareExclusive	F_WRLCK
fmShareDenyWrite	F_RDLCK
fmShareDenyNone	no SETLK call to fcntl()

Windows programmers should be sure to note that Linux has many more files that are effectively read-only than Windows does. While Windows, of course, has a read-only file attribute, even NT only supports file ownership if you use NTFS. Under Windows, you can almost always write every local file that's not marked read-only. Linux, however, is not only multitasking but also multiuser; users can routinely read but not write other users' files. The point, here, is that unless you really need to both read and write a file, you should use fmOpenRead, not fmOpenReadWrite.

> **Tip**
>
>
> *Before calling TFileStream.Create to open a file, you can use Libc.euidaccess() to see if you have permission to do so. This is cheaper than handling the exception you'll get when you try to open a file that you don't have permission to.*

Setting other users' access to a file you create is the point of the optional Rights parameter. This is just a standard file access mask (see Chapter 10), the same as you'd pass to Libc.chmod() or Libc.open(). You can use either a numerical constant or a bitwise combination of the standard S_Ix constants from Libc.pas.

> **Note**
>
>
> *The file access Rights parameter represents a sort of request. It will be and-ed with the process's umask, which the user can set to restrict the access rights on files created by your application. The Rights parameter is the broadest access your files may have, not necessarily the access that they will have. This is standard Linux, not a Kylixism. (See Chapter 10.)*

TMemoryStream

A TMemoryStream is, naturally enough, an in-memory stream. It has Load-FromFile and LoadFromStream methods, so it's particularly useful for caching a file stream that you will read several times. It also has SaveToFile and SaveToStream methods, which mean that you can write a whole stream to a TMemoryStream and then save it as a whole to a disk file. This lets you know exactly how big the stream will be before you try to save it to disk or stream it over a socket, and can be particularly convenient if the stream write may fail, as you don't have to worry about deleting a file with a partial stream in it.

TMemoryStream also has a Memory parameter that points to the heap block containing the stream, and that lets you examine and/or change the stream. A TStringStream is usually more convenient for this.

> **Note**
>
>
> *While streams can be a very good way to manage Inter-Process Communication [IPC] via shared memory, a TMemoryStream is not an appropriate class for this, as it expects to be free to reallocate Memory as need be. You'd need to write a TSharedMemoryStream, with a shared memory size and address that it could not change.*

TStringStream

TStringStream is perfect for turning a string into a stream or *vice versa*. The constructor takes a string, and the DataString property allows you to get the current stream contents as a string. Do note that you should really only use TStringStream if you need to stream to or from a string. TStringStream uses a string for its underlying stream storage, and every Write does a SetLength. By contrast, TMemoryStream 'chunks', or allocates more Capacity than it needs for its Size. Therefore, a series of Write() operations on a TMemoryStream involves fewer heap management calls (and so is faster) than the equivalent series of Write() operations on a TStringStream.

TResourceStream

TResourceStream allows you to read resources bound into your application's 'resource fork'. Kylix uses this internally to load forms, but you can use it to load bitmaps and/or arbitrary data from resource files that you create manually and explicitly link in via a pragma like {$R resource.res}. You might use resource files to include sound files in your application, or to assure that your application only contains one copy of a background bitmap. Similarly, you may want to include a license or README text file in your application's executable to simplify distribution, but to maintain it as a stand-alone file at development time (*ie*, not include it in a Pascal source file as a resourcestring.)

Kylix does not come with a resource compiler, but you can download wrc as part of the wine (Windows emulation) package from www.winehq.com. (You can also use the Gnu windres program, which is available as part of the binutils package.) The ResStream project in the ch7/Streams project group links in a file, paper.res, created with wrc, which contains a bitmap and the paper.rc source file. It uses a TResourceStream to load the paper.rc source into a TMemo, and uses the TBitmap LoadFromResourceName method to load the bitmap.

```
{$R paper.res} // Created with `wrc`, available from www.winehq.com

procedure TResStreamFrm.FormCreate(Sender: TObject);
var
  Stream: TResourceStream;
begin
  Stream := TResourceStream.Create(HInstance, 'Paper_rc', RT_RCDATA);
  try
    Paper_rc.Lines.LoadFromStream(Stream);
  finally
    Stream.Free;
  end;
  Bitmap.LoadFromResourceName(HInstance, 'Background');
end; // TResStreamFrm.FormCreate
```

HInstance is a global variable, set at program load time. RT_RCDATA is a constant, declared in Types.pas; you can also use RT_BITMAP, which is declared in QGraphics.pas. This code uses Bitmap.LoadFromResourceName and not Bitmap.LoadFromStream because LoadFromResourceName is a bit more forgiving; LoadFromStream complains about paper.bmp being in an unknown format.

IStream

The stream classes are, well, classes. As such, they're subject to all the ownership woes of any other class: Who should Free this stream? What if someone else has freed the stream I have a reference to? You can use IStream to avoid these issues. Although Classes.pas has a comment about "OLE IStream", there's really nothing particularly Windows specific about IStream; it's pretty much just the standard TStream contract in somewhat different terms.

To turn a TStream into an IStream, you use a TStreamAdapter. This is a small TInterfacedObject that implements IStream and contains a TStreamReference. The stream adapter can 'refer' to the TStream, which means that the stream is not freed when the last IStream reference goes away and the adapter is freed; or it can 'own' the TStream, which means that the stream **is** freed when the last IStream reference goes away. The default is actually soRefer, but this seems to me an artifact of the stream adapter's origins in OLE programming; if you're using an adapter only so you can take advantage of reference counting, you'll want the adapter to own the stream:

```
IStreamVar := TStreamAdapter.Create(StreamVar, soOwned) as IStream;
```

> **Note**
>
>
> *Remember, there's a bug in Kylix 1.0 that doesn't finalize global interface variables when the program shuts down. If a global interface variable represents an open file, any buffered writes may be lost. If you use global interface variables, be sure to set them to Nil in a* finalization *section.*

Streaming objects

Many applications need "persistent objects": Objects that can be streamed out to a file, then streamed in when the program next runs or when it loads a particular document. Three basic issues need to be addressed for this to work: saving the object's type, so you can create a new object of that type when you read the stream; saving and restoring its state; and saving and restoring references to other objects.

Saving and restoring object references is most often accomplished by "serializing" the object references. When an object needs to stream out an object reference, it actually streams an integer index into a table of all objects in the stream. When the objects are recreated from the stream, they convert these indices back into pointers to newly created objects. There's nothing particularly Kylix specific about this, so I'll pass blithely over the whole issue of how to implement serialization.

Saving and restoring the objects' state is mostly a matter of honoring the queue law: If you save properties in A, B, C order, then be sure to read them in A, B, C order.

The big issue, then, is saving and recreating the right type. The key to this is Object Pascal's "class of" variables. Every TObject can return its ClassType, which is a value of type TClass, or `class of TObject`. Class variables are implemented as pointers to the class's VMT [Virtual Method Table] and can be used to call class methods, including constructors. So, given these declarations from the Streamables unit of the ObjectStream project in the ch7/Streams project group,

```
type
  TStreamable = class
  protected
    procedure   SaveToStream(Stream: TStream);   virtual;
    constructor LoadFromStream(Stream: TStream); virtual;
  public
    class procedure RegisterClassname;
    class function CreateFromStream(Stream: TStream): TStreamable;
  end;
  CStreamable = class of TStreamable;
```

TStreamable.CreateFromStream needs to read the stream and somehow get the right CStreamable value. Then it can call LoadFromStream, which recreates the correct descendant type[4] and reads its state from the stream. So, the real issue is: How do you save a ClassType to a stream and get it back later?

Obviously, you don't want to save the binary value of the ClassType. This may change with every build of the program, and is likely to be different from run to run of programs that dynamically load runtime packages. The safe approach is to store ClassName, and be able to look that up at stream read time. If all your objects are TPersistent's, you can use RegisterClass and Find-Class to do this, but I don't like to do this for two reasons. First, TPersistent's have baggage like Assign() and GetNamePath() that are usually not appropriate. It's not right to say that a TStreamable is a TPersistent in the object

---

4.   LoadFromStream can recreate the correct descendant type because it's a virtual method. That is, if you have a `var Streamable: CStreamable`, the call Streamable.LoadFromStream goes through the VMT at Streamable^, and constructs the right type of object. If LoadFromStream were not virtual, Streamable.LoadFromStream would construct the base TStreamable type.

oriented analysis sense. Second, the Kylix form streaming mechanism (which RegisterClass and FindClass are part of) is designed for streaming forms and components; we have to do almost exactly as much work to stream our own TPersistent's using Kylix's mechanism as using our own. So, it seems better just to use our own, and not do semantic violence in the process.

Thus, the ch7/Streamables unit has a hidden TStringList, Registry. TStreamable.RegisterClassname saves the ClassName and the ClassType on to this list.

```
var
  Registry: TStringlist;

class procedure TStreamable.RegisterClassname;
begin
  Registry.AddObject(ClassName, TObject(Self));
end; // TStreamable.RegisterClassname
```

Within a class procedure, Self refers to the class that was used to call it. Thus, when a TStreamable descendent calls RegisterClassname within an initialization section, as TDemo does in ch7/ObjectStreamMain

```
initialization
  TDemo.RegisterClassname;
```

Self equals TDemo. Since TObject and TClass are not assignment compatible, RegisterClassname casts Self to TObject before passing it to AddObject.

At save time, TStreamable.SaveToStream uses StringToStream from lib/GrabBag to save the descendant class' ClassName to the stream as the first part of the object stream

```
procedure TStreamable.SaveToStream(Stream: TStream);
begin
  StringToStream(Stream, ClassName);
end; // TStreamable.SaveToStream
```

At read time, CreateFromStream looks up the ClassName in its Registry, casts the Objects[] value back to a CStreamable, and then uses the CStreamable to calls the virtual constructor LoadFromStream.

```
class function TStreamable.CreateFromStream(Stream: TStream): TStreamable;
var
  NewClassName: string;
  Index:       integer;
  NewClassType: CStreamable;
begin
  NewClassName := StringFromStream(Stream);
  Registry.Sorted := True; // Force IndexOf to use binary search
  Index := Registry.IndexOf(NewClassname);
  Assert(Index >= 0);
  NewClassType := CStreamable(Registry.Objects[Index]);
  Assert(Assigned(NewClassType));
  Result := NewClassType.LoadFromStream(Stream);
end; // TStreamable.LoadFromStream
```

And that's about all there is to it. Stream-out writes a ClassName, followed by the descendant class' properties. Stream-in converts the ClassName to a ClassType, creates a new object, and tells it to read in its own properties.

The ObjectStream project allows you to enter a number and a string in an "Original" group box. When you press the Clone button, it creates a TDemo object, streams it to a memory stream, and frees the TDemo object. Then it recreates the TDemo object from the memory stream, and uses it to populate the "Clone" group box.

```
constructor TDemo.LoadFromStream(Stream: TStream);
begin
  inherited; // not necessary, as TDemo descends directly from TStreamable
  Number := LongFromStream(Stream);
  Text   := StringFromStream(Stream);
end; // TDemo.LoadFromStream
```

```
procedure TDemo.SaveToStream(Stream: TStream);
begin
  inherited; // Necessary: Streams out ClassName
  LongToStream(Stream, Number);
  StringToStream(Stream, Text);
end; // TDemo.SaveToStream
```

As you can see, TDemo.SaveToStream calls inherited, which saves the ClassName, then streams out Number and Text. LoadFromStream in turn obeys the queue law by streaming in first Number and then Text.

The clipboard

The system clipboard allows users to cut and paste information within and between applications.[5] It can hold multiple views of the same data. This lets a word processor, for example, store a snippet both as plain text, for use by applications that can't handle formatted text, and as HTML formatted text, for applications that can handle formatted text. Similarly, an image editor might place an image on the clipboard in several different formats, to maximize the chances that another application will be able to read at least one of the formats it placed on the clipboard.

Logically, the clipboard contains multiple streams, each tagged with a MIME type. You can get a list of the MIME types on the clipboard, or you can query the clipboard to see if it contains a specific data type. You can read any stream on the clipboard, add a new stream to the existing collection, or Clear all streams from the clipboard. The Kylix clipboard object supplies an AsText property that lets you read and write plain text (*aka* the MIME type text/plain) simply by reading and writing the AsText property.

To use the clipboard in your applications, simply include the QClipbrd unit in a uses clause. QClipbrd exports the Clipboard function, which returns an instance of the TClipboard object. You should always use the Clipboard function instead of calling TClipboard.Create, as the Clipboard function guarantees that your application never has more than one instance of the TClipboard class. Table 7-12 summarizes the key functions of the Clipboard object.

Table 7-12. Key functions of the Clipboard object

Type	Notes
function AddFormat	Adds a named stream to the clipboard. Adding a format that's already on the clipboard replaces the existing stream.
procedure Assign	Primarily for copying Kylix graphics (TBitmap, TPicture) to and from the clipboard. (See the clipboard demo app, below, for an example.) Note that Assign uses custom MIME types, so that only other Kylix apps will be able to read the formats that Assign places on the clipboard.
procedure Clear	Deletes all streams from the clipboard.
function GetFormat	Reads a stream from the clipboard.

---

5. Inter-application copy and paste is a bit limited under Gnome. For example, Kylix's clipboard can 'see' data that gedit places on the clipboard, but gedit can't paste data that Kylix apps place on the clipboard. Similarly, The Gimp doesn't see anything a Kylix app places on the clipboard and *vice versa*.

Table 7-12. Key functions of the Clipboard object (Continued)

Type	Notes
procedure SetFormat	Clears the clipboard then adds a single stream.
function Provides	Tests whether the clipboard contains a particular MIME type.
function RegisterClipboardFormat	Not used on Linux.
procedure SupportedFormats	Adds all MIME format tags to a TStrings list. Note that Kylix 1 does not *set* the list but *appends to* it—if what you want is the format list and only the format list, be sure to Clear the list before passing it to SupportedFormats.
property AsText	Lets you read and write 'text/plain' data without bothering with creating and freeing a stream.

The Clipboard project in the ch7/Clipboard project group demonstrates some of these functions, as well as how to create a callback so that your application is notified whenever the clipboard changes.

Putting data on the clipboard

The TClipboardFrm.FormCreate method clears the clipboard and populates it with several versions of the same bitmap, as well as some totally unrelated text.

```
procedure TClipboardFrm.FormCreate(Sender: TObject);
var
  Bitmap: TBitmap;
  Stream: TMemoryStream;
  Text:   TStringStream;
begin
  fClipboard := Clipboard as TExClipboard;
  fClipboard.Clear;
  fClipboard.RegisterViewer(OnClipboardChange);

  Bitmap := TBitmap.Create;
  try
    Bitmap.LoadFromResourceName(HInstance, 'jon');
    QClipboard_setPixmap(fClipboard.Handle, Bitmap.Handle); // VERY slow
    Stream := TMemoryStream.Create;
    try
      Bitmap.SaveToStream(Stream);
```

```
      Stream.Position := 0;
      fClipboard.AddFormat(SDelphiBitmap, Stream);
    finally
      Stream.Free;
    end;
  finally
    Bitmap.Free;
  end;
  Text := TStringStream.Create(BlaaahBlaahBlaah);
  try
    fClipboard.AddFormat('text/plain', Text);
  finally
    Text.Free;
  end;
end; // TClipboardFrm.FormCreate
```

`fClipboard := Clipboard as TExClipboard` gets a reference to the clipboard object and stores it in an object field. (The application actually uses lib/XClipbrd instead of the stock QClipbrd, but TExClipboard is a TClipboard descendant that adds only clipboard viewing functionality.) The FormCreate method then wipes the existing contents of the clipboard, and installs a viewer, OnClipboardChange, that's called whenever the contents of the clipboard change.

After this setup code, the FormCreate method creates a bitmap and loads it with an old picture of me from the application's "resource fork". It then calls QClipboard_setPixmap to copy this picture to the clipboard.

Note

> *You don't have to use QClipboard_setPixmap to place bitmaps on the clipboard. I do it to demonstrate that you can, and to show how delphi.bitmap data can coexist with more portable image formats.*

No delayed rendering

Figure 7-6. The clipboard demo displaying a color delphi.bitmap stream

Note that QClipboard_setPixmap is really quite slow. The Qt documentation says that this is because it has to convert a QPixmap to a QImage, but there's something more going on. As you can see from these screenshots (or by running the demo), what gets placed on the clipboard for the xbm format is a monochrome image using a nice "error diffusion" dither (see Figure 7-7). Similarly, the pgm format is a grayscale version of the picture. These format conversions are done inside of QClipboard_setPixmap—the Qt clipboard does **not** support "delayed rendering" the way the Windows clipboard does. Every time you place data on the clipboard, you have to stream out a copy in every format that you support, even if some of those formats are rarely (or even never) used.

FormCreate next copies the bitmap to a memory stream, and places the stream on the clipboard in the same QConsts.SDelphiBitmap format that Clipboard.Assign(Bitmap) uses. This makes the bitmap available for a subsequent Bitmap.Assign(Clipboard) without wiping out the other formats on the

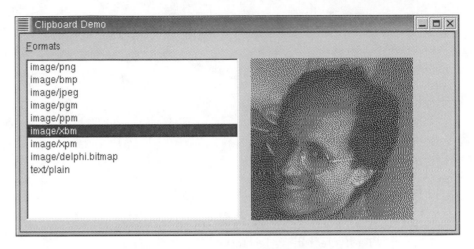

Figure 7-7. The clipboard demo displaying a dithered xbm stream

clipboard the way a Clipboard.Assign(Bitmap) would. Note that SaveToStream leaves Stream.Position at the end of the stream—if I didn't reset Stream.Position to 0 before placing it on the clipboard, the clipboard's SDelphiBitmap stream would be empty.

Finally, I create a TStringStream with some totally unrelated text and add that, too. As with the bitmap stream, I could have simply set the clipboard's AsText property, but that would have wiped out the various other formats on the clipboard. Setting AsText and using Clipboard.Assign save you having to create and Free streams, but they leave only the one format on the clipboard. If you want to place multiple formats on the clipboard, you have to use AddFormat.

Reading data from the clipboard

The TClipboardFrm.FormatsSelectionChange method is a simplistic clipboard viewer that's called whenever you change the selection in the Formats list. (Figures 7-6 and 7-7.) It decides whether the format is a bitmap or some text, and displays it accordingly.

```
procedure TClipboardFrm.FormatsSelectionChange;
const
  MimeText  = 'text/';
  MimeImage = 'image/';
var
  Selected:           string;
  IsText, IsImage: boolean;
  Stream:             TMemoryStream;
begin
  if Formats.ItemIndex >= 0
    then Selected := Formats.Items[Formats.ItemIndex]
    else Selected := '';
  IsText  := Copy(Selected, 1, Length(MimeText))  = MimeText;
  IsImage := Copy(Selected, 1, Length(MimeImage)) = MimeImage;

  Text.Visible  := IsText;
  Image.Visible := IsImage;

  if IsText
    then Text.Lines.Text := fClipboard.AsText
    else if IsImage then
      if Selected = SDelphiBitmap
        then Image.Picture.Bitmap.Assign(fClipboard)
        else begin
             Stream := TMemoryStream.Create;
             try
               fClipboard.GetFormat(Selected, Stream);
               Stream.Position := 0;
               Image.Picture.Bitmap.LoadFromStream(Stream);
             finally
               Stream.Free;
             end;
           end;
end; // TClipboardFrm.FormatsSelectionChange
```

As you can see, FormCreate's `fClipboard.AddFormat('text/plain', Text)` is compatible with the AsText property. FormatsSelectionChange reads the text into a Memo component with `Text.Lines.Text := fClipboard.AsText`. Similarly, `fClipboard.AddFormat(SDelphiBitmap, Stream)` is compatible with the Assign() method. FormatsSelectionChange reads the SDelphiBitmap format into the Image component with `Image.Picture.Bitmap.Assign(fClipboard)`.

For the portable image formats that QClipboard_setPixmap placed on the clipboard, you have to explicitly create a stream, read it from the clipboard, load the bitmap from the stream, and then Free the stream. As with SaveToStream and AddFormat, if you don't reset Stream.Position to 0 between GetFormat and LoadFromStream, the bitmap will try to load from the end of the stream, which will not work.

Clipboard viewers

It's common to want to know when the data on the clipboard changes. For example, we typically want a Paste action to be enabled only when there's data on the clipboard in a format we can paste. We could poll the clipboard in the action's OnUpdate handler, but OnUpdate is called often, and the clipboard typically doesn't change for seconds at a time.

Borland's TClipboard doesn't include any clipboard viewer functionality, but it's easy to add this, as in this code from lib/XClipbrd that is modeled on Borland's TClipboard code.

```
constructor TExClipboard.Create;
var
  ChangedEvent: QClipboard_dataChanged_Event;
begin
  inherited;
  Viewers := TNotifyList.Create;
  FHook := QClipboard_hook_create(Handle);
  ChangedEvent := ClipboardChangedNotification;
  QClipboard_hook_hook_dataChanged(FHook, TMethod(ChangedEvent));
end; // TExClipboard.Create

destructor TExClipboard.Destroy;
begin
  QClipboard_hook_destroy(FHook);
  Viewers.Free;
  inherited;
end; // TExClipboard.Destroy

procedure TExClipboard.ClipboardChangedNotification; cdecl;
begin
  Viewers.NotifyAll(Self);
end; // TExClipboard.ClipboardChangedNotification
```

The Qt clipboard provides a *signal* (see Chapter 12), dataChanged, that's emitted whenever the contents of the clipboard change. This signal can be sent to any number of *slots*, which are essentially registered signal handlers. To register a handler for the dataChanged signal, I create FHook, a QClipboard_hookH. I then create a `procedure of object` pointer pair, ChangedEvent, which points to my `cdecl` callback method, and tell the clipboard to add it to the chain. When the application terminates, QClipboard_hook_destroy unregisters my event handler.

TNotifyList is a simple list of TMethod's that you can find in lib/NotifyList. It provides functions to Add and Remove TMethod's, and to call every TMethod on the list. TExClipboard uses a TNotifyList so that an application's forms can register a clipboard viewer when they're created and unregister a clipboard viewer when they're freed; you may find it useful in similar situations in your own code.

Threads

Threads are ubiquitous. I'm sure all of my readers—except, possibly, the Visual Basic programmers—have written at least one multi-threaded program. Whether it's a Web server with a thread for every session, a Net client with a thread for every blocking socket, a database app with a thread for every long query, or even that traditional example of a word processor doing background printing and/or spell checking, just about every sort of program uses threads these days.

Accordingly, I'm going to cover threads pretty much the way I covered Object Oriented Programming in Section 1. I'll assume you've Been There, Done That, and will not belabor the fundamentals. Instead, I will concentrate on the specifics of thread programming in the Kylix environment.

Thread basics

Threads are special processes that allow an application to do more than one thing at once. On a single processor (or "uniprocessor"—UP) machine, this is always done through traditional timesharing. Each process gets a tiny slice of CPU time, and the CPU switches attention many times a second, creating the usually effective illusion that the machine is doing several things at once. By contrast, a multiprocessor (or "symmetric multiprocessor"—SMP) machine can run a different process on each processor, and can thus quite literally do more than one thing at a time.[6] This can make for a much more responsive

---

6.   Of course, when there are more active threads than processors, even SMP machines will do traditional timesharing.

server or workstation—but it can also mercilessly reveal any bugs in your synchronization code.

The difference between a thread and a "normal" process is simple: threads share their parents' address space, normal processes don't. That is, if you have two copies of the same program running as normal, separate processes, each has separate global variables and a separate heap. One process can't read or write the global variables or the objects of the other process, unless they've explicitly requested shared memory from the operating system. With threads, however, each process is part of the same program. Each thread can read or write any of its parent's global data structures and it can execute any of its parent's code. Similarly, the main program thread can read and write any global data structures created by any of its child threads.

Each thread has its own stack and register image, so that each thread can execute totally different code. Similarly, each thread's local variables are independent of every other thread's. (You can, of course, pass a pointer to a local variable to another thread—but you'd better be sure that that local variable will stay in scope (*ie*, the routine that created it won't return) until the other thread is done with it!)

Each thread can be assigned a different priority, so that a process can assign a lower priority to a long-running computation than to a short hand-shake over a socket. However, under Kylix, only processes running as root can use the TThread priority mechanism; normal processes need to use raw Libc calls to set their thread's priority. (See the *Priority* section, below.)

Kylix is not Delphi

Even on UP machines, threads can be executed in a thoroughly inter-leaved way—the processor can switch from one thread to another in the middle of an Object Pascal language statement. Thus, you have to exercise great care when reading and writing global data structures both to avoid reading a partially updated structure, and to prevent competing transactions from corrupting a structure.

Threads under Linux

Under some operating systems, threads and processes are very different entities. Threads may involve a "light weight", fast context switch, and/or be stored in different tables than processes. Linux, however, has a faster context switch than some older Unices, and under Linux a thread is just another sort of process; one that shares code and data pages with its parent.

```
[jon@BlueFat smp]$ ps
  PID TTY          TIME CMD
 4068 pts/0    00:00:02 bash
 5850 pts/0    00:00:16 M4L_smp
 5851 pts/0    00:00:00 M4L_smp
 5861 pts/0    00:00:01 M4L_smp
 5862 pts/0    00:00:01 M4L_smp
 5863 pts/0    00:00:00 ps
```

Figure 7-8. The results of a `ps` command

```
[jon@BlueFat smp]$ ps -H
  PID TTY          TIME CMD
 4068 pts/0    00:00:02 bash
 5850 pts/0    00:00:17   M4L_smp
 5851 pts/0    00:00:00    M4L_smp
 5861 pts/0    00:00:03     M4L_smp
 5862 pts/0    00:00:03     M4L_smp
 5864 pts/0    00:00:00   ps
```

Figure 7-9. The results of a `ps –H` command

This has little practical consequence, except that when you run the ps command, your multithreaded application will appear to be several different processes (see Figure 7-8). If you use the –H "hierarchy" switch, though, you will see your application's threads grouped together. You will often see an 'extra' thread, as in the ps -h illustration taken at a time when M4L_smp only had two non-GUI threads running (see Figure 7-9). This is an artifact of the pthreads library, which creates a 'management' thread the first time you create a thread.

One thing to be aware of is that when you run a multithreaded application in the Kylix IDE with "integrated debugging" turned on , terminated threads are not properly freed (see Figure 7-10). Thus, the ps command will show any dead threads as "<defunct>" processes until the application itself terminates. This does not indicate anything wrong with your application; it's purely a quirk in the interactions between the Kylix debugger and the pthreads (POSIX Threads) library. If you run your application outside of the IDE, you'll see that your threads disappear from ps as soon as they terminate.

Thread local storage

Most operating systems offer some mechanism for Thread Local Storage [TLS]. This is a chunk of memory accessible only to a single thread, which may be used to maintain thread state.

```
4007 ?          00:00:00    startkylix
4013 ?          00:00:04      Kylix
4016 ?          00:00:03        Kylix
4017 ?          00:22:19          Kylix
4026 ?          00:00:09            dbkexe
4027 ?          00:00:01             dbkexe
5879 ?          00:00:09            M4L_smp
5880 ?          00:00:00            M4L_smp
5882 ?          00:00:00            M4L_smp
5883 ?          00:00:00              M4L_smp <defunct>
5884 ?          00:00:00              M4L_smp <defunct>
5885 ?          00:00:04            M4L_smp
5886 ?          00:00:04            M4L_smp
4019 ?          00:05:56        Kylix
4020 ?          00:00:31        Kylix
4022 ?          00:07:03        Kylix
4029 ?          00:00:00        Kylix
5881 ?          00:00:00        Kylix
```

Figure 7-10. A multithreaded app running in the IDE

Object Pascal supports TLS through the `threadvar` keyword. Syntactically, a threadvar is like a normal var, with three important differences. First, a threadvar must be global. That is, it cannot be local to a procedure or function. It can have a very restricted scope—it can be declared in the implementation section of a unit (and even in the last few lines of a unit where it's only visible to the initialization and finalization code) or in a .dpr project file—but it must be declared outside of any routine. Second, a threadvar cannot have an initialization clause the way a normal global can. You have to explicitly set an initial value for any threadvars when your thread starts up. Third, a threadvar is thread local; each thread has its own copy. The first thread you explicitly create cannot read or write the values that the main (GUI) thread reads and writes; a subsequent thread can't read or write either of the other two thread's threadvars; and so on.

One glaring exception to the principle of thread locality involves pointers to threadvars. Be very wary of passing a threadvar as a var parameter, or assigning its address to a pointer variable. These pointers are **not** relative to the start of Thread Local Storage. As in the ThreadVars project in the ch7/Threads project group, if thread A sets a pointer to a threadvar and thread B dereferences the address, it will read or write thread A's copy of the threadvar, not its own. The compiler will not warn you of this, but this is a very dangerous, non-portable practice. It works under the standard Libc memory manager and it works in Delphi, but it doesn't work under stricter memory managers like Electric Fence (see Chapter 10). Similarly, this sort of violation of thread locality may not work under future versions of Libc, or on possible future Delphi/Kylix platforms like Solaris.

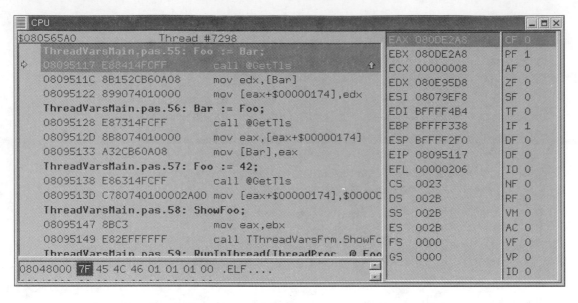

Figure 7-11. ThreadVar assembly code

The reason that pointers to threadvars can violate thread locality is that (as you can see in Figure 7-11) every read or write of a threadvar actually involves a call to GetTLS, which returns a pointer to the start of the current thread's storage. The threadvar is then read or written at an offset into TLS. As it happens, thread local storage is allocated sequentially, and each block is accessible to all the threads in the process—but neither of these **have** to be true. The memory manager could give each TLS block the same linear address and arrange the paging hardware to map the address appropriately; the memory manager could set the TLS blocks so that they were truly thread local.

This GetTLS implementation also means that threadvars are significantly slower than normal global vars, which are in turn normally somewhat slower than local vars. (Execution speed is largely determined by instruction length, and references to the 32-bit offsets of global variables make instructions that refer to globals longer than instructions that refer to locals, which are usually in registers or at a one or two byte offset relative to BP. Threadvars are even slower than normal globals, because they require function calls to get the variable's address.) As you can see from this sample run of the ThreadBench project in the ch7/Threads project group,

```
    Local:111746916
   Global:122568018
ThreadVar:922575701
```

reading and writing a global integer is about 10% slower than reading and writing a local integer—but reading and writing a threadvar integer is about 7.5 times slower than reading and writing a global integer.

A different drawback to threadvars is that every thread has a copy of every threadvar. While this is the whole **point** of threadvars and there are undoubtedly some cases where you do want every thread in the app to have its own copy of some variable, most apps have different threads for different uses. Why would a background spell check thread need the same threadvars as a background MIME encoder and a socket waiter?

In short, while threadvars have their uses, in most cases you're better off adding a member to your TThread descendant as *per* the next section.

TThread

Kylix's TThread class represents an operating system thread. Creating a TThread creates a thread and freeing a TThread deletes the thread. You can specify whether the thread should be created suspended or whether it should start running as soon as it's constructed; this is Windows behavior that's emulated on Linux with semaphores. The TThread's Execute method is the code that the thread runs. This is a virtual; abstract; method: You'll never directly create a TThread. Instead, you'll derive classes from TThread that override the Execute method and, perhaps, add fields that provide any thread local storage that this thread will need.

The Execute method can access any global data, including form objects. It can execute any code it can 'see', but it must be careful not to make any Qt calls or to call any library code that makes Qt calls. Making any GUI calls from a non-GUI thread (*ie*, a thread that you create manually) can crash your application and/or the X server. (Qt can be built in a threaded mode where it's safe for threads to make Qt calls so long as they acquire the QApplication::lock, but Kylix 1.0 does not build Qt this way, and there's no binding for QApplication_lock.) To update the display, you must either use the TThread.Synchronize method or post messages to the application's Qt message queue. (See the *Synchronization* section, below.)

Somewhat similarly, you must be careful not to let any exceptions propagate out of a thread. Application.OnException can only provide default exception handling for the main (GUI) thread. Most Execute methods wrap all thread code inside a try/except block that 'eats' any unhandled exceptions; you may prefer to log exceptions or redirect them to the main thread for display, perhaps using Synchronize.

If you set the TThread's FreeOnTerminate property to True before the Execute method returns, the TThread object will automatically Free itself when the thread finishes running, much like the caFree action in a form's OnClose event. Most threads Free themselves in this way; the exceptions are those that store results in their field variables, for other code to examine when the thread is done.

Suspend and Resume

Kylix is not Delphi

Threads can be created suspended. This allows you to set any thread field variables before the thread starts running and accesses them. Note that this is the **only** way that you should set field variables before the thread starts running; Delphi code that sets field variables in the thread's constructor before `inherited` `Create` is not safe. This may work most of the time but will fail some times. If you have any Delphi code that sets fields before calling `inherited` `Create` with the CreateSuspended parameter set False, be sure to rewrite your constructor to create the thread suspended, set the field variables, and then call Resume.

While the thread is suspended, its Suspended property will be True. Setting `Suspended := False` has the same effect as calling Resume. Similarly, while a thread is running you can suspend it either by calling Suspend or by setting Suspended to True.

Note, however, that there is a very important difference between creating a suspended thread and calling Resume, and suspending and resuming a running thread! When you create a TThread suspended, the ThreadProc that calls your Execute procedure waits on the FCreateSuspendedSem semaphore before calling your Execute procedure. If you are in this "initial suspend", Resume will simply post to the semaphore, allowing the ThreadProc to resume and call your Execute procedure. When you suspend a running thread, though, the implementation is quite different.

In general, POSIX threads cannot be suspended. Classes.pas says "Suspending a thread is [considered] dangerous since it is not guaranteed where the thread would be [suspended]. It might be holding a lock [or a] mutex or it might be inside a critical section." In order to simplify porting Delphi code to Linux, Borland has emulated the Windows Suspend/Resume behavior by sending a SIGSTOP and SIGCONT signals (see Chapter 10) to the thread. This works with the current implementation of the pthreads library, but it violates the POSIX standard, which calls for a SIGSTOP to a thread to stop the entire process. In other words, Kylix's Suspend and Resume implementation may not work with future versions of Linux, or on future Kylix platforms like Solaris.

Should you use Suspend and Resume? That's up to you, but it's probably not a very good idea. The pthreads signal behavior may be made more POSIX compliant at any time. If that time is some years out, using Suspend and Resume now may end up costing your company a lot of money as someone who wasn't involved with the port has to figure out why the application runs fine on older distributions but dies at "random times" on new distributions. It may make sense to use Suspend and Resume to get a port up and running, but to flag the dangerous methods with the deprecated directive or a custom {$message} so you can rewrite them before you release your port.

Note

 Rather than suspending a running thread, you should think in terms of having it wait on an event.

It's hard for me to give advice on how to convert code that suspends and resumes running threads, because I've never suspended a thread except to abort threads that don't use reference counted data (see the next section). However, I can imagine at least one class of problems where you might be tempted to suspend and resume a thread. You may have a "producer" thread that's continuously generating data, and a "consumer" thread that's doing something to each datum as it's produced. You might design the consumer thread to Suspend itself every time it finishes a datum and the queue is empty, and the producer thread to set the consumer thread's Suspended property to False every time it adds a datum to the queue. (As with most properties, setting Suspended to the current value has no side effects.) Such a design can easily be changed to avoid suspending and resuming the thread. Simply have the consumer thread wait on an event (see the Synchronization section, below) every time it's about to read from the queue, and have the producer thread set the event every time it adds to the queue.

Termination

Sometimes you need to abort a thread. Perhaps the user hit Cancel on the download, or changed the simulation's parameters, or just closed the app. In Delphi you can abort a thread by suspending it and then freeing it, but this doesn't work in Kylix. In Kylix, you can use Libc.pthread_cancel() to abort a thread.

Kylix is not Delphi.

By default, threads can be cancelled but cancellation is "deferred" until the thread reaches a cancellation point. As *per* the man page for pthread_cancel, there are relatively few of these. You can use pthread_setcanceltype to change this cancellation mode so that the cancel takes effect immediately. As in the ThreadAbort project[7] in the ch7/Threads project group, the thread needs to call pthread_setcanceltype itself—pthread_setcanceltype does not take a ThreadID parameter, but instead acts on the thread it's called from.

```
procedure TAbortFrm.SpawnBtnClick(Sender: TObject);
begin
  SpawnBtn.Enabled := False; // Visual feedback
  KillBtn.Enabled  := True;

  Thread := RunInThread(Sleepy, Nil);
end; // TAbortFrm.SpawnBtnClick

procedure TAbortFrm.Sleepy(Thread: TSimpleThread; Data: pointer);
begin
  // Allow this thread to be cancelled.
  pthread_setcanceltype(PTHREAD_CANCEL_ASYNCHRONOUS, Nil);

  // Sleep 15 seconds
  Sleep(15000);

  // Update the GUI
  Thread.Synchronize(NoThread);
end; // TAbortFrm.Sleepy

procedure TAbortFrm.NoThread;
begin
  SpawnBtn.Enabled := True;
  KillBtn.Enabled  := False;
  Thread := Nil;
end; // TAbortFrm.NoThread
```

By contrast, pthread_cancel is intended to be called from another thread—it takes a ThreadID parameter.

---

7.   This project uses the LThreads unit that I discuss below.

```
procedure TAbortFrm.KillBtnClick(Sender: TObject);
begin
  pthread_cancel(Thread.ThreadID);
  NoThread;
end; // TAbortFrm.KillBtnClick
```

Having shown you how to abort a thread, I should point out that this is just as unsafe as suspending a thread. If the thread is aborted while holding a lock, another thread may be deadlocked. Similarly, aborting a thread with open references to strings, interfaces, or dynamic arrays means that those objects will never be dereferenced and their memory will never be freed. You should only use pthread_cancel when you're **sure** that none of these problems will occur.

pthread cleanup routines

There **is** a way to protect resources even in threads that may be aborted, but it's not particularly easy to apply to reference-counted resources like strings. The pthread_cleanup_push procedure (in Libc as _pthread_cleanup_push) allows you to install a "cleanup handler" that will be called when the thread exits normally **or** when it is cancelled. The cleanup handler is a `procedure (Arg: pointer); cdecl;`, and you supply the Arg pointer when you "push" the handler onto the cleanup stack. The Arg pointer can, of course, point to a mutex to unlock, a file to close, or to an arbitrarily complex object or record.

If you don't call pthread_cleanup_pop to remove the most recently pushed handler from the chain, all installed cleanup routines are called in LIFO order when the thread terminates. Normally, though, you would pop the cleanup routine in a finally handler. The "pop" routine takes an Execute argument that allows you to either pop the routine without executing it or to pop and run the cleanup handler.

Thus, you might write code like

```
procedure Release(CriticalSection: pointer); cdecl;
begin
  TCriticalSection(CriticalSection).Release;
end; // Release
```

```
procedure TSomeObject.ThreadMethod( Thread: TSimpleThread;
                                    Data: pointer);
var
  Buffer: TPthreadCleanupBuffer;
begin
  CriticalSection.Lock;
  try
    _pthread_cleanup_push(Buffer, Release, CriticalSection);
    // ...
  finally
    _pthread_cleanup_pop(Buffer, 1); // calls Release
  end;
end; // TSomeObject.ThreadMethod
```

which releases the critical section even if you abort the thread. The cdecl
cleanup routines make for a fair amount of clutter, but it **is** a workable
solution.

One thing you should not do is to install a cleanup handler that raises an
exception, and uninstall it when you terminate normally. This **will** cleanly
unwind the Kylix stack if you abort the thread, dereferencings strings &c
and calling any finally blocks—but you will get a SIGSEGV when your
thread routine exits and Classes.ThreadProc calls pthread_exit. Pity.[8]

The only generally safe way to abort a thread is to have it periodically
poll an abort flag; perhaps at the bottom of every loop, or after every IO wait.
If you have many threads that you might want to abort simultaneously, you
might use a global abort flag—perhaps a field in a form object that all the
threads can see. If you will only be aborting single threads, you can use the
TThread.Terminate method. This does absolutely nothing but set the TThread's
Terminated property to True. If your Execute method returns when Terminated
(or your global abort flag) is True, your thread(s) will abort soon after you set
the flag.

See the Mandelbrot sample code (in the thread *Synchronization* section,
below) for an example of safely aborting a thread.

---

8.   The SIGSEGV can be fixed, but it requires stack tweaking on the order of what's
     done to map OS signals (Chapter 10) to Kylix exceptions, as well as tweaking
     Classes.ThreadProc. This sort of hackery is *definitely* "beyond the scope of this book!"

WaitFor

Some threads are "joined" to others: They wait for another thread to terminate before they resume. This is most commonly used to write "slow" code (like a request for a Web page) as if it were normal procedural code, without having to break it up into a state machine that's hard to write, hard to read, and hard to maintain. You may also use this technique as I do in the Mandelbrot code, to make sure that any aborted threads have terminated before you start any new ones.

The TThread.WaitFor method will wait for the thread to terminate before returning. Don't call this inside of the thread's own Execute method—call it only from another thread! The thread that calls WaitFor will be blocked until the thread that is waited for terminates.

Note

Calling Self.WaitFor will cause an endless loop.

WaitFor is a function that returns the TThread.ReturnValue. Many (most?) applications simply ignore the result, but you can use it to return a status code.

Note that WaitFor will most commonly be called when one secondary thread is waiting on another. (For example, a web spider thread waiting on a socket controlling thread.) You **can** call WaitFor from the main, GUI thread, but you should do so very sparingly. The main thread will not process any events while it's in WaitFor. This means it won't respond to mouse clicks and keypresses, and your application will appear hung.

ThreadId

Every thread has a Handle and a ThreadId. Under Windows, some system functions take a thread ID while others take a handle; under Linux, all system functions take a thread ID and Classes.pas never even sets TThread.Handle. In fact, it's hard to tell why Kylix's TThread even has a Handle. I suspect the likeliest explanation is just that no one noticed. I sort of doubt that it was a conscious decision to ease porting, as most porters would probably prefer that the compiler catch all references to a non-existent property.

Kylix is not Delphi

Priority

Threads and processes can have different priorities. High-priority processes run more often and/or run for longer when they run. Low-priority processes run less, and may only run when there are no higher-priority processes waiting to run.

Setting priorities properly can be a black art. You'll generally want to give compute-bound processes a lower priority than IO-bound processes. This can improve over-all system responsiveness without seriously affecting the long process's run-time; most systems have plenty of free cycles. Beyond that, though, things quickly get complicated. For example, imagine a producer thread that takes roughly twice as long to produce a datum as a consumer thread takes to process it. You might imagine that setting the producer thread's priority twice as high as the consumer thread's would balance the two, so that each takes roughly the same time. It might—or it might actually choke off the consumer thread so that it can't keep up with the producer, and data spends a long time in the queue. Be prepared to spend some time balancing priorities, and watch both total run time and queue lengths.

Caution

You should think twice before embarking on any process as murky and difficult as using thread priorities for load balancing. Beyond the clear-cut compute-bound vs *IO-bound cases, you may not see enough benefit to justify the time you spend getting priorities right.*

Kylix is not Delphi

Under Delphi, TThread.Priority is an enum, and priorities like THREAD_PRIORITY_LOWEST and THREAD_PRIORITY_ABOVE_NORMAL have obvious interpretations. Under Kylix, scheduling is much more complicated. To start with, Linux processes have both *static* and *dynamic* priorities. TThread.Priority affects only the static priority. The dynamic priority is automatically increased whenever a normal process is ready to run but has to wait for other processes, and can be manually altered with the Libc `nice()` or `setpriority()` system calls (below).

TThread.Priority is an integer from 0 to 99, where higher values have higher priority. In addition, Thread Priority is tightly bound to the scheduling Policy. Tasks running with superuser privileges can set Policy to SCHED_RR (real-time, round-robin scheduling), SCHED_FIFO (real-time, first-in first-out scheduling) or SCHED_OTHER (regular, non-real-time scheduling).

Tasks running without superuser privileges can only use the default SCHED_OTHER Policy.

In the two real-time policies, SCHED_RR and SCHED_FIFO, Priority can be set to a number from 1..99; in the standard policy, SCHED_OTHER, Priority must be 0. When a process with a high static priority becomes ready to run (emerges from a wait or a sleep), it preempts any running process with a lower static priority. SCHED_FIFO processes can only be preempted by higher priority tasks; they run until they block, yield, or terminate. SCHED_FIFO processes are not timeshared. SCHED_RR processes are much like SCHED_FIFO, except that they **are** timeshared and can be preempted by a waiting SCHED_RR task of the same priority. When the high priority process blocks, yields, terminates or is pre-empted, the next process of the same priority is run. If there is no process with the same priority ready to run, Linux gives the CPU (or "a CPU", on SMP machines) to the ready process with the next highest priority. Thus, normal SCHED_OTHER processes (with a static priority of 0) are only run if there are no real-time processes (which have a higher static priority) ready to run.

Table 7-13 summarizes the meaning of the three scheduling policies; see `man sched_setscheduler` for more information.

Table 7-13. Linux scheduling policies

Policy	Priority Range	Notes
SCHED_OTHER	0	The default Linux time-sharing policy. Processes are only run when there is no waiting real-time process. You can change the dynamic priority with the `nice()` and `setpriority()` system calls.
SCHED_FIFO	1..99	The basic real-time scheduling policy. The system maintains a FIFO queue for each process priority; a FIFO process runs until it surrenders control or is preempted by a higher-priority process. A preempted process stays at the head of its queue, and resumes execution as soon as there are no higher-priority processes waiting.

Table 7-13. Linux scheduling policies (Continued)

Policy	Priority Range	Notes
SCHED_RR	1..99	A more sophisticated real-time scheduling policy. RR processes are subject to preemption if they exceed their CPU time "quantum" and there is at least one task of the same priority waiting. RR processes preempted by higher-priority processes stay at the head of their queue and get the rest of their "quantum" before they time out. Processes that exceed their quantum are placed at the end of the queue, and are not executed again until all currently waiting processes of the same priority have had a chance.

When there are more than one normal processes (with a static priority of 0) waiting for execution, execution order is governed by the dynamic priority. Dynamic priority does not apply to processes with a non-zero static priority. A normal process's dynamic priority is automatically increased whenever the process is ready to run but has to wait for other processes. When the scheduler is selecting a process to run, it will choose the highest-priority waiting process; if there is more than process with the same high priority, it will choose the one that's been waiting longest. Dynamic priorities run from –20 to 20; unlike static priorities, a smaller number is a higher priority. That is, a dynamic priority of 0 is a higher priority than a dynamic priority of 20, and a dynamic priority of -20 is a higher priority than a dynamic priority of 0.

You can retrieve a process's dynamic priority with Libc.getpriority(ProcessID, 0), and—if your process is running as a superuser—you can set it with Libc.setpriority(ProcessID, 0, NewPriority). Normal user processes cannot use `setpriority()`, which allows them to raise priority, but they **can** use `Libc.nice()` to lower their priority. That is, applications running as (for) normal users can only lower their priority or their thread's priority; they can't raise it.

Note that a ThreadId is not the same as a process ID (PID). To get the thread's PID to pass to getpriority() or setpriority(), you can use Libc.getpid. This returns the current process's PID. If you call it from the main (GUI) thread, you will get a different result than if you call it from a background thread.

LThreads

I have one major gripe with the design of TThread: Instead of creating a thread by calling a function with a simple "procedure of object" parameter, we have to create an object that descends from TThread and which has a specialized Execute method. This encourages us to create a new thread type for each thread, and put the actual thread code in the Execute method.

What's wrong with that? It tends to violate encapsulation. Typically we want our threads to act with and on the program's existing objects—our forms and our data models. Putting the thread code into a separate thread object means that that thread object has to know an awful lot about other objects. Often, too, the other objects have to create special fields just for sharing data with the thread, so that thread creation can involve a lot of code. This is tedious. It's also a bad, dangerous coding practice for all the reasons that encapsulation is good, safe coding practice; making thread objects heavily dependent on other objects' internals creates opportunities for any small change in *this* object to break the thread running on *that* object, and creates the possibility of unrelated code breaking the 'contract'.

A far safer and simpler approach is to simply have the thread run a procedure of object, which is often called a *closure*. Because a closure contains both an object's instance pointer and a pointer to one of its methods, there's no need to break encapsulation or to write a potentially large set of communication methods; the object operates on itself. Additionally, the thread stays completely generic. It doesn't need to know *anything* about the other objects in the system, and there's no need to create a new thread type for each thread.

At first blush, though, this approach merely trades one evil for another. With thread objects, we have to hand-craft fragile communications channels to our other objects, but we get free thread local storage in the thread object. With generic threads that execute a closure, we get simpler, more robust communication at the expense of having to move any thread local storage into the object.

The lib/LThreads[9] unit in Listing 7-1 (below) avoids both evils by defining a TSimpleThread class that runs a closure. One of the closure's parameters is a reference to the thread that's running the procedure. This lets you call Thread.Synchronize (see below) for GUI updates—and if the thread is a TSimpleThread descendant, you can cast it to its own type and access any per-thread storage in the thread object.

Usually, you will create a TSimpleThread by calling one of the RunInThread procedures, whose parameters are the closure to run and an optional Data

---

9. LThreads is the Linux version of the Windows SynchedThreads unit I discussed in my 1998 magazine article http://www.midnightbeach.com/jon/pubs/MsgWaits/MsgWaits.html.

pointer or string. The RunInThread procedures (one for pointer Data and another for string Data) also have overloaded versions that allow you to specify a TSimpleThread descendant. Thus, when you just want to fire off a thread to run a closure (as in the Mandelbrot program of Chapter 14 and the *Synchronization* section below), you can use the simpler forms of RunInThread. When you need some thread local storage, you use one of the forms of RunInThread that allows you to specify both a closure and a thread to run it in.

Listing 7-1. The TPointerThreads part of the lib/LThreads unit

```
unit LThreads;

// This unit contains code for easy creation of threads that run methods of
// another object (typically a form) as well as integer and thread queues for
// use with Synchronize.

// Copyright © 1998..2001 by Jon Shemitz, all rights reserved.
// Permission is hereby granted to freely use, modify, and
// distribute this source code PROVIDED that all six lines of
// this copyright and contact notice are included without any
// changes. Questions? Comments? Offers of work?
// mailto:jon@midnightbeach.com - http://www.midnightbeach.com

interface

uses Classes, SysUtils, SyncObjs;

type
  TSimpleThread = class;

  TPointerThreadMethod =
    procedure (Thread: TSimpleThread; Data: pointer) of object;
  TSynchMethod      = Classes.TThreadMethod;

  TSimpleThread = class (TThread)
  public
    procedure AbortThread;
    procedure Synchronize(Method: TSynchMethod);
  end;
```

```
  TPointerThread = class (TSimpleThread)
  public
    constructor Create( CreateSuspended: boolean;
                        Action:          TPointerThreadMethod;
                        Data:            pointer = Nil );
    procedure Execute; override;
  private
    PointerMethod: TPointerThreadMethod;
    PointerData:   pointer;
  end;
  CPointerThread = class of TPointerThread;


function RunInThread( ThreadClass: CPointerThread;
                      Handler:     TPointerThreadMethod;
                      Data:        pointer = Nil ): TSimpleThread; overload;

function RunInThread( Handler:     TPointerThreadMethod;
                      Data:        pointer = Nil ): TSimpleThread; overload;


implementation

{ TSimpleThread }

procedure TSimpleThread.Synchronize(Method: TSynchMethod);
begin
  inherited Synchronize(Method); // TThread.Synchronize is protected
end; // TSimpleThread.Synchronize

procedure TSimpleThread.AbortThread;
begin
  pthread_cancel(ThreadID);
end; // TSimpleThread.AbortThread

// TPointerThread
```

```
constructor TPointerThread.Create( CreateSuspended: boolean;
                                   Action:          TPointerThreadMethod;
                                   Data:            pointer );
begin
  inherited Create(True);
  PointerMethod := Action;
  PointerData   := Data;
  if not CreateSuspended then
    Resume;
end; // TPointerThread.Create

procedure TPointerThread.Execute;
begin
  try
    // Allow this thread to be cancelled.
    pthread_setcanceltype(PTHREAD_CANCEL_ASYNCHRONOUS, Nil);

    PointerMethod(Self, PointerData)
  except
    // eat any exceptions
  end;
  FreeOnTerminate := True;
end; // TPointerThread.Execute

// RunInThread

function RunInThread( ThreadClass: CPointerThread;
                      Handler:     TPointerThreadMethod;
                      Data:        pointer = Nil ): TSimpleThread;
begin
  Result := ThreadClass.Create(False, Handler, Data);
end; // RunInThread

function RunInThread( Handler: TPointerThreadMethod;
                      Data:    pointer ): TSimpleThread;
begin
  Result := TPointerThread.Create(False, Handler, Data);
end; // RunInThread

end.
```

This listing elides the "string thread" methods, which are basically the same as the "pointer thread" methods except for the datatypes. The thread constructors call `inherited Create(True)` to create an initially suspended TThread. Then they set the procedure pointer and Data member, and Resume the thread, which lets it start to run the Execute procedure. The Execute procedure sets up an exception frame—remember, you can't allow exceptions to propagate outside of an Execute procedure—and then calls the thread procedure that was passed (as a closure) to the constructor. When the thread procedure exits, the Execute procedure sets FreeOnTerminate to True, and returns.

In turn, the RunInThread procedures simply call the constructors, passing along the procedure to run and the optional Data. The versions that take a thread class use the ThreadClass parameter to call the constructor; the others use a hardwired `class of TSimpleThread` constant (either TPointerThread or TStringThread) to call the constructor.

Synchronization

In a multithreaded program, you have to pay special attention to synchronization. You don't want two threads to try to change a value at once; you want them to take turns. You don't want a consumer to start eating until the producer has finished cooking—and you don't want the consumer to take any CPU cycles while it's waiting.

At the kernel level, both these examples are applications of *semaphores*, special flag variables that can be set "atomically", and can be waited on cheaply. Atomically means that raising or lowering the flag is an indivisible, uninterruptible operation. The result can't be distorted by two processes trying to do it at once.

At the application level, it's more convenient to think in terms of "critical sections" and "events". A critical section (also known as a "mutex", which is short for Mutual Exclusion) allows one and only one thread to pass at a time. If two or more threads need to read and write a shared value, they would use a critical section to be sure that only one is doing so at any one time. When one thread has the critical section locked, any other thread that tries to lock the critical section is suspended until the first thread unlocks the critical section.

An event lets a thread wait—without consuming CPU cycles—until it has something to do. A producer/consumer pair might use a critical section around queue operations to be sure that they don't scramble the data structure—and would use an event to let the consumer wait until the queue's not empty. The consumer starts life waiting to be fed. When the producer adds to the queue, it "posts" the event, which wakes up the consumer. In turn, every time the consumer finds the queue empty, it goes back to sleep by "waiting" on the event.

Critical sections

Critical sections are more commonly used than events. It's hard, in fact, to overstate their importance. The operating system can switch control from one thread to another between just about any pair of machine language instructions. The important thing, here, is that the OS does not know—or care—about statement boundaries in your source code. Control can switch from one thread to another within the middle of a statement like `This :=This + 1` just as easily as it can switch between statements. In fact, given that each statement generates several machine language instructions, the OS is actually considerably more likely to switch within a single Object Pascal statement than between them. The OS saves the registers and the stack, so that the thread picks up where it left off—but the global environment may have changed around it.

This can lead to a "race condition", where the result of the interaction between threads can depend on the exact order that each thread executes instructions. The race can come out differently every time it's run, which makes for a "Mandelbug" that can be hard to track down. Consider what can happen if two threads try to execute that `This := This + 1` statement simultaneously, as in Table 7-14. Assume that This is originally 0. The first thread reads This, and adds 1. But, before it can write it back, the second thread also read This, adds 1, and writes it back. This is now 1. When the first thread gets control back and writes This, it will also write 1.

Table 7-14. A race condition

Time	Thread 1	Thread 2
1	Read This (= 0)	-
2	Add 1	-
3	-	Read This (=0)
4	-	Add 1
5	-	Write This (=1)
6	Write This(=1)	-

Clearly, This should be 2 at this point, and yet it's 1. The results get more and more wrong the more threads you imagine to be racing. If you object that this is all so hypothetical, that the threads have to be aligned Just So for this to be an issue, remember that code that works 99.99% of the time will still average one failure a day if you have a thousand users, each of whom executes that particular part of the code ten times a day. That is, race conditions can easily slip past testing, only to bite you hard when the application is released.

The answer is to be vigilant, and to protect shared variables with a critical section. You don't have to protect **every** shared variable—if, for example, you've safely assured that *this* thread is beavering away on one row of a matrix while *that* thread is working on a different row, you don't need to protect matrix access—but you do need to protect every variable that two threads might try to change at the same time.

The name "critical section" is actually a bit of a misnomer. It does sort of suggest that what you're protecting is a section of code; that it only applies when two different threads might be executing the same code at the same time. What you are in fact protecting is a section of your program's state; you use the same critical section to guard against simultaneous updates to a variable from anywhere in your code.

Further, you can protect more than one variable at a time. For example, a dynamic array consists (at least conceptually) of two related variables: the length and the actual array. As you can see in this example from my lib/LThreads unit, you can manipulate both within the safety of the same critical section. The critical section has turned a complex series of events (which involves several function calls and perhaps some heap churning) into a single atomic transaction. Other threads can see the queue before and after the Enqueue operation, but not during it.

```
procedure TIntegerQueue.Enqueue(Number: integer; MultiThread: boolean);
begin
  if MultiThread then fLock.Acquire;
  try
    SetLength(Queue, Length(Queue) + 1);
    Queue[High(Queue)] := Number;
  finally
    if MultiThread then fLock.Release;
  end;
end; // TIntegerQueue.Enqueue
```

As you can see, the TCriticalSection object in Borland's SyncObjs unit is very easy to use. You Create it in your data structure's constructor, and Free it in your data structure's destructor. Before you read or write the contested data, you "Acquire" a lock on the critical section, and when you're done, you "Release" the lock. (Synonymously, you can "Enter" and "Leave" the critical section. While Enter and Leave are implemented in terms of Acquire and Release, which pair you use is up to you—though for clarity's sake you shouldn't pair Acquire with Leave or Enter with Release.) If no thread has a lock on the critical section, an Acquire operation is relatively cheap. However, if you try to Acquire a critical section that another thread has, you are blocked. Your thread waits, consuming no CPU cycles, until the lock has been released. At that point, you are given the lock, and your thread starts running again.

You may have noticed my weaselly characterization of Acquire (and Release) as "relatively cheap". They do involve OS calls, though, and the special LOCK instruction prefix that they use is not free. Use critical sections where you need them—and don't use them where you don't need them. Locking access unnecessarily will just slow down your application.

More importantly, holding a lock will block any thread that tries to acquire it. Lock as little code as possible; release the lock as quickly as possible. Note how this procedure from the Mandelbrot program (see Chapter 14 for a full walk-through; I'm only going to comment on the use of critical sections here, and on the use of PostInteger in the *GUI issues* section of this chapter, below) extracts pass-invariant data **before** acquiring the lock, and does the actual calculations **after** releasing the lock.

```
procedure TMainWindow.SparsePass;
var
  Rows, Grain, Col, Row: integer;
begin
  Rows  := Data.Rows; // read it once
  Grain := Calc.Sparse.Grain;
  Col   := Grain - 1;
  repeat
    LockCalc;
    try
      Row := Calc.Sparse.Row;
      if Row >= Rows then
      begin
        if not Calc.Sparse.Done then
        begin // 1st thread to get here
          Calc.Sparse.Done := True;
          PostInteger(wm_SparseDone, 0);
        end;
        EXIT;
      end;
```

```
      Inc(Calc.Sparse.Row, Grain);
    finally
      UnlockCalc;
    end;

    Data.CalcRow(Row, Col, Grain);
    if Calc.Abort then EXIT;
  until True = False; // We EXIT from this loop
end; // TMainWindow.SparsePass
```

The Mandelbrot application calls the Libc function `get_nprocs` to see how many CPU's the machine it's running on has, and fires off a calc thread for each CPU. On SMP machines, there might thus be two or more threads trying to read and write the Calc.Sparse record at the same time. The

```
LockCalc;
try
finally
  UnlockCalc;
end;
```

construct guarantees that only one thread can access Calc.Sparse at a time. Each thread reads the row it should work on, and updates the record to point to the row that the next thread to get the lock should work on. The first thread to get a Row >= Rows sets the Sparse.Done flag, and sends a message to the GUI thread. It then exits the procedure, as does every subsequent thread that sees the Sparse.Done flag, and the TMainWindow.Calculate routine proceeds to call the NormalPass routine.

Deadlock

Finally, I should at least briefly discuss the possibility of *deadlock*. Deadlock happens whenever one thread has locked a resource that another thread has locked and is waiting on a resource that the second thread has locked, while the second thread is waiting on a resource that the first thread has locked, as in Table 7-15.

As you can see, both threads are blocked, and will never be unblocked. The application as a whole may not be hung, but whatever these threads were doing will never be finished. The problem is that they tried to lock the

Table 7-15. Deadlock

Time	Thread 1 status	Thread 1 action	A locked by	B locked by	Thread 2 status	Thread 2 action
1	Running	Lock A	-	-	Running	Lock B
2	Running	Lock B	Thread 1	Thread 2	Running	Lock A
3	Blocked	-	Thread 1	Thread 2	Blocked	-

resources that they need in a different order. Had they both locked A and then locked B, as in Table 7-15, there could have been no deadlock.

Table 7-16. No deadlock

Time	Thread 1 status	Thread 1 action	A locked by	B locked by	Thread 2 status	Thread 2 action
1	Running	Lock A	-	-	Running	Lock A
2	Running	Lock B	Thread 1	-	Blocked	-
3	Running	(transaction)	Thread 1	Thread 1	Blocked	-
3	Running	Unlock B	Thread 1	-	Blocked	-
4	Running	Unlock A	Thread 2	-	Running	Lock B
5	Running	(whatever)	Thread 2	Thread 2	Running	(transaction)
6	Running	(whatever)	Thread 2	-	Running	Unlock B
7	Running	(whatever)	-	-	Running	(whatever)

Events

Critical sections are, well, critical, but they don't solve all your thread synchronization needs. The fLock variable in LThreads's TIntegerQueue class assures that Enqueue and Dequeue are atomic operations, that two threads can operate on the queue simultaneously without scrambling the data structure, but it isn't of much use to a consumer thread that needs to wait quietly until there's something for it to do. For that we need the related, but somewhat simpler, *semaphore*, or "event".

The most basic, or binary, semaphore is a flag that can have two states: *Pass* and *don't pass*. By default, the flag is in the *don't pass* state. When a thread tries to get through a flag in the *don't pass* state, it's blocked until some other thread sets the flag to the *pass* state. This unblocks the waiting thread, and usually resets the flag. (On Windows, you can choose whether flags "auto-reset" or not; on Linux, flags always auto-reset.)

Kylix is not Delphi

The Kylix interface to this functionality is contained in the SyncObjs unit's TEvent class. (Actually, most Kylix programs will use TSimpleEvent, as it defaults a number of arguments to TEvent's constructor that only apply to Windows semaphores.) As with TCriticalSection, there are really only two methods of interest, besides Create and Free. WaitFor(Timeout)—where Timeout is essentially ignored but **must** be the LongWord($FFFFFFFF)—blocks the calling thread until some other thread calls SetEvent.

Internally, TEvent calls the Linux API functions sem_wait and sem_post. These actually implement n-state semaphores: sem_post increases the value of the semaphore, and sem_wait blocks if (and until) the semaphore is non-zero. As a consequence, if *two* threads are waiting on the same event, only *one* will be released when a third thread does a post!

To have multiple threads released by a single event, you need to use the pthreads (POSIX threads) "condition variables" API. I've included an Object Pascal wrapper for these in the lib/ConditionVariables unit. (I wrote this wrapper for some CPU-counting code that I couldn't get working in time to use as an example.) This unit includes the following exports:

```
type
  ICondition = interface
  ['{E22861E6-6430-D511-8AAD-00A0C9E80506}']
    procedure Signal;    // wake at most one waiting task
    procedure Broadcast; // wake any waiting tasks

    procedure Reset;

    procedure Wait;                           overload;
    procedure Wait(const Time: TTimeSpec); overload;
            // Time is absolute, not relative - see FutureTime()
    procedure Wait(Milliseconds: integer); overload;

    function GetWaitCount: integer;
    property WaitCount: integer read GetWaitCount;
  end;

function Condition: ICondition;
```

As you can see, the API is a bit more complicated than TEvent's. The basic, niladic Wait will wait indefinitely for a Signal or Broadcast. You can also specify a Wait that will stop at a certain time, or one that will only last for a certain number of milliseconds. The Signal function will wake at most one waiting task, just like sem_post, while Broadcast will wake any waiting tasks. The WaitCount property is added by my OP wrapper to allow you to not Broadcast until all threads that should be waiting are waiting. The Reset procedure does nothing except reset the WaitCount. By now, you're all probably weary of me saying things like "exposing this as an interface means that you don't have to worry about ownership issues"—so I won't. Just call Condition to create a new condition variable, and pass it around as needed.

GUI issues

Finally, we come to the last and perhaps the least tractable issue you'll face writing multi-threaded Kylix programs: The GUI. Strange as it may seem (and it does seem very strange to me) Qt is not threadsafe by default. You might think that it would **have** to be, given that Unix has been a multiprocessing system ever since the days of ASR-33 teletypes and PDP-11's with less memory than a cell phone, but while X can handle connections from multiple processes, it can't handle requests from multiple threads within a Kylix process. You can easily crash X if you try, so don't.

Recent versions of Qt can be built in a multithreaded mode that avoids the issue by providing an Application::lock that you can call to assure that you're only making one X request at a time, but Kylix 1 doesn't do this. Instead, you have to rely on various mechanisms to ferry data from background threads to the GUI thread, and you have to be careful that you only do graphical operations from the GUI thread. (You can do some TBitmap manipulation within threads but not all; it's generally safest to just avoid the issue.) This is all a royal pain, and hopefully Kylix 2 will enable Qt thread support. In the meantime, if you want to write multi-threaded GUI apps, you have to play by the very strict rules.

A background thread can use two basic mechanisms to put something on the screen: Synchronize and the Qt message queue (see the *Asynchronous Processing* section of Chapter 6). Synchronize is simpler (and built-in) but its performance is not spectacular, and it's rather messy from an OOP point of view. Using the message queue takes a bit more work (which I've done for you) but is conceptually cleaner and operates asynchronously.

Synchronize

TThread.Synchronize is a protected method available to all TThread descendants. (My TSimpleThread redeclares it, so that you can call Synchronize using the TSimpleThread parameter to every thread procedure that you run with RunInThread.) Synchronize takes a single argument, Method of type

```
TThreadMethod = procedure of object;
```

which is a object method that takes no arguments. This niladic method can be a method of the thread object, form object, or indeed of any other object in your program.

Note

The ThreadAbort project in the ch7/Threads project group uses Synchronize.

When you call Synchronize, the Method is added to the internal SyncList, which is checked automatically after every message is dispatched. If there are no messages for a while (the user doesn't move the mouse or press a key) the SyncList may not get checked very regularly. You may need to add a TTimer to your application to generate a steady stream of messages.

The thread that calls Synchronize is blocked until the Method has been run by the GUI thread. This means that any background processing is seriously bottlenecked by the GUI update speed. Ideally, you'd like a long-running background thread to run at full speed, with any progress updates occurring asynchronously. You can do this using the Qt message queue, but not with Synchronize.

The fact that the Synchronize Method takes no arguments poses communication problems. How is the Method supposed to know what to do? If you have several Synchronize methods that are called at distinct points in the background operation, each one can be hard-coded to display exactly the right data. But if you want a single Synchronize method to periodically update a status indicator, or to display partial results, you need some way to pass parameters to it. The only channel open to you is to rely on global variables. These can be object fields, of course, in the thread object or in a form object, but they're still global variables, and this is still the same sort of encapsulation violation that I complained about in the LThreads section, above.

> **Note**
>
> *It might seem strange to refer to an object's private fields as global variables, but this is exactly what they are, when the object is as vague and diffuse as a form. Every event handler has full access to your Synchronize state variables.*

One relatively clean solution to this is to define a special object just for use in Synchronize calls. This would contain fields for whatever state data is necessary, and a single TThreadMethod that can 'talk to' the application's form(s) to display the state data. The background thread would create this with whatever state data it wants to display, then pass the display method to Synchronize. The last statement in the display method would then Free this 'synchronize packet'.

The synch packet is certainly an OOP-clean approach, but it's hard to avoid a feeling of baroque excess, especially if all you need to pass is a simple signal (you know, "been there, done that, tell the user") or a single value. For that, the Qt message queue (see the *Asynchronous processing* section of Chapter 6) seems better—and higher performance.

Posting messages

When you post a message to the Qt message queue, it will wake up the GUI thread if the queue was empty. This is a distinct contrast to the way the Synchronize procedure works. What's more, the Qt message can contain a single 32-bit value "for free", which makes it perfect for passing integers or pointers, and even strings and interfaces, from a background thread to the GUI thread.

This is what Chapter 14's Mandelbrot project does. The main window descends from lib/QMessages' TMessageForm, and handles four custom messages: wm_ShowColors, wm_SparseDone, wm_ShowRow, and wm_AllDone. ShowColors and ShowRow pass integers to their handlers, while SparseDone and AllDone are simple signals. The basic strategy is that the calc thread(s) build a Counts array, and send ShowRow messages to the GUI thread to show each row as it's done. The ShowRow handler then uses a ColorMap to map each count to a color and builds a single row bitmap, using Canvas.ScanLine, and copies this to an Image bitmap (which is used in an OnPaint handler, and to save pictures to disk) and to the screen. Because the PostInteger method does **not** block until the message has been processed, the calc thread can go on to work on another row even while the last row is being colored and displayed. (When the calculation runs very quickly, as in the initial picture with an "Infinity" of 100, the calc threads can flood the system with more messages than it can process. This isn't a problem with deeper zooms with higher values of Infinity.)

I won't include code here, because I'll cover it in Chapter 14, and because I've already listed the SparsePass method. (That method sends the wm_SparseDone message when it's done, which tells the GUI thread to build an initial ColorMap based on SparsePass's sampling of one sixteenth of the pixels.) The bottom line is that the calc threads work on off-screen data using a critical section to coordinate their activity, and send progress information to the GUI thread *via* Qt messages, which tell the GUI which bits of the off-screen data to format and display. The calc threads call Libc.nice(), so the system stays responsive to user input even though every available CPU cycle is being devoted to generating a notoriously compute-intensive fractal.

You may object that at a certain level sending a Qt message is just as much "baroque excess" as creating a synch packet. It's certainly true that calling QCustomEvent_create, as PostInteger ultimately does, does involve creating and then destroying an object, just as the synch packet does. Nonetheless, not only does posting messages offer higher performance than using Synchronize does, it's also taking advantage of an existing mechanism, rather than cobbling together a custom solution just to avoid using global state variables.

Library procedures

CHAPTER 8

Library procedures

THE PREVIOUS TWO CHAPTERS have moved from objects that you can see to objects that you can't. This chapter will continue the trend, moving on down to a sweeping overview of the various library procedures that are available to you. It's neither comprehensive nor exhaustive—I don't discuss every library routine, and I don't try to cover every facet of the routines that I do discuss. Rather, the intent is to highlight the most important uses of the most important routines with the expectation that you will know what sorts of things are available and where to look for more information.

I've grouped these routines functionally—Strings, Dates, Math, and so on. Within each functional section, each routine gets its own subsection that mentions which unit the routine is in. Many—but not all—of these routines are in either the System or SysUtils units. Remember, the System unit is a sort of virtual unit; you never actually include System in a uses clause, yet the routines it provides are always available.

System and SysInit[1] are the **only** units that are treated this way. To use a routine declared in any other unit, whether one of Borland's, one of mine, or one of your own, you have to explicitly include that unit in a uses clause. Kylix automatically includes SysUtils in the `interface` section's `uses` clause of visual (form and frame) units, but you have to explicitly add it to non-visual units. That is, a compiler message like "Undeclared identifier: Trim" means that you don't use SysUtils in the current unit; just add it to one of the uses clauses, and recompile. Similarly, a compiler message like "Undeclared identifier: Min" means that you need to use the Math unit.

Strings

I covered the System unit's standard string routines—Length, SetLength, Copy, Insert, Delete, and Pos—in Chapter 1. I won't cover them again, but will cover some of the higher-level functions, instead.

---

1. The SysInit unit is linked into every module–executables, libraries, and packages. It exports ModuleIsLib and ModuleIsPackage booleans, but the most generally useful export is the HInstance value that you use to load resources. (See chapter 7.)

AdjustLineBreaks   `SysUtils unit`

The **AdjustLineBreaks** function guarantees that any line breaks within a string are the Linux standard ^J (#10), not the Windows ^M^J ($13#10) or the Macintosh ^M (#13).

An optional second parameter allows you to specify either the tlbsLF or tlbsCRLF line break style. The default value of this parameter is tlbsLF on Linux and tlbsCRLF on Windows. Thus, a 'bare' AdjustLineBreaks(S) will adjust S to fit the conventions of the current platform, while you can always specify the second argument to fit S to the conventions of a different platform. (Neither Kylix 1 nor Delphi 6 support a tlbsCR line break style.)

AnsiUpperCase   `SysUtils unit`

The **AnsiUpperCase** function converts a whole string to UPPER CASE. It works with Latin-1 as well as with 7-bit ASCII. However, if you know that your string contains only 7-bit ASCII, the UpperCase function is faster.

> **Tip**
>
>
> *Obviously, there's also an AnsiLowerCase function that converts a whole string to lower case.*

Format   `SysUtils unit`

Kylix's `Format` function is very much like C's sprintf() function. It takes two arguments: a pattern string, which consists of a mixture of literal text and format 'pictures', and an `array of const` parameter, which contains the values to be interpolated in place of the pictures.

> **Note**
>
>
> *Using Format() can be much clearer—and faster—than concatenating a series of strings and numeric formatting functions.*

The format pictures are hardly models of self-documentation, but should be familiar to C and Perl programmers. See the online help for details.

An array of const is an open array that may contain any series of scalar values except enumerations. The compiler automatically converts an array like [1, 2, '3', 4] to an array of TVarRec records. Each TVarRec record contains a VType field and a 32-bit value, which is either the value itself or a pointer to it. (You can think of a TVarRec as a fast, lightweight version of a Variant.)

Note that despite the compiler magic involved in building the open array, an array of const parameter is a parameter like any other. You can easily write routines like Kylix's ShowMessage or Exception.CreateFmt that have the same (const Pattern: string; const Arguments: array of const) parameters as Format, and which pass the parameters on to Format *via* Format(Pattern, Arguments). Code like

```
raise Exception.CreateFmt('The %s function returned %.8x',
                          [FnName, GetLastError]);
```

is smaller and clearer than its functional equivalent

```
raise Exception.Create(Format( 'The %s function returned %.8x',
                          [FnName, GetLastError] ));
```

Tip

The online help for the Format function includes a link to the "string formatting routines" category that includes procedural and C-string variants like StrFmt and FmtBuf.

IntToHex   SysUtils unit

The **IntToHex** function converts a number to its hexadecimal representation—without a leading $ character. Thus, StrToInt('$' + IntToHex(Int, 8)) = Int. The second parameter is the minimum number of hexadecimal digits to produce; the result will be zero-padded as necessary, and may be longer than the requested width. Thus, IntToHex($100, 8) = '00000100', and IntToHex($1234, 2) = '1234', not '12' or '34'.

IntToStr   SysUtils unit

The **IntToStr** function is the inverse of the StrToInt function. IntToStr converts an integer to its string representation. That is, IntToStr(42) = '42'. IntToStr always returns the shortest, most compact representation of the number. To get a number that's zero padded, you need to use the Format function; to get a number that's right-aligned within a fixed-width 'cell', you need to use either the Format function or the Str procedure.

> **Tip**
>
> *There is also a FloatToStr function and a whole class of "floating point conversion routines".*

SetString   System unit

While you can always convert a C-string to an AnsiString just by saying `PascalString := CString`, this involves an inline StrLen operation, which walks the C-String looking for the trailing #0. When you already know the length of the C-string, you can use the **SetString** procedure.

StringReplace   SysUtils unit

Doubling quotes or escaping space characters (*ie*, replacing ' ' with '\ ') is a basic fact of a programmer's life. Whether you're constructing a SQL query or building a shell command line to pass to popen (see Chapter 10), you have to mangle strings to conform to other program's expectations. The StringReplace function does this for you, and prevents your having to write your own function.

Note

I mention StringReplace here both because it's broadly useful—and because it's a good illustration of the importance (and difficulty) of keeping up with Borland's library enhancements. They added StringReplace back in Delphi 4, but I didn't notice it until I was compiling the list of routines to mention in this section. Not only did this mean that I billed a customer for reinventing a wheel, it rendered my code a little less legible. A Borland library routine (that whoever inherits your code can press F1 on) is almost always preferable to a local library routine. (Almost—but not always. Borland's StringReplace is fine for small strings, but it's very slow on large strings with lots of replacements. The ReplaceAll function in lib/GrabBag is faster.)

Str System unit

The **Str** procedure converts an integer or float point value to its string representation. Compiler magic allows you to follow the value with an optional colon and a string width; float point values can also be followed by another optional colon and a decimal precision, just as in the Write and WriteLn procedures of the *Files* section, below. These three system procedures are the only place where you can use this colon notation—you cannot write procedures that do the same thing.

For both integers and floats, a zero width is the same as no width specifier at all; Str produces the most compact representation, with no leading blanks. When you specify width, the result will be left-padded as necessary; as with IntToHex, the result may be longer than the width.

Table 8-1. Str() width parameters

Str expression	S value
Str(12321, S)	'12321'
Str(12321: 0, S)	'12321'
Str(12321: 4, S)	'12321'
Str(12321: 8, S)	' 12321'

With float values, not specifying a precision is not the same as specifying a zero precision; no precision gives you scientific notation, while zero precision rounds to an integer.

Table 8-2. Str() precision parameters

Str expression	S value
Str(Pi, S)	'3.14159265358979E+0000'
Str(Pi: 0: 0, S)	'3'
Str(Pi: 0: 4, S)	'3.1416'
Str(Pi: 0: 8, S)	'3.14159265'

Note

The Str procedure ignores the locale information and so always uses '.' for the decimal point, even in locales that use, say, a comma.

StringOfChar   System unit

The **StringOfChar** function returns a string of a specified width, filled with a specified character. This is useful for right and left padding.

StrToInt   SysUtils unit

The **StrToInt** function is the inverse of the IntToStr function. StrToInt will either convert a string representation of an integer to the integer, or raise an EConvertError. This is very useful in expressions, but relying on exception handling to detect unexpected inputs can be very slow. You'd be better off using a function like Chapter 4's StrIsInt to validate lines from a large file.

Alternatively, **StrToIntDef** acts just like StrToInt, except that it returns a default value (that you supply) on any conversion error. If you can either supply a reasonable default, or can use some sort of flag value as the default, StrToIntDef is faster then either catching an exception **or** calling Val() twice, which is what the 'if StrIsInt then StrToInt' sequence does.

Note

StrToInt can handle hexadecimal numbers, so long as they start with a $ character and so look like Object Pascal hexadecimal constants. (The C-style '0x' radix prefix is also supported.) That is, StrToInt('$100') = 256, as does StrToInt('0x100').

Tip

The online help for the StrToInt function includes a link to the "type conversion routines" category that includes functions like StrToFloat and StrToDate.

Trim   SysUtils unit

The **Trim** function removes any leading and trailing white space and/or control characters. Thus, `Trim(Text) <> ''` tests whether Text contains anything besides white space, and Trim(NameEdit.Text) returns the parts of the contents of the NameEdit control that you actually care about.

Tip

There are also TrimLeft and TrimRight functions.

UniqueString   System unit

AnsiStrings and WideStrings use *copy on write* semantics. That means that if you do something like `S[1] := UpCase(S[1])`, only S is affected. If S referenced the same string as some other string variable, the assignment operation would first change S to point to a new copy of the string; the other copies would still point to the old value, which would now have a lower reference count.

This works totally transparently, and normally you don't have to pay any attention to it. However, if you cast a string to a PChar and then use PChar operations to modify the C-string, Kylix can't apply its copy on write semantics. Thus,

```
var
  This, That: string;

begin
  // Copy on write
  This := 'This';
  That := This;
  Assert(This = That);
  This[1] := 't';
  Assert(This = 'this'); // Changed This string
  Assert(That = 'This'); // Didn't change That string
  Assert(This <> That);

  // No copy on write
  That := This;
  Assert(This = That);
  PChar(This)[0] := 'T';
  Assert(This = 'This'); // Changed This string
  Assert(That = 'This'); // Changed That string, too!
  Assert(This = That);
end.
```

Under some circumstances, of course, you **want** to change any strings that refer to a given PChar buffer. Usually, however, you want the copy on write semantics; *eg*, if a Libc function modifies its C-string argument, you **don't** want every other copy of the string to be affected. UniqueString guarantees that a given value is referred to by only the string variable you pass to UniqueString. After calling UniqueString, you can safely cast the string to a PChar and modify the buffer.

UpperCase   SysUtils unit

The **UpperCase** function converts a whole string to UPPER CASE. It only works with 7-bit ASCII; use AnsiUpperCase to handle Latin-1 according to the current locale.

> **Tip**
>
> *Obviously, there's also a LowerCase function that converts a whole string to lower case.*

Val   System unit

The **Val** procedure converts a string to an integer or to a real, depending on the datatype of the second parameter. Unlike the StrToX functions, Val does **not** raise an exception when you feed it illegal input—it sets an error code. (Note that the online help is wrong—Val does not range check on bad data.) This makes it very useful for StrIsInt or StrIsFloat functions.

Dates

Kylix's TDateTime is a floating point double. The integer part is the number of days since December 30th, 1899, while the fractional part is the time since midnight. Programmers of a certain age still tend to flinch at the thought of using float point numbers, but floats have been fast ever since Intel started putting the FPU on the same chip as the CPU. Not only does a double have more then enough precision to register each clock tick as a fractional part of a day, it also has enough range that we're not going to face a Y2K or 2038 crisis anytime soon.[2]

The TDateTime is, of course, a sort of Julian date,[3] a count of the days since some point before any of the events that you want to date. As such it has three very useful properties:

---

2. OK, so you're the Extropian sort who plans to download yourself into a computer and live until the heat death of the universe and so you really care what the TDateTime format's Best By date is. Well, let's be pessimistic and assume that we only have 15 significant digits in a double. A millisecond is 1.1574E-8 days, so let's assume that we need ten of those digits for clock ticks. That leave five digits to the left of the decimal place for the day count—and day 99,999 is October 13th, 2173, which is about when my great-great-great-grandchildren will be turning 60. They may be thinking of retirement and letting their kids handle the tough decisions. If my great-great-great-great-grandchildren decide that timestamps don't really need 10 microsecond resolution, they can push the TDateTime format out to day 999,999, which is November 25, 4637. A lot can happen in 2600 years—it's really not much of an exaggeration to say that the TDateTime format will last forever.

3. Somehow, an urban legend has popped up to the effect that Julian dates have something to do with the Julian calendar, which everyone knows was supplanted by the current Gregorian calendar at various times after 1582. (Thomas Pynchon's 1997 bestseller, "Mason & Dixon" takes the eleven 'lost' days that the switch entailed as one of its recurrent motifs.) However, the original Julian date scheme was developed by Joseph Justis Scaliger in 1583 and named after his father, Julius Caesar Scaliger. Thus, Julian dates are named after a man named after the man that the Julian calendar was named after, not after the calendar itself.

1. It's easy to calculate the time between two events. Just subtract one TDateTime from another. The result will be the number of days between the two events, *eg* 0.5 is twelve hours. (A common mistake is to treat this difference as if it, too, were a TDateTime. It's not, of course, and trying to convert it to a Gregorian date will give absolutely ridiculous results.)

2. It's easy to do arithmetic like "three days from now": `Now + 3`.

3. It's easy to calculate the day of the week: `Trunc(Now) mod 7`. Saturday is 0, Sunday is 1, and so on.

Since a TDateTime also includes fractional days, it's easy to separate the date and time portions: Trunc(TimeStamp) is the date part, while Frac(TimeStamp) is the time part. In addition, the SysUtils unit contains the helpful constants HoursPerDay, MinsPerDay, SecsPerDay, and MSecsPerDay.

Kylix includes a number of date routines to encode and decode dates (turn Gregorian dates into Julian dates and *vice versa*); to convert a Unix `time_t` (another Julian date; the number of seconds since midnight, January 1, 1970) to and from a TDateTime; and to convert dates to and from string representations. The SysUtils unit also includes an array constant, MonthDays.

Many of the date formatting functions depend on various variables like the ShortDateFormat. These variables are automatically initialized at program startup from Linux locale information, and will generally reflect local custom and/or user preference. You **can** change them at run-time (to, for example, always display four-digit years, no matter what the local settings specify) but you really shouldn't, especially in multi-threaded applications. If you need to use some sort of canonical date format, you should use functions like DateToStr (below) which take an explicit format parameter.

Date   SysUtils unit

The **Date** function returns the current date; `Date = Trunc(Now)`. The various functions that work on dates (like DecodeDate and DateToStr) will generally ignore any fractional parts of the timestamp, but you may find it conceptually cleaner to use a date without a time for datestamps. (Calling Date is also somewhat faster than calling Now, as it involves one less system call.)

DateTimeToFileDate   SysUtils unit

Despite the name and the comments in the SysUtils interface section, this routine actually converts a Kylix TDateTime to a Linux `time_t`, which is used both for file timestamps and for functions like gettimeofday() which return the current time.

> **Tip**
>
> *FileDateToDateTime converts a* `time_t` *to a TDateTime*

DateTimeToStr   SysUtils unit

The **DateTimeToStr** function combines the functions of the DateToStr and TimeToStr functions. It formats the date part of its TDateTime argument according to the ShortDateFormat locale global, and formats the time part (if any) of its TDateTime argument according to the LongTimeFormat locale global. If the argument has no fractional part, DateTimeToStr produces the same result as DateToStr.

DateToStr   SysUtils unit

The **DateToStr** function formats the date (integer) part of its TDateTime argument according to the ShortDateFormat locale global. This is a good way to format a date in a user-friendly way.

> **Note**
>
> *If you need to format a date in a canonical way, one that's not dependent on the user's settings, you should use FormatDateTime or DateTimeToString, which take explicit format string parameters, rather than changing the global ShortDateFormat.*

DecodeDate SysUtils unit

The **DecodeDate** function converts a TDateTime to a Gregorian date (Year, Month, Day). The DecodeDateFully variant also gives you a Day Of The Week number, and returns True if the Year is a leap year.

> **Tip**
>
>
> *DecodeDate is the inverse of EncodeDate. The two are often used together to do date arithmetic. Kylix also supplies IncMonth and IncAMonth routines for date arithmetic.*

EncodeDate SysUtils unit

The **EncodeDate** function converts a Gregorian date (Year, Month, and Day) to a TDateTime. It raises an exception if the arguments don't specify a valid date; the TryEncodeDate procedure is similar but stores the result in an out parameter, and returns True if the date was valid.

> **Tip**
>
>
> *EncodeDate is the inverse of DecodeDate. The two are often used together to do date arithmetic. Kylix also supplies IncMonth and IncAMonth routines for date arithmetic.*

EncodeTime SysUtils unit

The **EncodeTime** function converts a 'clock time' (Hours, Minutes, Seconds, Milliseconds) to the fractional-day part of a TDateTime. Like EncodeDate, it raises an exception if the arguments are invalid, and has a TryEncodeTime variant that is similar but stores the result in an out parameter, and returns True if the time was valid.

FileDateToDateTime   SysUtils unit

Despite the name and the comments in the SysUtils interface section, this routine actually converts a Linux `time_t` to a Kylix TDateTime.

> **Tip**
>
> *DateTimeToFileDate converts a TDateTime to a `time_t`. FileAge and FileGetDate return a file's last-modified time as a `time_t`.*

FormatDateTime   SysUtils unit

The **FormatDateTime** function formats its TDateTime argument according to an explicit format string, which makes it the function of choice when you need to format a date to a fixed standard. You can also use the DateTimeToString procedure, which is what the FormatDateTime, DateToStr, TimeToStr, and DateTimeToStr functions all use internally.

> **Note**
>
> *Unfortunately, there's no form of StrToDateTime (UnformatDateTime) that takes the same format string as FormatDateTime. Thus, if you need to include a TDateTime in, say, an XML file, you have three somewhat less than thrilling choices: 1) You can write your own UnformatDateTime,[4] perhaps modeled on StrToDateTime, which reads an explicit format string; 2) you can just render the TDateTime as a float point value; or 3) you can diddle ShortDateFormat and LongTimeFormat before calling StrToDateTime. The first is … distinctly non-trivial; the second makes it hard for programs that aren't written in Kylix or Delphi to read your XML; and the third is, of course, not thread-safe.*

---

4.   Surprised that I haven't included such a function? Well, I'm running short on time.

IsLeapYear   SysUtils unit

The **IsLeapYear** function applies the now infamous rule 'a year is a leap year if it's divisible by four, unless it's a century year that's not also divisible by 400'. (Another one that I only found doing the research for this chapter. The Calendar.pas file in the date time picker component (see the next chapter) that I included on the Kylix Companion CD uses some old Turbo Pascal code I wrote back in the 1980s.)

Now   SysUtils unit

The **Now** function returns the current date and time as a TDateTime; Now = Date + Time. The resolution is system dependent (*ie*, it only changes when the clock ticks) but is more than adequate to benchmark relatively long events like file transfers. Remember, the difference between two Now calls is expressed in days: 0.25 is six hours.

StrToDate   SysUtils unit

The **StrToDate** function is a *partial* inverse of the DateToStr function. It reads the ShortDateFormat, but can only handle all-numeric dates. A ShortDateFormat like 'mmm d, yyyy' which (with US locale settings) produces dates like "Apr 28, 2001" will raise an EConvertError if you run code like StrToDate(DateToStr(Date)). (See the vfind projects in Chapter 13 for one solution to this problem.)

StrToDateTime   SysUtils unit

The StrToDateTime function combines all the features—and all the glitches—of the StrToDate and StrToTime functions.

StrToTime   SysUtils unit

The **StrToTime** function converts a timestamp string to a TDateTime or raises an exception. It does not read the LongTimeFormat locale variable, but *does* read the TimeSeparator global.

Time   SysUtils unit

The **Time** function returns the current time; `Time = Frac(Now)`. You can use this to timestamp transactions, but should use Now to measure elapsed time, as the difference between two calls to Now will automatically take any midnight-rollover into account.

TimeToStr   SysUtils unit

The **TimeToStr** function formats the time (fractional) part of its TDateTime argument according to the LongTimeFormat locale global. This is a good way to format a time in a user-friendly way.

> **Note**
>
>
>
> *If you need to format a timestamp in a canonical way, one that's not dependent on the user's settings, you should use FormatDateTime or DateTimeToString, which take explicit format string parameters, rather than changing the global LongTimeFormat.*

Math

For historical reasons, the math support in Kylix has a split personality. Some of the very most basic functions are in the System unit (*ie*, always available) while many equally fundamental functions are in the Math unit (which you have to explicitly use). For example, System includes Ln(), the natural log function, but not a base 10 log; Exp(), the e^x function but not a general x^y power function. After all, you learned in high school how to derive a base 10 logarithm from a natural logarithm, right?

Fortunately, Kylix does have the Math unit, and it's reasonably complete. It contains all the log, exponential, and trig functions you're ever likely to need; some basic statistics; a good suite of financial functions; and various miscellaneous float point comparison and selection routines, including a good set of equal-within-epsilon float point tests. If your programs do any math, use the Math unit and look through what it has to offer—this section is very brief, as I assume most of my readers *don't* do all that much scientific computing.

For that reason, it's probably appropriate to point out that the trigonometric functions use *radians*, not *degrees*. (New users frequently wonder why sin(90) <> 1.) Radians are measured in terms of the length of the arc the angle defines. That is, since the circumference of a circle is $2\pi R$, $360° = 2\pi$ radians and $90° = \frac{1}{2}\pi$ radians. Thus, sin(90) <> 1, but sin(Pi / 2) = 1. The Math unit contains routines to convert degrees to and from radians.

Abs   System unit

The **Abs** 'function' returns the *absolute value* of its numeric argument. You can pass Abs() either an integer or a float point number; Abs() acts as if it's an overloaded function, with integer Abs() generating inline integer code and float point Abs() generating inline FPU code.

ArcTan2   Math unit

The System unit's ArcTan function is rather unhelpful in many real-life applications of ArcTan, as it always returns a value between -Pi / 2 and Pi / 2. You have to decide for yourself whether or not the result should be in the second or third quadrants. The Math unit's ArcTan2 function is much better for applications like figuring out where (*ie*, what angle) the user clicked on a clock face or a pie chart, as you pass it X and Y values, and it returns an angle in the proper quadrant.

Ceil   Math unit

The **Ceil** function returns the smallest integer >= its argument. For negative numbers, this is the same as the Trunc function, but where Trunc(2.3) = 2, Ceil (2.3) = 3.

CompareValue   Math unit

Floating point values pose particular problems for programmers because they're inexact. Mathematically, $3 \times \frac{1}{3} = 1$, but using doubles it comes to 0.99999999999999994. That's close enough to 1 for all practical purposes—but it's not equal to 1, using simple FPU equality testing.

Thus, the float point CompareValue functions include an "Epsilon" parameter. If the difference between two numbers is less than Epsilon, they're considered to be the same number; otherwise one is greater than the other. (There are also integer CompareValue functions. All return –1..+1 (*ie*, Sign(A–B)) and are thus particularly suited to being called in sort comparison functions.) If you default Epsilon (*ie*, don't supply your own value) Kylix will generate a value based on the smaller (closer to zero) of the two parameters.

Tip

The Math unit also includes SameValue and IsZero functions that also take an Epsilon parameter.

Floor   Math unit

The **Floor** function returns the largest integer <= its argument. For positive numbers, this is the same as the Trunc function, but where Trunc(-2.3) = -2, Floor(-2.3) = -3.

Frac   System unit

The **Frac** function strips off anything left of the decimal place. The result has the same sign as the argument. Thus, Frac(-2.3) = -0.3 and Frac(2.3) = 0.3.

IfThen   Math unit

The **IfThen** functions return one of their two numeric arguments, depending on the value of their boolean argument. This can simplify and clarify your code, by avoiding an explicit branch and perhaps reducing parallelism. Unfortunately, because these functions *are* in the Math unit, there's no string version. (Delphi 6 adds a StrUtils unit which *does* include string versions, so presumably this will appear in Kylix 2.)

Note

For the special case where you want a particular Value or 0, depending on a boolean Test, you're still better off using the APL-ish Value * ord(Test) *idiom. This not only generates inline code, it avoids branching.*

Int   System unit

The **Int** function strips off the fractional part of a number—it rounds toward 0. Note that Int returns a float—to get the integral part of a float *as* an integer, use Trunc.

Max   Math unit

The **Max** function returns the larger of its two numeric arguments. (My lib/GrabBag unit has a string version.)

Tip

*The Math unit also contains **MaxValue** and **MaxIntValue** functions that return the largest value from an array of floats or integers.*

Min   Math unit

The **Min** function returns the smaller of its two numeric arguments. (My lib/GrabBag unit has a string version.)

Tip

*The Math unit also contains **MinValue** and **MinIntValue** functions that return the smallest value from an array of floats or integers.*

Round `System unit`

The **Round** function returns the nearest integer to its float point argument. If the fractional part is exactly ½, Round will choose the even number. (The Math unit contains float point control routines, **GetRoundMode** and **SetRoundMode**, which can change this behavior.)

Sqrt `System unit`

The **Sqrt** function returns the square root of its argument.

Sign `Math unit`

The **Sign** function reduces a number to its sign—an integer in the range $-1..1$. This can be very useful in `case` statements and in selecting from array constants.

Trunc `System unit`

The **Trunc** function strips off the fractional part of a number—it rounds toward 0. Note that Trunc returns an integer—to get the integral part of a float *as* a float, use Int.

Memory

Kylix contains three pairs of memory allocation/free routines: GetMem and FreeMem, New and Dispose, and Create and Free. GetMem and FreeMem are the most fundamental of the three; the other two use GetMem and FreeMem, and everything I say about the use and misuse of GetMem applies to data allocated with New as well as to TObject descendants.

GetMem(P, Size) allocates Size bytes, and sets P to point to them. GetMem does no initialization of the allocated memory; the allocated heap block will be full of random garbage. (TObject classes *are* filled with null bytes, but this is done after the GetMem; Kylix does not use `calloc`.) When you allocate blocks with GetMem, you can call ReallocMem to change their size. FreeMem frees the allocated memory; after calling FreeMem, you should no longer dereference P. FreeMem can optionally take a second parameter, which the documentation will tell you should be the exact same number that was passed to GetMem or the most recent ReallocMem. Kylix totally ignores this second parameter.

Kylix allows you to substitute your own procedures for GetMem, ReallocMem, and FreeMem by calling SetMemoryManager. These procedures will then be called for **all** memory management—from string addition on down to explicit allocations. You can use this facility to add debugging code or to log your program's use of dynamic memory. Also, if your application continually creates and frees heap blocks of a particular size, you may find that it makes sense to maintain a free pool of these blocks, rather than passing them to `free` only to `malloc` them again in a few moments.

The default memory manager implements GetMem, ReallocMem, and FreeMem by calling SysGetMem, SysReallocMem, and SysFreeMem. While your custom memory manager can call these routines, in most cases you should actually use GetMemoryManager to get the current memory manager, and implement your replacement routines in terms of the previous routines. This allows multiple debugging and/or specialized allocation layers to coexist.

New

Because GetMem works with untyped pointers and block sizes, GetMem and FreeMem are suitable for bulk allocation, such as buffers whose size varies with available memory or network speed. When you are working with fixed size structures, such as records or old-style objects, you will tend to use New and Dispose, which take a structured pointer type and get the size information from that. For example,

```
var
  I: PInteger;
  T: ^ TRect;

begin
  New(I); // allocates 4 bytes, Sizeof(I^)
  Dispose(I);
  New(T); // Allocates 16 bytes, SizeOf(TRect)
  Dispose(T);
end.
```

In addition to sparing you the need to specify a block size, New and Dispose automatically Initialize and Finalize reference-counted data in a way that GetMem and FreeMem do not.

> **Note**
>
> *I feel that to be thorough I should point out that when allocating old-style objects, New does still support the old Turbo Pascal syntax where the second argument to New can be the name of one of the object's constructors. Don't do this, though—even though I champion old-style objects' continued use as statically allocable "records with methods", I urge you not to use constructors and virtual methods with old-style objects: use new-style classes, instead.*

Suballocation

The default Kylix implementation of GetMem is a straightforward call to Libc.malloc(), which does "suballocation". That is, when you ask for a small block (like 1K), it will allocate a much larger block (like 64K) and carve the small block out of it. This minimizes fragmentation of the system heap, but also means that you will not necessarily get a SIGSEGV if you dereference a pointer after you free it.

Kylix is not Delphi

For example, the Suballoc project in the ch8/Memory project group deliberately dereferences freed memory.

```
procedure TSuballocFrm.OneKBtnClick(Sender: TObject);
var
  P: PInteger;
begin
  ClearLog;
  GetMem(P, 1024);
  LogLn('Allocated 1024 bytes');
  FreeMem(P);
  LogLn('Freed 1024 bytes');
  try
    F(P^);
    LogLn('No exception on deref');
  except
    on E: Exception do LogLn('Exception %s: "%s"', [E.ClassName, E.Message]);
  end;
end; // TSuballocFrm.OneKBtnClick
```

Yet, when you run the Suballoc project, you'll see that running OneKBtnClick by pressing the "1K" button does not generate a SIGSEGV (see Figure 8-1). However, pressing the "1M" button—which runs code that's identical except in that it allocates a much larger block—*does* generate a SIGSEGV, which Kylix reports to you as a EAccessViolation exception (see Figure 8-2).

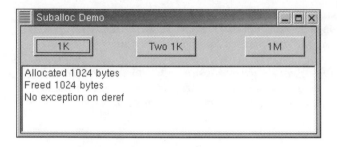

Figure 8-1. No SIGSEGV on a 1K alloc

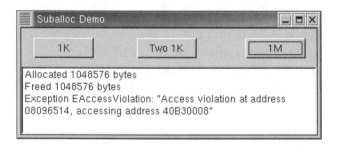

Figure 8-2. SIGSEGV on a 1M alloc

GetMem (or, rather, `malloc`) handled the 1K allocation by carving a chunk out of a larger block. When the 1K block was freed, it was added to a free list within that larger block, but the block as a whole stayed allocated and assigned to the Suballoc application. Thus, any pointer to any byte within that larger block remained a valid pointer that will not generate a hardware exception when dereferenced.

By contrast, the 1M allocation was handled by allocating a whole new block from the system free list. The allocation created a new entry in the hardware page tables for the 1M block belonging to the Suballoc application. When the 1M block was freed, the whole thing went back on the system free list, and the page table entry went away. Dereferencing the pointer generated a hardware exception.

Debugging

If you read man malloc, you'll see that glibc checks the MALLOC_CHECK_ environment variable when a program starts. Normally, (*ie,* when MALLOC_CHECK_ is not set) misuses of dynamic memory like freeing a heap block (calling FreeMem) twice or writing past the end of allocated memory are not necessarily caught immediately. As with suballocator abuse, sometimes these errors generate exceptions and sometimes they don't. Obviously, the sooner a bug shows up, the better.

If you set MALLOC_CHECK_ to 1 before you run your program, glibc can detect common programming mistakes, and write a message to StdErr. If you set MALLOC_CHECK_ to 2, glibc will raise a SIGIOT. If you're running within the IDE, Kylix will stop your program and report the SIGIOT, but it will **not** map it to an Object Pascal exception. If you press F9 after receiving a SIGIOT, your program halts.

The MallocCheck project in the ch8/Memory project group demonstrates this. If you run it in the normal (no MALLOC_CHECK_) environment, pressing the "Buffer Overrun" button causes no immediate problem (usually—this depends on the state of the suballocator). Similarly, pressing the "Double Free" button *may* cause an immediate SIGSEGV, or it *may* cause a SIGSEGV when you try to close the application, or it *may* not cause any problem at all.

However, if you bring up the Run ➤ Parameters dialog, select the Environment Block tab, and use the New button to set MALLOC_CHECK_ to 1 (Figure 8-3), you'll get very different behavior. When the program starts, you'll get a message on StdErr saying "malloc: using debugging hooks". When you press the Buffer Overrun or Double Free buttons, you'll get messages on StdErr about the mistakes these routines deliberately make. (Remember, you can select Use Launcher Application on the Run ➤ Parameters dialog's Local tab to capture StdErr output.)

Similarly, if you use the Run ➤ Parameters dialog to set MALLOC_CHECK_ to 2, you'll get a SIGIOT. Unfortunately, Kylix isn't able to show you which line generated the SIGIOT, but if setting MALLOC_CHECK_ to 1 or 2 reveals misuse of dynamic memory, you should find it reasonably straightforward to find where your error(s) is (are) by single-stepping and/or knocking out vast swatches of your application to pinpoint the offenders.

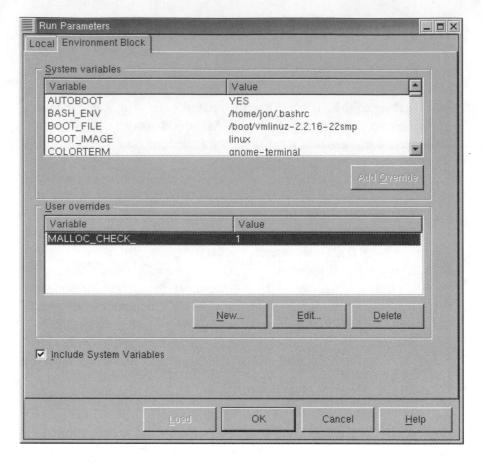

Figure 8-3. The Environment Block

Electric Fence

Linux also includes the Electric Fence memory checker, which forces each and every `malloc` to live on its own hardware memory page. This catches just about every sort of misuse of dynamic memory, at the cost of making your programs run **very** slowly and consuming vast quantities of memory.

If you suspect one of your programs is misusing dynamic memory, MALLOC_CHECK_ should be your first line of attack, because it won't slow your program down anywhere near as much as Electric Fence does. However, if MALLOC_CHECK_ doesn't report any suspicious behavior, you can run your program under Electric Fence by simply typing `ef MyApp &` instead of `MyApp &`.

For example, MALLOC_CHECK_ can't detect suballocator abuse like the MallocCheck project's "Deref Freed" button generates—but Electric Fence can.

FillChar   `System unit`

The **FillChar** procedure fills a buffer memory location with an arbitrary byte. Despite the name, you can pass it numeric fill patterns. Be careful! Kylix won't complain if you can pass it integers outside of the 0..255 range—it will 'just' change them to a 0.

In a somewhat different vein, despite the name, FillChar uses a 32-bit REP STOSD to do as much of the fill as it can, only using an 8-bit REP STOSB for any odd bytes at the end.

Move   `System unit`

The **Move** procedure moves an arbitrary number of bytes from one buffer to another. It can handle overlapping buffers, automatically employing "MoveLeft" and "MovcRight" logic as appropriate.

> **Note**
>
> *Be careful with Move. Its parameter list is **not** modeled on assignment, and you call it as Move(Source, Destination, Bytes), instead of Move(Destination, Source, Bytes).*

Just as FillChar uses a 32-bit STOSD as much as possible, so Move uses the 32-bit REP MOVSD for the bulk of the transfer, only using an 8-bit REP MOVSB for any odd bytes at the end.

SizeOf   `System unit`

The SizeOf function reports the size in bytes of a variable or type. Wherever possible, you should use SizeOf with bulk memory functions like GetMem, FillChar, and Move. This insulates your code from changes in type definition, as well as from any changes in alignment policies or in the size of generic types like integers and chars.

Files and directories

Kylix contains a full suite of routines for working with files and directories. While nothing prevents you from using raw Libc routines to do what these routines do, using the SysUtils routines will make your programs much more portable, as all these routines work under both Linux and Windows.

Similarly, if you want to write portable code, use the symbolic names PathDelim and PathSep instead of the hardcoded constants '/' and ':'. Under Kylix, PathDelim = '/' and PathSep = ':', while under Delphi 6 (and higher) PathDelim = '\' and PathSep = ';'.

> **Note**
>
>
> *The routines in this section deal with files and directories as opaque, static entities. To read and write files, you use the routines in the next section. Also, it seems particularly important to note here that these are only* some *of the available functions.*

CreateDir   SysUtils unit

The **CreateDir** function creates a new directory, returning True if it succeeds and False if it fails. CreateDir can fail because the immediate parent directory does not exist (*ie*, you can only `mkdir /foo/bar` if `/foo` already exists—the ForceDirectories function (below) can create intermediate directories.) It also can fail because your application's effective user ID ("euid" is not necessarily the same as the user running your application) or effective group ID does not have write privileges on the immediate parent directory.

DeleteFile   SysUtils unit

The **DeleteFile** function deletes an existing file, returning True if it succeeds and False if it fails. DeleteFile can fail either because the file does not exist or because your application's effective user ID does not have write privileges on the parent directory.

ExtractFileName   SysUtils unit

The **ExtractFileName** function returns the name and extension part of a filename—*ie*, anything after the last PathDelim.

ExtractFilePath   SysUtils unit

The **ExtractFilePath** function returns the path of a filename—*ie*, everything up to and including the last PathDelim, if any.

FileExists   SysUtils unit

The **FileExists** function returns True if the filename you pass it exists. Additionally, your application's effective user ID or effective group ID must have "execute" access on the file's directory—FileExists will return False if your application can't read the directory even if the file does exist.

FileIsReadOnly   SysUtils unit

The **FileIsReadOnly** function returns True if the file exists **and** your application's effective user ID can read it but can not write it.

FileSearch   SysUtils unit

The **FileSearch** function looks for a file in a PathSep delimited list of directory names. (Note that the comments in SysUtils are wrong in describing the DirList as a semicolon delimited list.) The result is either the full pathname (including the filename) or ''. For example, `FileSearch(Filename, GetEnvironmentVariable('PATH'))` will search $PATH for Filename.

FindFirst   SysUtils unit

The **FindFirst** function initiates a scan of a directory for files matching a pattern. The directory and the pattern are supplied as a single pathname—*eg*, FindFirst of '/foo/*bar*' scans /foo for *bar*. FindFirst uses `fnmatch()` internally, so the pattern can include any "shell wildcard pattern". The second argument is an Attr mask that must be matched; this is composed of a bitwise or of any of the file attribute constants in Table 8-3. The third argument is a TSearchRec where the actual file info will be placed as *per* Table 8–4.

> **Note**
>
>
>
> *You can* read *the TSearchRec, but don't change it while the scan is in progress. Doing so will have unpredictable—but probably not desirable—results. Especially, leave the FindHandle field alone: Messing with the FindHandle will leak resources or cause a crash in FindClose.*

Table 8-3. File Attributes constants

Name	Meaning
faReadOnly	Application's effective user ID can't write to this file
faHidden	File name starts with '.'
faSysFile	Not a regular file, *ie* lstat() doesn't show the S_IFREG bit
faVolumeID	*Not used under Linux*
faDirectory	File is a directory
faArchive	*Not used under Linux*
faAnyFile	All files in directory that match pattern are returned

Table 8-4. TSearchRec fields

Name	Meaning
Time	Last modified time—a Linux time_t
Size	32-bit file size
Attr	Bitmap of File Attributes constants as *per* Table 8-3
Name	File name *sans* path
ExcludeAttr	*Kylix internal*
Mode	Linux mode_t , as returned by lstat()
FindHandle	*Kylix internal*
PathOnly	Path part of FindFirst file pattern (ExtractFilePath)
Pattern	Filename part of FindFirst file pattern (ExtractFileName)

If FindFirst finds any matching files, it returns 0; otherwise it returns a system-dependent error code. To find all files that match a pattern, if FindFirst returns 0, you should call FindNext on the same TSearchRec until FindNext does not return 0, and then call FindClose. You don't need to call FindNext (and there won't be any point to doing so, if the FindFirst Path parameter didn't contain any wildcards) but you must **always** call FindClose if FindFirst returns 0; you do not need to call it if FindFirst does not return 0, but it can never hurt to do so.

For example, the following function from my lib/GrabBag unit returns a dynamic array of strings which contains all the files that match the FileMask.

```
function FindAll(const FileMask: string; Attr: integer = faAnyFile):
        TArrayOfString;
var
  Path:      string;
  SearchRec: TSearchRec;
  Len:       integer;
begin
  Path := ExtractFilePath(FileMask);
  Len := 0;
  SetLength(Result, Len);
  try
    if FindFirst(FileMask, Attr, SearchRec) = 0 then
      repeat
        SetLength(Result, Len + 1);
        Result[Len] := Path + SearchRec.Name;
        Inc(Len);
      until FindNext(SearchRec) <> 0;
  finally
    FindClose(SearchRec);
  end;
end; // FindAll
```

ForceDirectories   SysUtils unit

The **ForceDirectories** function will create a directory, creating intermediate directories if necessary. (That is, where CreateDir('/foo/bar') will fail if /foo doesn't exist, ForceDirectories will create /foo if necessary.) This function can fail (return False) if the disk is full, but the most likely failure mode is that your application's effective user ID doesn't have write privileges in the first directory that ForceDirectories tries to create a directory in.

GetCurrentDir   SysUtils unit

The **GetCurrentDir** function returns `` `pwd` ``.

IncludeTrailingPathDelimiter   SysUtils unit

The **IncludeTrailingPathDelimiter** function guarantees that a pathname
ends with a PathDelim character.

Tip

*The **ExcludeTrailingPathDelimiter** function does the
converse, stripping the PathDelim if it's the last character in
its pathname parameter.*

RemoveDir   SysUtils unit

The **RemoveDir** function deletes an existing directory, returning True if it
succeeds and False if it fails. RemoveDir can fail for any of three reasons:
the directory does not exist; the directory is not empty (*ie*, you can only
`rmdir /foo/bar` if there are no files in `/foo/bar`); or because your application's
effective user ID does not have write privileges on the directory, or its parent.

RenameFile   SysUtils unit

The **RenameFile** function renames a file, moving it as necessary. It calls
`rename()`, and returns True if `rename()` returns 0. You can call `GetLastError` to
retrieve the error codes listed in `man rename`.

Note

*On Windows, RenameFile will fail if the new file name already
exists. On Linux, RenameFile will do an "atomic replacement" of
the new filename. That is, any existing file with the new filename
will be unlinked (Chapter 10) and the renamed file will take its
place. The "atomic" part means that that there is no point in the
rename sequence where another process will not see a file with the
new name.*

Kylix is not Delphi

SetCurrentDir   SysUtils unit

The **SetCurrentDir** function changes the current directory, returning True if this was possible.

File IO

In addition to the file streams of Chapter 7, Kylix offers a 'cookie'-based file IO system. The 'cookies' are opaque types, `file` and `text`, that contain a file handle and various state information. In Turbo Pascal, the `file` functions were heavily used for files of records and for untyped (file stream) file IO. Arguably, new code should be using file streams for this sort of file access.[5] The `text` functions, however, remain useful for writing XML and/or log files, and for reading or writing the standard input, standard output, and standard error devices.

All text file operations begin by associating a `text` variable with a filename by calling AssignFile, and all end by calling CloseFile. In between, you can open the file with Reset, which opens an existing file for reading and positions the read pointer at the start of the file; Rewrite, which opens a file for writing and erases any existing contents; or Append, which opens a file for writing without erasing any existing contents. See Listings 8-1 and 8-2.

Listing 8-1. Reading a text file

```
var
  TextFile: text;
  Ln:       string;

begin
  AssignFile(TextFile, Filename);
  Reset(TextFile);
  try
    while not EOF(TextFile) do
    begin
      ReadLn(TextFile, Ln);
      // Process Ln
    end;
```

---

5. Especially since when you Reset() a file variable (open it for reading), Kylix uses the FileMode global variable to decide whether to open it in a read-only or read/write mode. This, of course, is not thread safe.

```
finally
  CloseFile(TextFile);
  end;
end.
```

You can actually use Read (as opposed to ReadLn) to read individual characters or numbers, but this is incredibly uncommon. See the documentation for details, if you're interested. Most text file input is done with ReadLn, which reads a line at a time and leaves you to bother with the line's internal structure.

Obviously, reading a line at a time is an inherently character-oriented protocol. The ReadLn procedure has to read the file character by character, looking for a newline character. The text variable contains a 128-byte buffer that is used to speed this process; for large files, or files with particularly long lines, you may wish to speed things up by giving the text cookie a larger buffer with the SetTextBuf procedure.

Listing 8-2. Writing a text file

```
var
  TextFile: text;
  Ln:       string;

begin
  AssignFile(TextFile, Filename);
  Rewrite(TextFile); // or Append(TextFile);
  try
    while DataToWrite do
    begin
      // Get Ln data
      WriteLn(TextFile, Ln);
    end;
  finally
    CloseFile(TextFile);
  end;
end.
```

Part of what makes text file operations so useful is that you can actually supply any number of values to be formatted and written on the same line. That is, you can write

```
WriteLn(TextFile, '<', XmlTag, ' ', XmlParams, '>');
```

or

```
WriteLn(TextFile, FunctionThatReturnsATimestampString, ^I,
                 FunctionThatReturnsALogMessage );
```

In addition, each WriteLn value can use the same Value: Width notation as the Str() procedure. You can specify a width for numeric *and* string values. As with the Str() procedure, float point values can also have a : Precision following the : Width. Thus, you can write a table with a series of statements like

```
WriteLn(TextFile, Tag, ^I, Value: Width);
```

where the Width value can either be a constant or a variable.

Standard input, output, and error

Kylix supplies three standard, pre-opened `text` file variables: Input, Output, and ErrOutput.

Reading from Input reads from the standard input device (or file). If you do not explicitly supply a `text` file variable as the first argument to Read or ReadLn, Kylix reads from the Input variable. A 'bare' `ReadLn;` is the same as `ReadLn(Input);` and will pause your program until a newline character appears on the standard input device.

Similarly, writing to Output writes to the standard output device (or file). If you do not explicitly supply a `text` file variable as the first argument to Write or WriteLn, Kylix writes to the Output variable. A 'bare' `WriteLn;` is the same as `WriteLn(Output);` and will write a newline character to the standard output device.

Obviously, writing to ErrOutput writes to the standard error device.

In addition to these predefined `text` file variables, you can associate any `text` file variable with standard input or standard output by doing an `AssignFile(TextVar, '')` before opening it.

Delphi programmers need to be aware that Linux and Windows handle text IO from GUI programs differently. Delphi GUI programs can only read or write Input, Output, and ErrOutput if the project file includes a {$APPTYPE CONSOLE} pragma, which forces the application to include some startup code to create a Windows console window. Under Linux, any GUI programs can write to Output and ErrOutput, even if they don't include the {$APPTYPE CONSOLE} pragma. If a program is started from a terminal window, any such output will appear in the window. (Redhat users, at least, are all too familiar with the way many standard Linux GUI programs litter the screen with

Kylix is not Delphi

various assertion failures &c.) If a program is not started from a terminal window, any output to the standard output or standard error devices will be lost unless it is redirected, or unless you select "Use Launcher Application" from the Run ➤ Parameters dialog. (See Figure 8-4—typos and all.)

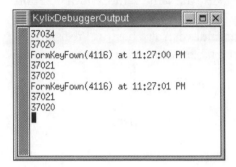

Figure 8-4. Capturing debug output with a Launcher Application

Similarly, GUI programs **can** read from the standard input device, though they really shouldn't try to get keyboard input this way. A ReadLn in a program started from a terminal window as a foreground task will block until the user hits Enter. A ReadLn in a program started from a terminal window as a background task (*ie*, with a trailing &) will be suspended until the user `fg`'s it. Not good!

Text file device drivers

Kylix retains Turbo Pascal's ability to create "text file device drivers". These allow you to use the great flexibility and convenience of WriteLn (and, to a lesser extent, Read and ReadLn) with any conceivable character stream. You might, for example, use a text file device driver to map a socket to a `text` file, so you can just `WriteLn(Socket, '<', XmlTag, ' ', XmlParams, '>')` and so on.

Text file device drivers are easy to write, as you can see from listing 8-3, my lib/StreamText unit, which associates a `text` file with any stream. You could use this to read and write to and from files, strings, sockets, or whatever. The ch8/Files project group contains two projects that demonstrate this. The TextStream project simply writes to and then reads from a TStringStream. The DriverDemo project defines a new stream type, TLinkedStream, which automatically keeps a TStrings.Text in synch with its DataString property; it uses this to WriteLn to a Log `text` file, and have the output automatically appear on screen in a TMemo.

Listing 8-3. The lib/StreamText unit

```
unit StreamText;

// A unit to map Text files to an arbitrary stream. When you call StreamAssign()
// instead of AssignFile (or Assign), all IO is done via the stream.

// Copyright © 2001 by Jon Shemitz, all rights reserved.
// Permission is hereby granted to freely use, modify, and
// distribute this source code PROVIDED that all six lines of
// this copyright and contact notice are included without any
// changes. Questions? Comments? Offers of work?
// mailto:jon@midnightbeach.com - http://www.midnightbeach.com

interface

uses
  Classes, SysUtils;

procedure StreamAssign( var    T:                       Text;
                        const TextStream:               TStream;
                              ClosingFileClosesStream: boolean = True );

implementation

type
  TPrivateData = record
    Stream:      TStream;
    FreeOnClose: boolean;
  end;
  PPrivateData = ^ TPrivateData;

function PrivateData(const Text: TTextRec): PPrivateData;
begin
  Result := Addr( Text.UserData ); // Addr() is {$T+} compatible
end; // PrivateData

function ReadText(var Text: TTextRec): Integer;
begin
  Text.BufPos := 0;
  Text.BufEnd := PrivateData(Text)^.Stream.Read(Text.BufPtr^, Text.BufSize);
  if integer(Text.BufEnd) = -1
    then begin
```

```
                    Text.BufEnd := 0;
                    Result    := -1; // error
                    end
            else Result := 0;
end; // ReadText


function WriteText(var Text: TTextRec): Integer;
begin
  if PrivateData(Text)^.Stream.Write( Text.BufPtr^,
                                Text.BufPos) < int64(Text.BufPos)
    then Result := -1 // error
    else begin
        Text.BufPos := 0;
        Result    := 0;
        end;
end; // WriteText


function Nop(var Text: TTextRec): Integer;
begin
  Result := 0;
end; // Nop


function CloseFile(var Text: TTextRec): Integer;
begin
  with PrivateData(Text)^ do
    if FreeOnClose then
      FreeAndNil(Stream);
  Text.Mode := fmClosed;
  Result := 0;
end; // CloseFile


function OpenFile(var Text: TTextRec): Integer;
begin
  Result := -1; // Error code
  case Text.Mode of
    fmInput:  Text.InOutFunc := @ReadText;  // called by Reset
    fmOutput: Text.InOutFunc := @WriteText; // called by Rewrite
    fmInOut:  Text.InOutFunc := @WriteText; // called by Append
    else      EXIT;
    end;
  Text.BufPos := 0;
  Text.BufEnd := 0;

  if Text.Mode = fmInput
```

```
      then Text.FlushFunc := @ Nop
       else Text.FlushFunc := @ WriteText;
    Text.CloseFunc := @ CloseFile;


    Text.Handle := -1; // We don't use it, and this should cause problems
                       // in any code that does
   with PrivateData(Text)^ do
   try
     if Text.Mode = fmInOut
       then begin
            Text.Mode := fmOutput;
            Stream.Seek(0, soFromEnd); // Position at end
            end
       else Stream.Position := 0; // Position at beginning
   except
     EXIT;
   end;
   Result := 0;
end; // OpenFile


procedure StreamAssign( var    T:                      Text;
                        const TextStream:              TStream;
                              ClosingFileClosesStream: boolean = True );
var
  Text: ^ TTextRec;
begin
  Text := Addr( T ); // Addr() is {$T+} friendly
  FillChar(Text^, SizeOf(Text^), 0);
  with Text^ do
  begin
    BufPtr   := Text.Buffer;
    Mode     := fmClosed;
    Flags    := tfCRLF * byte(DefaultTextLineBreakStyle);
    BufSize  := SizeOf(Text.Buffer);
    OpenFunc := @ OpenFile;
  end;
```

```
    Assert( SizeOf(TPrivateData) <= SizeOf(Text^.UserData),
            'TPrivateData bigger than TTextRec.UserData' );
    with PrivateData(Text^)^ do
    begin
      Stream := TextStream;
      FreeOnClose := ClosingFileClosesStream;
    end;
  end; // StreamAssign

end.
```

The keystone of any text file device driver is a custom Assign() procedure. There are really only two things that it **must** do: Set the TTextRec.Mode field to `fmClosed` and set the TTextRec.OpenFunc to point to a TTextIOFunc, which is a `function (var F: TTextRec): Integer`.

Note

We're dealing with parts of the RTL that are so old that they don't even know about procedural types. The OpenFunc and its relatives the InOutFunc, the FlushFunc, and the CloseFunc are all declared as pointer, *not* TTextIOFunc. *No one's ever taken the time to change the declaration! This is sort of stupid of Borland, as a trivial change would make it just that much harder for us to shoot ourselves in the foot, but hey—this is only the third text file device driver I've written in seventeen years, so maybe they're right not to bother. In any case, be careful, and make sure that you set the pointers right.*

TTextIOFunc's should return either a zero on success, or a non-zero error code. Any error code will be propagated up to IoResult. See the Borland documentation on IoResult for information on how to handle IO errors.

Whether in the custom Assign procedure or in the OpenFunc, you also need to set the BufSize, BufPos, BufEnd, and BufPtr fields of the TTextRec. BufSize and BufPtr normally refer to the TTextRec.Buffer; the SetTextBuf procedure may change this. BufPos represents a sort of read pointer, while BufEnd is the number of bytes that the last read operation actually placed in the buffer.

When you use Reset, Rewrite, or Append to open a `text` file that's been prepared with your custom Assign procedure, the RTL will call the OpenFunc that you specified. This needs to examine the Text.Mode field to determine whether it was called *via* Reset, Rewrite, or Append, which will govern whether

the InOutFunc needs to read or write. The OpenFunc should not leave
Text.Mode = fmInOut, which is a flag that indicates that you are Append()ing
to the file; it should change the Mode to fmOutput.

Once the file is opened, the RTL automatically calls the InOutFunc and
FlushFunc to fill or empty the buffer. These should update BufPos and BufEnd
as the ReadText and WriteText functions do, and return 0 or an error code.

The CloseFunc should make sure the buffer is flushed, and set the Mode
to fmClosed. Typically the CloseFunc would actually close the file or stream;
the StreamText unit makes this optional, so that you can do things like build
a string by WriteLn()ing to a StringStream and then use the string after
closing the text file.

Run time type information

When you Create a form at run-time, Kylix reads the names of all the form's
components from a resource stream. It uses the same sort of meta-class
pointers and virtual constructors that I covered in Chapter 6 and 7 to recreate
the components with all the right parentage, and then it reads the values of
those components' published properties and uses Run Time Type Information [RTTI] to set these properties by name. RTTI lets Kylix know the
names and datatypes of every published property. While this information is
a key part of what makes Kylix the wonderful, productive environment that it
is, manipulating RTTI isn't something that you'll need to do much of, except
perhaps in a custom component property editor. (Chapter 9 covers component writing, though not custom property editors.) Accordingly, in this
section I just cover a pair of routines that you may find helpful in monitoring
the state of an application as it runs, or persisting enumerated types.

The RttiDemo project in the ch8/RTTI project group provides a modest
demonstration of GetEnumName and SetToString.

GetEnumName   TypInfo Unit

The **GetEnumName** function takes two arguments, the PTypeInfo result of
calling TypeInfo() on the enum class name and the Ord() of an enum value,
and returns the enum string, capitalized just as in the source code. Thus,

```
type
  Colors = (Red, Green, Blue);

var
  Color: Colors;

begin
  for Color := Low(Color) to High(Color) do
    WriteLn(GetEnumName(TypeInfo(Colors), ord(Color)));
end.
```

will write

```
Red
Green
Blue
```

---

to the standard output device.

GetEnumValue   TypInfo Unit

The **GetEnumValue** function is just the opposite of the GetEnumName function; given a TypeInfo result and an enum string, it will return Ord() of the enum. That is, `Colors(GetEnumValue(TypeInfo(Colors), 'Red') ) = Red`. GetEnumValue will return –1 if the string doesn't match any of the tokens in the enumeration.

Packages

Kylix GUI apps run large. Where a minimal console app comes in at just under 15,000 bytes, a minimal GUI app comes to just under 385,000 bytes. What's more, it goes up fast; it's not very hard to have a rather modest GUI app tip the scales into the megabyte range just by using a wide variety of controls, even if it doesn't do all that much with them.

In terms of hard disk space in an era of multi-gigabyte drives, that's not a very big price to pay for all the power of the CLX. But it **does** make for a fairly hefty minimum download time for any of your users who still don't have a broadband connection. Especially if you plan to distribute updates with some regularity, or if you are distributing a suite of applications, you may want to consider using run-time packages. When you use run-time packages, your application links at run-time against the Borland CLX packages. This means that your application file is much smaller, as it only contains your code—not a statically linked copy of the CLX as well. When you select "Build with runtime packages" from the Packages tab of the SHIFT+CTRL+F11 (Project ➤ Options) Project Options dialog, that minimal GUI app goes down to just under 20,000 bytes, and grows much more slowly. (Of course, your app will run a bit more slowly, too, because of the PIC code overhead. See Chapter 4.)

If you use run-time packages, you only have to distribute the CLX packages once, on the distribution disk. After that, your users only need to download the comparatively tiny updated application. What's more, there's nothing at all preventing you from splitting your application into packages, too—so that users only need to download the parts that have changed.

When Windows loads libraries, it looks for them in a consistent and clearly defined order. It looks first in the directory of the application that's trying to load the library, then in the current directory, then in the Windows System directory, then in the Windows directory, then on the PATH. This makes it easy to bundle the libraries an application needs together with the application; just put them in the same directory. Linux doesn't work that way. Just as it won't look in the current directory for an executable file but only on the PATH, so it doesn't look for libraries (and packages) in the application's executable's directory (ExtractFilepath(ParamStr(0)); it only looks in /lib or /usr/lib and the directories named in either /etc/ld.so.conf or in the LD_LIBRARY_PATH environment variable. (Applications running as root ignore the LD_LIBRARY_PATH environment variable for security reasons.)

Kylix is not Delphi

Note

If your application uses packages and the directory the packages are in isn't /lib or /usr/lib and isn't in /etc/ld.so.conf or LD_LIBRARY_PATH, your application won't be able to load packages.

I think the best solution to this issue is to supply a script that runs your application. This script can add the package path to a local copy of LD_LIBRARY_PATH and then start your application. Your application will get a copy of LD_LIBRARY_PATH that includes the package path, yet no other environments will be affected. You won't be 'polluting the global environment' just to run a single program.

The best time to build such a script is at install time, when you know where the user wants the application and its packages to be installed. Chapter 11 covers how to 'brand' a generic loader script with the actual application name and directory; the Deployment appendix contains more information on library loading issues.

Dynamic packages and plugins

Breaking your application into small, easily updated modules is nice. Letting your application load plugins is one of the things that distinguishes a competent program from a potential category killer. Not only do plugins let you add incremental features (or support new hardware) without a full-fledged new release, a published plugin architecture creates the possibility that third parties will start to write plugins for your application, with all the positive feedback that such an active user community implies.

Creating plugins in Kylix is actually pretty easy. The package architecture means that both the application and the plugins can use the same services, and can easily share classes and other data. At a very high level, what you need to do is:

1. Separate the application's units into "services", which might be used by the plugins, and those specific to the application. Put the services into their own package, so that they can be used by both the application and the plugins.

2. Design a class (or, better, an interface) that lets a plugin describe itself to the application. What this description includes depends on your application; it can be as simple as a descriptive string and either a `class of TFrame` or `class of TForm` pointer. Put the description class (and interface) into the services package.

3. Add a plugin loader to the application. (You can choose to make users explicitly install plugins, in which case the loader can read a database, or you can simply scan a plugin directory, in which case users have only to install a plugin in the right directory.) The loader calls LoadPackage to load the package, then calls GetProcAddress to get a pointer to a registration function. The registration function returns either a plugin descriptor or a dynamic array of plugin descriptors.

4. Build plugins. Each plugin is a package that `requires` (Chapter 4) the services package and `exports` one registration function.

The plugin 'handshake'

To run the plugin demo, Linux has to be able to find the packages. In the IDE, select the DynamicPackageDemo and use the Environment Block tab of the Run ➤ Parameters dialog to "Add Override" (or "New …") the LD_LIBRARY_PATH string so that it includes ch8. *(On my system, this is* /home/jon/ch8.*) From the command line, you can use the* ch8/plugindemo *script, which prepends* `pwd` *to the LD_LIBRARY_PATH. This requires you to run the* plugindemo *script from the* ch8 *directory, and is obviously only suitable for a demo.*

The plugin demo, which constitutes the three packages in the ch8/Packages group as well as the DynamicPackageDemo application, uses the FindAll function from lib/GrabBag (see the *FindFirst* section, above) to scan the application directory for packages whose name begins with 'plugin-'. Using this naming convention means only that it won't waste time trying to find a registration function in BaseClass.so, the services package. For each package name, it calls LoadPackage, which returns an HModule or raises an exception. If LoadPackage succeeds, it calls GetProcAddress to find an exported routine whose name matches the RegisterFnName constant.

*GetProcAddress is not type safe; you have **no guarantee** that the pointer GetProcAddress returns is to a routine with the prototype that you expect. Your best protection is to use some long, non-generic name, perhaps including the application's name and plugin interface version number. 'Register' is a particularly bad choice; for that matter, so is 'RegisterPlugins' (which is what the demo uses).*

If GetProcAddress returns Nil, there is no routine whose name matches RegisterFnName in the package, so the loader closes the module and continues. If GetProcAddress returns a non-Nil pointer, the loader adds the package to a list of installed packages and then calls the package's registration function to get a dynamic array of IPlugIn's that describe the plugin(s) the package supports. The loader then loops over this array, calling AddPlugin to install each plugin in the UI. (See the next section for more about the UI.)

```pascal
procedure TDynamicPackageDemoFrm.FormCreate(Sender: TObject);
var
  Names:      TArrayOfString;
  Index:      integer;
  Name:       string;
  Package:    HModule;
  RegisterFn: TRegisterFn;
  Plugins:    APlugIns; // a dynamic "array of IPlugIn"
  Inner:      integer;
begin
  // Builtin(s)
  AddPlugin(TBuiltIn.Create);

  // Dynamic(s)
  Plugins := Nil;
  Names    := FindAll(ExtractFilePath(ExePath) + 'plugin-*.so');
  for Index := Low(Names) to High(Names) do
  begin
    Name     := Names[Index];
    try
      Package := LoadPackage(Name);
      RegisterFn := GetProcAddress(Package, RegisterFnName);
      if not Assigned(RegisterFn) then
      begin
        UnloadPackage(Package);
        Continue;
      end;
      SetLength(Packages, Length(Packages) + 1);
      Packages[High(Packages)] := Package;
      Plugins := RegisterFn; // Call the dynamically loaded
                             // registration function
      for Inner := Low(Plugins) to High(Plugins) do
        AddPlugin(Plugins[Inner]);
    except
    end;
  end;
end; // TDynamicPackageDemoFrm.FormCreate
```

At program shutdown, the demo clears the array of descriptors (which dereferences and thus frees the IPlugin's it contains) and then calls

UnloadPackage to close each package it has open. (I've snipped UI code out
of both the above FormCreate and the below FormDestroy procedures.)

```
procedure TDynamicPackageDemoFrm.FormDestroy(Sender: TObject);
var
  Index: integer;
begin
  // Free tabs, plugins; unload packages
  SetLength(PlugIns, 0);
  for Index := Low(Packages) to High(Packages) do
    UnloadPackage(Packages[Index]);
end; // TDynamicPackageDemoFrm.FormDestroy
```

The services package in the demo contains only the IPlugin interface
and an abstract class that implements it.

```
type
  IPlugin = interface
  ['{44CE3D7B-F440-D511-844E-00A0C9E80506}']

    function CreateFrame( FrameOwner:  TComponent;
                          FrameParent: TWidgetControl ): TFrame;

    function GetBitmap:  TBitmap;
    function GetCaption: string;
    function GetHint:    string;

    property Bitmap:  TBitmap read GetBitmap;
    property Caption: string  read GetCaption;
    property Hint:    string  read GetHint;
  end;
```

The demo's UI is a sort of tabbed dialog, something like what Microsoft uses
in Outlook and a few other programs. Rather than manila file folder style tabs
across the top, each tab is represented by an icon and a caption in a scrolling
pane on the left (Figures 8-5 through 8-7). Clicking on the icon highlights its
caption and brings its tab to the front. Hovering over the icon brings up a hint.
You can see how the IPlugin descriptor supports this; each has a Bitmap, a
Caption, and a Hint, and each can create a frame in the UI on command.

The demo contains one built-in tab. Thus, there's always at least one
icon on the left, even when the loader finds no plugins, as in Figure 8-5.

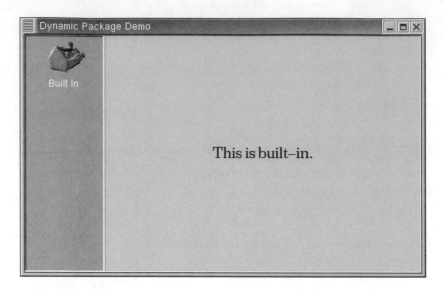

Figure 8-5. No plugins found

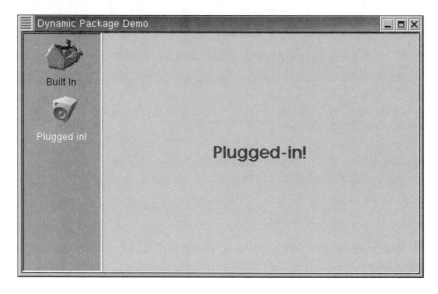

Figure 8-6. One plugin found

Figure 8-7. Both plugins found

```
unit BuiltIn;

interface

uses
  SysUtils, Types, Classes,
  QGraphics, QControls, QForms, QDialogs,
  DynamicPackages, QStdCtrls;

type
  TBuiltInFrame = class(TFrame)
    Label1: TLabel;
  private
    { Private declarations }
  public
    { Public declarations }
  end;

  TBuiltIn = class(TBaseClass)
  protected
    function GetHint:    string;  override;
    function GetCaption: string;  override;
    function GetFrame:   CFrame;  override;
```

```
public
  constructor Create;
end;
```

implementation

(This unit is stunning in its banality because the demo is stunning in *its* banality. The only real coding is in the plugin manager and the icon-tabs.)

The only real difference between the built-in tab and the plugins is that the UI is hardwired to add it; there's no RegisterFnName function. That is, the below Plugin1Main unit looks just like the above BuiltIn unit, except that it exports a RegisterPlugins function.

```
unit Plugin1Main;

interface

uses
  SysUtils, Types, Classes,
  QGraphics, QControls, QForms, QDialogs, QStdCtrls,
  DynamicPackages;

type
  TPlugin1 = class(TFrame)
    Label1: TLabel;
  private
    { Private declarations }
  public
    { Public declarations }
  end;


  TPlugIn = class(TBaseClass)
  protected
    function GetHint:    string;  override;
    function GetCaption: string;  override;
    function GetFrame:    CFrame;  override;

  public
    constructor Create;
  end;
```

```
function RegisterPlugins: APlugins;

exports RegisterPlugins;

implementation
```

That extra line—`exports RegisterPlugins;` —is all it takes to make the RegisterPlugins function visible to GetProcAddress. The RegisterPlugins function itself is just a perfectly ordinary Object Pascal function:

```
function RegisterPlugins: APlugins;
begin
  SetLength(Result, 1);
  Result[High(Result)] := TPlugIn.Create as IPlugIn;
end; // RegisterPlugin
```

At the risk of sounding like a wide-eyed groupie, I'd like to urge you to think for a moment about what a remarkable achievement packages are. Applications and packages have full access to the types that 'live' in other packages—without any extra effort on your part. You can move a unit between an application and a package just by changing the package declaration—you never have to change the unit or write glue logic. And you can implement a plugin manager with just three calls to LoadPackage, GetProcAddress, and UnloadPackage.

Can you do any of this in any other programming environment?

The plugin demo's GUI

The real point of the plugin demo is the plugin manager. However, there are a couple of points about the GUI worth mentioning here: the owner-draw list box that implements the icon-tabs, and the Application.OnShowHint handler that displays the appropriate hint for each icon.

Owner-draw list box

The icon pane, IconList, is more simplistic than it would be in a real app. I simply made sure that all four bitmaps were 48 by 48 when I wrote each tab, and didn't bother with any error checking code. Real code might want to reject plugins with improperly sized bitmaps and/or dynamically size the list box and center small bitmaps.

IconList is a TListBox, with ItemHeight = 68 and Style = lbOwnerDrawFixed. This allows 20 vertical pixels for the captions, which is plenty for a single line and some white space. The OnDrawItem event is a bit more complicated than the font dropdown in Chapter 6, but is still quite straightforward.

```
procedure TDynamicPackageDemoFrm.IconListDrawItem(Sender: TObject;
  Index: Integer; Rect: TRect; State: TOwnerDrawState;
  var Handled: Boolean);
var
  Plugin: IPlugin;
  Bitmap: TBitmap;
  X:      integer;
begin
  Assert(Sender = IconList);
  Plugin := Plugins[Index];
  Bitmap := Plugin.Bitmap;
  X := (IconList.ClientWidth - Bitmap.Width) div 2;
  IconList.Canvas.Draw(Rect.Left + X, Rect.Top + 2, Bitmap);

  Inc(Rect.Top, Bitmap.Height + 4);
  IconList.Canvas.TextRect( Rect, Rect.Left, Rect.Top,
                            IconList.Items[Index],
                            ord(AlignmentFlags_AlignHCenter) or
                            ord(AlignmentFlags_AlignTop) or
                            ord(AlignmentFlags_WordBreak) );
end; // TDynamicPackageDemoFrm.IconListDrawItem
```

I first Assert() that the Sender is the IconList component we expect it to be. This is less important in an event handler with such a distinctive prototype than in a more generic TNotifyMethod handler, but it still can't hurt. Second, I look up the IPlugin descriptor in the Plugins array, get its Bitmap, and draw the bitmap horizontally centered, two pixels below Rect.Top. Finally, I modify the Rect so that its Top is two pixels below the bitmap, get the caption from the list box's Items list, and draw the caption horizontally centered in what's left of the Rect. The list box itself takes care of changing the Font so that the current icon's caption is highlighted.

Tab selection is similarly straightforward.

```
procedure TDynamicPackageDemoFrm.IconListClick(Sender: TObject);
begin
  Tabs[IconList.ItemIndex].BringToFront;
end; // TDynamicPackageDemoFrm.IconListClick
```

I don't have to check that IconList.ItemIndex is >= Low(Tabs) and <= High(Tabs) because we simply don't get an OnClick event if we click outside the 'populated' area of the list.

And that's about all it takes to implement a novel UI device in Kylix.

Application.OnShowHint

The Application.OnShowHint event allows you to divide a control into functional regions, and to display a different hint for each region. The unfortunate aspect of it is that it's an Application event, not a per-control event or a per-form event. That means that you either have to place your OnShowHint handler in a central location, which can 'see' every unit that needs OnShowHint support—or you have to use a multiplexer which broadcasts the event to every control that cares about it.

Delphi programmers would use the ApplicationEvents component to do the multiplexing, but Borland didn't include this in Kylix 1. So, I reached way back into my archives and dusted off a unit I wrote for (I think) Delphi 2 that maintains a list of controls that care about OnShowHint events. On each Application.OnShowHint event,

Kylix is not Delphi

```
procedure TOnShowHintDispatch.OnShowHint( var HintStr:  THintStr;
                                          var CanShow:  Boolean;
                                          var HintInfo: THintInfo );
```

checks the HintInfo.HintControl against its list of registered controls. If it finds a match, it passes the event to the registered handler. I won't bother to list the lib/OnShowHint unit here, but it's available for you to use—full source, of course—in the tarball that you downloaded from the Apress website. (I do think it's worth noting that the only thing I had to do to port this old Delphi code to Kylix (besides commenting out a TListView truncated-caption expander that depended on Windows messages) was to change the declaration of THintStr from `string` to `WideString`.)

The registered handler has the same prototype as the Application.OnShowHint handlers itself. It walks the list of icons, using the IconList.ItemHeight to construct a TRect bounding box for each icon in the list, in control coordinates (*ie*, where the top-left pixel is [0, 0].) If the HintInfo.CursorPos (also in control coordinates) is in one of these rectangles, it sets the HintStr to the IPlugin's Hint property; sets HintInfo.HintMaxWidth so that long hints wrap and are easy to read; and sets HintInfo.CursorRect to the icon's bounding box. (When the cursor moves out of this rectangle, the hint window goes away.) Since IconList.Hint = '', there is no default hint, and so I don't have to do anything special if the cursor is outside of any of the icon's bounds boxes.

```pascal
procedure TDynamicPackageDemoFrm.OnShowHint(var HintStr: WideString;
var CanShow: Boolean; var HintInfo: THintInfo);
var
  ItemHeight, Index: integer;
  Rectangle:        TRect;
begin
  ItemHeight := IconList.ItemHeight;
  for Index := 0 to IconList.Items.Count - 1 do
  begin
    Rectangle := Rect( 0, Index * ItemHeight,
                       IconList.Width, (Index + 1 ) * ItemHeight);
    if PtInRect(Rectangle, HintInfo.CursorPos) then
    begin
      HintStr := PlugIns[Index].Hint;
      HintInfo.HintMaxWidth := IconList.Width * 2;
      HintInfo.CursorRect := Rectangle;
      BREAK;
    end;
  end;
end; // TDynamicPackageDemoFrm.OnShowHint
```

CHAPTER 9

Component creation

CHAPTER 9

Component creation

CHAPTERS 6, 7, AND 8 SHOULD have made it most abundantly clear how Kylix's components can simplify your programming life. Components represent standard functionality from the relatively simple to the relatively complex. Setting properties allows you to customize many aspects of a component's appearance behavior without writing code. Event handlers allow you to write only the code that's unique to your application, not mile after mile of tedious, error-prone boiler-plate.

One of the things that's most unique about Kylix is that it's written in Kylix. This goes beyond the already ample benefit of being able to CTRL+CLICK on a library identifier (like a component's class name) and jump straight to the library source code. You can write your own components—in Kylix. You don't have to switch gears to build a new component in C++; you don't have to spend hours fussing with translating header files and keeping them in synch. You write new components in the same environment that you'll use them in, and can test each incremental change as you make it.

Caution

*Component writing is for everyone—but don't get carried away. Projects have been cancelled because the developers spent too much time writing general-purpose components and not enough time writing the application itself! This is an easy trap to fall into, as most developers have a real soft spot for writing library code. Unless you plan to sell the component, try to focus on doing what you need and **only** what you need—you can always add features later—and be sure to see if someone's written a component that does just what you need before you start your own.*

Component writing can be a deep subject—there are at least two whole books on it—and I'm only writing a single, short chapter. This means that I skip relative esoterica like custom property editors and design-time packages. Instead, I focus on what you need to know to add features to existing components (or just change their default behavior) and to write basic components from scratch. Thus, this chapter contains three sections: the first provides the background that you need (the theoretical framework, if you will) to write components, while the latter two are basically extended examples, walkthroughs of an auto-complete combo box and of a dropdown date picker.

A component primer

If you ignore the sophisticated property discovery and access mechanism that allows components to be edited in the Object Inspector at design time and to be initialized from a resource stream at run-time, components are just objects that descend from TComponent. (This may seem like a big blind spot, but that mechanism is in place; it works just fine, and you don't need to think about it at all to write basic components.) Components live in design time packages so that Kylix can load and unload them dynamically, but they're statically linked into applications unless the user chooses to use run-time packages. A component's `published` properties appear in the Object Inspector, but of course a component can have `private`, `protected`, and `public` members, just like any other object.

A component package can contain several units, each of which can contain several components. Every component package must contain at least one public (interface) `procedure Register` that calls RegisterComponents to put component(s) on a component palette page. In many cases, each unit that exports components will contain a Register procedure that registers all the components in the unit; in other cases, a single Register procedure will register all the components in the whole package.

Note

*If you want to do it Right, you split your component into **two** packages—a design-time package and a run-time package. The design-time package contains the Register procedure(s) and the palette glyphs (see the* Component icons *section, below) as well as any design-time code like custom property editors or About boxes. In the simple examples in this chapter, the only effect of using a combined design-time and run-time package is that the palette glyphs get linked into the executable, bloating it a tiny bit more. This isn't a big deal, so I'll keep it simple and just use the combined package that Borland's New Component wizard creates—but you should certainly take the small trouble to split your components into two packages if you plan to distribute them, or if they contain more design-time only code than the Register procedure(s).*

Unlike the registration function of the plugins section of Chapter 8, the Register procedure does **not** have to be listed in an exports clause. It's not an error if your component source exports Register; the exported symbol is simply ignored. (See the *Components vs Plugins* sidebar if you're curious about how this works.)

Components *vs* Plugins

You'll recall that the plugin example in Chapter 8 relied on calling LoadPackage and then using GetProcAddress to find a registration function with a known, application-specific name. If that registration function didn't appear in an exports clause, GetProcAddress couldn't find the registration function and the plugin didn't load. Yet, component's Register functions don't have to appear in an exports clause. How do they do it?

If you use readelf -s (in a Linux shell) to look at the symbol table for a component you create, or for one of the dcl*.so.6 packages in Kylix's bin directory, you'll see that for every Unitname with a public procedure Register, there's a symbol @Unitname@Register$qqrv. (In addition to this mangled symbol, if Unitname exports Register, there will also be an umangled Register symbol. That's basically what exports does—puts an unmangled name in the symbol table.) The @Unitname@Register is obviously a 'quoted' form of Unitname.Register while the $qqrv appears to be a hashed prototype, as it changes with the symbol's prototype.

Clearly, if the component loader had a list of all the units in the package, it could construct strings like Format('@%s@Register$qqrv', [ThisUnitname]) and probe for them with GetProcAddress. I doubt you'll be very surprised to find that one of the SysUtil's "package support routines" is GetPackageInfo, which enumerates both the units that the package contains and the other packages that the package you're enumerating requires.

So, the component loader works by getting a list of contained units *via* GetPackageInfo; checking for an appropriately mangled Register symbol; and calling it if it exists. The big differences between this mechanism and the plugin mechanism in Chapter 8 are

1. Component loading has to support multiple Register functions in multiple units. The plugin registration functions in Chapter 8 return a list of plugin descriptions. The latter approach means that the registration function has to be able to 'see' all the plugins the package exports; the former approach means that each Register procedure only needs to 'know' about the components in the current unit. The tradeoff is between complexity in the loader and complexity in the packages.

2. The mangled name seems to include type information. The exported registration function name very definitely does not. Type safety is a serious issue, but I suspect that you're better off relying on non-obvious, application-specific names for a registration function than relying on name mangling to tell you that a given function is of the right type. You have absolutely no guarantee that the prototype hashing won't change from release to release.

The RegisterComponents procedure takes two arguments: a string containing the name of the component palette tab to put this (these) component(s) on, and an open array of TComponentClass (`class of TComponent`) values. If the palette tab doesn't exist, it will be created; if it does exist, the components will be added at the end. (Remember, you and anyone else who installs your component can always edit the component palette as you (they) like; the tab you specify in the Register procedure is just a default location.) If the unit contains more than one component, you can place more than one at a time by including multiple class names in the open array argument to Register-Components. Note that the arguments to RegisterComponents are **not** an array of tab names and an array of components; you need at least one RegisterComponents call for each tab you want to populate.

Creating a component

By far the easiest way to create a new component is to use the New Component wizard, Component ➤ New (Figure 9-1.) This will let you choose an ancestral type from a dropdown that contains all the currently installed components; specify a class name for your new component; which palette page to put it on; and what unit file to put it in. The wizard will then create the unit, with a minimal type declaration, and a valid Register procedure. The wizard can only create units with a single component in them, but it's not hard to either simply add another new component to the generated unit, or to manually merge two generated files.

Once you've created—and saved—the component's unit file, the Install Component wizard, Component ➤ Install, is the easy way to either add this unit to an existing package, or to wrap a whole new package around it. You can specify the name and location of the package file, as well as the unit search path that the compiler will use to make the package (Figure 9-2). When you click OK, the package dialog will appear, as will a dialog that asks you if it's OK to build and install the package. Saying No to this dialog will

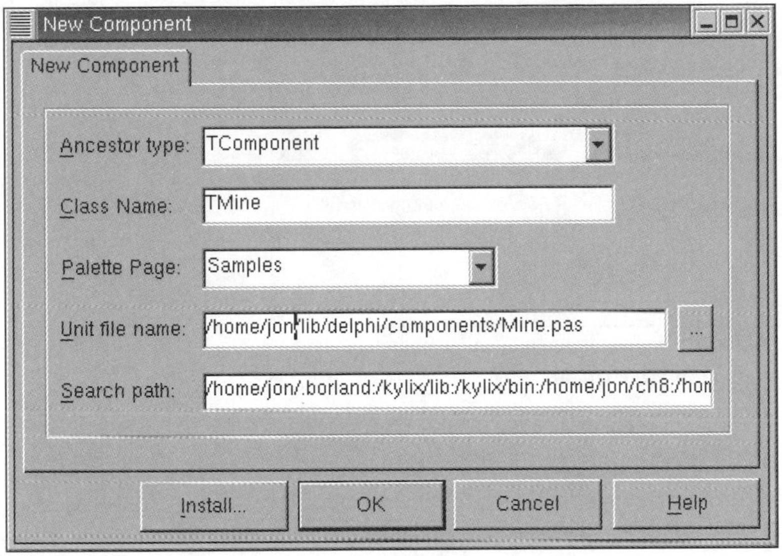

Figure 9-1. The New Component wizard

only abort the build and install, not the packaging process (the package dialog (Figure 9-3) will still be on the screen). It's a good idea to tell the dialog to go ahead and build and install the package, though, as this provides a good check of whether you have all the nit-picky stuff right.

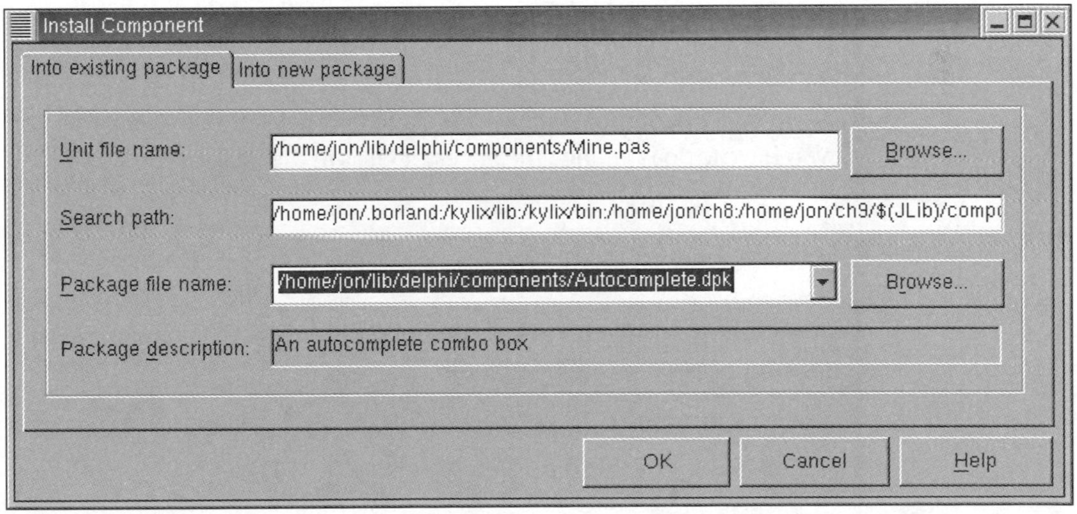

Figure 9-2. The Install Component wizard

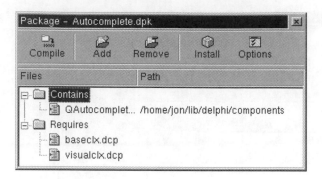

Figure 9-3. A package dialog

If you haven't made any mistakes, building and installing will result in a new icon appearing on the palette page you selected. If you select this icon and drop your new component on a form, you'll get a component with all the visual properties and Object Inspector behavior of its parent, as you haven't yet changed anything. It's a good idea to go ahead and do this because it provides a useful way to test your new component as you add features.

If you change your new component's source code and then run a test application that contains your new component, you will exercise the new code. You don't need to recompile or reinstall the design-time package; you only need to do that to change the list of published properties that the Object Inspector sees.

You'll probably go through a few iterations of changing the published properties and reinstalling before you get the published interface right. You may also find that your initial choice of ancestor was wrong—that you've inherited behavior that you don't want, or you haven't inherited behavior that you do want, or that you have published properties that you don't want. All you have to do is change the ancestor class in the declaration

```
type
  TMyNewComponent = class (TMyComponentsAncestor)
```

then click the Compile and Install buttons on the .dpk's dialog box, and your test component will act quite differently.

What ancestor?

Many non-visual components inherit directly from TComponent. This gives your component a design-time Top and Left, and not much else. Visual components will typically inherit either directly from TGraphicControl or indirectly from TWidgetControl[1] (*ie*, from a TWidgetControl descendant.) A TWidgetControl can receive the input focus and serve as a container (be a Parent) for other controls—a TGraphicControl can't do either, though it can get mouse events.

Kylix is not Delphi

TGraphicControl is the ancestor to use when you want a Canvas to draw on, and not much else. Because TGraphicControl's don't wrap a Qt object, they're lighter-weight than TWidgetControl's; they consume fewer resources, and they run faster. The flip side, of course, is that you have to implement every aspect of their behavior yourself.

> **Tip**
>
>
>
> *TCustomControl is a TWidgetControl that has a canvas. This is useful for eg custom containers that need full control over their appearance.*

It's probably fair to say most non-professional component developers—those developing components for use only in their own applications—will be working mostly with TWidgetControl's. You would use a TWidgetControl directly to wrap a Qt widget that Borland didn't, but more typically you'll work with a TWidgetControl descendant, either customizing an existing control or perhaps creating a composite control from two or more existing controls.

If you are customizing an existing control, you typically only have two choices of ancestors: the control itself, or its immediate ancestor, the "Custom" version of the component. Generally, the only real difference between a control and its Custom ancestor is that the Custom ancestor declares most properties as `protected` while the control redeclares them as `published`. Your best strategy is probably to initially base your customized component on the palette version of the control. Once you have your customizations working as you expect, you can change the ancestry to the Custom version, and copy only the property redeclarations (see *Inherited Properties* in Chapter 3) that you want.

---

1. TWidgetControl is the CLX equivalent of the VCL's TWinControl.

Kylix is not Delphi

Delphi programmers may be used to basing composite controls (like a spin edit or a calendar dropdown) on TPanel. Under Kylix, TFrameControl is a better bet. You get a wider range of BorderStyle's, and don't have any bevel to worry about.

Component icons

If you don't supply a bitmap for each component, Kylix will display a generic bitmap on the palette tab (Figure 9-4), and only the OnHover hint will let you (and/or your component's other users) know what component is 'behind' the generic icon. This is almost OK if there's just one such generic icon on a tab and you're the only one using it, but generally you do want a distinct icon for each component.

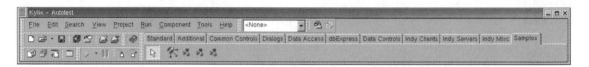

Figure 9-4. Generic icons on the Samples tab

To do this, just make sure that the (design-time) component package contains a 24x24 bitmap resource for each component, with the same name as the component. That is, the icon for a component named TMine will be loaded from the bitmap resource named TMINE. As *per* Chapter 7, Kylix does not come with any tools for creating resource files, but you can use wrc or windres to turn a file like

```
TMine bitmap "24x24_bitmap_for_tmine.bmp"
```

into a file TMine.res that you can link into your component package by including

```
{$R TMine.res}
```

in TMine.pas (or, more properly, into the design-time package that registers TMine).

Resource files normally have a .res extension. Resource files that contain component icons often have a .dcr [Delphi Component Resource] extension. You can link in either a .res or a .dcr file with {$R}—the only difference between the two extensions comes when you add a unit to a package. At that time, Kylix will check for a .dcr file with the same filename, and add a {$R} line to the package source if it found a matching .dcr file. Since creating the component glyph is typically one of the last things one does—after the design and implementation, and after all the iterations of testing and debugging—you might as well just ignore this feature, and always explicitly link the .res resource file into your (design-time) package.

Writing the component

Of course, all this is just preamble. Having chosen an ancestor and gotten Kylix to write most of the boilerplate, you have to fill in the blanks. Otherwise, your new component won't do anything its ancestor didn't.

The first thing to note here is that a component's constructor has some requirements and constraints that other Kylix code doesn't.

- The constructor needs to set all default property values (at least, all that it doesn't inherit from its ancestor) from generic properties like Height and Width, Color and Font, to component-specific properties like a TMemo's WantReturns and WantTabs.

- If the component has any object properties or fields (like a Font property) the constructor has to explicitly Create them.

- The constructor of a TWidgetControl descendant should not use the Handle in any way, either directly or by calling a method that uses the Handle. If you need to refer to the Handle in initialization code, you should override the InitWidget method.

This is very different from normal Kylix programming, where you just drop components on a form and they're automatically created and configured at run-time.

Of course, the usual "Free what you Create" rule applies to components: Anything you explicitly Create in the constructor, you should explicitly FreeAndNil in the destructor. And don't forget to call `inherited` in both the constructor and the destructor!

Properties

Properties, of course, are where it's at. Normal 'value' properties (scalars and classes) show up on the Properties tab of the Object Inspector, and let you control the appearance and behavior of your component. Procedural properties show up on the Events tab of the Object Inspector, and let your program respond appropriately as the user manipulates your component.

As *per* Chapter 3, properties can be simple aliases for private fields, or they can route reading and writing through setter and getter routines. See the *Storage Specifiers* section of Chapter 3 for a summary of the "default" and "stored" modifiers that affect how your properties are stored in form files. Remember that declaring that a property has a default value means that that value is one you can be certain will not be explicitly set at form load time. Be sure to set any default values in the component's constructor!

Class properties will automatically exhibit the sort of Object Inspector folding behavior as standard properties like Font and Constraints, subject to two big caveats. First, the property's type must be a class that descends from TPersistent. While you can have a TSize or TPoint property, these won't work in the Object Inspector. Similarly, you can have a published TStrings property— but not a TList property—because TStrings is a TPersistent and TList is not. You can see the difference in the CLX components; there are many published Lines and Items properties of type TStrings, but when a component uses a TList, suddenly there's a unpublished component pair, like ComponentCount and the Components[] array. Similarly, the TStatusBar has a published class-type property, Panels, which has two unpublished properties, Count and Items, that you manipulate at design-time *via* a custom property editor.

Second, class properties exhibit a somewhat paradoxical "read to write" behavior. That is, when an .xfm file contains a value for, say, Font.Color, what happens is that your Font property's **read** method gets called, to get a TFont reference, then that TFont's Color property is set. The effect is something like `GetFont.Color := XfmColor`. This actually makes a lot of sense when you think about it—you wouldn't want the form loading code to Create a temporary TFont just so it can be passed to your write method that Assign()s it to your Font property—but it certainly took me by surprise when I first ran into it back in 1995.[2] The key to dealing with it is simple: Make sure your class property read methods always return a valid class. Normally, you will create class properties in the constructor. If you want to use a "deferred Create" policy for rarely used properties, be sure that both the read and write method can Create the object behind the property. For example,

---

2. `http://www.midnightbeach.com/jon/pubs/persist.htm`

```
function TReadToWrite.GetFont: TFont;
begin
  // This property follows a "deferred Create" policy
  if not Assigned(fFont) then
    fFont := TFont.Create;

  Result := fFont;
end; // TReadToWrite.GetFont

procedure TReadToWrite.SetFont(const Value: TFont);
begin
  // Note that using Font - not fFont - uses the "deferred create" policy
  Font.Assign(Value); // Copy the contents, not the reference
end; // TReadToWrite.SetFont
```

> **Note**
>
>
>
> *"Read to write" does **not** mean that you do not need write methods for your class properties. Without a write method, any properties of the class property that you set in the Object Inspector will not be saved. Also, as per Chapter 6, the write method should Assign the Value to the property's object, not simply copy the object reference via code like* fFont := Value *which leaks memory **and** potentially leads to tombstoned pointers.*

Events

Any procedure of object property will appear on the Properties tab of the Object Inspector. These can have any arguments you like; though convention dictates that the first parameter is always Sender: TObject, this is not enforced in any way. ("Not enforced" by Kylix itself, that is. You might find other programmers are rather intolerant of any component that publishes events without a Sender parameter.)

The cardinal principle of events is that the component must work properly if the user does not handle them. This manifests itself in component code in two basic ways. First, you must always test to see if there is a handler before calling an event:

```
if Assigned(OnWhatever) then
  OnWhatever(Self);
```

Your component will be filled with #0 bytes on entry to the constructor, so any field that's not set will be 0 or Nil. An event field will be Assigned() only if the user sets a handler for it.

Second, whenever an event supplies a parameter that the user *may* change—like OnCloseQuery's CanClose boolean—it must be set to the default value before the if Assigned() test.

```
Allowed := True;
if Assigned(OnProceedNormally) then
  OnProceedNormally(Self, Allowed);
if Allowed then
  {proceed normally};
```

This way, your code will work properly even if there is no event handler, or the handler doesn't touch the parameter.

Loaded

Many components extract information from their published properties, both for internal use and for public use as a derived property. For example, an "alpha layer" component that overlays one bitmap on top of another might set Height and Width properties to the Min of its Foreground and Background bitmaps' Height and Width. But you don't have any control over the order your component's properties are set at form load time, so you can't rely on the Foreground property being set before the Background property, or *vice versa.*[3]

While the component is loading, csLoading in ComponentState is True, and your property write methods should just set their field and not execute any code that relies on other properties' values. Once the component is loaded, csLoading in ComponentState is no longer True, and you can assume that any activity in a write procedure is the result of a property change to your initialized component. In the alpha layer example, the Foreground and Background properties' write procedures should not try to set Height and Width when csLoading in ComponentState.

---

3. Strictly speaking, this is not true. Properties are streamed in and out in declaration order, and the CLX and VCL do rely on this in a few places. (This is why you'll see the occasional comment like "*this* property must be declared before *that* property.") However, this is a rather fragile mechanism, easily broken by careless use of a code beautifying program or a naive maintainer. In the absence of an explicit dependency syntax, I encourage you to write your code as if property streaming happens in a random order.

When can you safely derive information about the form's loaded state? In the Loaded procedure, which is called once not (csLoading in ComponentState). In general, you'll follow a pattern like

```
procedure TMyComponent.SetProperty(Value: ItsType);
begin
  // set it
  if not (csLoading in ComponentState) then
    ExtractPropertyData;
end; // TMyComponent.SetProperty

procedure TMyComponent.Loaded;
begin
  inherited; // Never forget to call "inherited Loaded"!
  ExtractPropertyData;
  // Call any other extractors
end; // TMyComponent.Loaded
```

That is, you split the write procedure into two parts. One part sets the field, while the other extracts any other data that also depends on other published properties. If your component is not loading, you can assume that the property is being changed, and go ahead and update your derived data. If your component **is** loading, you don't try to derive any data, but instead rely on the extract routine(s) being called in the Loaded procedure.

A customized component

The odds are good that most of the components that you write will be customized components that add some new behavior to an existing control or that replace some existing behavior with the behavior that you prefer. This is because this is a lot easier than writing a whole new component from scratch— and because a lot of public domain Delphi components (some of which are quite good) can be adapted to your Kylix needs relatively easily.

In this section, I'll walk through a TCustomComboBox descendant that implements auto-complete behavior, as in Netscape's URL and addressing widgets. I know the CLX combo box has an AutoComplete option, but this is a small customized component that I had lying around,[4] ready to use—and because the Qt AutoComplete behavior is *terrible*. If, for example, you type

---

4. I wrote the Windows version of this component for StationeryCentral.com, who have generously given me permission to rework their code and release it to the public on the same license terms as all the other sample code in the book.

"Di" and it auto-completes that to "Dick", it will highlight the "ck", as you'd expect. But, if you then hit backspace, it will only delete the highlighted "ck", not the last "i" you typed. You have to hit backspace a second time again to wipe out the last character you typed. See the Autotest project in the ch9/ Components project group (Figure 9-5) for an illustration of the difference between the TComboBox's AutoComplete behavior and my TAutocomplete-ComboBox's auto-complete behavior.

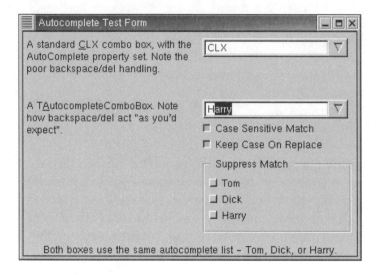

Figure 9-5. The Autotest project

The component is in `lib/components/Autocomplete.dpk`. The source code I'm excerpting here is from the `lib/components/QAutocomplete.pas` unit. Rather than include the whole file as Listing 9-1, I'll walk through the file from top to bottom, interleaving code snippets with commentary.

```
type
  TAutocompleteEvent = procedure( Sender: TObject;
                                  const Typed:       string;
                                  const Matched:     string;
                                  var   Replacement: string;
                                  var   Allow:       boolean ) of object;
```

The component introduces a new event, OnAutocomplete, so we need to create a procedure-of-object type for the event. (An object field can have the type `procedure of object`, but a property cannot. Therefore, I need the

type declaration so that the OnAutocomplete property can be of type
TAutoCompleteEvent.) You can probably tell just by looking at this type
declaration that the event allows the user to change the auto-complete text,
or to prevent the auto-completion.

```
TAutocompleteComboBox = class(TCustomComboBox)
private
  // property fields
  fAutoStart:          integer;
  fCaseSensitiveMatch: boolean;
  fKeepCaseOnReplace:  boolean;

  fOnAutocomplete:     TAutocompleteEvent;

private
  // private state
  fLastKey:   integer;
  fMatched:   boolean;
  fSelfChange: boolean;

  function FirstMatch(const Target: string): integer;
```

Here, I've divided the private members into two populations: the private
fields that stand behind the published properties, and the private fields and
methods that are used internally by the component. This has no syntactic
significance whatsoever, but I find it helps make the internal organization a
bit easier for a human to follow.

By convention, the name of a private field for a property is the property's
name preceded by a lower case 'f'. Thus, the private field for the AutoStart
property is fAutoStart; the private field for the OnKeyDown event is
fOnKeyDown; and so on. The protected section of the class declaration
contains LastKey, Matched, and SelfChange properties, so these fields are
prefaced with an 'f', too.

```
protected
  // Ancestral events that we need to handle
  procedure KeyDown(var Key: Word; Shift: TShiftState); override;
  procedure Change;                                     override;
```

This customized component needs to respond to its ancestor's
OnKeyDown and OnChange events—while leaving those events available to
the customized component's users. In most cases, we can handle this sort of

requirement by overriding the virtual (or dynamic) routines that actually call the event handler. So long as the override method calls `inherited` either before or after its event handling, the component acts just as if the override was a normal event handler—and it also calls any event handler set by the customized component's users.

Chaining event handlers

So far as I know, all CLX events are called from a method that you can override if you need to add to the standard event handling behavior. Still, there may be one or two that are not—and you may encounter third party components that do not follow this idiom. If so, you can "chain" event handlers as I do in `lib/components/QAutocomplete.chain.pas`.

First, you declare a new event field, just as if you were creating a new event.

```
private
  // property fields
  fOnKeyDown: TKeyEvent;
```

Second, you do a partial declaration (see the *Inherited properties* section of Chapter 3) of the event.

```
// OnKeyDown is a modification of an existing property, so it
// doesn't need a full declaration.
property OnKeyDown
        read fOnKeyDown write fOnKeyDown;
```

Third, you set the inherited event handler to a method of the chaining component.

```
inherited OnKeyDown := KeyDownHandler;
```

Finally, the event handler method calls the user event handler, if any.

```
if Assigned(fOnKeyDown) then // User event?
  fOnKeyDown(Sender, Key, Shift);
```

Caution

*While this chaining technique does work, it's a bit brittle and it results in bigger, slower code than simply overriding the method that call the event handler. You should **only** chain event handlers when the ancestral component doesn't call the event handler from a virtual (or dynamic) method that you can override.*

```
protected
  // New internal properties that descendants may need access to
  property LastKey:    integer read fLastKey    write fLastKey;
  property Matched:    boolean read fMatched    write fMatched;
  property SelfChange: boolean read fSelfChange write fSelfChange;
```

One of the most common complaints about Borland's VCL and CLX is that "too much" is private, making it hard to write derived components.

```
public
  property AutoStart: integer read fAutoStart;
  // 1st autocomplete char, if any

  constructor Create(AOwner: TComponent); override;
```

One of the hardest things about component writing is that—if your component is any good—people will use it in ways that you never expected. The more information you can expose, the better. The AutoStart property allows the component user to determine if the Text property contains any auto-complete characters; it's –1 if the application user typed the whole thing, or it's the index of the first auto-complete character, if the system supplied some of the Text.

This component has its own constructor—but no destructor—because while it needs to set defaults, as every component does, it doesn't have any class fields to Free.

```
published
  // The next 2 properties default TRUE, because Linux has a case sensitive
  // file system, but FALSE is more sensible for address book matches &c.
  property CaseSensitiveMatch: boolean // Case sensitive list matching?
          read fCaseSensitiveMatch write fCaseSensitiveMatch default True;
  property KeepCaseOnReplace:  boolean // Should "John Doe" replace "john d"?
          read fKeepCaseOnReplace  write fKeepCaseOnReplace   default True;

  property OnAutocomplete: TAutocompleteEvent
          read fOnAutocomplete write fOnAutocomplete;
```

Borland follows a convention of alphabetizing their declarations, but I prefer to use functional groupings.

The two boolean properties control the way auto-completion works—should "john d" match "John Doe" or not? If it does, should "john d" be replaced with "John D" or left as is? OnAutoComplete is a new event that uses the TAutocompleteEvent template, above.

```
  // TCustomComboBox properties that we want exposed. Same as TComboBox -
  // except we suppress the AutoComplete property.
```

I'll spare you the long list of property redeclarations that I copied from TCustomComboBox. Basically, I want all the same properties as a standard combo box except AutoComplete, so I use the same redeclaration list as TCustomComboBox, except that I comment out the redeclaration of AutoComplete.

```
implementation

{$R QAutocomplete.dcr}

procedure Register;
begin
  RegisterComponents('Samples', [TAutocompleteComboBox]);
end; // Register
```

This component links its TAutocompleteComboBox icon in from QAutocomplete.dcr. It could just as easily have been QAutocomplete.res—Kylix doesn't care.

I use the Samples palette page because that's a Delphi convention for 'miscellaneous' components—and because "Kylix: The Professional Developer's Guide And Reference" would have been a *bit* too long on a component palette tab.

```
constructor TAutocompleteComboBox.Create(AOwner: TComponent);
begin
  inherited;
  fCaseSensitiveMatch := True; // Have to explicitly set default values
  fKeepCaseOnReplace   := True;
end; // TAutocompleteComboBox.Create
```

Finally! Real code! About half the source file is 'just' declarations.

The constructor calls the inherited constructor—always important—and sets the default values for the two new properties.

```
type
  TStringEqualityTest = function (const S1, S2: string): boolean;

function TAutocompleteComboBox.FirstMatch(const Target: string): integer;
var
  TargetLength: integer;
  Equals:       TStringEqualityTest;
const
  Tests: array[boolean] of TStringEqualityTest =
         (AnsiSameText, AnsiSameStr);
begin // Returns index of 1st match, or -1 on no match
  TargetLength := Length(Target);
  Equals       := Tests[CaseSensitiveMatch];
  for Result := 0 to Items.Count - 1 do
    if Equals(Target, Copy(Items[Result], 1, TargetLength)) then EXIT;
  Result := -1; // no match
end; // TAutocompleteComboBox.FirstMatch
```

This function finds the first string in Items that matches Target, if any. It honors the CaseSensitiveMatch setting by using the property to select one of two string matching functions. AnsiSameText is case insensitive, while AnsiSameStr is case sensitive. The EXIT-on-match, negative-one-otherwise pattern is common in Kylix lookup code. Using Result as the for loop index variable simplifies the code by eliminating both the need to declare an index variable and the need to copy the index value to Result on a successful match.

```
procedure TAutocompleteComboBox.KeyDown(var Key: Word; Shift: TShiftState);
begin
  inherited;
  LastKey := Key;
  if SelLength = 0 then Matched := False;
end; // TAutocompleteComboBox.KeyDown
```

The KeyDown method overrides the ancestral method that's responsible for calling the OnKeyDown event. Thus, the first thing it does is to call the inherited method, which (among other things) triggers any user OnKeyDown event. It then saves the last key pressed (for the benefit of the Change method) and updates the Matched property, if necessary.

```
procedure TAutocompleteComboBox.Change;
var
  Caret, TextLength, Index: integer;
  NewText:                  string;
  Allow:                    boolean;
begin
  inherited;
  if SelfChange then EXIT;

  if LastKey <> Key_Delete then
  begin
    Caret      := SelStart;
    TextLength := Length(Text);
    if Caret = TextLength then // At end
    begin
      SelfChange := True; // Change Text on backspace or leading match
      try
        if LastKey <> Key_Backspace
          then begin // normal key
                Index   := FirstMatch(Text);
                if Index >= 0 then // A match?
                  begin
                  if KeepCaseOnReplace
                    then NewText := Text + Copy( Items[Index], TextLength + 1,
                                                 MaxInt )
                    else NewText := Items[Index];
                  Allow := True;
                  if Assigned(OnAutocomplete) then
                    OnAutoComplete(Self, Text, Items[Index], NewText, Allow);
```

```
    if Allow
      then begin
            Text        := NewText;
            SelStart    := Caret;
            SelLength   := Length(NewText) - Caret;
            end
        else Index := -1; // pretend there was no match
      end; // a match
    Matched := (Index >= 0) and (SelLength > 0);
    if Matched
      then fAutoStart := Caret
      else fAutoStart := -1;
    end // Normal key
  else begin// Backspace
    if Matched then // Wipe out char to left and any autocomplete
      begin
      Assert(Caret > 0);
      Assert(SelLength = 0);
      SelStart  := Caret - 1;
      SelLength := 1;
      SelText   := '';
    end;  // Backspace
    Matched := False;
    end;
finally
  SelfChange := False;
  end;
  end; // At end
  end; // LastKey <> Key_Delete
end; // TAutocompleteComboBox.Change
```

This overridden Change method is the real heart and soul of the component. This is the routine that supplies auto-match text on normal text, and that handles backspace properly.

The very first thing that it does is to call the inherited Change method, which (among other things) triggers any user OnChange event. Next, it does an Exit on "SelfChange". This is a common Kylix idiom, as many components do not differentiate between user changes and program changes. If you want to respond only to user changes (or only to program changes, for that matter), you need to maintain and inspect a SelfChange flag.

If this is indeed a user-triggered event, the Change method then checks that the last key was not the Del key, as the standard handling here is just fine. If the last key wasn't the Del key, it inspects SelStart to see where the caret (the insertion point) is. (When there is no selection, SelStart is the (origin 0) caret position. When there **is** a selection, there is no caret, and SelStart is the index of the first character in the selection, while SelLength is the number of characters in the selection. This is true for TEdit and TMemo, as well as for TComboBox.) SelStart uses origin 0, which means that SelStart = 0 indicates a caret before the first character, and `SelStart = Length(Text)` indicates a caret after the last character.

If the caret **is** after the last character, and the last key pressed was not a backspace, the component checks the typed text for a leading match against the Items list. Since the search is in Items list order, you have full control over how ambiguous matches are resolved. That is, if the Items are in alphabetical order, 'jo' will match 'John Doe', not 'Jon Shemitz'. If the items are in most-recently-used [MRU] order, as would be natural for an address book, whether 'jo' would match 'Jon Shemitz' or 'John Doe' would depend on who the user had sent mail to more recently.

If FirstMatch turns up a match candidate, NewText is set to the candidate replacement text, depending on the setting of the KeepCaseOnReplace property. The Allow boolean is initialized to True, and then the OnAutoComplete event is fired off, if there's a handler for it. If Allow is (still) True, the component's Text is replaced with the NewText, SelStart is placed after the last typed character, and SelLength is set to highlight all the auto-completed characters. Then I update the internal Matched property (in case the next character is a backspace) and the external AutoStart property, and that's that.

If, however, the last character typed **was** a backspace, we have to do a little fixup. The default handling has already wiped out the selected (auto-completed) text, but that by itself really doesn't feel right. You expect the backspace to wipe out the last character you typed, not just the auto-completed characters. So, on a backspace, if there was a match, I use SelStart and SelLength to select the last character typed, and then set `SelText := ''` to erase it. This is generally the best way to cut text from a TComboBox, TEdit, or TMemo, as it involves a **lot** less data movement than manipulating the Text property and resetting that.

Finally, I reset the SelfChange flag.

Patch required

SelText := '' doesn't work properly in Build 5.62, Kylix release 1. By the time you read this, Borland should have released a patch or three, and you've presumably installed them all, so this point should be moot. However, if SelText:= '' leaves the last character typed highlighted, then you either need to apply the Borland patches, or use mine.

You can either apply my patch to your 'global' copy of the CLX source, in which case you'll need to add that directory to your Kylix search path, or you can just copy QStdCtrls to a private directory in your Kylix search path, and edit that.

CTRL+CLICK on SelText, then CTRL+CLICK on the SetSelText write method. CTRL+DOWN should take you straight to the TCustomComboBox.SetSelText method. If it looks like

```
procedure TCustomComboBox.SetSelText(const Value: WideString);
begin
  if EditHandle <> nil then
    QLineEdit_insert(EditHandle, PWideString(@Value));
end;
```

then change it to

```
procedure TCustomComboBox.SetSelText(const Value: WideString);
begin
  if EditHandle <> nil then
    if Value <> ''
      then QLineEdit_insert(EditHandle, PWideString(@Value))
      else QLineEdit_clear(EditHandle);
end;
```

and SelText := '' should work as expected.

A custom component

The date picker I'm going to present in this section is a much more complex component than the customized combo box of the previous section—about three and a half times as many lines. Accordingly, I won't present the code in the same line-by-line detail, nor will I walk through the details of building a calendar dropdown. Rather, I'll focus on the mechanics of building a composite control that combines an edit box, a speed button, and a custom dropdown.

If you want to read the code more carefully, it's in the lib/components/ DatePicker.dpk package. The vfind projects in the ch13/vfind project group all use the TDatePicker component.

QDatepicker.pas

The component itself is in the QDatepicker unit, while the popup is in the Calendar unit.

```
TDatePicker = class(TFrameControl)
 protected
    procedure Resize; override;

  public
    constructor Create(AOwner: TComponent); override;
    destructor  Destroy;                    override;

  published
    property HeaderColor:      TColor read fHeaderColor   write fHeaderColor
                                    default DefaultHeaderColor;
    property CalendarColor:    TColor read fCalendarColor write fCalendarColor
                                    default DefaultCalendarColor;
    property FooterColor:      TColor read fFooterColor   write fFooterColor
                                    default DefaultFooterColor;
    property TodayColor:       TColor read fTodayColor    write fTodayColor
                                    default DefaultTodayColor;

    property DayNameFont:      TFont read fDayNameFont
                                    write SetDayNameFont;
    property GrayDateFont:     TFont read fGrayDateFont
                                    write SetGrayDateFont;
    property NormalDateFont:   TFont read fNormalDateFont
                                    write SetNormalDateFont;
    property SelectedDateFont: TFont read fSelectedDateFont
                                    write SetSelectedDateFont;
```

```
    property TodayCaption:      string read fTodayCaption write fTodayCaption;

    property Date: TDateTime read fDate write SetDate;

    property OnDateConvertError: TOnDateConvertError
             read fOnDateConvertError write fOnDateConvertError;

    property Enabled read fEnabled write SetEnabled;

    property TabStop;
    property TabOrder;

    property OnMouseDown;
    property OnMouseUp;
    property OnClick;
  end;
```

The date picker component is a TFrameControl. This gives us a BorderStyle property, keyboard and mouse events, and basic UI properties like TabStop and TabOrder, but not much else. There are no public properties; just the constructor and destructor. (Since this component has TFont properties, it needs a destructor to Free them.) The four color properties (which affect the dropdown's appearance) are pretty straightforward, but there are two things to note:

- The "default" clauses use symbolic values, declared earlier in QDatePicker.pas but not printed here. There's nothing very remarkable about using symbolic constants instead of literal ones (if you ever want to change the constant, you only have to make one change: your code doesn't get out of synch; and you never make the mistake of changing a functionally unrelated constant that just happened to have the same value) but it's worth noting that default clauses aren't limited to literal constants.

- Simply by virtue of having a TColor type, the color properties get the standard TColor property editor (ie, you can type in a literal hex value; select a named color from a dropdown; or double-click and get a color picker.) Custom property editors can apply to all properties of a particular type, or to a single property. While I don't cover them, they can be very useful if you're writing sophisticated components.

The four date fonts also affect the dropdown's appearance. As you can see from the vfind projects, they look and act like any other TFont property in the Object Inspector. I should point out again, though, that without their write methods, any font settings you made in the Object Inspector would not be saved and used.

The TodayCaption property is a FormatDateTime 'picture'. Note that you can't specify default values for string properties.

The Date property is the chief functional property. Visually, the component consists of an edit box that contains a date in DateToStr format and a button with a downward pointing arrow. The user can type in the edit box or click on the button to popup a calendar. (Figure 9-6.) The program can set or read the date at any time. (There's no OnDateChange event, though that wouldn't be a bad idea.)

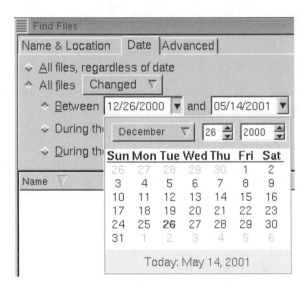

Figure 9-6. The date picker in action

The OnDateConvertError allows you to circumvent the limitations of the StrToDate function. StrToDate is called whenever the user presses Enter or focus leaves the control. If StrToDate can't handle the date the user typed, the OnDateConvertError event gives you a chance to decipher the date. The vfind project in chapter 13 uses this event to handle dates like "January 19, 2038", which StrToDate can't handle.

Finally, since the Enabled property is a standard TControl property, I don't need a full declaration, even though I'm not just changing visibility but also specifying the read and write methods.

```
constructor TDatePicker.Create(AOwner: TComponent);
begin
  inherited Create(AOwner);
  TabStop     := True;
  Height      := 25;
  Width       := 100;
  BorderStyle := bsSunken3D;

  // Create/initialize the button
  fButton              := TSpeedButton.Create(Self);
  fButton.Parent       := Self;
  fButton.OnMouseDown  := _OnMouseDown;
  fButton.OnMouseUp    := _OnMouseUp;
  fButton.OnClick      := OnButtonClick;

  // Create/initialize the edit control
  fEdit              := TEdit.Create(Self);
  fEdit.Parent       := Self;
  fEdit.AutoSize     := False;
  fEdit.BorderStyle  := bsNone;
  fEdit.OnKeyDown    := OnKeyDown;
  fEdit.OnExit       := OnExit;
  fEdit.OnMouseDown  := _OnMouseDown;
  fEdit.OnMouseUp    := _OnMouseUp;
  fEdit.OnClick      := _OnClick;
  fEdit.OnDblClick   := OnDoubleClick;

  // Set default properties
  Date    := Now;
  Enabled := True;

  // Create the dropdown fonts
  fDayNameFont        := TFont.Create;
  fDayNameFont.Assign(Font);
  fDayNameFont.Style := [fsBold];

  fGrayDateFont        := TFont.Create;
  fGrayDateFont.Assign(Font);
  fGrayDateFont.Color := clSilver;

  fNormalDateFont := TFont.Create;
  fNormalDateFont.Assign(Font);
```

```
fSelectedDateFont        := TFont.Create;
fSelectedDateFont.Assign(Font);
fSelectedDateFont.Style := [fsBold];
fSelectedDateFont.Color := clBlue;

// Default the dropdown colors
fHeaderColor   := DefaultHeaderColor;
fCalendarColor := DefaultCalendarColor;
fFooterColor   := DefaultFooterColor;
fTodayColor    := DefaultTodayColor;

// Only set default TodayCaption at design-time
if not Assigned(Owner) or
   (Owner.ComponentState * [csReading, csDesigning] = [csDesigning]) then
   fTodayCaption   := DefaultTodayCaption;
end; // TDatePicker.Create
```

Note again how a component's constructor looks so unlike other Kylix code. All that creating and initializing—it might almost be Perl/TK! The constructor sets TabStop, the default size, and the BorderStyle. (I used the Win32 date picker as my visual model, so I set BorderStyle to bsSunken3D.) Then it creates the button and edit components and sets the events it needs.[5] Be sure to note how the constructor has to explicitly set the child components' Parent properties—you have to do this whenever you programmatically create a visual component, but explicitly creating components is so rare in Kylix that not subsequently setting the Parent is a common mistake.

The rest of the constructor just creates class properties and sets various defaults. Can you predict the effect of the Date := Now line? Does it mean that a date picker will always show the current date at design time? No: a component's constructor is called and sets defaults before any property values are read from the resource stream, but saved values always replace default values. All that Date := Now really does is to set the initial Date to the day you dropped 'this' date picker on a form; that Date is then stored in the .xfm file along with the other published properties. If you never change the design-time

---

5. You might be wondering why I set event handlers rather than overriding methods as for 'chained' events. There are two reasons to do this: First, it takes less code to create a standard control and set event handlers than to create a specialized descendant control that overrides the virtual and dynamic methods. Second, and more importantly, these event handlers are methods of the composite control, TDatePicker, not of the contained TEdit or TSpeedButton controls. The TDatePicker methods are just as external to the contained controls as any form method would be to a normal, automatically created control.

date, it will always show the drop date; if you do change it, it will show whatever you set it to.

The last statement—the one that creates a default value for the TodayCaption property—is a bit complicated. Because you can't declare a default value for a string property, Kylix acts as if the default value is ' '. That is, any value except ' ' will be stored in the form resource and streamed in at form creation time, even if it's a value that you set in the constructor. Conversely, if you set a value in the constructor but the user resets it to ' ' at design-time (using the Object Inspector), the empty string will **not** be stored in the form resource. Thus, if you want to set a default string value, you have to be sure to set it only at design time—if you 'blindly' set a default string value in the constructor, the user won't be able to set the property to ' '. By not defaulting the string value at load time, the property will be ' ' unless the form resource contains an explicit value—which is exactly the right behavior.

```
destructor TDatePicker.Destroy;
begin
  inherited;

  FreeAndNil(fDayNameFont);
  FreeAndNil(fGrayDateFont);
  FreeAndNil(fNormalDateFont);
  FreeAndNil(fSelectedDateFont);
 end; // TDatePicker.Destroy
```

This component needs a destructor because the constructor creates classes. "Free what you Create." Component destructors should use FreeAndNil instead of simply calling Free, because that helps flush any code that refers to an object property after it's been freed.

```
procedure TDatePicker.Resize;
var
  FrameWidth, ButtonLeft, WidgetBottom, ButtonWidth: integer;
begin
  inherited;

  FrameWidth := QFrame_frameWidth(Handle);

  WidgetBottom := Height - FrameWidth;
  ButtonWidth  := (WidgetBottom - FrameWidth) * 2 div 3;
  ButtonLeft   := Width - FrameWidth - ButtonWidth;
```

```
      fButton.BoundsRect := Rect( ButtonLeft,                    FrameWidth,
                                   ButtonLeft + ButtonWidth, WidgetBottom);
      DrawGlyph;

      fEdit.BoundsRect := Rect(FrameWidth, FrameWidth, ButtonLeft - 1, WidgetBottom);
end; // TDatePicker.Resize
```

The inherited Resize method calls the OnResize handler, so this method is pretty much the equivalent of an OnResize handler. The Resize method is responsible for sizing and placing the edit control and the button, which is why there's no code to do that in the constructor. Perhaps the only thing unusual in the Resize method is the way I use QFrame::frameWidth to get the actual width of a bsSunken3D BorderStyle. While the value isn't likely to change, using the Qt call is just plain safer than a const FrameWidth = 2.

The DrawGlyph procedure (not shown) draws a bitmap with two downward pointing arrows (enabled and disabled) and sets the fButton.Glyph property.

```
procedure TDatePicker.OnKeyDown(Sender: TObject; var Key: Word;
  Shift: TShiftState);
begin
  case Key of
    Key_Return,
    Key_Enter:  if Shift = [] then ValidateText;
  end;
end; // TDatePicker.OnKeyDown

procedure TDatePicker.OnExit(Sender: TObject);
begin
  ValidateText;
end; // TDatePicker.OnExit
```

These two edit box event handlers take care of calling ValidateText whenever the user hits Return or tabs off the date picker.

```
procedure TDatePicker.ValidateText;
var
  ExceptionDate:  TDateTime;
  RaiseException: boolean;
begin
  try
    Date := StrToDate(fEdit.Text);
  except
    ExceptionDate  := Date;
    RaiseException := False;
    if Assigned(OnDateConvertError) then
      OnDateConvertError(Self, fEdit.Text, ExceptionDate, RaiseException);
    if RaiseException
      then raise
      else Date := ExceptionDate;
  end;
end; // TDatePicker.ValidateText
```

ValidateText itself is quite straightforward. On any exception in StrToDate, it sets ExceptionDate to the current contents of the component's Date property—the Date *before* the application's user entered a value that StrToDate couldn't understand. It defaults the RaiseException boolean to False, and calls the OnDateConvertError handler, if any. If the OnDateConvertError handler sets RaiseException, the component reraises the exception that StrToDate raised. If it doesn't, it sets the Date property to the ExceptionDate. Thus, if there is no OnDateConvertError handler, or it can't parse the application user's date string, the component's Date stays unchanged. On the other hand, any change the OnDateConvertError handler *does* make to its Date parameter becomes the new value of the component's Date property.

```
procedure TDatePicker.OnDoubleClick(Sender: TObject);
begin
  fButton.Click;
end; // TDatePicker.OnDoubleClick
```

TMTOWTDI.[6] For the user: It's our job to make it all hang together. It's 'natural' for double-clicking the edit box to dropdown the calendar—but it's not automatic.

---

6. That Perl slogan, again—"There's More Than One Way To Do It."

```
procedure TDatePicker.OnButtonClick(Sender: TObject);
begin
  _OnClick(Self);
  with Parent.ClientToScreen(Point(Left, Top)) do
    Date := TDropDown.GetDate( X, Y + Height, Date,
                               DayNameFont, GrayDateFont,
                               NormalDateFont, SelectedDateFont,
                               HeaderColor, CalendarColor,
                               FooterColor, TodayColor,
                               TodayCaption
                               );
end; // TDatePicker.OnButtonClick
```

The button click event handler passes the click on to the edit box's _OnClick handler, which calls the component user's OnClick event, if any. This passthrough means that clicking anywhere on the date picker generates an OnClick event; not just a click in the edit box. The real point of this method, though, is that it calls a TDropDown class method that pops up a calendar with the popup's top left corner right below the date picker's frame's bottom left corner.

Calendar.pas

The popup calendar is just a normal borderless[7] Kylix form (see Figure 9-7). It may not be obvious, but there's no reason that components can't include forms, whether as part of the component, as in this date picker; as an About box; or as a custom property editor like Kylix's standard string list editor. Kylix can handle forms and form resources in component packages just as easily as it handles forms in application packages.

When you drop a date picker on a form, Kylix will make sure that the form's unit uses QDatePicker, just as it does for every other unit. But it will **not** add Calendar to the uses list, even though QDatePicker depends on it. A component's internal structure is its own business. Dropping a component on a form means that the form's unit uses the component's unit and can see any of the component's unit's public declarations; it does not mean that the form unit automatically uses any units that the component uses. As always, inclusion is transitive but visibility is not—if program A uses unit B which uses unit C, building A builds and links B and C, but A cannot see any declarations in C unless it explicitly uses it.

---

7.   Which isn't as normal in Kylix as in Delphi. See the TDropDown.FormShow event handler.

Figure 9-7. The popup form at design time

Since component users won't normally see the Calendar unit, it can be designed with a much narrower, special-purpose interface. It's not part of the public face of a component that needs to support as many unplanned uses as possible. Thus, the TDropDown form class has only one public member: the class function which, as we've already seen, TDatePicker.OnButtonClick calls to create a popup in the appropriate place.

The GetDate function itself is very simple:

```
class function TDropDown.GetDate( X, Y: integer;
                                  StartDate: TDateTime;
                                  const DayFont, GrayFont,
                                      NormalFont, SelectedFont: TFont;
                                  HeaderColor, CalendarColor,
                                  FooterColor, TodayColor: TColor;
                                  const TodayCaption: string ): TDateTime;
begin
  with TDropDown.Create( X, Y, StartDate,
                         DayFont, GrayFont, NormalFont, SelectedFont,
                         HeaderColor, CalendarColor, FooterColor, TodayColor,
                         TodayCaption ) do
  try
    ShowModal;

    Result := Date;
  finally
    Free;
  end;
end; // TDatePicker.PopupAt
```

It passes the parameters (most of which are TDatePicker's published properties) on to the Create constructor; ShowModal()s the form, and returns the form's private Date property.

The constructor itself is so banal that I won't print it. It copies references to the fonts, copies the colors, uses the TodayCaption to set the 'quick click' label at the bottom of the popup, and sets its private Date property to draw the right month. The only even somewhat novel thing going on is

```
// Set month dropdown
Month.Items.Clear;
for Index := Low(LongMonthNames) to High(LongMonthNames) do
  Month.Items.Add(LongMonthNames[Index]);
```

which uses SysUtils.LongMonthNames to populate the Month dropdown with the names of the month in the application user's language. It similarly uses ShortDayNames to populate the top row of the calendar.

The calendar itself is a TDrawGrid, synched to an array of

```
type
  TCellDatum = record
               Display:   string;
               DayNumber: integer;
               DayFont:   TFont;
               end;
```

The OnDrawCell handler uses each DayFont to draw the Display string in the appropriate calendar cell. When the SetDate method is drawing a new month, it sets DayNumber to the integer portion of a date, and then uses that to set the DayFont to the GrayFont, the NormalFont, or the SelectedFont.

Voodoo

Most of the code in Calendar.pas actually involves generating, sizing, and/or drawing the calendar. I promised I'd skip that, so let's fast forward a bit to the 'voodoo' at the bottom of the file.

```
procedure TDropDown.FormShow(Sender: TObject);
begin
  QWidget_setActiveWindow(Handle);

  // Reset the Qt modal state, so form gets Deactivate event on click-off-form
  // (See TCustomForm.ShowModal)
  QOpenWidget_clearWState( QOpenWidgetH(Handle),
                           Cardinal(WidgetState_WState_Modal));
end; // TDropDown.FormShow
```

It turns out that Qt and X handle borderless windows very differently than Windows does. The assumption seems to be that borderless windows are only for tooltips and other non-interactive uses, because normally controls on a BorderStyle = fbsNone form don't get any keyboard activity. Fortunately, calling QWidget::setActiveWindow does fix this, albeit at the cost of a little weirdness.

Kylix is not Delphi

It appeared at first that the popup was losing the keyboard focus—you could use the cursor keys to change the selected date, and the calendar would flicker but show the same date. Or the date would jump, seemingly randomly. It turns out that if you click on the popup, then **some** keystrokes are followed by a bogus click event. It doesn't always happen. I *assume* that this is an artifact of the way that Qt creates borderless windows in a way that bypasses the window manager[8] (and this weirdness may be why Borland doesn't call QWidget::setActiveWindow for us) but I don't *know.*

What I did was to paper over the bug. The last thing the CalendarKeyDown and CalendarClick event handlers do is to 'latch' the current time

```
LastEvent := Time;
```

while the first thing the CalendarClick event handler does is to check that 'enough' time has passed since the last event:

```
if Time - LastEvent < 1E-6 then
  EXIT; // fake mouse clicks generally come 7E-8 after key down
```

The idea is that 'real' user events will be separated by tens of milliseconds, at least, and that anything faster is an artifact that we can ignore.

---

8. Qt has to do this because some window managers won't create borderless windows at all.

More voodoo

The QOpenWidget::clearWState call in TDropDown.FormShow is related to a straightforward design requirement; this popup calendar should act just like a popup list, and go away if the application user clicks off of the popup. This turned out to be hard to do without voodoo!

You might think that it's just a matter of setting Mouse.Capture. But it's not: The capture control does not get click events when the application user clicks off the form.

OK, how about the global event filter in Application.OnEvent? Nope: Application.OnEvent doesn't fire when the application user clicks off the form.

If the calendar was brought up with Show, not ShowModal, we could use

```
procedure TDropDown.FormDeactivate(Sender: TObject);
begin
  Close;
end; // TDropDown.FormDeactivate
```

to close the popup when the user took away its focus by clicking off the popup. But if we used Show, not ShowModal, how would TDropDown.GetDate block until the popup closed up? A Delphi programmer might use MsgWaitForMultipleObjects to do this sort of wait, but Linux and Qt don't have anything so integrated.[9]

I won't try to pretend that I really understand all the ramifications of calling the basically undocumented ("For internal use only") QOpenWidget::clearWState. I looked at TCustomForm.ShowModal and saw that Borland implemented ShowModal by 'bracketing' a Show call with

```
QOpenWidget_setWFlags( QOpenWidgetH(Handle),
                       Cardinal(WidgetFlags_WType_Modal) );
QOpenWidget_setWState( QOpenWidgetH(Handle),
                       Cardinal(WidgetState_WState_Modal) );
```

and

```
QOpenWidget_clearWFlags( QOpenWidgetH(Handle),
                         Cardinal(WidgetFlags_WType_Modal) );
QOpenWidget_clearWState( QOpenWidgetH(Handle),
                         Cardinal(WidgetState_WState_Modal) );
```

---

9. You can grumble about "embrace and extend" until you turn green—Windows will still have a better event and wait API than Linux.

So, I experimented a bit, and found that the QOpenWidget_clearWState call gave me the deactivate-on-click-off-popup behavior I wanted without seeming to cause any ill effects. *Caveat coder.*

Voodoo much?

I'm not quite sure what to make of the voodoo I've presented here. On the one hand, between Trolltech's documentation, Borland's source, and lots of WriteLn's to a Launcher Application window, it really wasn't that hard to make Qt and X11 do things that were obviously not expected. On the other hand, a borderless form that can get keyboard input and detect off-form clicks shouldn't take magic.

I guess this is just one example of something you'll find again and again as you look at Kylix's Qt underpinnings. In many ways, Qt is beautifully designed and really makes Windows look **old**. In other ways, Qt … gets it surprisingly wrong. At least some of the time, this is more X11's fault than Trolltech's, but arguably a cross-platform widget set should shield us from as much X11 nonsense as possible.

Component building necessarily takes us closer to Qt than application writing, and so I leave you with two specific talismans and, perhaps, a sense of how to approach the problems you'll run into.

Kylix

Postscript

WELL. I HOPE THAT WAS easier for you than for me. That might have taken more than a few evenings for you, but it took three and a half months for me. Walking in, I saw a forest. Walking out, my memories are dominated by trees.

Perhaps that's as it should be. After all, one of Kylix's greatest strengths is the way you can quickly jump from code that uses a feature to the code that implements it. CTRL+CLICK. CTRL+UP. CTRL+DN. Few questions are hard to answer when you can read the source. Kylix doesn't free you from the need to ask the right questions—but it sure makes it easy to get the answers. So, when you find yourself stuck with a great huge old tree in your path, look at its acorn. And move on.

Of course, all this beautiful "Kylix is written in Kylix", Smalltalk for the 21st Century stuff stops at the gates of Qt and Libc. Qt is very Delphi- like—and this can't be a coincidence—so the boundary layer between Kylix and Qt is thin and easy to see through. But it's there. You can't CTRL+CLICK into Qt or kernel source. It's a whole new world down there, with man pages and shell utilities and the occasional design flaw locked in by decades of tradition.

I have my Unix oldie credentials—I was writing C on a PDP-11 running Unix back in 1978, and I put in my time with a shell account as the Internet replaced BBSes—but really my Linux programming experience goes back no farther than December of 1999, when Kylix was announced and I agreed to write this book. So, the next section is pretty far from Authoritative. It's what I know, and only what I know. I can't promise to cover everything you need to know—but I do promise you that I don't make anything up to hide my ignorance, either.

Section 3

Linux

Taking full advantage of the "second system effect"

YOU KNOW THE STORY: Linux started as an independent rewrite of Minix, an independent rewrite of Unix. With the full benefit of decades of hindsight, the Linux kernel is a thing of beauty, an Open Source project fully the equal of any commercial operating system kernel. Add lots and lots of standard Unix utilities made freely available by the Gnu project, and you have a robust, open, Unix-like operating system to work with.

This section looks at Linux from a Windows programmer's perspective: What's different? What can you do under Linux that you can't do under Windows?

For example, the Linux *inode* is quite unlike the Windows notion of a file, so I spend a lot of time on files and file attributes. The Linux process model is reasonably similar to Windows, but the primitives are all different, so I cover those in some detail. Linux programming relies on regular expressions much more than Windows programming does, so I talk about *why* and *how* to use regexes in your Kylix code. Linux shell scripts are much more capable than Windows batch files, so I present an introduction to shell scripting that should take you through install scripts and into the sort of scripts that you might call as an integral part of your Kylix applications. I conclude with a quick look at the relationship between X, window managers, and desktops, and at Qt from a Kylix programmer's perspective.

CHAPTER 10

Unix

CHAPTER 10
Unix

STRICTLY SPEAKING, OF COURSE, Linux is not Unix. Linux is a variant of Unix—a rewrite of a rewrite. There are system calls in Libc that act differently than they do on a real Unix or on other common variants like Solaris or AIX; there are things in Libc that aren't on other Unices. Still, we all know that Linux got where it is because it's an Open Source Unix. It has a Unix file system, with inodes, symlinks, and permissions. It has a Unix process model, with fg and bg, process groups, and pipes. It has Unix shells, with command completion, job control, and scripting.

So it makes sense that the chapter about files, processes, and pipes is called "Unix".

This doesn't mean that I'm going to do what Linux programming books all seem to do and spend a lot of time talking about the differences between Linux and other Unices. For one thing, those of you who care already know. For another, Kylix only runs on Linux, so far, so there's not a lot of point to a Kylix book talking about cross-Unix incompatibilities. And finally, of course, I don't know much about the differences.

Another thing I'm not going to do is say much of anything about *using* Linux. I don't assume that all my readers have a lot of Linux experience—I'm quite sure that some of you bought this book along with Kylix and your first copy of Linux and are trying hard to make sense of it all—but that's what *Running Linux* (details in Bibliography) is for. Rather, this chapter focuses on the Linux API from a Windows programmer's view: what's new; what's different; and even a bit of what's the same.

As with Delphi, you have full access to the Linux API just by using Libc, but you only need to use it in special circumstances—and every API call you make reduces your portability. You should use System and SysUtils routines wherever you can. They're more accessible to other Kylix programmers than Libc routines are, and they're cross-platform, too. Code that eschews Libc will compile today with D6 on Windows, and will compile tomorrow, on Solaris or whatever other platforms Borland ports Kylix to.

Accordingly, this chapter focuses on what you can't do without Libc. For example, the section on files has an overview of inodes and links, and talks about the stat() and link() functions but not the open() and remove() functions, as it's generally better to access the latter *via* the portability layer in System and SysUtils.

Files

You already know, I'm sure, that it's all one big file system under Unix. There are no drive letters; every partition is mounted somewhere under /, as is every device from floppies and CD-ROMs to printers, mice, and sound cards, as well as the special 'files' like sockets, named pipes, and the whole /proc tree. You can use the same file functions to read and write every file in the file system—whether real file, device, or system status—though the symmetry is somewhat marred by the way that special files have a file size of 0, and can generally only be read *via* a line-oriented subset of the file functions.

Like most Windows programmers, I have some rather mixed feelings about the unified file system. On the one hand, it's a much simpler, cleaner name space without the drive letters. On the other hand, the physical reality of drives and partitions occasionally affects the file system semantics—you can't have a cross-partition hard link, and a file that uses up all the space on one partition will not automatically span to another—and it does seem like an abstraction that denies the very existence of discrete drives is missing the point in an important way. Still, the file system is the way it is, and nothing I say will have any effect on it.

Inodes

Unix files aren't strongly tied to their names, the way Windows files are. Where a Windows directory entry contains a name and a pointer to a sequence of disk blocks, a Unix directory entry contains a name and a pointer to an *inode*. The inode [Information Node] 'is' the file; it contains the file size, permissions, a pointer to a sequence of disk blocks, and one or two reference counts. On-disk inodes have only one reference count, which is the number of file names that the file has. (This count includes only *hard links*, not *soft* (or *symbolic*) links. A soft link is, essentially, a text file that contains the name of another file, which may itself be another soft link. I talk more about both types of links in the *Links* section, below.) When a file is opened, its on-disk inode is read and converted into an in-memory inode, which is functionally identical except that it also maintains a count of the number of open file descriptors (handles) that refer to the file.

Thus, deleting a file doesn't necessarily delete the inode and the associated storage. Rather, it deletes the directory entry and decrements the inode's name count. The inode is actually deleted only if both the name and handle count are zero. Otherwise, it sticks around. (One particularly interesting consequence of this architecture is that if an application opens a file and then deletes it, the application will still be able to read and write the open file—but no other application will be able to open the file.) Similarly, when the inode is closed, its handle count is decremented, and the inode will be deleted if the name and handle count are both now zero.

When you open a file, the system looks up the filename, and gets the inode from that. What actually gets opened is the inode. If the same inode is known as both ThisFile and ThatFile, it's entirely possible for one process to change ThisFile and have those changes seen by another process (or even the same process) that has ThatFile open.

This is actually rather similar to the way Object Pascal's dynamic arrays work: If A := B, then changing A[0] also changes B[0]. Like dynamic arrays, the links are one way, from the directory entry to the inode. The inode knows how many names it has, but there's no way to tell what they are, short of scanning (potentially) the whole directory tree. Similarly, the name that a file is created under is not privileged in any way. That is, there's no concept of "real name"—every hard link has the same status as every other hard link.

Another way that the inode 'is' the file and the filenames are just pointers is that permissions belong to the inode, not to the filename. Thus, you can't have two different hard links to the same file with different permissions.

The "stat" family of functions returns all there is to know about an on-disk inode: size, permissions, file type, and link count. There are six different stat functions: stat, fstat, and lstat, as well as stat64, fstat64, and lstat64. The 32-bit functions stat, fstat, and lstat fill in a TStatBuf record, while their 64-bit cousins fill in a TStatBuf64 which is basically identical except that it uses 64-bit file size and inode serial numbers. stat takes a file name and fills in a TStatBuf record. fstat is the same, except that it takes an open file's handle, not a file name. lstat, like stat, takes a file name; the difference is that if the file name is a symbolic link, lstat returns info for the inode that contains the soft link instead of info for the inode that the link ultimately points to.

Table 10-1. The TStatBuf

Field	Unix type	Pascal type	Interpretation
st_dev	dev_t	0..High(Int64)	The file's (63-bit) device number. The st_dev:st_ino pair uniquely identifies a file's storage.
st_ino	ino_t	LongWord	The inode's serial number on st_dev.
st_mode	mode_t	Cardinal	This is a bitmap, which contains both the file's permissions and the file's type. See below.
st_nlink	nlink_t	Cardinal	Link count—the number of hard links to this inode.

Table 10-1. The TStatBuf (Continued)

Field	Unix type	Pascal type	Interpretation
st_uid	uid_t	Cardinal	User ID of the file's owner—use getpwuid (next section) to turn this number into a recognizable name.
st_gid	gid_t	Cardinal	Group ID of the file's group—use getgrgid (next section) to turn this number into a recognizable name.
st_rdev	dev_t	0..High(Int64)	Major and minor device numbers, iff the file is actually a 'device' like a CD burner or a tape drive.
st_size	off_t	LongInt	File size, in bytes. 'Special' files, like /proc files, have a file size of 0.
st_blksize	blksize_t	LongInt	File system block size—the actual block size, as opposed to the 512-byte logical blocks of the st_blocks field. Writing a whole number of blocks, on block boundaries, is more efficient than writing fractional blocks or a st_blksize write that crosses a block boundary.
st_blocks	blkcnt_t	LongInt	Number of 512-byte logical blocks allocated. Normally, this is Ceil(st_size / st_blksize) * (st_blksize div 512), but Linux supports "sparse files" automatically, and the block count may actually be substantially smaller.
st_atime	time_t	LongInt	Access time—the time the file was last read or written. Use FileDateToDateTime to convert a time_t to a TDateTime.
st_mtime	time_t	LongInt	Modified time—the time the **file** (contents) was last changed.
st_ctime	time_t	LongInt	Changed time—the last time the **inode** (permissions, link count, &c) was changed.

Like most Unix functions, the stat family returns 0 (no error) on success. If there is any error, the stat functions return –1, and you can call GetLastError (which reads errno) to find why it failed. Kylix's Libc unit contains symbols for all the error codes listed on the man page (man 2 stat).

See the vfind projects in Chapter 13 for an example of using stat as well as more examples of the getpwuid and getgrgid functions than in the *Ownership* section below.

Permissions

Under Linux, all files have an *owner* and belong to a *group*, represented in the TStatBuf by the st_uid and st_gid fields. Groups are basically just lists of user names, used to grant access to department members or project teams. The owner and group are usually the same as the login account and *primary group* of the person who created the file (or who ran the program that created the file) but root can always change file ownership and group membership. Additionally, directories can be set so that any file created in them belongs to the same group as the directory.

The file's owner and group are used primarily to determine who may access a file, and how. When you[1] try to read a file, you can only do so if you are root, or the file grants all users read access, or you are the owner and the file grants the owner read access, or if you are a member of the file's group and the file grants group access. Similar access checks apply for writing and executing the file.

The file's access permissions are coded in the least significant (rightmost) twelve bits of the inode's sixteen-bit st_mode field, in four groups of three bits. (The four leftmost bits code the file's type, which I discuss in the *File types* section, below.) The three rightmost groups of permission bits are, from left to right, the file permissions for the file's owner, members of the file's group, and for all other users (*ie*, everyone besides the file's owner and members of the file's group). Within each group of permission bits, again reading from left to right, the permission bits are the read bit, the write bit, and the execute bit.

Fairly obviously, having read permission means that you can see the contents of the file. Having write permission means that you can change the file, while execute permission means that you can run the file. Unix doesn't use any special extensions to mark a file as an executable or a script; it relies on the execute bit. (Any executable file that's not in a recognized binary format is treated as a script. You can use the #! ("shebang") notation that I describe in the *Basic shell programming* section of Chapter 11 to force the

---

1. In the context of a running application, 'you' would more properly be 'the application's effective user ID', or euid. However, I will continue to speak of ''you' and 'your permissions' as if this were a chapter on using shell commands, as it's just plain simpler.

    Normally, the euid is the same as the person who launched the application, but this is not always the case. A "setuid" app runs as the file's owner, and there are other exceptions which I discuss in the *Processes* section of this chapter.

script to be interpreted by the Bourne Again Shell, or by Perl, or Python, or whatever. If a script doesn't start with #!, it's passed to the current shell for interpretation.) A binary executable, like a Kylix program, can be execute only; a text executable (a script) must also be readable.

Permissions are slightly different for directories than for files. A directory you can read is one you can get the contents of, with ls or FindFirst. A directory you can write is one that you can create files in, while a directory you can execute is one that you can cd to.

Note

To cd to a directory, it must be executable—and any intermediate directories must also be executable. Thus, if /locked is not executable for you, you can't cd to /locked/unlocked, even if /locked/unlocked is executable for you. Conversely, you do not have to be able to read a directory to cd 'through' it. Thus, you can cd to /hidden/directory (assuming both /hidden and /hidden/directory are executable for you) even if /hidden is not readable by you. The lack of readability just means that you have to know that /hidden/directory exists.

The three bits in the leftmost (most significant) group of access bits are known as "file permission modifiers"—the setuid, setgid, and "sticky" bits. For the most part, these modifiers only apply to binary executables and directories: Except for the special setgid combination (below) that keys for mandatory locking, they are ignored for scripts and non-executables.

A setuid program runs with the permissions of its owner, instead of the permissions of the user who's running the program. In particular, this allows you to write programs that run as root and have all root's privileges—from erasing every file on the system to creating a .pid file in /var/run—but that can be run by normal users. Setuid programs need to be especially careful about system security; obviously, a setuid root program that can run arbitrary (user specifiable) scripts is a huge security hole. Similarly, a setuid root program that downloads and installs software should go to extraordinary lengths to be sure that the source can be trusted and that the software hasn't been tampered with. Less obvious security risks are equally real—you should only write setuid programs if you're quite sure that you have to, and if you've carefully examined every operation for security risks.

> **Tip**
>
> *Setuid programs are why Linux maintains more than one* uid *("user ID") for each process. The "effective user ID" (or* euid*) is the uid that controls the program's permissions. This is usually the uid of the user who started the program, but in a setuid application it's actually the uid of the application's owner. The "real user ID" (or* ruid*) is the uid of the user who started the program. Similar distinctions apply to the real and effective* gid*, or group IDs. See the* Effective user ID *section (below) for more information.*

Somewhat similarly, a setgid program runs with the permissions of its group, rather than the permissions of the user's group(s). This presents fewer security issues than setuid, but a setgid program that belongs to a group that includes root **can** generally modify more files than a normal user program. When a non-executable file has the setgid bit set (and the file system is mounted to allow mandatory locks), any file locking (see the *File Locking* section of this chapter) is "mandatory", not "advisory".

The "sticky" bit has no meaning for files (as opposed to directories). Historically, Unix systems loaded the entire executable into memory at program load time, which could be a lengthy process for large programs. The sticky bit told the system to keep the loaded program around as long as possible, so that subsequent invocations could be faster. Linux uses demand loading, *ala* Windows, where code pages are loaded on an as-needed basis. This speeds program loading considerably, and the sticky bit is now mostly just a historical artifact.

The file permission modifiers have completely different meanings for directories than for files. Setuid has no meaning for directories, and is ignored. Setgid on a directory means that any files created in the directory belong to the same group as the directory, rather than the primary group of the user running the application. You can use this to guarantee that any files saved in a shared Object Repository (Chapter 5) will be visible to everyone working on the project.

In a directory without the sticky bit set, anyone who can create a file in the directory can also erase any file in the directory. You do **not** need write access to delete a file! By contrast, in directories with the sticky bit, only the file's owner (and root, of course) can delete a file. Again, this may be useful for a shared Object Repository.

Octal

Permissions are customarily written in octal (base 8) as each octal digit represents three bits. Octal was widely used in programming circles through the 1970's or so, as most people find it easy to remember the eight bit patterns of

Table 10-2, and the eight-bit byte hadn't become quite so universal. (For example, the PDP-8, which was the first computer that I (and most people my age) ever programmed) had a twelve-bit word.)

Table 10-2. Octal, binary, and permissions

Octal	Binary	Permissions
0	000	---
1	001	--x
2	010	-w-
3	011	-wx
4	100	r--
5	101	r-x
6	110	rw-
7	111	rwx

Hexadecimal has almost entirely supplanted octal, though, and Kylix has little support for octal. There is no general equivalent of $1234 that will force a constant to be interpreted as octal; Borland supplies no functions like IntToHex that will format a number in octal; and neither StrToInt nor Val has any support for octal strings. The best way to construct file permission bitmaps to pass to the chmod or umask API functions (below) is to or together the symbolic names (Table 10-4) like S_IRUSR (read by user) and S_IWUSR (write by user) in Libc. These are more readable than the equivalent octal constants for those who simply can't be bothered learning which bit is which—and they are much more legible than hexadecimal.

However, while you can't use octal constants in Object Pascal code, you **can** use octal in BASM code. Within an asm block, any number ending in O or o is interpreted as octal. (BASM is case insensitive, and using 'o' instead of 'O' for a radix specifier will help avoid any 0/O ambiguity, which can be pretty common with fixed-pitch fonts.) Thus, though it's somewhat awkward, you can use asm blocks to support octal constants using code like

```
procedure DefaultUmask;
var
  Mask: mode_t;
begin
  asm mov Mask,022o end;
  umask(Mask);
end; // DefaultUmask
```

Finally, my lib/GrabBag unit—in the tarball you can get from the Downloads section at www.apress.com—does include

```
function IntToOctal(Int: integer; Width: integer = 0): string; overload;
function IntToOctal(Int: int64;   Width: integer = 0): string; overload;

function OctalToInt(const Octal: string): integer;

function OctalToInt64(const Octal: string): int64;
```

functions. There aren't many places where I'd use code like OctalToInt('777') instead of an actual octal constant, but there are certainly places where the inefficiency just docsn't matter.

access

All these access bits can make a program's job difficult. Simply seeing a file in a directory is no guarantee that you can read it, while it's common to be able to read files but not change them. You could use the information I've presented here to roll your own tests—but clearly that's not a trivial task. Fortunately, the system exposes its internal tests *via* the access and euidaccess functions.

```
function access(Name: PChar; Mode: Integer): Integer; cdecl;
function euidaccess(Name: PChar; Mode: Integer): Integer; cdecl;
```

The first argument is a filename, either fully qualified or relative to the current directory, while the Mode argument is a bitmap constructed from one or more of the access bits in Table 10-3.

Table 10-3. Access "Mode" parameter bit names

Name	Meaning
R_OK	Can I read this file?
W_OK	Can I write this file?
X_OK	Can I execute this file?
F_OK	Does this file exist?

As with most API functions, a zero result code means the function succeeded, while a non-zero result code means the function failed. In this case, success means that you have the desired access to the file while failure means that you do not. Generally, that's all you care about, but you can examine errno to find **why** you can't access the file in the desired way.

The difference between the two functions is that access checks permissions for the application's 'real' user ID—the user who actually started the program—while euidaccess checks permissions for the effective user ID. If the program is not running setuid, or has not otherwise changed its effective user ID, the two functions are essentially identical.

In general, you should use euidaccess() and not access(). Even in a normal program (one which doesn't have the setuid bit set), calling euidaccess expresses the semantics of the operation better than access: "Will I be able to do this?" Also, using access to check permissions means that the code will break if it does become necessary to make the program setuid. You should only call access in setuid programs that need to know the difference in permissions for their real and effective user ids.

Note

Many Unix API functions have identical names to their shell counterparts, which presumably makes it easier to move from writing scripts to writing programs and vice versa. *For example, there is an* access *shell command as well as an* access *API function. However, this can make it harder to read* man *pages, as shell pages will shadow API pages. Within Kylix, F1 may either show you an 'index' dialog that lets you select the appropriate page, or it may simply show you first the shell page, then the API page. At a shell prompt, you can use, eg,* man -k access *to get a list of pages that refer to* access, *then* man 2 access *to read the API page.*

---

chmod

No permission bits govern setting permissions. You can always change a file's permissions if you are (running as) the file's owner or if you are (running as) root. You don't have to have write permission on the directory that contains the filename—permissions belong to the inode, not to the filename. Here, too, the API function name—chmod—is the same as the shell command.

```
function chmod(FileName: PChar; Mode: __mode_t): Integer; cdecl;
function fchmod(FileDes: Integer; Mode: __mode_t): Integer; cdecl;
```

The chmod function allows you to set any file's Mode by file name, while fchmod takes a file handle and allows you to set the mode for an open file. You can only set the low (rightmost) twelve bits of the inode's st_mode *via* chmod; the file type in the four high order bits can't be changed after the file is created. You can specify the Mode numerically, or you can use any bitwise combination of the symbolic constants in Table 10-4.

Table 10-4. Chmod "Mode" parameter bit names

Name	Meaning	Shell equivalent
S_ISUID	setuid	+s
S_ISGID	setgid	+g
S_ISVTX	sticky	+t
S_IRUSR	owner read	u+r
S_IWUSR	owner write	u+w
S_IXUSR	owner execute	u+x
S_IRWXU	owner read, write, and execute	u+rwx
S_IRGRP	group read	g+r
S_IWGRP	group write	g+w
S_IXGRP	group execute	g+x
S_IRWXG	group read, write, and execute	g+rwx
S_IROTH	other read	o+r
S_IWOTH	other write	o+w
S_IXOTH	other execute	o+x
S_IRWXO	other read, write, and execute	o+rwx

umask

When you create a file, you specify its initial access bits. (Some Kylix routines read a global (and thus not thread-safe) FileAccessRights, while others take an explicit parameter.) The appropriate access is a function of both the program's needs and the user's desires. For example, there might be no technical reason why your program's log files should not be world readable and world writable, but a user might prefer that they only be group readable and owner writable.

Rather than make every program get and set the appropriate permissions in its own incompatible way, Unix uses the concept of a user settable mask, the *umask*. When an application creates a file requesting, say, a+rwx access, the actual access is Request and not umask. That is, the bits set in the mask are the bits that are cleared (masked off) in a created file's permissions bitmap. A program can always create a file with narrower permissions than the umask allows, but can never create a file with wider permissions than the umask allows. (The umask applies only to file creation—once the file has been created, a program can always change the file permissions with chmod.) Thus, a user can set the umask in their profile to set the default access for the files that they create, and they can wrap specific programs in a script that sets a different umask for that program. (As with environment variables, child processes inherit their parent process's umask, but changing the umask in a child process—as is created to run a script—does not affect the parent process.) The umask is most likely to be set by the user, *via* the umask shell command, but you will sometimes find

```
function umask(Mask: __mode_t): LongWord; cdecl;
```

useful in your Kylix programs. It always returns the old value, so this function

```
function GetUmask: mode_t;
begin
  Result := umask($01FF); // $01FF = 777o = no access
  umask(Result);
end; // GetUmask
```

returns the current umask. You might want to check the umask to see if you will be able to create files with the access you need.

If the user's umask is too restrictive, you can use the umask function to loosen it. As you can see from the chkumask project of the ch10/Files project group,

```
begin
  WriteLn('umask = ', IntToOctal(GetUmask, 3));
  umask(OctalToInt('777'));
  WriteLn('umask = ', IntToOctal(GetUmask, 3));
  umask(0);
  WriteLn('umask = ', IntToOctal(GetUmask, 3));
end.
```

the umask is **not** cumulative and ever more restrictive;

```
umask = 022
umask = 777
umask = 000
```

you can go from a very restrictive umask that allows nobody to read, write, or execute the file (777o) to a very loose one that allows whatever access the app wants to grant.

Of course, many users will think that an app that does this is 'ill behaved' and refuse to use it. A more typical use of umask in Kylix apps will probably be to condition the environment for a utility you're running. That is, you might call umask before you run another program to ensure that any files it creates are only visible to you, the owner.

File ownership and the user database

Files are owned by login accounts, which are normally defined in the file /etc/passwd. Groups in turn consist of a list of user accounts, and are normally defined in the file /etc/groups. Both files contain a mapping of the uid and gid numbers to user and group names, along with other information about the account or the group. You can convert uid and gid numbers to and from the human-readable names by reading these files directly— except that there are Linux systems that do not use /etc/passwd and /etc/groups. Some systems, for example, use password and group files on a network file server, while others use local files in non-standard locations. This is why you should use the Libc user and group database functions. These functions hide the details of *where* the user and passwords files are, and provide a standardized interface that lets you either scan the files record by record or simply locate the record that matches either a particular uid or gid, or a particular user or group name.

The uid functions all populate a passwd (*aka* TPasswordRecord) record:

```
type
  passwd = {packed} record
    pw_name: PChar;              { Username.  }
    pw_passwd: PChar;            { Password.  }
    pw_uid: __uid_t;             { User ID.  }
    pw_gid: __gid_t;             { Group ID.  }
    pw_gecos: PChar;             { Real name.  }
    pw_dir: PChar;               { Home directory.  }
    pw_shell: PChar;             { Shell program.  }
  end;
```

As you can see, the names all start with pw_, for passwd. It's pretty obvious what some of the fields do; others are a bit more obscure (see Table 10-5).

Table 10-5. The passwd (TPasswordRecord) record

Field	Interpretation
pw_name	The login name; the name that utilities like ls display as a file's owner. At least in theory, the login name is unique; there will only be one instance of each name in the passwd file. In practice, an inept system administrator (perhaps someone who just installed Linux on their personal machine) may manage to break this rule.
pw_passwd	For obvious reasons, this will **not** be a plain-text version of the user's password. In fact, by default the actual password is stored, encrypted, in /etc/shadow, which is a file that only root can read. The password field in /etc/passwd, which is what you get in a passwd record, is just a placeholder. Apparently, the actual contents vary from version to version and/or distribution to distribution, but on my Red Hat 7.0 system, it's a '*'.
pw_uid	The number that corresponds to pw_name. This is usually unique, but it's possible to set up aliases; multiple login names that actually refer to the same account. Each alias has its own password, group memberships, and so on, but shares file ownership.
pw_gid	The number of the user's primary group. As *per* the above Permissions section, any files the user creates belong to this group, unless they are created in a directory with its setgid bit set, in which case they belong to the same group as the directory.

Table 10-5. The passwd (TPasswordRecord) record (Continued)

Field	Interpretation
pw_gecos	This field's name is an unfortunate historical oddity.[2] At a minimum, it contains the user's real (*eg,* my real name is 'Jon Shemitz' as opposed to my login name of 'jon'); some systems add a comma-separated list of fields that includes `finger` information like phone numbers.
pw_dir	The user's home directory. Reading this *via* `getpwuid(getuid)^.pw_dir` (or the thread-safe `getpwuid_r` alternative that I discuss below) is better than reading the HOME environment variable, as there's at least some chance that the environment variable has been accidentally or maliciously corrupted.
pw_shell	The user's shell program. This will typically be a valid shell program (like `/bin/bash`) only for actual user accounts; those that people use to login. Accounts like `named` that are only used for daemons will typically list an invalid shell program like `/bin/false`.

Similarly, the gid functions populate a `group` (*aka* TGroup) record (see Table 10-6):

```
type
  group = {packed} record
    gr_name: PChar;        { Group name.}
    gr_passwd: PChar;      { Password.}
    gr_gid: __gid_t;       { Group ID.}
    gr_mem: PPChar;        { Member list.}
  end;
```

---

2. Some of the very first Unix machines at Bell Labs used mainframes running GCOS [General Comprehensive Operating System], a successor to GECOS [GE Comprehensive Operating System, a System/360 DOS knock-off,] for batch jobs and print spooling. The "GECOS field" was added to the passwd file to contain GCOS login information, and managed to survive as a catch-all field for account information that's useful to users but not necessary for system operation.

Table 10-6. The group (TGroup) record

Field	Interpretation
gr_name	The name of the group, as you'd see it in ls or pass to chown.
gr_passwd	This field is largely vestigial. Once upon a time, Unix didn't really understand the notion that any particular user could belong to several different groups. Your access was defined by your UID and a single GID. To switch from project to project, you had to change your GID by using newgrp to switch from your current group to another group. To newgrp, you had to either be listed in the new group's /etc/group line or know the group's password. Now that access is based on primary and secondary group membership, newgrp and the group password are so unnecessary that there's no /etc/gshadow analog to /etc/shadow. The contents of this field, if any, are the actual encrypted password, in the same format as /etc/shadow.
gr_gid	The gid as returned by stat.
gr_mem	A pointer to a Nil terminated list of PChar's—**not** a comma-separated string as in the /etc/group file. Each non-Nil entry in the list points to a user name. This list includes only those users for whom this is a secondary group. (A user's primary group is stored in the /etc/passwd file.) That is, an empty (Nil) gr_mem is either a group with no members or a "user private group" whose only member is the user for whom this is their primary group.

Changing file ownership

Just as the chmod function does the programmatic equivalent of the chmod shell command, so the chown functions mirror the chown shell command, and allow you to programmatically change a file's owner and/or group.

```
function chown(  FileName: PChar;
                 Owner: __uid_t; Group: __gid_t ): Integer; cdecl;
function fchown( FileDes: Integer;
                 Owner: __uid_t; Group: __gid_t ): Integer; cdecl;
function lchown( const FileName: PChar;
                 Owner: __uid_t; Group: __gid_t ): Integer; cdecl;
```

All share the same core functionality.

- Specifying Owner or Group as –1 means "no change". (There's no chgrp function.)

- Only a process running as root can change a file's ownership. (No, you can't give away your files—this prevents you from writing a malicious program, chown-ing it to root, and wreaking havoc.)

- Unless the process is running as root, you can only change your file's group to one that you belong to.

The differences between chown, fchown, and lchown are relatively minor. Obviously, fchown operates on an open file, while chown and lchown operate on file names. The difference between chown and lchown is that if the FileName specifies a symbolic link, then chown changes ownership of the linked-to file, while lchown changes ownership of the link.[3]

UID and GID lookup

Probably the most common operation on the user and group files is mapping a uid and a gid to the corresponding strings. The getpwuid function looks up a UID and returns a pointer to a passwd record. Similarly, the getgrgid looks up a GID and returns a pointer to a group record. The me project in the ch10/ Files project group uses these functions to report on the current user (which it gets *via* getuid) like this:

```
with getpwuid(getuid)^ do
  WriteLn(   'Login:'^I^I,          pw_name,
          ^J'Real name:'^I,         pw_gecos,
          ^J'Home directory:'^I, pw_dir,
          ^J'Shell:'^I^I,          pw_shell,
          ^J'Primary group:'^I,  getgrgid(pw_gid)^.gr_name );
```

The getpwuid and getgrgid functions are easy to use, but they suffer from a huge flaw: They store strings in a (hidden) global buffer, and return a pointer to a (hidden) global record that contains pointers into this buffer. There are two problems with this. First, each call to getpwuid or getgrgid overwrites both the string buffer and the global passwd or group records. If

---

3. There's a bug in Kylix 1.0 whereby chown is misbound to lchown, so that both chown and lchown operate on the link file, not the linked-to file. By the time you read this, Borland will almost certainly have issued patches that fix this behavior. If chown acts like lchown, download and install all patches—or shadow Libc with my lib/LibcX, which contains a correct declaration

you don't copy the strings right away (copy the contents by assigning to an AnsiString; don't simply copy the PChar value) they're lost. Second, using global variables like this is not thread-safe (*aka* "not reentrant," though the two are not identical). If two or more threads call, say, getpwuid, it's entirely possible that one thread will call getpwuid before the other thread has finished interpreting the results of its prior call to getpwuid, thus mingling the results. Similarly, if one thread calls getpwuid while another thread is waiting for its call to getpwuid to return, about the best you can hope for is a seg fault. It's probably somewhat more likely that you'd get scrambled results without any error indication.

While many applications are single-threaded, and even many multi-threaded applications may only need to format UID's and GID's in a single thread, if your application has more than one thread formatting UID's and GID's, you should use the reentrant versions of getpwuid and getgrgid: getpwuid_r and getgrgid_r.

'Use the source' *vs* 'Use the web'

One of Linux's dirty little secrets is that the programmer's documentation is not exactly complete. Unlike commercial operating systems, where people are paid to document the API and a lack of documentation is often the result of a conscious decision[4]—'this is an internal and/or provisional routine which may change'—this is usually an accidental result of the fact that Linux is a volunteer effort. Kernel hacking is "sexy", and people who'll add the functionality that they're used to from other Unices are relatively common. Writing man pages is "boring", and people who'll document the API are relatively scarce.

'The source is the documentation.'

You can go there, of course, but it's not necessarily the fastest way to answer a basic question like "what are the parameters to the `getpwuid_r()` function?"

Fortunately, many Unix systems have better documentation, and there are plenty of installations running simple cgi-man scripts that can serve up any man page on request. If you find functions in Libc that don't have a man page (you press F1 and get "No help found for 'getpwuid_r'") try searching on Google (or your favorite search engine). When I did that for getpwuid_r, two out of the top ten hits were man page servers. The individual man page servers may come and go, but with any luck Google will be a permanent feature of the online world.

---

4.   Or, yes, anti-competitive practices.

Of course, you must remember that while Linux is **like** other Unices, it is still a different system, with independent source code. While most Linux API functions will act *much like* the various standards suggest that they should, and *similarly* to how the equivalent functions act on a different Unix, a man page that you find online is not likely to tell you how the Linux version differs. You may find that some combinations of parameters don't work as the man page suggests that they should, because the Linux version doesn't implement certain features that the other version does. Conversely, an online man page is unlikely to tell you about any useful enhancements the Linux function may have. You should be wary of using an man page from a different Unix for anything but the most basic questions.

These both have a somewhat strange interface.

```
function getpwuid_r(uid: __uid_t; var ResultBuf: TPasswordRecord; Buffer: PChar;
  BufLen: size_t; var __result: PPasswordRecord): Integer; cdecl;
function getgrgid_r(gid: __gid_t; var ResultBuf: TGroup; Buffer: PChar;
  BufLen: size_t; var __result: PGroup): Integer; cdecl;
```

The first parameter is the UID or GID to lookup, while the second parameter is the passwd or group record to fill in. The third and fourth parameters are the string buffer to populate. It's the fifth parameter that's weird—a pointer to a pointer to the result record. On a successful return, `__result = @ ResultBuf`; on an unsuccessful return, `__result = Nil`. I suppose this was intended to make it a little easier to write functions that emulate getpwuid and getgrgid and return a record pointer—but you already know the address of the ResultBuf, and you have the function result code to tell you whether or not the function failed.

In any event, these functions are basically identical to their non-reentrant cousins, except that you have to supply the storage for both the string buffer and the record that contains pointers into it. You do have to be careful to make sure that the string buffer has the same 'lifetime' as the record of pointers into it! Code like

```
function GetPasswordRecord(UID: uid_t): TPasswordRecord;
var
  Buffer:     array[0..NSS_BUFLEN_PASSWD] of char;
  ResultPtr: PPasswordRecord;
begin
  getpwuid_r(UID, Result, Buffer, SizeOf(Buffer), ResultPtr);
end; // GetPasswordRecord
```

will work—some of the time. But, since the string buffer is on the stack, it can be wiped out by any subsequent routines you call. You might want to explicitly allocate a string buffer if you will be calling getpwuid_r or getgrgid_r in a loop, but the best strategy for 'one offs' is to return a record that bundles a string buffer and PChar record together, as in this function from lib/GrabBag.

```
type
  TReentrantPasswordRecord = record
    Password: TPasswordRecord; // ptrs into Buffer
    Buffer:   array of char;
  end;

function GetPasswordRecord( UID:    uid_t;
                            BufLen: integer = 0 ): TReentrantPasswordRecord;
var
  ResultPtr: PPasswordRecord;
begin
  if BufLen <= 0 then
    BufLen := sysconf(_SC_GETPW_R_SIZE_MAX);
  SetLength(Result.Buffer, BufLen);
  ELinuxFn.Check( 'getpwuid_r',
                  getpwuid_r( UID, Result.Password,
                              PChar(Result.Buffer), BufLen,
                              ResultPtr ));
  Assert(ResultPtr = @ Result.Password);
end; // GetPasswordRecord
```

The TReentrantPasswordRecord contains an array of char field that will be freed automatically when the record goes out of scope. Thus, the PChar's in the passwd record will be valid as long as the TReentrantPasswordRecord is in scope, whether this is just for a single statement as in this code from the me project in the ch10/Files project group:

```
with GetPasswordRecord(getuid).Password do
    WriteLn(   'Login:'^I^I,         pw_name,
            ^J'Real name:'^I,        pw_gecos,
            ^J'Home directory:'^I, pw_dir,
            ^J'Shell:'^I^I,          pw_shell,
            ^J'Primary group:'^I,  GetGroupRecord(pw_gid).Group.gr_name );
```

or until a function returns, or an object is freed.

The optional second parameter to GetPasswordRecord allows you to specify a string buffer size. (Too small a buffer will cause getpwuid_r to fail with an ERANGE.) A default value results in a call to sysconf() to get the system's actual maximum buffer size. Once the buffer is allocated, the call to getpwuid_r is wrapped within a call to ELinuxFn.Check, a procedure that raises an exception on a non-zero return code.

ELinux and ELinuxFn

Many of the Libc calls in lib/GrabBag are wrapped within a call to ELinux.Check or ELinuxFn.Check. Both take a function name string and a result code, and raise an exception if the result code is non-zero.

```
type
  ELinuxFn = class (Exception)
  protected
    fResultCode: integer;
  public
    constructor Error(const Fn: string; Code: integer); virtual;

    class procedure Check(const Fn: string; Code: integer);
    // raises exception on non-zero Code

    property ResultCode: integer read fResultCode;
  end;


  ELinux = class (ELinuxFn)
  protected
    fErrNo:    integer;
    fErrString: string;
  public
    constructor Error(const Fn: string; Code: integer); override;

    property ErrNo:    integer read fErrNo;
    property ErrString: string  read fErrString;
  end;
```

ELinux is for functions that set errno on failure. The exception constructor reads errno and calls strerror to get a description of the error, and saves the return code, the error number, and the error string as properties of the exception object. The simpler ELinuxFn is for functions that simply return a non-zero error code on failure but that do not set errno. (Unfortunately, there's no easy way to predict which group a given function is in—you have to RTFM.) The class procedure ELinuxFn.Check

```
class procedure ELinuxFn.Check(const Fn: string; Code: integer);
begin
  if Code <> 0 then
    raise Self.Error(Fn, Code);
    // Uses Self, not ELinuxFn, so can call Elinux.Check (for fns that set
    // errno) or ELinuxFn.Check (for fns that do not set errno).
end; // ELinuxFn.Check
```

calls the constructor Self.Error—not ELinuxFn.Error—so it will raise an
ELinux exception if you call it as ELinux.Check, and it will raise an ELinuxFn
exception if you call it as ELinuxFn.Check.

Using ELinux.Check or ELinuxFn.Check makes the code that calls API
functions smaller and clearer than if each API call included inline checks
on the result code. The tradeoff is that it links in the exception handling
mechanism from SysUtils, which adds about 130,000 bytes to the executable
if you aren't already using SysUtils and exceptions. Of course, if you
are already using SysUtils and exceptions, using ELinux.Check or
ELinuxFn.Check will have an absolutely negligible effect on your executable's size.

Other user database applications

If the most common operation on the user and group files is mapping a uid
and a gid to the corresponding strings, the second most common operation
is probably mapping a given user or group name back to a uid or gid, as utilities like su and login, chown and chgrp have to do. This is just as easy as id lookup;
the functions getpwnam and getpwnam_r, getgrnam and getgrnam_r are
exactly analogous to getpwid and getpwid_r, getgrid and getgrid_r except
that they lookup a PChar name pointer instead of an integer ID value.

All of the user and group functions I've mentioned so far are shortcut
wrappers for the six[5] lower level routines—get??ent, set??ent, and end??ent—
that provide line-by-line access to the /etc/passwd and /etc/groups files. You
might use the lower level functions for tasks like compiling a list of all the
groups that a given user belongs to.

The functions getpwent and getgrent return a record pointer just as
getpwnam and getgrnam do. The big difference is that they take no arguments.
The first call will open the appropriate file, while subsequent calls will read
the next line of the file, returning Nil when you've read the last record. The

---

5.   Libc also includes getpwent_r and getgrent_r functions which can be used
     interchangeably with getpwent and getgrent. In fact, getpwent calls getpwent_r.

procedures setpwent and setgrent rewind the file pointer to the first record. They do **not** return a record pointer; you need to follow them with a call to getpwent or getgrent to reread the first record. Be sure to call endpwent or endgrent to close the file when you're done!

Links

File links are a Unix feature that has no Windows counterpart. They create opportunities and problems—in a development environment and in a deployment environment, and of course you can manipulate hard links and soft links from your Kylix programs just as you can from a shell prompt.

In a development environment, you can use links to maintain a 'deployment image'. That is, development directories always have a huge number of files that are not part of the finished product, from *.~* backup files, *.dcu files, and all the various Kylix project files to all the little throw-away test apps that any reasonably involved project requires. You don't really want to send all these files to QA every time they ask for a snapshot—and you certainly don't want to install them on customers' systems—yet you don't want to purge the 'dross' every time you need to do a preliminary deployment, either.

Building a parallel directory of soft links into the development directory is a nice, clean solution. You can just tar the links directory when you need to send off a snapshot—and you can use it for other purposes, too, like testing or periodic footprint checks. Compare this flexibility to a script file that tars only specified files. You can't browse the tarball as easily; you can't use it to test your code; and so on. The links directory is easier to modify than a script, too.

Note

It's important to use soft *links in your links directories. A hard link is to the inode; a soft link is to the file name. A hard link to an executable goes stale as soon as you recompile, while a soft link always points to the newest build. (Also, that stale hard link keeps the stale build 'alive', taking up disk space.) A hard link to a text file may point to a backup copy, or to a stale copy that's since been deleted from the development directory, while a soft link always points to the current text.*

In a deployed environment, it's common to install an arbitrarily complex directory tree wherever the user wants it,[6] and then to just install a link to the main executable in some directory in the PATH. This keeps the PATH directories as small and fast to read as possible, and hides the details of your program from casual inspection.

Linux is not Windows   It also creates a new problem. Where is your application? That is, Windows programmers are used to looking at ExtractFilePath(ParamStr(0)) or Application.ExeName to see where their executable is. They then load database and/or configuration files in the executable path or in a subdirectory. This doesn't work under Linux! The contents of ParamStr(0) are not mandatory, and apparently can vary even between versions of bash. Thus, you and your users may or may not get the same behavior that I get, whereby I only get an absolute path in ParamStr(0) if that's the way I start the program; I get a relative path (*ie*, foo/appname) if that's the way I start the program; and I get no path information at all if I simply type the name of a program that's somewhere in my PATH environment variable.

More, even if ParamStr(0) (or System.GetModuleFileName) could reliably return path information, it would suffer from a more basic problem: What the user typed to start the program may simply be a link from a PATH directory to the application's executable. Getting the path where the link lives wouldn't help at all with finding the application directory! (You can use readlink to read soft links, but there's no way to do the same for hard links. Remember, a file has no "real name"—every hard link is just as real as every other hard link.)

This combination of imperfect information and hard links means that while it still makes sense to store data files in the application directory (or in a subdirectory of the application directory), you can't use the Windows technique of using the application's path to find your configuration and/or data files. (As *per* Chapter 8, Linux won't automatically load any .so's or packages from the application directory, either. You have to explicitly add the application directory to LD_LIBRARY_PATH *via* a 'branded' script that knows where the application was installed. See the *Basic shell programming* section of Chapter 11 for an example.) The Linux approach is to store configuration files in a fixed, or *privileged* location. Thus, an application called "turboschadenfreude" would normally be installed in /opt/turboschadenfreude, and would read global configuration data (like where the data files are) from /etc/opt/turboschadenfreude.[7] Also, it would read and write user configu-

---

6. A "Filesystem Hierarchy Standard", endorsed by leading Linux lights like Eric Raymond, recommends that you deploy Kylix applications to /opt/YourKylixApp. Like most such Unix standards, it's advisory, not mandatory, and doesn't appear to have gained much traction yet. Still, you should at least read the standard— http://www.pathname.com/fhs/—and consider it in your deployment decisions.

7. Yes, this only works if there aren't two or more different programs with the same name.

ration data (like window positions and a Most Recently Used files list) from and to the ~/.turboschadenfreude (or perhaps ~/.turboschadenfreude.ini) file or directory.

Hard links

A hard link is a pointer to an inode. The inode keeps track of the number of incoming hard links to it, and is only actually deleted when the link count is zero and no processes have the file open.

You create a hard link to an existing file with

```
function link(FromName, ToName: PChar): Integer; cdecl;
```

provided FromName exists and ToName does not, and provided that you have write permission on ToName's path and execute permission on FromName's path. (You can link to a file even if you don't have read or write permissions on it.) The syntax of the link function is similar to that of the ln shell command in that FromName (*aka* origpath) is the name of an existing file, while ToName (*aka* newpath) is the link that you're creating to it.

You can rename an existing hard link with rename, which Libc binds as

```
function __rename(OldName, NewName: PChar): Integer; cdecl;
```

to avoid name collisions. Most applications will use SysUtils.RenameFile instead of __rename, as it's just an imperceptibly thin wrapper and provides a measure of portability.

One key difference between Linux's rename() and Windows' MoveFile() is that while MoveFile fails if the target name already exists, rename does not. Rather, rename "atomically" replaces NewName with OldName, so that other processes will never be unable to open NewName, and will never be able to open the inode as either OldName or NewName. This replacement behavior is very useful and if you depend on it, you may prefer to emphasize the point by using __rename directly, rather than through the RenameFile wrapper.

Linux is not Windows

You can delete a hard link with

```
function unlink(const Name: PChar): Integer; cdecl;
```

although most of the time you will probably use SysUtils.DeleteFile, which provides portability and calls

```
function remove(Filename: PChar): Integer; cdecl;
```

which works on either files *or* directories.

Symbolic links

A symbolic link is a pointer to a file name. It's essentially a text file that contains another file's name. Where hard links cannot span partitions or cross file systems, soft links can; a soft link can be to any file or device, anywhere in the name space. Where hard links are tied to inodes, and can go stale when the file is replaced with a new version, soft links are automatically 'updated' when the file is replaced. Conversely, where a hard link **always** points to an inode, a soft link can point to a file that has been deleted. There's no direct way to detect such *dangling links*—you need to readlink and then see if the linked-to file actually exists.

You create a soft link with

```
function symlink(FromName, ToName: PChar): Integer; cdecl;
```

which acts much like link, except that while you do still need execute permission in FromName's path, there's no requirement that FromName actually exist—there's nothing to stop you from creating a dangling link.

You can read the filename that a soft link points to with

```
function readlink(PathName: PChar; Buf: PChar; Len: size_t): Integer; cdecl;
```

but you need to be aware that readlink is a very strange function that does not append a trailing null (#0) to the result buffer! (That is, a successful call to readlink will not result in Buf being a 'proper' PChar that you can assign to an AnsiString.) Rather, readlink returns the number of characters written to Buf (the string length), or –1 on an error. You should always call it from a wrapper like this one from my lib/GrabBag:

```
function readlink(const LinkName: string): string;
var
  Code:   integer;
  Buffer: MAX_PATH_STRING; // array[0..MAX_PATH] of char
begin
  Code := Libc.readlink(PChar(LinkName), Buffer, SizeOf(Buffer));
  if Code < 0
    then raise ELinux.Error('readlink', Code)
    else SetString(Result, Buffer, Code);
end; // readlink
```

File types

An inode's sixteen-bit st_mode field combines the file's access permissions in the least significant (rightmost) twelve bits with a file type code in the four most significant (leftmost) bits. The type code is actually a rather strange beast. It's neither a bitmap nor an enumeration; seven of the sixteen possible combinations are meaningful, but the meaningful combinations are not $1000 to $7000.

You can get an inode's type by st_mode and S_IFMT (S_FMT = $F000), which will yield a value that matches one of the seven S_IFxxx constants in Libc. Alternatively, you can use any of the seven S_ISxxx functions to see if a given inode is or is not of a given type. (Each is basically just shorthand for st_mode and S_IFMT = S_IFxxx—in C, they're macros.) Table 10-7 lists the seven file type constants and their corresponding classification functions.

Table 10-7. File types

Type constant	Classification function	Interpretation
S_IFDIR	S_ISDIR	The inode is a directory.
S_IFCHR	S_ISCHR	The inode is a character device (like a serial port).
S_IFBLK	S_ISBLK	The inode is a block device (like a disk drive).
S_IFREG	S_ISREG	The inode is a regular file.
S_IFIFO	S_ISFIFO	The inode is a pipe, or FIFO [First In, First Out].
S_IFLNK	S_ISLNK	The inode is a soft link.
S_IFSOCK	S_ISSOCK	The inode is a socket.

Ordinary files

Ordinary files are, well, ordinary files. Aside from the ubiquitous line end differences, a file is a stream of bytes, whether on Linux, Windows, or a Mac. You can write it, you can read it, you can seek within it. For the most part, you can and should—for portability's sake—use the Turbo Pascal text file system (Chapter 8) or a TFileStream. Code that uses the low-level, handle-oriented functions (FileOpen &c) in SysUtils should also port between Delphi and

Kylix without much difficulty (if any), as these utilities have always hewed pretty closely to the Unix file semantics.

Of course, Libc does include bindings for the native Linux handle and stream-oriented file functions. (The handle-oriented ones take an integer "filedes" argument, while the stream-oriented functions usually start with f and take a PIOFile argument.) However, you should generally avoid using the native functions except under a few special circumstances:

- You're doing something explicitly non-portable (like using popen to capture a program's output, or redirecting a child process's standard IO—examples of both are below) which absolutely requires the use of low-level handle or stream-oriented functions.

- Having tried existing components and found them wanting in some way that really matters to your application, you're writing low-level socket code.

- You're trying to port some existing code to Object Pascal. For verification's sake, you want the port to be as close as possible to a line-by-line, statement-by-statement port, with a minimum of translation.

- You're writing a command line utility, where size really matters for some reason.

Scatter/Gather

There *are* two low-level Linux handle-oriented file functions that you ought to know about:

```
function readv(__fd: Integer; __vector: PIoVector; __count: Integer): ssize_t;cdecl;
```

and

```
function writev(__fd: Integer; __vector: PIoVector; __count: Integer): ssize_t;cdecl;
```

The readv and writev functions take a "vector" of buffer locations and sizes, instead of the more normal Buffer: pointer; Bytes: Cardinal argument pair. Thus, a single read operation can be 'scattered' all along the vector of buffers, while a single write operation can be 'gathered' from all the different buffers in the vector. As you can see from the "benchv" project of the ch10/Files project group, this is slightly faster than multiple writes.

The real point, though, is that a writev is a single, *atomic* operation. If you're writing to a socket, all the information in the vector will go out as a single packet (subject to packet size limits, of course) which can be important with protocols that require that a complete message arrive in a single packet. If you're writing to a named pipe, all the information in the vector will be placed in the pipe as a single unit, not intermixed with data from other processes that may be filling the pipe at the same time. You could, of course, gather the information into a single buffer yourself, but it can be easier (and faster) to construct the vector than to alloc and free memory and do all the copies.

As you can see from this procedure from the ch10/benchv project,

```
procedure WriteV(Handle: integer; Vector: array of iovec);
begin
  Libc.writev(Handle, Addr(Vector[Low(Vector)]), Length(Vector))
end; // WriteV
```

readv and writev are quite compatible with Object Pascal open arrays. (Which, in turn, are assignment-compatible with dynamic arrays, as *per* Chapter 3.) The project defines a function that returns an iovec

```
function IOV(const Buffer; Size: Cardinal): iovec;
begin
  Result.iov_base := @ Buffer;
  Result.iov_len  := Size;
end; // IOV
```

and simply passes an open array of IOV() calls to a procedure that expects a Vector: array of iovec parameter.

Sparse files

One thing worth knowing about the Linux file system is that it automatically supports "sparse files". That is, if you seek past the end of the file, to byte 1,000,000 say, and write a thousand bytes, ls will report your file size to be 1,001,001 bytes—but stat may report a good deal less than 1956 512-byte logical blocks. What gets written onto the disk amounts to the actual data plus a description of the space not explicitly written. If you read from a location that you haven't written, you will get back zeroes.

As you can see from the Sparseness project in the ch10/Files project group, you get sparse files whether you use Linux-native functions like fseek and fwrite or Kylix routines like Seek and BlockWrite. Don't be fooled by the fact that reading an unwritten area returns $00 bytes—you don't get a sparse file if you write zero-filled blocks, you get a large file that's filled with zeroes. The only way to get a sparse file is to seek to an area that's never been written and write to it.

Sparse files are a great feature, and you might want to design algorithms that take advantage of them. For example, when there are few hash collisions that require a secondary search, a hashing algorithm will make a faster index to a large collection of strings than any sort of tree. In general, the more bits in the hash function's result, the less likely you are to have collisions, and so lookups and insertions perform better. (Assuming reasonably uniform distribution over that result space, of course.) But, without sparse files, storing a large hash space on disk makes for a huge data file, and few users are willing to dedicate a sixteen gig (four billion 32-bit addresses) file to the index file for, say, the few hundred entries in their email address book. With sparse files, though, the file will be quite tiny.

Of course, you need to keep in mind that sparseness is not 'free'. A sparse file may take much less room than a normal file, but seek time in a normal file is essentially a constant speed operation, unless the file is fragmented, while presumably seek time in a sparse file is a function of the complexity of the pattern of holes and data. That is, the more you write to it, the slower it will get. In the end, you may not see much run-time difference between using a sparse hash file and using some sort of a tree file—but it will probably take you a lot less time to write the hash file version.

You should also bear in mind that while you can infer sparseness from the fact that the physical size is less than the logical size, there are no system calls that will tell you anything about how sparse the file is, or whether a given $00 byte is a 'real' zero byte or an unset location. Thus, a naïve copy (as with TStream.Copy) does not preserve sparseness—you can end up with a very large file, composed mostly of zero bytes.

As far as portability goes, Windows 9*x* and NT4 do not support sparse file, but Windows 2K does. The implementations are different, of course (apparently sparseness is not automatic under Windows 2K, and there are ways to tell the OS that previously used space is no longer needed) but the differences should be relatively minor.

/dev

Unix sweeps most peripherals into the file system, as /dev 'files'. There are a lot of these—6,228 on my machine—and they're not all meaningful. For example, I have only one SCSI tape drive, yet my /dev hierarchy contains /dev/st0 through /dev/st31, as well as a, l, an m variants of all 32 (*ie*, /dev/st0a, /dev/st0l, and /dev/st0m) plus the 128 "non-rewind" variants, /dev/nst0 through /dev/nst31m. For the most part, Kylix apps will have little or no need to read or write /dev files directly, as Qt and the CLX provide canonical access to the mouse and keyboard.

For those few of you who need access to, say, a serial port, all that you really need to know is that you can open character devices with any file functions you prefer, and that you then read and write them, just as if they were normal files. Reading a serial port will block until there's input—just like reading the standard input will—so you would normally do this in a thread, and roll your own mechanism to alert the other threads to serial port events.

The TwoDevices project in the ch10/Files project group demonstrates using the Turbo Pascal `file` functions to read integers from /dev/zero and /dev/random. Of course, the Turbo Pascal `file` functions are not thread safe (see Chapter 8), so this isn't a particularly good model for you to follow, but it does illustrate that there's nothing magical about /dev files.

One use that you may want to make of device files is to replace the standard Pascal function Randomize—which simply sets the RandSeed to the current time_t—with this function from lib/GrabBag

```
procedure SlashDevSlashRandomize;
begin
  with TFileStream.Create('/dev/random', fmOpenRead) do
  try
    Read(RandSeed, SizeOf(RandSeed));
  finally
    Free;
  end;
end; // SlashDevSlashRandomize
```

which sets RandSeed from /dev/random, a source of high-quality random numbers based on unpredictable external events like the timing of keyboard and mouse IO. While the standard Randomize is adequate for most purposes, it's not perfect. For example, two Kylix apps started from the same cron script could easily end up with the same RandSeed. Thus, replacing Randomize with a routine that gets a genuinely random seed may improve the randomness of your simulations, or may make for a hash function with more uniformly distributed results.

/proc

You probably know that the /proc 'files' are a great source of all sorts of information about the state of a Linux system. Some of them can even be written to, to control various aspects of the system, such as whether or not IP masquerading is enabled.

From a programmer's point of view, though, they are more than a little weird. Stat reports that they're normal files, not devices, yet while they always have a file size of zero, they contain text. This means that you can't use a function like lib/GrabBag's ReadFile, which reads the file size, sets the Result length, and then reads the whole file in one operation. Rather, you have to do a line-by-line read while not EOF as in this function from lib/GrabBag.

```
function ReadPseudoFile(const FileName: string): string;
var
  PseudoFile: text;
  Line:       string;
begin
  Assign(PseudoFile, FileName);
  Reset(PseudoFile);
  try
    Result := '';
    while not EOF(PseudoFile) do
    begin
      ReadLn(PseudoFile, Line);
      Result := AddLns(Result, Line);
    end;
  finally
    Close(PseudoFile);
  end;
end; // ReadPseudoFile
```

(AddLns is a lib/GrabBag function that concatenates two strings, interpolating a NewLn iff the left string is not empty.)

/proc has a subdirectory for every running process, with files that represent various aspects of the process's state. Your apps might find their cmdline file—Format('/proc/%d/cmdline', [getpid]) to be particularly useful. This file contains an "ARGV-style" string—the file consists of one or more sub-strings, separated by #0 characters—that contains the whole command line in one string. For some purposes, it may be easier to read cmdline from /proc than to work with the ParamCount and ParamStr functions. For example, if you want to check for a –switch, you could use a for loop to check each ParamStr in turn, or you could simply use Pos to scan the whole command line as a single unit, as in this slashproc project from the ch10/Files project group:

```
program slashproc;

uses
  Libc, SysUtils, GrabBag;

var
  CmdLine: string;

begin
  CmdLine := ReadPseudoFile('/proc/' + IntToStr(getpid) + '/cmdline');
  WriteLn('Command line = ', CmdLine);
  WriteLn( '"-switch" present (case sensitive) '^I'= ',
           Pos(#0'-switch'#0, CmdLine) <> 0);
  WriteLn( '"-switch" present (case insensitive) '^I'= ',
           Pos(#0'-switch'#0, LowerCase(CmdLine)) <> 0);

  ReadLn; // not good in 'real' projects—fine within IDE, when
          // Run-Parameters "Use Launcher Application" is checked.
end.
```

> **Note**
>
>
> *There's also a* Format('/proc/%d/environ, [getpid]) *file, but this is not the easiest way to find what variables are set in your application's environment. Instead, you should use System.envp, a pointer to a Nil-terminated array of PChar's.*

Finally, if you're writing software that will be distributed beyond machines that you control, you should be aware that the /proc files are not always available. A sysadmin can disable all or part of the /proc file system, and may do so for various security reasons.

Pipes

Pipes are special files that are used for interprocess communication [IPC]. What makes them special is that they're designed to be used only as First-In, First-Out queues, or FIFO's. You can only open a pipe to read or to write; you can't open a pipe for reading *and* writing, nor can you seek within a pipe. One (or more) process(es) writes to a pipe; one (or more) usually different process(es) reads the pipe.

Pipes come in two basic flavors: named and unnamed. Named pipes are used for communication between cooperating processes, which is a subject that's beyond the scope of this book. Most advanced Unix programming book—like Stevens' *Unix Network Programming: Volume 2, Interprocess Communications* (see Bibliography)—treat it quite adequately.

Unnamed pipes are most commonly used for communication between child and parent processes. Unnamed pipes are what are involved in familiar shell sequences like `ls -l | less`, but of course we can manipulate unnamed pipes in code. I'll return to this in the *Processes* section, below.

Sockets

Sockets are not necessarily files, but a socket handle can be passed to `read()` and `write()`—or `readv()` and `writev()`—in exactly the same way that a file handle can. Linux sockets come in two basic flavors, or "domains"—inet and unix—though some systems will also have ipx, ax25, netrom, and ddp. Inet sockets are the Internet sockets everyone's at least somewhat familiar with; they're used primarily for communication with other machines, over a network. Inet sockets are also beyond the scope of this book, especially since Kylix comes with the Indy suite of Open Source socket components that covers all the standard protocols and provides tools for constructing custom protocols. Most people will find the Indy components more than adequate; those who don't, should investigate third-party components or consult a standard text like Stevens' *Unix Network Programming, Volume 1*.

Unix sockets, too, are basically beyond the scope of this book, but I'll say a little about them because they typically seem quite novel to a Windows programmer. As with named pipes, they're essentially special files with custom semantics. They differ from named pipes in that any number of processes can open a named pipe and write to it, and any number of processes can open a named pipe and read from it, but only a single pair of processes can communicate through any given Unix domain socket. Every time a new client tries to connect to the socket, the server gets a distinct socket handle to talk to that client with. That is, Unix sockets are private and "connection oriented", where named pipes are communal and "connectionless". Both named pipes and Unix sockets are restricted to IPC between processes running on the same machine; the connection differences between the two are what would make one or the other more suited for a given IPC task.

File locking

Just as multithreaded programs need mutexes or critical sections (see Chapter 7) to keep their data structures coherent, so programs that share files need some sort of file or record locking to make sure that only one program is changing a given (part of a) file at a time. Unix uses three different systems of file locking. The oldest system, based on the use of "lock files", locks a whole file at a time and is based strictly on convention. The two newer methods involve API functions, flock() and fcntl(), that can mostly assure that only one process at a time is writing to a file, or to a part of a file.

Lock files provide what is known as "advisory locking", which means that they work perfectly well so long as everybody plays by the rules, but that they are helpless against both deliberate cheaters and against hapless innocents who are unaware of the locking conventions. The API functions normally operate in the advisory mode as well, but under Linux fcntl can also be made to provide "mandatory locking", where ignorance of the law is no excuse, and no other application can access the parts of a file that you have locked, even if they don't try to lock it themselves. Mandatory locking affects performance, is not available over many network file systems, and many Unices do not support it.

Lock files

The basic idea between lock files is every file that may need to be locked is paired with a lock file. Every application that may want to change the lockable file uses the same lock file name. When an application wants to lock a file, it tries to open its lock file using the O_WRONLY or O_CREAT or O_EXCL flags, which guarantees that the open() call will fail if the lock file already exists. When the application wants to remove the lock, it simply deletes the lock file, allowing some other application to create the lock file.

There are a number of weaknesses to this approach. Most obviously, perhaps, is that if the application crashes before it deletes the lock file, the lock file will remain. (For that matter, a lock file will survive a system restart.) Expecting the locking application to write its PID to the lock file doesn't help all that much—while a lock file with an invalid PID is a reliable sign that the application crashed before removing the lock file, PID's are reused, so a valid PID might not actually belong to the application that created the lock file before it crashed.

Just about as obviously, the system is quite fragile in that it relies on every programmer knowing about the lock file convention. Where you can reasonably expect all but the least experienced programmers to automatically consider concurrency issues and to seek out record locking calls, it requires a fair amount of Unix knowledge to know that *this* file is protected by *that* lock file. All it takes is one naïve application to corrupt a file …. Worse, sometimes there isn't even a single lock file name: different programs use different names. (For example, try doing a search for /etc/passwd lock file names.)

The lock file system also increases security risks. Many lock files are supposed to 'live' in /var/lock, which is normally not writable by normal users. This means that, in many cases, an application has to be setuid root just to create a lock file. This increases the amount of damage a buggy program can do—and presents a target for hacker attacks.

Somewhat less obviously, a lock file locks the *whole file*. It doesn't allow for any subtleties like "I'm writing record 759 and she's writing record 6578, but you're free to read any of the other records". This affects the performance of every other application that might want to share the file, as they have to sit and wait for exclusive access to the file.

Finally, and least obviously, the whole system relies on the O_EXCL flag, which turns out to work only on local file systems.

These are five big problems, and you'd be foolish to rely on lock files for a new lockable file. However, there are subsystems out there that rely on lock files, and you do need to know how to play by their rules if you want to modify the common files.

File locking API's

The weaknesses in the lock file approach were visible long ago. A file locking API is the obvious answer to the most glaring problems, as it cures the two biggest problems: Anyone who wants to lock a file can do so, without having to know the lock file name; and the system is responsible for the locks, and can remove them if the locking process crashes.[8] In addition, you can have more flexibility in specifying either a read lock (where other processes can

---

8.   That is, a process can't crash and keep a file locked. This is generally a Good Thing, but it does mean that a buggy application can crash partway through a transaction, leaving behind a corrupt file for other processes to deal with.

also apply read locks, but no process can apply a write lock; this is also known as a "shared" lock) or a write lock (where no other process can apply a read or write lock; this is also known as an "exclusive" lock). You can choose whether to block until your lock can be applied, or whether to simply get an error indication and try again later.

Of course, this being Unix with all its long, complex history, there are two different ways to apply locks: fctnl (and lockf, which is just syntactic sugar for fctnl) and flock. Naturally, under Linux, the two are incompatible: fcntl locks don't affect flock locks and *vice versa*. Charming, eh?

Fortunately, in most cases the apparent choice is just an illusion: fcntl is POSIX-compatible and flock is not. fcntl supports record locking, while fluck supports only file locking. On Linux, fcntl can do mandatory locking, while flock can only do advisory locking. You'd be foolish to use flock for any other reason than that you need to write to a file that other applications lock with flock. Accordingly, most of this "File locking" section talks about fcntl, with a short subsection on flock at the end.

You need to pass a file *handle* to all of the file locking functions. Every file you open on Linux has a handle, though if you use the Turbo Pascal file system you will have to cast the opaque type to a (System unit) record to read the handle. Table 10-8 lists the ways to get a handle from the various structures used to read and write files under Kylix.

Table 10-8. File structures and file handles

Subsystem	Structure	Handle
Turbo Pascal file system	F: file	TFileRec(F).Handle
Turbo Pascal text files	T: text	TTextRec(T).Handle
C streams	Stream: PIOFile	Stream^._fileno
Kylix streams	Stream: TFileStream	Stream.Handle

lockf and fcntl

The lockf function is significantly simpler—and less flexible—than fcntl. lockf always creates an exclusive, or write lock. You have to use fcntl to create shared, or read locks. Similarly, you have to use fcntl to specify an arbitrary region to lock, as lockf always locks a region that starts at the file pointer (seek location), and runs for Len bytes.

```
function lockf(FileDes: Integer; Cmd: Integer; Len: __off_t): Integer; cdecl;
function lockf64(FileDes: Integer; Cmd: Integer; Len: __off64_t): Integer;
      cdecl;
```

Obviously enough, lockf takes a 32-bit Len, while lockf64 takes a 64-bit Len. A zero Len means 'to the end of the file'; any appended data will automatically be added to the locked region. Somewhat similarly, it is not an error to lock a region that overlaps a region that you already have locked; the kernel just adds the new region to the existing lock.

The Cmd parameter must be one of the following four values:

Cmd	Meaning
F_LOCK	Lock a region, blocking until you get the lock.
F_TLOCK	Try to lock a region, but return an error code if some other process already has it locked
F_ULOCK	Release your lock on a region.
F_TEST	Test the region's lock state.

While lockf is fairly straightforward and obvious, it has a performance cost that should lead you to shun it: It can only create exclusive locks. A shared lock allows you to say "I need to do some reading here—I don't care who else reads along with me, but don't let anyone change this region until we're all done". Using an exclusive lock where you only need a read lock increases the chances that other processes will be blocked, waiting for you to finish.

You have to use fcntl to create shared locks. This requires you to fill in the first four fields of a flock (TFlock) record, and pass it to fcntl with a F_SETLK, F_SETLKW or F_GETLK command.

```
type
  flock = {packed} record
    l_type: Smallint;    { Type of lock: F_RDLCK, F_WRLCK, or F_UNLCK. }
    l_whence: Smallint;  { Where `l_start' is relative to (like `lseek'). }
    l_start: __off_t;    { Offset where the lock begins. }
    l_len: __off_t;      { Size of the locked area; zero means until EOF. }
    l_pid: __pid_t;      { Process holding the lock. }
  end;
  TFlock = flock;
```

```
function fcntl(Handle: Integer; Command: Integer; var Lock: TFlock): Integer;
cdecl; overload;
```

The TFlock record should be pretty obvious. In the l_type field, you specify whether you are creating a read or write lock, or whether you are releasing an existing lock. The l_whence and l_start fields let you specify a starting position relative to either the start of the file (SEEK_SET), the current file pointer (SEEK_CUR), or the end of the file (SEEK_END), just as with lseek. The l_len field is the lock length, with 0 again meaning to the end of the file.

The Command parameter must be one of F_SETLK, F_SETLKW or F_GETLK:

Command	Meaning
F_SETLK	Tries to lock on F_RDLCK or F_WRLCK; returns error code if another process has a conflicting (overlapping) lock. Removes process's lock on F_UNLCK.
F_SETLKW	Tries to lock on F_RDLCK or F_WRLCK; blocks ("waits") if another process has a conflicting lock. Removes process's lock on F_UNLCK.
F_GETLK	Tests to see if lock could be granted. The test results are returned in the flock record, not the fcntl result code. If the region is unlocked, l_type is set to F_UNLCK; if the region is locked, l_pid is set to the (a) PID that has a conflicting lock.

Tip

With a 2.4 kernel, you can use fcntl() to lock large files by using a TFlock64 record with the F_SETLK64, F_SETLKW64, or F_GETLK64 commands. (My lib/LibcX contains an alternate fcntl() binding that supports the TFlock64 parameter.) You can use the 64-bit locking syntax with (at least the latest) 2.2 kernels, but the calls will fail if you try to lock a region beyond the 2G boundary.

Mandatory vs *advisory*

Record locks might seem like pretty sturdy mechanisms, in that you can say 'suspend me until I have exclusive access to this region', but they're still "advisory", in the sense that they offer you no protection from the naïve program that tries to write to shared files without doing any locking. Linux does offer a way to make record locks "mandatory": if the locked file has its setgid (S_ISGID) bit set but *not* its group execute (S_IXGRP) bit set, all record locks become mandatory.

What this means is that only the process with the lock can `read()` from an exclusively locked region, and no process can `write()` to a region that's locked by another process. Processes that try to cheat are blocked until the lock is released.

Before concluding that you should always use mandatory locking, you should consider that

1. It imposes a performance hit. *Every* read and write has to be checked against the lock table, not just the comparatively few lock requests.

2. It doesn't offer perfect protection. An ill-behaved program that doesn't use locking calls will be prevented from changing your locked region until your multiple-write transaction is complete and you release the lock, but there's no way that mandatory locking can keep you from getting a lock in the middle of a non-locking program's multiple-write transaction.

3. Mandatory locking isn't as portable as advisory locking. Many network file systems do not support mandatory locking.

Caution

In addition to these three caveats, Linux supports mandatory locking only when the file system is mounted with the undocumented "mand" mount option. The default is "nomand", so most systems don't actually support mandatory locking without some reconfiguration. Many sysadmins will be reluctant to tweak system configuration just to install your application, so you should probably restrict your use of mandatory locking to turnkey systems where you have full control over the configuration—and you have a need to write to system files that are also touched by poorly behaved applications that don't use explicit locking.

Locks and threads

One little bit of advanced Linux programming that you **need** to know about is that while locks are acquired and released on regions of files, where the file is specified by a file handle, the kernel lock table is keyed on pid+inode pairs. Since each thread has its own pid, this means is that while threads can share open file handles, they don't share locks!

The Locks project of the ch10/Files project group, Figure 10-1, demonstrates this. It has a timer that does a `lockf(F_TEST)` five times a second, setting a label to report on the result. Normally, this shows "unlocked". But, when you press the "Lock in thread" button, the label shows that the file is locked by a different thread than the GUI.

Figure 10-1. The Locks project

In some ways, of course, this is really desirable behavior. One thread can block while another thread is writing, just as you'd expect other programs to block. It allows a multithreaded program to use file locks for internal coordination of file IO in exactly the same way that it might use mutexes to maintain the coherence of in-memory structures.

It does mean, though, that some possible architectures just won't work. For example, you can't have Thread A block until it gets a write lock on a region, then spawn Thread B to write to the region and release the lock when done—because *Thread B doesn't have the lock*, Thread A does.

Caution

This is Linux specific behavior. The Windows lock table, for example, is keyed on file handles, so that locks can be shared across threads. Any Kylix code that relies on the fact that file locks are not shared across threads should be flagged with platform *directives, or perhaps* {$ifNdef Linux} {$message 'This code may not work on this OS'} {$endif} *messages, so that you can be sure to check it carefully when porting.*

flock

There are good reasons not to use `flock`: It only supports file locking, not record locking; it can't do mandatory locking; it's not POSIX-compatible. Unfortunately, there's also one reason to use `flock` that can trump the others: Some existing Linux applications use `flock`. If you need to write to a file that's locked with flock, you have to use flock yourself, as flock and fcntl are orthogonal—fcntl locks don't affect flock locks and *vice versa*.

It's entirely possible that the documentation for an application that uses flock to lock its files will say so clearly. It's just not all that likely. Fortunately, you can look at /proc/locks to see what sort of locking is in use. You don't need to understand all the information in it to see whether or not you need to use flock—what really matters are the second column, which specifies whether a given lock uses the POSIX (fcntl) or FLOCK API's; the fourth column, which specifies the locking PID, for POSIX locks; and the fifth column, which specifies the device ID and inode number of the locked file. (The sample /proc/locks below is truncated after the fifth column, because the full listing won't fit on the page.)

```
1: POSIX  ADVISORY  WRITE 18886 08:06:639453
1: -> POSIX  ADVISORY  WRITE 25793 08:06:639453
1: -> POSIX  ADVISORY  WRITE 18885 08:06:639453
2: POSIX  ADVISORY  WRITE 749 08:06:655263
3: POSIX  ADVISORY  WRITE 739 08:06:655261
4: FLOCK  ADVISORY  WRITE 0 08:06:720355
5: POSIX  ADVISORY  WRITE 473 08:06:720350
```

As you can see, the fourth lock is a flock lock on inode 720355 on device 806. To see whether or not you need to use flock, just stat the file you want to lock and watch /proc/locks until you see it being locked.

If you do need to use flock, you face a bit of a problem. In Kylix 1.0, Libc doesn't include a binding for flock. This may be fixed by the time you read this; if not, you can use my lib/LibcX, as the flocktest program in the ch10/Files project group does. This project displays /proc/locks; then creates a temporary file; locks it with both flock and lockf; displays /proc/locks with the locks in effect; then unlocks, closes, and deletes the file.

```
flock(Handle, LOCK_EX or LOCK_NB);
try
  lockf(Handle, F_WRLCK, 0);
  try
    WriteLn('/proc/locks = '^J, ReadPseudoFile('/proc/locks'));
  finally
    lockf(Handle, F_UNLCK, 0);
  end;
finally
  flock(Handle, LOCK_UN);
end;
```

Deadlock

Finally, using file locking is a lot like using mutexes (Chapter 7). You use either when you want to make sure that only one process at a time is changing a shared data structure. If you need to lock two or more different resources, you must be sure that all processes that lock multiple resources lock them in the same order. If one process locks A before B, while another locks B before A, both can *deadlock* when one locks A and waits for B while the other locks B and waits for A. If both processes lock A and then lock B, they can't deadlock; one will lock A and then B, while the other will block until the first one unlocks A.

Memory mapping

At its most basic, memory mapping involves loading a file into memory in such a way that changing the disk image changes the memory image, and changing the memory image changes the disk image. In addition, the memory map can be shared between processes, just as a file can be shared. A shared memory map can involve a real file, or it can be based on a special, file-like "shared memory object" which allows you to create or open a named bit of shared memory.

Probably the most common reason to use a memory mapping is to speed up file processing. This is especially true of text files with their variable length lines. When you use ReadLn (Chapter 8), you're effectively reading each character at least twice; once as ReadLn finds the next line break, and again as you process each line. You can minimize the costs of line break detection by using SetTextBuf to read the file in large chunks, but ReadLn still has to deal with 'soft page faults' at the end of each buffer, and the overhead of assembling a single line from two (or more!) different buffers. With memory mapping, all the overhead is incurred when the mapping is set up, and after that you can 'read' the 'file' with normal PChar or array operations. In addition to avoiding all the issues with lines that span buffer boundaries, memory mapped IO avoids the cost of moving file data from kernel space to user space.

The other common reason to use memory mappings is to let two or more different programs share a chunk of memory, almost as if they were different threads sharing the same heap and global variables. Obviously, two different programs that share binary data in RAM need to agree on exactly how that data is structured. However, this isn't a very big problem in the common case of a single system being partitioned into multiple programs to make it easier to sell more or less capable systems to different segments of the market, or to minimize the size of upgrades. Each program just needs to use the same shared memory definition unit.

There are other, more specialized uses of "anonymous" memory mappings that are useful in systems-level tasks like loading libraries, allocating memory, and debugging, but fast file access and shared memory are the two that are most likely to be useful in Kylix applications.

Creating memory mappings

You create a memory mapping with either the mmap or mmap64 functions:

```
function mmap( __addr: __ptr_t; __len: size_t; __prot: Integer;
               __flags: Integer; __fd: Integer; __offset: __off_t): __ptr_t;
           cdecl;
```

The result is either a pointer to the newly created memory mapping, or the special value MAP_FAILED. Note that MAP_FAILED <> Nil! (For what it's worth, MAP_FAILED equals pointer(-1).)

The __addr parameter will almost always be Nil. If it's not, it specifies a requested starting address for the memory mapping. The address is normally a "hint", but you can specify MAP_FIXED, which will cause mmap to fail if __addr is not page-aligned (an integral multiple of getpagesize) or if it is already in use as a memory mapping.

The __len parameter allows you to create mappings bigger or smaller than the underlying file. The actual allocation will be rounded up to the next integral multiple of getpagesize, and as much of the file as will fit in that allocation will be mapped. (That is, if you request a 32-byte mapping of a 40960-byte file, you'll actually get the first 4096 bytes.) If the mapping is bigger than the file, the 'tail' of the mapping will be filled with zero bytes. Subject to a few serious *caveats*, you can use any of the memory in the mapping—even the "round up" memory between the requested length and the page boundary—but changing mapping bytes beyond the end of the file will not grow the file.

Note

In general, changing the mapping beyond the end of the file is a risky proposition. On my 2.2.16 system, you will get a SIGSEGV if you try to write beyond the end of the mapping, and if the mapping is shared (MAP_SHARED) you will get a SIGBUS if you try to write beyond the end of the page that contains the end of the file. This behavior may not be universal, and this is certainly far into "undocumented" territory, where the behavior may well change from release to release.

(The mmaptest project in the ch10/Files project group plays with these concepts a bit. It creates a short text file with no trailing 0. When it maps this, the mapping is a valid PChar, because the first "fill in" byte is a 0. It successfully writes more memory than was allocated, with both private and shared mappings—until it tries to write beyond a page boundary—but the file never grows.)

Basically, you should avoid using memory beyond the requested length. Whatever behavior you see on your development system(s) may not be the same behavior your users will see on their systems. Play by the rules, and use ftruncate() to change the mapping's size as necessary.

The _prot parameter to mmap() is a bitmap, consisting of one or more of PROT_READ, PROT_WRITE, and PROT_EXEC. (The last allows you to write self-modifying code, a program loader, or a just-in-time compiler.) You can also use PROT_NONE (0), which doesn't let you read or write the mapping. PROT_NONE is most likely to be useful in conjunction with mprotect, which allows you to change the mapping's protection bitmap. You may want to disable access to a memory map when the underlying file is being changed radically, or you may want to build some sort of system whereby only one process at a time has access to a shared memory map.

Note

The _prot parameter must be compatible with the file open mode—you can't map a O_WRONLY file as PROT_READ.

The mmap() _flags parameter is also a bitmap (see Table 10-9).

Table 10-9. mmap flags

Bit name	Portability	Interpretation
MAP_SHARED	POSIX	Writing to mapped memory changes the file, and can be seen by other processes that are also mapping the file. (You must have PROT_WRITE to change the mapped memory.) You must specify either MAP_SHARED or MAP_PRIVATE.
MAP_PRIVATE	POSIX	Changes to the mapped memory are **not** mirrored to the file. You must specify either MAP_SHARED or MAP_PRIVATE.
MAP_FIXED	POSIX	The __addr parameter is a requirement, not a hint.
MAP_ANONYMOUS	POSIX	The mapping is not associated with a file, and the __fd parameter is ignored. This amounts to a way to allocate memory with a specific set of protections—executable, read-only, write-only, &c.
MAP_GROWSDOWN	Not POSIX	The kernel uses this for stacks. If you try to access memory *below* the mapped region, Grows Down maps will expand instead of giving you a SIGSEGV.
MAP_DENYWRITE	Not POSIX	Changes to the file are normally reflected in the memory map. A Deny Write mapping causes write()s to the inode to fail with an ETXTBSY.
MAP_EXECUTABLE	Not POSIX	Not documented except in passing. While mmap.c source does not appear to make actual use of this flag, MAP_EXECUTABLE is used internally by the kernel.
MAP_LOCKED	Not POSIX	Processes running as root can use this to keep the pages from getting swapped out.
MAP_NORESERVE	Not POSIX	Does not check for memory availability before allocating private, writable mapping.

The __fd parameter is the handle of the file to map. This is ignored for MAP_ANONYMOUS mappings. You do **not** have to keep the file open after you have created the mapping.

The final parameter, __offset, allows you to map only the 'tail' of a file, omitting the first __offset bytes from the mapping. This **must** be an integral multiple of getpagesize—the most common multiple is zero.

Closing and flushing memory mappings

Memory maps are closed when the process that creates them terminates or calls exec (below). If you want to close one before that, you can use munmap.

```
function munmap(__addr: __ptr_t; __len: size_t): Integer; cdecl;
```

Normally, you would unmap the whole mapping. Under Linux, you can unmap part of a mapping, but this is a non-POSIX feature that may not be supported on future Kylix platforms.

Finally, while changes to a shared mapping are always written to disk—eventually—synchronization normally happens at the system's discretion. If you want to force synchronization, you can call msync. In particular, munmap does not imply msynch, and it's possible that unmapping without first synching can result in a loss of changes.

```
function msync(__addr: __ptr_t; __len: size_t; __flags: Integer): Integer;
cdecl;
```

Obviously, the first two parameters allow you to specify which parts of the mapping to synch to disk. The __flags parameter is a bitmap consisting of either MS_ASYNC or MS_SYNC—synch "soon", or synch before returning from msynch—and possibly MS_INVALIDATE, which forces any other mappings of the same file to be invalidated and reloaded before they're next read.

Shared memory objects

A shared memory object is a special, file-like structure that allows you to create and share a memory mapping *via* a file name, without a file actually being involved. Unlike Windows, where you can create either a file mapping or a shared memory segment *via* different parameters to CreateFileMapping(), under Linux you must always pass a file descriptor (handle) to mmap() to create a mapping (unless you're using MAP_ANONYMOUS). Also, where Windows file-mapping objects can be shared between processes either by handle or by name, under Linux the only way to share a mapping is by name.

Linux is not Windows

> **Note**
>
>
>
> *I'm describing the POSIX shared memory API, here. There's also a System V API—*shmget()* &c—but I suggest that you avoid it for the simple reason that shmget() requires that you 'name' shared memory via an integer 'key' while shared memory objects have pathnames, as if they were files. While there are many ways of picking a reasonably unique key—like the time_t of the moment you choose a key; a random number generator; or some sort of 32-bit hash of a pathname—it is still all too easy to have a collision, and end up with unrelated programs trying to share memory. With shared memory objects, your shared memory can have a unique name based on where your application is installed, or where it stores its data files.*
>
> *As of the time I'm writing this, Linux support for POSIX shared memory is new enough that there are no man pages for shm_open and shm_unlink. For more information than I present here, you'll have to use Google to get Unix man pages, or read the Stevens IPC book, or read the source. Note also that shm_get and shm_unlink are only present in glibc 2.2 (and later), and only actually supported in 2.4 (and later) kernels. More, support is still ...problematic ... in most early 2.4 distributions. Still, these functions are the way to go, and with any luck all the teething pains will be over by the time you actually need shared memory.*

Shared memory objects are created and destroyed *via* the Libc functions `shm_open()` and `shm_unlink()`:

```
function shm_open(__name: PChar; __oflag: Integer; __mode: mode_t): Integer;
        cdecl;
function shm_unlink(__name: PChar): Integer; cdecl;
```

The basic idea is that you create or open a shared memory object with shm_open, then pass the descriptor to mmap() as the __fd parameter. The shm_open() function is modeled on the basic file open() function, and takes similar arguments. It returns –1 on an error, and a non-negative file descriptor on success. Once you've created the mapping, you can __close() the shared memory object, just like any other file descriptor that you pass to mmap(). shm_unlink deletes the pathname from the system, so that the shared memory is not available to any processes that don't already have it open. Just as with the eponymous file unlink() function, calling shm_unlink deletes only the filename, and has no effect on any open file mapping or shared memory objects.

You should usually use fully qualified pathnames (*ie*, ones that start with PathDelim), as the behavior of shm_open() with unrooted pathnames is undefined, or "implementation-dependent." The actual choice of name is subject to the same complications outlined in the *Links* section, above, but generally if you choose a shared memory object name somewhere in the same directory that you use for your data and/or global configuration files, you can be pretty sure that no other application will be trying to use the same name.

The __oflag parameter to shm_open() can contain a subset of the flags that you can pass to open(). It *must* contain either O_RDONLY or O_RDWR, and *may* be modified with any of O_CREAT, O_EXCL, and O_TRUNC.

O_CREAT	Create the shared memory object if it doesn't already exist. Trying to open a shared memory object that doesn't exist with O_CREAT will fail, returning −1. O_CREAT has no effect if the object already exists; the call simply returns a handle to the existing object.
O_EXCL	Meaningless except in conjunction with O_CREAT, where it means "don't open an existing object"—*ie*, fail unless this call actually creates the object.
O_TRUNC	Meaningless except in conjunction with O_RDWR; resets the size of the share memory object to 0.

The __mode parameter to shm_open() is always required, but is only read when the flags parameter includes O_CREAT. This is a file permissions bitmap—777_8 &c—just as you pass to open() when you're creating a file.

When you create a shared memory object, or when you specify O_TRUNC, the object will be zero bytes long—and so will the memory mapping that you get from mmap(). You can call ftruncate() to set the size of shared memory object before you call mmap(), or you can call ftruncate() on the memory map descriptor after creating the mapping.

How to use the shared memory is, like all IPC, largely beyond the scope of this book. In general, you will either treat the shared memory as a record, with a fixed structure, or as a memory stream that different processes read and write, much as if it were a file. (The stream approach is probably the best way to pass strings and other variable length data.) You will need some way to alert the other processes sharing the memory to changes you make (you could use a named pipe, a Unix-domain socket, the message queue API (mq_open() &c), or you could send a *signal*) and you need some way to synchronize access to the shared memory. You can either use mutexes to assure that only one process at a time has write access to the shared memory, or you can employ a brute force system where each communicating process has a shared memory buffer that only it can write but that all the other cooperating processes can read.

Processes

Linux doesn't have as strong a separation between "processes" and "threads" as both Windows and older Unices do. Threads *are* processes, with their own PID and so on. There aren't two different types of scheduling entities; everything's a process to the Linux scheduler. This is largely because the Linux context switch is so fast that there was nothing much to gain by creating a "lightweight process", and obviously a system with one entity is much simpler and more reliable than a system with two entities. Still, threads share their parent process's memory, open files, and so on—so it does still make sense to think of a "process" as a group of threads sharing various resources.

Accordingly, this Processes section begins with two of the basic process resources, the environment and effective user ID. After a short discussion of these, it moves on to somewhat more advanced topics, like process creation, shared memory, and signals.

Environment

As under Windows,[9] the environment is a collection of strings of the form Name=Value. Each process has its own environment; changing a process's environment affects any processes that the process subsequently creates, but can never affect the parent process.

Environment strings affect all sorts of things in the Linux environment. For example, you've undoubtedly found by now that Linux will only search directories listed in the current PATH string when you try to run a program without an explicit pathname. That is, unlike Windows, Linux won't look in the current directory unless . is explicitly included in the PATH. Similarly, we've already seen that Linux won't load .so's and/or packages unless they're in a directory in /etc/ld.so.conf or the LD_LIBRARY_PATH environment variable. Finally, various user-level commands can be strongly affected by the setting of other environment variables. You should always look for envi-

---

9.   This is a poor—if simple—way to put it, as Microsoft copied the idea from Unix, and not the other way around.

ronment dependencies (which are usually documented in the utility's man or info pages) before calling another program from one of your applications.

You can get the value of an environment value by calling the Libc function

```
function getenv(Name: PChar): PChar; cdecl;
```

This function takes the name of an environment variable and returns the value. If the variable does not exist, getenv() will return Nil, while if the variable is '', getenv() will return an empty string (a pointer to a #0). Remember that while you can always assign a PChar such as getenv() returns to a Kylix AnsiString or WideString, Kylix treats both Nil and a pointer to a #0 as empty strings whose string representation is a Nil pointer. If you want to use getenv() to test for an environment variable existence, be sure to code your test as Assigned(getenv(Name)) (or getenv(Name) <> Nil), **not** getenv(Name) <> ''.

If you need to know about every environment variable, you can use the System unit's envp variable. This is declared as a PPChar, a pointer to a PChar, but it's actually a pointer to an ARGV-style, Nil-terminated array of PChar's. Thus, the best way to access it is to cast it to a PPCharArray

```
type
  TPCharArray = array[0..MaxInt div SizeOf(PChar) - 1] of PChar;
  PPCharArray = ^ TPCharArray;
```

as in the "listenv" project in the ch10/Environment project group.

```
var
  Index:             integer;
  EnvironmentString: PChar;

begin
  Index := 0;
  repeat
    EnvironmentString := PPCharArray(envp)^[Index];
    if Assigned(EnvironmentString) then
      WriteLn(EnvironmentString);
    Inc(Index);
  until not Assigned(EnvironmentString);
end.
```

Note that each pointer in the envp PChar array is to a 'Name=Value' string. You can parse this yourself, but you may prefer to simply add each line to a TStringList and use the TStringList's associative array abilities as in Chapter 7.

You can set an environment string with the Libc function

```
function setenv(Name: PChar; const Value: PChar; Replace: Integer): Integer;
cdecl;
```

If the Name does not currently exist, setenv() will create it and set it to Value. If the Name does exist, setenv() will only replace it if the Replace parameter is non-zero. That is, the Replace parameter acts like an Object Pascal LongBool.

Note

Changing environment variables won't necessarily affect a running program. Many of the functions that are controlled by environment variables only 'see' the values the environment variables had at program start-up. For example, changing LD_LIBRARY_PATH at runtime doesn't affect subsequent calls to LoadLibrary or Load-Package—they'll still only search the LD_LIBRARY_PATH in effect when your program was loaded. What changing environment variables affects most reliably is the behavior of programs that you call from your app.

As *per* the ZapEnv project in the ch10/Environment project group, using setenv() to set an environment variable's Value to Nil sets it to an empty string—it doesn't delete it. To delete an environment entirely, you need to either use

```
procedure unsetenv(Name: PChar); cdecl;
```

which deletes the variable named Name, or use a truly weird function,

```
function putenv(AString: PChar): Integer; cdecl;
```

When you call putenv() with a 'bare' 'Name' string (*ie*, not a 'Name=Value' string), it will delete the current variable named Name, just like unsetenv. As per the putenv project in the ch10/Environment project group, it's perfectly safe to thus 'delete' an environment string that doesn't exist. When you call putenv() with a 'Name=Value' string, you create a variable Name and set it to Value.

So, what's so weird? It's that the PChar you pass to putenv() is actually added to the environment. This means that any changes to the buffer it points to will be reflected in the environment! Thus, when the putenv project does

```
var
  EnvVar: array[0..1024] of char = 'New=Value';

begin
  Libc.putenv(EnvVar);
  WriteLn(getenv('New'));

  StrCopy(EnvVar, 'New=Old');
  WriteLn(getenv('New'));

  StrCopy(EnvVar, 'Old=New');
  WriteLn(getenv('New') = Nil); // New doesn't exist
  WriteLn(getenv('Old'));
end.
```

the output is

```
Value
Old
TRUE
New
```

That is, setting the EnvVar to 'New=Old' sets the New variable's value to 'Old', while setting the EnvVar to 'Old=New' both deletes the New variable and creates an Old variable.

> **Note**
>
>
> *Because the PChar you pass to* putenv() *is actually added to the environment, it's a very bad idea to pass* putenv() *a local variable—and neither Kylix nor Linux has any way to detect this.*

In case you're wondering, setenv() and putenv() are not orthogonal. That is, if you create a variable named Foo with putenv and then set a variable named Foo with settenv—or *vice versa*—the second operation will change the existing Foo. You will **not** end up with two variables named Foo.

Effective user ID

In most cases, your applications run with the same permissions as the user who launched them. This means that they can only read and write files that the user can read and write; and they can only create files in directories where the user can create files. Similarly, it doesn't generally matter which user owns the executable, so long as the user can run it. However, executables with the "set user ID" (setuid) are a special case. A setuid application runs with the same permissions as its owner. This will generally be root, as root can do just about anything. Thus, an application that needs to create a file in /var/lock or in /var/log will generally be *setuid root*, which means simply that it's owned by root and has its setuid permission bit set.

> **Tip**
>
>
>
> *Being root is an all or nothing proposition. A program that's setuid root can call any privileged function and can change or delete any file on the system. A buggy setuid program can do a lot of damage, and any program that's setuid root represents a security risk. You should do anything you can to avoid needing to run setuid root. For example, installation could create a subdirectory of /var that's owned by an application-specific, unprivileged account like "mymail" or "mynews". If your setuid application is owned by this special account, it can write to its /var subdirectory without having all root's special privileges.*

A setuid root application has to be especially careful about security. Any user configurability it offers—from where it puts its log files to scripts that it runs when various events are triggered—represents opportunities for crackers to overwrite system files or run code as root. Accordingly, Unix provides mechanisms for setuid root applications to surrender privileges that they don't need most of the time, and to regain them in the very few places that they do need them.

These mechanisms revolve around a set of four uid's: The *fsuid*, or file system uid; the *euid*, or effective uid; the *ruid*, or real uid; and the *suid*, or saved uid. The file system uid controls your file permissions. An application can do anything with files and directories that the user with its fsuid can do. The effective uid controls all your other permissions. Many Linux API functions are only available to a process running as root, or act differently when called by a process running as root; it's an euid of 0 that marks a process as one that's running as root.[10]

When you want to voluntarily lower your program's access, you can change the euid and the fsuid. Changing the euid also changes the fsuid, but you can change the fsuid separately. One scenario where you might want to do this is where you need root's file permissions (to create lock and/or log files, for example) but you neither need the special privileges nor want the special responsibilities that come with an euid of 0 and running as root.

A process running as root can change any of its four uid's however it likes. Having done so, however, it's subject to the same restrictions on changing uid's as any other user.

- A normal process (with a non-root euid) can only change its euid to a uid that matches its real uid or its saved uid.

- A normal process can only change its fsuid to a uid that matches its euid, suid or ruid.

- All processes can freely change their ruid to either the euid or the suid.

What makes this work is that setuid programs start with their suid set to their euid (which is the uid of the file's owner), and with their ruid set to the uid of the user who started the application. Thus, they can always lower their privilege level to that of the user who launched the app, or raise it back to that of the user who owns the executable file.

The getuid function returns the current real uid, and geteuid returns the effective uid. There's no getsuid or getfsuid, but there is a function getresuid[11] that returns ruid, euid, and suid.

The setreuid function allows you to set the real and/or effective uid's. That is, you have to pass it new real and effective uid's, but if either parameter is –1, the corresponding uid is not changed. The setfsuid allows you to set the fsuid.

---

10. Apparently, Linux is the only Unix system that thus splits the euid into a fsuid and an euid.

11. The getresuid function is not declared in the Libc unit in the initial Kylix release, but **is** declared in my lib/LibcX unit.

Note

There is a setuid *function, but you have to be careful with it, as it acts differently for processes running as root than it does for normal user processes. When a user process calls* setuid, *it changes only the euid. However, when a root process (one running as root) calls* setuid, *it sets all four uid's. Thus, a program that uses* setuid *to surrender privileges can never regain them. In many cases, this is exactly what a setuid program wants: it does some setup using its root privileges, and then surrenders them permanently to avoid any danger that a malicious attack might use its root privileges to subvert the system. A program that uses* setreuid *to surrender privileges temporarily needs to be even more carefully designed than a normal setuid program.*

As you might expect, there are four parallel gids—egid, fsgid, rgid, and sgid—and parallel functions to get and set gids that operate under rules that parallel the uid rules.

Caution

*Security is no light subject. There are plenty of Linux-knowledgeable people out there with nothing better to do than to seek out vulnerabilities and write scripts that exploit them. There are even more people with nothing better to do than to use these scripts to take over systems. (It's something like spraying graffiti on walls, without even ever being pretty.) Basically, any weakness in a setuid program **will** be exploited someday. Avoid writing setuid programs as much as you can. If you really need to, treat the material here as an introduction and do a lot more research before putting any setuid program on a publicly accessible machine!*

Creating processes

You can't use Linux without creating a lot of processes. Typing less README at a shell prompt creates a process that runs the less program and waits for it to terminate. Typing GuiApp & creates a process that runs the GuiApp program "detached", so that the shell program doesn't wait for the GuiApp process. Typing readelf -s /lib/libc.so.6 | grep fcntl creates one process to run readelf and another process to run grep, and creates a pipe to transfer the standard output of the readelf process to the standard input of the grep process. Nothing new here, I'm sure—and I'm equally sure you won't be surprised to hear that your Kylix apps can do all this programmatically.

Basic process creation

Linux supplies two high-level functions that cover perhaps 99% of your process creation needs: system() and popen(). The system function—which you'll usually have to call as Libc.system because of an unfortunate name collision with Kylix's System unit—executes a command and returns the exit code. The popen function allows you to run a command, and either capture the standard output or supply the standard input. For more complicated scenarios, such as setuid programs that shouldn't use system or popen because of their dependency on easily-hacked environment strings, or where you need to tailor the environment of the new process, you need to use the lower level fork and exec functions in the next section, *Advanced process creation*.

The system function

The Libc.system() function

```
function system(Command: PChar): Integer; cdecl;
```

is the simpler of the two high-level process creation functions. It invokes /bin/sh[12] and passes your Command to it. Because the Command is run by the shell, it can use all the features available at the shell prompt, like filename expansion (~'s and shell regular expressions) and redirection with >, <, and |. If the system() function is able to return your Command, it will return the Command's exit code. If system() can't exec the shell, it will return 127, and it will return –1 on any other error. (That's right, there's no way to tell the difference between a system() failure and a Command that returns 127 or –1. Fortunately, almost all programs return only small, non-negative exit codes.) Normally, the system() function will block until the command returns, but if the command ends with an & character, the Command will run "detached", just as at the shell prompt, and the system() function will return 'immediately'. When you create a detached process, it's completely independent of your application: ps -AH won't show the new process as a child of the application process, the way that it does for threads and non-detached

---

12. /bin/sh is **usually** bash, the Bourne Again Shell, but may actually be any shell the sysadmin prefers.

processes, and closing the application has absolutely no effect on the detached process.

The Recursive project of the ch10/ProcessCreation project group uses detached processes to launch a new copy of the application whenever you press the "Do It!" button, without hanging the application until the spawned process terminates.

```
procedure TRecursiveFrm.DoItBtnClick(Sender: TObject);
begin
  Libc.system(PChar(ParamStr(0) + '&'));
end; // TRecursiveFrm.DoItBtnClick
```

Kylix is not Delphi 5

> **Note**
>
>
>
> *Long-time Delphi programmers might think that* `Libc.system(PChar(ParamStr(0) + '&'))` *is wrong because the result of the string expression is dereferenced before the system() call—especially in a multithreaded application, the memory that the PChar points to might be overwritten before the system() function had a chance to act on it. Kylix (and Delphi 6) have fixed this: string expressions are saved to anonymous local variables, and thus have a reference count of 1. (Yes, I've mentioned this before. But it's important enough to mention again—and I don't assume that all of you are reading this book from cover to cover.)*

Setuid root programs should never use system() (or popen) because the use of the shell (and all its environment string dependencies) represents a security hole. Instead, they should manually code a fork and exec, which gives them full control over the spawned program, without the mediation of the shell program.

The popen function

The system() function only returns the spawned process's exit code. Obviously, this can be useful, but often we want the output of the command— what in the shell or Perl would be `Command`. Less often, we want to run a command, supplying its standard input. The Libc popen() function

```
function popen(const Command: PChar; Modes: PChar): PIOFile; cdecl;
```

allows us to handle both these situations. The Command is a string that's passed to /bin/sh, as with the system() function, while the Modes string must be either 'r' or 'w' to specify whether the returned PIOFile (a C text stream) is used to *read from* or *write to* the spawned process. Note that while the PIOFile is a perfectly normal stream pointer that you write to or read from with the standard functions fwrite() and fread() or fputs() and fgets(), you **must** close it with pclose() instead of fclose(). The pclose() function will not only close the stream but will also terminate the child process, if it is still running, and will return the child process's exit code.

When you are writing to the spawned process, you're done when you're done. When you're reading from the spawned process, you should read until feof() or until the fgets() function returns Nil. The following function from lib/GrabBag demonstrates the basic idea. (This function is used in the ch8/DriverDemo project.)

```
function Eval(Cmd: string; ForceExec: boolean = True): string;
var
  Handle: PIOFile;
  Line:   PChar;
  Buffer: array[0..1024] of char;
const
  Exec = 'exec ';
begin
  if ForceExec and (System.Copy(Cmd, 1, Length(Exec)) <> Exec) then
    Cmd := Exec + Cmd;
  Handle := popen(PChar(Cmd), 'r');
  if not Assigned(Handle) then
    raise Exception.Create('popen() returned Nil');
  try
    Result := '';
    repeat
      Line := fgets(Buffer, SizeOf(Buffer), Handle);
      Result := Result + Line;
    until Line = '';
  finally
    pclose(Handle);
  end;
end; // Eval
```

The first line assures that the Command will normally start with 'exec '. As *per* the bash man page, this reduces popen()s resource consumption a bit by allowing the Command to replace the shell, instead of requiring the shell to stick around. This isn't always what you want, as passing *eg* 'exec w; w' to popen() will only run the first w command. Accordingly, the optional ForceExec parameter allows you to disable the exec-adding behavior as needed.

Next, I call popen() and read it within a try/finally block that pclose()s the handle when done. I initialize the Result to '' and append to it, line by line. Note that it's safe, here, to check for Nil by comparing Line to '' as fgets() will only return '' at the end of the file—an empty line will be returned as a newline (^J) character.

It's important not to be blindsided by the way that standard input is normally the keyboard and standard output is normally the console. Neither redirection nor the popen() function are in any way limited to ASCII text or keyboard characters! Many Linux filter programs read or write 8-bit binary data *via* stdio, and you can read or write 8-bit binary data with popen().

For example, in one of my Kylix projects, I was using POV-Ray to generate some bitmaps. The version of POV-Ray I was using couldn't write .bmp or .jpg files, nor could it reliably write .png files. The best I could do was to have it write .ppm files to standard output, and pipe that to ppmtobmp. I used the BinEval function from lib/GrabBag

```
procedure BinEval(Result: TStream; Cmd: string; ForceExec: boolean = True);
overload;
var
  Handle: PIOFile;
  Buffer: array[1..10240] of char;
  Read:   integer;
const
  Exec = 'exec ';
begin
  Result.Position := 0;

  if ForceExec and (System.Copy(Cmd, 1, Length(Exec)) <> Exec) then
    Cmd := Exec + Cmd;
  Handle := popen(PChar(Cmd), 'r');
  Assert(Assigned(Handle), 'popen() returned Nil');
  try
    repeat
      Read := fread(@ Buffer, SizeOf(char), SizeOf(Buffer), Handle);
      if Read > 0 then
        Result.Write(Buffer, Read);
    until feof(Handle) <> 0;
  finally
```

```
    pclose(Handle);
  end;
  Result.Position := 0;
end; // BinEval
```

to read the .bmp file into a stream with

```
BinEval(Stream, 'x-povray +i' + PovFile +
                ' +W800 +H600 -P +FP +O- +Q9 2> /dev/null ' +
                '| ppmtobmp 2> /dev/null' );
```

and then read the stream into a TBitmap object with the
TBitmap.LoadFromStream method.

You can see the benefits of popen's using the shell, here; my Kylix application constructs a complex process sequence (with two processes, one
redirection of standard output, and two redirections of standard error) just
as easily as at a shell prompt or in a shell script. Of course, the drawbacks of
popen's using the shell are the same as with the system() function—setuid
programs should avoid popen.

Advanced process creation

Setuid programs and those with complex file or environment conditioning
needs can't use the high-level system() and popen() functions. They need to
use the low-level fork and exec family of functions.

The basic idea is that you call fork to create a new process that's a nearly
exact copy of the original. The most noticeable difference is that the fork
function returns a special exit code (0) in the child process that it will never
return in the parent process. In the parent process, the fork function returns
either an error code (-1) or the pid of the child process. The other difference
between the parent and child processes is subtler but just as real: The child
process appears to have all the same files open as the parent, but all the
handles are actually duplicates. Closing a handle in the child will not close
the handle in the parent or *vice versa*, though of course, closing either does
decrement the in-memory inode's handle count.

Within the child process, you do any environment conditioning that you
need to, like redirecting an inherited open file handle to standard input or
standard output, and then you call one of the exec functions to *replace* the
current process's executable with a new one. That is, after the exec, the pid
and the parent pid are still the same, and the environment variables are still
the same, and any files that weren't set to "close on exec" are still open—but

everything that we think of as a "program" has been replaced. The old global variables are no longer accessible; the new ones are. The old code is no longer mapped into the process's address space; the new code is. The old stack is no longer valid; a new, empty stack is. The EIP register points to the new code's entry point (the main() function, in a C program).

In every way except the open files, it's as if the new program had just been launched from a shell. This, of course, makes sense, because the shell programs themselves use fork and exec to execute commands.

Now, of course, there is a lot of possible complexity behind this three-paragraph overview—all of which is well beyond the scope of this book. I'm going to present an extended example of a manual implementation of popen()—the ManualPopen project of the ch10/ProcessCreation project group—and move on. If you find you need more, or you're just curious and have the time to scratch the itch, I recommend Johnson & Troan's *Linux Application Development* (to which this chapter owes a great deal) or, of course, Google and the man pages.

An extended example

The main program block of the ManualPopen program is simply

```
begin
  WriteLn(Evaluate(CmdLine));
end.
```

where the CmdLine function rather simplistically reconstructs the command line, using the Kylix ParamCount and ParamStr functions:

```
function CmdLine: string;
var
  Index: integer;
  This:  string;
begin
  for Index := 1 to ParamCount do
  begin
    This := ParamStr(Index);
    if AnsiPos(' ', This) <> 0 then
      This := '"' + This + '"'; // Quote params with embedded spaces
    if Index = 1
      then Result := This
      else Result := Result + ' ' + This;
  end;
end; // CmdLine
```

(The CmdLine function can't know if the actual command line was something like find / "*"—the shell strips the quotes.)

The heart of the program is the Evaluate function

```
function Evaluate(const Command: string; Status: PInteger = Nil): string;
var
  ThePipe:   TPipeDescriptors;
  PID:       pid_t;
  {$ifdef FD_CLOEXEC}
    Handle: integer;
  {$endif}
begin
  ELinux.Check( 'pipe', pipe(ThePipe) ); // Create a pipe pair before we fork
  PID := fork();
  if PID = -1
    then begin
        __close(ThePipe.WriteDes);
        __close(ThePipe.ReadDes);
        raise ELinux.Error('fork', PID);
        end
    else if PID <> 0
      then begin // parent
          __close(ThePipe.WriteDes); // If we don't close this,
                                     // we won't get EOF on .ReadDes
          Result := ReadAll(ThePipe.ReadDes);
          __close(ThePipe.ReadDes);
          wait4(PID, Status, 0, Nil);
          end
      else begin // child
          // redirect standard output to the pipe
          dup2(ThePipe.WriteDes, STDOUT_FILENO);

          {$ifdef FD_CLOEXEC}
            // We don't want any other open handles to survive
            for Handle := STDERR_FILENO + 1 to sysconf(_SC_OPEN_MAX) do
              fcntl(Handle, F_SETFD, FD_CLOEXEC);
          {$endif}

          // Exec
          Exec(['/bin/sh', '-c', 'exec ' + Command, '']);
          end;
end; // Evaluate
```

The first thing I do is to call the Libc function `pipe()`, raising an ELinux exception if it fails. What pipe() does is to create a pipe, and fill in a pipe record containing a pair of file handles, one to write to the pipe and the other to read from it. The child process will redirect standard output to this pipe's write descriptor (handle) before calling exec, while the parent process will read the pipe's read descriptor, and then wait for the child to terminate.

Next, I call the Libc function `fork()`, raising an ELinux exception (and closing the pipe) if it fails. If the PID is not equal to 0 or –1, the fork() succeeded, and we are in the parent process.

The parent process first closes the pipe's WriteDes handle, because otherwise we'll never get a zero-bytes-read indication when we read the ReadDes handle; we'll just block indefinitely. Next, the parent process calls the ReadAll function to empty the pipe. (ReadAll is a pretty straightforward function that I won't list here—it's in the ManualPopen program itself, not in lib/GrabBag or some other unit in the tarball.) The parent process then closes the pipe's ReadDes handle, and finally uses the Libc function `wait4()` to wait for[13] PID (the child process) to terminate. wait4()'s first argument is the process to wait for; the second argument is an optional parameter to the process's return (status) code; the third parameter is a bitmap that controls how to wait for non-existent or stopped processes; while the fourth and last parameter is an optional pointer to an `rusage` structure that can be filled with information on the process's resource consumption.[14]

Note

The read-then-wait sequence is important. I first coded this as wait-then-read, which works just fine when there's not much output. However, as soon as a process returned more than PIPE_BUF (4096) bytes, the ManualPopen project deadlocked: the child process couldn't terminate, because it was waiting for the pipe to be emptied before it could be refilled; the parent process never read the pipe, because it was waiting for the pipe to empty.

---

13. No, `wait4()` is not so named because it 'waits for' a PID—it is the wait function with four arguments. See, for example, `wait3()`.

14. `wait4()` is misbound in Kylix 1.0—the ManualPopen project uses lib/LibcX.

Pipes and the inode process count

It's important that the parent process close the pipe's WriteDes handle because, with pipes, the behavior of the Libc function __read() function depends on the inode's handle count; the number of different open handles there are to the inode. When any process has the pipe's write handle open, the process count is non-zero and a __read() call for more data than is in the pipe will block, waiting for more data to be written. However, if no process has the pipe's write handle open, the process count is zero and a __read() call for more data than is in the pipe will return all the data in the pipe, while subsequent calls will not block but will return zero-bytes-read.

If the parent process explicitly closes its copy of the pipe's write handle, the only writable handles will be the child process's copy of the pipe's write handle, and any duplicates it makes, whether to standard output or to some other handle. When the child process terminates, its copy of the pipe's write handle (and any copies it made of that copy) is closed. This will set the inode's process count to 0, and so __read()s of the pipe's ReadDes handle will eventually return zero.

The child process is a bit more complicated. It does three things: It redirects its standard output to the pipe's WriteDes; it, in effect, closes all files except standard input, standard output, and standard error; and it calls exec().

Redirecting standard output is done by calling the Libc function dup2() to force the STDOUT_FILENO to be a duplicate of the pipe's WriteDes handle. This duplication means that every subsequent write to standard output will actually be done to the pipe. Note that it's not necessary to close the existing STDOUT_FILENO, as dup2() will do that automatically.

Whether or not you want the exec()ed program to inherit the current program's open files depends on your application's particular requirements, of course. In this simple case, there is no reason for the child process to share any files with the parent except the pipe—and every reason not to share things like X server sockets (Chapter 12)—so we mark all possible files with handles greater than STDERR_FILENO as "close on exec". This point—between recognizing that we're in the child process and calling exec—is where you would insert any more complex process conditioning code, like setting environment variables or whatever. Once the child process calls exec(), the parent application's code is no longer in control.

The Evaluate function calls an Exec procedure from lib/GrabBag.

```
procedure Exec(const Params: array of string);
begin
  if Params[High(Params)] <> ''
    then Exec(DynArrayOfString(Params, 1))
    else begin
        Assert(Params[High(Params)] = '');
        ELinux.Check( 'execv',
                        execv(PChar(Params[0]), Addr(Params[0])) );
        end;
end; // Exec
```

There are several different Libc exec() functions. This procedure uses the execv() variant, which is a good match for an array of string parameter. The first parameter to execv is the fully qualified name of the command to exec()—execv won't search the PATH. The second parameter to execv is a pointer to an ARGV-style, Nil-terminated array of pointers to strings. This, of course, is exactly what an array of string that ends with a '' *is*: An array of some base type consists of a stream of the base type. AnsiString's are stored as pointers to null-terminated strings, with the length and reference count 'to the left', where C functions won't see them; and an empty AnsiString is stored as a Nil pointer.

Thus, the lib/GrabBag Exec procedure first checks that the last string is ''. If it's not, it calls the lib/GrabBag DynArrayOfString procedure to copy the open array to a dynamic array that *does* end with an empty string, and passes the dynamic array to a largely identical overloaded Exec procedure. If the open array passes muster, it's passed straight to execv(), and the new code starts executing.

> **Note**
>
> *It doesn't matter that there may seem to be pending try/finally or try/except blocks that the child process will never return through—the parent process returns through them. Similarly, it doesn't matter if the child process allocates memory (strings, objects, dynamic arrays, or whatever) between the fork and the exec—its heap goes away when it calls exec, just as it would when the process terminated. Freeing the child process's heap has no effect on the parent process, as it's just a collection of copy-on-write pages.*

Since the Evaluate function is a manual implementation of
popen(PChar(Command), 'r'), what it passes to Exec is ['/bin/sh', '-c',
'exec ' + Command, '']. That is, it runs the program /bin/sh with two parameters, '-c' and 'exec ' + Command. The –c is a bash shell switch that says 'run
this command as if it were typed in'. The exec prefix says that the shell should
call its standard filename expansions on Command, and then exec() the
expanded Command, rather than calling fork and waiting on the shell's child
process as it normally would. (If you run `ManualPopen ManualPopen ps –
AH` from the command line, you'll see that the second ManualPopen's PID
differs from the first by 1, not 2.)

Obviously, those of you doing manual fork and exec from your setuid
root programs will **not** want to exec a shell. Similarly, you will need to be
careful of the environment you pass to your child process. For example, you
wouldn't want to pass a compromised PATH or LD_LIBRARY_PATH to your
child process. You should either check each and every environment string—
or use execve instead of execv, as this allows you to pass a custom environment to your child process, instead of a copy of the current environment.

Signals

You're almost certainly familiar with the shell commands kill and killall,
which let you terminate hung processes. You're probably also aware that
those commands work by sending the SIGTERM *signal* to the process or processes that you're trying to kill, and that they let you send a different signal if
you wish. For example, most Linux services treat a SIGHUP as a request to
reread a changed configuration file.

Naturally, you can send signals from within your Kylix applications, too.
The Libc function

```
function kill(ProcessID: __pid_t; SigNum: Integer): Integer; cdecl;
```

sends the signal number SigNum to ProcessID, which normally specifies a
single PID. There's a full list of signals in Libc and in Table 10-13. The ProcessId
parameters allows you to send the signal to a single PID or to a *process
group*[15] as *per* Table 10-10, subject to the limitation that unless you are

---

15. Since I assume that *most* Kylix apps will be GUI or web server apps, I'm not going to
cover process groups. Briefly, though, a process group is a set of processes that act as a
single unit for the purposes of job control. That is, when you press ^Z, you bg all
processes in the group. When you run fg, you reactivate the whole process group.
Normally, a process group is a set of processes created together, *via* a sequence like
foo | bar, but this can be manipulated *via* the setpgid() function.

running as root (euid = 0) you can only send a signal to processes with the same euid as yours.

Table 10-10. The kill() function's ProcessID parameter

ProcessID	Interpretation
> 0	Send the signal to the single PID, ProcessID. This is the most normal use.
= 0	Send the signal to all PID's in the current process group.
= -1	Send the signal to all processes except the init process. You are not likely to ever do this.
< -1	Send the signal to all processes in the process group Abs(ProcessID).

To the receiving process, a signal is much like a hardware interrupt; you can mask it off, and a handler is simply a procedure whose one argument is a signal code. The analogy is not perfect, but it's pretty good:

- Signals can happen at any time.

- Signals can happen while you're handling other signals.

- You can choose to ignore signals, on a signal-by-signal basis.

- You should make your signal handlers as short and simple as possible.

- You can structure your program around signals, blocking until the next signal.

Of course, since signals are generated and handled by software, the analogy to hardware interrupt handlers breaks down, as does any analogy, if you look at it too closely. In particular, where a masked interrupt is a lost interrupt, masked signals are simply deferred until the mask is removed. There are two types of signal mask, a process-wide mask and a per-signal mask. The process-wide mask allows you to read or make updates to data structures that signal handlers read or write, without the danger that a signal handler will occur in the middle of the transaction. The per-signal masks allow you to specify, for each signal handler, the signals that should be deferred until the handler returns.

One thing that you need to be aware of is that signal masks can be set on a per-thread basis, but signal handlers are a process-wide resource. A multi-threaded application can't have different signal handlers for different threads.

The signal API

Unix is old. Unix may well be older than you are. Here and there you can see signs of that age in 'old' and 'new' API's, where the old API is crippled in some fundamental way, and only supported under Linux for the sake of making it easier to port old code to Linux. While you may be in the position of trying to port an old Unix program from C to Object Pascal, for the most part as Kylix programmers we have the great luxury of being able to ignore all the old, broken API's, and only use the newer (and usually better designed) API's.

Signal processing is one of those areas. You may see old code or old Unix texts that sets signal handlers with the signal() function, but you should never use it. The ANSI C signal() function specifies a 'one shot' behavior; before your handler is invoked, the kernel sets the handler to the default action. If you want to keep handling the signal, your handler needs to call signal() to grab the signal again. Unfortunately, this makes for *unreliable* signal handling behavior. If the same signal arrives twice in rapid succession, the second signal might get the default behavior—either process termination or a simple no-op—instead being passed to your signal handler. The new POSIX signal API fixes this problem, so use it and not signal().

The POSIX signal API can be broadly divided into two groups: low-level utility functions to manipulate signal sets (masks) and higher-level functions that use signal sets to control signal handling behavior.

Signal set functions

All the signal set functions manipulate sigset_t variables. This is defined in Libc as an array of 1024 bits (32 LongWord's), but you would be very foolish to manipulate it directly. Treating it as an opaque type and only accessing it *via* the Libc signal set functions means your code will still work in the future, with different versions of the kernel and glibc, and it will help make your code more portable should Kylix be ported to other Unices or to Mac OS X.

```
function sigemptyset(var SigSet: TSigset): Integer; cdecl;
```

Clears the set; removes all signals. Analogous to SigSet := [].

```
function sigfillset(var SigSet: TSigset): Integer; cdecl;
```

Fills the set; adds all signals. Analogous to `SigSet :=` `[Low(Signals)..High(Signals)]`.

```
function sigaddset(var SigSet: TSigset; SigNum: Integer): Integer; cdecl;
```

Adds SigNum to the set. Analogous to SigSet := SigSet + [SigNum] (or Include(SigSet, SigNum)).

```
function sigdelset(var SigSet: TSigset; SigNum: Integer): Integer; cdecl;
```

Removes SigNum from the set. Analogous to `SigSet := SigSet - [SigNum]` (or `Exclude(SigSet, SigNum)`).

```
function sigismember(const SigSet: TSigset; SigNum: Integer): Integer;
cdecl;
```

Returns 0 if SigNum is not in the set, and 1 if it is. Analogous to `SigNum in SigSet`.

```
function sigisemptyset(const SigSet: TSigset): Integer; cdecl;
```

Returns 0 if the set is not empty, and non-zero if the set is empty. Analogous to `SigSet = []`.

```
function sigandset(var SigSet: TSigset; const Left: TSigset;
  const Right: TSigset): Integer; cdecl;
```

Does a logical AND of the Left and Right sets. Analogous to `SigSet := Left *` `Right`. (Returns non-zero iff any of the pointers is Nil, which can't happen with the Object Pascal `var` and `const` bindings.)

```
function sigorset(var SigSet: TSigset; const Left: TSigset;
  const Right: TSigset): Integer; cdecl;
```

Does a logical OR of the Left and Right sets. Analogous to `SigSet := Left +` `Right`.

Basic signal handling

The most basic signal handling function is

```
function sigaction( SigNum: Integer;
                    Action: PSigaction;
                    OldAction: PSigaction ): Integer; cdecl;
```

which allows you to set a signal handler, get the signal handler, or both. That is, if Action is non-Nil, sigaction() will set the signal handler for SigNum. If OldAction is NonNil, sigaction() will get the existing signal handler for SigNum. A PSigaction is a pointer to a __sigaction record

```
type
  { Signal handler. }
  __sigaction = {packed} record
    __sigaction_handler: TSigActionHandler;

    { Additional set of signals to be blocked.  }
    sa_mask: __sigset_t;

    { Special flags.  }
    sa_flags: Integer;

    { Restore handler.  }
    sa_restorer: TRestoreHandler;
  end;
```

The __sigaction_handler is either a procedure(Signal: Integer); cdecl or one of the special values SIG_IGN or SIG_DFL.[16] SIG_IGN means that the signal should be ignored, while SIG_DFL means that the kernel should take the default action for the signal, as *per* Table 10-12 (below).

By default, a signal is blocked while it's being handled. That is, if you are handling, say, SIGHUP, a SIGHUP that arrives before your handler returns will not interrupt your signal handler. Rather, it will be deferred until the handler returns. (You can override this with the SA_NODEFER flag.) The sa_mask field allows you to specify a set of additional signals that should be deferred until your handler returns. This can be useful in two different ways. First, you might use the same handler for two or more different signals. If this updates any data structures, the handler probably isn't reentrant; you **don't** want signal A to be handled while you're handling signal B. Second, different handlers might read or write the same data structures. You generally don't want A's handler to read or write the data that B's handler is updating.

---

16. Actually, under the first release of Kylix, SIG_IGN and SIG_DFL are declared as integer constants, which are not assignment-compatible with the __sigaction_handler: TSigActionHandler field. Thus, you have to write *eg* __sigaction_handler := TSigActionHandler(SIG_IGN) instead of just __sigaction_handler := SIG_IGN. It's possible that this will have been fixed by the time you read this.

The sa_flags field is a bitmap.

SA_NOCLDSTOP	Child processes can either *terminate* normally or *stop* when they receive a SIGSTOP, a SIGTSTP, a SIGTTIN or a SIGTTOU. Normally, the parent process receives a SIGCHLD signal in either case. However, if the SA_NOCLDSTOP is set when you assign a SIGCHLD handler, you will only receive a SIGCHLD when your child processes terminate.
SA_NOCLDWAIT	This is complicated. When you wait() for a child process, it passes its status code to you when it dies. However, if you are not waiting for the child process when it dies, it becomes a "zombie process" (you can see them in ps when you're debugging multithreaded Kylix apps) until you collect its status code with a wait() function **unless** you either set your SIGCHLD handler to SIG_IGN or set the SA_NOCLDWAIT in the SIGCHLD handler's flags. You do **not** need to do this if your child processes are threads created *via* a Kylix TThread.
SA_SIGINFO	Specifies that you are using a new signal handler syntax that passes a pointer to a siginfo record to the handler in addition to the signal number parameter. The siginfo record contains information on which user process sent the signal, or detailed information about the cause of a kernel-generated signal. Note that the man page is wrong where SA_SIGINFO is concerned. Under Linux, the __sigaction_handler field of the sigaction struct is actually a *union* (or a *variant record* in Pascal) of a pointer to either a TSigActionHandler function or to a procedure(Signal: Integer; const SigInfo: siginfo_t; const Context: ucontext_t); cdecl;. To use this ternary form, use the overloaded forms of sigaction() from my lib/LibcX that allow you to pass either a PSigAction or a PSigInfo, and be sure to include the SA_SIGINFO bit in the sa_flags bitmap.
SA_ONSTACK SA_STACK	Obsolete. A BSD-compatible feature that appears to have been abandoned.
SA_RESTART	By default, signals received during a "slow" system call, like a socket or pipe read, abort the call with an EINTR error. If this flag is set, the call is automatically restarted.

SA_NODEFER	Allow the signal handler to be called recursively.
SA_NOMASK	
SA_RESETHAND	In some special cases, you may **want** the old signal() 'one
SA_ONESHOT	shot' behavior of resetting the signal handler to SIG_DFL.

The sa_restorer field appears to be obsolete. It was meant to be a pointer to a stack swapping procedure that would be invoked before the interrupt handler. The value of sa_restorer doesn't matter; it should only be read if the SA_ONSTACK flag is set. According to the man pages, this flag doesn't appear to actually be read, but it would still be wise to avoid setting it.

Advanced signal handling

Every process has a *signal mask*—the set of signals whose handling is being deferred. This is usually set automatically as the logical or of all the sa_mask's of any signals being handled, but you can also change it manually with

```
function sigprocmask( How: Integer;
                      SigSet: PSigset; OldSigSet: PSigset ): Integer; cdecl;
```

If the SigSet parameter is not equal to Nil, the How parameter should be one of SIG_BLOCK, SIG_UNBLOCK, or SIG_SETMASK. SIG_BLOCK adds the SigSet's signals to the current mask; SIG_UNBLOCK removes the SigSet's signals from the current mask; and SIG_SETMASK replaces the current mask with SigSet. In all cases, any pending signals that are unmasked will execute more or less immediately. If the SigSet parameter is Nil, then sigprocmask() has no effect on the signal mask. If the OldSigSet parameter is not Nil, sigprocmask() sets it to the signal mask before any How/SigSet mandated changes.

Some specialized non-GUI applications may want to block until they receive a particular signal.

```
function sigsuspend(const SigSet: TSigset): Integer; cdecl;
```

temporarily sets the signal mask to SigSet, and doesn't return until one of the signals in SigSet has been handled. On return, the signal mask is reset to its state before the call to sigsuspend(). Note that if SigSet contains more than one signal, there is no way to tell from the sigsuspend() call which signal unblocked it, though of course the signal handler itself could save this information if you need it. You might also look into the functions sigwait(),sigwaitinfo(), and sigtimedwait().

Finally, if you need to find out what signals are pending,

```
function sigpending(var SigSet: TSigset): Integer; cdecl;
```

fills in SigSet with all pending signals.

Signal handlers

Like interrupt handlers, signal handlers should be as short and simple as possible. As with threaded code, you have to always be alert to the fact that a signal handler may execute in the middle of **any** statement. However, where threaded code can use mutexes to protect critical sections, mutexes are worse than useless with signal handlers. A signal handler executes as an interruption of a specific process; it's not an independent thread that can block and then resume. If a process uses a mutex to protect a critical section and is interrupted by a signal handler that tries to lock the mutex, the signal handler will never get the lock and the process will hang.

The key to safely modifying global data structures from a signal handler is to use the process's signal mask to make sure that any updates can't be interrupted by a signal that may also want to change the structure. That is, before starting to update any structure that's also updated in a signal handler, you block those signals, using code like

```
// Blocks signals in Signals array; returns CURRENT signal mask
function BlockSignals(const Signals: array of integer): TSigSet; overload;
var
  NewMask: TSigSet;
  Index:   integer;
begin
  sigemptyset(NewMask); // initialize set
  for Index := Low(Signals) to High(Signals) do // add Signals
    sigaddset(NewMask, Signals[Index]);
  sigprocmask(SIG_BLOCK, @ NewMask, @ Result);
end; // BlockSignals

// Sets signal mask; may be used to restore mask after BlockSignals()
procedure SetSignalMask(const SigSet: TSigSet);
begin
  sigprocmask(SIG_SETMASK, @ SigSet, Nil);
end; // SetSignalMask
```

```
procedure Update;
var
  SignalMask: TSigSet;
begin
  // Block ALL signals that update the structure
  SignalMask := BlockSignals([SIGHUP, SIGALRM]);
  try
    // update the data structure
  finally
    SetSignalMask(SignalMask);
  end;
end; // Update
```

You might think at first blush that you don't want to thus block signals within the signal handler, that the signal handler should just go ahead and update the data structures without changing the signal mask. However, signal handlers can be interrupted by other signals (though the current signal is blocked, unless you specified SA_NOMASK in sigaction's sa_flags parameter) so it's actually just as important to block signals within signal handlers as within normal code. The only time you might consider not protecting an update by masking off signals is when you are quite sure that you are only doing this update within a single signal handler. However, even this is a dubious practice; you may only be handling a single signal today, but next year whoever inherits your code may find it necessary to handle another signal.

In general, the safest course is to wrap **all** updates of structures that may be changed in a signal handler within code that temporarily blocks those signals. You have two different ways you can do this: You can include all signal handlers that affect the data that *this* signal handler touches in the sa_mask parameter to sigaction(), or you can simply use the same mask/modify/unmask routines in your signal handler that you use in your regular code. The former makes for shorter, faster-returning signal handlers, as the mask is built when you install the handler; the latter is probably somewhat safer (*ie*, less subject to 'code rot'), as you're defining the mask at the point of use, rather than at the point where you install the handler. Also, since a mask/modify/unmask routine keeps the mask in effect for a shorter time than a sigaction mask (which is in effect the whole time the signal handler is running), you can use a 'maintenance-free' mask like

```
// Blocks ALL signals; returns CURRENT signal mask
function BlockSignals(const Signals: array of integer): TSigSet; overload;
var
  NewMask: TSigSet;
begin
  sigfillset(NewMask); // initialize set
  sigprocmask(SIG_BLOCK, @ NewMask, @ Result);
end; // BlockSignals
```

which blocks all signals, thus ensuring that your code can never break because someone adds or modifies a signal handler without properly updating all signal masks.

Reentrant functions

Function calls present an issue related to global data: Some are reentrant; other are not. Note that reentrancy is not entirely the same thing as "thread safe". A reentrant routine is one that can be called while it's still in progress—it uses no global state. A thread-safe routine may be reentrant, or it may use critical sections to serialize access to global data. You can call reentrant routines from a signal handler, but you can't call routines that use locking unless you wrap *all* calls to that routine within a try/finally block that masks all signals before the call, and then restores the original signal mask when it returns.

```
procedure CallLockingRoutine;
var
  SignalMask: TSigSet;
begin
  // Block ALL signals
  SignalMask := BlockSignals;
  try
    // call the locking routine
  finally
    SetSignalMask(SignalMask);
  end;
end; // CallLockingRoutine
```

A signal handler can wait for another thread to release a global resource, just like the interrupted process can. What it can't do is wait for the interrupted thread to release a lock. Making locking calls in a 'no signal' environment means that a signal handler will never hang a process by trying to lock a mutex that the interrupted process has locked. (Linux supports optional recursive mutexes, which allow the same process to lock the mutex more than once. A process won't hang if a signal handler tries to lock a recursive mutex that the interrupted process had locked—but the signal handler probably will scramble the data that the lock was meant to protect.)

In general, it's very hard to be absolutely sure you know every routine that any given high-level routine will ever call, as *this* routine may call *that* routine which in turn calls *these* routines and *those* routines, and so on. This in turn means that it's very hard to be absolutely sure that you know if a given routine is signal safe or safe. While you can use `CallLockingRoutine`'s signal-blocking technique for a few key routines that you need to call from signal handlers, this can slow down your whole program. The safest course is to keep your signal handlers as short and simple as possible, with a minimum of subroutine calls that you need to check for safety.

That said, you obviously should not call any Kylix library routines that are explicitly described as not thread-safe. Conversely, if a Kylix library routine is described as thread-safe, it *may* be safe to call from it a signal handler. Unfortunately, the Kylix documentation is written in terms of thread-safety, not signal handler safety, so you do need to think carefully—and read the source—before using any Kylix library routines in a signal handler. Remember, too, that there are large classes of inline code—like string expressions—that actually entail 'magic' procedure calls and/or dynamic memory management.

You should avoid using AnsiString's in signal handlers. Similarly, you should not call SetLength() on a dynamic array or Create or Free an object. If you really need to do any of this, you can install SetMemoryManager routines (see Chapter 7) that block signals *ala* `CallLockingRoutine`, but Kylix apps use so much dynamic memory that this will probably have a very significant effect on your application's performance.

Similar issues apply to the Linux API calls in Libc, but it can be even harder to tell what's safe and what is not. To be absolutely safe, you should limit yourself to the guaranteed reentrant functions in Table 10-11, which is taken from the sigaction page of The Single UNIX® Specification, Version 2 [SUS v2] at `http://www.opengroup.org/onlinepubs/7908799/xshix.html`.

Table 10-11. Libc functions that are signal-handler safe as per SUS v2

_exit()	fork()	read()	stat()
access()	fpathconf()	rename()	sysconf()
aio_error()	fstat()	rmdir()	tcdrain()
aio_return()	fsync()	sem_post()	tcflow()
aio_suspend()	getegid()	setgid()	tcflush()
alarm()	geteuid()	setpgid() tcgetattr()	tcgetpgrp()
cfgetispeed()	getgid()	setsid()	tcsetattr()
cfgetospeed()	getgroups()setuid()	tcsendbreak()	tcsetpgrp()
cfsetispeed()	getpgrp()	sigaction()	time()
cfsetospeed()	getpid()	sigaddset()	timer_getoverrun()
chdir()	getppid()	sigdelset()	timer_gettime()
chmod()	getuid()	sigemptyset()	timer_settime()
chown()	kill()	sigfillset ()	times()
clock_gettime()	link()	sigismember()	umask()
close()	lseek()	signal()	uname()
creat()	mkdir()	sigpause()	unlink()
dup()	mkfifo()	sigpending()	utime()
dup2()	open()	sigprocmask()	wait()
execle()	pathconf()	sigqueue()	waitpid()
execve()	pause()	sigset()	write()
fcntl()	pipe()	sigsuspend()	
fdatasync()	raise()	sleep()	

Now, this is a rather restrictive list, and it doesn't completely agree with Johnson & Troan's (see the Bibliography) Table 13.2 of signal handler safe "Reentrant Functions". When I asked them how they generated that table, they said that the *rule of thumb* under Linux is that "system calls[17] are safe, other calls may be." So, how to tell which is a system call and which is not? The easiest way to tell is that system calls have man pages in section 2, while user space calls have man pages in section 3. Thus, when you type man malloc and get a page headed MALLOC(3), you know that malloc is a user space call, and thus should be avoided within signal handlers. Similarly, when you type man sigprocmask and get a page headed SIGACTION(2), you know that sigprocmask is a system call, and so safe to use within a signal handler. Of course, the way that many Libc calls are also shell commands means that you may get a page in section 1, which doesn't help at all, here. If you type something like man chown and get a page headed CHOWN(1), try typing man 2 chown to see if it has a page in section 2. If it doesn't try man 3 chown. You can also use man -k chown, though in many cases this will return too many matches to be entirely useful.

As you know by now, though, the man pages are far from perfect. It's entirely possible that there isn't a man page in section 2 or section 3. If so, your only real recourse is to examine the list of "syscall numbers" in /usr/include/bits/syscall.h. If the function has a syscall number, it's a system call; if it doesn't, it's a user-space call.

Signals under Kylix

When you use the SysUtils unit, Kylix automatically maps the SIGINT, SIGFPE, SIGSEGV, SIGILL, SIGBUS, and SIGQUIT to exceptions.[18] Since all GUI apps use SysUtils, as do all but the tiniest Kylix console apps, essentially all Kylix applications install signal handlers that map these six signals to Kylix exceptions.

---

17. System calls are calls to kernel code, executed with kernel permissions. They look exactly like normal C function calls, but that's just a wrapper around a messy "syscall" interface that handles the protection switch &c. The other functions in Libc are normal, "user space" calls; they execute with normal, user permissions. (Don't confuse hardware permissions, like the kernel *vs* user distinction, with software permissions like the root *vs* user distinction. When you run as root, you're still running as a user from the hardware's point of view; setuid root programs can't execute privileged instructions any more than normal programs can.)

18. It will not do this mapping in a library. In a Kylix library called from a Kylix application, the mapping will be done anyway. If your library will be called from a non-Kylix application, the mapping will not be done automatically. Conversely, using a non-Kylix library **may** cause trouble for the Kylix signal mappings. See the comments about "HookSignals" in the SysUtils unit for more information.

This mapping of signals to exceptions is really very useful. For example, a SIGFPE can be any of: division by zero; float point stack overflow; a denormal operand; or result overflow or underflow. The exception mapping examines the FPU status, and converts the relatively uninformative SIGFPE into a more specific exception. Similarly, the SIGSEGV exception mapping examines the "trap number" and separates the signal into numeric overflow, range errors, page faults, and stack errors. Generally, you won't want to override the Kylix signal handlers except in very specialized situations.

Note

 *Mapping signals to exceptions does not mean that the exception is raised within a signal handler. The SysUtils code includes some clever hacks that edit the signal handler's context so that it 'returns' to a routine that raises the exception. This means that you do **not** face the same restrictions on what you can do in a mapped exception handler that you do in a signal handler.*

Kylix's handling of SIGINT and SIGQUIT is a bit different than its automatic demultiplexing of SIGFPE, SIGSEGV, SIGILL, and SIGBUS.

SIGINT is generated when the user sends the interrupt character, which is normally ^C but which can be reconfigured by the user. Similarly, SIGQUIT is generated when the user sends the quit character, which is normally ^\ but which can also changed by the user. Kylix maps SIGINT to EControlC and SIGQUIT to EQuit—if DeferUserInterrupts is False, which is its default state.

However, if you set DeferUserInterrupts to True, Kylix won't generate exceptions on either SIGINT and SIGQUIT. Instead, it will simply set SIGINTIssued or SIGQUITIssued to True. It becomes your responsibility to poll these variables. One way to do so is to use a nested pair of try/finally blocks, like

```
try
  DeferUserInterrupts := True;
  try
    // execute code without getting EControlC or EQuit
  finally
    DeferUserInterrupts := False;
  end;
finally
  if SIGINTIssued   then {handle ^C};
  if SIGQUITIssued then {handle ^\};
end;
```

Of course, especially in GUI apps, you may not want SIGINT and SIGQUIT
to either raise an exception or set a flag that you have to poll. You may well
prefer to have these (and other) signals post messages to the GUI thread, as
per Chapter 6. How can you do this, when Qt is not reentrant and thus not
signal-handler safe?

The simplest solution is probably to create a special "signal mapping
thread" that spends most of its life in a sem_wait. The signal handler would
set a flag that indicates which signal just happened, then does a sem_post,
which is the only signal safe semaphore function. When the mapping thread
wakes up, it would examine the flag, and either just call a TMessageForm's
PostMessage method, or call some sort of *per* signal callback. Handling
thread-signal coordination will not be trivial in a multi-threaded (*ie*, other
threads beside the GUI thread and the signal mapping thread) application,
but I leave this as an exercise for the reader.

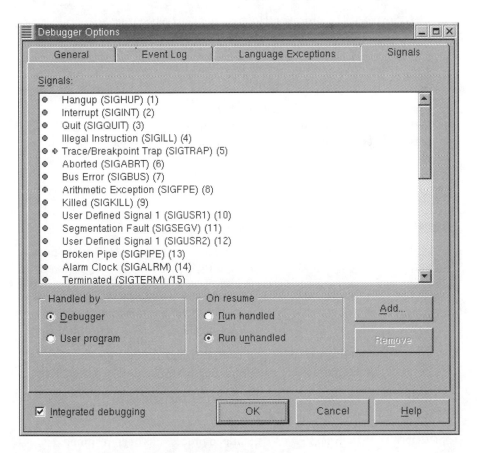

Figure 10-2. Signal handling options

Finally, the Kylix debugger's normal response to a signal is much like that to an exception: it suspends the program, and returns control to the debugger. Just as you can disable this on an exception-by-exception basis, so can you configure the debugger's handling of each signals on a signal-by-signal basis using the Signals tab of the Tools ➤ Debugger Options dialog (Figure 10-2).

Signals and default actions

You can install handlers for all signals except SIGKILL and SIGSTOP. The handler can be an actual procedure pointer, or one of the special values SIG_IGN (ignore) or SIG_DFN (default action). The default action depends on the signal, but will always be one of

- Ignore: The signal is ignored.
- Suspend: The process is stopped, but can be restarted.
- Terminate: The process aborts.
- Dump core: The process aborts and generates a core file, if the system policies permit core files.

Signals that are handled by Kylix have "Mapped" under their Default Action. Some signals have more than one name for various historical reasons; these are shown together, on the same row of Table 10-12, in alphabetical order.

Table 10-12. Signals and default action

Signal	Default action	Cause
SIGABRT SIGIOT	Dump core	A C function called abort(). This happens on assertion violations.
SIGALRM	Terminate	You can request that a SIGALRM be sent at some future time with various functions, including alarm(), setitimer(), and sleep().
SIGBUS	Terminate Mapped	Process ran afoul of some hardware protection besides memory protections.
SIGCHLD SIGCLD	Ignored	Child process terminated.
SIGCONT	Ignored	Stopped process has been resumed; see SIGSTOP.

Table 10-12. Signals and default action (Continued)

Signal	Default action	Cause
SIGFPE	Dump core Mapped	Float point exception.
SIGHUP	Terminate	Originally, terminal disconnect, or "hang up". Commonly used by system services as a message to reread their configuration file(s).
SIGILL	Dump core Mapped	Illegal hardware instruction. This might be either a privileged instruction or a genuine nonsense bitstream.
SIGINT	Terminate Mapped	^C, or whatever the user has mapped the interrupt character to.
SIGIO SIGPOLL	Terminate	As an alternative to blocking on a socket, you can set it to send you a SIGIO whenever it needs attention. Stevens has a whole chapter on this in *Unix Network Programming*, vol 1.
SIGKILL	Terminate	The user killed your process. Cannot be caught.
SIGPIPE	Terminate	You wrote to a pipe that no process is reading.
SIGPROF	Terminate	Profiling timer expired.
SIGPWR	Terminate	Power failure. Normally, this is sent only to the init process by a daemon monitoring the system's UPS; you are not likely to ever need to trap this.
SIGQUIT	Dump core Mapped	^\, or whatever the user has mapped the quit character to.
SIGSEGV	Dump core Mapped	Your process has tried to read or write memory that it does not have permission to read or write.
SIGSTKFLT	Terminate	Coprocessor stack fault
SIGSTOP	Suspend	Cannot be caught. Only generated by explicit kill command.
SIGTERM	Terminate	Usually sent by user *via* shell kill command. You should shut down gracefully.

Table 10-12. Signals and default action (Continued)

Signal	Default action	Cause
SIGTRAP	Dump core	Breakpoint.
SIGTSTP	Suspend	Sent when user sends ^Z, or whatever they have mapped the suspend key to. Has no effect on GUI apps!
SIGTTIN	Suspend	Background (bg) process tried to read from the 'terminal'.
SIGTTOU	Suspend	Background (bg) process tried to write to the 'terminal'.
SIGURG	Ignored	Out-of-band data on a socket.
SIGUSR1	Terminate	Provided for you to send to your processes. You might use this to tell a cooperating process to read shared memory, for example.
SIGUSR2	Terminate	Like SIGUSR1, meant for simple communication between cooperating processes.
SIGVTALRM	Terminate	A setitimer() timer has expired.
SIGWINCH	Ignored	Terminal window has changed size.
SIGXCPU	Terminate	Process has exceeded sysadmin-set CPU limit.
SIGXFSZ	Terminate	Process has exceeded sysadmin-set file size limits.

Extending and correcting Libc

I've referred you a few times to my lib/LibcX unit that contains both corrections for Libc misbindings and functions that Libc simply doesn't supply Pascal bindings for. Naturally, I've reported all these to Borland, so there's a good chance that LibcX will be obsolete by the time you read this—but that doesn't mean that Libc will be absolutely complete and correct. Even if Borland managed to supply correct bindings for every function in glibc 2.2—and history suggests that that's not overwhelmingly likely—Linux is a fast-moving target and the chances are good that there will be at least one new version of glibc between every Kylix release. There's nothing to prevent you from using new functions—provided that you're willing to distribute an updated libc with your application and provided that you're willing to write Pascal bindings.

Probably few of you will want to go that route, but it's not impossible that you will run into misbindings and/or omissions. The most common misbindings are optional pointers declared as var parameters, or non-optional pointers declared as simple pointer parameters. A var parameter is a non-optional pointer because you can't pass Nil, while conversely a pointer parameter is an optional parameter, because you **can** pass Nil.

To correct a misbinding, all you need to do is shadow it with a correct prototype (in the interface of your own version of LibcX, for example) and copy the external implementation from Libc. For example, wait3() is declared in Libc as

```
function wait3( __stat_loc: Integer; __options: Integer;
               usage: PRUsage): pid_t; cdecl;
```

while the man pages (and any Unix programming text) will tell you that the first parameter should actually be a pointer to an integer, which may be Nil if you don't care about the status code. As *per* lib/LibcX, the correct prototype is thus

```
function wait3( Status: PInteger; Options: Integer;
               Usage: PRUsage): pid_t; cdecl;
```

which would be 'implemented' as either

```
function wait3(Status: PInteger; Options: Integer; Usage: PRUsage): pid_t;
       cdecl; external libcmodulename name 'wait3';
```

or, more simply,

```
function wait3; cdecl; external libcmodulename name 'wait3';
```

Correcting omissions is really just as easy—construct a prototype and declare it external—but you do have to be sure you know which library the function 'lives' in. Most Linux API functions are in libc.so.6 (*aka* libcmodulename), but thread functions are in libpthread.so.0 (*aka* libpthreadmodulename), dynamic library functions are in libdl.so.2 (*aka* libdlmodulename), and so on. If you misdeclare the function, your program will compile, link, and load just fine—and die when it tries to call the misbound function.

To find where a function lives you can try to RTFM, but the best resource is the readelf program, whose –s option dumps all the symbols in a program or library. You'll see all sorts of interesting stuff in a symbol dump, but for present purposes, just pipe it to grep to narrow it down to the symbol you're looking for, as in

```
readelf -s /lib/libc.so.6 | grep flock
```

to verify that flock() is indeed defined in libcmodulename.

readelf can also give you clues to more complicated problems, like the way Release 1 conflated chown() with lchown(), but I rather hope that that was a unique case, as I don't want to talk about it here.

Finally, you may run across references to various global variables supplied by libraries that you're using, but that Kylix doesn't expose. For example, I kept reading about an environ variable that, like System.envp, is a pointer to an ARGV-style, Nil-terminated array of PChars. I wanted to get access to it, because there were hints (that didn't pan out) in the man pages that setenv() and putenv() would reset environ; that environ wasn't a static pointer to the starting environment, the way envp is.

It turns out that you can use dlsym() to get the address of any symbol in a shared object (library) that you load with dlopen()—or in the current program. That is, when you pass dlsym() an open handle that you got from dlopen(), it will search the shared object for the symbol. However, if you pass it Nil, it will search the current program—your running program. Thus,

```
dlsym(nil, 'environ')
```

gives the address of the environ pointer, and

```
type
  TPCharArray  = array[0..MaxInt div SizeOf(PChar) - 1] of PChar;
  PPCharArray  = ^ TPCharArray;
  PPPCharArray = ^PPCharArray;

var
  environ: PPCharArray = Nil; // set in init code

initialization
  environ := PPPCharArray( dlsym(nil, 'environ') )^;
end.
```

gives you the actual environ pointer—which, alas, turns out to be identical to envp.

CHAPTER 11
Regexes & Scripts

Regexes & Scripts

REGULAR EXPRESSIONS AND SCRIPTS are much more common in Linux programming than in Windows programming. Regular expressions let you match strings, and extract or replace substrings. They offer a lot of power—a one-line regex can replace several screens of hand-written string code. Because many Windows programmers have little or no experience with regular expressions, this chapter covers the *why* as well as the *how*.

Linux shell scripts have much more powerful operators and control structures than Windows batch files. The traditional Unix programming methodology is to combine small utilities to create new utilities as much as possible, and shell scripts are the glue that holds them together. A Kylix programmer will need to write shell scripts, so I include an introduction that should cover all you'll need to know.

Regular expressions

Regular expressions are much more central to Unix programming than they are to Windows programming. Many Delphi programmers, for example, use regular expressions only to form the occasional complex search/replace string in the code editor—if they use regular expressions at all. There are a few Delphi regular expression libraries, but they're not widely used and there's no standard syntax. Under Unix, on the other hand, regular expressions are everywhere, from vi to less, and from Perl and grep to shell wildcards. (Of course, while regular expressions are widely used under Unix, there's still no standard syntax. The grep program's regular expression syntax is not wholly compatible with egrep or Perl, and all three are quite incompatible with—and much more powerful than—shell wildcards.) There's even a POSIX regular expression API so that C—and Kylix!—applications can easily use regular expressions. I'll turn to this API after a bit of background on what regular expressions are and what they're good for.

A regular expression [or *regex*] is an expression formed according to the rules of a "regular language" (as opposed to a "context-free" or "context-sensitive" language). The rules specify a syntax for describing pieces of text: A regex is a description of a search term. What makes regexes so popular in

Unix circles is that the syntax allows you to do much more than just search for 'foo'. You can search for 'foo' followed by any one of a specific set of characters (*eg*, you could match 'fool' and 'foot' but not 'food' or 'foos') or for 'foo' followed by 's' or 't' and then maybe '-' and then 'ball', which would match 'foosball', 'football', 'foos-ball', and 'foot-ball' but not 'the **food** fight after the **ball** game.'

In general, a regular expression consists of literal text—which must be matched exactly—mixed freely with various expressions that describe which characters are acceptable at this point in the match. The expressions can be as specific as 'match this character only' or as broad as 'match any character'. You can specify sets of characters to match, and there are various predefined sets for matching alphanumeric characters, white space, and so on. In addition, each wild card can be followed by a repeat count. The repeat count defaults to 'one and only one', but you can specify 'at least one', 'any number', or even 'at least *this* many but no more than *that* many'.

What's more, a regular expression can do more than simply return match/no-match. If a regex contains parenthesized subexpressions, a match will also return the substrings that matched each parenthesized subexpressions. Thus, a regex can easily extract everything between a valid HTML file's <body> and </body> (a regex can't handle invalid HTML, with nested <body> and </body> tags), or the last unquoted tag value in an <a> tag. (See *More regex syntax examples*, below, for these regexes.)

One thing that you can do with parenthesized subexpressions is to use regexes as inverse functions for Format() or WriteLn(). Those routines take a 'picture' of the output and pour data into it; regexes take a 'picture' of the input and pull data out of it. Neither 'picture' is a model of clarity, but both save significant amounts of your time.

With this sort of expressive power, a single regular expression can often replace two or three screens worth of hand-coded string matching code. While regexes, like C, can be easier to write than to read, the sheer economy of expression can make a regex easier to write and maintain than complex string matching code. You have to read a regex carefully—but there's less to read. What's more, 'code' in a regex is localized in a way that hand-coded string code isn't. The bits between the 'foo' and the 'ball' may be wrong, but it's clear that they're describing what may come between 'foo' and 'ball'. The same simply isn't true for hand-made code. A state machine or recursive descent parser may invoke code anywhere in a sea of predicates and actions. While Kylix stands ready to help you navigate, with CTRL+CLICK &c, you just have to do less jumping around with regexes. While a hand-coded parser can handle patterns that a regex cannot, anything that you **can** do with a regex will be easier to implement and maintain as a regex than as a hand-coded parser.

Finally, all this power and flexibility is pretty cheap. When you first use a regular expression, it gets compiled to a finite state machine so that most regular expressions (generally those without "back references") can be evaluated quickly. (See Table 11-1, below.) This does mean that first use is more expensive than subsequent use, but the compile cost is pretty modest even on today's slower machines. Subsequently, a regular expression will certainly be faster than a naïve Pos/Delete string ripper, and will generally be more than competitive with—perhaps even faster than—a more sophisticated, offset based search-and-extract using something like the FindString() function in Chapter 1. The tradeoff is that the state machine's tables do consume many kilobytes of RAM (exactly how many depends on the type of wildcards and repeat counts you use)—but even the largest regex state machine doesn't really have much impact on a turn-of-the-century machine with hundreds of megabytes.

Table 11-1 is the output of the RegexBenchmark project in the ch11/ Regex project group. This project constructs a Text string

```
'We had a great <a '^I^I' href=http://f00df1ght.com  name="f00df1ght">food '
+ 'fight</a> yesterday'
```

and then prepends either 0, 1K, 4K, 256K, or 1024K pad bytes (repeats of either the partial-match string 'football' or ParamStr(1), if ParamStr(1) is not blank) to construct a string to search in. The header row of table 11-1 contains the total length of the search string. The "PosRatio" row compares the speed of a regex match for 'food' to a Pos('food', Text) match, for each length of Text. The "Regex(1)" row compares that same trivial regex match with a more complicated match that looks for 'food' followed by 'day' ('food.*day'). The "Regex(2)" row compares the trivial regex with a much more complicated regex that not only looks for valid HTML anchor tags with a href= clause that's not in double quotes, but also returns the unquoted string as a subexpression, for possible remediation - '<a[[:space:]]+[^>]*href=([^"][^[:space:]">]+[^"])[^>]*>.+</a>'. I won't try to pretend that what this regex does is obvious on inspection (I dissect it in the next section), but neither would be the equivalent hand-written Pascal code—and the Pascal code would be many times as long and would take significantly longer to write.

Table 11-1. Output of the ch11/RegexBenchmark project

	90	1114	4186	16474	262234	1048666
PosRatio	504%	239%	236%	235%	232%	235%
Regex(1)	196%	112%	103%	101%	100%	100%
Regex(2)	22290%	2219%	605%	184%	44%	41%

As you can see, for very short strings, the regex match takes about five times as long as Pos, but this decreases asymptotically towards a 'mere' two and a third times as the string being searched gets longer. That is, there's a setup cost going into the regex matcher but, once in, the per-char searched cost is not all that much worse than a simplistic char-by-char match. Importantly, though, while the regex search for 'food' followed by 'day' takes about twice as long as the trivial regex search for 'food', the ratio drops to near equivalence for relatively long target strings. Similarly, while the more complex regex search—for HTML anchor tags with unquoted href= clauses—is a whopping 223 times as long as the simple regex search for short strings, the ratio also decreases asymptotically to the point where it's actually faster to do the complex regex search on a quarter meg string than to do the simple one. These numbers depend heavily on the pad string that you use, but this is some pretty impressive scaling behavior.

Obviously, the exact cost will depend on how complex the regex is, how many partial matches there are, and how far into the regex the evaluator gets before meeting a mismatch. But basically, regexes scale well against complexity of regex when you measure CPU time, and they scale spectacularly against complexity of regex when you measure programmer time. This makes regexes ideally suited for real-world text processing tasks like decoding formatted dates; parsing data from an .ini file; parsing a mini-language in a more free-form configuration file; or spidering web sites.

Regexes can't do everything. For example, you can't write a regex that can recognize an improperly nested <a><a></a></a> tag. But, within the (rather generous) limits of their abilities they're definitely the technology of choice.

The POSIX regex syntax

The POSIX regex API uses essentially the same regex syntax as the grep and egrep utilities. (This isn't particularly surprising, considering that the GNU versions of these programs use the GNU regex library, which is basically a superset of the POSIX regex API.) This regex syntax is more verbose and not quite as powerful as Perl's regex syntax, but is still quite useful and capable.

You can use `egrep` to experiment with the "extended" regex syntax, or you can use the Syntax project of the ch11/Regex project group (Figure 11-1) to experiment interactively, loading various text files and seeing the results of various search expressions (Figure 11-2).

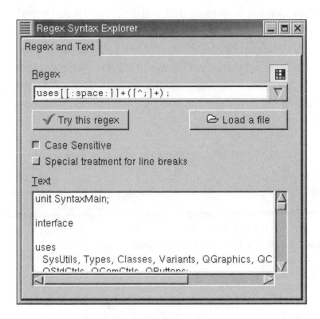

Figure 11-1. The Syntax project

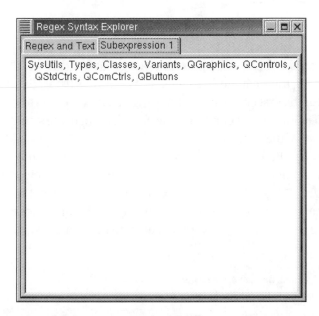

Figure 11-2. Extracting subexpressions

Now, regular expression syntax is actually a surprisingly deep subject. Some seemingly fine distinctions can mean the difference between your regex matching as you expect it to and not. More, mismatching is often not an all or nothing proposition: Just as with a hand-coded string parser, you can write a regex that matches some of the strings that you want it to, but not all of them. Or that matches some of the strings that you don't want it to. Or both.

But you're more likely to run into problems with fancy, subtle regexes than with simple ones, and you're more likely to write simple regexes than complex ones, so I'm not going to try to cover every detail here. When a regex doesn't work as expected, just take your regex one element at a time. At each step, compare what you actually told the regex to do with what you wanted it to do, and you'll be fine.

Tip

For more information about writing and debugging regexes, see the Programming Perl *"camel book." For more information on how regexes are evaluated, see the famous* Compilers *"dragon book." Both are in the Bibliography. There's also an O'Reilly book I haven't read,* Mastering Regular Expressions, *which may be helpful. Finally, ActiveState's "Komodo" at* http://www.activestate.com/ASPN/Downloads/Komodo *includes a Perl regex debugger,* Rx. *The Perl regex syntax is not the same as the POSIX regex syntax, but the two are close enough that you may be able to use Rx to get some insight into faulty POSIX regexes.*

A regular expression is a stream of *elements*. A string that matches the regex contains a substring that matches each element in turn.[1] That is, the regex evaluator looks for the first character of the string that matches the first element of the regex. If it finds one, it compares the next element of the string with the second element of the regex, and so on.

Each element may be a literal character or a *description* of a set of characters. A trivial regex that consists of nothing but literal characters matches any string that Pos(Regex, TargetString) would. Certain characters, like the dot, ., have special meanings in the regex pattern language. For example, the dot matches any single character.[2] If you want to specify a literal match on

---

1. The 'substring' may, of course, be the whole string.
2. Whether the dot matches a newline character depends on the flags you pass to the regex compiler.

one of these special characters, you have to *escape* it, or precede it with a backslash, like \. .

Some elements match empty strings, the strings between characters. This sounds a little strange, I know, but it allows you to 'anchor' a search term at the start of a word or line. That is, '\<verb\>' matches the string 'verb' when it's a stand-alone word, but not when it's part of another word, like 'verbose'.

Table 11-2. Regex 'singleton' elements

Element	Interpretation
.	Matches any one character.
\w	Matches any one alphanumeric (or "word") character.
\W	Matches any one non-alphanumeric character.
^	Matches the empty string at the beginning of a line.
$	Matches the empty string at the end of a line.
\<	Matches the empty string at the beginning of a word (a "word" is a sequence of alphanumeric characters).
\>	Matches the empty string at the end of a word.
\b	Matches the empty string at the edge (beginning or end) of a word.
\B	Matches an empty string that's **not** at the edge of a word.

In addition to the 'singletons' in Table 11-2, you can specify that a particular element must match one of a set of characters by enclosing the characters in square brackets. For example, [tT] will match either 't' or 'T'. You can specify a range of characters by separating them with a hyphen, or dash. For example, [a-z] will match any characters in the range 'a'..'z'. If a set starts with a caret, ^, it matches any characters **not** in the set. For example, [^;] matches any character except a ';'.

There are 11 named groups of characters, like [:alnum:], that you can include in sets. (These are the 11 names on the Palette form of the Syntax project, as well as in Table 11-3, below.) The names are rather ridiculously verbose, but they not only save you from the possibility of making mistakes in specifying a set like [a-zA-Z0-9], they also work across locales in a way that a 'literal set' like [a-zA-Z0-9] does not. You can only use these named groups in character sets—[[:alnum:]] is the same as \w, while a 'bare' [:alnum:] is a set containing the six literal characters ':', 'a', 'l', 'n', 'u', and 'm'.

Table 11-3. Regex named, locale-dependent character groups

Name	Interpretation
[:alnum:]	Alphanumeric characters.
[:alpha:]	Alphabetic characters.
[:cntrl:]	Control characters.
[:digit:]	Numeric digits.
[:graph:]	Non-space characters.
[:lower:]	Lower-case characters.
[:print:]	Printable characters—the opposite of [:cntrl:].
[:punct:]	Punctuation.
[:space:]	White space.
[:upper:]	Upper-case characters.
[:xdigit:]	Hexadecimal digit.

Any regex element can be followed by one of the *repetition operators* in Table 11-4. When a regex element is **not** followed by a repetition operator, it's mandatory—it must be present for the match to succeed. A repetition operator can make an element optional and/or specify the maximum number of allowable repeats.

Table 11-4. Regex repetition operators

Operator	Interpretation
?	The preceding element is optional: It may appear zero or one times.
+	The preceding element is mandatory but may repeat: It may appear one or more times.
*	The preceding element is optional but may repeat: It may appear zero or more times. Note that .* will match anything—even an empty string.
{n}	The preceding element must appear *n* and only *n* times.

Table 11-4. Regex repetition operators (Continued)

Operator	Interpretation
{n,}	The preceding element must appear at least *n* times. {1,} is the same as +.
{n,m}	The preceding element must appear at least *n* times but no more than *m* times.

You can group elements together with parentheses and then apply a repeat count to the group. For example,

```
(\$[[:xdigit:]]{1,8}[[:space:]]*,[[:space:]]*){3}\$[[:xdigit:]]{1,8}
```

will match a list of four 32-bit hexadecimal digits (in Object Pascal $ format) separated by commas and optional white space. If you take it element by element, it's not so daunting:

- The (starts a group.

- Since $ is the *metacharacter* that matches the end of a line, it's escaped here, \$, to match a literal '$'.

- [[:xdigit:]]{1,8} specifies from one to eight hexadecimal digits, immediately following the '$'.

- [[:space:]]*,[[:space:]]* is a three element group that specifies optional white space, followed by a mandatory comma, followed by more optional white space.

-){3} closes the group which started on the first (, and specifies that the whole group must repeat three times. Three 32-bit hexadecimal digits, separated by commas.

- \$[[:xdigit:]]{1,8} simply repeats the hexadecimal digit 'picture' again, for the fourth list element.

The parentheses can be described as creating *subexpressions*, which can be used for more than complex repeats. For example, \0 will match the last string that matched the first parenthesized subexpression in the regex. If the subexpression has no repeat count, the *back reference* will simply match the string that matched the subexpression. However, if the subexpression does have a repeat count, as in the above hexadecimal list regex, the back reference is to the last string that matched. For example, if the hexadecimal list regex matched $1234, $4567, $34, $56, \0 would match "$34, ". (Because ,[[:space:]]* is within the parentheses, the back reference would include the comma and the white space.)

Note

Using back references makes your regular expressions very slow and hard to read. Avoid them if you possibly can.

A more common use for subexpressions is extracting and/or replacing strings from a larger string. For example, if we enclose the whole hex list regex in parens

((\$[[:xdigit:]]{1,8}[[:space:]]*,[[:space:]]*){3}\$[[:xdigit:]]{1,8})

it will still match a list of four hexadecimal digits, but now \0 will contain the whole list that matched. (\1 will contain the third element in the list.) That is, if you apply the regex to a string, you will get a Boolean that tells you whether or not there is a list of four hex digits in it—and you can also extract the list. See *The POSIX regex API* and *The IRegEx Object Pascal wrapper* sections, below, for more information.

Finally, while regexes normally consist of a stream of elements, each linked by an implicit (imaginary!) *concatenation operator*, and each of which must be matched in turn, you can use the *alternation operator*, |, to say that the regex must match *this* stream or *that* stream. The repetition operators have a higher precedence than the concatenation operator (*ie*, repetition applies only to a single element, unless the elements are grouped with parens) and both take precedence over the alternation operator. What that means is that foo|bar will match 'foo' or 'bar'. If you wanted something more like fo[ob]ar, you would use fo(o|b)ar. You wouldn't actually do this, because fo[ob]ar is faster than fo(o|b)ar, but you might use something like f(ri|l)ed to match 'fried' or 'fled'.

More regex syntax examples

By now, some of the regexes I mentioned earlier should seem pretty trivial. To extract everything between a HTML <body> and </body>, use

```
<body>(.*)</body>
```

—and the case insensitive flag I mention in the regex API section, below. Similarly, the example in Figure 11-2

```
uses[[:space:]]+([^;]+);
```

should be pretty clear. It returns the contents of the first uses clause by matching everything between the first non-white space after a uses string and the next semicolon. Perhaps, though, you want only the implementation section's uses clause, if any. In that case, you can either match again, starting after the first match point—or just change the regex to either

```
implementation.+uses[[:space:]]+([^;]+);
```

or (more carefully)

```
\<implementation\>.*\<uses\>[[:space:]]+([^;]+);
```

Getting the last unquoted attribute value in an <a> tag is more complicated. Broadly, we want to look (ignoring case) for an opening <a, followed by a tag= that's not followed by a quoted value, followed by the >. But this simplistic description illustrates the most common cause of regex bugs: It ignores key features of the problem space. As a result, my first pass at some elements was too restrictive while others were too accepting, resulting in a regex that didn't recognize some tags that it should have, and/or returning more than it should. After a bit of perfectly normal fiddling, I ended up with

```
<a[[:space:]]+[^>]*[[:alnum:][:space:]_]+=[[:space:]]*([^'"> ]+)[^>]*>
```

The element-by-element analysis is revealing:

- Obviously, it starts by looking for <a.

- The next pair of elements is where I made my first mistake. Initially, I coded it as simply [[:space:]]+, since there must be some white space between the <a and the first *tag=value* pair. But this ignores the possi-

bility that the first tag(s) is (are) quoted, but a subsequent one is not! By using [[:space:]]+ [^>]*, the subsequent tag matching elements can match anything between the <a and the >. An expression like this will have to *backtrack* because the [^>]+ will initially try to match everything up to the >. After doing this *greedy match*, it will find that there's nothing left to match the unquoted tag elements, so it will repeatedly release the rightmost character from the greedy match and try again to match the next element. If it finds a match for the next element, matching proceeds from there; otherwise, the matching backs up to the <a elements and tries to match them further on in the target string.

- The [[:alnum:]][:space:]_]+=[[:space:]]* element triple also contained plenty of room for error. My first pass was simply [[:alnum:]]+=, which ignored the facts that tags can contain underscores, and that there can be spaces between the attribute name, the = character, and the attribute value. Many regex errors are of this simple sort.

- ([^'">]+) matches and returns an arbitrary length string of characters containing no quotes, spaces, or right angle brackets. (Would you have remembered the >? I didn't.)

- There may be any number of tags and values after the last unquoted one—[^>]* matches everything from the end of the unquoted value to the closing >.

- Finally, of course, all this is moot if there's no closing >.

For the final example in this section, I return to the complex regex from the ch11/RegexBenchmark project,

```
<a[[:space:]]+[^>]*href=([^"][^[:space:]">]+[^"])[^>]*>.+</a>
```

This is obviously similar to the above regex, though a bit simpler because it's looking specifically for unquoted href= clauses, not any unquoted value, and because it doesn't support either single-quoted attribute values or spaces around the = sign. Thus, this regex can match href= instead of [[:alnum:]_]+=. The next difference is revealing, in its way. Is there any real difference between ([^"][^[:space:]">]+[^"]) and ([^'">]+)? Not really— except that the latter is smaller and presumably faster. There's More Than One Way To Do It, but some ways are more equal than others. The final difference is that this regex won't accept a 'bare' <a> tag. Instead, it also looks explicitly for at least one character followed by a </a>.

> **Note**
>
>
> *There are more regex examples in the projects in Section 4.*

The POSIX regex API

Linux (and Kylix) actually supports two different regex API's—the Gnu API that revolves around the `re_pattern_buffer`, and the POSIX API that revolves around the `regex_t`. The two are actually the same datatype (the POSIX API is implemented by the GNU regex library), and it's possible—I haven't tried it— that they are intercompatible, that you can use both sets of calls with the same regex_t. The Gnu API seems to offer a bit more capability, especially when it comes to optimizing matches and searching subsets of a PChar string. The Gnu API is well documented in Libc, which is good, because there aren't any man pages for it—and I'm not going to talk about it. The POSIX API is quite a bit simpler, and it's probably more portable, but the real reason is that I already have IRegEx code (below) that uses the POSIX functions.

The POSIX regex API is really quite simple, containing four functions, two data structures, and a couple of sets of bitmap bit names. The basic idea is that you compile a regex string "pattern" to a regex_t (or TRegEx in Kylix-speak) with regcomp(). If regcomp() succeeds, it fills in the regex_t, which you can treat entirely as an opaque type, except for the `re_nsub` field, which holds the number of subexpressions the compiler found in the pattern. (It's equally valid to think of `re_nsub` as holding the number of substrings you can extract from the target string after a match.)

Once you've compiled a regex, you apply it to a target string with regexec(). This takes a regex_t, a target string, an optional substring information buffer, and a couple of flags.

When you're done with the compiled regex, you should free it with regfree. You can call regerror to get a human readable text version of any regex error code.

Compiling a regex

Before you can use a regex to test a string or to extract substrings, you have to compile it with the regcomp() function,

```
function regcomp( var __preg:    TRegEx;
                      __pattern: PChar;
                      __cflags:  Integer ): Integer; cdecl;
```

which takes a regex string and a "compile flags" [cflags] bitmap, and fills in a regex_t (TRegex) structure. As with most Linux API functions, regcomp() returns 0 on success, or one of several non-zero error codes. Note that these are **not** drawn from the usual errno.h name space, but will instead be members of the Libc.reg_errcode_t enum. It's possible for regcomp to fail because the system ran out of memory, but almost all the error codes involve poorly formed regexes, or regexes that are so complex that the compiled pattern breaks the implementation limit of 2^{16} bytes *per* compiled pattern.

Note

I don't cover regcomp error codes here, because I recommend that you avoid using the API directly and use my IRegEx wrapper (below) where possible.

You can set four bits in the cflags argument. Note that the lib/RegEx unit redefines these (and the eflags bits, below) so that you can use an IRegEx without using Libc.

| REG_EXTENDED | Use "extended" regex syntax instead of "basic" regex syntax. The difference seems to revolve mostly around the { character, but I confess to finding the documentation baffling. Rather than investigate the differences, I usually just specify REG_EXTENDED. |

| REG_ICASE | Regex matches are case sensitive by default; this switch allows you to make them case insensitive. Note that even case insensitive source code (like Object Pascal or HTML) may contain case sensitive filenames or URL's. Note also that character classes are **not** affected by this switch; even with the REG_ICASE switch, [xy] will match only the lowercase letters x and y. To make a character class ignore case, you have to explicitly code something like [xyXY]. |

REG_NEWLINE	If REG_NEWLINE is set, newline characters within the string are treated specially; otherwise, they act like any other whitespace character. If REG_NEWLINE is **not** set, ^ and $ match only the beginning and end of the string you're searching with regexec(). If it **is** set, they match the beginning and end of lines within the string. Also, if REG_NEWLINE is set, the 'dot' singleton will not match a newline character, and a "non-matching list", [^list], will not match a newline character.
REG_NOSUB	If set, parens in the regex serve only for grouping and overriding the normal operator precedence; regexec() will not fill in the pmatch array. If all you want is a Boolean match/no-match indicator, using this flag will presumably save you a few cycles.

Running a regex

Having successfully compiled a regex to a regex_t with regcomp, you can apply it to strings with regexec().

```
function regexec( const __preg:   TRegEx;
                        __string: PChar;
                        __nmatch: size_t;
                        __pmatch: PRegMatch;
                        __eflags: Integer): Integer; cdecl;
```

This takes a pointer to a compiled regex_t (*aka* TRegEx); a null terminated string to search; the number of entries in the pmatch array; a pointer to an array of regmatch_t records; and an "execute flags" [eflags] bitmap.

The nmatch parameter, which contains the number of entries in the array pmatch points to, will generally be equal to preg.re_nsub + 1. The re_nsub field contains the numbers of substrings that you can extract, but the pmatch^[0] entry will contain 'match' info for the whole string. You can pass a larger array or a smaller array; regexec will set any unused entries in the array to –1.

The pmatch parameter is a pointer to an array of regmatch_t records.

```
type
  regmatch_t = {packed} record
    rm_so: regoff_t;  { Byte offset from string's start to substring's start.}
    rm_eo: regoff_t;  { Byte offset from string's start to substring's end.  }
  end;
```

Object Pascal dynamic arrays (`array of regmatch_t`) work perfectly well here, which obviously makes allocation very easy.

```
SetLength(fPositions, fRegEx.re_nsub + 1); // Positions[0] is whole __String
regexec( fRegEx, PChar(__String),
         fRegEx.re_nsub + 1, PRegMatch(fPositions), Flags );
```

The rm_so field is the offset of the first byte [start offset] of the substring within the string being searched. That is, the first byte of the string has a start offset of 0, not 1 as with AnsiString indexing. The rm_so field is the end offset, the offset of the first byte not in the substring. That is, `rm_eo - rm_so` is the length of the substring.

The eflags bitmap has only two possible members, `REG_NOTBOL` and `REG_NOTEOL`, which govern how the ^ and $ metacharacters work. Normally, these will match the beginning and end of the string (as well as the beginning and ends of lines within the string, if the regex was compiled with REG_NEWLINE). It's possible, though, that sometimes you will apply a regex to a string that represents a whole line, where the first and last characters are indeed the beginning and end of lines, while other times you will apply the same regex to a string cut out of a line, where the first and last characters are not the beginning or end of a line. Include REG_NOTBOL in the eflags if you don't want ^ to match the start of the search string, and include REG_NOTEOL in the eflags if you don't want $ to match the end of the search string.

The IRegEx Object Pascal wrapper

My lib/RegEx unit contains an IRegEx interface that gives you access to all the functionality in the POSIX regex API, as well as supporting substring replacement *ala* Perl's s/// [substitute] operator. The RegularExpression() function either compiles a regex string to an IRegEx or raises an ERegEx exception. The IRegEx lets you Match() and extract substrings, or match and Replace() substrings.

I know it's *my code*, but I do recommend that you use my IRegEx wrapper rather than the Libc functions. The IRegEx API is more Pascal oriented, and the fact that it revolves around an interface means that you don't have to worry about regfree()—the interface, and its regex_t, is freed when the interface goes out of scope or is reassigned.[3]

The RegularExpression() function

---

3. Subject, of course, to the *caveat* that Kylix 1.0 doesn't dereference global interfaces when the program terminates.

```
function RegularExpression( const Expression: string;
                            Flags:       CFlags = [REG_EXTENDED] ): IRegEx;
```

is the only public way to create an IRegEx. RegularExpression() takes a regex Expression and an optional CFlags set. If you don't supply the CFlags set, it defaults to [`REG_EXTENDED`]. Because RegularExpression() returns an interface, it's perfectly safe to use it in expressions like

```
if RegularExpression(SomeRegex).Match(SomeText) then {whatever};
```

You might use a one-shot regex like this in situations where you are computing the regular expression at run-time.

If you don't want to use a compile flags set of [`REG_EXTENDED`], you can create one either by explicitly including other REG_x enums, or by using the StrToCFlags() function. This is a case-sensitive, position-insensitive (*ie*, `StrToCFlags('xi')` = `StrToCFlags('ix')`) function that allows you to specify the flags symbolically, much as you do with the Perl `m//` [match] and `s///` [substitute] operators.

'x'	REG_EXTENDED
'i'	REG_ICASE
's'	REG_NEWLINE
'-'	REG_NOSUB

The match group

Conceptually, the IRegEx interface is divided into two groups, the match group and the replace group, that correspond to Perl's match and substitute operators. The match group consists of the two Match() functions and a handful of substring routines.

The basic Match() function

```
function Match( const __String:     string;
                      Flags:        EFlags = [];
                      ExtractMatches: boolean = True): boolean; overload;
```

takes a string to match against the compiled regex, an optional EFlags set, and an optional boolean that allows you to skip substring extraction. There is also a basically identical overloaded version that takes a PChar instead of a string. This is supplied just so you can find subsequent matches without having to explicitly Copy() a tail string. That is, you would `Match(@Target[LastMatch])` rather than `Match(Copy(Target, LastMatch, MaxInt))`.

As with the CFlags parameter to RegularExpression(), you can specify the optional EFlags parameter to Match() either as a compile time constant, or by calling the StrToEFlags function.

'^'	REG_NOTBOL
'$'	REG_NOTEOL

Obviously enough, Match() returns True if the regex matches the __String, and False if it does not. You can use the substring routines

```
function  SubStringCount: integer;
function  SubString(N: integer): string; // N in [0..SubStringCount-1]
function  SubStrings: TArrayOfString;
procedure GetSubStrings(const List: TStrings);
```

whether or not the regex matches, but if Match() returns False (or you passed False for the optional ExtractMatches parameter), then SubStringCount will return 0, and SubStrings will return an empty `array of string`. The rt project in the ch11/Regex project group demonstrates the use of SubStrings and SubStringCount.

The list of substring routines may appear a bit repetitive—because it is. Each application is different, and one application may only need one or two of the substrings where another application may need all of them. One application may more naturally use a dynamic array, where another application more naturally uses a TStrings. Thus, IRegEx supplies three different ways to get the same substring information.

1. The SubStringCount returns the number of substrings extracted. This will always be either 0 or re_nsub. The SubString function allows you to read the extracted strings one by one, from 0 to SubStringCount—1. (There are also MatchCount and MatchString properties that correspond to the SubStringCount and SubString functions.)

2. The SubStrings function returns an `array of string`, which may be empty.

3. The GetSubStrings procedure sets a TStrings list to the extracted substrings, if any. GetSubStrings expects you to pass it an existing list—the `const` parameter means that it can't create one for you if the List parameter is Nil—which it will Clear and then set.

Finally, the RegMatches function

```
function  RegMatches: TArrayOfRegMatch;
```

gives you direct access to the `array of regmatch_t` that regexec() sets. This will always contain `re_nsub + 1` elements, even if you told the Match function not to ExtractMatches.[4] You might use the RegMatches array if you really only want to extract one or two substrings, but the regex needed several sets of parens for grouping or controlling precedence.

The replace group

The IRegEx replace group consists of six overloaded functions that all do basically the same thing, differing only in how you specify the replacement strings, and in what the functions return. For example, the basic

```
function Replace( const __String:     string;
                  const Replacements: array of string;
                        Flags:        EFlags = [] ): string;
```

takes a string to apply the regex to; an `array of string` that must contain re_nsub elements; and the same optional EFlags set as with Match(). If the regex matches, it replaces all the substrings with the corresponding string from the Replacements array, and returns the new string. If the regex doesn't match, Replace() simply returns the original string.

This function is simple, but you 'lose' the information about whether the regex matched or not. Of course, unless all the replacements equal the matched text, the information is present in the sense that the Result either equals the input __String or it doesn't—but the comparison is not free. Accordingly,

```
function Replace( var    Replacement:  string;
                  const __String:      string;
                  const Replacements:  array of string;
                        Flags:         EFlags = [] ): boolean;
```

---

4. If you created the IRegEx with a REG_NOSUB flag, re_nsub will be 0 and RegMatches will return an array with one regmatch_t. However, regexec will ignore its pmatch parameter, and the regmatch_t you get from RegMatches will contain random values.

sets the Replacement string as a `var` parameter, and returns True or False, matched and replaced or not matched and replaced. You might use this form in a `while` loop to replace all substrings that match the regex.

Similarly, the third form

```
function Replace( var   Replaced:     boolean;
                  const _String:      string;
                  const Replacements: array of string;
                        Flags:        EFlags = [] ): string;
```

returns the new string, but also stores the Replaced state in a boolean variable.

All three are overloaded with identical functions that take a Transform parameter of

```
type
  TTransformer = function (const A: array of string): TArrayOfString;
```

instead of an actual Replacements array. Obviously, the Transform versions are the ones to use when you want to modify the substrings, not replace them with constants. A Transform function can add double quotes to a HTML tag's value; change case; or 'unescape' a string, as in the rt project in the ch11/Regex project group. Similarly, the Transform versions are the way to go when your regex uses parens for grouping or controlling precedence and you don't want to change them all.

For example, the regex `'(&#[[:digit:]]+;)'` matches and returns HTML &# escape sequences. Given a Transform function like

```
function Unescape(const A: array of string): TArrayOfString;
var
  Index: integer;
  This:  string;
begin
  SetLength(Result, Length(A));
  for Index := Low(A) to High(A) do
  begin
    This := A[Index];
    Result[Index] := char(StrToInt( Copy(This, 3, Length(This) - 3) ));
  end;
end; // Unescape
```

you can unescape all &# sequences with

```
PoundEscapes := RegularExpression('(&#[[:digit:]]+;)', cflags('x')));
while PoundEscapes.Replace(HTML, HTML, Unescape) do ;
```

One striking feature of writing Transform functions is how 'bare' the code can be. For example, the Unescape() function can safely contain code like StrToInt(Copy(This, 3, Length(This) - 3)) that 'knows' it will only see HTML &# escape sequences, because those are the only strings that will match. All the bullet-proofing that normally takes at least a few lines of hand-coded checks is embedded in the regex.

Basic shell programming

It may seem strange to include a section on shell programming in a Kylix book. I'm doing so for two reasons: First, you'll probably need to write install scripts, and scripts to run your applications. Second, you can use system() and popen() to run scripts just as easily as to run 'raw commands'. If a Kylix application needs to set some environment variables before it runs a utility, you could either manually fork(), set the environment in the new process, and then exec()—or you could just use system() to run a script that sets environment variables and runs the utility. Somewhat similarly, shell scripts have much more capable control structures than batch files. If you need to run a sequence of Linux commands with some branching or repetition, you could hard-wire that into your Pascal source—or you might find it more sensible to just use a single system() call to run a single script that handles the whole process.

Everything I'm going to say in this section applies to the bash, or Bourne Again Shell, which is the most common shell on Linux systems. Other shells are similar but different. Rather than learn the ins and outs of every common shell, and try to write scripts that can work on all of them, you can force Linux to use bash to execute a script by placing the special comment

```
#! /bin/bash
```

on the first line. Since many Unix types call the # character "sharp" and the ! character "bang", this is commonly called the "shebang notation". The way it works is that when you execute a text file, the system looks at the first line. If that first line contains a shebang and the name of a program, the filename is passed to that program to be executed. (Specifically, the file name is passed on the command line, following any command line options that you specified on the #! line.) Otherwise, the script is executed by the current shell. This is how Unix knows whether to use bash, or the C shell, or Perl, or

Python, or whatever—even though it doesn't use a system of known file extensions the way Windows does.

Note

If you use Libc.system() to run a script, it will always be run by /bin/sh, *which is a symlink to the user's (or their sysadmin's) choice of shell. This may or may not be bash. It's just as important to 'shebang bash' (ie,* #! /bin/bash*) in scripts that your applications will call as it is in scripts that users will call.*

Just as Object Pascal tucks pragmas inside comments, so the shebang is a special comment. In general, anything between a # ('sharp', or 'pound' sign) and a newline is a comment to bash. There are no block comments, analogous to { } and (* *); every line in a comment block must start with #.

Variables

The way the shell handles variables is almost straightforward. You just have to remember that there are, in effect, two name spaces: The shell name space, which contains variables that are seen only by the current shell and/or the current script; and the environment name space, which contains the variables that will be seen by any child processes.[5] Variable names in both the shell and environment name space must be alphanumeric and must start with a letter or underscore, as in Pascal; in addition they're case sensitive, as in C.

To create a shell variable, just assign to it:

```
x=7
foo='numbers are actually saved as strings'
bar=foo
```

---

5. It's tempting to think of the shell and environment name spaces as "local" and "global", but this is inaccurate and misleading. Global implies a single name space that can be read and written by every process, which is certainly not the way environment variables work. A better analogy is to "static" and "dynamic" scoping of local variables. Pascal's statically scoped locals can only be seen within the routine which declares them, much as shell variables are not visible to either parent or child processes. Dynamically scoped locals in languages like APL and Lisp are visible within the routine which declares them and to the routines they call, much as environment variables are visible to child processes but not to parent processes.

Note

You can set variables like this at the shell prompt, not just in a script. In general, anything you can do in a script, you can do at a shell prompt. This makes experimenting very easy.

The shell handles variable values much the way it handles command line parameters; any sequence of characters without white space is a single 'word'. If a value consists of a single word it doesn't *need* to be quoted; if a value contains white space, it does need to be quoted. The shell supports single quotes, as above, as well as double quotes (") and back quotes (`). The three quoting mechanisms are not identical by any means; each has a different meaning, which I describe below.

To get the contents of a variable, you dereference the name by putting a $ character in front. For example, given the above three assignments, `echo $bar` would print `foo` while `echo bar` will print `bar`. If you set `bar=$foo`, `echo $bar` would print `numbers are actually saved as strings`.

It's not an error to dereference a name that hasn't been set; you just get an empty string value. Since the shell is case sensitive, the script

```
foo=foo
echo "foo='$foo', Foo='$Foo'"
```

will print

```
foo='foo', Foo=''
```

As you can see, when you dereference a variable within double quotes, the value is inserted into the string. (If you need a literal $ in a double-quoted string, you have to *escape it*, as \$.) In this example, the shell could easily tell the boundary between variable name and string literal because variable names can't contain quote characters. In more complex cases, like where you want to concatenate `$typeof` and the string `bear`, you'd have to enclose the variable name in 'curly braces', like `${typeof}bear`.

As the `${}` example may suggest, there's no special concatenation operator, and you only actually need double quotes when a string contains space characters.

```
foo=foo
bar=$foo$foo
echo $bar
```

will print

```
foofoo
```

If you don't want variable interpolation, use single quotes, not double quotes. That is, the value of `"this $string"` will depend on the value of the `string` variable, while the value of `'this $string'` will always be the twelve-character string `this $string`. You can freely combine both unquoted words, single-quoted strings, double-quoted strings, and dereferenced variables, subject only to the bounds of your common sense. Thus, if `foo=bar`, `Ba$foo`, `'Ba'$foo`, `"Ba$foo"`, and `'B''a'"$foo"` all equal `Babar`.

Back-quoted strings (using `` ` ``, the key to the left of the 1 key on standard US 104-key keyboards) are used for Unix commands. The value of a back-quoted string is the command's standard output. That is, `` w=`w` `` will not set `w` to a one-character string containing the 'w' character, but will instead execute the `w` command and set the `w` variable to the command's output. Back-quoted strings do variable interpolation just like double-quoted strings, so `` filecontents=`cat filename` `` will set the `filecontents` variable to the contents of the file named `filename`, while `` filecontents=`cat $filename` `` will set the `filecontents` variable to the contents of the file whose name is stored in the `filename` variable.

Note

`$(value)` *is equivalent to* `` `value` ``. *Note the difference between* `$(name)` *and* `${name}`*!*

As in Perl, and unlike Pascal, string constants can include line breaks.

```
long='this string
has line breaks in it'
```

When you're dealing with strings that contain line breaks, you need to know that `echo "$long"` acts differently than `echo $long`. The double-quoted version preserves line ends and other white space; the unquoted version translates them to spaces. See *Word Splitting* in `man 1 bash` for more information.

The export command

Shell variables are local to a particular instance of a shell, running in a particular process. That is, they're not visible to any child processes, and they disappear when the script terminates, or when you type `exit` to close a shell session. If you want to set an environment variable that can be seen by programs that your script runs, you use the `export` command. You can either just `export foo` to export the current value of `foo`, or you can use a shorthand `export foo=bar` form to both set and export a variable in the same operation.

What makes this confusing is that if you set an environment variable like HOME or LD_LIBRARY_PATH, the assignment **is** seen by child processes. That is, sometimes you have to use `export` and sometimes you don't. The rules are really pretty simple, though:

1. If *name* is not an environment variable, setting it won't change the environment.

2. If *name* **is** an environment variable, setting it will change the environment.

The easiest way to deal with this is to just **always** use `export` to set environment variables. This not only guarantees that your assignment is to an environment variable, whether or not the variable already exists, it also serves to make your (dynamic, inheritable) environment variable assignments stand out from your (static, private) shell variable assignments.

The source command

Since the shell runs each command in a new process, any changes a script makes to environment variables are visible only within the script and to any programs it runs. That is, a script can set the environment seen by any programs it runs, because the programs run in a child process of the script process, and child processes automatically inherit a copy of their parent's environment. But a child process cannot affect its parent's environment; you can not run a script that changes the current environment.

In other words, if you have a set of scripts that all need to condition the environment the same way, you can't put the common code into a script that each runs. What you **can** do, though, is to use the `source` command. Where running a script in a script starts a whole new process and a whole new copy of the shell program, sourcing a script merely runs the shell's script interpreter recursively, within the current process. Thus, while a sourced script can have its own command line parameters (below) just like a normal script, it executes in the current process and the current process's name space. That is, any shell or environment variables that it creates or changes will still have their new values when the `source` command finishes and control returns to the original script.

An example may make this clearer. The ch11/sourceme script simply does

```
foo=bar
```

while the ch11/sources script does

```
echo "before calling sourceme, \$foo=$foo"
sourceme
echo "after calling sourceme, \$foo=$foo"
source sourceme
echo "after sourcing sourceme, \$foo=$foo"
```

and produces the output

```
before calling sourceme, $foo=
after calling sourceme, $foo=
after sourcing sourceme, $foo=bar
```

That is, when the `sources` script starts up, `foo` is undefined. Within the call to `sourceme`, `foo` is defined, but this has no effect on the `sources` process. However, after `source sourceme`, `foo` **is** defined in the `sources` process.

> **Note**
>
> *You can use* source *from a shell prompt to help debug scripts. While running a script normally leaves no trace on the calling environment, sourcing it leaves all its variables available in the shell for inspection.*

Finally, you can think of the `source` command as the shell's equivalent of Perl's `do` or (interpreted) Basic's `eval` command. Just as these commands let you run a bit of data as if it were code, so source does not require that the file you source be executable. In fact, unless the file does something useful by itself, it probably **shouldn't** be executable.

Script parameters

Although scripts do not have formal prototypes the way an Object Pascal routine does, you can pass parameters to them, just as you can to any other executable file. The special variable $# contains the argument count, and is almost precisely analogous to Kylix's ParamCount function. The special variable $* contains the whole command line, while $0 contains the name of the script and $1 through $9 contain the first nine parameters.

> **Note**
>
> *There's also a $@ which is almost identical to $*, except that "$*" is a single word, while "$@" yields as many words as parameters. This is useful if you need to forward all the current script's parameters to another script; it's also useful when you use for to iterate over the script parameters. See the* The for statement *section, below.*

If a script has more than nine command line parameters, there's no way to read the tenth (and subsequent) parameters. You can, however, use the shift command to discard the first parameter and shift all the others over. That is, $1=$2 and $2=$3 and so on. The shift command affects both $* and $#: After a shift, $# will be one less[6] (unless it was already zero) and the new value of $1 will be the first token in $*.

Arithmetic

Though variables are saved as strings, you can do arithmetic with the let command, using the same operators as in C.

---

6.   The way that shift affects $# is the principle difference between $# and Kylix's ParamCount function: Since you can pass any number to Kylix's ParamStr function, Kylix has no equivalent to shift and the ParamCount never changes while the program is running.

```
result=fee
let hours=24*7
let $result=$hours*$rate # yes, this sets fee
let fee+=$latefee
```

Also as in C, boolean operators return zero or one, and treat zero as False and non-zero as True. Unlike C or Pascal, white space is **not** allowed in a `let` expression, unless you quote the expression—the `let` command expects a single string value.

Those who find typing `let` to be unpleasantly reminiscent of BASIC can use the equivalent `(( ))` syntax: `let foo=6*4` and `((foo=6*4))` have absolutely identical effects. Don't be fooled by the way the `(( ))` 'looks like a value', though. The `let` command acts like Pascal's assignment operator, not C's assignment operator. That is, `let` does not return a value, and you cannot write `echo ((6*7))` or `foo=((bar=2+2))`. Within the `let`, though, the assignment operator works as in C, and you can write `let foo=(bar=2+2)+2`.

Note

Just to make things confusing, `$((expr))` **does** *evaluate expr and return its value, so you can write* `foo=$((6*7))` *or* `echo $(($foo+$bar))`.

Table 11-5. Shell arithmetic operators, by precedence

Operator	Interpretation
+, -	Unary plus and minus
!, ~	Logical and bitwise `not`
*, /, %	Multiplication, integer division (`div`), and modulus (`mod`)
+, -	Addition and subtraction
<<, >>	Bitwise shifts—`shl` and `shr`
<, <=, >=, >	Integer (**not** string) comparisons
==, !=	Equality and inequality - = and <>
&	Bitwise and
^	Bitwise xor
|	Bitwise or

Table 11-5. Shell arithmetic operators, by precedence (Continued)

Operator	Interpretation
&&	Logical and
||	Logical or
=, +=, -=, *=, /= <<=, >>=, &=, |=, ^=	Assignment

String manipulation

The bash shell offers a nice range of string operators. The syntax is as execrable
as it gets, though, so you might want to stick a placeholder in the book right here.
Note that all these operators return values, but only the ${varname:=value}
operator can actually change the variable *varname*.

Table 11-6. Shell string operators

Syntax	Semantics	Comments
${varname}	Returns the value of *varname*.	Useful in concatenating variables and constants.
${#varname}	Returns the string length of the value of *varname*.	Analogous to Length(*Varname*).
${varname:-value}	Returns $varname unless that's '', in which case it returns value.	Lets you supply a default value.
${varname:=value}	Just like ${:-}, except also sets *varname* to *value* iff $varname is currently ''.	Make sure a value is defined; or flag it as undefined (as opposed to '').
${varname:+value}	The converse of ${:-}—returns '' iff $varname is '', and *value* if it is not empty.	Preserves defined/undefined status, while converting arbitrary defined value to something more appropriate for the part of the script.
${varname:?string}	Returns $varname, if that isn't an empty string; otherwise echoes varname: string to stderr and aborts the script.	Not unlike an Assert().
${varname#pattern}	Deletes the **shortest** leading match to *pattern* from *varname*'s value. Returns the result, without affecting the contents of *varname*.	The pattern can include shell wildcard patterns like ?, *, and [a-z] character sets.

Table 11-6. Shell string operators (Continued)

Syntax	Semantics	Comments
`${varname##pattern}`	Deletes the **longest** leading match to *pattern* from *varname*'s value.	
`${varname%pattern}`	Deletes the shortest **trailing** match to *pattern* from *varname*'s value.	`${filename%/*}` returns the path part of `filename`.
`${varname%%pattern}`	Deletes the longest trailing match to *pattern* from *varname*'s value.	
`${varname/pattern/replacement}`	Replaces the first instance of *pattern* in the value of *varname* with the *replacement* string and returns the result, without changing the value of *varname*.	As with the deletion operators, the pattern can include shell regex patterns.
`${varname//pattern/replacement}`	Replaces **all** instances of *pattern*.	

The bash shell also supports a `printf` command that's very like Kylix's Format() function.

```
printf pattern parameter(s)
```

Naturally enough, `printf` 'prints' to stdout, but you can capture this with backquotes or `$()` to do arbitrary formatting. For example, `james_bond=`printf '%03d' 7`` sets `james_bond` to 007. The shell `printf` command uses Libc's printf() function. While Kylix's Format() has been patterned on printf() and the two are very similar, they're not identical; see `man 3 printf` for the details of the pattern language.

Control structures

The shell supports standard control structures like `if`, `case`, `for`, `while`, and `until`. The `if`, `while`, and `until` constructs are very much like those in Pascal, allowing you to use a (conceptually!) simple boolean test to control execution. The `case` and `for` constructs are more novel, being built around pattern matching and lists, so I'll cover those after I cover the simpler constructs.

Simple boolean structures

The if, while, and until structures are built around boolean tests. Do *this* if the test is true, else do *that*. Do *this* while the test is true. Do *that* until the test is true. Directly analogous to the Pascal control structures of Chapter 2.

The big difference between a Kylix program and a shell script is that shell scripts are (or at least originally **were**) vehicles for stringing together small executables. Over the years they've grown features, including functions that let you write some reasonably sophisticated programs entirely as shell scripts, but you can still see the original orientation in the way that the control structures work on the *result code* of the last program executed. In Kylix terms, a program that does a halt(0) returns True, while a program that halts with any other status code returns False.

The tst project in the ch11/Scripts project group illustrates this.

```
program tst;

var
  Return, Error: integer;

begin
  Val(ParamStr(1), Return, Error);
  if Error <> 0 then
    Return := 0;
  halt(Return);
end.
```

This trivial little program returns 0, unless ParamStr(1) is an integer, in which case it returns that. The ch11/showtst script calls the tst application.

```
if ./tst $1
  then
    echo 'True'
  else
    echo 'False'
fi
```

If you run it as showtst 0, it will print True. If you run it as showtst 1, it will print False.

Scripts can set a return code by using the exit statement, which also halts the script. It's exactly analogous to the Kylix Halt() function.

This ability to treat programs as subroutines means that you can write a script that detects a failure code and reacts appropriately. More to the point of the sort of basic scripting that most Kylix programmers will need to do, evaluation of the sort of conditions that a script might branch on—like string and numeric tests, or the settings of various file properties—were not originally built into the shell. Rather, they were handled by a special executable, test, whose sole purpose was to set a result code that script could branch on.

That is, you can't say something like if $foo = $bar. Instead, you have to say if test $foo = $bar. The test command has long since been moved into bash itself, so it doesn't incur the overhead of creating a process and running a program, but the ungainly syntax remains. You can use [ ] as a sort of shorthand for test, but you **have** to remember that it's a shorthand: if [$foo = $bar], with spaces between the square brackets and the condition, will work, but the more normal looking if [$foo = $bar] will not work.

The things that test can test fall into four groups: string comparisons, integer comparisons, file properties, and boolean combinations of the other three. Be sure to note that, as in Perl, you use different operators for string testing than for integer testing. The following four tables—especially table 11-9—are not exhaustive, but represent my best guess at the most useful tests. See *Conditional Expressions* under man 1 bash for more tests.

Table 11-7. Shell string tests

Test	Interpretation
[string]	The string is not null (*ie*, not equal to ' '). This is the same test as [-n string]
[-n string]	The string's length is greater than zero.
[-z string]	The string's length is zero. This is the same test as [! string]
[string1 = string2]	String1 and string2 are equal. Note the use of a single =, as in Pascal, not the double == as in C.
[string1 != string2]	String1 and string2 are not equal. Note the use of != as in C, not <> as in Pascal.

Table 11-8. Shell integer tests

Test	Interpretation
`[ number1 -lt number2 ]`	Number1 is less than number 2. Note that you need white space before and after the –lt.
`[ number2 -le number2 ]`	Number1 is less than or equal to number2.
`[ number2 -eq number2 ]`	Number1 is equal to number2.
`[ number2 -ge number2 ]`	Number1 is greater than or equal to number2.
`[ number2 -gt number2 ]`	Number1 is greater than to number2.
`[ number2 -ne number2 ]`	Number1 is not equal to number2.

Table 11-9. Shell file property tests

Test	Interpretation
`[ -e filename ]`	The file exists
`[ -f filename ]`	The file exists and is a regular file.
`[ -d filename ]`	The file exists and is a directory.
`[ -r filename ]`	The file exists and can be read by the script's euid.
`[ -w filename ]`	The file exists and can be written by the script's euid.
`[ -x filename ]`	The file exists and can be executed by the script's euid.
`[ file1 -ef file2 ]`	File1 and file2 are exactly the same file—they have the same device and inode numbers.
`[ file1 -ot file2 ]`	File1 is older than file2.
`[ file1 -nt file2 ]`	File1 is newer than file2.

Table 11-10. Shell booleans

Code	Interpretation
`[ ! condition ]`	True if the condition is False; logical **not**.
`[ condition1 -a condition2 ]`	True iff both conditions are true; logical **and**.
`[ condtion2 -o condition2 ]`	True if either condition is true; logical **or**.

The precedence rules that control boolean combinations are complex and can easily trip you up. (Note, for example, that –a is both a boolean operator and a file test.) You can't go wrong, though, if you always group tests with explicit parentheses.

Note

The shell syntax starts to get pretty messy around parens. For one thing, you need to escape them—\(and \)—to avoid shell expansion. For another, as per man test, *you need to put spaces around parenthesis characters. Thus, you have to write parenthesized tests like*
`[ \( -n "$filename" \) -a \( -e "$filename" \) ]`, *not*
`[ (-n "$filename") -a (-e "$filename") ] or`
`[ (-n $filename)-a(-e $filename) ].`

The if statement

The basic form of the shell if statement is

```
if test
then
  statements
else
  statements
fi
```

where the else and its statements are optional. Normally, the if, then, the optional else, and the fi are all on separate lines, as above. You can combine one or more of these elements onto a single line by separating them with a semicolon, ;, but the shell can be awfully picky about this:. For example,

```
if [ 1 -gt 2 ]; then echo gt; else echo lte; fi
```

is valid, but

```
if [ 1 -gt 2 ]; then; echo gt; else; echo lte; fi
```

is **not**.

You can nest two or more if statements, but this can make for a lot of syntax to plow through. In the common case where the else clause is another if statement, you can use an elif instead of an else ; if. The elif clause can have its own else clause; the combined three-way statement needs only a single fi.

The ch11/brandit script uses string substitution to 'brand' a loader script template with the directory where the user installed the Kylix libraries like `libqtintf.so` and the name of the Kylix executable to load. It then saves the 'branded' script to $1, creating a loader script that either prepends to an existing LD_LIBRARY_PATH environment variable or creates a new one.

```
#!/bin/bash

# The loader script template
export Template='#!/bin/bash

if [ "$LD_LIBRARY_PATH" ]
  then
    export LD_LIBRARY_PATH="<path>:$LD_LIBRARY_PATH"
  else
    export LD_LIBRARY_PATH="<path>"
fi
<program>'

# Replace all <path> in the template with $2
Template="${Template//<path>/$2}"

# Replace all <program> in the template with $3
Template="${Template//<program>/$3}"

# Write the branded template to $1, make it executable
echo "$Template">"$1"
chmod +x "$1"
```

Running this as `./brandit rundemo /kylix/bin demo` produces the following `rundemo` script:

```
if [ "$LD_LIBRARY_PATH" ]
  then
    export LD_LIBRARY_PATH="/kylix/bin:$LD_LIBRARY_PATH"
  else
    export LD_LIBRARY_PATH="/kylix/bin"
fi
demo
```

Thus, if $LD_LIBRARY_PATH is defined and has a non-empty value, `rundemo` prepends `/kylix/bin:` to it. Otherwise, `rundemo` simply sets LD_LIBRARY_PATH to `/kylix/bin`. In both cases, `rundemo` uses export to be sure that the modified

LD_LIBRARY_PATH can be seen by the demo program. A branded loader script like this is probably the best way to have users run your Kylix programs, as it doesn't require them to 'pollute' their global environment with a LD_LIBRARY_PATH, and it prevents any possible conflicts with different versions of the Kylix libraries that other applications may have installed.

The while and until statements

The basic form of the while statement is

```
while test
do
   statements
done
```

That is, the body of the while consists of one or more statements between do and done lines. Similarly, an until looks like

```
until test
do
   statements
done
```

Don't be fooled by the vague similarity to the Pascal repeat Body until Test construct which does its Test at the bottom, and will always execute the Body at least once. The shell until statement has its test at the top, and may not execute the body at all. It's just syntactic sugar for while [! \(condition \)].

The for statement

The shell's for statement is very different from its counterpart in Pascal. Where Pascal's for statement steps a ordinal loop control variable from one value to another, bash's for statement iterates through a list, setting the control variable to each value in turn.

The simplest form of the for loop is

```
for variable
do
   statements
done
```

which sets the `variable` to each command line parameter in turn, and executes the `statements` with each value. The more general form is

```
for variable in list
do
    statements
done
```

which sets `variable` to each element of `list` and executes the `statements`.

The `list` can use any of the shell regular expression patterns (`*`, `?`, and `[a-z]` type characters sets), in which case it is expanded to a list of all matching files in the current directory, just as at the command line.[7] (Bash contains primitives to build and manipulate lists, but that's an advanced topic that I don't cover.) You can also specify a list constant:

```
for token in this that 'the other'; do
echo $token; done
```

will produce the output

```
    this
    that
    the other
```

The `for` statement is one of the only places where the difference between `$*` and `$@` becomes obvious. In a list context, like after a `for variable in`, `"$@"` preserves the parameter boundaries properly, where `$*`, `"$*"` or `$@` do not. That is, if the script's parameter were `this that` and `'the other'`, `$#` would be 4, and `$4` would be `the other`. But, if you were to iterate over `$*`, `"$*"` or `$@`, you would get five tokens, with `the` and `other` being ripped apart. If you iterate over `"$@"` you get the four tokens that you expect.

This is awfully esoteric and may seem sort of pointless—"Why not just use `for variable; do`?" The reason is really quite simple: `"$@"` might just be one element of a list.

---

7.   This is true for your Kylix applications, too. If you run a program, `kylixapp`, with the command line `kylixapp *`, you won't get a single parameter, `'*'`, you'll get a list of every file in the current directory.

```
for token in first "$@" last; do
echo $token; done
```

will 'wrap' the command line parameters in the tokens `first` and `last`.

The case statement

The bash shell's `case` statement is really sort of cool.

```
case selector in
  pattern1) statements;;
  pattern2) statements;;
esac
```

That is, it consists of a `case selector in` line (much like Pascal's `case selector of`) followed by one or more statement blocks consisting of a regular expression (in an extended form of the shell wildcard language), followed by a `)`, followed by one or more statements, and ending in `;;`, and finishing with an `esac`. The statement blocks are not unlike Pascal's: They consist of a pattern, a separator, and a possibly compound statement. The differences are

- Pascal's case patterns are ordinal constants and ranges. The shell's case patterns are regular expressions. As in Pascal, though, only the first matching block will execute; there's no fall-through behavior as in C.

- There's no explicit **else** syntax. Use a `*` pattern to match anything that hasn't already matched.

- Pascal separates patterns from code with a `:`. The shell uses a `)`.

- Pascal expects a single statement to follow the `:`. If you need a compound statement, you need an explicit `begin` and `end`. The shell expects a series of statements, which may be separated by semicolons. Even if you only have a single statement in a case statement block, it has to end with a pair of semicolons, `;;`.

Note that a case pattern can include a `|`, so that the selector can match any of a series of regexes. This is the sense in which `case` regular expressions use an extended form of the shell wildcard language, as you can't include a `|` in a shell wildcard at the command line.

The ch11/finfo script illustrates the case statement, as well as some of the string operators, and some of the problems you can encounter when dealing with strings that contain white space.

```
#!/bin/bash

for filename
do
  if [ -f "$filename" ]; then
    length=$(wc -c "$filename")
    length=${length%$filename}

    extension=${filename##*\.}
    if [ "$extension" - "$filename" ]; then
      extension=''; fi
    case $extension in
      pas)  extension='Kylix unit file';;
      xfm)  extension='Kylix form file';;
      dpr)  extension='Kylix project file';;
      ?o*f) extension='Kylix configuration file';;
      txt)  extension='Plain text file';;
      *)    extension='';;
    esac

    printf '%-40s %10d %s\n' "$filename" $length "$extension"
  fi
done
```

I check every token on the command line to see if it's a normal file. I have to use [-f "$filename"] to check filenames that may contain white space. If I didn't, the $filename would be expanded, and I'd get error messages about too many arguments to [whenever $filename contained white space.

If the token does represent a normal file, I first get the length with $(wc -c "$filename"). I have to use "$filename" to make sure that the filename appears as a single string to the wc command. The wc -c command returns the character count followed by the file name, so I use ${length%$filename} to strip off the trailing filename. The length string still contains whitespace, but that doesn't matter to printf when I format it as %10d.

After I get the length, I get the extension, with ${filename##*\.}, which strips off the longest leading string ending in a dot. Since this doesn't affect filenames with no dot, I have to then compare this 'extension' to the original filename, double quoting the variables so that [ ] only 'sees' two strings and an operator. Once I have the extension, I use a `case` statement to classify a few known extensions. (Note how the shell regex pattern `?o*f` matches both `.conf` and `.kof` files. If this were a "real" script and not just a demo, I'd probably want to use something like `conf|kof` instead of `?o*f`, so that I didn't match .roof, .motif, .soundproof, and so on.)

Finally, I pass the filename and the two computed values to printf. I have to quote the format pattern, because it contains white space, and the format pattern has to end in an explicit `\n` to print a newline. Also, both the $filename and the #extension may contain white space, so both have to be quoted, so that they appear to `printf` as single strings.

CHAPTER 12
X & Qt

X & Qt

THIS IS A SHORT CHAPTER. Kylix applications have pretty much the same relation to X as Delphi applications have to Windows device drivers, and Kylix programmers have about as much need to know about X as Delphi programmers have to know about device drivers.

Not much.

The very lowest-level GUI services a Kylix application would normally ask for—like "create a window, with an event loop"—are about the highest level of services that X provides. X doesn't provide even trivial UI elements like buttons and scrollbars; it leaves that to you and your choice of *X toolkit*. An X toolkit is a library that builds standard widgets from X primitives, and is thus responsible for the application's "look and feel."

There are many X toolkits in Unix land, from OpenLook and Motif to GTK+ and Qt. They all have a different look and feel, and their API's are structured differently, but they have one key point in common: It makes more sense to speak of an app that uses a toolkit as, say, "a Qt app" than as "an X app". That is, while a Kylix GUI app **is** an X app, it will almost certainly not talk directly to X, while it will contain plenty of code that talks to Qt, either directly or *via* CLX.

Accordingly, the X section of this chapter is basically just enough of an architectural overview of X for you to understand how that architecture affects your Kylix applications. There's a bit more about Qt, simply because Kylix developers need to occasionally make Qt calls, just as they occasionally need to make Libc calls. Still, I covered some of the most common Qt calls in Chapters 6 and 7, so the Qt section of this chapter is also mostly an architectural overview, with an emphasis on the interface between Qt and CLX. For the most part, though, this chapter is more background information than anything you really *need* to know to write Kylix applications.

X

In the beginning, Unix was a timesharing system. The contemporary distinction between "workstations" and "servers" lay far in the future; computers were big, expensive things that required a dedicated staff and an air-conditioned room. The only way to keep the cost reasonable was to load as many users as possible onto each machine.

The height of interactivity was an ASR-33 teletype [TTY], a big, noisy sort of electric typewriter. These were soon supplanted by Video Display Terminals [VDT], which allowed Full Screen Editing of the sort that we still use today in Kylix's code editor. There were soon lots and lots of different terminals, and Unix hackers developed packages like Curses that allowed applications to work with a sort of virtual terminal that could be mapped at run-time to an actual terminal *via* an environment variable and a "terminal capabilities" file.

Thus, when mice and bitmapped screens came along, the terminal was deeply entrenched in the Unix world, and it was only natural that the new paradigm would be shoehorned into the old, much as the first VDT's were basically just "glass TTY's". The X model is basically a terminal model, with communication *via* sockets instead of serial lines. This structure allowed you to use your account on the departmental machine either from your expensive new workstation or from a comparatively cheap "X terminal". Even now, when single-user workstations are the norm and not the exception, the X model allows you to run Linux applications over the network, using an X terminal program on another machine—even a Windows or Mac machine—if you've set permissions properly.

Architecture

X uses a client/server architecture. GUI applications are clients that get GUI services from the X server. The server is responsible for relaying mouse and keyboard events to the focused window and for drawing on the screen; the client is responsible for handling the inputs and telling the server to draw the right outputs.

Client and server communicate *via* sockets. In the normal case, where you are running a GUI application on a Linux workstation, the GUI client and the X server are independent processes running on the same machine, and they use *Unix domain* sockets to communicate. In the special case, where you are running a GUI application on a remote machine, the remote GUI client and the local GUI server use *Inet domain* sockets to communicate. This socket creation is handled automatically by Qt *via* calls to the *Xlib* client/server communication API. Your Kylix apps don't have to do anything special to run over a network, nor should they act any differently.

Given that X was written for Unix, which has always been a multiprocessing system, it may seem surprising that the X communication protocol is fundamentally single-threaded. But multiprocessing is not multithreading, and Unix actually had X before it had threads. If a non-GUI thread makes a method call or sets a property that causes Qt to talk to X, you'll get "serialization" error messages on stderr. Qt does provide an optional locking mechanism (QApplication::lock and QApplication::unlock) that allows applications to be sure that only a single thread is talking to X at a time, but this option is not available in Kylix 1.0. This may change in the future; for now, see Chapter 7 for details on how to marshal events from a non-GUI thread to the GUI thread.

Window managers and desktops

Just as X doesn't provide user interface widgets, so it doesn't offer any pre-scriptions about how the various windows should look or act. The catch phrase here is "mechanism, not policy".[1] Basic user interface ("policy") deci-sions—which window has the focus, what window frames look like, and what widgets should be on those frames and what those widgets should do—are usually made by the *window manager*.

The window manager is a perfectly ordinary application—you can write one in Kylix—that has a special relationship with X. The window manager doesn't put windows on the screen, the way other applications do; it tells X how those other applications' windows should look and act. While X doesn't require a window manager and can run *sans* window manager in a trivial, single window way, X will only talk to one window manager at a time.

Note

The X jargon gets a little strange in the neighborhood of window managers. A window manager is really a sort of policy server to the X server's policy client, but speaking of the same piece of software as both client and server is an obviously dangerous source of ambiguity. Since a window manager is an independent process (that may even be running on a different machine) that talks to the X server over a socket, just like your Kylix GUI apps are, window managers are described as special sorts of X clients. Weird but true.

This reliance on a policy server to provide look and feel is the key to X's survival since the mid 1980s.[2] X provides only the GUI version of stdin and stdout—mouse and keyboard services, and bitblt and font services—and it

---

1. RFC 1013.

2. Of course, it didn't hurt that MIT gave X away. "Free" is a pretty good price.

got these basic abstractions close enough to right that no one ever felt compelled to replace it. By not taking a stand on content, X permitted user interfaces to evolve. By sleeping with anyone, X survived the fragmentation of the Unix world in the late '80s and early '90s.

In the 21st century, in a specifically Linux context, window managers provide the big benefit of allowing users to make choices—both functional and cosmetic—for themselves. On the other hand, the basic window manager API was defined a long time ago, and there are an awful lot of things it doesn't cover. It's been extended in various ways over the years, but "the great thing about standards, [is that] there are so many to choose from."

No matter how broken or stripped down the window manager, you can count on at least one of your users using it, unless you're working in a standardized corporate environment. (For that matter, the more broken or stripped down the window manager, the more the users will resist changing. They already know it's old and crufty, or flashy but incomplete, but there's something about it that they like, or they would already have switched.) Every window manager your apps will run under may or may not implement all the basic and extended protocols properly; your app can "hint" that a given window shouldn't be resizable or that it shouldn't have a maximize button, but you can't know whether the user's window manager actually takes the hint.

Desktops

The window manager is responsible for how windows look and act, and how focus changes when you move and/or click the mouse. It doesn't handle things like the panel at the bottom or top of the screen, and the various virtual screen arrangements. These higher-order functions are the responsibility of the desktop, which is typically either Gnome or KDE.

As a general rule, desktops are layered on top of window managers. Desktops need window managers; window managers don't need desktops. In practice, though, the relationship is a bit more symbiotic than hierarchical; some of the newer window managers are written for either KDE or Gnome, and either won't work at all without the right desktop or will only work in a minimal way.

While Linux isn't incredibly useful without a window manager, you *can* run Kylix apps on Linux with an old, minimal window manager and no desktop. You might want to do this in embedded situations, or if you are selling turnkey systems to a vertical market.

Qt

From X's perspective, Qt is just another X toolkit that uses X primitives to build user interface widgets. This is true enough, but Qt can also run on Windows or on embedded Linux systems without an X server. That is, Qt is a portable widget library that survived in a competitive environment that killed products like Zinc by virtue of being reasonably well designed and reasonably well implemented. By basing the CLX on Qt, Borland can offer us the opportunity to write applications that can run on either Linux or on Windows with little or no conditional compilation.

Qt's no more perfect than any other software, but it's certainly better than most. It combines occasional bits of unfathomable stupidity with a generally high level of cleanliness and sensibility. From Borland's point of view, a key inducement must have been that Qt is very Delphi-like. From the use of properties and events to the way it caches drawing tools like pens, brushes, and fonts, Qt shows a strong Delphi influence. This must have been very flattering, of course, but perhaps more importantly, it means that the CLX can be as VCL compatible as it is without mile after mile of complex protocol translation code.

Signals and slots

For the most part, there's a one-to-one correspondence between Kylix objects and Qt objects. Thus, every Qt application has a QApplication object that handles app-wide things like the event loop, and every form as well as every control on every form is backed by a QWidget. The single biggest difference between the Qt architecture and the Kylix architecture is that where under Kylix no event can have no more than one handler, any Qt *signal* can be dispatched to any number of *slots*.

That is, a Qt signal is really almost exactly the same as a Kylix event. (It definitely has nothing to do with the Unix signals (SIGSEGV &c) of Chapter 10.) A component emits a signal when something happens that it thinks an application or another component might be interested in. Where a Kylix component is responsible for either calling an event handler or not, using inline code like

```
if Assigned(fEventHandler) then
  fEventHandler(Self);
```

the Qt documentation says that an object emitting a signal "does not know if anything is receiving the signal at the other end." Presumably this means that calling slots is handled by templates or macros that walk some sort of slot list.

Similarly, a Qt slot is basically the same thing as a Kylix event handler: an object method (with a specific prototype). Just as several events can share a single event handler, so may a slot be connected to more than one signal.

One relatively minor difference between Qt signals and Kylix events is that Qt signals don't include a Sender parameter; just an implicit `This` pointer and perhaps some parameters. The Qt equivalent of Kylix's TNotifyProc—an event handler with no special parameters—is a method like `void QLabel::clear ()`.

Qt and Kylix

Qt is a C++ class hierarchy. Kylix applications can't just use C++ declarations directly, they have to use units that translate C++ header files into their Object Pascal equivalents. C++ typedefs and function declarations pose little problem, but objects, macros, and templates present various issues.

The Qt unit is a mostly mechanical translation of Qt declarations into Object Pascal. The most striking feature of the Qt unit is the way it 'flattens' the Qt class hierarchy. Presumably, this was done out of some combination of concerns about vtable formats, name mangling, Self/This parameter order, and/or portability. The effect of the flattening is that `QThis::that()` is not called as `Handle.that`, but as `QThis_that(Handle)`.

This flattening is verbose and annoying, but really won't affect you much since the CLX covers so many aspects of GUI programming. To the extent that curiosity or necessity does drive you to dig into Qt, you'll find that the translation from Qt documentation (or previous Qt experience) to OP implementation quickly becomes routine.

Somewhat more violence has been done to the Qt signal and slot API. If you read the Qt documentation on *Signals and Slots*, you'll see that it relies on SIGNAL() and SLOT() macros. While straightforward inline code macros like the S_ISREG file type macro of Chapter 10 can readily be turned into function calls, some of the more "template-like" macros cannot. I call a macro template-like if it uses its arguments to generate type names. Templates and template-like macros can't be implemented as statically typed subroutines but basically have to be hand expanded, to boiler plate inline code and/or overloaded routines with the appropriate type declarations.

Thus, where C++ signal and slot code would use QObject::connect and the SIGNAL() and SLOT() macros, Kylix signal and slot code has to use a two-step process that looks totally unlike its C++ counterpart, but which presumably corresponds pretty closely to what is actually being done by the SIGNAL() and SLOT() macros.

Most Qt objects have a corresponding "hook" object. To connect a signal and a slot, you have to pass both the appropriate hook and the slot method to a *QObjectName*_hook_hook_*Signal* procedure [a *_hook_hook_* procedure]. For example, in this code from the ch7/Clipboard project

```
constructor TExClipboard.Create;
var
  ChangedEvent: QClipboard_dataChanged_Event;
begin
  inherited;
  {snip}
  FHook := QClipboard_hook_create(Handle);
  ChangedEvent := ClipboardChangedNotification;
  QClipboard_hook_hook_dataChanged(FHook, TMethod(ChangedEvent));
end; // TExClipboard.Create
```

I create a specialized clipboard hook, then use it to connect my ClipboardChangedNotification slot to the clipboard's dataChanged signal. The connection takes two steps:

```
ChangedEvent := ClipboardChangedNotification;
```

and

```
QClipboard_hook_hook_dataChanged(FHook, TMethod(ChangedEvent));
```

because all the *_hook_hook_* procedures take a generic TMethod, instead of the appropriate *QObjectName_Signal_*Event type.[3] Since you can't cast a method name to a procedural type (*ie,* you can't code TMethod (ClipboardChangedNotification)) you have to first create a procedure of object variable (TExClipboard.Create's ChangedEvent) and then cast that variable to a TMethod.

The signal and slot code in TExClipboard.Create looks rather different from the various HookEvents methods throughout the CLX. There are two reasons for this. First, every THandleComponent has a protected Hooks property, of the generic type QObject_hookH. Every THandleComponent descendant sets its Hooks property to the appropriate specialized hook in its CreateWidget method. Thus, the various HookEvents methods don't have to

---

3. It's not obvious **why** Borland went this route, though I presume 'ease of mechanical translation' had a lot to do with it.

create a hook object, but instead cast their generic Hooks property to the appropriate specialized descendant type.

```
procedure TCustomEdit.HookEvents;
var
  Method: TMethod;
begin
  inherited HookEvents;
  QLineEdit_textChanged_Event(Method) := TextChangedHook;
  QLineEdit_hook_hook_textChanged(QLineEdit_hookH(Hooks), Method);
end;
```

Note

The various HookEvents methods **have** *to use code like* `QLineEdit_hookH(Hooks)` *instead of* `Hooks as QLineEdit_hookH`. *Even though the generic* `QObject_hookH` *is declared as* `class(TObject)` *and the specialized hooks are declared as* `class(QObject_hookH)`, *they're Qt objects, not Object Pascal objects. The internal layout is different, and the* as *operator can't be used to do safe casts.*

TExClipboard can't follow this model because it's based on TClipboard, which descends directly from TPersistent and doesn't have a Hooks property. Although TClipboard does create a QClipboard_hookH, it stores this in a `private` FHook property that TExClipboard can't read. Thus, TExClipboard both has to explicitly create a specialized hook and also doesn't have to (unsafely!) cast a generic property to a specialized descendant. Use the Hooks property where it's available, but use a more specific property wherever Hooks is not available and you have to explicitly declare, create, and destroy the hook object yourself.

The second way in which TExClipboard.Create (and TClipboard.GetHandle, for that matter) differs from the various HookEvents methods is that it declares its 'slot pointer' variable, `ChangedEvent`, as a specialized *_Event type, and casts that to a TMethod in the call to the *_hook_hook_* procedure. This is different from the HookEvents methods, which declare their slot pointer variable as a TMethod, and do a 'left cast' like

```
QLineEdit_textChanged_Event(Method) := TextChangedHook;
```

at the point where they set it. They then pass Method to the _hook_hook_ procedure without having to do any casting.

Since the *_hook_hook_* procedures all take TMethod's, not the appropriate *_Event types, connecting signals to slots under Kylix inevitably involves the use of casting. Given that, the difference between left casting a TMethod on assignment or right casting a *_Event on connection is very nearly a six of one, half dozen of the other situation:

- You can argue that it's clearer to assign to a *_Event type, without any casts, and only do the right-cast to a generic TMethod in the *_hook_hook_* procedure call. "It's the *_hook_hook_* procedures that are misbound, so keep the violence there."

- Conversely, the left-cast puts the *_Event type in the same statement as the assignment, not several lines up in a var declaration. The assignment is both type-safe and self-documenting.

Personally, I find the first argument more convincing, and think the right-cast model is better overall. What I suspect tipped Borland towards the left-cast model in the HookEvents methods is that many of them do multiple connect operations. The left-cast model allows them to reuse the same Method local for each connection. If you haven't skipped ahead in disgust ("I mean, *who cares*? This Shemitz guy is really beating a dead horse here!") I recommend that you follow the right-cast model (explicit *_Create variables, not generic TMethod variables) for your own signal and slot connection needs, unless you find that you need to do several connections in the same routine.

Whether you'll ever actually *have* any signal and slot connection needs is an open question. While the CLX doesn't map the clipboard's dataChanged signal to an event, thus forcing us into signal and slot land to create clipboard viewers, that's the only such lapse I've found. There may be others, or you may find that you want to manually connect a signal to a slot so that you can have more than one slot receive the same signal without having to write event multiplexing code—but I can't come up with any less contrived example of (non-clipboard) signal and slot programming than the SignalsAndSlots project in the ch12/Qt project group.

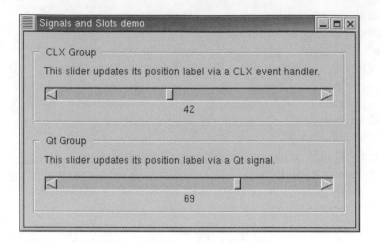

Figure 12-1. The SignalsAndSlots project

This project, based shamelessly on the Qt tutorials, has two scrollbars, each associated with a label. (See Figure 12-1) When you move the scrollbar, the associated label shows the scrollbar's position. The top scrollbar does this with a standard CLX event handler:

```
procedure TSignalsAndSlotsFrm.ClxScrollBarChange(Sender: TObject);
begin
  ClxPosition.Caption := IntToStr(ClxScrollBar.Position);
end; // TSignalsAndSlotsFrm.ClxScrollBarChange
```

while the lower scrollbar connects the scrollbar's valueChanged signal to the label's setNum slot.

```
type
  QScrollBar = class (TScrollBar)
  public
    property Hooks; // expose the protected Hooks property
  end;

procedure TSignalsAndSlotsFrm.FormCreate(Sender: TObject);
var
  SetInt: procedure (handle: QLabelH; p1: Integer); cdecl;
  Method: TMethod;
```

```
begin
  SetInt       := QLabel_setNum;
  Method.Data := QtPosition.Handle;
  Method.Code := @ SetInt;
  QScrollBar_hook_hook_valueChanged(
    QScrollBar_hookH(QScrollBar(QtScrollBar).Hooks), Method );
end; // TSignalsAndSlotsFrm.FormCreate
```

The signals and slots approach does takes a **lot** more code than
its CLX counterpart. In addition to setting the TMethod and calling
QScrollBar_hook_hook_valueChanged, I have to publicize the protected
Hooks property, and I have to use the SetInt variable to select the proper overloaded SetNum procedure—but the code is only executed once. Presumably,
directly executing a Qt slot in this way is faster than setting a label's Caption
in a CLX event handler.

Of course, the speed is basically irrelevant, here, but you may find situations
where it does matter. Probably, though, the way that manually connecting
signals and slots leaves the CLX event available—and takes advantage of Qt
functionality that Borland ignored, like QLabel_setNum—is more important
than saving a few microseconds.

Qt documentation

You can find the Qt documentation at www.trolltech.com. The *Getting Started*
and *Overviews* sections contain useful information, but the most generally
useful bit is the *Classes* list, which is an alphabetical list of every class. If
you're trying to understand why a particular control works as it does, or you
want to see if there's some way you can get the control to do what you want
by using raw Qt calls, you can read the CLX source to see what Qt class the
control wraps. Generally, a CLX control's Handle property is of the type
*QName*H [QName Handle] where the *QName* part is the name of a Qt class
that you can look up in the Qt documentation.

You can also find lots of interesting and useful tidbits just by browsing
the class list and clicking on names that sound promising.

Each class description has a list of *Public Members* which **should** all be
present in Qt.pas, as should any *Public Slots, Static Public Members,*
and *Protected Members.* (Remember that a function like, say,
QMultiLineEdit::isOverwriteMode will be bound in Qt.pas as
QMultiLineEdit_isOverwriteMode.) It may seem a little strange at first, but
you **can** call protected Qt member functions from your Kylix applications.

Feel free to think of CLX controls as descendants of the Qt objects, if that helps ease any theological pain.

As *per* the previous (*Qt and Kylix*) section of this chapter, any names listed in the *Signals* are accessed from Kylix *via* the *QName*_hook_hook_*Signal* connection procedure. For example, you'd call QMultiLineEdit_hook_hook_textChanged to connect to what the Qt documentation describes as "void QMultiLineEdit::textChanged () [signal]".

Of course, Kylix is a 1.0 product, and as with Libc, there are some missing and/or erroneous bindings in Qt.pas. For example, sometimes you want to know which line breaks in a TMemo are 'real' (or 'hard') line breaks, where the user hit Enter; and which are just 'soft' line breaks, artifacts of the current window size that will change if the user resizes the form. Perhaps you want to save the text as a paragraph stream, with the soft breaks turned into spaces. Or perhaps you just want a 'real' line count, as in the WordWrap project in the ch12/Qt project group.

The TMemo class doesn't offer any way to tell, but since a TMemo is 'just' a wrapper for Qt's QMultiLineEdit object, you can comb the documentation for helpful-looking methods. As it turns out, the protected function QMultiLineEdit::isEndOfParagraph looks tailor-made for this problem. But, there's no QMultiLineEdit_isEndOfParagraph in Qt.pas. What to do?

As with Libc, the `readelf` program's –s switch is your friend. If you `cd` to the Kylix `bin` directory and do

```
readelf -s libqtintf.so.2 | grep -i isendofparagraph
```

you'll find that there's no `isEndOfParagraph` symbol in libqtintf.so.2. However,

```
readelf -s libqt.so.2 | grep -i isendofparagraph
```

reveals that libqt.so.2 *does* contain a symbol `isEndOfParagraph__C14QMultiLineEditi`

```
12228: 00368c1c 51 FUNC GLOBAL DEFAULT 16 isEndOfParagraph__C14QMultiLineEditi
```

---

and a little experimentation reveals that

```
const
  _QMultiLineEdit_isEndOfParagraph_ = 'isEndOfParagraph__C14QMultiLineEditi';

function QMultiLineEdit_isEndOfParagraph( Handle: QMultiLineEditH;
                                          Row:    integer ): Boolean; cdecl;
external QtLibName name _QMultiLineEdit_isEndOfParagraph_;
```

works exactly as we'd like it to.

Tip

The __C14Q and the trailing i *are name-mangling artifacts. In a case like this, where* readelf -s *produces only one match to* isendofparagraph, *it's pretty safe to assume that the mangled symbol is the one we want. But, where there is more than one match, binding to the right one can take a lot of trial and error. You can avoid the trial and error by using the* nm *command line utility instead of* readelf. *While* nm -D libqt.so.2|grep -i isendofparagraph *gives the same mangled symbol that* readelf -s *does, adding the* —C *switch—*nm -D -C libqt.so.2|grep -i isendofparagraph— *shows that the unmangled name for the symbol at address 00368c1c is* QMultiLineEdit::isEndOfParagraph(int) const.

If you open the ch12/WordWrap project and CTRL+CLICK on the call to QMultiLineEdit_isEndOfParagraph in TWordWrapFrm.ParagraphCount, you'll see that it gets the QMultiLineEdit_isEndOfParagraph function from my QGrabBag unit. QGrabBag wraps its declaration of QMultiLineEdit_isEndOfParagraph within an

```
{$if not Declared(QMultiLineEdit_isEndOfParagraph)}
```

statement. This is because correspondence with Borland R&D suggested that future releases of Kylix *would* wrap the function, and I didn't want my binding to shadow the 'real' binding. I use this {$if not Declared()} technique in my LibcX unit (see Chapter 10), too.

Linux

Postscript

I HOPE THAT HELPED. Without a doubt, this was the hardest section for me to write. Section 2 presented lots of chicken and egg, organizational issues—but I've been using Object Pascal for 17 years, ever since it was Turbo Pascal. Section 2 presented lots of challenges both because there was so much to cover and because Kylix is not Delphi—but it's close, and it was easy to research the differences. But Section 3 presented novel challenges.

There's nothing like writing to show you what you don't know. You may know something well enough to do it routinely—but when you have to explain it from first principles, you quickly find that you only know about *this* as a sort of magic incantation ("it only works if I do it like this") or that you really haven't the least idea why *that* is structured as it is. "Because" and "I dunno" are not acceptable explanations!

You have to do research and you have to experiment. Then you write up what you knew and what you've found, and you find that there's something else you don't know. So you repeat the process. It's hard work, but it's satisfying, too.

But in writing Section 3, I didn't have the benefit of years of Linux experience. It was all very well to promise myself not to get caught up in tangents, not to do any more research than I'd done for the previous sections—but there was so much I didn't know! It always felt like a cop-out to say "that's beyond the scope of this book," but I really tried to restrict myself to the core Linux knowledge that you *need* to deliver sophisticated Kylix applications on time and under budget.

I'm sure you'll let me know if I succeeded. You can always contact me through Apress.

This has been the last of the "tutorial and reference" sections. Section IV consists of two very extended examples, each more-or-less complete apps that involve more code than even the longest examples so far. It gives me an opportunity to show Kylix in action in a way that the narrow and contrived examples of the first three sections could not.

Section 4

Projects

Two extended examples

WAY BACK WHEN I started this book, this section was going to be the heart of the book—maybe 40% to 60% of the page count. Detailed walkthroughs of a wide variety of complete applications would let me show Kylix in action, not just as isolated bits of sample code.

Two things changed that. First, the first three sections turned out much bigger than I ever imagined that they would. Second, between the time it took to write the first three sections and the very short time in which Kylix went from unusable to ready to ship, I simply don't have a large stable full of working Kylix apps that I can write about.

Thus, there are only two chapters in this section. Chapter 13 covers vfind, a visual wrapper for the venerable find utility. It illustrates the use of a few standard controls, the Libc.popen() and Libc.system() commands, and basic thread/GUI synchronization. In addition, I present three slightly different versions, primarily to show how much simpler regular expressions can make some common tasks and secondarily showing incremental development in action.

Chapter 14 covers m4l, a Mandelbrot explorer. It's not exactly a polished application—in fact, there are more than a few big bugs, still—but it does a good job of illustrating the use of critical sections to guard inter-thread communications, advanced thread/GUI synchronization, inter-form communication, and some of the pitfalls you face doing direct pixel manipulation *via* the TBitmap.ScanLine property.

A visual find utility

A visual find utility

I'M SURE IT WOULD be nice if the era of putting GUI shells on command line utilities was over, if all the little GUI applets were simple and easy to use. But it doesn't seem to be. The applets that do exist aren't very good, and there's still too much need to tweak text configuration files by hand.

Maybe it's got something to do with the amount of work pre-Kylix GUI toolkits made you do—manually creating and positioning each widget, for example, or writing reams of boilerplate code—but all too many seem simply to map command line options to GUI widgets or otherwise assume that you really know what you're doing. The best Windows applets can basically educate an intelligent but naïve user—and that's good, in a world that changes so fast and where no one can know everything—where most Linux applets still seem to require both intelligence and experience.

It's still just too easy to misconfigure Linux, and too hard to get it right and keep it right. Every change and every addition seems to take more work than under Windows. There seems to me to be a lot of room for public-spirited Kylix programmers to ease this tremendous sysadmin burden with applets and configuration tools that explain every option.

My visual find utility, vfind, is a small effort along these lines. It doesn't try to provide a GUI interface to each of the find utility's options; it simply imitates the Windows 98 Find Files (FLAG+F) applet, as that's both familiar to many users and as it seems to me that Find Files does a good job of focusing on files as the user thinks of them, not as a program does.

The first pass

There are actually three different projects in the ch13/vfind project group: vfind1, vfind2, and vfind. All three versions use popen() to run the standard find utility and differ both in how they implement the "Containing Text" function (Figure 13-1) and in how they save and load run-time settings. Initially, I used system() to call the grep utility to see whether or not a given file contained the desired text. After implementing IRegEx (Chapter 11), I realized that I could move this test inline, saving both the cost of creating a new process for every file and the expense of compiling a search pattern for every file.

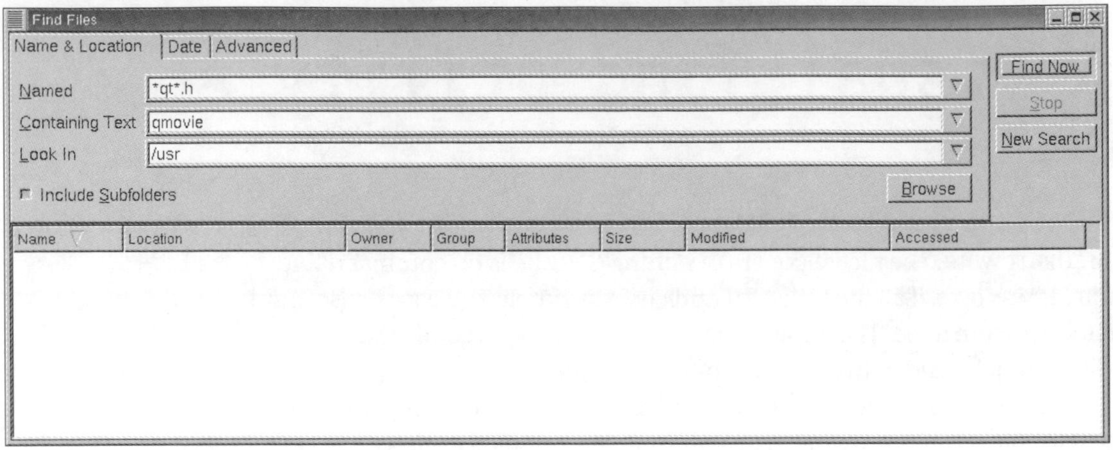

Figure 13-1. The 'Containing Text' function

This was relatively major surgery, so I did what I'm sure you've done in similar circumstances: I checkpointed the project. Once I had the IRegEx code working, it was smaller, faster, and clearer, so there was no real question of my going back to the original system() code, but I decided to keep it around, primarily as an example of the utility of the regex functions. I continued development a little while after the split, so that vfind2 contains some improvements over vfind1, but the two are pretty similar in the way they save and load settings and the way the UI works, so I'll walk through those aspects of vfind1 and primarily discuss vfind2 in terms of how it differs from vfind1.

As I was writing about vfind1, I realized that the way I'd been handling persistent settings for a few years was really unbelievably clunky, so I checkpointed vfind2 as well, and implemented a much cleaner persistence architecture in the final vfind project.

Form design

The 'specification' here is really simple: a fixed-height set of three tabs that specifies what to look for, with three buttons to the right that start, stop, or reset the search. The tabs should grow horizontally with the form, while all remaining space should go to the search results. Thus, the basic layout is a top-aligned panel, TopPnl, on which is a right-aligned panel, ButtonPnl, and a client-aligned page control, PageControl, which gets any space on the TopPnl that the ButtonPnl doesn't take. Below that is a client-aligned list view, Results, which gets any space on the form that the TopPnl doesn't take. (Figure 13-2.)

```
┌─────────────────────────────────────────────┐
│            The TFileFinder form               │
│  ┌─────────────────────────────────────────┐ │
│  │          The top-aligned TopPnl          │ │
│  │ ┌─────────────────────┐ ┌──────────────┐ │ │
│  │ │ The client-aligned  │ │ The right-   │ │ │
│  │ │ PageControl         │ │ aligned      │ │ │
│  │ │                     │ │ ButtonPnl    │ │ │
│  │ └─────────────────────┘ └──────────────┘ │ │
│  └─────────────────────────────────────────┘ │
│  ┌─────────────────────────────────────────┐ │
│  │ The client-aligned                      │ │
│  │ "Results" list view                     │ │
│  │                                         │ │
│  │                                         │ │
│  └─────────────────────────────────────────┘ │
└─────────────────────────────────────────────┘
```

Figure 13-2. The 'Find Files' form layout

On the page control, only the "Name & Location" tab can really take any advantage of increased width. The three combo boxes are anchored Top, Left, and Right, so that they grow (and shrink) horizontally, and the Browse button is anchored Right, so that it's always lined up with the right edge of the three combo boxes.

This simple layout assures that the three search buttons always stay in the top-right; that the tab control gets as much width as possible; and that the list view expands to fill all available space. Without a single line of code.

The rest of the form design is similarly straightforward, with only a few things worth commenting on.

- The combo boxes on the "Name & Location" tab have the csDropDown style, while the combo boxes on the "Date" and "Advanced" tabs have the csDropDownList style. The difference is that the dropdown combo boxes have an edit box that the user can edit, while with the dropdown list combo boxes, the user can only choose from entries in the Items list.

- The Results list view has a ViewStyle of vsReport. This is the only way that the list view can have column headings.

- The VCL list view lets you toggle between four view styles: small icons, large icons, list view, and report view. Under the CLX, the list view has been split off from the icon view. If you're porting code that lets the user select any of the four styles, you'll have to create a tab control with two pages and the tsNoTabs Style, and put an icon view on one tab and a list view on the other.

Kylix is not Delphi

- You set a report's columns (Figure 13-3) by selecting the list view's Columns property and clicking on the …

Figure 13-3. The 'Columns' property

button. This lets you specify the header captions, as well as each column's default, minimum, and maximum widths.

- I don't have to do anything special to draw the sorted-column indicator (Figure 13-4); I just set ShowColumn-SortIndicator to True, and the CLX does it for me.

Figure 13-4. The ColumnSortIndicator

Conversely, I have **no control** over sort order, and even numeric columns are sorted in alphabetical order.

- In vfind2 and vfind, the date pickers on the Date tab have a regex-based OnDateConvertError handler that can handle dates like "July 13, 2001".

Persistence framework

Most real-world applications need to save settings between runs. At a minimum, bringing up a window where it was when the user last closed it allows the user to arrange her desktop as she likes. Saving the most recently used file names (or the entries in a dropdown list) makes the user's life easier. Saving the state of various options can spare the user the necessity of recreating her preferred working state each time she loads your application.

Windows applications typically store this information in the registry. Linux applications typically store configuration information in a 'hidden' file (one whose name starts with a dot) in the user's home directory. This difference is one reason why it can make sense for applications to maintain a single Configuration object that hides the details of how and where the information is stored. A single Configuration object means that there's only one place that needs to be changed.

Another reason to use a central Configuration object is that it makes it easier to change your persistence strategy. There's a range of strategies that you may follow. At one extreme, you can load each persistent datum as it's needed and save it whenever it's changed. At the other extreme, you can read the whole configuration at startup and only save it at shutdown. Or you can be somewhere in between, like reading all the common data at startup but only reading the less common data as needed. Or perhaps you might load everything at startup and save everything on any change. The on-demand/ as-changed extreme is a bit slower overall, but minimizes startup time—and is less subject to losing state information in the event of a power failure or program crash. The *en masse* extreme is a bit faster and simpler, but is also more fragile. By using a central Configuration object, you can easily change the way you handle each datum.

For a few years, I handled persistence rather stupidly: Every time I started a new project, I'd hunt down the most recent project in which I remembered using a Configuration object, copy it into the new project's directory, and strip out the project specific stuff. Eventually, I realized what a waste of time this was, and factored some of the common code into a BaseConfig unit that could live in a library directory. Each new project would simply derive its TConfig from TBaseConfig, adding the properties the new project needed to persist, and simply inheriting the routines that saved form size &c. (I mention this only by way of pointing out that even those of us who preach about Best Practices don't *always* follow them.)

Except for the final version of vfind, all of the projects I discuss in this Projects section—vfind, and the Mandelbrot explorer of Chapter 14—use the lib/BaseConfig framework. This is a rather stripped down version of my Windows registry code, and it provides five basic services:

1. It exports the user's HomeDirectory string.

2. It provides a TBaseConfig class, which descends from TIniFile and can thus save and load strings, numbers, dates, and booleans.

3. It provides a base (ancestral) form which saves its non-maximized size, so it can save both WindowState and the wsNormal size.

4. It provides routines to save and restore the position and WindowState of these TBaseForm's.

5. It provides routines to save and restore string lists.

Note

The vfind1 project uses a checkpointed copy of BaseConfig that does not use a regex to unpack a TBaseForm's saved size. I present both versions, by way of showing how regexes can simplify many common programming tasks. The final version of vfind uses a newer module, lib/IConfig, that provides a better way to persist UI settings.

Home directory

The chief reason that lib/BaseConfig exports the HomeDirectory string is that units that implement TBaseConfig descendants need to know where to put their *.appname*.ini file. You are, of course, free to use this string in any other way you want. The vfind projects, for example, use it to start a directory browse operation in the user's home directory.

HomeDirectory is set as

```
HomeDirectory := IncludeTrailingPathDelimiter(getpwuid(getuid).pw_dir);
```

because reading the HOME environment variable is susceptible to malicious spoofing by a virus or Trojan Horse application, or to accidental munging by the sort of user with just enough knowledge to make them dangerous.

Ini files

Ini files consist of a series of named sections. Each section name appears in square brackets, and is followed by zero or more lines in the form *Name=Value*. Section names must be unique, and value names must be unique within a section. Comments, if any, start with a semicolon, and run to the end of the line. For example,

```
; This file was last changed at 9:17 PM on July 7, 2001, by user jon.

[This is a section name]

This is a value=Value names can include spaces
* This is also a value *=and other non-alphanumeric characters.
No Quotes=String values don't have to be quoted.
```

When you set a value, you specify a section name, a value name, and the value itself. (At the lowest level, all values are strings, but TIniFile includes methods for reading and writing numbers, dates, and booleans.) Setting a value will either create a new entry or replace any existing value in that section with that name; there's no special API for creating *vs* replacing values.

You can read individual values by specifying the section and value name, along with a default value to use if the ini file doesn't contain that section or if that section doesn't have a value with that name. Alternatively, you can read all the values in a section into a TStrings object, and use the TStrings' associative array properties (Names and Values) to read individual values.

> **Note**
>
>
> *Kylix's TIniFile class stores the whole ini file—and any changes— in memory. This makes updates much faster, but you **must** remember to call the UpdateFile method before freeing the object. The TBaseConfig class does this automatically.*

The base form

Probably the most basic sort of persistent setting is window position. This borders on a frill for a simple, single form application like vfind, but becomes more important with applications that may have several windows open at once. Saving the windows' size and positions reduces the amount of fiddling that users have to go through every time they run your application—thus making it more likely that they'll actually get something done with it.

It's not enough just to save the BoundsRect, though. This is because there are two basic differences between maximizing a window and setting the BoundsRect to the BoundsRect of a maximized window. The first difference is that most window managers will either draw a maximized window with no frame, or will ignore any attempts to resize a maximized window. If you merely set the BoundsRect to fill the non-panel area of the desktop, you do not get this behavior. The second difference is that many window managers supply a fictitious value for a maximized window's BoundsRect. The BoundsRect may include a Top and Left that's off the screen, or the Top and Left may correspond to where the restored window would be—but setting the BoundsRect to this value will not necessarily draw a window that fills the non-panel area of the desktop.

In addition, even if you *could* maximize a window just by setting its BoundsRect, you really wouldn't want to. Ideally, if a user closes a window maximized, you want to record that fact—along with the un-maximized size. Then, the window is maximized on the next run, but it can resume the same size and position that it had on the previous run. A small detail, yes, but it's precisely such attention to small details that distinguishes a pleasant application from an annoying one.

Thus, the BaseConfig unit defines a TWindowSize record

```
type
  TWindowSize = record
    Bounds: TRect;
    State:  TWindowState;
  end;
```

that includes both a BoundsRect and a WindowState. It then declares a TBaseForm that exports a WindowSize property

```
TBaseForm = class(TForm)
  procedure FormResize(Sender: TObject);
private
  fNormalSize: TRect;
  function GetWindowSize: TWindowSize;
  procedure SetWindowSize(const Value: TWindowSize);
protected
  property NormalSize: TRect read fNormalSize write fNormalSize;
public
  property WindowSize: TWindowSize read GetWindowSize write SetWindowSize;
end;
```

and has an OnResize handler that sets NormalSize iff the WindowState is wsNormal.

```
procedure TBaseForm.FormResize(Sender: TObject);
begin
  if WindowState = wsNormal then
    NormalSize := BoundsRect;
end; // TBaseForm.FormResize
```

By saving NormalSize only when WindowState is wsNormal, a maximized or minimized TBaseForm should always know what its un-maximized size will be. The WindowSize property allows it to export and import the normal size and current state.

```
function TBaseForm.GetWindowSize: TWindowSize;
begin
  Result.State  := WindowState;
  if Result.State = wsNormal
    then Result.Bounds := BoundsRect  // Current position & size
    else Result.Bounds := NormalSize; // last wsNormal position & size
end; // TBaseForm.GetWindowSize
```

```
procedure TBaseForm.SetWindowSize(const Value: TWindowSize);
var
  NewRect: TRect;
begin
  WindowState := wsNormal;

  NewRect := Value.Bounds;
  if not (BorderStyle in [fbsSizeable, fbsSizeToolWin]) then
    // Not resizable - just adjust Top and Left
    OffsetRect( NewRect,
                Value.Bounds.Left - NewRect.Left,
                Value.Bounds.Top - NewRect.Top );
  BoundsRect  := NewRect;

  WindowState := Value.State;
end; // TBaseForm.SetWindowSize
```

The GetWindowSize function should be pretty much self-explanatory. It returns both the current window state, and a bounding box. When the window state is normal (neither maximized nor minimized), GetWindowSize returns the current BoundsRect, which includes the form's current Top and Left properties. When the window state is not normal (either maximized or minimized), GetWindowSize returns the last normal size.

SetWindowSize is a tad more complex. It first sets the WindowState to wsNormal, as some window managers will ignore an assignment to BoundsRect if the form is maximized or minimized. If the window is resizable, SetWindowSize then sets the BoundsRect to the saved size. If the window is not resizable, SetWindowSize just changes the window's Top and Left. Finally, SetWindowSize sets the WindowState to the saved state. Thus, SetWindowSize sets both the current window state and the size that the window should have when restored.

Unfortunately, there's a **huge** fly in this ointment. Worse, it's still alive and buzzing and eager to sting. By now you may even be anticipating it: Some window managers are far from cooperative. Your forms may not ever 'know' that they are actually maximized. Instead, they'll just get a wsNormal WindowState with a bizarre BoundsRect. Under these window managers, TBaseForm's that persist WindowSize (using the code in the next section) will not restore themselves properly if the user closes them while they're maximized. Instead, they'll restore themselves as a large window, partially off the screen.

You don't really have much recourse against such inept windows managers except to 1) provide your users with a list of window managers that **do** work properly with your application(s) and 2) to push the authors of broken windows managers to bring them up to snuff.

Persistent form positions

The TBaseConfig class includes a pair of routines that can save and load a TBaseForm's WindowSize.

```
function FormSection: string;
begin
  // Includes Screen size in [Form Positions] heading, so can have different
  // preferences for different resolutions
  Result := Format('Form Positions - %d x %d', [Screen.Width, Screen.Height]);
end; // FormSection


procedure TBaseConfig.SaveFormSize(const Form: TBaseForm);
begin
  with Form, WindowSize, Bounds do
    WriteString( FormSection, {Form.}Name,
                 Format( '%d %d %d %d %d',
                         [Left, Top, Right, Bottom, ord(State)]) );
end; // TBaseConfig.SaveFormSize
```

As you can see, SaveFormSize rather straightforwardly saves the WindowSize as an ASCII 'stream' of five integers separated by single spaces, using the form's Name property as a key. If your application creates several copies of a form, Kylix automatically appends a 'serial number' (*ie*, while the first copy of TThisForm is named ThisForm, as you specified at design time *via* the Object Inspector, the second and third copies are named ThisForm_1 and ThisForm_2) so using the Name property means that your apps automatically maintain different sizes for each copy of a form. The form sizes are stored in an ini file section that includes the screen size, so that users who switch between multiple screen sizes get the application layout that they find most appropriate to the current screen size.

The inverse routine, LoadFormSize, isn't quite so straightforward.

```
procedure TBaseConfig.LoadFormSize(Form: TBaseForm);
// Sets WindowSize or throws an exception
var
```

```
  FmtdRect: string;
  Offset,
  Index,
  Delim:    integer;
  This:     string;
  Result:   record
              case byte of
                1: (Size: TWindowSize);
                2: (A:    array[0..4] of integer);
              end;
begin
  FmtdRect := ReadString(FormSection, Form.Name, '');
  Offset := 0;
  for Index := Low(Result.A) to High(Result.A) do
  begin
    Delim := FindChar(FmtdRect, ' ', Offset);
    This := Copy(FmtdRect, Offset + 1, Delim - Offset - 1);
    Result.A[Index] := StrToInt(This);
    Offset := Delim;
  end;
  Form.WindowSize := Result.Size;
end; // TBaseConfig.LoadFormSize
```

This loops through the retrieved string, looking for the spaces between numbers, using the FindChar() function from lib/GrabBag. It converts each token to a number with StrToInt, which will raise an exception if the string can't be converted to a 32-bit integer. This code is straightforward enough, but rather bulky; the equivalent code in lib/BaseConfig and lib/IConfig uses a regex to extract the five substrings, and is much smaller and clearer.

Persistent string lists

The TBaseConfig routines that persist string lists save each string list in its own section. TIniFile's can load a whole section into a string list, which makes it easy to restore the lists.

```
  function ZeroPadFmt(Width: integer): string;
  begin
    Result := '%.' + IntToStr(Width) + 'd';
  end; // ZeroPadFmt
```

```pascal
procedure TBaseConfig.SaveStrings( const SectionName:   string;
                                         List:          TStrings;
                                         AllowBlankLns: boolean = True;
                                         MaxEntries:    integer = 12 );
var
  Index:          integer;
  Entries, Digits: integer;
  Fmt:            string;
begin
  EraseSection(SectionName);

  with TStringList.Create do
  try
    // Prune
    Assign(List);
    if not AllowBlankLns then
      for Index := Count - 1 downto 0 do
        if Trim(Strings[Index]) = '' then
          Delete(Index);

    Entries := Min(Count, MaxEntries);
    Digits  := Length(IntToStr(Entries));
    Fmt := ZeroPadFmt(Digits);
    for Index := 0 to Entries - 1 do
      WriteString(SectionName, Format(Fmt, [Index]), Strings[Index]);
  finally
    Free;
  end;
end; // TBaseConfig.SaveStrings
```

The SaveStrings method begins by calling EraseSection, which wipes out any existing section. I do this so I don't have to store a list length line and can just store a line stream like

```
[Look In]
0=/usr
1=/
2=/kylix/source
3=/var
4=/tmp
```

If I didn't call EraseSection, it would be hard for a list to shrink: If I tried to store only four lines, the 0 through 3 values would overwrite the old ones, but the 5 value would still be there. Next time I loaded the list, it would have four values from the last run—and one from the run before that.

Next, the SaveStrings method copies the input list to a temporary TStringList, and optionally eliminates any blank lines. It then imposes an optional limit on the number of lines to save (most MRU lists have a limited length, as it's just overwhelming to see every file you ever opened, or every search term you ever used) and uses the number of entries to decide how wide the line names should be.

```
Digits  := Length(IntToStr(Entries));
Fmt := ZeroPadFmt(Digits);
```

I use leading zeroes on the line 'names', both because then the equal signs all line up when you look at an ini file in the Kylix code editor and because then they sort properly if you ReadSectionValues() and sort the string list.

Finally, the SaveStrings method just writes the pruned list, line by line.

The LoadStrings method, obviously enough, is SaveStrings' inverse function.

```
procedure TBaseConfig.LoadStrings(     List:       TStrings;
                                const SectionName:  string;
                                      AllowBlankLns: boolean = True );
var
  Section:      TStringList;
  Count, Digits: integer;
  Fmt:          string;
  Index:        integer;
  This:         string;
begin
  List.Clear;
  Section := TStringList.Create;
  try
    ReadSectionValues(SectionName, Section);
```

```
    Count   := Section.Count;
    Digits  := Length(IntToStr(Count));
    Fmt     := ZeroPadFmt(Digits);
    for Index := 0 to Count - 1 do
    begin
      This := Trim(Section.Values[Format(Fmt, [Index])]);
      if AllowBlankLns or (This <> '') then
        List.Add(This);
    end;
  finally
    Section.Free;
  end;
end; // TBaseConfig.LoadStrings
```

The LoadStrings method begins by clearing the result List, then reads all the values in the SectionName into a temporary string list. It derives the name format from the Section.Count in just the same way that SaveStrings generated it from the Count of the pruned list, and reads the Values[] property, entry by entry, optionally pruning blank lines. (Both procedures have AllowBlankLns parameters, as it's not impossible that two programs would share the same ini file, with one saving blank lines and the other not wanting to load them.)

You can use these routines to save and restore the values of any CLX component that publish its contents as a TStrings, though they're most useful in conjunction with a TListBox or a TComboBox. Storing a TMemo line-by-line in an ini file seems sort of gratuitously wasteful. The vfind project uses these routines to persist the dropdowns on the main, "Name & Location" tab; I show this in the next section.

Persistent settings

Projects that use the persistence framework, as the vfind1 and vfind2 projects do, declare a TConfig object that descends from TBaseConfig. This TConfig object has a property for each value that the application wants to persist, and is a 'singleton' that's instantiated as a global Configuration variable in the Config unit's initialization code. Applications that maintain both a global configuration (for things like server and/or plugin locations) and a *per* user configuration (for various UI preferences) would use two different TBaseConfig descendants, instantiated as global variables named something like GlobalConfiguration and PerUserConfiguration.

```
initialization

  Configuration := TConfig.Create;

finalization

  Configuration.Free;

end.
```

The actual TConfig code tends to be fairly repetitive, so I'm showing only a tiny extract, here.

```
type
  TConfig = class (TBaseConfig)
  private
    // Name & Location tab
    fNamed:             TStringList;
    fIncludeSubfolders: boolean;

    constructor Create;

  public
    // Name & Location tab
    property Named:              TStringList read  fNamed;
    property IncludeSubfolders: boolean      read  fIncludeSubfolders
                                             write fIncludeSubfolders;

    procedure  Save; override;
    destructor Destroy; override;
  end;
```

Loading settings

In addition to normal chores like creating string lists and any other member objects, the TConfig constructor is responsible not only for passing a file name to the inherited constructor, which reads the whole ini file into memory, but also for reading values from the ini file into the appropriate properties.

```
const
  ConfigFilename = '.vfind.ini';

  NamedSection        = 'Named';
  IncludeSubfoldersKey = 'Include Subfolders';

constructor TConfig.Create;
begin
  inherited Create(HomeDirectory + ConfigFilename);

  // Date & Location tab
  fNamed := TStringList.Create;
  LoadStrings(Named, NamedSection);

  IncludeSubfolders := ReadBool(SettingsSection, IncludeSubfoldersKey, True);
end; // TConfig.Create;
```

Maintaining a lengthy section of string constants outside of any routines that actually save or load write values to or from the ini file ensures that there's no risk of two string constants getting out of synch. (As I mentioned in Chapter 5, I set the syntax highlighting (using the Color tab of the Tools ➤ Editor Options dialog) to make strings really garish, so that it's really obvious when I use an inline string constant.)

The constructor's first line, `inherited Create(HomeDirectory + ConfigFilename)`, opens the file ~/.vfind.ini. If the file doesn't exist, it will not be created at this time; instead, the TIniFile object will simply initialize its internal lists so that all Read operations will fail and return the default value. Subsequent lines create the objects behind the properties, and read them from the ini file. Note that all the TInfiFile Read methods allow you to specify a default value as the last parameter. The Read functions will return this default value if the key does not exist, or if the key does exist but does not contain a string that can be converted to an integer, boolean, or date.

Using a global configuration object means that you then have to copy the persistent data from the configuration object to each form as it's created.[1]

---

1. This is unquestionably annoying and wasteful, but until I wrote this section I didn't really think much about just how annoying and wasteful it was. The ability to easily change your persistence technology and/or your persistence strategy seemed to more than make up for the inconvenience. The final project in this chapter offers a new approach to persistence that retains the flexibility of the approach I'm describing here while losing the cumbersome replication of data and boilerplate code.

```
  procedure LoadDropdown(ComboBox: TComboBox; List: TStrings);
  begin
    ComboBox.Items.Assign(List);
    if ComboBox.Items.Count > 0 then
      ComboBox.ItemIndex := 0;
  end; // LoadDropdown

procedure TFileFinder.FormCreate(Sender: TObject);
begin
  // create vars
  DisplayQueue := TStringQueue.Create;

  GrepQueue    := TStringQueue.Create;
  GrepWait     := TEvent.Create(Nil,True, False, '');

  // get form size, col widths
  try
    Configuration.LoadFormSize(Self);
  except
  end;
  RestoreWidths(Results.Columns, Configuration.ColumnWidths);
  PageControl.ActivePage := NameAndLocationTab;
    // no matter which was left active in the IDE

  // Name & Location tab
  LoadDropdown(Named,          Configuration.Named);

  IncludeSubfolders.Checked := Configuration.IncludeSubfolders;
end; // TFileFinder.FormCreate
```

The form's OnCreate handler, TFileFinder.FormCreate, creates three
objects—DisplayQueue, GrepQueue, and GrepWait—that the search code
uses; I'll describe them in the *Searching* section, below. Next, FormCreate
loads the saved form size, if any, and loads the TListView's saved column
widths. I'm not going to print the SaveWidths and RestoreWidths code
because it's very similar to the LoadFormSize code that I do print, but of
course the tarball includes full source and you can easily check out the array
of integer code on your own machine. FormCreate then sets the page control's
ActivePage. This is something that I find I do in just about every program that
uses a page control, as that way you can't break the program by working on a
'secondary' tab and leaving it selected when you compile the program. You
may actually prefer to save the tab that was visible when the user closed the
app with the rest of the user's preferences, and use that instead of the first tab.

Finally, FormCreate restores the user's settings, from the global Configuration object. (I've elided quite a few of them, in the interests of clarity and not wasting trees.)

Question: Did you notice the bug in the LoadDropDown procedure?

It sets the ItemIndex to 0 whenever the dropdown isn't empty. That is, it doesn't distinguish between, say, a Containing Text dropdown with a populated MRU list and an empty Text, and one whose Text property is the top dropdown entry. This could easily be fixed, simply by adding new persistent properties that contain the actual current Text of each dropdown.

> **Note**
>
>
>
> *I could certainly just fix this bug, instead of commenting on it. But I'm not going to do that, for two reasons. First, I could easily spend weeks polishing demos that no one will ever really use. Second, it's just too good an example of a general principle to pass up: Many, perhaps even most, bugs aren't pieces of code that don't do what you mean; they're pieces of code that do the wrong thing. Poor analysis, not poor implementation.*

Saving settings

At program startup, we walk the 'persistence chain' in three steps:

1. TIniFile reads the ini file into memory when it's created.

2. The Configuration object reads various properties from the in-memory ini file.

3. The application's form(s) read their persistent settings from the Configuration object as they're created.

At shutdown, we take the same three steps—in reverse—to save the (possibly changed) settings for the next program run:

1. The application's form(s) save their persistent settings to the Configuration object as they're destroyed.

2. The Configuration object writes its properties back to the in-memory ini file.

3. The Configuration object calls the TIniFile UpdateFile method to save the in-memory changes to the on-disk ini file.

Thus, vfind's OnDestroy handler frees the objects that OnCreate created, then saves form size and all the persistent settings.

```
procedure TFileFinder.FormDestroy(Sender: TObject);
begin
  // Free vars
  GrepQueue.Free;
  GrepWait.Free;

  DisplayQueue.Free;

  // Save positions &c
  Configuration.SaveFormSize(Self);
  Configuration.ColumnWidths := SaveWidths(Results.Columns);

  // Name & Location tab
  Configuration.Named.Assign(Named.Items);
  Configuration.IncludeSubfolders := IncludeSubfolders.Checked;
end; // TFileFinder.FormDestroy
```

Since the applications in this section take a lazy, *en masse* approach to saving settings to disk, Configuration object properties just stay in memory until the Configuration object is freed. The TBaseConfig destructor

```
destructor TBaseConfig.Destroy;
begin
  Save;
  inherited;
end; // TBaseConfig.Destroy
```

calls the virtual procedure Save

```
procedure TBaseConfig.Save;
begin
  UpdateFile;
  // Descendants should write changes BEFORE calling inherited
end; // TBaseConfig.Save
```

which in turn calls the TIniFile UpdateFile method. The idea, here, is that the Configuration object overrides the Save method, saving all its properties to the in-memory ini file. The override procedure should call Save at the end, thus copying the changes to disk.

```
procedure TConfig.Save;
begin
  // Name & Location tab
  SaveStrings(NamedSection,      Named);
  WriteBool(SettingsSection, IncludeSubfoldersKey, IncludeSubfolders);
  inherited;
end; // TConfig.Save
```

Note that one consequence of this design is that TConfig.Destroy **must** call inherited Destroy before freeing any data structures.

```
destructor TConfig.Destroy;
begin
  inherited;
  Named.Free;
end; // TConfig.Destroy
```

Do you see why? TBaseConfig.Destroy calls the Save procedure, which in this case reads the string lists. If TConfig.Destroy followed an inherited-last strategy, the string lists would no longer exist by the time Save tried to read them. Arguably, this is a stupid and even reprehensible design: In the name of keeping the finalization simple—

```
finalization

  Configuration.Free;

end.
```

—I've created an object that breaks if you write the destructor in the wrong order.

Note

As it happens, inherited-first is the way I've normally written destructors. It's never caused any problems for me. However, several people who read the manuscript of this book commented on this practice, and pointed out that inherited-last should be the normal destructor strategy, as that eliminates the possibility of problems should an object's cleanup code depend in any way on inherited object fields.

Event handlers

Though Kylix will always place new event handlers (and methods that SHIFT+CTRL+C builds the implementation stubs for) at the end of the unit, I always try to keep my units grouped functionally. Kylix is great at showing you the source for a routine, but not so great at taking you back where you were.[2] Keeping related code together makes it easier to read. If you're reading the code from the top to the bottom, you get all the different aspects of a subsystem in one place, instead of some here and some there. Similarly, if you can PGUP and PGDN to see the other code that uses *this* data structure, or the code *that* calls that routine, you'll grasp the code faster than if you have to keep jumping around and using CTRL+F.

Thus, I followed my usual practice in laying out vfind1/Main.pas and setup regions for "Name & Location tab events", "Date tab events", "Advanced tab events" and "Button (start/stop/reset search) events". While not a perfect division of the code—several widgets share the same ViableSearch method, for example—it still makes a good order to discuss the code in.

Name & Location tab events

There's only one Name & Location tab event, the Browse button's OnClick handler.

```
procedure TFileFinder.BrowseBtnClick(Sender: TObject);
var
  NewDir: string;
begin
  NewDir := HomeDirectory;
  if SelectDirectory('Search Directory', PathDelim, NewDir) then
    LookIn.Text := NewDir;
end; // TFileFinder.BrowseBtnClick
```

This procedure very simply calls the QDialogs.SelectDirectory function. The first parameter is the popup window's caption. (The popup will always appear in the center of the screen; you can't make it line up with the button or anything like that.) The second parameter is the 'local root' for the search. If you set it to the user's home directory, for example, she can only select her

---

2. You can use Undo (ALT+BACKSPACE, or CTRL+Z) but, obviously, that will also undo any changes. You can use bookmarks to record your current position, but they don't help you if you forgot to set one, or if all ten are already in use and you don't want to overwrite any of them.

home directory or one of its subdirectories; she can't select / or /usr/share or any other system directory. As you can see, the third parameter does double duty: It specifies both which dialog should be highlighted initially, and also which directory the user selected. (If the initial directory is not under the local root, the function will 'mostly work, most of the time', but the result may be missing a leading / or be malformed in some other way.)

SelectDirectory returns True iff the user presses OK. In that case, this event handler sets the LookIn combo box's Text field to the returned directory and returns.

Date tab events

The Date tab (Figure 13-5) is a curious beast, in its way. At the top level, it has two radio buttons that let you either ignore file dates in the search or specify a range of dates. The "All files, regardless of date" caption is part of the top radio button, and clicking anywhere on the caption will select the top radio button. But, while logically all the other controls on the tab are part of the second, date-limited search radio button, and clicking on any of them (or using the keyboard shortcuts) should select that second radio button, that's not the way it works on its own. To make the tab work that way takes event handlers.

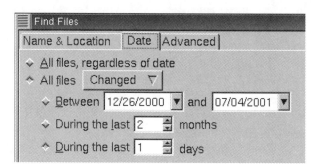

Figure 13-5. The Date Tab

Thus, clicking on any of the three type of date ranges calls the DateFiltering event handler

```
procedure TFileFinder.DateFiltering(Sender: TObject);
begin
  Filtered.Checked := True;
end; // TFileFinder.DateFiltering
```

which makes sure that the Filtered radio button is also checked. (Note that a radio button's OnClick—the DateFiltering method, in this case—is also called when the user uses a keyboard shortcut to select a radio button.)

Similarly, clicking on (or using the keyboard shortcuts for) either of the date dropdowns, or the "and" label in between them, will check both the Between dates radio button and the Filtered (by dates) radio button. There's similar logic for the filter by months and filter by days spin edits and labels.

Note

*This sort of attention to detail represents a bit of a Catch-22. Time spent building a good, There's More Than One Way To Do It user interface is time not spent building more visible features that a customer and/or boss will see as signs of progress. Yet, if you **don't** include details like this, everyone will find the UI frustrating and/or confusing, without being able to offer any specific suggestions.*

Advanced tab events

Actually, there aren't any event handlers specific to the Advanced tab (Figure 13-6)—the dropdown shares the ViableSearch event handler (below) with other search specifiers, but otherwise all the action on the advanced tab happens when you click Find Now, and the search function builds a `find` argument line from the various widgets.

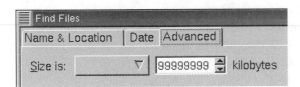

Figure 13-6. The Advanced Tab

Button events

Strangely enough, the first of the "button events"

```
procedure TFileFinder.ViableSearch(Sender: TObject);
begin
  FindNowBtn.Enabled := (NameTests <> '') or
                        (DateTests <> '') or
                        (AdvancedTests <> '');
end; // TFileFinder.ViableSearch
```

doesn't fire when any of the buttons are pressed. Instead, it fires when the value in any of the "search content" widgets (on the page control) changes. In vfind1, the ViableSearch method makes sure that the Find Now button is only enabled when the search has been narrowed down a bit. In general, of course, it's a lot better to disable a button than to let users press it and then popup a message box saying "Sorry, that operation is not available at this time" —but in this case, it turned out to be unnecessary. find / is a perfectly valid command, and the later versions of vfind comment out the tests in ViableSearch, leaving the FindNowBtn always Enabled.

The three actual OnClick events are all pretty straightforward.

```
procedure TFileFinder.FindNowBtnClick(Sender: TObject);
begin
  RunInThread(Find);
end; // TFileFinder.FindNowBtnClick
```

The Find Now button creates a thread ["the Find thread"] which runs the search. This lets the UI stay responsive, even when popen('find', 'r') goes long seconds (or even minutes) without returning control to the calling thread. I'll walk through the Find routine in the *Searching* section, below.

```
procedure TFileFinder.StopBtnClick(Sender: TObject);
begin
  StopSearch := True;
end; // TFileFinder.StopBtnClick
```

The StopBtn is only enabled when a search is in progress. As you can see, all it does is set a flag that tells the search thread to break out of its loop.

```
procedure TFileFinder.NewSearchBtnClick(Sender: TObject);
begin
  // Name & location tab
  Named.Text               := '';
  ContainingText.Text      := '';
  LookIn.Text              := '';
  IncludeSubfolders.Checked := True;

  // Date tab
  Unfiltered.Checked := True;

  // Advanced tab
  SizeType.ItemIndex := 0;
end; // TFileFinder.NewSearchBtnClick
```

The New Search button is only enabled when a search is **not** in progress. It clears all the search terms, selecting the equivalent of find /. Returning every file on the system isn't a very useful search—but if you want to do a totally different search, it can be easier to clear all widgets and just set a few than to set a few and clear the rest by hand.

Searching

The TFileFinder.Find routine (Listing 13-1), which runs in the Find thread, is the heart of the program. This is the routine that gathers the search parameters from the various widgets; translates them into find parameters; uses popen() to run find; optionally passes each found file to grep for a content check; and finally displays the results. My discussion of the Find routine basically ignores all the parameter translation, and focuses on the use of popen() and system() as well as on inter-thread communication.

Listing 13-1. TFileFinder.Find

```
procedure TFileFinder.Find(Thread: TSimpleThread; Data: pointer);
var
  RootDir,
  Contains,
  Cmd:      string;
  Handle:   PIOFile;
  Line:     PChar;
  Buffer:   array[0..MAX_PATH] of char;
  Filename: string;
```

```
const
  Limit: array[boolean] of string = ('-maxdepth 1', '');
begin
  // setup
  Thread.Synchronize(GuiSetup);

  RootDir := ComboText(LookIn);
  if RootDir = '' then RootDir := PathDelim;

  Contains := ComboText(ContainingText);
  if Contains <> '' then
    Contains := Format('exec grep -qie "%s" "%%s"', [Contains]);
  GrepTemplate := Contains;

  if GrepTemplate <> '' then
  begin
    GrepWait.ResetEvent;
    GrepKill := False;
    GrepQueue.Purge;
    RunInThread(Grep);
  end;

  // run
  Cmd    := Format( 'exec find %s %s %s %s %s 2> /dev/null',
                    [ RootDir, Limit[IncludeSubfolders.Checked],
                      NameTests, DateTests, AdvancedTests ]);
  Handle := popen(PChar(Cmd), 'r');
  try
    repeat
      Line     := fgets(Buffer, SizeOf(Buffer), Handle);
      Filename := Trim(Line); // make a Pascal string of the PChar,
                              // sans trailing LF

      if Filename <> '' then
        if GrepTemplate <> ''
          then begin
               GrepQueue.Enqueue(Filename, True);
               GrepWait.SetEvent;
               end
          else ShowThis(Thread, Filename);
    until StopSearch or (Line = Nil);
  finally
    pclose(Handle);
  end;
```

```
// teardown
{ TODO : This can happen before GrepQueue is empty! }
Thread.Synchronize(GuiCleanup);
end; // TFileFinder.Find
```

The first line, `Thread.Synchronize(GuiSetup)` suspends the thread and
requests that GUI thread run the GuiSetup procedure as soon as possible. In
principle, this could have been done in TFileFinder.FindNowBtnClick, before
calling `RunInThread(Find)`, but it seemed best to keep that routine simple, and
to keep the whole search process in the same procedure. The GuiSetup procedure itself is pretty unexceptional: It clears any previous results; resets the
StopSearch flag; and sets the three search button's Enabled state
appropriately.

The second and third lines

```
RootDir := ComboText(LookIn);
if RootDir = '' then RootDir := PathDelim;
```

are really only interesting for the ComboText function, which both returns
the Text property and manages the MRU list.

```
function ComboText(Box: TComboBox): string;
// Returns Box.Text, makes it first entry in Items
var
  IndexOf: integer;
begin
  Result := Trim(Box.Text);
  if Result <> '' then
  begin
    IndexOf := Box.Items.IndexOf(Result);
    case Sign(IndexOf) of
      0: Exit; // already first entry
      1: Box.Items.Delete(IndexOf);
      end;
    Box.Items.Insert(0, Result);
  end;
end; // ComboText
```

ComboText sets `Result := Trim(Box.Text)`, which deletes any leading or trailing
white space and/or control characters. If the trimmed Result is non-empty,
ComboText looks up Result in the Box parameter's Items list. If the Result is
already in the first position, the ComboText function exits; if the Result is in
any other non-negative position, ComboText deletes the old string from the

Items list. (If IndexOf is negative, the Result text is not currently in the Items list.) If the Result text wasn't empty or already in the MRU position, ComboText inserts Result at the start of the Items list and returns.

The next four lines of the TFileFinder.Find method

```
Contains := ComboText(ContainingText);
if Contains <> '' then
  Contains := Format('exec grep -qie "%s" "%%s"', [Contains]);
GrepTemplate := Contains;
```

set GrepTemplate to either an empty string or a Format template—note how the use of %%s (which formats to %s) means that the GrepTemplate contains the ContainingText search term, but only a "%s" 'slot' for the filename. (The alert reader may have noticed that this code will fail if the search term contains a double-quote character. The later vfind projects use an IRegEx for their content search, and so don't have this problem.)

The next block of lines

```
if GrepTemplate <> '' then
begin
  GrepWait.ResetEvent;
  GrepKill := False;
  GrepQueue.Purge;
  RunInThread(Grep);
end;
```

is more interesting. The find command can grind away for quite awhile before spitting out another line for the popen() thread to handle. Since the find command is generally file bound, and since Linux is quite good about running other processes while one process is blocked waiting for file IO, there are generally plenty of CPU cycles to spare while find is keeping the popen() thread waiting. Thus, rather than calling system() to run grep from within the popen() thread (which risks letting the pipe fill up and block the find process) I start a second thread whose only task is to grep the candidate files that find spits out. I'll go into this in more detail after I finish discussing the Find thread; for now, I'll just say if there is a grep template, I reset the thread communication variables and start up a new Grep thread.

We've now come to the heart of the routine, where the Find thread spends almost all of its time.

```
Handle := popen(PChar(Cmd), 'r');
try
  repeat
    Line     := fgets(Buffer, SizeOf(Buffer), Handle);
    Filename := Trim(Line); // make a Pascal string of the PChar,
                            // sans trailing LF

    if Filename <> '' then
      if GrepTemplate <> ''
        then begin
             GrepQueue.Enqueue(Filename, True);
             GrepWait.SetEvent;
             end
        else ShowThis(Thread, Filename);
  until StopSearch or (Line = Nil);
finally
  pclose(Handle);
end;
```

The Cmd string contains a complete find command, which I pass to popen(). As *per* Chapter 10, popen() spawns a new process ["the find process"], and returns the new process's stdout to the originating process, line by line. I Trim() each line I get back, and pass each non-empty line to either the Grep thread or the ShowThis procedure. I drop out of the loop when the StopSearch flag is set by the Stop button, or when fgets() returns Nil, which signals that I've read all the output from the popen()ed command. Finally, I pclose() the Handle I got from popen()—as *per* Chapter 10, this is important to prevent "zombie processes."

The last lines of the Find procedure

```
// teardown
{ TODO : This can happen before GrepQueue is empty! }
Thread.Synchronize(GuiCleanup);
```

mostly undo the GuiSetup at the start. They also contain a serious bug—the Grep thread might still be running after the find process terminates, yet GuiCleanup contains code

```
GrepKill := True;
GrepWait.SetEvent; // wake up and let die
```

to kill the Grep thread. This first version, vfind1, is the only version that has this bug.

Thread-safe string queues

If there's no GrepTemplate, the Find thread calls ShowThis

```
procedure TFileFinder.ShowThis(Thread: TSimpleThread; const Filename: string);
begin
  DisplayQueue.Enqueue(Filename, True);
  Thread.Synchronize(ShowFoundFileWrapper);
end; // TFileFinder.ShowThis
```

directly. If there **is** a GrepTemplate (and hence a Grep thread) the Grep thread calls ShowThis on any filename that passes the `grep` test.

Remember, both routines that call ShowThis are running in a non-GUI thread. They have to marshal any display requests over to the GUI thread. The TThread.Synchronize() routine can only take a `procedure of object`—the synchronized procedure can't have any arguments. The only way to pass data from a non-GUI thread to a synchronized procedure running in the GUI thread is to stick it in a global (or at least global to the form object) data structure. Accordingly, ShowThis places the filename in a thread-safe string queue, and then uses Synchronize to call a GUI-thread procedure that empties the queue.

The TStringQueue class is in lib/LThreads. It combines a critical section and an `array of string` to produce a thread-safe string queue.

```
procedure TStringQueue.Enqueue(const S: string; MultiThread: boolean);
begin
  if MultiThread then fLock.Acquire;
  try
    SetLength(Queue, Length(Queue) + 1);
    Queue[High(Queue)] := S;
  finally
    if MultiThread then fLock.Release;
  end;
end; // TStringQueue.Enqueue
```

As you can see, there's nothing special about the Enqueue method, except the way that it makes locking optional. Usually, of course, you would lock all queue operations, so that an enqueue interleaved with a dequeue in another thread can't leave the queue scrambled. There are some special cases, though, where you don't need to lock the queue. For example, a producer might pre-load the queue before a consumer has begun reading it, or a consumer might know that the producer is all done. Any time that you know that only one thread is using the queue, you can pass False to the MultiThread parameter and use the queue in an unlocked mode.

The Dequeue method is more complicated, using some of the dynamic array techniques from Chapter 3.

```
function TStringQueue.Dequeue(MultiThread: boolean): string;
var
  NewLength: integer;
begin
  if MultiThread then fLock.Acquire;
  try
    NewLength := Length(Queue) - 1;
    if NewLength < 0 then raise ERangeError.Create('Empty queue');
    Result :- Queue[0];
    Finalize(Queue[0]); // deref string that's being deleted
    if NewLength > 0 then
    begin
      Move(Queue[1], Queue[0], NewLength * SizeOf(Result));
      pointer(Queue[NewLength]) := Nil; // No deref on SetLength() ....
     end;
    SetLength(Queue, NewLength);
  finally
    if MultiThread then fLock.Release;
  end;
end; // TStringQueue.Dequeue
```

The Dequeue method calculates the new queue length, then sets Result to the first string in the queue. It calls Finalize() on this first slot, to decrement the first string's reference count. Then, if there are any strings left in the queue (Figure 13-7, Stage 1), Dequeue uses Move() to shift them all one slot to the left. The Move operation doesn't affect the reference count of the last string in the Queue array, yet there are now two references to it (Figure 13-7, Stage 2). Dequeue has to fix this before calling SetLength to wipe out the slot, and it does so by casting the last slot to a pointer and setting it to Nil (Figure 13-7, Stage 3).

Displaying the results

The TFileFinder.ShowFoundFileWrapper method that TFileFinder.ShowThis passes to Synchronize simply calls an overloaded dequeue method

Stage 1: The Queue array before the Move()

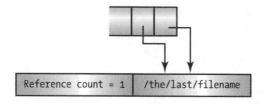

One pointer to the last string:
all is well.

Stage 2: The Queue array before the Move() left

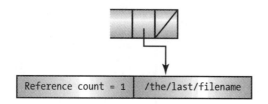

Two pointers to the last string,
which still only has a reference
count of 1. Freeing the last slot
with SetLength[] would be a
disaster.

Stage 3: The Queue array after Nil-ing the last slot

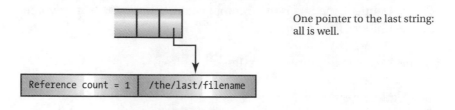

One pointer to the last string
again, and the last slot doesn't
point to a string at all. All is
well again.

Figure 13-7. Dequeuing strings

```
while DisplayQueue.Dequeue(Filename, True) do
  ShowFoundFile(Filename);
```

to display as many filenames as possible in a single Synchronize() operation.
The ShowFoundFile method

```
procedure TFileFinder.ShowFoundFile(const Filename: string);
var
  GoodInfo: boolean;
  Info:     TStatBuf;
begin
  GoodInfo := stat(PChar(Filename), Info) = 0; // get file info
```

```
with Results.Items.Add do
  begin
    Caption := ExtractFileName(Filename);        // name
    SubItems.Add( ExtractFilePath(Filename) );   // path

    if GoodInfo then
    begin
      SubItems.Add( getpwuid(Info.st_uid).pw_name ); // owner
      SubItems.Add( getgrgid(Info.st_gid).gr_name ); // group
      SubItems.Add( ModetToStr(Info.st_mode) );    // permissions
      SubItems.Add( IntToStr(Info.st_size) );      // file size
      SubItems.Add( TimetToStr(Info.st_mtime) );   // modified
      SubItems.Add( TimetToStr(Info.st_atime) );   // accessed
    end;
  end;
end; // TFileFinder.ShowFoundFile
```

is interesting primarily as an example of how to add data to a list view. (See
Chapter 10 for details on all of the Libc calls that ShowFoundFile makes.)

Remember, Results is the client aligned list view at the bottom of the
form. The Results.Items property is a list of TListItem's, each of which represents a line of the report. Calling Results.Items.Add adds a new, empty item
to the report, and returns a reference to it. The Caption property is the 'primary'
string associated with the Item; in the vsList state, only the Caption is shown,
not any of the SubItems. The SubItems property is a TStrings list of strings,
one for each 'secondary' column of the report. You can set it either as I do here,
via a series of successive Add() operations, or you can set it *en masse*, perhaps
using some open array code like lib/GrabBag's AssignStrings procedure.

The Grep thread

The Grep thread runs the TFileFinder.Grep procedure.

```
procedure TFileFinder.Grep(Thread: TSimpleThread; Data: pointer);
var
  Filename: string;
  GoodInfo: boolean;
  Info:     TStatBuf;
  Cmd:      string;
begin
  repeat
    GrepWait.WaitFor($FFFFFFFF);
    if GrepKill then EXIT;
```

```
      while GrepQueue.Dequeue(Filename) do
      begin
        GoodInfo := stat(PChar(Filename), Info) = 0; // get file info

        if (not GoodInfo) or (Info.st_mode and S_IFDIR = 0) then
          // file (or unknown)
          if euidaccess(PChar(Filename), R_OK) = 0 then // we can read it
          begin
            Cmd := Format(GrepTemplate, [Filename]);
            if Libc.system(PChar(Cmd)) = 0 then // show this file
              ShowThis(Thread, Filename);
          end;
      end;
  until True = False;
end; // TFileFinder.Grep
```

This thread spends its life in an endless loop (`repeat {body} until True = False`) with a semaphore wait at the top. When the Find thread enqueues a file name for the Grep thread to check, it calls GrepWait.SetEvent, which wakes up the Grep thread. When the Find thread calls GuiCleanup, the GUI thread executes

```
GrepKill := True;
GrepWait.SetEvent; // wake up and let die
```

which wakes the Grep thread and cause it to Exit from the endless loop.

Once woken it dequeues filenames, and checks to see if they're file or directory names. If it **is** a file, and euidaccess() says that the file is one that this user can read, Grep interpolates the filename into the GrepTemplate and uses system() to call the grep command.

The second pass

The biggest single change between vfind1 and vfind2 is that I discarded the whole Grep thread in favor of an inline regex search. Since using an inline regex search avoids both the overhead of a system() command and the lesser overhead of not having to recompiling the regex each time I spawned an independent `grep` command, I decided that there wasn't much chance of the pipe between the `find` process and my Find thread filling up and blocking the `find` process.

As you can see from Listing 13-2, even though vfind2 is doing an inline content scan, the Find procedure is shorter than in vfind1, because Find no longer has to setup and talk to the Grep thread. In addition to that simplification, the GrepTemplate is no longer a string, but a case-insensitive IRegEx.

Most significantly, the content test has been moved into the fgets() loop:

```
if not Assigned(GrepTemplate) or
   GrepTemplate.Match( ReadFile(Filename), [], False) then
  ShowThis(Thread, Filename);
```

That is, show the file if there's no GrepTemplate or if the GrepTemplate matched the file contents returned by the lib/GrabBag ReadFile function. Note that the Match() operation specifies False for the last parameter, ExtractMatches: this speeds things up by not extracting any substrings (regex parenthetical expressions) that the regex might match.

All three versions of vfind use the same ShowThis mechanism, which adds the filename to a TStringQueue and calls the ShowFoundFileWrapper method *via* Synchronize(). You can get some idea of the inefficiency of the Synchronize() mechanism by doing a search for, say, qt*.h in the directory /usr, either containing some text like qmovie or not. The search for files containing qmovie will stop fairly quickly, with only one or two results. By contrast, when Containing Text is blank, the search for all qt*.h files will take much longer, as the results appear one by one. I'm sure vfind could be optimized to work better with Synchronize(), but synchronization *via* lib/QMessages will generally be both faster and more flexible than synchronization *via* Synchronize().

Listing 13-2. A simpler TFileFinder.Find

```
procedure TFileFinder.Find(Thread: TSimpleThread; Data: pointer);
var
  RootDir, Contains, Cmd: string;
  GrepTemplate:           IRegEx;
  Handle:                 PIOFile;
  Line:                   PChar;
  Buffer:                 MAX_PATH_STRING; // array[0..MAX_PATH] of char;
  Filename:               string;
  const
  Limit: array[boolean] of string = ('-maxdepth 1', '');
begin
  // setup
  Thread.Synchronize(GuiSetup);
```

```
      RootDir := ComboText(LookIn);
      if RootDir = '' then RootDir := PathDelim;

      Contains := ComboText(ContainingText);
      if Contains <> ''
        then GrepTemplate := RegularExpression( Contains,
                                                [REG_EXTENDED, REG_ICASE] )
        else GrepTemplate := Nil;

      // run
      Cmd    := Format( 'exec find %s %s %s %s %s 2> /dev/null',
                        //'find %s %s %s %s %s',
                        [ RootDir, Limit[IncludeSubfolders.Checked],
                          NameTests, DateTests, AdvancedTests ]);
      Handle := popen(PChar(Cmd), 'r');
      try
        repeat
          Line     := fgets(Buffer, SizeOf(Buffer), Handle);
          Filename := Trim(Line); // make a Pascal string of the PChar,
                                  // sans trailing LF

          if Filename <> '' then
            if not Assigned(GrepTemplate) or
               GrepTemplate.Match( ReadFile(Filename), [], False) then
              ShowThis(Thread, Filename);
        until StopSearch or (Line = Nil);
      finally
        pclose(Handle);
      end;

      // teardown
      Thread.Synchronize(GuiCleanup);
    end; // TFileFinder.Find
```

Better form state handling

The second vfind project includes two enhancements to the persistence
framework. The first one replaces the manual string parsing in LoadFormSize
with a regular expression. The second enhancement loads and saves form
state to and from an IWindowSize instead of TBaseForm. Working with an
interface instead of a specific form class makes it possible to use the same

code to persist the window state of both TBaseForm descendants and forms that need a different ancestor, such as QMessage's TMessageForm.[3]

Regular expression parsing

You'll recall that vfind1's TBaseConfig.LoadFormSize looped through the string it read from the ini file, looking for the spaces between numbers. Not exceptionally difficult code to read or write, but not quite trivial, either. Also, changing it so that, say, the four BoundsRect numbers were visually distinct from the trailing WindowState ordinal—perhaps `Format( '(%d %d %d %d) <%d>',` `[Left, Top, Right, Bottom, ord(State)])` instead of `Format( '%d %d %d %d %d',` `[Left, Top, Right, Bottom, ord(State)])` would have required a major rewrite.

However, using a regex to verify that the form size string is in the right format and to extract the five numbers means that adding decorations to the format string would only require adding the same decorations to the regex. Also, with a regex, we know if we have the right number of elements before we've done a single StrToInt.

The line count in lib/BaseConfig is actually slightly higher, because I 'cache' the compiled regex

```
var
  IExtractFormSizeElements: IRegEx = Nil;

const
  ExtractFormSizeElementsRegEx =
    // This regex uses [0-9] instead of [[:digit:]], as Kylix's StrToInt won't
    // work with any locale-dependent digits.
    '([0-9]+) ([0-9]+) ([0-9]+) ([0-9]+) ([0-9]+)';

function ExtractFormSizeElements: IRegEx;
begin
  if not Assigned(IExtractFormSizeElements) then
    IExtractFormSizeElements :=
      RegularExpression(ExtractFormSizeElementsRegEx);
  Result := IExtractFormSizeElements;
end; // ExtractFormSizeElements
```

but the actual LoadFormSize code is much simpler.

---

3. Chapter 14 includes an example of a persistent TMessageForm.

```
function TBaseConfig.ReadFormSize(const FormName: string): TWindowSize;
var
  RegEx: IRegEx;
  Return:   record
              case byte of
                1: (Size: TWindowSize);
                2: (A:    array[0..4] of integer);
              end;
  Index: integer;
begin
  RegEx := ExtractFormSizeElements;
  if not RegEx.Match(ReadString(FormSection, FormName, '')) then
    raise EBaseConfig.Create('Invalid form size string');
  Assert(RegEx.SubstringCount = High(Return.A) + 1);

  for Index := Low(Return.A) to High(Return.A) do
    Return.A[Index] := StrToInt(RegEx.Substring(Index));
  Result := Return.Size;
end; // TBaseConfig.ReadFormSize

procedure TBaseConfig.LoadFormSize(const Window: IWindowSize);
begin
  Window.SetWindowSize(ReadFormSize(Window.GetWindowSizeName));
end; // TBaseConfig.LoadFormSize
```

The ReadFormSize method gets the regex—five integers, each separated by a single space—and matches the loaded string against it. The regex uses [0-9] instead of [[:digit:]] because Kylix's StrToInt does not honor locales, and only recognizes characters in the range '0'..'9' as digits. After Assert()ing that the regex and the Result declaration are in synch, it converts the extracted substrings to numbers, and returns the resulting TWindowSize record. The LoadFormSize method then passes this record to the form, *via* a new IWindowSize interface, which I describe in the next section.

Delegated interfaces

The original TBaseConfig LoadFormSize and SaveFormSize methods work well, but they do have a problem: They take a TBaseForm parameter, and set its WindowSize property. That is, vfind1's persistence framework supplies a root form for application forms to inherit from, and the framework can only persist the window state of forms that descend from its root form.

The problem this poses may not be immediately obvious. You can base an application-specific root form on TBaseForm, and add any specialized functionality that you need. Even if you want to graft the persistence framework onto an existing application, it's easy to change a form's ancestry (see Chapter 5). But what if you want a form to inherit both lib/QMessages' TMessageForm's EventFilter and PostMessage code and the persistence framework's WindowSize abilities? Both forms are intended to be the root of a hierarchy —which should be changed?

Well, LoadFormSize and SaveFormSize could be written in terms of an interface that can read and write a WindowSize value. The lib/QMessages' TMessageForm's message sending code can also be written as an interface that application forms support—but this is **not** true of the lib/QMessages' TMessageForm's EventFilter. EventFilter is an override of an inherited method, and passing messages to a form will only work if the form overrides (or descends from a form that overrides) TCustomForm's EventFilter. You can't just add an EventFilter method with the right prototype.

That is, you can persist the window state of any form that "can do" the right sort of window state maintenance, but you can only pass messages to a form that "is a" TMessageForm. This suggests that the persistence framework should be redesigned a bit to work with lib/WindowSize's

```
type
  IWindowSize = interface
  ['{7839F982-267A-D511-8654-00A0C9E80506}']
    function  GetWindowSizeName: string;
    function  GetWindowSize: TWindowSize;
    procedure SetWindowSize(const Value: TWindowSize);
  end;
```

instead of TBaseForm. In turn, TBaseForm should be rewritten so that it supports the IWindowSize interface—but in a way that's easy to add to other forms.

The persistence framework in vfind2 does this by defining a

```
type
  TManageWindowSize = class (TAggregatedObject, IWindowSize)
  // A utility class to simplify adding IWindowSize to forms
  private
    fForm:      TForm;
    NormalSize: TRect;
  protected
    function  GetWindowSizeName: string;
    function  GetWindowSize: TWindowSize;
```

```
      procedure SetWindowSize(const Value: TWindowSize);
    public
      procedure OnResize;                        overload;
      procedure OnResize(NewRect: TRect); overload;
      constructor Create(Form: TForm);
    end;
```

and adding it to TBaseForm as

```
type
  TBaseForm = class(TForm, IWindowSize)
    procedure FormCreate(Sender: TObject);
  private
    fManageWindowSize: TManageWindowSize;
  protected
     property WindowSize: TManageWindowSize read fManageWindowSize
                                          implements IWindowSize;
  public
    procedure SetBounds(ALeft, ATop, AWidth, AHeight: Integer); override;
  end;
```

As *per* Chapter 3, the `implements` keyword means that TBaseForm *delegates* the IWindowSize interface to the WindowSize property, which is a TManageWindowSize object field. The TManageWindowSize class descends from TAggregatedObject, which is an interfaced object designed specifically to be used for delegation: it relies on an 'outer' class to manage reference counts. Adding the IWindowSize abilities to TBaseForm *via* an aggregated object means that it's easy to add them to other base classes. Aside from the declarations, the new TBaseForm only needs a couple of statements to setup and maintain the WindowSize property. Thus, the FormCreate method creates the fManageWindowSize class field

```
procedure TBaseForm.FormCreate(Sender: TObject);
begin
  inherited;
  fManageWindowSize := TManageWindowSize.Create(Self);
end; // TBaseForm.FormCreate
```

while the overridden SetBounds method passes the current size and position on to the aggregated object.

```
procedure TBaseForm.SetBounds(ALeft, ATop, AWidth, AHeight: Integer);
begin
  inherited;
  fManageWindowSize.OnResize(Rect(ALeft, ATop, ALeft + AWidth, ATop + AHeight));
end; // TBaseForm.SetBounds
```

> **Note**
>
>
>
> *While the OnResize event is only called when the form is resized, SetBounds is also called when the form is moved. Overriding SetBounds allows the form to save its position more reliably.*

The flip side of this convenience is that putting the IWindowSize implementation into an outboard object means that TManageWindowSize has to have a rather intimate relationship with the form that it's managing. It's true that it only reads and writes published properties, but even that may be enough of an encapsulation violation to make you uneasy. I think the proper way to think of this relationship, though, is that the TManageWindowSize object is a symbiote that can no more live without its host than a mitochondrion can: An aggregated object is less "another object" than a bolt-on part.

The constructor

```
constructor TManageWindowSize.Create(Form: TForm);
begin
  inherited Create(Form);
  fForm := Form;
end; // TManageWindowSize.Create
```

'marries' the two objects by saving a fForm reference that the other methods all use to read and write fForm properties. For example, the IWindowSize.GetWindowSizeName method reaches into the form and reads its Name property in order to return a name to save the form state under.

```
function TManageWindowSize.GetWindowSizeName: string;
begin
  Result := fForm.Name;
end; // TManageWindowSize.GetWindowSizeName
```

Similiarly, the OnResize handler that I called above in TBaseForm.SetBounds sets NormalSize when the WindowState is wsNormal, much as vfind1's TBaseForm.FormResize event handler did:

```
procedure TManageWindowSize.OnResize(NewRect: TRect);
begin
  if fForm.WindowState = wsNormal then
    NormalSize := NewRect;
end; // TManageWindowSize.OnResize
```

Finally, the TManageWindowSize objects GetWindowSize and SetWindowSize methods differ from the old TBaseForm methods only in that they read and write fForm's BoundsRect and WindowState instead of Self's BoundsRect and WindowState. If you're interested, you can read the source in lib/WindowSize, so I don't think it's necessary to print it here.

Handling symbolic dates

Perhaps the coolest, most generally applicable thing I do in vfind2 is handle dates like `'July 12, 2001'` that StrToDate() can't. I once spent days and hundreds of lines of code writing complex Windows code that could only handle symbolic dates in the users' ShortDateFormat. By contrast, the Linux regex code is simpler, clearer, and more flexible (it can handle either American (M D, Y) or European (D M, Y) formats); it took only a couple of hours to write; and it comes in at under a hundred lines.

First, I 'cache' compiled regexes, as in the ExtractFormSizeElements function, above.

```
var
  IAmerican, IEuropean: IRegEx;

function American: IRegEx; // Month Day, Year
const
  //       month must be first non-white
  RegEx = '^[[:space:]]*' +
  //       ------month-----    --whitespace--    -------day------
           '([[:alpha:]]+)' + '[[:space:]]+' + '([0-9]+)' +
  //       --whitespace--    -opt-    --whitespace--    ------year------
           '[[:space:]]*' + '[,]?' + '[[:space:]]*' + '([0-9]+)';
```

```
begin
  if not Assigned(IAmerican) then
    IAmerican := RegularExpression(RegEx, [REG_EXTENDED]);
  Result := IAmerican;
end; // American


function European: IRegEx; // Day Month, Year
const
  //      day must be first non-white
  RegEx = '^[[:space:]]*' +
  //      -------day------   --whitespace--   -----month-----
          '([0-9]+)' + '[[:space:]]+' + '([[:alpha:]]+)' +
  //      --whitespace--   -opt-    --whitespace--   ------year------
          '[[:space:]]*' + '[,]?' + '[[:space:]]*' + '([0-9]+)';
begin
  if not Assigned(IEuropean) then
    IEuropean:= RegularExpression(RegEx, [REG_EXTENDED]);
  Result := IEuropean;
end; // European
```

Next, a single function tries to match either the American or European regex, and extract the Month, Day, and Year strings.

```
function GetMDY(var Month, Day, Year: string; const Date: string): boolean;
var
  RegEx: IRegEx;
begin
  // Month day, year?
  RegEx := American;
  Result := RegEx.Match(Date);
  if Result then
  begin
    Assert(RegEx.SubStringCount = 3);
    Month := RegEx.SubString(0);
    Day   := RegEx.SubString(1);
    Year  := RegEx.SubString(2);
    EXIT;
  end;
```

```
    // Day month, year?
    RegEx := European;
    Result := RegEx.Match(Date);
    if Result then
    begin
      Assert(RegEx.SubStringCount = 3);
      Day   := RegEx.SubString(0);
      Month := RegEx.SubString(1);
      Year  := RegEx.SubString(2);
    end;
  end; // GetMDY
```

The GetMDY function first matches the date string against the American MDY pattern. If the American pattern matches, GetMDY sets the Month, Day, and Year parameters appropriately and exits. If the American pattern doesn't match, GetMDY tries to match the European DMY pattern. If the European pattern matches, GetMDY sets the Day, Month, and Year parameters appropriately and returns normally. If neither pattern matches, GetMDY returns False and leaves the var parameters untouched.

The OnDateConvertError event handler, LookForMonthNames, uses GetMDY to see if the date is in a format it can make sense of. If so, and if the LookupMonth function

```
function LookupMonth(var iMonth: integer; const sMonth: string): boolean;
var
  Index: integer;
begin
  Assert(Low(ShortMonthNames)  = Low(LongMonthNames));
  Assert(High(ShortMonthNames) = High(LongMonthNames));
  for Index := Low(ShortMonthNames) to High(ShortMonthNames) do
  begin
    Result := (AnsiCompareText(sMonth, ShortMonthNames[Index]) = 0) or
              (AnsiCompareText(sMonth, LongMonthNames[Index]) = 0)  ;
    if Result then
    begin
      iMonth := Index + 1 - Low(ShortMonthNames); // 1..12
      EXIT;
    end;
  end;
end; // LookupMonth
```

can find the month string in either the LongMonthNames or ShortMonthNames arrays,[4] LookForMonthNames converts the string to a date and returns the result to the date picker component.

```
procedure TFileFinder.LookForMonthNames(Sender: TObject;
  const DateString: String; var Date: TDateTime;
  var RaiseException: Boolean);
// Handles dates like "February 18, 2001" and "18 Feb, 01". Doesn't handle dates
// like "May 12", but probably should.
var
  Month, Day, Year: string;
  iMonth, iYear:    integer;
begin
  if GetMDY(Month, Day, Year, DateString) and LookupMonth(iMonth, Month) then
  begin
    iYear := StrToInt(Year);
    if iYear < 100 then Inc(iYear, 2000);
    Date := EncodeDate(iYear, iMonth, StrToInt(Day));
  end;
end; // TFileFinder.LookForMonthNames
```

Extending this code to handle dates like 'July 12' would be pretty straightforward. You'd change the regexes to make the year string optional—'([0-9]*)' instead of '([0-9]+)'—and you'd convert Year to iYear using a new function like StrToYear that used DecodeDate and Now to get the current year, if the year string was blank.

The final program

Incremental development is the only reliable way to get from "File ➤ New Application" to the singing, dancing category killer that you've mapped out in loving detail with the help of market research and years of design experience. Step by tiny step; one working, testable state to another. For that matter, it's the only way to get to a goal that you may only have articulated in broad strokes, trusting that your experience and raw ability will let you devise solutions to each problem that comes up.

In the process, sometimes you put up with compromises—or kluges—for a relatively long time, because the cost of replacing the code seems higher than the cost of putting up with it. Or because the kluge evolved over time,

---

4. These locale dependent arrays are in the SysUtils unit.

and you don't necessarily see it as a whole. Once something pushes you over the hump, though, and you actually rewrite your code, you're more apt to see only the drawbacks of the old code, and not the history and/or cost-benefit analysis that kept you with it.

What I'm leading up to, here, is that writing about the 'three-step persistence chain' brought out its true ugliness. I feel rather like I've been stupid in public.

A *better persistence framework*

You'll remember that to persist a UI setting, I had to declare a property in a Configuration object, and write code to transfer that property to and from a persistence store. Then I had to write more code to transfer that property to and from the UI. Between the Configuration object's private field variables, the Configuration object's public property, the key name constant, the Configuration object's read code (which is where the setting's default value was buried), the Configuration object's write code, the form's read code, and the form's write code, each additional persistent setting required changing the source in seven different places!

Seeing it like that naturally made me ask if there wasn't some better way, some way that didn't require adding code in many different places and that didn't bury a persistent setting's default value in a global configuration unit. My first thought was that an interfaced object would let me declare the persistence information once, when I loaded a setting. Because of reference counting, the information would stick around in a little self-contained 'state packet' until the form was destroyed and the interface dereferenced, at which point the interfaced object could save the current UI setting to the persistence store. My second thought was that I could use RTTI to get and set any published property. Since most—if not all—the UI settings that one might want to persist **are** published properties, I suddenly had a much cleaner, more localized persistence architecture.

Each UI setting that I want to persist can be linked by an interfaced object to a 'persistence server'. There's enough parallelism between an ini file's section and key name, a database's table and field name, and the Windows registry key and value name that a single pair of strings and an IPersistenceServer reference serves to define a persistent value that might reside in a local (*per* user) or global ini file, a database, or the Windows registry. Specifying the IPersistenceServer reference when I create the link allows me to still easily change my persistence technology, and also to still easily mix local and global configurations where necessary.

Now, my first thought was that each link would be stored in an I*Datatype*Link field of the form object. This would make it possible to assign a value to both the run-time property and the persistent setting in a single operation, if necessary. It would also allow each link to offer BeginUpdate and EndUpdate methods that would allow you fine-grained control over your persistence strategy; any changes to *this* link should be written immediately, while any changes to *that* link should only be written when the form is destroyed. What quickly developed, though, was not only that declaring all those link fields was an annoyance, but also that it didn't work as I'd like it to. The reason wasn't very surprising, in retrospect: Forms free their components before they dereference any interface reference fields. By the time a link's destructor was called, there wasn't any UI component around to get the current setting from!

Thus, instead of relying on interface dereferencing to save any changed settings to a persistence server, I needed to explicitly save each link. The simplest way to do this is to create an explicit list of settings links. As I create each link in a form's OnCreate handler, I add the new link to the list; in the form's OnDestroy handler, I tell the list to tell each setting link to save itself. Where I had originally conceived of relying on reference counting to save the state when the form was destroyed, in the end it just became a convenience: I never have to Free the settings links that I Create.

Without the need for individual fields for each link, I also realized that there wasn't really a *need* to set the link independently of the published property. The point of persistent settings is to save the user's changes, not the program's. Similarly, the whole notion of BeginUpdate and EndUpdate came to seem like unnecessary overkill. If a particular application does need fine-grained control over persistence strategy, it can easily save explicit references to some of the links, and 'flush' them as necessary.

In the end, I only had three interfaces. An object that implements ISettingsLink can ReadPropertyFromStorage and WritePropertyToStorage, while an object that implements ISettingsLinkList can Add(Link: ISettingsLink), LoadAllSettings,[5] and SaveAllSettings. An object that implements IPersistenceServer is a bit more complicated, but it can basically do what the TBaseConfig object can do: read and write strings, integers, booleans, dates, string lists, and window size records. The lib/IConfig unit only implements an ini file IPersistenceServer, but it wouldn't be hard to write database or Windows registry versions.

---

5. You might call LoadAllSettings or ReadPropertyFromStorage if you got some sort of signal that a global configuration had changed, and you wanted the running application to show the effect.

To use this new framework, you do still need a certain amount of boiler-plate code. First, you need to create at least one IPersistenceServer. The vfind project Config unit does this as

```
initialization

  Configuration := TIniPersistenceServer.Create(HomeDirectory + ConfigFilename)
                     as IPersistenceServer;

finalization

  Configuration := Nil;

end.
```

Second, you have to declare an ISettingsLinkList field in your form variable,

```
SettingsLinks: ISettingsLinkList;
```

and then actually create the list in the OnCreate handler

```
SettingsLinks := CreateSettingsLinkList;
```

and explicitly save the current settings in the OnDestroy handler

```
SettingsLinks.SaveAllSettings;
```

However, that's pretty much all the boilerplate you need. Adding a new persistent setting now takes only a single statement like

```
SettingsLinks.Add(TWideStringLink.Create( Named, 'Text',
                                          Configuration,
                                          SettingsSection, Named_Text ));
```

instead of the seven steps that my old persistence framework took. The link constructor automatically reads the persistence server, and sets the linked property if the persistence server contains a setting for the property that differs from the design time default.

The first two parameters to the link constructor are a component and the name of one of its `published` properties. That is, the example above links Named.Text to the Named_Text key in the SettingsSection. The link constructor will raise an exception if the named property does not exist or if it is not of the right type.

The third parameter to the link constructor is an IPersistenceServer reference. Again, passing an explicit IPersistenceServer reference means that *this* setting can be read from and written to a user-specific preferences file, while *that* setting can be read from and written to a system or network-wide preferences file. If you want to be able to load settings from a global preference file but not allow this user to change the file, you would simply never call WritePropertyToStorage; the easiest way to do this would be to just not add the new link to the list.

The final pair of parameters to the link constructor are the section (key) and value names for the persistent setting. The link saves these, along with the other parameters, and can use them to store the current value at any time.

> **Note**
>
>
> *The vfind project does use the same list of string constants in its Config unit as the vfind1 and vfind2 projects, but this is only because I wanted it to be able to use the same ~/.vfind.ini file as the other two projects. Since the persistent value name is only used in the link constructor, you could very well just use inline constants. You're no more likely to use the same string twice than you are in a separate 'table' of string constants, and you can assure that* this *form's* 'Date filter'*, say, doesn't conflict with* that *form's* 'Date filter' *simply by using different section names. The form's Name or ClassName would work very well.*

The lib/IConfig unit only implements links for integer, boolean, date, string, and wide string properties. (Perhaps I should implement string list and form state links as well, but I'll exercise an author's prerogative and Leave That As An Exercise For The Reader.) All the link objects descend from TAbstractLink.

```
type
  TAbstractLink = class (TInterfacedObject)
  protected
    fInstance:      TComponent;
    fPropName:      string;

    fStorage:       IPersistenceServer;
    fSection, fIdent: string;
```

```
        constructor Create( Instance: TComponent; const PropName: string;
                            Storage: IPersistenceServer;
                            const Section, Ident: string;
                            TypeKind: TTypeKind );

    procedure ReadPropertyFromStorage; virtual; abstract;
    procedure WritePropertyToStorage;  virtual; abstract;
  end;

constructor TAbstractLink.Create(Instance: TComponent; const PropName: string;
  Storage: IPersistenceServer; const Section, Ident: string;
  TypeKind: TTypeKind);
begin
  // Make sure we're creating the right sort of link
  if not PropIsType(Instance, PropName, TypeKind) then
    raise ELink.Create(Instance, PropName, TypeKind);

  // If so, save link state
  inherited Create;

  fInstance    := Instance;
  fPropName    := PropName;

  fStorage     := Storage;
  fSection     := Section;
  fIdent       := Ident;

  // Read saved value, if any
  ReadPropertyFromStorage;
end; // TAbstractLink.Create
```

The PropIsType function (from the standard TypInfo unit) raises an exception if Instance doesn't have a published property named PropName, and otherwise returns a TTypeKind enum. The ELink.Create constructor

```
constructor ELink.Create(         Instance: TComponent;
                            const PropName: string;
                                  TypeKind: TTypeKind );
begin
  inherited CreateFmt(
    'Property type mismatch on %s.%s: Is %s, link expects %s',
    [ Instance.Name, PropName,
      GetEnumName( TypeInfo(TTypeKind),
                   ord(PropType(Instance, PropName) )),
      GetEnumName(TypeInfo(TTypeKind), ord(TypeKind)) ]);
end; // ELink.Create
```

uses the GetEnumName function (Chapter 8) to construct an informative message like 'Property type mismatch on Named.Text: is tkWString, link expects tkString' if you try to attach the wrong link to a property.

The TAbstractLink.Create constructor is otherwise pretty unremarkable. It saves its parameters in field variables, and then calls the abstract method ReadPropertyFromStorage to read the persistence store and update the property as necessary. Naturally, each type of link implements ReadPropertyFromStorage differently; equally naturally, for the most part all that differs is the type information. Accordingly, I'll only present the TIntegerLink in full, and leave you to read the code for the other links if you're interested.

```
type
  TIntegerLink = class (TAbstractLink, ISettingsLink)
  private
    function ReadProperty: integer;
  protected
    procedure ReadPropertyFromStorage; override;
    procedure WritePropertyToStorage; override;

  public
    constructor Create( Instance: TComponent; const PropName: string;
                        Storage: IPersistenceServer;
                        const Section, Ident: string );
  end;

constructor TIntegerLink.Create(Instance: TComponent; const PropName: string;
  Storage: IPersistenceServer; const Section, Ident: string);
begin
  inherited Create(Instance, PropName, Storage, Section, Ident, tkInteger);
end; // TIntegerLink.Create
```

Each specific link constructor simply passes on all its arguments to `inherited`, only tacking on a TTypeKind constant.

```
function TIntegerLink.ReadProperty: integer;
begin
  Result := GetOrdProp(fInstance, fPropName);
end; // TIntegerLink.ReadProperty
```

GetOrdProp is a function from the TypInfo unit that allows you to read any published ordinal property (that is: characters; wide characters; enumerations; and all integers except int64's) by name. There are routines like GetStrProp and GetFloatProp for other datatypes, while GetEnumProp allows you to read enumerated properties as strings.

```
procedure TIntegerLink.ReadPropertyFromStorage;
var
  State, Setting: integer;
begin
  // Get the design-time value - this is the default
  State := ReadProperty;

  // Read the persistent setting
  Setting := fStorage.ReadInteger(fSection, fIdent, State);

  // Write it to the component, if necessary
  if State <> Setting then
    SetOrdProp(fInstance, fPropName, Setting)
end; // TIntegerLink.ReadPropertyFromStorage
```

ReadPropertyFromStorage first reads the current property State, which will normally be the design-time setting. It then reads the persistent Setting, if any, using the current State as the default value. If the Setting and the State differ, it calls SetOrdProp to change the ordinal property. This changes the form, just as if you'd set the property directly.

```
procedure TIntegerLink.WritePropertyToStorage;
begin
  fStorage.WriteInteger(fSection, fIdent, ReadProperty);
end; // TIntegerLink.WritePropertyToStorage
```

Finally, WritePropertyToStorage reads the current property value, and writes it back to the persistence store. Normally, this only happens when the form is destroyed and you call SaveAllSettings in the OnDestroy handler, but you can always call WritePropertyToStorage (or SaveAllSettings) on an as-needed basis.

Don't forget that TIniFile doesn't write changes to disk until you call UpdateFile. If you want to save changes while the program is running (perhaps as each form in a multi-form application closes), call the IPersistenceServer's CommitChanges method.

Note

I took advantage of the ease of creating new persistent values to fix the LoadDropdown bug I mentioned earlier. The vfind program's version of LoadDropdown doesn't set the combo box's ItemIndex property; instead, I explicitly save and load both the Text and Items properties.

Other changes

The first two vfind projects use the find program's default –print action. This allows the popen code to use a simple fgets() call to read the output line-by-line—but then the find process sees filenames that contain newline characters as two (or more) non-existent different files. The find program's –print0 action avoids this issue, but as it separates filenames with #0 characters, not newline characters, I can no longer use fgets(). Instead, I have to use fread(), as in the BinEval example of Chapter 10.

```
Cmd    := Format( 'exec find %s %s %s %s %s -print0 2> /dev/null',
                  [ RootDir, Limit[IncludeSubfolders.Checked],
                    NameTests, DateTests, AdvancedTests ]);
Handle := popen(PChar(Cmd), 'r');
try
  repeat
    Filename := '';
    if feof(Handle) = 0 then
      repeat
        fread(@ NextChar, SizeOf(char), SizeOf(NextChar), Handle);
        if NextChar <> #0 then
          Filename := Filename + NextChar;
      until (NextChar = #0) or (feof(Handle) <> 0);
```

```
      if Filename <> '' then
        if not Assigned(GrepTemplate) or
           GrepTemplate.Match( ReadFile(Filename), [], False) then
           ShowThis(Thread, Filename);
   until StopSearch or (feof(Handle) <> 0);
 finally
   pclose(Handle);
 end;
```

As you can see, this isn't all **that** different from Listing 13-2. I assemble the line a character at a time using fread() rather than using fgets(), and test for feof() instead of a Nil fgets() result. Building the Filename a character at a time **is** very inefficient—but since this inefficiency has essentially zero effect on total runtime, I can't see any great reason to replace it with, say, code that builds the Filename in an array[0..MAX_PATH] of char.

Mandelbrot 4

CHAPTER 14

Mandelbrot 4

THE MANDELBROT SET AND ME, we go way back. In 1985, A. K. Dewdney covered the Mandelbrot set in his "Computer Recreations" column in *Scientific American.* Along with half a thousand other readers, I promptly threw together my own Mandelbrot explorer, using Turbo Pascal 6-byte reals, CGA 4-color graphics, and an amazingly hard-to-use interface. Not long after, I did a second version that used fixed-point math for higher speed, and the CGA 160x100 16-color mode. When I got a new machine with an EGA, one of the first things I did was to write an EGA Mandelbrot to take advantage of the higher resolution. This third version had an "incremental draw" that gave you an idea where you were even before you were done, so you could zoom in on promising details without waiting for the whole picture to emerge. This feature wowed everyone who saw it, and before long I'd applied lots of polish and was selling the program as MANDELBROT 3.

Over the course of a few versions, MANDELBROT 3 got mentioned a couple of times in both *The New York Times* and in Jerry Pournelle's column in *Byte.* I took booths at computer shows, wrote fast floppy duplication software, and generally had fun. I also sold only a little over a thousand copies in about two and a half years. So, eventually I went on to other things and never did a Windows version, though there were certainly times when I was tempted by all that available memory and by the portable support for high-res graphics modes.

Come 1999, I had both a contract to write this book and a dual CPU machine to run Linux on. Wanting a good SMP project, and knowing that writing compute-bound GUI apps under Kylix presents all sorts of complications worth writing about, I decided to finally write yet another Mandelbrot explorer. Now, m4l [MANDELBROT 4—Linux] is still a lot more "prototypy" than I'd like, and in the best of all possible worlds I'd spend a few months getting this little demo app up to shrink-wrap standards. But there are tradeoffs in writing books, just as there are in writing software, and since I don't have a time machine I have to conclude that this prototype is "good enough". The parts that are worth writing about work; while the app lacks polish and features and even has a few known bugs, those aren't the parts that I'd write about.

As with the vfind projects, I'll try to skim quickly over the most application specific code, and focus on the parts of the application that are most likely to be of use to you in your applications: inter-form communication;

bitmap manipulation; the use of critical sections to protect shared data structures; and (relatively) high-performance thread-GUI synchronization.

Main window

MANDELBROT 4 is a more complex application than vfind in that it has multiple forms where vfind has only one. Still, m4l basically has a single main form and three modeless forms that report on and/or control the main form's contents. I'll discuss the main form first, then briefly cover the auxiliary forms and their communication channels.

Background information

You probably know that Mandelbrot images are generated by repeatedly evaluating a polynomial expression on a complex number.[1] Each point in the image is used as a seed point, the first complex number fed into the polynomial. After each iteration, the polynomial's result is fed back into the polynomial as the new input value. With some seed points, you can repeat this process indefinitely; those points are *in* the Mandelbrot set. With other seed points, sooner or later the polynomial result becomes infinite. What makes this process interesting is that the shape of the Mandelbrot set is very complex, consisting of endless series of repetitions of the basic shape in Figure 14-1, all joined by ever tinier repetitions of rotated and skewed versions of the basic shape. More, some points take longer than others to shoot off to infinity. When you color these neighboring points depending on how long they take to go infinite (by convention, points in the set itself are colored black), you get pretty pictures, like Figures 14-2 and 14-3 .

Note

These pictures are included in the tarball as m4l .mpf [Mandelbrot Position File] files, which specify the image coordinates. You can generate high-res, full-color images on your own Linux machine by running m4l and opening the files SpiralWheel.mpf *and* PinwheelMolecule.mpf.

---

1.   A complex number is a pair of numbers, of which one is *real* and the other is *imaginary*. The basic imaginary number, *i*, is the square root of -1. That is, i^2=-1.

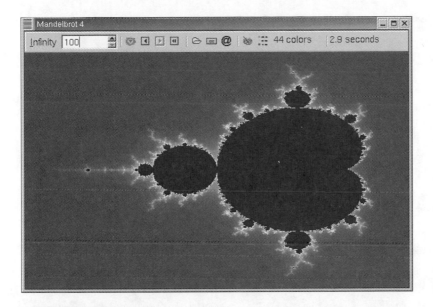

Figure 14-1. The basic shape

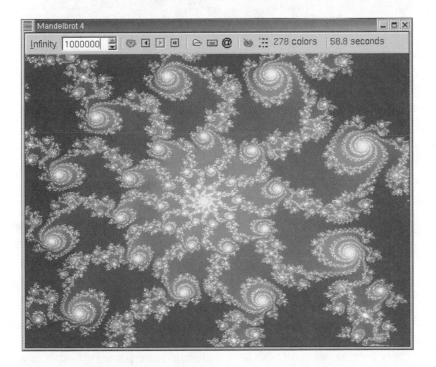

Figure 14-2. Spiral wheel

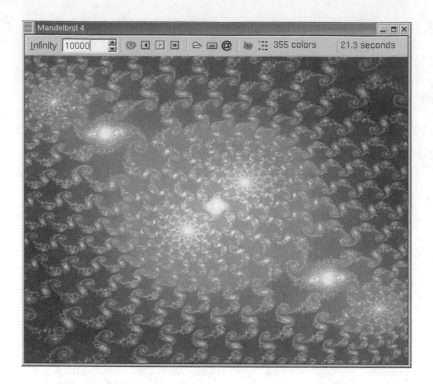

Figure 14-3. Pinwheel molecule

As a practical matter, you can't loop an infinite number of times to tell if a given point is in the set or not. You have to pick some reasonable number of iterations. Too low, and you lose the fine detail near the set; too high, and you just waste time coloring the black islands in a low-count sea. Accordingly, any given image of the Mandelbrot set is specified by five numbers: The bounding box and the value for "Infinity". In m4l, these five numbers are bundled together in the Calculations unit as a TMandelWindow record.

```
TMandelWindow = record
          Top, Left, Bottom, Right: extended;
          Infinity:               Cardinal;
          end;
```

Each TMandelWindow specifies a region of the complex plane as well as the appropriate infinity value. These MandelWindows are used throughout m4l: an .mpf file consists of a TMandelWindow and some palette information; maintaining a dynamic array of recent windows allows m4l to offer a history trail (*via* the 'VCR buttons' on the toolbar); the top-level calculation routine,

CalcWindow, draws a TMandelWindow that might have come from an on-screen selection, an .mpf file, the interactive Location window, or the history trail.

The TMandelView object maps this window information to a specific screen size. Accordingly, it contains methods to set the window

```
procedure SetWindow(const Window: TMandelWindow); overload;
```

and the 'grain', or number of pixels,

```
procedure SetGrain(NewRows, NewColumns: Cardinal);
```

as well as methods to map pixels to coordinates.

```
Coordinate =    record
                R, i: extended;
                end;
```

```
function PixelToCoord(X, Y: integer): Coordinate;
```

The TMandelView object maintains an array of Counts as an `array of integer`. Because two-dimensional arrays are inherently slower than one-dimensional arrays (see Chapter 3) and because most access to the Counts array is row-oriented (*eg*, a calculation thread might be calculating every fourth point in the row), m4l maintains the count information as a simple linear array. Code that reads or writes a Counts row calculates an offset of the first point that it's interested in, and the distance between that first offset and the offset of the next point that it's interested in. For each successive point on that row, m4l just steps the offset by the inter-point distance, and reads or writes `Counts[Offset]`.

To support incremental drawing, TMandelView provides a function

```
procedure CalcRow(Row, FirstCol, SkipCols: integer);
```

which calculates a subset of the points on the Row. The first, sparse pass calculates every eighth dot on every eighth row. This gives m4l enough of a sample of the final image to build a tentative color map, which it will use while it's drawing. Once it's done this sampling pass, it displays the first pass using the tentative color map, and then goes back and draws every fourth dot on every fourth row, skipping the dots that have already been calculated. A third and fourth pass fill in every dot on every other row, and then every unset dot on each row. A little bit of logic in the Main form's NormalPasses method keeps CalcRow from repeating any work; the incremental draw adds little overhead, and allows you to both quickly get an idea of where you are and also to zoom in before the whole image has been calculated.

Color mapping relies on TMandelView's Histogram, another `array of integer` that records how many elements in the Counts array have a given value. That is, the value of the 0th element in Histogram is the number of positions in the Counts array that have a value of 0; the value of the $1,000^{th}$ element in Histogram is the number of positions in the Counts array that have a value of 1000; and so on. The TMainWindow.SetColorMap method uses the histogram and a WhiteBasis to divide the range of Counts values into a series of bands that each has roughly the same number of pixels. The WhiteBasis represents a target for the percentage of pixels that should be colored bright white to show that they're very near the target. Each band accumulates discrete count values until it has more than this target number of pixels. A low WhiteBasis thus makes for many narrow bands, while a higher WhiteBasis makes for fewer, wider bands.

SetColorMap maps these bands to actual colors by reading a palette. Each palette consists of a stream of color/length pairs that specify a series of gradients. That is, the first gradient is between the first color and the second color, and takes up a given portion of the whole palette. The second gradient is between the second color and the third color, and so on. The last length is simply ignored. Thus, the same palette can be applied to a low-count image with 30 or 40 colors and to a high-count image with hundreds of colors. For example, if a given band is the 45th band out of 200 and the first gradient should take up 25% of the total, the band's color would be the color 90% of the way between the first and second palette colors. If the same palette were being used to color the 45th band out of 400, the band's color would be the color 45% of the way between the first and second palette colors

Actual display is handled by a private View bitmap and an on-form PaintBox. As the background calculation threads finish each pass over a row, they send a message to the GUI thread. The GUI thread's message handler reads the Counts data for that row, and fills in a ViewRow bitmap (using direct pixel access *via* ScanLine) and then copies the ViewRow to both the View bitmap and to the PaintBox. Copying the ViewRow to the PaintBox does an immediate draw, while the View bitmap is used both for saving images as .png, .jpeg, or .bmp files and also for repainting the PaintBox as necessary.

Calculation architecture

The actual calculation is done in background threads, so as to both maximize calculation speed and retain GUI responsiveness. The threads and the incremental drawing are coordinated by the main form's Calc record:

```
Calc: record
        Threads:        array of TSimpleThread;
        StartTime:      TDateTime;
        Abort:          boolean;
        UseLocking:     boolean;
        Lock:           TCriticalSection;

        Sparse,
        Normal:         record
                        Pass:   integer;
                        Grain:  integer;
                        Row:    integer;
                        Done:   boolean;
                        end;
        end;
```

The lib/SMP unit exports a variable, CpuCount, and the unit's `initialization` section contains ifdef-ed code that sets CpuCount to the number of processors in the system under either Linux or Windows. The Main form's FormCreate procedure initializes Calc as

```
SetLength(Calc.Threads, CpuCount);
Calc.UseLocking := CpuCount > 1;
if Calc.UseLocking
  then Calc.Lock := TCriticalSection.Create
  else Calc.Lock := Nil; // should be anyway, but it can't hurt to be explicit
```

which creates one thread reference 'slot' for each CPU, and creates a critical section if there is more than one CPU. The other fields in the Calc record are (re)initialized in the StartCalc routine, which is called from CalcWindow to setup every calculation.

The calculation threads' state machine code (below) wraps all access to the Sparse and Normal records in calls to LockCalc and UnlockCalc

```
procedure TMainWindow.LockCalc;
begin
  if Calc.UseLocking then
    Calc.Lock.Acquire;
end; // TMainWindow.LockCalc

procedure TMainWindow.UnlockCalc;
begin
  if Calc.UseLocking then
    Calc.Lock.Release;
end; // TMainWindow.UnlockCalc
```

which lock and unlock the Calc.Lock critical section iff the UseLocking flag is set because there is more than one calc threads.

The Sparse and Normal records support parallelized incremental drawing. That is, while TMandelView.CalcRow provides parameters that allow the calling code to do an incremental draw, there is no incremental draw logic in CalcRow itself. (A more complete version of M4 might offer a 'batch' mode that lets you generate an arbitrary resolution bitmap or animation, without actually drawing anything as it works. There'd be no point in a batch mode working in anything but a full-row-at-a-time manner.) The incremental draw logic is in the code that the calc threads run, but a parallelized computation can't use local variables and a doubly nested loop the way a single-threaded computation can. A parallelized computation needs to maintain some global state—the Sparse and Normal records—so that each time a thread finishes one row, the thread can calculate which pixels on which row to calculate next.

The calculation sequence

In the interest of simplicity, m4l creates a new set of threads for each calculation. Thus, when a user starts a new calculation, the CalcWindow method calls KillCalc to make sure that the old threads no longer exist.

```
procedure TMainWindow.KillCalc;
var
  Index: integer;
begin
  // Various window managers' "show contents while dragging" settings causes a
  // string of OnResize events as the user resizes the window: We have to make
  // the slow redraw abortable.
```

```
    Calc.Abort := True; // Can't call AbortThread because of use of dynamic arrays
                        // (and strings)


    // (Calculate's last action is "Calc.Threads[] := Nil;")
    for Index := Low(Calc.Threads) to High(Calc.Threads) do
      while Assigned(Calc.Threads[Index]) do
        Application.ProcessMessages; // Yes, a vile active wait - but a short one
end; // TMainWindow.KillCalc
```

KillCalc sets the Calc.Abort flag, then does an active wait for each thread to terminate and set its 'slot' to Nil. (If the threads have already terminated normally, the slots will already be cleared.) Now, in general an active wait **is** a very bad thing, but these waits will never last longer than it takes to calculate a single row and, after all, what is the alternative? Some sort of fragile hand-shaking protocol that could stop a calculation; assure the GUI thread that the calculations were stopped and that it is safe to update the current window and the Calc record; then start a new calculation. And it would also have to handle shutting down the calc threads when you shut down the app. This would be a lot more complexity for very little gain.

The CalcWindow method then pushes the new TMandelWindow onto the history list and calls StartCalc. StartCalc in turn clears labels and the elapsed time machinery; resets the View bitmap and the PaintBox, adding a message about sampling the count distribution; initializes the incremental draw state machine; and finally starts the calc threads *via*

```
for Index := Low(Calc.Threads) to High(Calc.Threads) do
    Calc.Threads[Index] := RunInThread(Calculate, @ Calc.Threads[Index]);
```

This creates one or more calc threads, each of which runs the Calculate method.

```
procedure TMainWindow.Calculate( Thread:             TSimpleThread;
                                 SimpleThreadPointer: pointer );
begin
  try
    Libc.nice(20); // We're going to take every spare cycle, anyway -
                   // allow the GUI thread to keep up with the message stream

    // First, sparse pass
    SparsePass;
```

```
    // Subsequent passes, using initial color map
    NormalPasses;
  finally
    Assert(Assigned(SimpleThreadPointer));
    Assert(TObject(SimpleThreadPointer^) is TSimpleThread);
    PPointer(SimpleThreadPointer)^ := Nil;
  end;
end; // TMainWindow.Calculate
```

The Calculate method really only does four things:

1. Call `Libc.nice()` to drop the new thread's dynamic priority. (As *per* Chapter 7, a higher value is a lower priority. A thread with a dynamic priority of 0 will run before a thread with a dynamic priority of 20.)

2. Do the SparsePass.

3. Do the NormalPasses.

4. Set the Calc.Threads 'slot' to Nil, which lets the GUI thread know that the thread has terminated.

The SparsePass method

```
procedure TMainWindow.SparsePass;
var
  Rows, Grain, Col, Row: integer;
begin
  Rows  := Data.Rows; // read it once
  Grain := Calc.Sparse.Grain;
  Col   := Grain - 1;
  repeat
    LockCalc;
    try
      Row := Calc.Sparse.Row;
      if Row >= Rows then
      begin
        if not Calc.Sparse.Done then
        begin // 1st thread to get here
          Calc.Sparse.Done := True;
          PostInteger(wm_SparseDone, 0);
        end;
```

```
        EXIT;
      end;
      Inc(Calc.Sparse.Row, Grain);
    finally
      UnlockCalc;
    end;

    Data.CalcRow(Row, Col, Grain);
    if Calc.Abort then EXIT;
  until True = False; // We EXIT from this loop
end; // TMainWindow.SparsePass
```

begins by reading and calculating the three data that don't change while the calc threads are running: Rows, Grain, and Col. The Data field is the current TMandelView, and the MandelView's Row field corresponds to the number of rows in the PaintBox component on the main form. The Grain is the number of rows and columns to skip between every pixel, and is set in StartCalc as

```
const
  Passes = 4;

  with Calc.Sparse do
  begin
    Grain := 1 shl (Passes - 1);
    Row   := Grain - 1;
    Done  := False;
  end;
```

That is, Calc.Sparse.Grain is 1 shl (4 - 1), or 8; the sparse pass calculates every eighth pixel on every eighth row. The value of the Calc.Sparse.Row field is always the next row to work on. As each thread gets the lock, it reads what it should do, and sets Calc.Sparse.Row to the next row that will need attention. Thus, Calc.Sparse.Row is initialized to 7, or the eighth row; the first thread to get the Calc.Lock will start calculating on row 7, and will set Calc.Sparse.Row to 15, which is the sparse pass's second row. When one of the calc threads starts on the sparse pass's last row, it sets the next row to a non-existent row. Any thread that gets this non-existent row will know that it should exit SparsePass and proceed to NormalPasses. The first thread to detect this pass-done state sets the Calc.Sparse.Done flag; sends a wm_SparseDone message to the GUI thread; and exits the SparsePass method. Any other threads that detect the Row >= Rows state will see that the Calc.Sparse.Done flag is already set, and thus will simply exit the SparsePass method.

> **Note**
>
>
> *All this state manipulation is protected by the LockCalc and UnlockCalc calls, which turn the multi-step update into a single atomic transaction. Only one thread at a time sees Calc.Sparse in an incoherent state; all other threads have to wait until that thread releases the lock. Data.CalcRow sets the Data.Counts array, but this does **not** have to be protected by a critical section, because the Calc.Lock code ensures that only one thread is writing to any given row at any given time.*

The wm_SparseDone message handler resets the View to clear the Sampling message; creates a color map and draws each sparse row to the View bitmap (see the *Graphics issues* section, below); and calls the PaintBox's OnPaint handler to do a

```
PaintBox.Canvas.Draw(0, 0, View); // full refresh
```

> **Note**
>
>
> *The background threads write the Data.Counts array but they never touch the View bitmap or the on-screen PaintBox. All graphics work is done by the GUI thread.*

The NormalPasses method is really quite similar to the SparsePass method, with the extra complication that it has to handle three passes, at successively finer Grain's, and that it needs to Skip over the pixels that have already been calculated on the rows that have already been visited. I don't really think it's necessary to print it here, as the SparsePass method is already a pretty good example of turning a simple loop into a state machine. The extra complications involved in turning a doubly nested loop into a state machine are really just "more of the same": If you find yourself in need of pointers on doing something similar, you can always look at the NormalPasses code in ch14/Main.pas.

The chief difference worth commenting on is that where SparsePasses works invisibly, only updating the screen at the end of the whole sparse pass, NormalPasses calls ShowRow(Row)

```
procedure TMainWindow.ShowRow(Row: integer);
begin
  PostInteger(wm_ShowRow, Row);
end; // TMainWindow.ShowRow
```

after every CalcRow, to send a wm_ShowRow message to the GUI thread.
As you might imagine, the wm_ShowRow handler colors a single row, and
writes it to both the off-screen View bitmap and the on-screen PaintBox. In
general, whenever a custom message is not a simple signal—whenever it
contains parameters—I like to use the idiom of pairing a custom message
handler with a custom message sender. The two can be implemented right
next to each other, thus minimizing the chance that the handler will read
the parameters in a different way than the sender sent them. Obviously,
this is more important when you're using lib/QMessage's Windows-style
SendMessage and PostMessage (with their lParam and wParam arguments)
than when you're using PostInteger or one of the other methods that send a
single value, but I find using custom message senders improves clarity even
in these simpler, safer cases.

On efficiency

To recap, m4l creates one low-priority ('nice') calculation thread for each
CPU in the machine. These set the Data.Counts array, using a global state
machine and a critical section to coordinate the activity of the threads. In the
three normal passes, each calculation thread sends a message to the GUI
thread after every row it works on.

As you can see by running the application, the thread priorities work
nicely. A load monitor like the Gnome CPULoad panel applet will show that
your machine is fully loaded, but any other applications you have running
on your machine stay very responsive.

Note

*Because the Qt messages are actually being routed through a
Synchronize procedure (see Chapter 6) m4l runs **much** faster from
the command line or with integrated debugging (Tools ➤ Debugger
Options) turned off. With integrated debugging turned on, an SMP
machine will not be fully loaded.*

The same is not really true for the GUI thread and its message handling. Especially when you're drawing a low-count image (like the 'zoomed out' starting image in Figure 14-1) in a small window, m4l can easily get flooded with messages. Rows may get drawn out of order; the label that shows the number of colors may take a noticeable amount of time to update itself; buttons may react sluggishly to mouse clicks. You may not see this behavior at all, as I have an older, relatively slow machine (dual P200), and the sluggishness does go away as the images get more complex and the message *per* second rate drops—but the Qt message loop does not seem to be a very high-performance mechanism. It's more suited to hundreds of messages a second than to thousands of messages a second.

Still, it offers much higher performance and better encapsulation than the Kylix TThread.Synchronize mechanism. Not only does the Synchronize mechanism block the thread until the Synchronize procedure returns in a way that PostInteger() does not, and not only does the Synchronize mechanism require you to pass data from background thread to GUI thread *via* global variables, the Synchronize mechanism is **slow**. (In Chapter 13, I mentioned how Synchronize makes a file search that returns a lot of files much slower than a search that only returns a few.)

In general, passing messages is a better way to pass data from your background threads to your GUI thread than calling Synchronize. If you need to pass even more data than m4l does and you start to suffer severe message flooding problems, you could probably follow a simple strategy whereby you place your data on a locked list, and only send a message if the list was empty when you locked it. The message handler would then just lock the list; extract an item; unlock the list; process the extracted item; and repeat until the list is empty, perhaps calling Application.ProcessMessages between each item.

Graphics issues

m4l's basic display architecture is that the background thread(s) call TMandelView.CalcRow, which writes the raw counts for each row into the TMandelView's Counts array. The background thread(s) then call TMessageForm.PostInteger to send a Qt message to the GUI thread, telling the GUI thread which row to draw. The GUI thread maps the raw counts to specific colors; draws these colors to a one-row bitmap, ViewRow, using the ScanLine property for direct pixel access; and then copies ViewRow to both the off-screen View bitmap and to the screen.

This message passing architecture has three consequences. First, only the GUI thread ever draws to the screen. Second, only one thread at a time is ever updating the View bitmap. While some bitmap operations **are** thread-safe, doing (potentially) simultaneous Canvas.Draw operations to different parts of the same bitmap just seems to be asking for trouble. Finally, having the single GUI thread manipulate the ViewRow bitmap means that the app only needs one copy of it. Even if it were perfectly safe for each calc thread to color its row and update the View bitmap, passing messages to the GUI thread only for screen updates, this sort of 'distributed' approach would mean that each calc thread needed its own ViewRow bitmap.

The background thread(s) call TMainWindow.ShowRow (listing above) to tell the GUI thread which Row to color and draw. The GUI thread's wm_ShowRow handler

```
procedure TMainWindow.wmShowRow(var Msg: TIntegerMessage);
var
  Row: integer;
begin
  Row := Msg.Data;
  ColorRow(Row, 0, 1);

  PaintBox.Canvas.Draw(0, Row, ViewRow);
end; // TMainWindow.wmShowRow
```

calls ColorRow (below) to update the View and ViewRow bitmaps, and then calls Draw to copy the whole ViewRow to the screen. (I could also CopyRect the row from the View bitmap, but using Draw is much simpler and, presumably, correspondingly faster.)

The ColorRow method uses ViewRow.ScanLine for direct, pixel-by-pixel access.

```
procedure TMainWindow.ColorRow(Row, FirstCol, SkipCols: integer);
type
  TImageRow = array[0..High(integer) div SizeOf(LongWord) - 1] of LongWord;
var
  Column, Offset: integer;
  ThisLine:       ^ TImageRow;
  Index, Count:   integer;
  Color:          LongWord;
begin
  Column   := FirstCol;
  Offset   := Row * Data.Columns + FirstCol; // Offset into Counts^ array
```

```
with ViewRow do
  Canvas.FillRect(Rect(0, 0, Width, 1));
ThisLine := ViewRow.ScanLine[0];
for Index := 1 to (Data.Columns - FirstCol) div SkipCols do
begin
  Count := Data.Counts[Offset];
  if Count > 0
    then Color := ColorMap[Count]
    else Color := UnsetColor;
  ThisLine^[Column] := Color;
  Inc(Column, SkipCols);
  Inc(Offset, SkipCols);
end;

  View.Canvas.Draw(0, Row, ViewRow);
end; // TMainWindow.ColorRow
```

ColorRow spends most of its time in a for loop which reads from Data.Counts and writes to ViewRow, stepping a read pointer (Offset) and a write pointer (Column). ColorRow initializes the Column write pointer to a copy of the FirstCol parameter; within the for loop, ColorRow steps Column while leaving FirstCol untouched. ColorRow then initializes the Offset read pointer to the index of what would be Data.Counts[Row, FirstCol] were Data.Counts actually a two-dimensional array. Of course, Data.Counts is actually a one-dimensional array, so m4l has to explicitly do the sort of row/col addressing that Kylix would do automatically for a two-dimensional array: Offset is set to Row * Data.Columns (the offset of the first column in the Row) + FirstCol (the offset of the FirstCol within the Row).

When the ViewRow bitmap is created in the CreateView method (which is called by TMainWindow.FormCreate), its Brush.Color is set to the UnsetColor, or $00505050. Thus, when ColorRow does a FillRect on ViewRow, it has the effect of setting every pixel in ViewRow to the dark gray UnsetColor. ColorRow next reads the ViewRow's ScanLine property, and assigns the untyped pointer ViewRow.ScanLine[0] to the local ThisLine pointer, which is declared as a typed pointer to an array of 32-bit LongWord's.

The for loop then uses the local ThisLine pointer to color pixels in the ViewRow bitmap, and finally ColorRow copies the updated ViewRow to the View bitmap.

ScanLine and QPixmap issues

Whenever you write code to read or write a bitmap's ScanLine property, you have to pay attention to QPixmap issues. You'll recall from Chapter 6 that a TBitmap maintains both a device-independent QImage, which is comparatively easy to read and write, and a device-dependent QPixmap, which is comparatively easy to copy to and from the screen. The ScanLine property calls FreePixmap and returns a pointer to a QImage row. You can then freely change the QImage *via* the ScanLine pointer, because the QPixmap will be automatically recreated the next time you do any operation that requires a QPixmap.

Kylix is not Delphi

There are two QPixmap issues that affect the ColorRow method. The first issue is that it's important that ColorRow reads ScanLine **after** it does the FillRect, as FillRect affects both the QImage and the QPixmap. If ColorRow read ScanLine before calling FillRect, reading ScanLine would implicitly destroy the QPixmap and explicitly get a pointer into the QImage, and then calling FillRect would implicitly recreate the QPixmap before the for loop modified the QImage. That is, all the changes made *via* ThisLine^[Column] := Color would not show when the ViewRow was drawn on the View bitmap or the PaintBox! However, since ColorRow **does** call FillRect before it reads ScanLine, it sets both the QPixmap and the QImage to the dark gray UnsetColor; then implicitly destroys the QPixmap and explicitly modifies the QImage; and finally implicitly recreates the QPixmap when it calls Draw to copy the new ViewRow to the View bitmap.

> **Tip**
>
>
>
> *If your ScanLine code doesn't seem to be having any effect, check it carefully to make sure that you aren't inadvertently recreating the QPixmap between getting the ScanLine pointer and using it to modify the QImage.*

The second issue is a simple matter of efficiency. I could have written ColorRow to modify View.ScanLine[Row] and, in fact, that's exactly what I did at first. (This meant that wmShowRow had to do a CopyRect instead of a Draw, but the increased complexity there was more than offset by the way that I didn't have to create and destroy ViewRow along with View and keep their Width's and PixelFormat's in synch.) The problem is that the View bitmap can be rather large, and at even moderately high resolutions, destroying and recreating View's QPixmap every time I redrew a row actually took longer than it did to generate the Counts for the row! As *per* Chapter 6, using ViewRow is much more efficient. ViewRow's QPixmap is continually being created and destroyed, but it's much faster to recreate a 1 row QPixmap than a 100 or a 1,000 row pixmap.

Selection

The Mandelbrot explorer allows you to zoom in on a picture by clicking and dragging a selection marquee. Since m4l needs to update the selection marquee as you drag it about, the mouse event code is a bit more complex than the schematic example in the *Mouse Events* section of Chapter 6.

The selection code uses two private form fields,

```
private // Selection
  MouseDownAt:  TPoint;
  MouseFocus:   TRect;
```

and event handlers for the PaintBox's OnMouseDown, OnMouseMove, and OnMouseUp event handlers.

```
procedure TMainWindow.PaintBoxMouseDown(Sender: TObject;
  Button: TMouseButton; Shift: TShiftState; X, Y: Integer);
begin
  Mouse.Capture := PaintBox;
  MouseDownAt := Point(X, Y);
  MouseFocus  := Rect(X, Y, X, Y);

  PaintBox.Canvas.DrawFocusRect(MouseFocus);
end; // TMainWindow.PaintBoxMouseDown
```

The mouse down handler sets Mouse.Capture so that the PaintBox mouse event handlers get mouse events even when the mouse isn't over the PaintBox; stores the click point (which is in PaintBox client coordinates); initializes the MouseFocus field as a one-pixel rectangle; and then uses MouseFocus to DrawFocusRect. It might seem silly to draw a one-dot marquee, but DrawFocusRect is designed to be used in paired calls. That is, it uses an XOR drawing mode, so that the second call will erase the first call's rectangle. The MouseMove event handler, below, starts by erasing the previous marquee. By drawing a one-dot marquee in the MouseDown handler, I avoid the need for an additional "MarqueeDrawn" state variable, or for testing that Mouse-Focus has a height and a width.

```
procedure TMainWindow.PaintBoxMouseMove(Sender: TObject; Shift: TShiftState;
  X, Y: Integer);
begin
  if Mouse.Capture = PaintBox then
  begin
    PaintBox.Canvas.DrawFocusRect(MouseFocus);
    MouseFocus := Rect( Min(X, MouseDownAt.X), Min(Y, MouseDownAt.Y),
                        Max(X, MouseDownAt.X), Max(Y, MouseDownAt.Y) );
    PaintBox.Canvas.DrawFocusRect(MouseFocus);
  end;
end; // TMainWindow.PaintBoxMouseMove
```

The MouseMove event handler undraws the previous marquee, then sets the current MouseFocus rectangle to the rectangle defined by the MouseDown point and the current mouse location, and finally draws a new marquee. There are three things to note, here:

1. The event handler doesn't need to check that the mouse button is still down: If the mouse button had been released, the PaintBox would no longer have the Mouse.Capture.

2. Because the PaintBox does have the Mouse.Capture, the X and Y coordinates may be off the PaintBox. 'Out of range' coordinates cause no problems with the DrawFocusRect call—which simply clips—and allow you to select parts of the Mandelbrot set which are not in the current window.

3. Because DrawFocusRect uses an XOR drawing mode to undraw the previous MouseFocus rectangle, you can get some funny-looking results by dragging while m4l is still calculating. A visually better—but much slower and more complicated—way to undraw would be to CopyRect from the View bitmap onto the Paintbox. With large MouseFocus rectangles, a single copy out of the View bitmap probably couldn't keep up with mouse movement very well: you'd probably want to use four copies, one for each side of the rectangle.

```
procedure TMainWindow.PaintBoxMouseUp(Sender: TObject; Button: TMouseButton;
  Shift: TShiftState; X, Y: Integer);
begin
  PaintBox.Canvas.DrawFocusRect(MouseFocus);
```

```
  if Mouse.Capture = PaintBox   then
    begin
    Mouse.Capture := Nil;
    CalcWindow(MandelWindow( Data.PixelToCoord( MouseFocus.Left,
                                                MouseFocus.Top ),
                             Data.PixelToCoord( MouseFocus.Right,
                                                MouseFocus.Bottom),
                       Infinity.Value));
    end;
end; // TMainWindow.PaintBoxMouseUp
```

The MouseUp handler undraws the marquee one last time, then resets Mouse.Capture and uses TMandelView.PixelToCoord to map the MouseFocus rectangle to Mandelbrot set coordinates.

Resizing

m4l's resizing code faces unusual problems and so is a bit more complex than the resizing code in most applications. At the same time, long-running event handlers that need to be abortable are not uncommon, and so the resizing code is interesting in that it illustrates an idiomatic solution to the general problem.

m4l needs to do three things when the main window is resized:

1. Call KillCalc to stop any existing calculations.

2. Call ResizeView to resize both the View[2] and ViewRow bitmaps, and to resize the Data.Counts array.

3. Call RecalcClick to redraw the existing window on the Mandelbrot set with a new view size.

The first operation can take hundreds of milliseconds, if it has to wait for a calc thread to do most of a wide row before noticing the Calc.Abort flag. Similarly, the second operation has to release several heap blocks, allocate several new heap blocks, and (indirectly) make several Qt calls. It's not fast, either.

The problem is that with many window managers you don't just get a single OnResize event when the resizing is done; you get a continuous stream of events

---

2. Actually, it resizes the BlankView bitmap, which I don't talk about elsewhere. I use the BlankView bitmap so that I can clear View by calling `View.Assign(BlankView)` instead of having to do a brush fill every time.

at various intermediate sizes. This means that the OnResize event handler needs to be abortable, both because the later resize event contains more accurate size information and also because the Application.ProcessMessage calls in KillCalc give rise to some really poor resize behavior (like restarting the whole calculation after it's done) if a resize at time t1 interrupts a resize at time t0.

The solution is really pretty simple. I define three new custom message numbers,[3]

```
const
  wm_KillCalc   = qtm_Simple + 4;
  wm_ResizeView = qtm_Simple + 5;
  wm_Recalc     = qtm_Simple + 6;
```

a ResizeSerialNumber field, and three custom message handlers,

```
private // Resize sub-messages
    ResizeSerialNumber: integer;

    procedure wmKillCalc(  var Msg: TIntegerMessage); message wm_KillCalc;
    procedure wmResizeView(var Msg: TIntegerMessage); message wm_ResizeView;
    procedure wmRecalc(    var Msg: TIntegerMessage); message wm_Recalc;
```

and break the resize code into a chain of four message handlers, starting with the standard OnResize handler, FormResize.

```
procedure TMainWindow.FormResize(Sender: TObject);
begin
  inherited;
  Inc(ResizeSerialNumber);
  PostInteger(wm_KillCalc, ResizeSerialNumber);
end; // TMainWindow.FormResize
```

The FormResize 'entry point' increments the ResizeSerialNumber. It then passes ResizeSerialNumber to the wm_KillCalc event in an integer message.

---

3. A series of constants like qtm_Simple + N might look like a great use for assigned enums. Instead of a series of constant + constant lines–which is just an open invitation to careless errors–the whole series might be defined as type ResizeMessages = (wm_KillCalc = qtm_Simple + 4, wm_ResizeView, wm_Recalc). Unfortunately, assigned enums are still enums, and can't be used in message clauses or PostInteger calls unless you turn them into integers *via* code like ord(wm_KillCalc), which seems really clunky.

```
procedure TMainWindow.wmKillCalc(var Msg: TIntegerMessage);
begin
  if Msg.Data = ResizeSerialNumber then
  begin
    KillCalc;
    PostInteger(wm_ResizeView, Msg.Data);
  end;
end; // TMainWindow.wmKillCalc

procedure TMainWindow.wmResizeView(var Msg: TIntegerMessage);
begin
  if Msg.Data = ResizeSerialNumber then
  begin
    ResizeView;
    PostInteger(wm_Recalc, Msg.Data);
  end;
end; // TMainWindow.wmResizeView

procedure TMainWindow.wmRecalc(var Msg: TIntegerMessage);
begin
  if Msg.Data = ResizeSerialNumber then
    RecalcClick(Self);
end; // TMainWindow.wmRecalc
```

Each of the three subsequent links in the 'resize chain' check the serial number that they were passed against the 'global' (to the form) serial number that FormResize updates. If the two numbers are the same, the custom event handlers know that no subsequent resize event has come along since the resize chain was started, so they do their bit of the task and then pass the serial number on to the next link, if any. If the passed serial number does not match the global serial number, the custom event handler knows that it's a link in a resize chain that has been superceded by a later resize event, so the custom event handler simply returns without doing any work and without posting a message to invoke the next link.

The Location window

The Location window (Figure 14-4) is associated with the @ button on the toolbar, because it shows where you're "at". The Location window is one of m4l's three modeless "tool" windows. All three act in basically the same way: When you click a toolbar button, the tool window comes up. The button stays down until you click it again, at which point the tool window is hidden, or until you close the tool window by clicking on the close button on the window frame. While the tool windows are up, they're updated when the main window changes; changes to the Location window and the Palette window can also affect the main window.

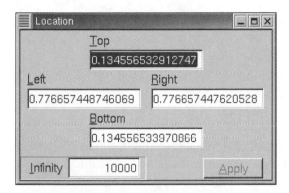

Figure 14-4. The Location window

This is a common enough pattern for auxiliary windows, so I'll walk quickly through the Location window code that implements this behavior. Since the tool windows are all modeless, I don't bring them up by calling ShowModal. Instead, I simply toggle their Visible state. (As *per* Chapter 6, setting Visible to True is the equivalent of calling Show, while setting Visible to False is the equivalent of calling Hide.)

```
procedure TMainWindow.LocationBtnClick(Sender: TObject);
begin
  LocationWindow.Visible := not LocationWindow.Visible;
end; // TMainWindow.LocationBtnClick
```

The Main unit has a circular "uses" relationship with the three tool window's units: It includes all three in its implementation section's uses clause, while they all include Main in **their** implementation section's uses clause. This allows the main window to call public methods and to read or write public properties on the tool windows, and in turn it allows the tool windows to call public methods and to read or write public properties on the main window. (Yes, it also allows the main form to fool around with any of the published components on the tool windows or *vice versa*, but you wouldn't do *that*. Right?) Thus, when the Location window is closed, it lets the main form know by calling the main form's public LocationWindowClosed method.

```
procedure TLocationWindow.FormClose(Sender: TObject;
  var Action: TCloseAction);
begin
  inherited;
  MainWindow.LocationWindowClosed;
end; // TLocationWindow.FormClose
```

The LocationWindowClosed method simply raises the location button.

```
procedure TMainWindow.LocationWindowClosed;
begin
  LocationBtn.Down := False;
end; // TMainWindow.LocationWindowClosed
```

Now, obviously creating the LocationWindowClosed method is a *bit* more work than just putting `MainWindow.LocationBtn.Down := False` inline in the Location window's FormClose event handler, but by using SHIFT+CTRL+C it's not a *lot* more work—and by calling a public method, the Location window is insulated from any changes to the main window's UI. For example, adding a menu and an action list to the main window would mean only that the TMainWindow.LocationWindowClosed method had to be changed to update the TMainWindow visuals when the Location window closed; it wouldn't be necessary to change the Location window at all.[4]

The main window's CalcWindow method updates the Location window every time the TMandelWindow changes.

```
  if Assigned(LocationWindow) then
    LocationWindow.Window := Window;
```

The Location window's Window property is a public property

```
public
  property Window: TMandelWindow read GetWindow write SetWindow;
```

that updates the various controls

---

4. I know that this is a really basic point and that I've made it in several places already, but it really never ceases to amaze me how many people don't get it. "Oh, I don't have the time to do it right"–so, when the program changes, they spend *more* time tracking down all the places that are affected than they would have spent doing it right in the first place.

```
procedure TLocationWindow.SetWindow(const Value: TMandelWindow);
begin
  Top.Value      := Value.Top;
  Bottom.Value   := Value.Bottom;
  Left.Value     := Value.Left;
  Right.Value    := Value.Right;
  Infinity.Value := Value.Infinity;
  ApplyBtn.Enabled := False;
end; // TLocationWindow.SetWindow
```

The Top, Bottom, Left, Right and Infinity controls are all specialized TCustomEdit controls that know if they contain a Valid integer or float point number; reading or writing their Value property is just a convenient shorthand for code like Top.Text := FloatToStr(Value.Top). (I cover these custom controls, briefly, in the *Validated edit components* section, below.)

The TLocationWindow.GetWindow function is the exact inverse of the SetWindow function, reading off the control values into its TMandel-Window Result. The edit controls on the Location window all share an OnChange handler

```
procedure TLocationWindow.ValueChange(Sender: TObject);
begin
  inherited;
  ApplyBtn.Enabled := Top.Valid and Left.Valid and
                      Bottom.Valid and Right.Valid and
                      Infinity.Valid and (Infinity.Value >= MinInfinity);
end; // TLocationWindow.ValueChange
```

that only enables the Apply button when all five edit controls contain valid values. When the Apply button is pushed, the Location window uses the main form's public CalcWindow to tell the main form to draw the changed TMandelWindow.

```
procedure TLocationWindow.ApplyBtnClick(Sender: TObject);
begin
  inherited;
  ApplyBtn.Enabled := False;

  MainWindow.CalcWindow(Window);
end; // TLocationWindow.ApplyBtnClick
```

In summary, the Location window maintains two two-way communication channels with the Main window, *via* public methods and properties.

The LocationBtn hides and shows the Location window *via* the public Visible property, while the Location window tells the main form when it closes *via* the public LocationWindowClosed method. The main window sets the Location window's public Window property to update the status display, and the Location window calls the main window's CalcWindow method to change the current fractal.

The validated edit components

Many applications need controls that only allow certain types of text input: integer or float point numbers, Social Security numbers, telephone numbers, dates, and so on. The CLX includes the TMaskEdit component which will only allow the user to enter strings that fit a mask that you specify, but this component is … not very user friendly. (Try it and see.)

In my opinion, a better solution is a free-form edit control that can 'pass judgement' on the contents—*ie*, that has a Valid property that lets you know if the contents match your expectations, but that otherwise acts like a perfectly normal edit control. You can then write an OnChange handler that disables the OK or Apply button(s) until all the fields on the dialog are Valid.

The TCustomValidatedEdit control in the lib/components/ValidatedEdit package is the root of an object hierarchy (Figure 14-5) that supports validation by adding both a protected IRegex field, and a read-only boolean property named Valid.

```
public
  property Valid: boolean read GetValid;
```

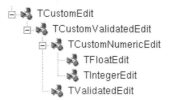

Figure 14-5. The inheritance tree

Reading the Valid property calls the GetValid method (below), which calls the IRegEx Match function on the edit control's Text.

The TCustomValidatedEdit has three registered descendants that appear on the Sample tab: TValidatedEdit, TIntegerEdit, and TFloatEdit. TValidatedEdit adds a published RegEx string property that lets you specify exactly what makes for Valid Text. TIntegerEdit and TFloatEdit use hard-coded regexes; are always right-aligned; and add a published numeric Value property.

I don't use TValidatedEdit in m4l, so I won't discuss it here, but the Location window uses both TIntegerEdit and TFloatEdit. The two are very similar, so I'll just briefly discuss TIntegerEdit and let that stand for both of them.

The numeric edit controls both set their protected Compiled: IRegEx in their constructor.

```
const
  OptionalWhiteSpace = '[[:space:]]*';

var
  IntegerRegEx: IRegEx;

function CompiledIntegerRegEx: IRegEx;
begin
  Result := IntegerRegEx;
  if Result = Nil then
  begin
    Result := RegularExpression( '^' + OptionalWhiteSpace +
                                 '[0-9]+' +
                                 OptionalWhiteSpace + '$',
                                 [REG_EXTENDED, REG_NOSUB] );
    IntegerRegEx := Result;
  end;
end; // CompiledIntegerRegEx


constructor TIntegerEdit.Create(AOwner: TComponent);
begin
  inherited;
  Compiled := CompiledIntegerRegEx;
end; // TIntegerEdit.Create
```

As you can see, TIntegerEdit.Create calls the inherited constructor, then calls CompiledIntegerRegEx which 'caches' the compiled regex so that all TIntegerEdit's in the application use the same compiled regex. (I used the same idiom with vfind2's American and European date regexes.) The regex matches the beginning of the string followed by optional leading white space, followed by at least one digit, followed by optional trailing white space, and the end of the string. Do you see why I needed to match the beginning and end of the string? If I didn't match the beginning and end of the string by including the '^' and the '$' in the regex string, a string like 'x 88 ' would match just as well as a string like ' 88 ': the leading 'x' wouldn't match, but the optional leading white space would match the second character, and the regex would be happy. By including the beginning and end of the string in the regex, I assure that it's not enough for the string to contain one all-digit 'word'. A string that matches the regex consists of one *and only one* all-digit 'word.'

You probably noticed that the regex is optimized a bit by compiling it with the REG_NOSUB flag, which disables substring support. Similarly, the GetValid method

```
function TCustomValidatedEdit.GetValid: boolean;
begin
  Result := Assigned(Compiled) and Compiled.Match(Text, [], False);
end; // TCustomValidatedEdit.GetValid
```

explicitly requests that Match not extract any substrings, even if the regex contains parenthesized subexpressions. Explicitly telling Match not to ExtractMatches is not really necessary, as the IRegEx object 'remembers' that it was compiled with the REG_NOSUB flag, but it never hurts to be explicit.

Finally, as I said in the previous section, the numeric Value properties are just a shorthand for StrToInt() and IntToStr().

```
function TIntegerEdit.GetValue: integer;
begin
  Result := StrToInt(Trim(Text));
end; // TIntegerEdit.GetValue
```

```
procedure TIntegerEdit.SetValue(const Value: integer);
begin
  Text := IntToStr(Value);
end; // TIntegerEdit.SetValue
```

The Value properties are not really *necessary*, but they certainly make the code smaller and clearer. You probably noticed that GetValue does no validation—the thinking here is that you wouldn't read Value unless Valid is True (or unless you can handle an exception.)

Projects

Postscript

THIS CONCLUDES THE regularly scheduled part of our program. I hope you have enjoyed the show.

The Appendices that follow are a collection of free-standing overview and reference material. The first two appendices are specialized overviews—*Kylix for Visual Basic programmers* and *Kylix for Delphi programmers*—that will only be interesting to some of my readers. Thus, I thought it best to place them at the back, and not at the front with Chapter 0.

Conversely, the reference material is at the back to make it easy to find. Some, like the *Glossary* and *Bibliography*, is material that you may want easy access to while reading the book. Others, like the *BASM Quick Reference*, *Optimization*, and *Deployment* appendices, simply seemed to be the reference material you'd most want easy access to once you were done with the book as a guide.

Section 5

Appendixes

APPENDIX I

Kylix for Visual Basic programmers

by Paul Bonner

BACK BEFORE THE WEB rendered computer magazines more or less pointless, I used to write a monthly column about "visual programming" for *Windows Sources* magazine. In theory, the column was supposed to cover the whole gamut of rapid application development tools: tips and techniques for one tool one month, a different tool the next, and yet another tool the third. In fact, the publisher would have been thrilled if I'd covered twelve different tools every year, and never repeated one. That kind of "impartiality" is considered good for business in the publishing world, because it maximizes the number of potential advertisers who have reason to be happy about the press they're getting.

In practice, though, no matter how much I tried to pursue diversity, for several of those years the column might as well have been called *Visual Basic Programming*. It seemed like three months out of every four I would end up coding some little system utility in VB, and then devoting my column to the techniques I'd used to do so. Even when I managed to use some other interesting programming environment or macro language or scripting tool, almost inevitably my column would include a passage to the effect that "Of course, if I'd built this in Visual Basic, it would have been better because...blah, blah, blah." I truly was trying to be fair, but back in those days, VB was so far superior to anything else on the market for rapid development of Windows applications that anything beyond a token acknowledgement of the competition was a stretch.

Then two things happened, more or less simultaneously as I recall, to change that. First, Microsoft released the long-awaited 32-bit version of Visual Basic. The VB community had been anticipating Visual Basic 4.0 for a long time, expecting a product that would blow away all the limitations of its predecessors and set the standard for 32-bit Windows development. But instead of a paradigm, Microsoft delivered a slow bloated pig of a product: clumsy, cumbersome, and in no way any fun to use. For those of us who wondered how Microsoft would manage to come up with approaches to encapsulating new technologies, like remote automation and networking, as creative and revolutionary as VB 1.0's encapsulation of the Windows API, the answer was suddenly clear: They wouldn't.

At about the same time, however, I became aware of Borland's Delphi. From the start, Delphi was a beautiful product that duplicated and generally improved upon all the best parts of Visual Basic, while delivering the kind of speed and power that had previously been the sole province of C programmers. Visual Basic made a few complex things very simple by limiting the things you could do. Delphi didn't impose any limits, but achieved nearly the same simplicity and ease of development by virtue of its elegant architecture and the strength of the VCL object model. Delphi 3.0 was, as I and many others wrote at the time, the upgrade to Visual Basic that VB programmers *wished* Microsoft had given them.

The tone and content of my column changed overnight. Delphi became my preferred development tool, and I found myself writing about it almost every month. Often, I would recreate projects that I'd originally created in VB, and then write in my column about how I was able to replace 50 lines of Visual Basic code with three lines of Object Pascal, or about how Delphi had enabled me to replace some awful kludge that I'd been forced to employ just to make something work in VB with a few simple operating system calls in Delphi.

That was, of course, long ago. But maybe not so far away, for once again, as I write this, Visual Basic programmers are faced with a tough choice about the next upgrade to their development tool of choice. On the one hand, Microsoft is about to release Visual Basic.Net, a new-from-the-ground-up interpretation of Visual Basic that introduces so many incompatibilities, and will break so much existing code, that many Visual Basic developers and analysts have taken to calling it "Visual Fred"—suggesting that it is not, in fact, Visual Basic at all. Borland, meanwhile, has made its play for those developers with an enticing multi-platform combination: a new release of Delphi for Windows, and the brand new Kylix for Linux.

If you're reading this, I imagine that you're already considering the Visual Basic versus Delphi/Kylix question, or perhaps have already made your decision. Either way, I'm not going to try to influence that decision one way or the other. The criteria that go into making a decision about which development tool to use are complex, and vary wildly from one individual to another, one project to another, one development organization to another. For that reason, I'm not even going to attempt to advocate one tool over another here. Rather, my purpose is simply to inform the reader of some of the issues, and some of the surprises (good and bad) that await any Visual Basic programmer who makes the decision to move to Kylix.

With that goal in mind, I'm going to restrict my comments to the differences between a traditional Visual Basic coding environment (for example, Visual Basic 6.0) and Kylix. Some of what I say might not still be true in the forthcoming Visual Basic.Net environment, but remember, I'm not trying to influence your upgrade decision here. My only goal is to give you an idea of what to expect moving from the Visual Basic environment you already know to Kylix.

Also, I should point out that the criteria I use to evaluate development environments have changed considerably since the days when I so eagerly embraced Delphi 3.0. Back then, I was writing small, relatively simple applications. I constituted a one-man development team, and the code I wrote was largely procedural in nature. It was event-driven, of course, as good client-side code must be, but even when I was using Delphi, the code I produced was a long way from being object oriented.

Nowadays, I work on a 20-member development team, writing completely object-oriented code in Java for a server-side development project. I hadn't done more than a smattering of VB or Delphi work in a year when I was asked to write this piece, but I've very much enjoyed my subsequent exploration of Kylix. In fact, I've come to appreciate it on a deeper or richer level than before; whereas before I viewed it largely from the perspective of a solo programmer engaged in short-term projects, today my primary interest is in a development environment's applicability to team development and long-term projects. Factors like performance and gee-whiz technology are still important, but what really gets me jazzed today is what I used to call the boring stuff: reliability, scalability, and above all, maintainability. And, I'm happy to say that it appears that Kylix is just as good at being boring as it is at the glamorous stuff.

Enough introductions. Let's dive in and see what Kylix holds for Visual Basic programmers.

I'll start by talking about the Kylix IDE (Integrated Development Environment—its code editor and support tools), what it has in common with Visual Basic, and how they vary from one another. Then I'll look at the underlying languages, and discuss the adjustments that a Visual Basic programmer has to make to become proficient at Object Pascal. Finally, I'll look at what's similar and what's different about the programming styles that the two tools encourage.

The Kylix IDE

I start with the obvious: In Visual Basic, your control palette presents its selection of the components and controls available to you in a floating properties-style window. In Kylix, your components appear in a series of tabbed-panels that are part of Kylix's main toolbar. While Visual Basic shows you only those components that you've explicitly added to your application, Kylix shows you all available components at all times. (The component set is editable, but all components in the active set are available without having to add external references to your project.)

That's it. Aside from that, the Kylix IDE and the Visual Basic IDE appear, at least at first glance, to be near twins of one another. Kylix's Object Inspector looks very much like Visual Basic's Properties window, the buttons for Run and Pause differ only in color, their respective Form editors appear to work in identical fashion, etc.

Look closer, however, and you'll discover some more significant, and qualitative, differences between the two.

The differences reflect different origins. The Kylix IDE, like that of Delphi, was built using the same model and object-oriented component library—originally the Windows-specific VCL in Delphi, now the operating system independent CLX for both Delphi and Kylix—that you use to build applications within it.[1] Every piece of Kylix, and every component built within it, is ultimately a subclass of TObject. This has enormous practical impact, especially when compared to Visual Basic, which has been assembled in a rather piecemeal fashion over the years.

Consider, for instance, a popup properties menu that appears when you right-click on a window or component. Microsoft endorsed them as a standard part of the Windows user interface as far back as Windows 95. Yet Visual Basic still makes it difficult or impossible to add popup menus to most of its forms and components. Why? Because the Visual Basic form component, and its menu editor and message-handling code, were all written in C and interwoven into the main VB run-time DLL long before anyone at Microsoft had gotten the OOP religion. In contrast, it is simple to add a popup menu to any UI component in Kylix, because TControl, the class from which they all descend, has had a popup menu property since the days of Delphi 1.0. So everyone of its descendents automatically gains access to that property.

---

1. Strictly speaking, this isn't totally true. The Delphi IDE **is** built using the same VCL that Delphi applications use. However, to speed the port from Delphi to Kylix, parts of the Kylix IDE still use the Windows-only VCL on top of Windows emulation libraries. Kylix applications, however, do not use the VCL or these Windows emulation libraries.

That's exciting in itself—Visual Basic just doesn't have that kind of clear class hierarchy. But even more exciting is the implication that if the TControl in Delphi 1.0 hadn't had a popup menu property—if it hadn't been added until Delphi 3.0 or 4.0—every component recompiled for that version of Delphi would still automatically gain access to the popup menu property. That's the power of the coherent object model at work, and it's something that Visual Basic developers just aren't used to seeing. To achieve the same thing in Visual Basic, Microsoft would have had to go back and modify the code of dozens of components individually, and provide a method better than Visual Basic's antiquated menu editor for creating those menus (something like, for instance, Kylix's TMenu component). Evidently, they haven't thought it a worthwhile project thus far.

Many other examples leap out at you as you begin to work in the Kylix IDE—places where it's evident that Kylix was designed from the start to be flexible and extendable, and that at least the early versions of Visual Basic—from which many of its core elements still derive—were not. The limitations of Visual Basic's properties window, for instance, force many component developers to put all the complex custom configuration features of their components on a separate dialog box reachable only by selecting the blandly named "Custom" property in the properties window. Kylix, and Delphi before it, offers an API that makes it simple to build custom configuration elements into the Object Inspector.

Another example is the Align property shared by all Kylix UI elements, which makes it possible to create forms utilizing multiple panels that resize themselves and react correctly to movement of a splitter bar without any coding on your part. Most Visual Basic codes still don't have any self-alignment capabilities (and those that do lack the alClient setting that enables codeless operations). Again, the difference is that in Kylix, there are common base classes to which a developer can easily add system-wide capabilities, while in Visual Basic there are not.

No ActiveX

Most Visual Basic components outside of the basic textbox, listbox, and other relics of the Windows 3.0 era are ActiveX controls that live outside of Visual Basic in OCX files. When you distribute a Visual Basic application, you need to distribute all of the OCX's it uses. That reduces the resources your application consumes if it shares its OCX's with other applications, because it makes your core EXE small and you only need one copy of an OCX no matter how many applications share it. (However, the unfortunate side effect of this sharing is an increase in version compatibility issues).

At one time, all OCX controls were written in C or C++, and were totally immutable as far as the Visual Basic programmer was concerned. But since Visual Basic programmers can now create their own OCX controls, it's possible to extend the capabilities of an existing OCX by encapsulating it in a new OCX control. Doing so lets you add new properties or methods to an OCX fairly easily. Actually modifying the original OCX's core operations, on the other hand, remains problematic in Visual Basic.

Kylix's CLX components, of course, follow a considerably different model. They're built out of Object Pascal, just like the rest of Kylix; they follow a strict class hierarchy; and they benefit from true inheritance and polymorphism. So when you create a new CLX component that inherits from an existing one, you have the ability to override or extend any of its methods, properties, or functions.

Moreover, since Kylix components are written in Kylix, the components you use (and only those) are included in your application's EXE at compile time. This undoubtedly inflates your EXE size a bit, but it also simplifies distribution and eliminates many version conflict issues.

There's another subtle benefit to Kylix's component model. In Visual Basic, many component properties are visible only through the properties window, and there is no easy way to tell which properties reflect default values for that component and which have been modified. This can make it quite difficult to go back and debug some odd behavior months after you've coded a form, or when working in a team setting on a form that was initially designed by another programmer. In Kylix, you can view a form, and all the components you've added to it, either as a form, like in the VB IDE, or as text. When you select the "view as text" option, you are presented with a listing of all the components on the form, as well as any properties that have been modified from the component's default. For instance, a *Cancel* button might look like this when viewed as text:

```
object Button1: TButton
  Left = 16
  Top = 64
  Width = 81
  Height = 25
  Hint = 'Close this form'
  Cancel = True
  Caption = 'Cancel'
  TabOrder = 2
end
```

(What we're seeing here, by the way, is a simple declaration that the form includes an object named "Button1" that is an instance of the class TButton, and that has been assigned a number of specific property settings through the Object Inspector.)

This visible record of all your actions in the Object Inspector is a real boon to the maintainability of a Kylix application.

This isn't to suggest that the move to Kylix will be an absolutely smooth one for Visual Basic developers. There are definitely adjustments to be made— although they're as much a factor of the operating system as of differences in the IDE and language. One is the simple lack of ActiveX controls. If you have a set of components that you've developed or purchased and have grown comfortable with in Visual Basic, you'll need to find or build equivalents or replacements for them in Kylix. Fortunately, Kylix comes with a rich collection of standard components, including obvious matches for most of Visual Basic's standard components, but the process of making the switch isn't painless by any stretch of the imagination.

The largest issues in this area revolve around databases. The tools a Visual Basic developer is used to in this area simply aren't available under Kylix: no ADO, no Access, and no local instances of SQL Server. As the *Kylix Programmer's Guide* puts it: "An application that makes heavy use of Windows-specific technologies such as ADO will be more difficult to port than one that uses Delphi database technology."

That said, Kylix has amazingly good database technology and components, with out-of-the-box support for DB2, Interbase, MySQL, and Oracle databases. The bad news is that, if you're used to building a lot of database-access features into your applications, you'll have to learn some new tricks to be able to do so in Kylix. The good news is that the tools you'll have to work with are first-rate.

Coding: syntax and style

This one is easy. When you move from Visual Basic to Object Pascal, the main thing you've got to remember is to end every statement with a semicolon.

So, a Visual Basic statement like

```
Text1.Left=30
```

becomes the Object Pascal statement

```
Text1.Left := 30;
```

If you can remember that much, you're halfway to becoming a champion Kylix programmer. Oh, there are a few other things to remember—a lot, actually—but it doesn't take much time to become comfortable with the basic language differences.

Undeniably, of course, there are significant differences between BASIC and Pascal. Their datatypes are different, their conditional and looping structures are different, their operators are different, their comment styles are different, and their error-handling is different. But as those core languages have evolved in Visual Basic and Delphi/Kylix to become vehicles for manipulating objects, they have followed a similar course—focusing more and more on the business of automating components. So to the extent that your code consists largely of reading and writing and otherwise manipulating object properties and methods, you'll find that there are far fewer significant syntactical differences than you'd imagine. A Visual Basic code snippet like

```
With Text1
  .Text="This is a test"
End With
```

could be rendered in Kylix like this:

```
with Text1 do
  Text := 'This is a test';
```

The code isn't identical by any means, but if you understand one you should be able to decipher the other and figure out the rules behind it relatively easily.

Just like Visual Basic, Kylix is case-insensitive, so in moving to Kylix you'll avoid one of the more aggravating aspects of most other languages for Visual Basic programmers. However, unlike VB, Kylix *is* strongly typed. How much of an impact this has on you will depend a lot on your Visual Basic coding style. If you habitually use *Option Explicit* to force you to declare the types of all variables, the transition will be easy. If you—well you should anyway, but the adjustment [from VB to Kylix] will be rougher in that case.

Only two areas of Kylix syntax and language differences qualify as truly nasty surprises for Visual Basic developers: strings and garbage collection. If you've never coded in any language other than BASIC, you have no idea how good you've got it in these areas.

Let's start with strings. Just about any implementation of BASIC will let you create strings on the fly, append them to one another, extract substrings, copy them into other strings, etc., all without doing anything special. Unless you're doing COM work where Unicode is important, there is only one type of string, and you never need to do anything special to create one or to carry out any of the operations you want to with it.

Kylix, on the other hand, offers not one, not two, but three different String types, each with different capabilities. The first, known as the `AnsiString` or *long string,* can be of any length, and behaves pretty much exactly like a standard Visual Basic string. The second is the `WideString`, which is basically a *long string* for Unicode characters. Finally, there is the `ShortString`, which is really a length byte plus an array of individually addressable characters, between 0 and 255 characters long.

This multiplicity of string types can be confusing if you've always believed that a string is a string is a string. However, Kylix makes it as simple as possible. By default, the `string` datatype gives you an `AnsiString`—the Visual Basic-like, general purpose string. Kylix also automatically converts strings from one type to another, allowing you to simply assign the contents of a string of one type to a string of another type, or to pass any type of string to a function that takes a specific type of string as a parameter.

A more significant issue waiting for Visual Basic programmers in Kylix (and, in fact, in just about every other language I've encountered except for Java), is garbage collection, or the lack thereof for objects. Visual Basic programmers *know* that when an object or variable goes out of scope—when the last reference to it dies—the variable is freed, and the memory it uses is reclaimed. Of course, from time to time that faith is misplaced (form-level variables, for one, have been known to persist between instances of the form when by rights they should have been destroyed). Still, Visual Basic's automatic garbage collection works well enough that, for all of its faults, Visual Basic has seldom been a major cause of memory leaks in Windows applications.

Kylix doesn't work like that, not for object references at least. As you read this book, you'll encounter the phrase "Free what you Create" in many different places. That's because Kylix, like most languages, doesn't count how many references you make to an object, and doesn't automatically free the memory used by the object when it goes out of scope (when there is no longer any way for your program to access it.) It's not that Kylix's designers see any value in objects that are no longer accessible, but that they faced backward-compatibility constraints—the imperative that they not break existing code—when they added reference-counted datatypes.

That is, Kylix does do reference counting and automatic garbage collection for some datatypes, just not for all datatypes. There are sound technical reasons for this. It makes sense, kind of. Still, it's one of those things that takes a long time to feel right to someone brought up in the world of Visual Basic.

Programming styles and OOP

Visual Basic programmers who choose to program in Kylix have two choices: They can continue to write Visual Basic-style applications in their new language, or they can learn how to write true object-oriented code.

Visual Basic has had the ability to create objects for years. But make no mistake about it: Visual Basic is not an object-oriented language. It doesn't support true inheritance or polymorphism (wherein an object of type *Cow* can be passed to a function that expects an object of type *Ruminant* or *Mammal* or *Animal* because the *Cow* type is a subclass of the *Ruminant type* which is a subclass of the *Mammal* type which is a subclass of the *Animal* type, and thus as far as your program is concerned, a *Cow* is a *Ruminant*, and a *Cow* is a *Mammal*, and a *Cow* is an *Animal.*)

Moreover, even if Visual Basic did comply completely with the definition of an object-oriented language, history would still prevent it from being used as such. Visual Basic programmers were brought up to write event-driven code, modular and procedural in style, not object-oriented code. Most Visual Basic developers may create a class from time to time and make use of it like a complex data type, but no matter how much object awareness Visual Basic has, I doubt that anyone is writing true object-oriented code—where an application revolves entirely around its internal object model—in VB. And certainly, anyone who does so is engaging in the technical equivalent of choosing a pogo stick for a downhill race when plenty of mountain bikes are available. Visual Basic simply isn't the tool of choice for object-oriented development.

Kylix, on the other hand, could be. It fully complies with the definition of an object-oriented language, and every element you encounter in Kylix other than primitive data types descends from TObject.

At the same time, as demonstrated by my magazine-writing antics described above, you're not forced to write object-oriented code in Kylix. You do need to make a few more nods to it than in Visual Basic—Kylix insists on referring to all those forms and components, etc. as objects—but you can still proceed down pretty much the same development path as you would in Visual Basic: create broad, general purpose code modules, use Types (Records in Kylix) and Arrays to hold data, and generally avoid any OOP notions that data and code should be merged into entities known as objects. You'll have to finesse it a bit here and there—but it's not hard. What you'll end up with is a Kylix application structured very much like the Visual Basic applications you used to write.

Or you could do it the right way.

The right way is to embrace object-oriented programming to a degree that just isn't possible with Visual Basic. Why? Because it will make you a better programmer. The code you produce will be easier to code, easier to debug, and easier to maintain. Plus, Kylix is practically begging you to do so—it's a wonderful environment for object-oriented programming, and the richness of that environment is a wonderful advertisement for the riches that will befall you if you embrace object-oriented programming.

Evolutionary biologists like to talk about the ability of a species to learn or acquire a "good trick". For example, camouflage is a good trick—members of a species that develops effective camouflage should live longer and reproduce more than members of a species that doesn't, all else being equal. So acquiring good tricks is a valuable thing for a species.

The same holds true in the world of programming, where we've acquired a number of good tricks over the years: the keyboard (you're probably too young to remember punch cards, but I'm not), modular programming, event-driven programming for windowing environments, client-server, SQL, multi-tiered applications, and many more. But of all the good tricks we've learned, none may be more important than objects.

Once you truly figure out what object-oriented programming is, once your entire conception of an application begins with and revolves around its object model (and that, I daresay, is a stage you'll never reach working with Visual Basic alone), then the truly amazing benefits begin to roll in. The most important of them is this: Every operation, no matter how complex, becomes simple to understand and work through once you can break it down into the atomic objects that make it up.

Have you ever coded a tree control? I did recently, and it's not easy. In fact, I know that if I had proceeded the way I used to code in Visual Basic—from the user-interface in, mixing the code that maintains the hierarchy with the code that displays it—I would have failed. I'm not a good enough programmer to get the job done going that route. Instead, I started with an object model, and concentrated first on defining two or three classes that handle the task of populating and maintaining a hierarchy. Not just the hierarchy for that control, in fact, but any hierarchy. And by proceeding along that route, the task became almost like child's play.

1. It started with defining a HierarchyNode class, which does nothing other than track its own ID and that of its parent.

2. Then, I built a container class, which doesn't do much more than keep a list of all the nodes you add to it, and sort it on demand. That doesn't sound like much, but it's the core I needed to build a tree control, or a hierarchical Gaant chart, or any number of hierarchical structures.

3. Once the core was in place, all I had to do was add a class to populate the hierarchy from a flat dataset, and another class to loop through the hierarchy and feed it to my tree component for display.

So objects allow you to break down the most complex parts of your application into granular units, each in itself simple. Moreover, adapting an object-oriented approach to development opens the door for you to make use of many of the exciting concepts in programming today, among them UML (the Unified Modeling Language, a tool for visually describing object hierarchies, application use cases, sequential operations, and many other aspects of application design), and patterns (essentially a way for developers and architects to exchange tribal wisdom describing proven solutions to common development problems).

The transition to object-oriented programming is like the transition to relational databases. It's hard to entirely explain to someone who, for instance, is running his or her application off of flat files or unrelated Access tables why SQL Server might be better, but once you make the switch you'll never consider going back. And Kylix, by virtue of its ability to support any transitional stages you go through on your way to becoming a fully committed OOP developer, is a great place to make that transition.

Conclusion

I started this piece off promising to be unbiased. Obviously, however, I think that Kylix is a wonderful tool, and recommend it strongly to Visual Basic programmers who are looking for new worlds to conquer. The transition isn't effortless, but the rewards are significant—the chief one being a better tool with which you can write better code. Enjoy.

Kylix for Delphi programmers

IN GENERAL, THE BETTER you know Delphi, the easier you'll find learning Kylix. The Qt API is quite different from the Windows graphics and controls API, but you'll find that while the CLX is not identical to the VCL, it **is** quite similar. Still, there are differences, even before you drop below the CLX to the system API level.

This appendix has three main sections that roughly parallel the first three sections of this book. These sections group the most important differences functionally, and then very roughly prioritizes them. That is, within each functional section, the first points are the ones that will affect the most people or that will require the most effort in porting. Each point is briefly summarized, and I provide references to the chapters that discuss them. For production reasons, I can't provide actual page numbers, but the detailed table of contents at the start of each chapter should make it pretty easy to find where I discuss each point—and most of these points are flagged with margin notes.

Within the 14 chapters of sections 1 through 4, most of these points are flagged with margin notes like this.

I expect that you expect big differences between Windows and Linux in file handling and the process model, so I only mention a few of the very biggest points, there. If you're the type of programmer who routinely drops to the Windows API for these services, plan to read Chapter 10 carefully.

Object Pascal

For the most part, Kylix is a port of Delphi 5, so this section uses Delphi 5 as its point of reference. All of these core language changes are also present in Delphi 6.

- In old versions of Delphi you could write to typed constants, as in pre-Delphi Borland Pascal's. In Delphi 5, this was made subject to a compiler switch. By default, you could write to typed constants as before— {$J+} or {$WRITEABLECONST ON}. In Kylix, the default is that typed constants are true, unwriteable constants—{$J-} or {$WRITEABLECONST OFF}. (Chapter 2.)

- Kylix supports a new {$IF} conditional compilation construct. With {$IF}, you can test the existence and value of Pascal identifiers, not just pragmas as with {$IFDEF}. (Chapter 4.)

- BASM now supports processors newer than the 386. (Chapter 2.)

- Kylix supports operator overloading *via* custom variants. (Chapter 3.)

- Kylix includes a portable implementation of Microsoft's variants, but this does not include VarArrayRedim. (Chapter 3).

- Kylix offers you fine-grained control over record alignment, not just packed or aligned as in older versions of the compiler. (Chapter 4.)

- You can still use `absolute VarName`, but the eponymous `absolute Address` form is no longer available. (Chapter 2.)

Kylix

This section is divided into subsections that roughly parallel the structure of the book's Section 2.

Visual code

- The way the "non-client" areas of your forms behave is much less standardized—and much less under your control—under Linux than under Windows. (Chapters 6, 9, and 12.)

- You can't place configuration files in the "application's directory." (Chapter 10.)

- Any `OnKeyDown` or `OnKeyUp` event handler that uses `VK_x` key names will have to be rewritten to use the new `KEY_x` names from the Qt unit. Kylix forms do not automatically use Qt the way Delphi forms automatically use Windows—you'll have to manually add Qt to the form's `uses` clause. (Chapter 6.)

- TBitmap has no MaskHandle property. Instead, it always maintains a QImage and QPixmap, which are analogous to DIB's and DDB's, respectively. This creates complications for ScanLine code. (Chapters 6 and 14.)

- "Form in form" code, where you embed one form in another form by setting the embedded form's Parent, will not work. Any such code will have to be changed to use frames. (Chapter 6).

- There's no standard PostMessage API—though I supply a replacement. (Chapter 6.)

- Application.Icon and Application.Title act differently. (Chapter 7.)

- Most components now have a Bitmap property that overrides their Color. (There is no ParentBitmap property, though.) This lets you build 'pretty', textured forms. (Chapter 6.)

- Components have more choices in BorderStyle's than bsSingle and bsNone. More components—like labels—can be bordered than under the VCL. Many forms that used panels or bevels to frame some text will no longer need to. (Chapter 5.)

- There is no TPrintDialog or TPrinterSetupDialog. (Chapter 6.)

- There's no ApplicationEvents component. (Chapter 7.)

- TCanvas's TextRect() and TextExtent() properties take an optional TextFlags parameter. (Chapter 6.)

- TCanvas's CopyMode is an enum, not an arbitrary 32-bit "ternary raster op" specification. (Chapter 6.)

- Font.Height is always positive. (Chapter 6.)

- KeyPreview does not work on borderless (fbsNone) forms without heroic efforts. (Chapters 6 and 9.)

Library code

- The search order for packages and libraries is quite different from under Windows. In particular, the system does **not** first look in the "application's directory." (Chapter 8.)

- Any GUI program can write to Output (Linux standard output) and ErrOutput (Linux standard error) without having to create a console. (Chapter 8.)

- There is no system-wide registry. You'll have to roll your own persistence mechanisms. (Chapter 13.)

- TList.Assign has been enhanced—you can now optionally combine two different lists, using a variety of binary operators. (Chapter 7.)

- TThread.Priority is both different from Windows and basically useless. (Chapter 7.)

- TEvent's are always auto-reset. (Chapter 7.)

- You can't abort a TThread with Suspend and Free. (Chapter 7.)

- TThread's Handle property is meaningless. (Chapter 7.)

- Kylix does not do its own suballocation of heap blocks—it lets Libc do that. (Chapter 8.)

Writing components

- Kylix does not include any tools to create `.dcr` files. (Chapters 7 and 9.)

- You generally have to {$R} your `.dcr` files. (Chapter 9.)

- The new TFrameControl is a better option for composite controls than TPanel. (Chapter 9.)

- TWinControl has been replaced by TWidgetControl. (Chapter 9.)

Linux

- X11 leaves most user interface "policy" decisions to plug-in "window managers." There are a lot of window managers to choose from, and they are often chosen more on the basis of eye-appeal than standards compliance. The result is that key aspects of form behavior—like their resize and maximize behavior, the border appearance, and the presence or absence of system buttons—vary from system to system. (Chapters 6, 9, and 12.)

- Many things, like semaphores, thread and process creation, thread priorities, and shared memory, work much as they do under Windows—but the API's are very different. (Chapters 7 and 10.)

- File attributes and permissions are much more fine-grained than under Windows 9*x*, while being somewhat coarser grained than under Windows NT/2000. (Chapter 10.)

- Linux shell scripts are much more capable than Windows batch files. They have relatively sophisticated control structures and can do arithmetic and string manipulation. When you write Kylix applications that call standard Linux commands, you can use shell scripts to provide some of the 'glue' that binds various commands into something useful to your application. (Chapter 11.)

- Regular expressions are common in Linux programming. There's an API that lets you include them in your Kylix applications. (Chapter 11.)

- Security is handled very differently than under either Windows 9*x*, which basically has no security at all, or Windows NT/2000, which allows for very fine-grained control over access. There is a class of operations that can only be done by the root user (or by a normal user running a *setuid* application owned by root) but if you can do any of these privileged operations, then you can do **all** of them. (Chapter 10.)

- Filenames are not as tightly bound to the file contents as under Windows. Directory entries contain pointers to an *inode*, which represents the contents, and there's no concept of 'real' or 'primary' name: each filename is as real as any other. For the most part, this is a good feature, but it does have some unpleasant consequences. (Chapter 10.)

- ParamStr(0) is not reliable, due both to linking and the way that calls to exec() can 'lie'. (Chapter 10.)

- There's no equivalent to Windows' MsgWaitForMultipleObjects() function. (Chapters 6, 9, and 10.)

Optimization

OPTIMIZATION IS A DANGEROUS, macho subject; *yang* to maintainability's *yin*. We all know that Knuth said that *premature optimization is the root of all evil*—but how many of us really act as if it's true? We see clear code and have a sort of "Gee, that's obvious" reaction, while we see fast code and have a sort of "Gee, that's clever" reaction.

That's why the conventional advice is worth repeating: Get it right, first. Write simple, clear code that does the job. Once it works is the time to start thinking about performance issues—and then only if performance **is** an issue. When your working code is too slow, measure it to find the bottlenecks, and then work on those.

Don't think that you can identify the bottlenecks with a little *a priori* reasoning. Sometimes you can—but usually you can't. Benchmarks have a way of surprising even the cleverest, most experienced programmers.

Be careful not to be tempted by the seductive allure of what I used to call *heuristic programming*, the notion that keeping efficiency in mind as you code makes for more efficient programs. It does, but clarity should always trump efficiency. If you have a choice between a fractionally clearer approach and a fractionally faster approach, go for the clearer approach. Only let efficiency concerns break ties between two equally clear approaches. Always remember that *it's easier to optimize correct code than to correct optimized code*.

Having said that, here are some specific tips, broken into three broad categories: General principles, CPU-dependent tips, and Kylix/Delphi specific tips. For more information, see the *High Performance Delphi* web site at www.optimalcode.com.

General principles

While these all have a Kylix spin, for the most part, these are general algorithmic tips that will apply in any language, on any CPU.

Algorithms beat optimization

When we find a bottleneck, we lick our lips and start spotting places where we can shave a few cycles. This might be our first reaction—but it shouldn't be the first thing that we do. It's relatively unusual for "bumming cycles" to speed up a routine by as much as ten to one. Yet, problem routines are often routines that work fine with small data sets, but not with large ones. If a routine has performance proportional to N^K—or, worse, K^N— (where N is the size of the data set and K is some arbitrary constant) then shaving 90% off the runtime might be irrelevant. 10% of "geological time" is still way too long.

The first thing to do with a slow routine is to look to see if it can be rewritten using a better algorithm. Get the theoretical performance as good as it can be before you start to worry about the actual performance. Going from N^K to N^{K-1} will make more of a difference than going from N^K to $N^K \div 10$, for even relatively low values of N.

Benchmark—don't guess

This applies in two different ways. First, you should only put your optimization efforts into routines that benchmarking shows are the bottlenecks, not the routines that you *think* are the bottlenecks. (I'm repeating this because it's worth repeating. Programmers are bright, analytic people who tend to rate analysis over experimentation.)

Second, when you do set out to optimize a routine, test your results. We tend to build up mental models of what various constructs cost, and to use these to guide our optimization efforts. This is fine, but it's no substitute for actual tests. Not only does the relative cost of various constructs change as CPU architecture changes, but also the compiler does not do a simple mechanical translation of *this* source construct to *that* object code. In many cases, the generated code depends on the context, and will thus be different in a real routine than in simple test cases that you write to check out the generated code with CTRL+ALT+C (*aka* View ➤ Debug Windows ➤ CPU).

The best approach to benchmarking is to use a *source code profiler* that can benchmark individual statements without requiring any source code changes. There aren't (yet?) any such tools for Kylix, so you'll have to rely on explicitly logging timestamps before and after an operation. The Pentium RDTSC instruction is fine for this, as it gives you a 64-bit count of clock cycles since the last CPU reset. You can use it inline in asm blocks, but it's more convenient to call

```
function RDTSC: int64;
asm
  RDTSC;
end;
```

from my lib/Pentium unit.

Keep in mind that alignment issues affect code just as much as they affect data, but that you have much less control over them. A simple change *here* can easily relocate code *there*, affecting its performance for good or ill. If you have to repeat a pair of operations tens or hundreds of thousands of times to see a significant difference, then you should really conclude that they're equivalent, as any difference will be swamped by code alignment issues.

Avoid "heap churning"

Strings and dynamic arrays are wonderfully convenient, but you pay a price for that convenience. Resizing a string or dynamic array involves creating a new heap block, copying data from the old block to the new block, and freeing the old block. Adding two strings involves creating a new heap block, copying data from both old strings to the new string, and possibly freeing the old heap block.

These are relatively expensive operations. Computers are so fast these days that you can get away with dozens of string ops in, say, a button click event handler—but you still don't want to do something like process a 10K (let alone 10M) text file word-by-word by repeatedly "popping" the leading word off of the string! You should instead step a Start and Stop pointer, and either Copy the word from Start to Stop out of the larger string, or work with PChar(BigString)[Start].

Factor out invariants

Sometimes "functions" like Length() and High() are really compile-time constants. The Length() of a compile-time constant string is itself a compile time constant. Referring to the string's length doesn't generate a subroutine call. Similarly, a "call" to get High() of an ordinal type or variable doesn't generate a real subroutine call. But when these functions are applied to string variables, or to dynamic arrays, then they do generate real subroutine calls.

The compiler won't optimize away repeated calls to these (or other) functions, even where the result doesn't change within the loop. Calling them *once* before the loop and saving the result to a local variable can make a big difference.

Rearrange your code

Somewhat similarly, while the compiler will *generally* manage to rearrange expressions so that, say, adding one constant and subtracting another will be implemented as adding the difference between the two, it won't always do this. Write your code so that it's clear what you're doing (and where the constants come from) but on occasion you may find that you need to introduce new constants like

```
const
  Difference = This - That;
  Ratio      = This / That;
```

to save a step or two.

As *per* Chapter 1, the compiler will make no attempts at algebraic simplification of your expressions. It's up to you to recast an expression like X * K + Y * K to (X + Y) * K.

Avoid branching

Branching is a relatively expensive operation for modern processors that pipeline their instruction decoding. They make heroic efforts to predict branches, but these can be foiled when a loop goes down a different branch every time around. Keeping if and case statements out of loops will maximize performance. You can do this by:

- Using table-driven programming. You can often replace a conditional statement with code that looks up pre-computed values from an array.

- Using ordinal expressions. Doing arithmetic with Ord(BooleanExpression) does not involve a branch because Kylix will use the SETcc instructions to turn a test's results into a 0 or a 1.

- Using Break, Continue, and Exit. While these involve jumps, the alternative is often something like if not BooleanStateVar then {...}. It's faster to jump out of a loop than to have every iteration check whether it should continue. (This is one of the few places where optimization can actually make your code clearer.)

CPU architecture

CPU's keep changing, and if you're still optimizing Pentium code as if it were an 8088, you're actually "pessimizing", in many cases. You also always face tough tradeoffs between optimizing for the slowest machine that may run your code (where your efforts are most needed) and optimizing for the newest, fastest machine (such as those who really care about speed will buy.)

To be modern without tying yourself to a specific CPU model, follow the rule of thumb *Keep It Short, Stupid*. An object code sequence's run-time is generally pretty directly proportional to its length.

Avoid globals

Every reference to a global variable requires object code that includes a 32-bit offset into the data segment. (With PIC code, this is a 32-bit offset relative to EBX, which doesn't directly slow things down that much—but maintaining EBX and not being able to use it as a general purpose register takes its toll.) By contrast, references to local variables will often be nice, fast register references; if they **are** memory references, they'll typically be 8-bit offsets relative to EBP.[1] Instructions that read and write local variables are shorter than instructions that read and write global variables; local variables are faster than global variables.

> **Note**
>
>
>
> *This has nothing to do with scope. References to a "unit private" global, or a typed constant "static local" generates exactly the same 32-bit offset instructions as references to a true "unit public" global.*

---

1. Some locals in routines that allocate large amounts of local data will have 16-bit offsets to EBP. In the 16-bit days, it made sense to declare small locals before large locals, so that they could be compiled to 8-bit offsets from BP, not 16-bit offsets. Kylix's optimizer seems capable of ignoring declaration order, and giving a local an 8-bit offset, even when it follows a large array or record.

Any way that you can avoid using global variables will speed up your code.

- A loop that needs to repeatedly read or update a global will probably be sped up by reading the global to a local variable before the loop, and saving changes after the loop.

- Dereferencing a local pointer is actually faster than reading and writing a global variable. If you need to refer to a global repeatedly, doing so through a local pointer will pay for the extra cost of explicitly saving the address to the local.

- Since object methods keep the Self pointer in EAX, referring to a global by dereferencing an object field that points to it can also be faster than a direct reference to the global.

Virtual methods aren't slow

If you're over 30 or so, you probably remember that when object oriented languages first started to be popular, the dinosaurs always objected that virtual methods were slow. Well, under 16-bit implementations, they were. If you haven't managed to purge that bit of mental dross yet, you might be in for a bit of a shock. Not only aren't virtual methods slow, they can actually be faster than static methods.

A static method always includes a 32-bit offset to the method in the CALL instruction. That makes for a six-byte instruction. By comparison, the first method in the VMT is called as

mov edx,[eax]	2 bytes	Load the VMT pointer into edx
call dword ptr [edx]	2 bytes	Do an indirect call through the first VMT slot

which only takes four bytes, and is actually faster than a static method call. Similarly, the second method in the VMT is called as

mov edx,[eax]	2 bytes	Load the VMT pointer into edx
call dword ptr [edx+$04]	3 bytes	Do an indirect call through the second VMT slot

Virtual method calls don't get to be as long as static calls until you get to the 65th VMT slot—edx+$0100.

Use arrays

As *per* the *Performance issues* section of Chapter 3, it's often faster to use array indexing than to step a pointer to the array's base type. Array indexing is very fast—especially for 1, 2, 4, or 8 byte base types—and does not take much longer than dereferencing a pointer. The time difference can be smaller than the cost of incrementing the pointer, even when the pointer 'lives' in a register.

Avoid 16-bit data

References to 16-bit data are always slower than references to 32-bit or 8-bit data. Use the generic Integer and Cardinal datatypes as much as possible.

- Don't use the word or smallint datatypes except in records that you pass to library code that requires 16-bit fields.

- Even 16-bit hashing code that discards the high-order word of intermediate calculations is faster using 32-bit variables and explicitly discarding the high-words (*via* and $FFFF) than using 16-bit variables with overflow checking off ({$Q-}—see Chapter 4) to do automatic discarding of the high-word.

- Enums take a performance hit when they have between 256 and 65535 elements. Use {$Z4} (Chapter 4.)

- Consider avoiding subranges in performance critical code. Kylix offers no way to force a subrange to take 32-bits. You can still step a 32-bit Index variable from Low(SubrangeType) to High(SubRangeType). This loses the safety of stepping from Low(SubrangeVariable) to High(SubrangeVariable), but also avoids the performance hit.

Kylix specific tips

This last category includes the tips that have to do with Object Pascal language features, or with details of the Kylix environment.

Use the CPU window

I can't place enough emphasis on the importance of experimentation—actual benchmarking—as opposed to *a priori* theorizing. Still, you need to have a mental model of what various constructs compile to, in order to be able to generate ideas about which alternate ways of expressing something might be faster. The very best way to build this mental model is to use the CPU window, CTRL+ALT+C (*aka* View ➤ Debug Windows ➤ CPU).

Set breakpoints, and look at the generated code. Try to always remember the *Heisenberg Uncertainty Principle* as applied to optimizing compilers: The very act of creating a test case can change the generated code. For example, the compiler will optimize away expressions that result in values that aren't subsequently used. It assumes that any value that's passed to a subroutine is used, even if that routine has an empty body, so I used to routinely pass expression results to an empty procedure, just to make sure that the expression code actually made it into the object code. However, it turns out that a subroutine call can change the way that the compiler uses registers. My test cases **were** telling me something about Kylix's code generation—just not quite what I thought they were!

Minimize register pressure

In general, the optimizer performs best when it doesn't have to push locals onto the stack. Keep your "working set"—the variables in play—as small as possible. At the extreme, two simple passes over the same array may actually be faster than one complex pass; array indexing is cheap, and the *per* item overhead of a loop pass that requires locals on the stack may cost more than doing the array indexing again.

Remember that a routine's first three parameters are passed in registers, and that object method's Self pointer and a function's Result pointer (if any) count as parameters. If you can rewrite a complex routine that takes five or six parameters as a suite of simpler routines that take no more than three parameters, it may be faster.

Avoid expensive constructs

"Absolute" variables have no place in a bottleneck routine. While I think `absolute` aids clarity, the optimizer can't handle absolute variables at all. Use explicit casts.

Similarly, while nested routines aid clarity and avoid namespace pollution, they're more expensive than normal, un-nested routines. A bottleneck routine should replace any nested routines with un-nested routines that use `var` parameters to change its locals.

Include and Exclude are faster than `SetVar := SetVar + [Value]` or `SetVar := SetVar - [Valuc]`.

APPENDIX IV

BASM quick reference

Using **BASM** means you have to know details about registers, parameters, and results that are normally hidden deep within the compiler. These minutiae are easy to forget and can be hard to find.

Register usage

All BASM blocks, whether they're compound statements within an Object Pascal routine or whether they're stand-alone assembler routines, may freely modify EAX, EDX, and ECX. All other registers must be unchanged on exiting the asm block.

BASM code in a package or a library must be Position Independent Code, or PIC. You can use {$ifdef PIC} to test for this.[1] PIC code must address all global variables relative to the Global Offset Table [GOT] pointer in EBX—*eg,* mov eax, [ebx+GlobalVar] instead of mov eax, [GlobalVar]. In PIC mode, any Pascal routine not flagged as local sets EBX to point to the GOT; PIC assembler code should either avoid using global variables, avoid all-assembler routines, or use a function like SysUtil's GetGOT to set EBX. In addition to leaving EBX unchanged on exit, any PIC code must be sure that EBX has its original value before using the CALL instruction.

Parameter passing

BASM code may refer to any subroutine parameter by name, even in routines that use the default register calling convention and pass the first three parameters in registers. You only need to pay attention to which parameters are passed in which register if you need to modify EAX, EDX, or ECX.

The first parameter that will fit in a 32-bit register, if any, is passed in EAX. The second register parameter is passed in EDX, and the third register parameter is passed in ECX.

---

1. Kylix 1.0 does not {$define PIC} when a **package** or **library** file is being compiled, though it does {$define PIC} when a **unit** is being compiled in PIC mode.

In object methods, the implicit Self parameter is always passed as the **first** parameter. That is, EAX contains Self in all object methods that use the `register` calling convention. The first explicit method parameter that will fit in a 32-bit register is in EDX.

When a function result will not fit in an ordinal or float point register, Kylix passes a pointer to the result as the **last** parameter, `@Result`. This may be passed in a register. For example, in

```
function Rectangle(HeightAndWidth: integer): TRect;
```

HeightAndWidth is passed in EAX, and @Result is passed in EDX, while in

```
function TSomeObject.Rectangle(HeightAndWidth: integer): TRect;
```

Self is passed in EAX, HeightAndWidth is passed in EDX, and @Result is passed in ECX.

Function results

Pointers and ordinal values are returned in the A register. That is, 8-bit ordinals are returned in AL, 16-bit ordinals are returned in AX, and all pointers and 32-bit ordinals are returned in EAX.

Float point values are returned on the FPU stack, in st(0).

Records with a SizeOf 1, 2, or 4 bytes are returned in the A register, just like ordinals.

All other results—including records with a SizeOf 3 bytes and records with a SizeOf greater than 4 bytes—are returned *via* an implicit @Result parameter.

Deployment

THE #1 KYLIX DEVELOPER'S FAQ may be "Why can I run my app in the IDE, but not at the command line?" A close runner-up is "Why can't I just run my Kylix apps from visual shells by double-clicking on them like I do on other apps?"

The short answer is that Kylix apps require a couple of Borland-supplied libraries that aren't (yet) included in all the standard distributions, the way older user interface libraries are. If Linux can find these Borland libraries, it can run your apps just fine. If you installed Kylix in /kylix, putting a line like

```
export LD_LIBRARY_PATH="/kylix/bin:$LD_LIBRARY_PATH"
```

in your ~/.bash_profile (or functional equivalent) file will let you run your Kylix GUI apps from the command line. (Alternatively, you can source the kylixpath script, just as the startkylix script does.)

Of course, it's not likely that you want to ask your users to edit their profile just so they can run your applications. Nor is it likely that they'd do so if you did ask. And, even if they did, they probably won't have the Kylix libraries on their system, unless they're also Kylix developers. So, what connection does the developer's FAQ and its short answer have with the issues of deployment, of writing a script that installs your app on a customer's system so that they can just run it without any further fiddling? Understanding this is going to take a bit of background.

Linux and libraries

You probably know that libraries can be *static* or *dynamic*. A static library is a collection of object files that's linked, in whole or in part, into your executable. You don't need to deploy the static library: The part(s) that your application needs get linked into the application. (Kylix 1 can't do this. It can link individual .o files,[1] just as it can link .dcu or .dpu files, but it can't link against static libraries.) The primary reasons to use a static library are link speed and linker stupidity. On some systems, opening and closing files is slow, and linking against a single library is faster than linking against a large collection

---

1. Though, as *per* Borland's README, **not** C++ .o files.

of individual object files. More importantly, while linkers always include **all** of a .o file, linkers can pick and choose from static libraries, as libraries have a symbol table in addition to their collection of object files.

By contrast, a dynamic library is linked at run-time. The application loads the library and looks up the symbol(s) it needs. This lets the application file be smaller, as it can load standard library functions from the dynamic library. Dynamic libraries can also shrink the amount of memory that a running program takes, as more than one application can be using the same library at once. That is, dynamic libraries are *shared object* files, which is why Linux's dynamic libraries have a .so extension.

All library loading under Linux is done by the `dlopen()` function. This includes both explicit dynamic linking and the sort of implicit dynamic linking that's done by the program loader. The dlopen() function takes a filename, and returns a handle. You then pass this handle to functions like `dlsym()` to find specific symbols.[2] If you pass a fully qualified filename to dlopen(), it will either open that file or fail. However, you'll rarely want to do this. Despite the various standardization efforts, different distributions still use different directory structures; you generally don't want to change your application to reflect the user's choice of installation directory; and so on. More typically, you'll just pass dlopen() a file name, and expect it to find the library.

Importantly, this is what Kylix does. If you look at Libc.pas or Qt.pas, you'll see lots of functions implemented as `external QtShareName` or `external libcmodulename`, where QtShareName is the unqualified filename `'libqtintf.so'` and libcmodulename is the unqualified filename `'libc.so.6'`. When you run a Kylix application, the system's run-time linker reads these library names from the ELF [Executable and Linking Format] header, and expects dlopen() to be able to resolve them.

When dlopen() is passed an unqualified file name, it looks for it in one of three groups of places.

1. Any of the directories in the LD_LIBRARY_PATH environment variable. LD_LIBRARY_PATH is a colon-separated list of directory names, just like the PATH variable. (For security reasons, programs running as root (that is, either being run **by** root or a setuid program owned by root) ignore LD_LIBRARY_PATH.)

---

2. The LoadLibrary() and GetProcAddress() functions of Chapter 4 call dlopen() and dlsym(). Chapter 8's LoadPackage() function also calls dlopen().

2. The libraries listed in /etc/ld.so.conf. More accurately, dlopen()
   looks in /etc/ld.so.cache, which is compiled from /etc/ld.so.conf
   by the ldconfig program, usually at boot time. Files that you add to
   a directory in /etc/ld.so.conf, or directories that you add to
   /etc/ld.so.conf won't be seen by dlopen() until you run ldconfig.

3. /lib, then /usr/lib.

Any match stops the search: *ie*, if dlopen() finds the library in a
LD_LIBRARY_PATH directory, it won't look in /etc/ld.so.conf or /usr/lib.
Similarly, if dlopen() finds the library in the first LD_LIBRARY_PATH, it
won't look in the second or third LD_LIBRARY_PATH directory.

A normal (as opposed to setuid) application that uses a special version
of a standard library can thus 'shadow' the standard library by supplying a
loader script that places the directory containing the right version in
LD_LIBRARY_PATH, ahead of any other entries. The special version will be
found before the standard version, and the application will load properly.
Since the change to the environment variable can only be seen within the
script and any processes it launches (Chapter 10), there's no danger of this
application's special needs affecting other applications.

Using a loader script that sets LD_LIBRARY_PATH also means that the
user doesn't have to edit her ~/.bash_profile (or "pollute the global environment" in any other way) to run your application. Note that this is the
approach that Borland takes with the startkylix script.

Note

*Because setuid-root programs ignore LD_LIBRARY_PATH, you can't
use a loader script to run a setuid program. You'll only be able to
run your setuid Kylix applications on "Kylix ready" systems. (See the*
Detecting "Kylix ready" systems *section, below.)*

Kylix libraries

Most Linux applications make some use of dynamic libraries, if only
libc.so.*n*. You can use the ldd program to list the libraries that an application
uses. If a program doesn't use any libraries, ldd will report "not a dynamic
executable". Typically, though, ldd will report a list of the libraries that the
application uses, followed by the location that it found them in.

For example, on my system `ldd ch14/m4l` reports

```
/lib/libNoVersion.so.1 => /lib/libNoVersion.so.1 (0x40017000)
libqtintf.so => /kylix/bin/libqtintf.so (0x40019000)
libX11.so.6 => /usr/X11R6/lib/libX11.so.6 (0x401a8000)
libpthread.so.0 => /lib/libpthread.so.0 (0x40276000)
libdl.so.2 => /lib/libdl.so.2 (0x4028d000)
libc.so.6 => /lib/libc.so.6 (0x40290000)
libqt.so.2 => /kylix/bin/libqt.so.2 (0x403b1000)
/lib/ld-linux.so.2 => /lib/ld-linux.so.2 (0x40000000)
libXext.so.6 => /usr/X11R6/lib/libXext.so.6 (0x40a48000)
libSM.so.6 => /usr/X11R6/lib/libSM.so.6 (0x40a56000)
libICE.so.6 => /usr/X11R6/lib/libICE.so.6 (0x40a5f000)
libjpeg.so.62 => /usr/lib/libjpeg.so.62 (0x40a76000)
libstdc++-libc6.1-1.so.2 => /usr/lib/libstdc++-libc6.1-1.so.2 (0x40a96000)
libm.so.6 => /lib/libm.so.6 (0x40ad8000)
```

This is a lot of libraries, but most of them are system libraries, in /lib, /usr/lib, and /usr/X11R6/lib. With the possible exception of libjpeg.so.62, these should all be on every Linux workstation, so you don't have to worry about deploying them. (Certainly you can leave it up to the user to install these files, if they don't have them.)

The only files that you do need to make deployment decisions about are the Kylix libraries. Since I installed to /kylix, `ldd ch14/ m4l | grep kylix` reports

```
libqtintf.so => /kylix/bin/libqtintf.so (0x40019000)
libqt.so.2 => /kylix/bin/libqt.so.2 (0x403b1000)
```

That is, I piped ldd's output to grep, and looked for lines mentioning my Kylix directory. You can use this technique to compile a list of the libraries that your application needs. While console apps do not normally require any Borland libraries, all GUI apps need at least libqtintf.so and libqt.so.2 to run. Database applications may need additional libraries.

If you install the libraries that your application needs into the same directory as the application, you can use the `ch11/brandit` script to create a loader script that the user will call to run your application. The loader script sets a local copy of LD_LIBRARY_PATH to point to the library directory, then runs your application. As *per* Chapter 11, the loader script will look something like

```
if [ "$LD_LIBRARY_PATH" ]
  then
    export LD_LIBRARY_PATH="/opt/myapp:$LD_LIBRARY_PATH"
  else
    export LD_LIBRARY_PATH="/opt/myapp"
fi
/opt/myapp/myapp
```

That is, it checks to see if the user has a LD_LIBRARY_PATH environment variable. (Most users won't.) If the user **does** have a LD_LIBRARY_PATH environment variable, the loader script prepends the directory where the GUI libraries are to the existing value, so that you can be sure that your application will see the versions of the libraries that you tested it with and that you installed along with it. More typically, the script simply sets LD_LIBRARY_PATH to point to the directory that you installed the libraries to. The loader script runs your application, and then exits, taking its local copy of LD_LIBRARY_PATH with it.

By using a loader script, your application can load the libraries it needs, and the user doesn't have to make any changes to the system configuration.

Note

 Avoid the temptation to install libqtintf.so and libqt.so.2 to a /etc/ld.so.conf directory! Doing so might break other applications that depend on libqt.so.2

Detecting "Kylix ready" systems

The two libraries, libqtintf.so and libqt.so.2, come to about eight megabytes, or three meg as a .tgz file. While this is not a problem for a CD distribution, it's obviously quite a large minimum file size for online distribution. (It's also a waste of your users' systems' memory to have two or more identical copies of libqt.so.2 open.) It would be nice to not have to install Borland's libqtintf.so and libqt.so.2 along with your application.

The problem is that most systems will already have a copy of libqt.so.2. As of the time of writing, this might be libqt.so.2.2.0, while the Borland patched libqt.so.2 is libqt.so.2.2.4. Kylix and Kylix apps will not run with 2.2.0, while most (or all) existing Qt apps (like KDE) will not run with the Borland patched 2.2.4.

"Kylix ready" distributions include a libqtintf.so and a libqt.so.2 that the vendor built with the same gcc version.

Early reports are that Kylix applications run just fine with `libqt.so.2.3.0` and higher—so long as both libqtintf.so and libqt.so.2 have been compiled with the same version of `gcc`. (The ABI—Application Binary Interface—has a way of varying from version to version.) This would be true of a "Kylix ready" distribution, one that ships with both libqtintf.so and libqt.so.2.3.0 (or higher). That is, if the system already has libqtintf.so in a `/etc/ld.so.conf` directory, and if libqt.so.2 is version 2.2.4 or higher, then you can **probably** safely conclude that the system is "Kylix ready" and that you don't need to install the Borland libraries and create a loader script.

Note

Distributor-compiled Qt 2.3 libraries haven't been Borland-tested the way that Borland's 2.2.4 has. Bizarre choices of unstable gcc versions, and/or unfortunate choices of compile options can always cause problems—and, as we all know, code isn't always as backward compatible as it's meant to be. (Delphi programmers undoubtedly remember the headaches that Microsoft gave us with all the different versions of `comctl32.dll`.) Even if a system seems to be "Kylix ready", be sure to give the users a way to install Borland's libqtintf.so and libqt.so.2 to the application directory, and to create a loader script. Using Borland's libqtintf.so and libqt.so.2 will always be your safest route.

Checking for libqtintf

You can use a simple little console app like the qtintf project in the deployment/deployment project group to test for the existence of a 'globally visible' copy of libqtintf.so:

```
program qtintf;

uses Libc;

function CanLoad(const ModuleName: string): boolean;
var
  Module: pointer;
begin
  Module := dlopen(PChar(ModuleName), RTLD_LAZY);
  Result := Module <> Nil;
  if Result then
    dlclose(Module);
end; // CanLoad

begin
  Halt(ord(not CanLoad('libqtintf.so')));
end.
```

This sets a result code of 0 if `dlopen('libqtintf.so')` succeeds, and 1 if it fails. You can easily detect this in a script like

```
#! /bin/bash

if qtintf ; then
echo 'qtintf found'; else
echo 'qtintf not found'; fi
```

While obviously a real install script would want to install the Borland libraries and create a loader script if qtintf returns False, my point here is that it's easy to write a script to detect qtintf's result code.

The qtintf program is only 15,584 bytes, so it won't add appreciably to download time. If you're using online distribution, you can have the installer script download the Borland libraries iff qtintf returns False.

Checking the libqt version

If you can open libqtintf.so without setting LD_LIBRARY_PATH, it's probably safe to conclude that the system is "Kylix ready". Still, it's safest to also make sure that you can open libqt.so.2, and that it's version 2.2.4 or higher. The qversion project in the deployment/deployment project group

```
program qversion;

function Version: PChar; external 'libqt.so.2' name 'qVersion__Fv';

begin
  WriteLn(Version);
end.
```

is a console application that simply writes the qVersion string to standard output. (This program does assume that there is **a** libqt.so.2 on the system— if you're **really** cautious, you might prefer to write a LoadLibrary version of qversion.)

The deployment/chkqversion script

```
# Get the qversion string - on my Redhat 7.0 system, this is '2.2.0-beta2' if
# LD_LIBRARY_PATH is not set
qversion=`qversion`

# Extract the major version number
nomajor=${qversion#*.}
major=${qversion%.$nomajor}

# Extract the minor version number
nominor=${nomajor#*.}
minor=${nomajor%.$nominor}

# Extract the release number
norelease=${nominor##[0-9]}
release=${nominor%$norelease}

echo $major $minor $release
```

captures the version string from standard output and extracts the major (first), minor (middle), and release (last) codes. It's relatively straightforward as shell scripts go; see Chapter 11 (and Table 11-6, in particular) if you can't read it. Obviously, a real install script would want to test the major, minor, and release numbers, not just print them out. A major code greater than 2 should be fine, as should a major code equal to 2 and a minor code greater than 2, or a major and minor code equal to 2 with a release code greater than or equal to 4.

Deploying GUI applications

If you need to install Borland libraries like libqtintf.so and libqt.so.2 along with your application, you probably should just install them into the application directory, or possibly a /usr/lib/MyCompany/shared directory. Avoid the temptation to add them to a /etc/ld.so.conf directory, or to add your new Kylix library directory to /etc/ld.so.conf. While making the libraries globally accessible would thus spare subsequent installs of Kylix apps the need to install the Kylix libraries, you might break existing apps that use libqt.so.2, as above—or subsequent installs might overwrite your libqtintf.so with an earlier or later version.

Linux uses a system of soft links and library versioning[3] that's supposed to avoid this sort of "DLL hell", and allow multiple versions of a library to coexist—but it requires cooperation on all sides. Many Kylix programmers are new to Linux; while most of them are bright and capable, just like you, prudence suggests that you avoid putting yourself in a situation where any mistake by any other Kylix programmer can damage your application.

You should create the versioning links even when you're installing the Borland libraries to a private directory. Why? Mostly to prevent mysterious errors if it turns out that code you use depends in some way on the link structure.

That is, you'd copy `libqt.so.2.2.4` and `libqtintf.so.2.2.4` to your private directory, and then create the following three soft links:

File name	Links to
libqt.so.2	libqt.so.2.2.4
libqtintf.so	libqtintf.so.2
libqtintf.so.2	libqtintf.so.2.2.4

Deploying packages

Deploying applications that use packages is much like deploying any other application, except that you also have to be sure that dlopen() can load the packages. (Packages are 'just' special libraries.) For dlopen() to be able to load your packages, they must be in either /lib or /usr/lib, or in a LD_LIBRARY_PATH directory: They can't be in an /etc/ld.so.config directory.

---

3. See the "Program Library HOWTO" at
   `www.linuxdoc.org/HOWTO/Program-Library-HOWTO/`.

You might be willing to install your custom packages into /usr/lib, but you should refrain from installing the Borland run-time packages into a system library, for fear of wandering into DLL Hell, as above. If you want to use Borland's run-time packages, you'll **have to** use a loader script that sets LD_LIBRARY_PATH, even on a "Kylix ready" system. (Yes, this means that a setuid-root program can't use Borland's run-time packages.)

As *per* the above section on *Kylix libraries*, you can use ch11/brandit to create a loader script. It doesn't matter if you want to put your packages in a different directory than the GUI libraries, or if you have more than one package directory: brandit will work just as well if its library path parameter contains a single directory name as it will if its library path parameter contains several directories, separated by colons.

What won't work

The loader scripts that brandit produces may seem fragile. They contain the installation directory, and if the user moves your application, the scripts won't work. You might be tempted to use a script like

```
filename=`readlink $0`      # if it's a symlink, this will return base name
filename=${filename:-$0}    # base name, if any; else $0
namepart=${filename##*/}    # filename part
path=${filename%$namepart}  # path part
```

that attempts to examine $0—the script name—to see where the script 'lives'. You can then set LD_LIBRARY_PATH to $path, or to something like ${path}/lib.

Unfortunately, this is just as fragile:

- The user may call the loader script from a hard link that has a totally different path than the library files.

- While $0 *normally* contains the full path and script name, it doesn't *always* contain the full path and script name. What you see in $0 is up to the exec() call that loads the program. This may be stripped for security reasons, or it may be a flat-out lie.

The bottom line is that using brandit to create a loader script is the best way to deploy any Kylix application that uses libraries that didn't come with the user's Linux distribution.

Bibliography

Compilers: Principles, Techniques, and Tools

Aho, Sethi, & Ullman, Addison-Wesley, 1986. ISBN 0-201-10088-6.
Commonly known as the "Dragon Book," a good source of insight into how regular expressions are evaluated. Some people prefer Hopcroft, Motwani and Ullman's: Introduction to Automata Theory, Languages, and Computation *(ISBN 0-201-44124-1).*

Delphi Component Design

Thorpe, Addison-Wesley, 1997. ISBN 0-201-43136-6.
Out of print, but available used; said to be excellent on Delphi internals, much of which applies to Kylix. Definitely worth tracking down if Chapter 9 left you wanting more.

Delphi in a Nutshell

Lischner, O'Reilly, 2000. ISBN 1-56592-659-5.
The best Delphi book in print. A good language overview, with a different approach and organization than mine; a detailed reference to every keyword and fundamental library procedure.

Developing Custom Delphi 3 Components

Konopka, Coriolis, 1997. ISBN 1-57610-112-6.
Out of print, but available used (or as PDF from raize.com); worth tracking down if Chapter 9 left you wanting more.

Linux Application Development

Johnson & Troan, Addison-Wesley, 1998. ISBN 0-201-30821-5.
A good overview of Libc programming, though obviously written from a C perspective. This was my introduction to the Linux API, and there's plenty of material here that's not in Chapter 10.

Programming Perl

Wall, Christiansen, & Orwant, 3e, O'Reilly, 2000. ISBN 0-596-00027-8.
The "Camel Book" is a charming—at least in the second edition that I have— if dense introduction to a language that's very different from Object Pascal. It also includes more material on regular expressions than Chapter 10 does, though Perl regexes use a somewhat different syntax than POSIX regexes. If you don't already know Perl, get a copy of Programming Perl *and learn it; it's probably already installed on your Linux machine, and getting a different perspective on common problems will make you a better Object Pascal programmer.*

Running Linux

Welsh, Dalheimer, & Kaufman. 3e, O'Reilly, 1999. ISBN 1-56592-469-X.
An indispensable guide for the Linux newbie; helps you understand what various options mean.

Unix Network Programming

Stevens, Volume 1: "Networking APIs" 2e, Prentice Hall, 1998. ISBN 0-13-490012-X. Volume 2: "Interprocess Communication" 2e, Prentice Hall, 1999. ISBN 0-13-081081-9.
The standard reference on sockets and IPC.

Glossary

Term	Meaning
BASM	Built-in Assembler.
BSD	Berkeley Software Distribution. In the early '80's, Unix development forked between UC Berkeley and AT&T (*System V* &c.) The two streams were merged in the '90's, but left a legacy of multiple incompatible ways of doing the same thing that you can still see in Linux today.
client area	The part of a GUI window that you are responsible for, below the caption and within the frame. While you can (try to!) specify what is on the caption and what the frame looks like, drawing in these *non-client areas* is the responsibility of the window manager.
CLX	Component Library Cross-platform—the portable component library that makes Kylix so powerful.
control	A discrete part of a user interface, like a button or text editor. Under X and Qt, controls are often spoken of as *widgets*.
Delphi	Kylix for Windows.
desktop	An optional layer of Linux software above the window manager and the X windowing system that provides services like system menus, workspaces, and themes.
euid, effective user id	While normally programs run with the same permissions as the user who started them, setuid programs run with the permissions of the program's owner, which is usually root. The effective user id, or euid, is the user id that governs the process's privileges.

Term	Meaning
finalize	When a reference to huge string, dynamic array, or interface is changed or goes out of scope, the data structure's reference count is decremented; if the reference count is now 0, the data structure is freed. This is a common operation, and it's unwieldy to have to describe it in full every time you refer to it. I use "finalize" as a shorthand, as you have to explicitly call the Finalize procedure in the few cases where Kylix doesn't automatically finalize a data structure for you.
focus	When you pay attention to something, you "focus on it". Analogously, the window and/or widget that gets keystrokes and mouse clicks "has the focus".
form	The object that represents an on-screen window and contains the code for the window's event handlers.
IDE	Integrated Development Environment. A programming environment, like Kylix's, that combines a compiler, an editor, a debugger, and cross-referencing tools.
iff	In formal logic, this is short for "if and only if". *Iff* is a much stronger assertion than *if*. When you say "if A then B", you are not saying anything about other conditions under which B might be true. You are merely stating a *sufficient* condition. By contrast, when you say "iff A then B", you are saying that A is not just a *necessary* and sufficient condition for B, it is also a *complete* condition. B is true when A is true and only when A is true.
inode	A data structure that represents what we normally think of as a "file": Contains permissions, sizes, timestamps, and a pointer to the file's stream of disk sectors. A single inode may have several different names, and hence may appear to exist in several different places in the directory tree.
Julian date	A timestamp based on a *Julian calendar*, where dates are represented by the number of days (or other unit of time) since the start of an *epoch*. Kylix's TDateTime is a Julian date, as is the standard Unix time_t.
Mandelbug	An intermittent, hard to reproduce bug that only occurs in very specific parts of your program's state space. A pun on Benoit Mandelbrot, a pioneer of chaos theory.

Term	Meaning
mechanism, not policy	Cynically, this is X jargon for "Somebody Else's Problem". Officially, it refers to the way that X11 servers only deal with the mechanics of reading keyboards and mice and of putting images on the screen, while leaving all user interface decisions ("policy") to the *window manager*.
memory leak	Allocating memory without later freeing it.
MIME	Multipurpose Internet Mail Extensions. Originally a standard (RFC 2046), extensible way to describe how to interpret email attachments; used in Linux to describe clipboard datatypes.
multiprocessor	A computer design where more than one processor shares a common bus, memory, and peripherals. Particularly useful in servers, as the computer can literally do more than one thing at once.
nice	A Unix command that lowers a (usually long-running) process's *priority*. As in "be nice, and let the other processes go first, because they'll be done soon."
non-client area	The parts of a GUI window that you don't usually draw on yourself, such as the caption, frame, and the various buttons on the frame. These are the responsibility of the window manager. Under Windows, you can customize the non-client area by responding to various messages; this is not possible under Linux. In general, you can only give the window manager "hints" about the appearance and behavior of the non-client area, and the window manager is entirely free to ignore you.
overload	To use an operator or routine in two or more distinct but related ways. For example, Object Pascal overloads +, the addition operator, to do string concatenation. You can do operator overloading with custom Variants, and can overload any subroutine.
owner	Every *control* (or *widget*) has an owner. When the owner is freed, it will free every control it owns. (You can always explicitly free a control before its owner is freed.) Controls are generally owned by the forms that they appear on; forms are generally owned by the application that they're part of.

Term	Meaning
parent	Every control has a parent. The control is only visible when the parent is visible, and any part of the control that lies outside of the parent's visible area is clipped. All controls that belong to a form ultimately trace their parentage to the form, but their actual parents may be *container controls* which group various controls together. Examples of container controls include panels, group boxes, and the various pages of tab controls.
PITA	Pain In The Ass.
POSIX	Portable Operating System Interface. Originally, IEEE-IX or "IEEE Unix"; an attempt to standardize API's across all the different Unices. Generally, Linux API's are converging towards POSIX compliance, but they're not always 100% there. See also *Single Unix*.
pragma	A compiler directive. A special sort of comment that affects either how the compiler generates code, or whether it will allow certain sorts of code.
priority	Every process and thread has a priority: High priority tasks run before low priority. Standard Linux priorities run from —20 to 20, with higher numbers representing lower priorities. (This may seem paradoxical, but it's just another one of those cases where there's more than one way to look at things, and both make sense. Yes, 20 is higher than 1—but would you rather be first in line or twentieth?) See also *nice*.
process	Under Linux, a process is a group of *threads* that share memory, open files, and so on.
process group	A set of processes that stay together when suspended (usually by CTRL+Z, but this is user-configurable) or made the *background* or *foreground task* with bg or fg. A process group is **usually** composed of a series of linked processes, like the two in ps -a	less, but there are various API calls that control process groups.
regex	A common shorthand for *regular expression*.

Term	Meaning
regular expression	A sort of program in a language that describes text patterns. A regular expression can be used to match, extract, and/or replace substrings in a piece of text. Regular expressions are very common in Linux use and in Linux programming; see Chapter 11. You can also use regular expressions in the Kylix code editor.
root	The super-user, or system administrator. Some API functions are only available to the root user, or to a process running as root (*ie*, a setuid program), while other API functions offer more options to root users than to normal users.
RTL	Run Time Library—the low-level, Borland-supplied code that manages memory, files, and so on.
RTTI	Run Time Type Information—info about the identity of objects, their properties, the display names of enumerations, and so on.
setuid	A file permission bit that means that the process running this program should run with the permissions of the program's owner, not the user who's actually running the program. Since the usual reason to do this is to gain root permissions, "a setuid program" is often used as a shorthand for "a setuid program owned by root."
shell	A shell is a program responsible for loading other programs, running scripts, maintaining a command history, and so on. Though bash is the most common, you have a choice of several different shells, each of which is more capable than the Windows command processor.
shell prompt	Essentially synonymous with "command line"—what you see in a terminal window. The shell prompt is not quite synonymous with the shell itself, as you can interact with the shell in ways that don't involve a prompt, like shell scripts or the Libc system() and popen() functions.

Term	Meaning
Single Unix	A Unix standardization project, much like *POSIX*. The Single Unix standard slightly predates the IEEE's POSIX standard; efforts are being made to bring them into synch. The version 2 standard document at `www.opengroup.org/onlinepubs/7908799/xshix.html` is a good place to look for information on undocumented (or poorly documented) Linux API functions, so long as you never forget that the actual Linux behavior may not precisely match the Single Unix committee's specification.
SMP	Symmetric Multi Processing. A computer system with two or more identical processors sharing a common memory, bus, and peripherals. See also *multiprocessor* and *uniprocessor*.
System V	The culmination of the AT&T line of Unix development (as distinct from the *BSD* line.) You'll most often run into references to System V and/or BSD in the "Compatibility" section of various Libc functions' `man` pages.
tar	Tape Archive and Retrieval—the standard Unix archive program.
tarball	The colloquial name for a "tar file".
thread	A unit of program execution. A process can contain several threads. They all share memory, code, and files, but each has its own stack (and hence its own local variables), register image, and priority.
TLA	Three Letter Acronym.
TMTOWTDI	There's More Than One Way To Do It. The Perl motto, and also a fine rule for user interfaces: mouse *or* keyboard; select and click a button *or* double-click; menus *or* hotkeys; and so on.
tombstone	A pointer that refers to memory that has already been freed, or "dead" memory.
uniprocessor	As opposed to *multiprocessor*—a conventional computer, with a single "central" processing unit.
unit	Object Pascal's modules. Contains a public (*interface*) part and a private (*implementation*) part.
UP	Uniprocessor; usually only seen in opposition to *SMP*.

Term	Meaning
VCL	Visual Component Library—the Windows version of CLX.
vtable	C++ shorthand for "virtual method table" [or VMT]— each object class's table of pointers to virtual method handlers.
widget	The X/Qt name for what under Windows are called *controls*: discrete bits of a user interface, like scroll bars or menus.
window	A usually rectangular screen region backed (in Kylix) by a form object. Each application consists of several windows, each of which may contain multiple *controls*, and may be fully or partially obscured by other windows. Only one window at a time has the input *focus*.
window manager	A special X client that's responsible for user interface "policy", or how *windows* look and act. It controls default window placement, keyboard *focus*, and the appearance and behavior of each window's *non-client area*. Many windows managers ignore Kylix's BorderStyle and BorderIcons requests.
workspace	1) Various Linux desktops allow you to maintain groups of virtual desktops called workspaces, which can be a great way to organize your work. 2) A (mostly Windows) synonym for *client area*.

Index

B

back-quoted strings, in shell programming, 722

back references, in regular expressions, 707–708

base form in vfind, 769–772

base type, pointer reference to, 102

BaseConf unit, 767

    TWindowSize record, 769–770

bash (Bourne Again shell), 719

BASM (built-in assembler), 61–62. *See also* Appendix IV

    octal digits for code, 618–619

    routines implemented in, 92

begin/end block, 59–60

BeginUpdate, 458

bevel control, 303

bindings, correcting, 694–695

BinEval function, 670–671

Bit Block Transfer (bitblt), 391–392

Bitmap project, 394–395

Bitmap property, 275

bitmapped font, 382

bitmaps

    of Brush, 379

    for menus, 316

    sharing, xxxix–xl

    TBitmap class for, 393–400

    transparency-related properties, 396

bitwise operators in Pascal, 49

block commands, in code editor, 329

block indent, 267

.bmp file, reading into stream, 671

bookmarks, in code editor, 329

boolean datatypes, 7, 8–10

boolean expressions, 312

boolean structures in shell programming, 729–734

    file property tests, 731

    integer tests, 731

    string tests, 730

borderless windows, 599

BorderStyle property

    of group box, 302

    of panel, 302

bounds rectangle, 271

BoundsRect, vs. maximizing window, 769

branches, avoiding with boolean expressions, 9

brandit script, 733

break statement (Pascal), 70

breakpoints in debugging, 337

BringToFront method

    of Application variable, 434

    to display controls, 312–314

Browser, 333–334

Brush tool, 379–382

    Assign() method, 375–376

Brushes project, 379–380

bugs, 780. *See also* debugging

buttons, xxxv–xxxvi

    adding to toolbars, 319

    anchoring, xxxvi–xxxviii

    Cancel property of, 298

    Default property of, 298

    events in vfind, 786–787

Byte type, 16

    casting to Integer, 41

ByteBool, 9–10

E

N

Q